STRATEGIC MANAGEMENT

@H6StrategicMgr

STRATEGIC MANAGEMENT

@H6StrategicMgr

A customised edition of

Exploring Strategy
Tenth Edition
Gerry Johnson, Richard Whittington, Kevan Scholes,
Duncan Angwin and Patrick Regnér

PEARSON

Harlow, England • London • New York • Boston • San Francisco • Toronto • Sydney • Auckland • Singapore • Hong Kong
Tokyo • Seoul • Taipei • New Delhi • Cape Town • Sao Paulo • Mexico City • Madrid • Amsterdam • Munich • Paris • Milan

Pearson Education Limited
Edinburgh Gate
Harlow
Essex CM20 2JE

And associated companies throughout the world

Visit us on the World Wide Web at:
www.pearson.com/uk

Compiled from:

Exploring Strategy
Tenth Edition
Gerry Johnson, Richard Whittington, Kevan Scholes,
Duncan Angwin and Patrick Regnér
ISBN 978-1-292-00254-5
© Simon & Schuster Europe Limited 1998 (print)
© Pearson Education 2002, 2011 (print)
© Pearson Education Limited 2014 (print and electronic)

ISBN 978-1-78448-101-8

Printed and bound in Great Britain by CPI Group.

CONTENTS

PART I
THE STRATEGIC POSITION

PART II
STRATEGIC CHOICES

10 MERGERS, ACQUISITIONS AND ALLIANCES   328

Commentary on Part II Strategic Choices   360

STRATEGIC MANAGEMENT

@HrStrategicMgr

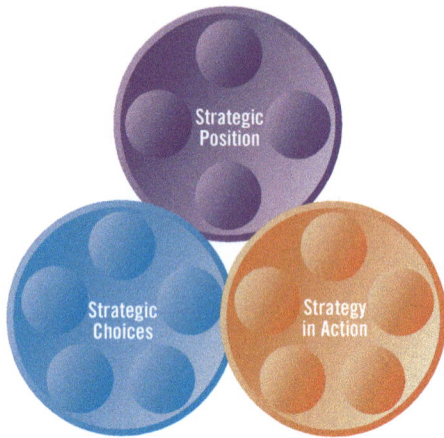

1

INTRODUCING STRATEGY

Learning outcomes

After reading this chapter you should be able to:

● Summarise the strategy of an organisation in a *'strategy statement'*.

● Distinguish between *corporate*, *business* and *operational* strategies.

● Identify key issues for an organisation's strategy according to the *Exploring Strategy* model.

● Understand different people's roles in *strategy work*.

● Appreciate the importance of different *organisational contexts*, *academic disciplines* and *theoretical lenses* to practical strategy analysis.

Key terms

business-level strategy p. 7

corporate-level strategy p. 7

Exploring Strategy **Model** p. 10

operational strategies p. 7

strategic choices p. 12

strategic position p. 11

strategy p. 3

strategy in action p. 13

strategy lenses p. 20

strategy statements p. 8

three-horizons framework p. 4

MyStrategyLab

MyStrategyLab is designed to help you make the most of your studies. Visit **www.pearsoned.co.uk/mystrategylab** to discover a wide range of resources, including:

• A personalised **Study plan** that will help you understand core concepts

• **Audio and video clips** that put the spotlight on strategy in the real world

• **Online glossaries and flashcards** that provide helpful reminders when you're looking for some quick revision.

(1.1) INTRODUCTION

Strategy is about key issues for the future of organisations. For example, how should Apple, primarily a devices company, compete in the computer and tablet market with Google, primarily a search company? Should universities concentrate their resources on research excellence or teaching quality or try to combine both? How should a small video games producer relate to dominant console providers such as Microsoft and Sony? What should an arts group do to secure revenues in the face of declining government subsidies?

All these are strategy questions, vital to the future survival of the organisations involved. Naturally such questions concern entrepreneurs and senior managers at the top of their organisations. But these questions matter more widely. Middle managers also have to understand the strategic direction of their organisations, both to know how to get top management support for their initiatives and to explain their organisation's strategy to the people they are responsible for. Anybody looking for a management-track job needs to be ready to discuss strategy with their potential employer. Indeed, anybody taking a job should first be confident that their new employer's strategy is actually viable. There are even specialist career opportunities in strategy, for example as a strategy consultant or as an in-house strategic planner, often key roles for fast-track young managers.

This book takes a broad approach to strategy, looking at both the economics of strategy and the people side of managing strategy in practice. It is a book about 'Exploring', because the real world of strategy rarely offers obvious answers. In strategy, it is typically important to explore several options, probing each one carefully before making choices. The book is also relevant to any kind of organisation responsible for its own direction into the future. Thus the book refers to large private-sector multinationals and small entrepreneurial start-ups; to public-sector organisations such as schools and hospitals; and to not-for-profits such as charities or sports clubs. Strategy matters to almost all organisations, and to everybody working in them.

(1.2) WHAT IS STRATEGY?[1]

In this book, **strategy is the long-term direction of an organisation**. Thus the long-term direction of Amazon is from book retailing to internet services in general. The long-term direction of Disney is from cartoons to diversified entertainment. This section examines the practical implication of this definition of strategy; distinguishes between different levels of strategy; and explains how to summarise an organisation's strategy in a 'strategy statement'.

1.2.1 Defining strategy

Defining strategy as the long-term direction of an organisation implies a more comprehensive view than some influential definitions. Figure 1.1 shows the strategy definitions of three leading strategy theorists: Alfred Chandler and Michael Porter, both from the Harvard Business School, and Henry Mintzberg, from McGill University, Canada. Each points to important but distinct elements of strategy. Chandler emphasises a logical flow from the determination of goals and objectives to the allocation of resources. Porter focuses on deliberate choices, difference and competition. On the other hand, Mintzberg uses the word 'pattern' to allow for the fact that strategies do not always follow a deliberately chosen and logical plan, but can emerge

Figure 1.1 Definitions of strategy

'the determination of the long-run goals and objectives of an enterprise and the adoption of courses of action and the allocation of resource necessary for carrying out these goals'

Alfred D. Chandler

'Competitive strategy is about being different. It means deliberately choosing a different set of activities to deliver a unique mix of value'

Michael Porter

'a pattern in a stream of decisions'

Henry Mintzberg

'the long-term direction of an organisation'

Exploring Strategy

Sources: A.D. Chandler, *Strategy and Structure: Chapters in the History of American Enterprise*, MIT Press, 1963, p. 13; M.E. Porter, What is Strategy?, *Harvard Business Review*, 1996, November–December, p. 60; H. Mintzberg, *Tracking Strategies: Towards a General Theory*, Oxford University Press, 2007, p. 3.

in more ad hoc ways. Sometimes strategies reflect a series of incremental decisions that only cohere into a recognisable pattern – or 'strategy' – after some time.

All of these strategy definitions incorporate important elements of strategy. However, this book's definition of strategy as 'the long-term direction of an organisation' has two advantages. First, the long-term direction of an organisation can include both deliberate, logical strategy and more incremental, emergent patterns of strategy. Second, long-term direction can include both strategies that emphasise difference and competition, and strategies that recognise the roles of cooperation and even imitation.

The three elements of this strategy definition – the long term, direction and organisation – can each be explored further. The strategy of Vice Media illustrates important points (see Illustration 1.1):

● *The long term*. Strategies are typically measured over years, for some organisations a decade or more. The importance of a long-term perspective on strategy is emphasised by the 'three-horizons' framework in Figure 1.2 (below). The three-horizons framework suggests **organisations should think of themselves as comprising three types of business or activity, defined by their 'horizons' in terms of years.** *Horizon 1* businesses are basically the current core activities. In the case of Vice Media, Horizon 1 includes the original *Vice* magazine. Horizon 1 businesses need defending and extending but the expectation is that in the long term they will likely be flat or declining in terms of profits (or whatever else the organisation values). *Horizon 2* businesses are emerging activities that should provide new sources of profit. For *Vice*, that might include the new China business. Finally, there are *Horizon 3* possibilities, for which nothing is sure. These are typically risky research and development

ILLUSTRATION 1.1

Vice pays

Beginning in 1994 as a government subsidised free 'zine' in Montreal, Vice Media now pursues an ambitious strategy of diversification and globalisation.

Vice Media is a global business, with a declared ambition to be the largest online media company in the world. But at its heart is still the original print magazine, *Vice*, specialising in fashion, music, lifestyle and current affairs. With a good deal of nudity, satire and violence, the magazine is regarded as edgy by some, puerile by others. An early spin-off book, *The Vice Guide to Sex, Drugs and Rock and Roll*, gives an idea of its market position. *Vice* magazine is paid for by advertising and distributed free via style-conscious clothing retailers.

However, since the late 1990s, the company has steadily diversified into a number of businesses, including clothing retail, web video, a record label, book publishing, live events, an advertising agency, television and film production, and even a London pub. By 2012, Vice Media was operating in 34 countries around the world. Revenues were approaching $200 m, with an estimated company value of around $1 bn (€750 m; £600 m).

The magazine had been started as a government work-creation scheme by three friends with no publishing experience, Suroosh Alvi, Gavin McInnes and Shane Smith. The magazine had originally been *The Voice of Montreal*, a newspaper for the local community. It soon drifted from its mission, and the three founders each borrowed $5,000 Canadian (€4,000; £3,000) to buy it out. It was said that the magazine got its title '*Vice*' because the *Village Voice* magazine of New York threatened to sue them over its name. True or not, *Vice* was a very good fit with the magazine's provocative content and style.

Outside investors were soon attracted to the magazine's strong connection with its youth audience. The first investor was the Normal Network, which in 1998 bought one quarter of the group for $1 m (US), implying a total value of $4 m. This injection of capital allowed *Vice* to move its base to New York and helped its diversification into clothing retail. When Normal Network went bust in 2000, another investor, Barrontech, stumped up more capital. In 2007, the media giant Viacom helped *Vice* into video. This partnership was said to have provoked the departure of co-founder Gavin McInness, distrustful of corporate constraints on creative freedom. In 2011, a consortium of external investors that included the world's largest advertising agency, WPP, injected a sum rumoured at between $50 and $100 m. These new funds helped launch *Vice* in China and India. New ventures were also envisaged in gaming and sports.

Co-founder Suroosh Alvi explained to the *Financial Times* the advantages to advertising partners of Vice Media's wide range of businesses and territories: 'Diversification of our media and pushing quality content through it on a global level has played massively for us. It's created a deep engagement with our audience and made a compelling story for brand partners as well, who are signing up platform-wide and doing international buy-ins. It's a bit better than publishing a magazine in a single territory.'

Vice's approach is informal, however. Another co-founder, Shane Smith, recalled the early days: 'We didn't have a business plan or any idea of what we were doing. We just loved magazines and loved making the magazine. And we didn't have anything else to do, so we kept doing it.' As for *Vice* today: 'It's a totally insane working environment. It's like an incestuous family. It's a weird culture and we love it. Keeping that culture is one of our big challenges going forward.'

Sources: National Post, 19 July 2000; Financial Times, 19 November 2009; Forbes, 1 January 2012.

Questions

1 How does Vice Media's strategy fit with the various strategy definitions of Alfred Chandler, Michael Porter and Henry Mintzberg (see Figure 1.1)?

2 What seems to account for Vice Media's success and is it sustainable?

Figure 1.2 Three horizons for strategy

Note: 'profit' on the vertical axis can be replaced by non-profit objectives; 'business' can refer to any set of activities; 'time' can refer to a varying number of years.

Source: M. Baghai, S. Coley and D. White, *The Alchemy of Growth*, Texere Publishers, 2000. Figure 1.1, p. 5.

projects, start-up ventures, test-market pilots or similar: at Vice Media, these might be the gaming and sports initiatives. For a fast-moving organisation like Vice Media, *Horizon 3* might generate profits only a couple of years from the present time. In a pharmaceutical company, where the R&D and regulatory processes for a new drug take many years, *Horizon 3* might be a decade ahead. While timescales might differ, the basic point about the 'three-horizons' framework is that managers need to avoid focusing on the short-term issues of their existing activities. Strategy involves pushing out Horizon 1 as far as possible, at the same time as looking to Horizons 2 and 3.

- *Strategic direction*. Over the years, strategies follow some kind of long-term direction or trajectory. The strategic direction of Vice Media is from the original print magazine to diversified youth media services. Sometimes a strategic direction only emerges as a coherent pattern over time. Typically, however, managers and entrepreneurs try to set the direction of their strategy according to long-term *objectives*. In private-sector businesses, the objective guiding strategic direction is usually maximising profits for shareholders. However, profits do not always set strategic direction. First, public-sector and charity organisations may set their strategic direction according to other objectives: for example, a sports club's objective may be to move up from one league to a higher one. Second, even in the private sector profit is not always the sole criterion for strategy. Thus family businesses may sometimes sacrifice the maximisation of profits for family objectives, for example passing down the management of the business to the next generation. The objectives behind strategic direction always need close scrutiny.

- *Organisation*. In this book, organisations are not treated as discrete, unified entities. Organisations involve complex relationships, both internally and externally. This is because organisations typically have many internal and external *stakeholders*, in other words people and groups that depend on the organisation and upon which the organisation itself depends. Internally, organisations are filled with people, typically with diverse, competing and more or less reasonable views of what should be done. At Vice Media, the three co-founders had clashed over corporate partnerships, leading to the departure of Gavin McInness. In strategy, therefore, it is always important to look *inside* organisations and to consider the people involved and their different interests and views. Externally, organisations are surrounded by important relationships, for example with suppliers, customers, alliance partners, regulators and investors. For Vice Media, relationships with investors and advertisers were crucial. Strategy therefore is also crucially concerned with an organisation's external *boundaries*: in other words, questions about what to include within the organisation and how to manage important relationships with what is kept outside.

Because strategy typically involves managing people, relationships and resources, the subject is sometimes called 'strategic management'. This book takes the view that managing is always important in strategy. Good strategy is about the practicalities of managing as well as the analysis of strategising.

1.2.2 Levels of strategy

Inside an organisation, strategies can exist at three main levels. Again they can be illustrated by reference to Vice Media (Illustration 1.1):

- **Corporate-level strategy is concerned with the overall scope of an organisation and how value is added to the constituent businesses of the organisational whole.** Corporate-level strategy issues include geographical scope, diversity of products or services, acquisitions of new businesses, and how resources are allocated between the different elements of the organisation. For Vice Media, diversifying from the original magazine into retail, publishing and video are corporate-level strategies. Being clear about corporate-level strategy is important: determining the range of businesses to include is the basis of other strategic decisions, such as acquisitions and alliances.

- **Business-level strategy is about how the individual businesses should compete in their particular markets** (for this reason, business-level strategy is often called 'competitive strategy'). These individual businesses might be standalone businesses, for instance entrepreneurial start-ups, or 'business units' within a larger corporation (as the magazine is within Vice Media). Business-level strategy typically concerns issues such as innovation, appropriate scale and response to competitors' moves. In the public sector, the equivalent of business-level strategy is decisions about how units (such as individual hospitals or schools) should provide best-value services. Where the businesses are units within a larger organisation, business-level strategies should clearly fit with corporate-level strategy.

- **Operational strategies are concerned with how the components of an organisation deliver effectively the corporate- and business-level strategies in terms of resources, processes and people.** For example, Vice Media had to keep raising external finance to fund its rapid growth: its operational strategy is partly geared to meeting investment needs. In most businesses, successful business strategies depend to a large extent on decisions that are taken, or activities that occur, at the operational level. Operational decisions need therefore to be closely linked to business-level strategy. They are vital to successful strategy implementation.

This need to link the corporate, business and operational levels underlines the importance of *integration* in strategy. Each level needs to be aligned with the others. The demands of integrating levels define an important characteristic of strategy: strategy is typically *complex*, requiring careful and sensitive management. Strategy is rarely simple.

1.2.3 Strategy statements

David Collis and Michael Rukstad[2] at the Harvard Business School argue that all entrepreneurs and managers should be able to summarise their organisation's strategy with a 'strategy statement'. **Strategy statements** should have three main themes: the fundamental *goals* (mission, vision or objectives) that the organisation seeks; the *scope* or domain of the organisation's activities; and the particular *advantages* or capabilities it has to deliver all of these. These various contributing elements of a strategy statement are explained as follows, with examples in Illustration 1.2:

- *Mission.* This relates to goals, and refers to the overriding purpose of the organisation. It is sometimes described in terms of the apparently simple but challenging question: '*what business are we in?*'. The mission statement helps keep managers focused on what is central to their strategy.

- *Vision.* This too relates to goals, and refers to the desired future state of the organisation. It is an aspiration which can help mobilise the energy and passion of organisational members. The vision statement, therefore, should answer the question: '*what do we want to achieve?*'.

- *Objectives.* These are more precise and ideally quantifiable statements of the organisation's goals over some period of time. Objectives might refer to profitability or market share targets for a private company, or to examination results in a school. Objectives introduce discipline to strategy. The question here is: '*what do we have to achieve in the coming period?*'.

- *Scope.* An organisation's scope or domain refers to three dimensions: customers or clients; geographical location; and extent of internal activities ('vertical integration'). For a university, scope questions are twofold: first, which academic departments to have (a business school, an engineering department and so on); second, which activities to do internally themselves (vertically integrate) and which to externalise to subcontractors (e.g. whether to manage campus restaurants in-house or to subcontract them).

- *Advantage.* This part of a strategy statement describes how the organisation will achieve the objectives it has set for itself in its chosen domain. In competitive environments, this refers to the *competitive* advantage: for example, how a particular company or sports club will achieve goals in the face of competition from other companies or clubs. In order to achieve a particular goal, the organisation needs to be better than others seeking the same goal. In the public sector, advantage might refer simply to the organisation's capability in general. But even public-sector organisations frequently need to show that their capabilities are not only adequate, but superior to other rival departments or perhaps to private-sector contractors.

Collis and Rukstad suggest that strategy statements covering goals, scope and advantage should be no more than 35 words long. Brevity keeps such statements focused on the essentials and makes them easy to remember and communicate. Thus for Vice Media, a strategy statement might be: 'to build the world's largest online media group, focused on youth and with competitive advantages in terms of the diversity and international range of our businesses and the strength of our relationships with key partners'. The strategy statement of American financial advisory firm Edward Jones is more specific: 'to grow to 17,000 financial advisers by 2012 by offering trusted and convenient face-to-face financial advice to conservative individual investors through a national network of one-financial adviser offices'. Of course, such strategy statements

ILLUSTRATION 1.2

Strategy statements

Both Samsung Electronics, the Korean telecommunications, computing and TV giant, and the University of Utrecht, a leading Dutch university, publish a good deal about their strategies.

Samsung Electronics

At Samsung, we follow a simple business philosophy: to devote our talent and technology to creating superior products and services that contribute to a better global society.

Every day, our people bring this philosophy to life. Our leaders search for the brightest talent from around the world, and give them the resources they need to be the best at what they do. The result is that all of our products – from memory chips that help businesses store vital knowledge to mobile phones that connect people across continents – have the power to enrich lives. And that's what making a better global society is all about.

As stated in its new motto, Samsung Electronics' vision . . . is, 'Inspire the World, Create the Future'. This new vision reflects Samsung Electronics' commitment to inspiring its communities by leveraging Samsung's three key strengths: 'New Technology', 'Innovative Products', and 'Creative Solutions'. As part of this vision, Samsung has mapped out a specific plan of reaching $400 billion in revenue and becoming one of the world's top five brands by 2020. To this end, Samsung has also established three strategic approaches in its management: 'Creativity', 'Partnership', and 'Talent'.

As we build on our previous accomplishments, we look forward to exploring new territories, including health, medicine, and biotechnology. Samsung is committed to being a creative leader in new markets and becoming a truly No. 1 business going forward.

Utrecht University, Strategic Plan 2012–16

The University's core mission is to: educate young people; train new generations of researchers; produce academics who have both specialist knowledge and professional skills; conduct groundbreaking research; and address social issues and work towards solving them.

Education targets

- Utrecht University will manage to retain third place in the top six of [Dutch] general research universities with the highest number of Bachelor's programmes rated good/excellent.
- The percentage of (permanent) lecturers with a basic teaching qualification will grow from 20 per cent in 1999 via 60 per cent in 2010 to a projected total of 80 per cent in 2016.
- By 2016, the number of scheduled contact hours and other structural education-related hours in . . . full-time Bachelor's programmes will total 12–18 hours per week.
- The percentage of students enrolled in entrepreneurship courses will increase from 1 per cent in 2006, via 3 per cent in 2010 to a projected total of 5 per cent in 2016.

Strengths	
A university-wide education model and a broadly supported educational culture.	A broad range of instruments for the professionalisation and assessment of teaching staff.
Innovative educational developments that are adopted by institutions around the country.	The largest Summer School in Europe, serving as a centre for internationalisation.

Sources: Edited extracts from www.samsung.com and the University of Utrecht Strategic Plan, 2012–16, www.uu.nl.

Questions

1 Construct short strategy statements covering the goals, scope and advantage of Samsung and the University of Utrecht. How much do the different private- and public-sector contexts matter?

2 Construct a strategy statement for your own organisation (university, sports club or employer). What implications might this statement have for your particular course or department?

are not always fulfilled. Circumstances may change in unexpected ways. In the meantime, however, they can provide a useful guide both to managers in their decision making and to employees and others who need to understand the direction in which the organisation is going. The ability to give a clear strategy statement is a good test of managerial competence in an organisation.

As such, strategy statements are relevant to a wide range of organisations. For example, a small entrepreneurial start-up can use a strategy statement to persuade investors and lenders of its viability. Public-sector organisations need strategy statements not only for themselves, but to reassure clients, funders and regulators that their priorities are the right ones. Voluntary organisations need persuasive strategy statements in order to inspire volunteers and donors. Thus, organisations of all kinds frequently publish materials relevant to such strategy statements on their websites or annual reports. Illustration 1.2 provides published materials on the strategies of two very different organisations: the technology giant Samsung from the private sector and the Dutch University of Utrecht from the public sector.

(1.3) THE *EXPLORING STRATEGY* MODEL

This book is structured around a three-part model that emphasises the interconnected nature of strategic issues. The *Exploring Strategy* Model includes understanding *the strategic position* of an organisation; assessing *strategic choices* for the future; and managing *strategy in action*. Figure 1.3 shows these elements and defines the broad coverage of this book. Together, the three elements provide a practical template for studying strategic situations. The following sections of this chapter will introduce the strategic issues that arise under each of these elements of the *Exploring Strategy* Model. But first it is important to understand why the model is drawn in this particular way.

Figure 1.3 could have shown the model's three elements in a linear sequence – first understanding the strategic position, then making strategic choices and finally turning strategy into action. Indeed, this logical sequence is implicit in the definition of strategy given by Alfred Chandler (Figure 1.1) and many other textbooks on strategy. However, as Henry Mintzberg recognises, in practice the elements of strategy do not always follow this linear sequence. Choices often have to be made before the position is fully understood. Sometimes, too, a proper understanding of the strategic position can only be built from the experience of trying a strategy out in action. The real-world feedback that comes from launching a new product is often far better at uncovering the true strategic position than remote analysis carried out in a strategic planning department at head office.

The interconnected circles of Figure 1.3 are designed to emphasise this potentially non-linear nature of strategy. Position, choices and action should be seen as closely related, and in practice none has priority over another. It is only for structural convenience that this book divides its subject matter into three sections; the book's sequence is not meant to suggest that the process of strategy must follow a logical series of distinct steps. The three circles are overlapping and interdependent. The evidence provided in later chapters will suggest that strategy rarely occurs in tidy ways and that it is better not to expect it to do so.

However, the *Exploring Strategy* Model does provide a comprehensive and integrated framework for analysing an organisation's position, considering the choices it has and putting strategies into action. Each of the chapters can be seen as asking fundamental strategy questions and

Figure 1.3 The *Exploring Strategy* Model

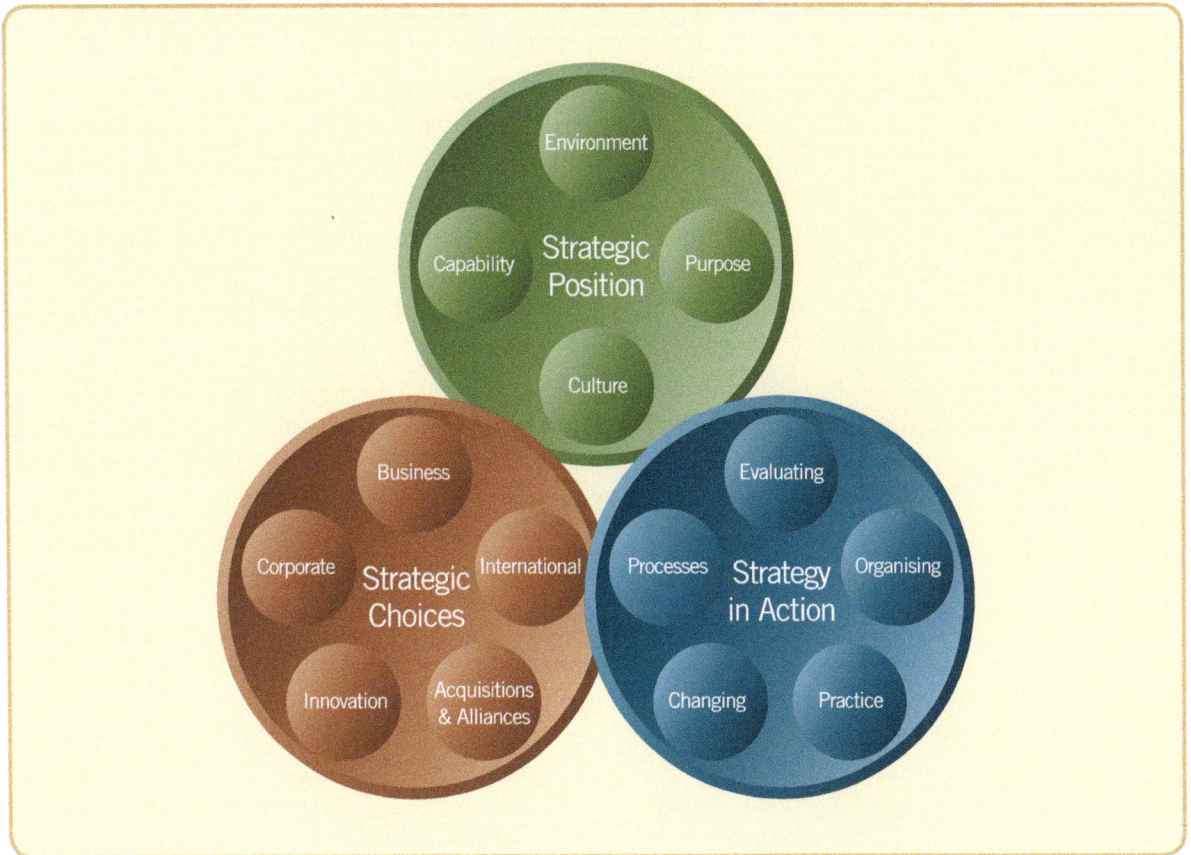

providing the essential concepts and techniques to help answer them. Working systematically through questions and answers provides the basis for persuasive strategy recommendations.

1.3.1 **Strategic position**

The strategic position is concerned with the impact on strategy of the external environment, the organisation's strategic capability (resources and competences), the organisation's goals and the organisation's culture. Understanding these four factors is central for evaluating future strategy. These issues, and the fundamental questions associated with them, are covered in the four chapters of Part I of this book:

- *Environment.* Organisations operate in a complex political, economic, social and technological world. These environments vary widely in terms of their dynamism and attractiveness. The fundamental question here relates to the *opportunities* and *threats* available to the organisation in this complex and changing environment. Chapter 2 provides key frameworks to help in focusing on priority issues in the face of environmental complexity and dynamism.

- *Strategic capability.* Each organisation has its own strategic capabilities, made up of its *resources* (e.g. machines and buildings) and *competences* (e.g. technical and managerial skills). The fundamental question on capability regards the organisation's *strengths* and *weaknesses* (e.g. where is it at a competitive advantage or disadvantage?). Are the organisation's capabilities adequate to the challenges of its environment and the demands of its goals? Chapter 3 provides tools and concepts for analysing such capabilities.

- *Strategic purpose.* Most organisations claim for themselves a particular purpose, as encapsulated in their *vision, mission* and *objectives*. But often this purpose is unclear, contested or unrealistic. The third fundamental question therefore is: what is the organisation's strategic purpose; what does it seek to achieve? Here the issue of *corporate governance* is important: how to ensure that managers stick to the agreed purpose? Questions of purpose and accountability raise issues of *corporate social responsibility* and *ethics*: is the purpose an appropriate one and are managers sticking to it? Chapter 4 provides concepts for addressing these issues of purpose.

- *Culture.* Organisational cultures can also influence strategy. So can the cultures of a particular industry or particular country. These cultures are typically a product of an organisation's *history*. The consequence of history and culture can be *strategic drift*, a failure to create necessary change. A fundamental question here, therefore, is: how does culture fit with the required strategy? Chapter 5 demonstrates how managers can analyse, challenge and sometimes turn to their advantage the various cultural influences on strategy.

The *Exploring Strategy* Model (Illustration 1.1) points to the following positioning issues for Vice Media. What is the future of *Vice* magazine given the environmental shift from print to internet media? Are its distinctive capabilities in youth media sustainable, given the ageing profiles of its two remaining founders? Is Vice Media's dedication to rapid growth funded by corporate partners consistent with the kind of creativity defended by departing co-founder Gavin McInness? Is the original 'weird' culture, as championed by Shane Smith, still a source of advantage, or is it now a constraint on what is fast becoming a diversified, global media conglomerate?

1.3.2 Strategic choices

Strategic choices involve the options for strategy in terms of both the *directions* in which strategy might move and the *methods* by which strategy might be pursued. For instance, an organisation might have a range of strategic directions open to it: the organisation could diversify into new products; it could enter new international markets; or it could transform its existing products and markets through radical innovation. These various directions could be pursued by different methods: the organisation could acquire a business already active in the product or market area; it could form alliances with relevant organisations that might help its new strategy; or it could try to pursue its strategies on its own. Typical strategic choices, and the related fundamental questions, are covered in the five chapters that make up Part II of this book, as follows:

- *Business strategy.* There are strategic choices in terms of how the organisation seeks to compete at the individual business level. For example, a business unit could choose to be the lowest cost competitor in a market, or the highest quality. The fundamental question here, then, is how should the business unit compete? Key dilemmas for business-level strategy, and ways of resolving them, are discussed in Chapter 6.

- *Corporate strategy and diversification.* The highest level of an organisation is typically concerned with issues of corporate scope; in other words, which businesses to include in the portfolio. This relates to the appropriate degree of *diversification*, with regard to products offered and markets served. Corporate-level strategy is also concerned both with internal relationships, both between business units and with the corporate head office. Chapter 7 provides tools for assessing diversification strategies and the appropriate relationships within the corporate portfolio.

- *International strategy.* Internationalisation is a form of diversification, but into new geographical markets. Here the fundamental question is: where internationally should the organisation compete? Chapter 8 examines how to prioritise various international options and key strategies for pursuing them.

- *Innovation and entrepreneurship.* Most existing organisations have to innovate constantly simply to survive. Entrepreneurship, the creation of a new enterprise, is an act of innovation too. A fundamental question, therefore, is whether the organisation is innovating appropriately. Chapter 9 considers key choices about innovation and entrepreneurship, and helps in selecting between them.

- *Acquisitions and alliances.* Organisations have to make choices about methods for pursuing their strategies. Many organisations prefer to build new businesses with their own resources. Other organisations develop by acquiring other businesses or forming alliances with complementary partners. The fundamental question in Chapter 10, therefore, is whether to buy another company, ally or to go it alone.

Again, issues of strategic choice are live in the case of Vice Media (Illustration 1.1). The *Exploring Strategy* Model asks the following kinds of questions here. Should Vice Media compete predominantly with cheap web video or move up market with film and TV? How far should it widen the scope of its businesses: does the London pub really belong in the portfolio? How should Vice Media manage its partnerships with the various corporate giants, already the cause of disputes over creativity? And should Vice Media be allowed to continue to innovate in its 'insane' free-wheeling style?

1.3.3 Strategy in action

Managing strategy in action **is about how strategies are formed and how they are implemented.** The emphasis is on the practicalities of managing. These issues are covered in the five chapters of Part III, and include the following, each with their own fundamental questions:

- *Strategy performance and evaluation.* Managers have to decide whether existing and forecast performance is satisfactory and then choose between options that might improve it. The fundamental evaluation questions are as follows: are the options *suitable* in terms of matching opportunities and threats; are they *acceptable* in the eyes of significant stakeholders; and are they *feasible* given the capabilities available? Chapter 11 introduces a range of financial and non-financial techniques for appraising performance and evaluating strategic options.

- *Strategy development processes.* Strategies are often developed through formal *planning* processes. But sometimes the strategies an organisation actually pursues are *emergent* – in other words, accumulated patterns of ad hoc decisions, bottom-up initiatives and rapid responses to the unanticipated. Given the scope for emergence, the fundamental question is: what kind of strategy process should an organisation have? Chapter 12 addresses the question of whether to plan strategy in detail or leave plenty of opportunities for emergence.

- *Organising.* Once a strategy is developed, the organisation needs to organise for successful implementation. Each strategy requires its own specific configuration of *structures* and *systems*. The fundamental question, therefore, is: what kinds of structures and systems are required for the chosen strategy? Chapter 13 introduces a range of structures and systems and provides frameworks for deciding between them.

- *Leadership and strategic change.* In a dynamic world, strategy inevitably involves change. Managing change involves *leadership*, both at the top of the organisation and lower down. There is not just one way of leading change, however: there are different *styles* and different *levers* for change. So the fundamental question is: how should the organisation manage necessary changes entailed by the strategy? Chapter 14 therefore examines options for managing change, and considers how to choose between them.

- *Strategy practice.* Inside the broad processes of strategy development and change is a lot of hard, detailed work. The fundamental question in managing this work is: who should do what in the strategy process? Chapter 15 thus provides guidance on which *people* to include in the process; what *activities* they should do; and which *methodologies* can help them do it. These kinds of practicalities are a fitting end to the book and essential equipment for those who will have to go out and participate in strategy work themselves.

With regard to strategy in action, the *Exploring Strategy* Model raises the following kinds of questions for Vice Media. Should the firm move towards a more disciplined strategy development process rather than continuing with the unplanned processes of the early years? Does the 'insane' environment of Vice Media need more structure and systems? How should the surviving co-founders lead any changes that may be necessary as Vice Media grows?

Thus the *Exploring Strategy* Model offers a comprehensive framework for analysing an organisation's position, considering alternative choices, and selecting and implementing strategies. In this sense, the fundamental questions in each chapter provide a comprehensive checklist for strategy. These fundamental questions are summed up in Table 1.1. Any

Table 1.1 The strategy checklist

Fourteen fundamental questions in strategy		
Strategic position	**Strategic choices**	**Strategy in action**
• What are the environmental opportunities and threats?	• How should business units compete?	• Are strategies suitable, acceptable and feasible?
• What are the organisation's strengths and weaknesses?	• Which businesses to include in a portfolio?	• What kind of strategy-making process is needed?
• What is the basic purpose of the organisation?	• Where should the organisation compete internationally?	• What are the required organisation structures and systems?
• How does culture fit the strategy?	• Is the organisation innovating appropriately?	• How should the organisation manage necessary changes?
	• Should the organisation buy other companies, ally or go it alone?	• Who should do what in the strategy process?

assessment of an organisation's strategy will benefit from asking these questions systematically. The frameworks for answering these and related questions can be found in the respective chapters.

The logic of the *Exploring Strategy* Model can be applied to our personal lives as much as to organisations. We all have to make decisions with long-run consequences for our futures and the issues involved are very similar. For example, in pursuing a career strategy, a job-seeker needs to understand the job market, evaluate their strengths and weaknesses, establish the range of job opportunities and decide what their career goals really are (positioning issues). The job-seeker then narrows down the options, makes some applications and finally gets an offer (choice issues). Once they have chosen a job, the job-seeker sets to work, adjusting their skills and behaviours to suit their new role (strategy in action). Just as in the non-linear, overlapping *Exploring Strategy* Model, experience of the job will frequently amend the original strategic goals. Putting a career strategy into action produces better understanding of strengths and weaknesses and frequently leads to the setting of new career goals.

(1.4) WORKING WITH STRATEGY

Strategy itself is a kind of work, and it is something that almost all levels of management have to engage in, not just top decision-makers. Middle and lower-level managers have to understand their organisation's strategic objectives and contribute to them as best they can. Managers have to communicate strategy to their teams, and will achieve greater performance from them the more convincing they are in doing so. Indeed, as responsibility is increasingly decentralised in many organisations, middle and lower-level managers play a growing part in shaping strategy themselves. Because they are closer to the daily realities of the business, lower-level managers can be a crucial source of ideas and feedback for senior management teams. Being able to participate in an organisation's 'strategic conversation' – engaging with senior managers on the big issues facing them – is therefore often part of what it takes to win promotion.[3]

For many managers, then, strategy is part of the job. However, there are specialist strategists as well, in both private and public sectors. Many large organisations have in-house strategic planning or analyst roles.[4] Typically requiring a formal business education of some sort, strategic planning is a potential career route for many readers of this book, especially after some operational experience. Strategy consulting has been a growth industry in the last few decades, with the original leading firms such as McKinsey & Co., the Boston Consulting Group and Bain joined now by more generalist consultants such as Accenture, IBM Consulting and PwC, each with its own strategy consulting arm.[5] Again, business graduates are in demand for strategy consulting roles.[6]

The interviews in Illustration 1.3 give some insights into the different kinds of strategy work that managers and strategy specialists can do. Galina, the manager of an international subsidiary, Masoud, working in a governmental strategy unit, and Chantal, a strategy consultant, all have different experiences of strategy, but there are some common themes also. All find strategy work stimulating and rewarding. The two specialists, Masoud and Chantal, talk more than Galina of analytical tools such as scenario analysis, sensitivity analysis and hypothesis testing. Galina discovered directly the practical challenges of real-world strategic planning, having to adapt the plan during the first few years in the United Kingdom. She emphasises the importance

ILLUSTRATION 1.3

Strategists

For Galina, Masoud and Chantal, strategy is a large part of their jobs.

Galina

After a start in marketing, Galina became managing director of the British subsidiary of a Russian information technology company at the age of 33. As well as developing the strategy for her local business, she has to interact regularly with the Moscow headquarters: 'Moscow is interested in the big picture, not just the details. They are interested in the future of the business.'

The original strategic plans for the subsidiary had had to be adapted heavily:

'When we first came here, we had some ideas about strategy, but soon found the reality was very different to the plans. The strategy was not completely wrong, but in the second stage we had to change it a lot: we had to change techniques and adapt to the market. Now we are in the third stage, where we have the basics and need to focus on trends, to get ahead and be in the right place at the right time.'

Galina works closely with her management team on strategy, taking them on an annual 'strategy away-day' (see Chapter 15): 'Getting people together helps them see the whole picture, rather than just the bits they are responsible for. It is good to put all their separate realities together.'

Galina is enthusiastic about working on strategy:

'I like strategy work, definitely. The most exciting thing is to think about where we have come from

and where we might be going. We started in a pub five years ago and we have somehow implemented what we were hoping for then. Strategy gives you a measure of success. It tells you how well you have done.'

Her advice is: 'Always have a strategy – have an ultimate idea in mind. But take feedback from the market and from your colleagues. Be ready to adjust the strategy: the adjustment is the most important.'

Masoud

Aged 27, Masoud is a policy advisor in a central government strategy unit in the United Kingdom. He provides analysis and advice for ministers, often on a cross-departmental basis. He typically works on projects for several months at a time, continuing to work with responsible service departments after the delivery of recommendations. Projects involve talking to experts inside and outside government, statistical analysis, scenario analyses (see Chapter 2), sensitivity analyses (see Chapter 11), hypothesis testing (see Chapter 15) and writing reports and making presentations. As he has progressed, Masoud has become increasingly involved in the management of strategy projects, rather than the basic analysis itself.

Masoud explains what he likes most about strategy work in government:'I like most the challenge. It's

of flexibility in strategy and the value of getting her managers to see the 'whole picture' through involving them in strategy making. But Masoud and Chantal too are concerned with much more than just analysis. Chantal emphasises the importance of gaining 'traction' with clients, building consensus in order to ensure implementation. Masoud likewise does not take implementation for granted, continuing to work with departments after the delivery of recommendations. He sees strategy and delivery as intimately connected, with people involved in delivery needing an understanding of strategy to be effective, and strategists needing to understand delivery. For him, strategy is a valuable stepping-stone in a career, something that will underpin his possible next move into a more operational role.

Strategy, therefore, is not just about abstract organisations: it is a kind of work that real people do. An important aim of this book is to equip readers to do this work better.

working on issues that really matter, and often it's what you are reading about in the newspapers. They are really tough issues; these are problems facing the whole of society.' He thinks people should get involved in strategy: 'I would encourage people to do strategy, because it gets to the heart of problems. In all organisations, having some experience of working on strategy is very valuable, even if it is not what you want to major on your whole career.'

Masoud is considering moving into service delivery as the next step of his career, because he sees knowledge of strategy and knowledge of operations as so interconnected: 'Part of doing strategy is you have to understand what can be delivered; and part of doing delivery is you have to understand the strategy.'

Chantal

Chantal is in her early thirties and has worked in Paris for one of the top three international strategy consultancies since graduating in business. Consulting was attractive to her originally because she liked the idea of helping organisations improve. She chose her particular consultancy because 'I had fun in the interview rounds and the people were inspiring. I pictured myself working with these kinds of topics and with these kinds of people.'

Chantal enjoys strategy consulting: 'What I like is solving problems. It's a bit like working on a mystery case: you have a problem and then you have to find a solution to fit the company, and help it grow and to be better.' The work is intellectually challenging:

'Time horizons are short. You have to solve your case in two to three months. There's lots of pressure. It pushes you and helps you to learn yourself. There are just three to four in a team, so you will make a significant contribution to the project even as a junior. You have a lot of autonomy and you're making a contribution right from the start, and at quite a high level.'

Consulting work can involve financial and market modelling (see Chapters 2 and 11), interviewing clients and customers, and working closely with the client's own teams. Chantal explains:

'As a consultant, you spend a lot of time in building solid fact-based arguments that will help clients make business decisions. But as well as the facts, you have to have the ability to get traction. People have to agree, so you have to build consensus, to make sure that recommendations are supported and acted on.'

Chantal summarises the appeal of strategy consulting: 'I enjoy the learning, at a very high speed. There's the opportunity to increase your skills. One year in consulting is like two years in a normal business.'

Source: Interviews (interviewees anonymised).

Questions

1 Which of these strategy roles appeals to you most – manager of a business unit in a multinational, in-house strategy specialist or strategy consultant? Why?

2 What would you have to do to get such a role?

(1.5) STUDYING STRATEGY

This book is both comprehensive and serious about strategy. To understand the full range of strategy issues – from analysis to action – it is important to be open to the perspectives and insights of key disciplines such as economics, sociology and psychology. To be serious about strategy means to draw as far as possible on rigorous research about these issues. This book aims for an evidence-based approach to strategy, hence the articles and books referenced at the end of each chapter.[7]

This book therefore covers equally the three main branches of strategy research: conventionally, these are known as strategy *context*, strategy *content* and strategy *process*. In terms of

Figure 1.4 Strategy's three branches

Context (internal and external)	Content (strategic options)	Process (formation and implementation)
Research: Industry analysis Cultural analysis Resource-based view	**Research:** Strategy and performance	**Research:** Strategic planning Choice and change Strategy-as-practice

the *Exploring Strategy* Model (Figure 1.3), context broadly relates to positioning, content to choice and process to action. Each of these branches contains various research streams whose lessons can be readily applied to practical questions of strategy issues. Figure 1.4 shows the three branches and their respective research streams: these are listed in the approximate historical order of their emergence as strong research streams, the arrows representing the continuously developing nature of each. In more detail, the three branches and the characteristic analytical approaches of their main research streams are as follows:

- *Strategy context* refers to both the internal and the external contexts of organisations. All organisations need to take into account the opportunities and threats of their external environments. *Industry analysis* took off as a research tradition in the early 1980s, when Michael Porter showed how the tools of economics could be applied to understanding what makes industries attractive (or unattractive) to operate in.[8] From the 1980s too, *cultural analysts* have used sociological insights into human behaviour to point to the importance of shared cultural understandings about appropriate ways of acting. In the internal context, cultural analysts show that strategies are often influenced by the organisation's specific culture. In the external context, they show how strategies often have to fit with the surrounding industry or national cultures. *Resource-based view* researchers focus on internal context, looking for the unique characteristics of each organisation.[9] According to the resource-based view, the economic analysis of market imperfections, the psychological analysis of perceptual or emotional biases, and the sociological analysis of organisational cultures should reveal the particular characteristics (resources) that contribute to an organisation's specific competitive advantages and disadvantages.

- *Strategy content* concerns the content (or nature) of different strategies and their probability of success. Here the focus is on the merits of different strategic options. *Strategy and Performance* researchers started by using economic analysis to understand the success of different types of diversification strategies. This research continues as the enduring central core of the strategy discipline, with an ever-growing list of issues addressed. For example, contemporary Strategy and Performance researchers examine various new innovation strategies, different kinds of internationalisation and all the complex kinds of alliance and networking strategies that organisations adopt today. These researchers typically bring a tough economic scrutiny to strategy options. Their aim is to establish which types of strategies pay best and under what conditions. They refuse to take for granted broad generalisations about what makes a good strategy.

● *Strategy process*, broadly conceived, examines how strategies are formed and implemented. Research here provides a range of insights to help managers in the practical processes of managing strategy.[10] From the 1960s, researchers in the *Strategic Planning* tradition have drawn from economics and management science in order to design rational and analytical systems for the planning and implementing of strategy. However, strategy involves people: since the 1980s, *Choice and Change* researchers have been pointing to how the psychology of human perception and emotions, and the sociology of group politics and interests, tend to undermine rational analysis.[11] The advice of these researchers is to accept the irrational, messy realities of organisations, and to work with them, rather than to try to impose textbook rationality. Finally, *Strategy-as-Practice* researchers have recently been using microsociological approaches to closely examine the human realities of formal and informal strategy processes.[12] This tradition focuses attention on how people do strategy work, and the importance of having the right tools and skills.

From the above, it should be clear that studying strategy involves perspectives and insights from a range of academic disciplines. Issues need to be 'explored' from different points of view. A strategy chosen purely on economic grounds can easily be undermined by psychological and sociological factors. On the other hand, a strategy that is chosen on the psychological grounds of emotional enthusiasm, or for sociological reasons of cultural acceptability, is liable to fail if not supported by favourable economics. As underlined by the four strategy lenses to be introduced later, one perspective is rarely enough for good strategy. A complete analysis will typically need the insights of economics, psychology and sociology.

(1.6) DOING STRATEGY DIFFERENTLY

So far we have stressed that strategic issues are typically complex, best explored from a number of points of views. There is no simple, universal rule for good strategy. This section introduces two ways of exploring strategy differently: one depending on context, the other depending on perspective.

1.6.1 Exploring strategy in different contexts

Although the basic elements of the *Exploring Strategy* Model are relevant in most circumstances, how they play out precisely is likely to differ according to organisational context. To return to Illustration 1.2, both Samsung and the University of Utrecht share some fundamental issues about how to compete and what activities they should have in their portfolio. However, for a Korean electronics company and a Dutch university, the role of the government, the freedom to choose and the ability to change all vary quite widely. In applying the *Exploring Strategy* Model, it is therefore useful to ask what kinds of issues are likely to be particularly significant in the specific context being considered. To illustrate this general point, this section shows how issues arising from the *Exploring Strategy* Model can vary in three important organisational contexts:

- *Small businesses.* With regard to positioning, small businesses will certainly need to attend closely to the environment, because they are so vulnerable to change. But, especially in small entrepreneurial and family businesses, the most important positioning issue will often be strategic purpose: this will not necessarily just be profit, but might include objectives such as independence, family control, handing over to the next generation and maybe even a pleasant lifestyle. The range of strategic choices is likely to be narrower: it is rare for a small business to make an acquisition itself, though small businesses may have to decide whether to allow themselves to be acquired by another business. Some issues of strategy in action will be different, for example strategic change processes will not involve the same challenges as for large, complex organisations.

- *Multinational corporations.* In this context, positioning in a complex global marketplace will be very important. Each significant geographical market may call for a separate analysis of the business environment. Likewise, operating in many different countries will raise positioning issues of culture: variations in national culture imply different demands in the marketplace and different managerial styles internally. Strategic choices are likely to be dominated by international strategy questions about which geographical markets to serve. The scale and geographical reach of most multinationals point to significant issues for strategy in action, particularly those of organisational structure and strategic change.

- *Public sector and not-for-profits.* Positioning issues of competitive advantage will be important even in these contexts, but have a different flavour. Charitable not-for-profits typically compete for funds from donors; public-sector organisations, such as schools and hospitals, often compete on measures such as quality or service. The positioning issue of purpose is likely to be very important too. In the absence of a clear, focused objective such as profit, purpose in the public sector and not-for-profits can be ambiguous and contentious. Strategic choice issues may be narrower than in the private sector: for example, there may be constraints on diversification. Strategy-in-action issues often need close attention, leadership and change typically being very challenging in large public-sector organisations.

In short, while drawing on the same basic principles, strategy analysis is likely to vary in focus across different contexts. As the next section will indicate, it is often helpful therefore to apply different lenses to strategy problems.

1.6.2 Exploring strategy through different 'strategy lenses'

Exploring means looking for new and different things. Exploring strategy involves searching for new angles on strategic problems. A comprehensive assessment of an organisation's strategy needs more than one perspective. We introduce 'the strategy lenses' as distinct, theoretically informed ways of thinking about strategy. **The strategy lenses are ways of looking at strategy issues differently in order to generate additional insights.** Looking at problems in different ways will raise new issues and new solutions. Thus, although the lenses are drawn from academic theory, they should also be highly practical in the job of doing strategy.

The four lenses are described fully at the end of Part I, after you have had a chance to take on board some key strategy frameworks for analysing strategic position. We shall return to them as well through brief *commentaries* at the end of Parts II and III. This section is therefore just a brief introduction to the lenses, as follows:

- *Strategy as design*. This takes the view that strategy development can be 'designed' in the abstract, as an architect might design a building using pens, rulers and paper. The architect designs, and then hands over the plans for the builders actually to build. Thus the design lens encourages a detached approach to planning and analysis, valuing hard facts and objectivity. It tends to exclude improvisation in strategy development and gives little credit to the unpredictable, conservative or political aspects of human organisations. Taking a design lens to a strategic problem means being systematic, analytical and logical.

- *Strategy as experience*. The experience lens recognises that the future strategy of an organisation is often heavily influenced by its experience and that of its managers. Here strategies are seen as driven not so much by clear-cut analysis as by the taken-for-granted assumptions and ways of doing things embedded in people's personal experience and the organisational culture. Strategy is likely to build on and continue what has gone on before. Strategic dilemmas will be resolved not simply through rational analysis, as in the design lens, but also by rules of thumb, appeals to precedent and standard fixes. The experience lens suggests that the biases and routines of key decision-makers need to be understood. It sets low expectations of radical change.

- *Strategy as variety*.[13] Neither of the above lenses is likely to uncover radical new ideas in strategy. Design approaches risk being too rigid and top-down; experience builds too much on the past. How then are radical new ideas discovered? The variety lens sees strategy not so much as planned from the top as emergent from within and around organisations as people respond to an uncertain and changing environment with a variety of initiatives. New ideas bubble up through unpredictable selection processes. The variety lens therefore emphasises the importance of promoting diversity in and around organisations, in order to allow the seeding of as many genuinely new ideas as possible. Somebody with a variety lens would look for future strategies at the bottom and the periphery of organisations. They should be ready for surprises.

- *Strategy as discourse*. Managers spend most of their time talking, persuading and negotiating. They are always using language, or what is here called 'discourse'. Adopting the discourse lens focuses attention on the ways managers use language to frame strategic problems, make strategy proposals, debate issues and then finally communicate strategic decisions. Strategy discourse becomes a tool for managers to shape 'objective' strategic analyses in their favour and to gain influence, power and legitimacy. For believers in the discourse lens, strategy 'talk' matters. The discourse lens tries to look under the surface of strategy to uncover the personal interests and politicking in organisations. Taking a discourse lens encourages a sceptical view.

None of these lenses is likely to offer a complete view of a strategic situation. The point of the lenses is to encourage the exploration of different perspectives: to look at the situation first from one point of view (perhaps design) and then from another. These lenses help in recognising how otherwise logical strategic initiatives might be held back by cultural experience; in checking for unexpected ideas from the bottom or the periphery of the organisation; and in seeing through the formal strategy discourse to ask whose interests are really being served.

SUMMARY

- Strategy is the *long-term direction* of an organisation. A *strategy statement* should cover the *goals* of an organisation, the *scope* of the organisation's activities and the *advantages* or *capabilities* the organisation brings to these goals and activities.

- *Corporate-level strategy* is concerned with an organisation's overall scope; *business-level strategy* is concerned with how to compete; and *operational strategy* is concerned with how corporate- and business-level strategies are actually delivered.

- The *Exploring Strategy*Model has three major elements: understanding the *strategic position*, making *strategic choices* for the future and managing *strategy in action*.

- Strategy work is done by *managers* throughout an organisation, as well as specialist *strategic planners* and *strategy consultants*.

- Research on strategy *context*, *content* and *process* shows how the analytical perspectives of economics, sociology and psychology can all provide practical insights for approaching strategy issues.

- Although the fundamentals of strategy may be similar, strategy varies by *organisational context*, for example small business, multinational or public sector.

- Strategic issues are best seen from a variety of perspectives, as exemplified by the four *strategy lenses* of *design*, *experience*, *variety* and *discourse*.

VIDEO ASSIGNMENTS

Visit **MyStrategyLab** and watch the British Heart Foundation case study for Chapter 1.

1 Refer to section 1.2.3 and Illustration 1.2 as a guide and use the video to help you write a strategy statement for the British Heart Foundation. Why is such a statement useful to the BHF?

2 Show how the *Exploring Strategy* Model (Figure 1.3) can be used to map key strategic management issues for the BHF. Identify the key challenges facing the BHF.

WORK ASSIGNMENTS

✱ *Denotes more advanced work assignments.*
* *Refers to a case study in the Text and Cases edition.*

1.1 Drawing on Illustration 1.2 as a guide, write a strategy statement for an organisation of your choice (e.g. the Glastonbury chapter case, or your university), drawing on strategy materials in the organisation's annual report or website.

1.2 Using the *Exploring Strategy* Model of Figure 1.3, map key issues relating to strategic position, strategic choices and strategy into action for the Lego case*, Glastonbury, or an organisation with which you are familiar (e.g. your university).

1.3 Go to the website of one of the major strategy consultants such as Bain, the Boston Consulting Group or McKinsey & Co. (see reference 5 below). What does the website tell you about the nature of strategy consulting work? Would you enjoy that work?

1.4✱ Using Figure 1.3 as a guide, show how the elements of strategic management differ in:

   (a) A small or family business (e.g. Adnams*, Feed Henry*, Leax* or Hotel du Vin*).

   (b) A large multinational business (e.g. Vodafone*, SABMiller*, Unilever*).

   (c) A non-profit organisation (e.g. AIDS Alliance*, GMB* or Queensland Rail*).

RECOMMENDED KEY READINGS

It is always useful to read around a topic. As well as the specific references below, we particularly highlight:

- Two stimulating overviews of strategic thinking in general, aimed particularly at practising managers, are C. Montgomery, *The Strategist: Be the Leader your Business Needs*, Harper Business, 2012; and R. Rumelt, *Good Strategy/Bad Strategy: the Difference and Why it Matters*, Crown Business, 2011.

- Two accessible articles on what strategy is, and might not be, are M. Porter, 'What is strategy?', *Harvard Business Review*, November–December 1996, pp. 61–78;

and F. Fréry, 'The fundamental dimensions of strategy', *MIT Sloan Management Review*, vol. 48, no. 1 (2006), pp. 71–5.

- For contemporary developments in strategy practice, business newspapers such as the *Financial Times*, *Les Echos* and the *Wall Street Journal* and business magazines such as *Business Week*, *The Economist*, *L'Expansion* and *Manager-Magazin*. Several of these have well-informed Asian editions. See also the websites of the leading strategy consulting firms: www.mckinsey.com; www.bcg.com; www.bain.com.

REFERENCES

1. The question 'What is strategy?' is discussed in R. Whittington, *What Is Strategy – and Does it Matter?*, International Thomson, 1993/2000; and M.E. Porter, 'What is strategy?', *Harvard Business Review*, November–December 1996, pp. 61–78.

2. D. Collis and M. Rukstad, 'Can you say what your strategy is?', *Harvard Business Review*, April 2008, pp. 63–73.

3. F. Westley, 'Middle managers and strategy: microdynamics of inclusion', *Strategic Management Journal*, vol. 11, no. 5 (1990), pp. 337–51.

4. For insights about in-house strategy roles, see D. Angwin, S. Paroutis and S. Mitson, 'Connecting up strategy: are strategy directors a missing link?', *California Management Review*, vol. 51, no. 3 (2009).

5. The major strategy consulting firms have a wealth of information on strategy careers and strategy in general: see www.mckinsey.com; www.bcg.com; www.bain.com.

6. University careers advisors can usually provide good advice on strategy consulting and strategic planning opportunities. See also www.vault.com.

7. For reviews of the contemporary state of strategy as a discipline, J. Mahoney and A. McGahan, 'The field of strategic management within the evolving science of strategic organisation', *Strategic Organisation*, vol. 5, no. 1 (2007), pp. 79–99; and R. Whittington, 'Big strategy/Small strategy', *Strategic Organisation*, vol. 10, no. 3, (2012), pp. 263–8.

8. See M.E. Porter, 'The five competitive forces that shape strategy', *Harvard Business Review*, January 2008, pp. 57–91.

9. The classic statement of the resource-based view is J. Barney, 'Firm resources and sustained competitive advantage', *Journal of Management*, vol. 17, no. 1 (1991), pp. 91–120.

10. A recent review of strategy process research is H. Sminia, 'Process research in strategy formation: theory, methodology and relevance', *International Journal of Management Reviews*, vol. 11, no. 1 (2009), pp. 97–122.

11. Psychological influences on strategy are explored in a special issue of the *Strategic Management Journal*, edited by T. Powell, D. Lovallo and S. Fox: 'Behavioural strategy', vol. 31, no. 13 (2011).

12. For a review of Strategy-as-Practice research, see E. Vaara and R. Whittington, 'Strategy-as-practice: taking social practices seriously', *Academy of Management Annals*, vol. 6, no. 1 (2012), pp. 285–336.

13. In earlier editions, this lens was called the 'ideas lens'.

Glastonbury: from hippy weekend to international festival

Steve Henderson, Leeds Metropolitan University

Following on from Woodstock in 1969, many have been inspired to create their own music festival. While some of these events have come and gone, the longevity and location of Fuji Rock Festival in Japan, Roskilde in Denmark, Coachella in the USA, Rock al Parque in Colombia illustrate the established international nature of this market (see Table 1). One of the longest established is Glastonbury Festival where, in 2013, the Rolling Stones were added to the long list of acts (from Paul McCartney to Oasis) that have appeared there. It started in 1970 when 1,500 hippy revellers paid £1 (€1.2; $1.5) for their ticket and gathered on a farm near Glastonbury Tor to be plied with free milk and entertainment from a makeshift stage. Now, Glastonbury is a major international festival that attracts over 150,000 attendees. Without any information about the performers, the 2013 festival tickets – priced at over £200 – sold out within a few hours.

In those early days, the vision was developed by local farmer, Michael Eavis, whose passion for music and social principles led to a weekend of music as a means of raising funds for good causes. It was a social mission rooted in the hippy counter-culture of the 1960s and events such as the Woodstock Festival. Today, the Glastonbury Festival attendee finds that those early days

Source: Neil Lupins/Redferns

of hippy idealism are a long way off. The scale of the organisation demands strong management to support the achievement of the festival's social aims.

At first, the statutory requirements for an event held on private land were minimal. Jovial policemen looked over hedges while recreational drugs were sold from tables near the festival entrance as if this was just a slightly unusual village fête. Needless to say, the festival began to attract the attention of a number of different groups, especially as legislation around the running of events tightened. Eavis struggled with local

Table 1 International music festivals

Festival	Country	Started	Estimated capacity[1]	2013 pricing
Woodstock	USA	1969	400,000	Price/free
Glastonbury	UK	1970	130,000	£205 (weekend)
Reading/Leeds Festival	UK	1971[2]/1999	162,000	£197.50 (weekend)
Roskilde	Denmark	1971	103,000	£195 (three days)
Rock am Ring/Rock im Park	Germany	1985/1993	150,000	£150 (weekend)
Rock al Parque	Colombia	1995	88,000	Free
Benicassim	Spain	1995	55,000	£150 (four days)
V Festival – Weston Park/Hylands Park	UK	1996	160,000	£185 (weekend)
Fuji Rock	Japan	1997	More than 100,000	£305 (three days)
Coachella	USA	1999	75,000	£220 (three days)
Peace & Love	Sweden	1999	22,000	£170 (five days)

[1] Based on daily capacity
[2] Existed from 1961 as a Jazz Festival

residents who hated the invasion of their privacy; with hippy activist groups whose contribution in helping at the festival gave them a sense of ownership; with drug dealers carrying on their activities on the fringes of the festival; and with fans climbing over the fences to get free access.

The continued expansion has resulted in a festival with over ten stages covering jazz, dance, classical, world music and other genres. Added to this, there is comedy, poetry, circus, theatre and children's entertainment alongside more esoteric street theatre performances. Much of this is organised into specific grassy field areas where, for example, the DanceVillage uses a number of tents dedicated to different types of dance music. Indeed, such is the range of entertainment on offer that some attendees spend the whole weekend at the festival without seeing a single live music act. Though the Eavis family remain involved with the main programme, much of the other entertainment is now managed by others. Reflecting this shift towards more diverse entertainment, the name of the festival was changed from Glastonbury Fayre (reflecting the ancient cultural heritage of the area) to the Glastonbury Festival for Contemporary Performing Arts.

In some years, like 2012, the festival is forced to take a year off to allow the farmland to recover from the trampling of thousands of pairs of feet. Not only is this wise for agricultural reasons but it also gives the local residents a rest from the annual invasion of festival goers. Despite this, the festival has met with a number of controversies such as when a large number of gatecrashers spoilt the fun in 2000. This caused the festival to be fined due to exceeding the licensed attendance and excessive noise. Furthermore, health and safety laws now impose on event management a 'duty of care' to everyone on the festival site. To address these health and safety concerns, support was sought from Melvin Benn who ran festivals for the Mean Fiddler events organiser. With a steel fence erected around the perimeter, Melvin Benn helped re-establish the festival in 2002 after a year off.

In 2006, Mean Fiddler was taken over and renamed Festival Republic by major music promoters, Live Nation and MCD Productions. In a worrying move, Live Nation announced that it would entice a number of major artists to appear on the weekend normally used by Glastonbury at a new festival called Wireless. Based in London, this seemed set to offer a city-based alternative to Glastonbury. Later, in 2010, Live Nation acquired Ticketmaster in a controversial move that extended its control over the ticketing of its own and other events.

This shift among the major music promoters indicated not only their interest in the ownership of key events but their desire to control income streams and the customer interface.

Elsewhere in the world of live entertainment, the success of Glastonbury had not gone unnoticed and the music festival market showed considerable growth. Some of the other festivals tried to capitalise on features that Glastonbury could not offer. For example, Glastonbury was famous for its wet weather with pictures of damp revellers and collapsed tents being commonplace. Live Nation's city-based Wireless Festival offered the opportunity to sleep under a roof at home or hotel, as opposed to risking the weather outdoors. Alternatively, Benicassim in southern Spain offered a festival with an excellent chance of sunshine and top acts for the price of a low-cost airline ticket. Other festivals noted that Glastonbury attendees enjoyed the wider entertainment at the event. In doing this, they realised that many festival goers were attracted by the whole social experience. So, sidestepping major acts and their related high fees, smaller festivals were created for just a few thousand attendees. These offered entertainment in various formats, often in a family-friendly atmosphere. Freddie Fellowes, organiser of the Secret Garden Party, describes this 'boutique' type of festival as a chance 'to be playful, to break down barriers between people and create an environment where you have perfect freedom and perfect nourishment, intellectually and visually'. Festival Republic, the rebranded Mean Fiddler, created a boutique festival on a larger scale with its Latitude Festival. Similarly, Rob da Bank, a BBC DJ, put together Bestival on The Isle of Wight where the attendees are encouraged to join in the fun by appearing in fancy dress. Quite clearly, audiences are now being presented with a wide range of festivals to consider for their leisure-time entertainment.

Many of these festivals attract sponsors with some becoming prominent by acquiring naming rights on the festival, e.g. the Virgin brand's support of V Festival. Others have low-profile arrangements involving so-called 'contra' deals as opposed to sponsorship payments. For example, Glastonbury has official cider suppliers who typically boost their brand by giving the festival a preferential deal on their products in exchange for publicity. Though these commercial relationships are sometimes spurned by the smaller festivals that see the branding as an intrusion on their social environment, larger festivals often need such relationships to survive. In order to attract sponsors, large festivals are turning to radio and television broadcasters as a means to expand the audience and offer wider exposure for the sponsor. Indeed, in 2011, the BBC sent around 250 staff members down to Glastonbury for broadcasting aimed at satisfying the interest of the armchair viewer/listener.

With such huge demand for their talents, artists can have a lucrative summer moving between festivals. Similarly, audiences can make lengthy treks to their favourite festivals. For some, this has caused environmental concerns with Glastonbury's rural location, poor transport links and large audience being cited as a specific problem. On the other hand, artists are not only finding that the festivals offer a good source of income but that private parties and corporate entertainment have emerged as alternative, often greater, income opportunities. One newspaper claimed that George Michael pocketed more than £1.5 m to entertain revellers at the British billionaire-retailer Sir Philip Green's 55th birthday party in the Maldives. Hence, for major artists, the summer has become a case of 'cherry picking' their favourite festivals or seeking out the most lucrative opportunities.

Over time, the shift from small, homespun event to corporate-controlled festival has provided awkward situations for Michael Eavis – from the difficulties with establishment politicians who felt the event was out of control to the demands of counter-cultural groups such as the travelling hippies. However, along the way, the festival has maintained its aim of supporting charities like CND and, later, Greenpeace, Oxfam and a number of local charities. In the mind of the audience, this helps position the festival as a fun event with a social conscience.

In recent years, Glastonbury has sold all its tickets and is relatively highly priced to many competitors (Figure 1). Indeed, since 1979, Glastonbury has been moving its prices up significantly faster than both inflation and the comparable Danish Roskilde Festival (see Case Example Figure 1). At the same time, it continues to make donations to favoured causes, confirming the financial viability of the current business model. Indeed, the festival's iconic status has helped it to become a rite of passage for many young music fans. Yet, in 2008, Eavis publicly registered concern over the ageing nature of the Glastonbury audience and announced that Jay-Z, an American rap artist, was to headline in order to help attract younger people. Reflecting on the 2008 festival, Michael Eavis displayed concerns over the future, saying: 'Last year I thought that maybe we'd got to the end and we'd have to bite the bullet and fold it all up. A lot of the bands were saying Glastonbury had become too big, too muddy and too horrible.'

Audiences and artists are the two key factors that underpin financial success at these events, as successful festival promoters are well aware. Despite the fact that Michael's daughter, Emily Eavis, and her husband were taking on more of the workload and Michael himself has become more of a figurehead for this event, these comments from the festival's founder highlight worries in key strategic areas that would be troubling for management. Others pointed to the strong relationships Live

Figure 1 Glastonbury ticket price trend, 1979–2013, relative to Roskilde festival prices and inflation (all rebased to 1979)

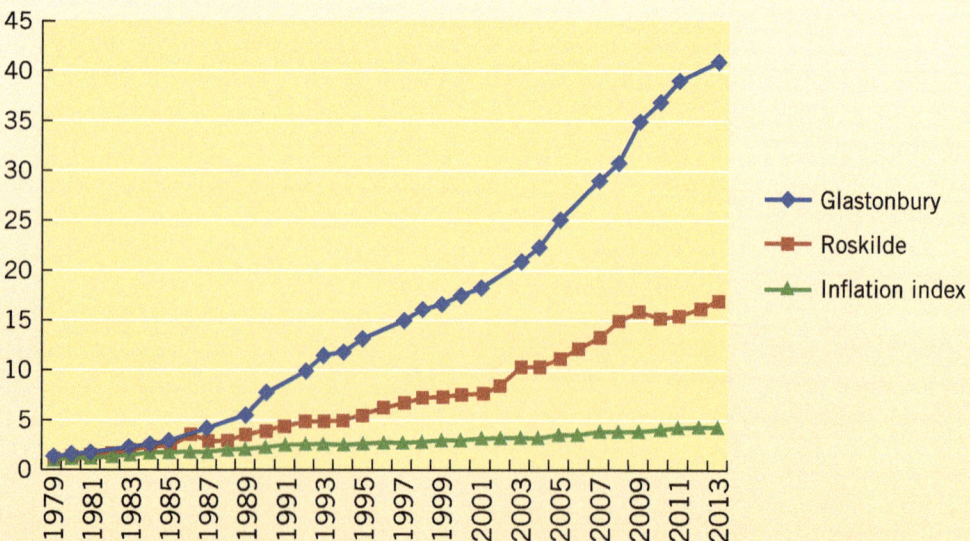

Nation were developing with artists via 360 degree deals that meant both parties would profit not only from live performances but from some combination of merchandise, publishing and recordings too. Both Jay-Z in 2008 and U2 who headlined in 2011 had such relationships and encouraged some observers to accuse the festival of adopting corporate elements that took them away from their core social image.

In 2012, the year of the London Olympics when Glastonbury took a break, Melvin Benn and Festival Republic amicably parted company with the festival. Citing the demands of expanding international festival responsibilities on Benn, the separation of the two seems aimed at re-establishing independence and removing some of the more recent corporate aspects to the festival. Thanking Melvin Benn for his efforts, the Eavis family find themselves firmly back in control and planning the way forward for this iconic festival in a market that is facing difficult recessionary times.

Sources: The history of Glastonbury is charted on the website, www.glastonburyfestivals.co.uk/history, while details of ownership and finances are available through Companies House; most of the background to the festival and related market has been drawn from online news resources such as the BBC, *Times Online*, *the Independent* and *the Guardian*, or industry magazines such as *Music Week*. See also: *Watchmojo: The History of the Glastonbury Festival*: https://www.youtube.com/watch?v=b2bXzuB7sZw.

Questions

1 Sticking to the 35 word limit suggested by Collis and Rukstad in section 1.2.3, what strategy statement would you propose for the Glastonbury Festival?

2 Carry out a 'three-horizons' analysis (section 1.2.1) of the Glastonbury Festival, in terms of both existing activities and possible future ones. How might this analysis affect its future strategic direction?

3 Using the headings of environment, strategic capability, strategic purpose and culture seen in section 1.3.1, identify key positioning issues for the Glastonbury Festival and consider their relative importance.

4 Following on from the previous questions and making use of section 1.3.2, what alternative strategies do you see for the Glastonbury Festival?

5 Converting good strategic thinking into action can be a challenge: examine how the Glastonbury Festival has achieved this by considering the elements seen in section 1.3.3?

PART I

THE STRATEGIC POSITION

This part explains:

- How to analyse an organisation's position in the external environment.

- How to analyse the determinants of strategic capability – resources, competences and the linkages between them.

- How to understand an organisation's purposes, taking into account corporate governance, stakeholder expectations and business ethics.

- How to address the role of history and culture in determining an organisation's position.

INTRODUCTION TO PART I

This part of the book is concerned with understanding the strategic position of the organisation. There are four chapters, organised around two themes. The first theme is the organisation's strategic *potential*, in other words, what it *can* do. The second theme is the organisation's strategic *ambitions*, what it actually *seeks* to do, sometimes deliberately and sometimes not so deliberately (see Figure I.1).

Strategic potential is addressed as follows:

- Chapter 2 considers how different environments can be more or less rich in opportunities or hostile, imposing threats and constraints.
- Chapter 3 considers how each organisation has its own particular strategic capabilities (resources and competences), and how these can enable or constrain strategies.

Organisational ambitions are addressed in the following two chapters:

- Chapter 4 is about ambition in terms of the organisation's fundamental purpose, often expressed in terms of vision and mission statements for example.
- Chapter 5 examines how an organisation's history and culture may shape the ambitions of an organisation, often in taken-for-granted and hard-to-change ways.

There is an important strategic dilemma that runs through Chapters 2 and 3. How much should managers concentrate their attention on the external market position and how much should they focus on developing their internal capabilities? On the external side, many argue that environmental factors are what matter most to success: strategy development should be primarily about seeking attractive opportunities in the marketplace. Those favouring a more internal approach, on the other hand, argue that an organisation's specific strategic capabilities should drive strategy. It is from these internal characteristics that distinctive strategies and superior performance can be built. There can be a real trade-off here. Managers who invest

Figure I.1 Strategic position

time and resources in developing their external market position (perhaps through acquiring companies that are potential competitors) have less time and resources to invest in managing their internal capabilities (e.g. building up research and development). The same applies in reverse. This trade-off between the internal and the external is discussed explicitly in Chapter 2's Key Debate at the end of that chapter.

Chapters 4 and 5 raise another underlying issue. To what extent should managers' ambitions for their organisations be considered as free or constrained? Chapter 4 explains how the expectations of investors, regulators, employees and customers can often influence strategy. Chapter 5 raises the constraints on managers exercised by organisational history and culture. Managers may be only partially aware of these kinds of constraints and are often in danger of underestimating the hidden limits to their ambitions.

Understanding the extent of managers' freedom to choose is fundamental to considering the issues of strategic choice that make up Part II of this book. But first Part I provides a foundation by exploring the question of strategic position.

2

THE ENVIRONMENT

Learning outcomes

After reading this chapter, you should be able to:

- Analyse the broad macro-environment of organisations in terms of political, economic, social, technological, ecological and legal factors (*PESTEL*).

- Construct alternative *scenarios* in order to address possible environmental changes.

- Use *Porter's five forces* analysis in order to define the attractiveness of industries and markets and to identify their potential for change.

- Analyse strategic and competitor positions in terms of *strategic groups*, *market segments* and '*Blue Oceans*'.

- Use these various concepts and techniques in order to recognise *threats* and *opportunities* in the marketplace.

Key terms

Blue Oceans p. 58

complementor p. 49

critical success factors p. 58

industry p. 41

market p. 41

market segment p. 56

PESTEL framework p. 34

Porter's Five Forces Framework p. 41

strategic groups p. 54

strategy canvas p. 58

value net p. 49

MyStrategyLab

MyStrategyLab is designed to help you make the most of your studies. Visit **www.pearsoned.co.uk/mystrategylab** to discover a wide range of resources, including:

- A personalised **Study plan** that will help you understand core concepts
- **Audio and video clips** that put the spotlight on strategy in the real world
- **Online glossaries and flashcards** that provide helpful reminders when you're looking for some quick revision.

$\left(2.1\right)$ INTRODUCTION

The environment is what gives organisations their means of survival. It creates opportunities and it presents threats. For example, the success of Facebook's platform created rich market opportunities for online games publishers such as Zynga. On the other hand, the rise of online encyclopaedias such as Wikipedia forced the traditional market-leader *Encyclopaedia Britannica* to cease publishing its print editions after nearly two-and-a-half centuries of production. Although the future can never be predicted perfectly, it is clearly important that entrepreneurs and managers try to analyse their environments as carefully as they can in order to anticipate and – if possible – influence environmental change.

This chapter therefore provides frameworks for analysing changing and complex environments. These frameworks are organised in a series of 'layers' briefly introduced here and summarised in Figure 2.1.

- *The macro-environment* is the highest-level layer. This consists of broad environmental factors that impact to a greater or lesser extent on almost all organisations. Here, the PESTEL framework can be used to identify how future issues in the *political, economic, social, technological, ecological and legal* environments might affect organisations. This PESTEL analysis provides the broad 'data' from which to identify *key drivers of change*. These key drivers can be used to construct *scenarios* of alternative possible futures.

- *Industry*, or *sector*, forms the next layer within this broad general environment. This is made up of organisations producing the same sorts of products or services. Here the *five forces*

Figure 2.1 Layers of the business environment

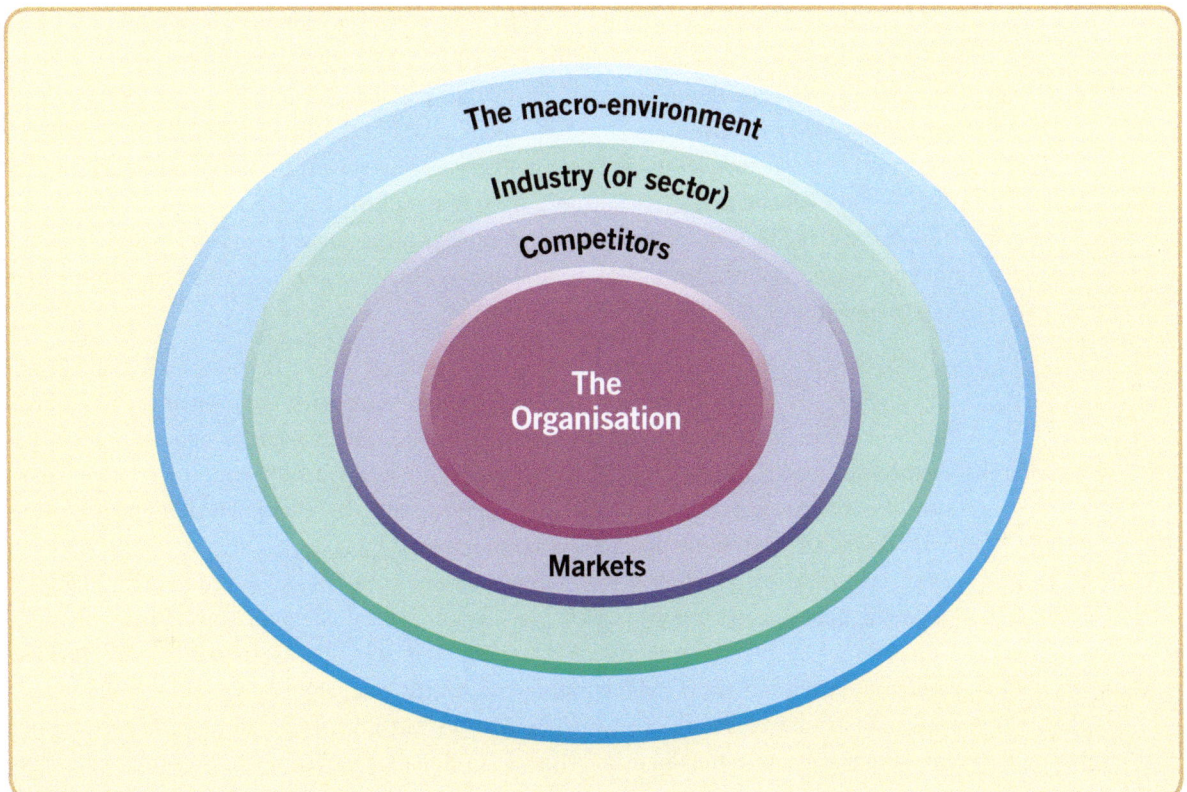

framework is particularly useful in understanding the attractiveness of particular industries or sectors and potential threats from outside the present set of competitors. The Key Debate at the end of this chapter addresses the importance of industry factors, rather than business-specific factors, in determining success.

● *Competitors and markets* are the most immediate layer surrounding organisations. Here the concept of *strategic groups* can help identify different kinds of competitors. Similarly, in the marketplace, customers' expectations are not all the same, which can be understood through the concept of *market segments*. Finally, competitors' relative positions can be analysed using the *strategy canvas*, helping also to identify 'Blue Ocean' opportunities in the marketplace.

This chapter works through these three layers in turn, starting with the macro-environment.

(2.2) THE MACRO-ENVIRONMENT

This section introduces two interrelated tools – PESTEL and scenarios – for analysing the broad macro-environment of an organisation. PESTEL provides a wide overview and scenarios build on this in order to consider how the macro-environment might change. Both PESTEL and scenarios, however, can be overwhelming in the amount of issues and possibilities that they uncover. So throughout this section we shall emphasise techniques and concepts that help focus the analysis on what is likely to matter most.

2.2.1 The PESTEL framework

The **PESTEL framework** is one of several frameworks (including the similar 'PEST' and 'STEEPLE' frameworks) which categorises environmental factors into key types.[1] PESTEL highlights six environmental factors in particular: political, economic, social, technological, ecological and legal. This range of factors underlines that the environment is not just about economic forces: there is an important *non-market* environment. Organisations needs to consider both market and non-market aspects of strategy (Illustration 2.1).[2]

In practice, political, economic, social, technological, ecological and legal factors are often interconnected. Nevertheless, going through each of the six PESTEL factors helps raise a wide range of potentially relevant issues, as follows:

● *Politics* highlights the role of the state and other political forces. The state is often important as a direct economic actor, for instance as potential customer, supplier or owner of businesses. But there are also influences from various political movements, campaign groups or concerned media. Figure 2.2 (p. 36) is a matrix that helps identify both the relative importance of the state as direct economic actor and exposure to other political influences. Thus the defence industry for instance of course faces highly involved states that are both customers and often owners of key companies, while also being exposed to political groups campaigning against the arms trade, for instance. Food companies are mostly privately owned and operate in private-sector markets, but are still be exposed to great political pressures from fair trade, labour rights and health campaigners. Canals are often state-owned but nowadays are not usually politically sensitive. Industries can rapidly change positions: thus after the financial crisis of 2008, banks moved towards both greater state ownership and increased political criticism.

ILLUSTRATION

ILLUSTRATION 2.1

Oil's troubled waters

In 2013, the controversial oil giant BP faced a complex environment.

BP is one of the world's largest oil and gas companies. It operates right across exploration, production, refining, distribution and marketing. It has about 21,000 service stations worldwide, half in the United States, 40 per cent in Europe. The largest sources of its oil production are Russia (about 45 per cent) and the USA (20 per cent); the USA accounts for about a quarter of its natural gas production and Russia about 10 per cent. Since 2005, BP has had a small alternative energy business, active in biofuels and windpower. In 2010, BP's Deepwater Horizon oil rig exploded, causing 11 deaths and an oil slick in the Gulf of Mexico covering 180,000 km^2. In 2012, the US government fined BP more than \$4 bn. (about £2.5 bn; €3 bn) for the disaster, and many court cases are still pending.

Some headline features of BP's environment include:

Political: More than 80 per cent of the world's oil reserves are owned by state-controlled enterprises, the largest being Saudi Aramco and the Iranian National Oil Company. In 2013, BP's oil business in Russia was transferred from a controversial alliance with a group of leading Russian businessmen to a partnership with Rosneft, the state-controlled Russian oil company, in which BP would hold 18 per cent of the shares.

Economic: *Forbes* magazine reports predictions of economic growth between 2012 and 2020 of 7 per cent per annum for China, about 2 per cent for the United States and 1 per cent for Europe. Oil prices peaked at about \$120 a barrel in 2008, before dropping to around \$30 as recession took hold in 2009, and recovering to around \$100 in 2012. New extractive technologies led natural gas prices in the USA to fall 30 per cent between 2011 and 2013.

Social: Car usage is falling in many European economies. After having doubled in the preceding 30 years, miles travelled in the United Kingdom by motor vehicles have fallen by about 1 per cent between 2008 and 2012; miles travelled by train reached a record in 2012, having increased by 50 per cent since the mid-1990s. From 2008 to 2012, the number of driving tests taken in the United Kingdom fell by about 17 per cent.

Technology: New technologies include the exploitation of 'fire ice' (gas hydrates under the sea) and 'fracking', the extraction of gas by fracturing underground rock to produce 'shale gas'. Fire ice might eventually equal 4,000 times all the natural gas consumed in the US in 2010; fracking offers the prospect of doubling the world's available natural gas supply by 2020.

Ecological: Fracking is liable to pollute local water supplies and even trigger small earthquakes. According to Cornell University, about 8 per cent of the gas extracted by fracking is released direct into the atmosphere, potentially a major contribution to global warming. In the USA, natural gas costs about \$50 per megawatt hour to produce; wave \$500; tidal \$450; biomass \$130; on-shore wind \$80.

Legal: The Deepwater Horizon disaster has led to new safety regulations for deepwater drilling. The European Union, where 90 per cent of oil extraction is from the sea, has imposed stricter exploration licensing procedures, risk assessment and financial guarantees against the costs of accidents. New regulations in the USA are estimated to increase costs by \$1.5 m per oil well. In 2012, the USA banned BP from tendering for all government contracts.

Sources: BP Annual Report, 2012; *Business Week*, 7 March 2013; *Forbes*, 26 March 2012.

Questions

1 Which of the above PESTEL factors offer the most important opportunities to BP, and which the most important threats?

2 Which of the above factors spill over from one PESTEL category to another? Does this matter?

Figure 2.2 The political environment

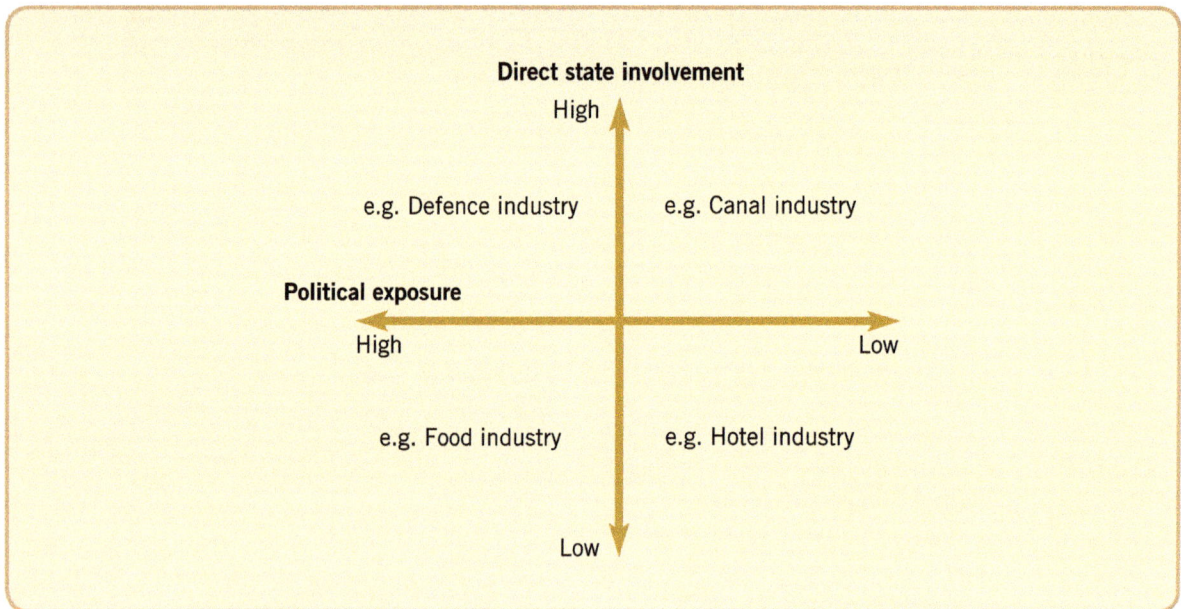

- *Economics* refers to macro-economic factors such as exchange rates, business cycles and differential economic growth rates around the world. It is important for a business to understand how its markets are affected by the prosperity of the economy as a whole. Managers should avoid over-confidence at the top of the business cycle, and excessive caution at the bottom. They should have a view on how changing exchange rates may affect viability in export markets and vulnerability to imports.

- *Social* influences include changing cultures and demographics. Thus, for example, the ageing populations in many Western societies create opportunities and threats for both private and public sectors. Changing cultural attitudes can also raise strategic challenges: for example, new ethical attitudes are challenging previously taken-for-granted strategies in the financial services industry.

- *Technological* influences refer to influences such as the internet, nano technology or the rise of new composite materials. As in the case of the internet in retailing, new technologies open up opportunities for some (e.g. Amazon), while challenging others (traditional stores).

- *Ecological* stands specifically for 'green' environmental issues, such as pollution, waste and climate change. Environmental regulations can impose additional costs, for example with pollution controls, but they can also be a source of opportunity, for example the new businesses that emerged around mobile phone recycling.

- *Legal* embraces legislative and regulatory constraints or changes. For example, legal changes might include restrictions on company mergers and acquisitions or new tax treatments of profits earned overseas. On the other hand, legal changes can provide opportunities, as for example the liberalisation of foreign investment in India.

As can be imagined, analysing these factors and their interrelationships can produce long and complex lists. Rather than getting overwhelmed by a multitude of details, it is necessary to step back eventually to identify the *key drivers for change*. Key drivers for change are the environmental factors likely to have a high impact on the future success or failure of strategy. Typical key drivers will vary by industry or sector. Thus a retailer may be primarily concerned with social changes driving customer tastes and behaviour, for example forces encouraging out-of-town shopping, and economic changes, for example rates of economic growth and employment. Public-sector managers are likely to be especially concerned with social change (e.g. rising youth unemployment), political change (e.g. changing government priorities) and legislative change (new training requirements). Identifying key drivers for change helps managers to focus on the PESTEL factors that are most important and which must be addressed most urgently. Without a clear sense of the key drivers for change, managers will not be able to take the decisions that allow for effective action.

Three concepts are useful for focusing on change while at the same time avoiding too much detail:

● *Megatrends* are large-scale social, economic, political, ecological or technological changes that are typically slow to form, but which influence many other activities and views, possibly over decades.[3] A megatrend typically shapes other trends. Thus the megatrend towards ageing populations in the West influences other trends in social care, retail spending and housing. The megatrend towards rapid economic growth in Asia drives employment patterns in the advanced economies and commodity prices worldwide. It is important to identify major megatrends because they influence so many other things.

● *Inflexion points* are moments when trends shift in direction, for instance turning sharply upwards or downwards.[4] For example, after decades of stagnation and worse, in the early twenty-first century sub-Saharan Africa may have reached an inflexion point in its economic growth, with the promise of substantial gains in the coming decade or so. Town-centre retailing may also have reached an inflexion point, where the rise of internet shopping and out-of-town retail parks has put urban shopping on a path to significant decline in advanced economies. Clearly it is valuable to grasp the inflexion point at the moment when trends just start to turn, in order either to take advantage of new opportunities early or to act against escalating decline as soon as possible.

● *Weak signals* are advanced signs of future trends and are particularly helpful in identifying inflexion points.[5] Typically these weak signals are unstructured and fragmented bits of information, often perceived by observers as 'weird'. A weak signal for the worldwide financial crisis that began in 2008 was the rise in mortgage failures in California the previous year. An early weak signal foreshadowing the current success of Asian business schools was the first entry of the Hong Kong University of Science and Technology into the Financial Times' ranking of the top 50 international business schools in the early 2000s. It is important to be alert to weak signals, but it is also easy to be overwhelmed by 'noise', the constant stream of isolated and random bits of information without strategic importance. Some signs of truly significant weak signals (as opposed to mere noise) include: the repetition of the signal and the emergence of some kind of pattern; vehement disagreement among experts about the signal's significance; and an unexpected failure in something that had previously worked very reliably.

2.2.2 Building scenarios

When the business environment has high levels of uncertainty arising from either complexity or rapid change (or both), it is impossible to develop a single view of how environmental influences might affect an organisation's strategies – indeed it would be dangerous to do so.

Scenario analyses are carried out to allow for different possibilities and help prevent managers from closing their minds to alternatives. Thus scenarios offer plausible alternative views of how the business environment might develop in the future.[6] Scenarios typically build on PESTEL analyses and key drivers for change, but do not offer a single forecast of how the environment will change. The point is not to predict, but to encourage managers to be alert to a range of possible futures. Effective scenario-building can help build strategies that are robust in the face of environmental change.

Illustration 2.2 shows an example of scenario planning for the global fashion industry to 2025. Rather than incorporating a multitude of factors, the authors focus on two key drivers which (i) have high potential impact; (ii) are uncertain; (iii) are largely independent from each other. These two drivers are the extent to which the world becomes more interconnected and the speed with which society, and fashion, changes. Both of these drivers may produce very different futures, which can be combined to create four internally consistent scenarios for the next decade and a half. The authors do not predict that one will prevail over the others, nor do they allocate relative probabilities. Prediction would close managers' minds to alternatives, while probabilities would imply a spurious kind of accuracy.

While there are many ways to carry out scenario analyses, five basic steps are often followed:[7]

- *Defining scenario scope* is an important first step. Scope refers to the subject of the scenario analysis and the time span. For example, scenario analyses can be carried out for a whole industry globally, or for particular geographical regions and markets. While businesses typically produce scenarios for industries or markets, governments often conduct scenario analyses for countries, regions or sectors (such as the future of healthcare or higher education). Scenario time spans can range from a decade or so (as in Illustration 2.2) or for just three to five years ahead. The appropriate time span is determined partly by the expected life of investments. In the energy business, where oil fields, for example, might have a life span of several decades, scenarios often cover 20 years or more.

- *Identifying the key drivers for change* comes next. Here PESTEL analysis can be used to uncover issues likely to have a major *impact* upon the future of the industry, region or market. In the fashion industry, key drivers range from demographics to technology. However, the scenario cube suggests two additional criteria are relevant (see Figure 2.3): *uncertainty*, in order to make different scenarios worthwhile; and *mutual independence*, so that the drivers are capable of producing significantly divergent or opposing outcomes. In the oil industry, for example, political stability in the oil-producing regions is one major uncertainty; another is the capacity to develop major new oil fields thanks to new extraction technologies. These could be selected as key drivers for scenario analysis because both are uncertain and regional stability is not closely correlated with technological advance.

- *Developing scenario 'stories'*: as in films, scenarios are basically stories. Having selected opposing key drivers for change, it is necessary to knit together plausible stories that incorporate both key drivers and other factors into a coherent whole. Thus in Illustration 2.2, the 'Techno-chic' scenario brings together in a consistent way a more global and integrated culture with a rapid rate of social, technological and economic change. But completing the story of 'Techno-chic' would also involve incorporating other consistent factors: for example, rapid development in China and India where low cost becomes supplanted by technological sophistication as source of advantage; free markets to allow rapid growth and international trade; and the creation of an under-class whose cheap labour and outdated technological skills are no longer needed.

Figure 2.3 The scenario cube: selection matrix for scenario key drivers

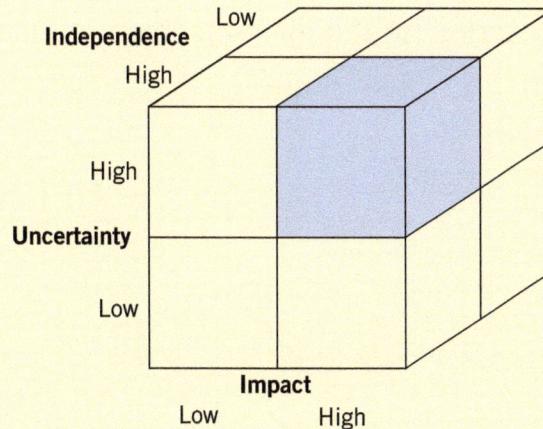

Select key drivers in the high-impact, high-uncertainty, high-independence box

- *Identifying impacts* of alternative scenarios on organisations is the next key stage of scenario building. 'Techno-chic' might have a very negative impact for many traditional fashion labels and retailers who could not keep up with hi-tech clothing and distribution. On the other hand, 'Community couture' could see the strengthening of local craft producers. It is important for an organisation to carry out *robustness checks* in the face of each plausible scenario and to develop *contingency plans* in case they happen.

- *Establishing early warning systems*: once the various scenarios are drawn up, organisations should identify indicators that might give early warning about the final direction of environmental change, and at the same time set up systems to monitor these. Effective monitoring of well-chosen indicators should facilitate prompt and appropriate responses. In Illustration 2.2, indicators of a 'Slow is beautiful' trend might be low wage growth and rises in religious observance.

Because debating and learning are so valuable in the scenario-building process, and they deal with such high uncertainty, some scenario experts advise managers to avoid producing just three scenarios. Three scenarios tend to fall into a range of 'optimistic', 'middling' and 'pessimistic'. Managers naturally focus on the middling scenario and neglect the other two, reducing the amount of organisational learning and contingency planning. It is therefore typically better to have two or four scenarios, avoiding an easy mid-point. It does not matter if the scenarios do not come to pass: the value lies in the process of exploration and contingency planning that the scenarios set off.

ILLUSTRATION 2.2

Scenarios for the global fashion industry, 2025

Levis uses students to investigate alternative futures.

During 2009–10, the clothing company Levi Strauss & Co., known worldwide for its jeans, worked with Masters students at the London College of Fashion to produce four scenarios for the global fashion industry in the coming 15 years. Levi Strauss knew that fashion was facing massive changes in fabric technologies, manufacturing locations, retailing and much more. It wanted to understand what kinds of futures it might have to deal with.

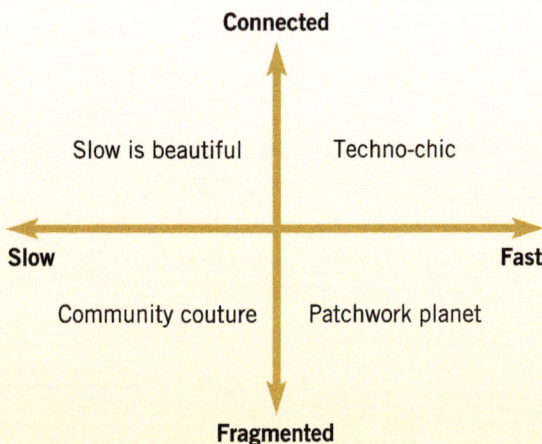

The students identified many important drivers that could simply be taken for granted: for instance, an ageing population and increasing natural resource constraints. However, they highlighted two key drivers that involved high uncertainty and that were largely independent of each other, and so could create divergent scenarios: interconnectivity and speed of change. The first driver offers two extreme points: on the one hand, a highly connected world with low trade barriers, integrated communications internationally and a homogenisation of cultures; on the other hand, a fragmented world with falling long-distance trade and strengthening regional identities. The second driver offers a range between fast change

and slow change: a fast world would be one in which media and communications are increasingly instant, capital moves easily and people live hectic lives; a slow world would imply less emphasis on consumption and more conservatism in cultures.

The divergent directions of the two key drivers define four scenarios for 2025. The first is 'Slow is beautiful', based on a slow world with high interconnectivity. In this scenario, durability and sustainability would be highly important, but interconnectivity would allow people to swap and refurbish old clothes very easily: 'vBay' (like eBay) would emerge as a hugely popular website dedicated to vintage clothing. The second scenario, 'Community couture', would also be slow because of growing resource constraints, climate change and poverty, while political barriers would reduce interconnectivity in the form of international trade: new, fashionable clothes would only be for the privileged. 'Techno-chic' on the other hand would be the product of a fast-paced interconnected world: clothes would be 'smart', changing colour, carrying embedded media and even controlling bodily health. Pharmaceutical companies could be in the clothing business. Finally, the 'Patchwork planet' scenario imagines low interconnectivity but rapid change. In a 'Patchwork planet', fast-growing emerging economies would be culturally confident, so that national rather than global fashions would prevail: Western clothes might even be banned in some countries.

Source: http://www.forumforthefuture.org/project/fashion-futures-2025/overview.

Questions

1 Which scenario would Levi Strauss most desire and which would it most fear?

2 What are the implications of these fashion industry scenarios for other industries, for example hotels or retail?

(2.3) INDUSTRIES AND SECTORS

The previous section looked at how forces in the macro-environment might influence the success or failure of an organisation's strategies. But the impact of these general factors tends to surface in the more immediate environment through changes in the competitive forces surrounding organisations. An important aspect of this for most organisations will be competition within their industry, sector or market. **An industry is a group of firms producing products and services that are essentially the same.**[8] Examples are the automobile industry and the airline industry. Industries are also often described as 'sectors', especially in public services (e.g. the health sector or the education sector). Industries and sectors are often made up of several specific markets. **A market is a group of customers for specific products or services that are essentially the same (e.g. a particular geographical market).** Thus the automobile industry has markets in North America, Europe and Asia, for example.

This section concentrates on industry analysis, starting with Michael Porter's *five forces framework* and then introducing techniques for analysing the *dynamics* of industries. However, while the following section will address markets in more detail, this section will refer to markets and most of the concepts apply similarly to markets and industries.

2.3.1 Competitive forces – the Five Forces Framework

Industries vary widely in terms of their attractiveness, as measured by how easy it is for participating firms to earn high profits. One key determinant of profitability is the extent of competition, actual or potential. Where competition is low, and there is little threat of new competitors, participating firms should normally expect good profits.

Porter's Five Forces Framework[9] **helps identify the attractiveness of an industry in terms of five competitive forces: (i) threat of entry, (ii) threat of substitutes, (iii) power of buyers, (iv) power of suppliers and (v) extent of rivalry between competitors.** These five forces together constitute an industry's 'structure' (see Figure 2.4), which is typically fairly stable. For Porter, an attractive industry structure is one that offers good profit potential. His essential message is that where the five forces are high, industries are not attractive to compete in. Excessive competitive rivalry, powerful buyers and suppliers and the threat of substitutes or new entrants will all combine to squeeze profitability.

Although initially developed with businesses in mind, the five forces framework is relevant to most organisations. It can provide a useful starting point for strategic analysis even where profit criteria may not apply. In the public sector, it is important to understand how powerful suppliers can push up costs; among charities, it is important to avoid excessive rivalry within the same market. Moreover, once the degree of industry attractiveness has been understood, the five forces can help set an agenda for action on the various critical issues that they identify: for example, what can competitors do to control excessive rivalry in a particular industry? The rest of this section introduces each of the five forces in more detail. Illustration 2.3 on the evolving steel industry provides examples.

Competitive rivalry

At the centre of five forces analysis is the rivalry between the existing players – 'incumbents' in an industry. The more competitive rivalry there is, the worse it is for incumbents. *Competitive rivals* are organisations with similar products and services aimed at the same customer group

Figure 2.4 The Five Forces Framework

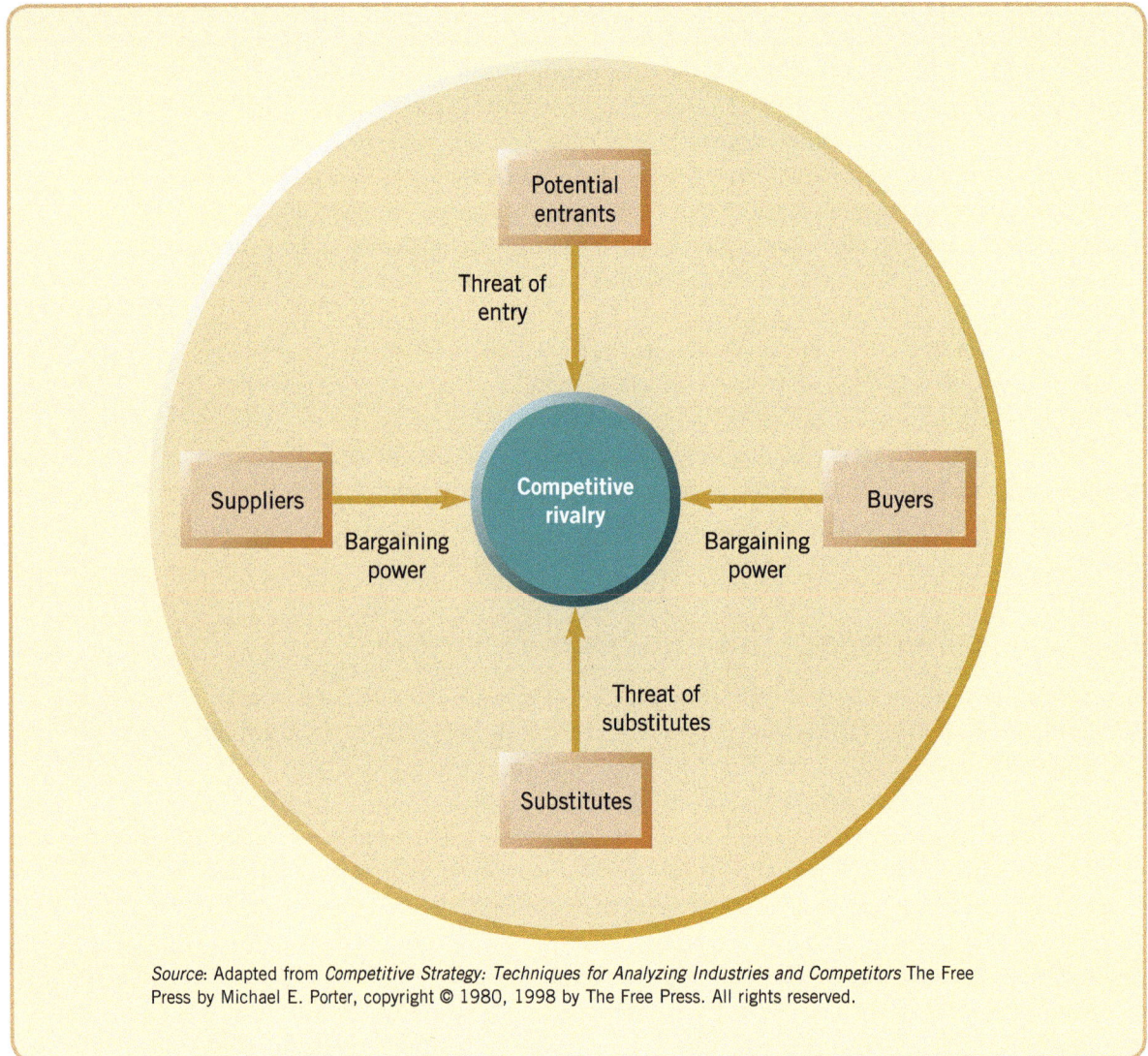

(i.e. not substitutes). In the European airline industry, Air France and British Airways are rivals; high-speed trains are a 'substitute' (see below). Five factors tend to define the extent of rivalry in an industry or market:

- *Competitor balance.* Where competitors are of roughly equal size there is the danger of intensely rivalrous behaviour as one competitor attempts to gain dominance over others, through aggressive price cuts for example. Conversely, less rivalrous industries tend to have one or two dominant organisations, with the smaller players reluctant to challenge the larger ones directly (e.g. by focusing on niches to avoid the 'attention' of the dominant companies).

- *Industry growth rate.* In situations of strong growth, an organisation can grow with the market, but in situations of low growth or decline, any growth is likely to be at the expense of a rival, and meet with fierce resistance. Low-growth markets are therefore often

ILLUSTRATION 2.3

The consolidating steel industry

Five forces analysis helps understand the attractiveness of an industry.

For a long time, the steel industry was seen as a static and unprofitable one. Producers were nationally based, often state-owned and frequently unprofitable – the early 2000s saw 50 independent steel producers going into bankruptcy in the USA alone. But there then followed a surge in confidence. During 2006, Mittal Steel paid $35 bn (€24.5 bn) to buy European steel giant Arcelor, creating the world's largest steel company. The following year, Indian conglomerate Tata bought Anglo-Dutch steel company Corus for $13 bn. But these acquisitions were made just before the onset of the Great Recession in 2008 and further turmoil in the world steel industry.

New entrants

In the last two decades, China has become a major force in the world steel industry. Between the early 1990s and 2011, Chinese producers increased their capacity seven times. Although the Chinese share of world production reached over 45 per cent by 2011, most of this was directed at the domestic market. None the less, China was the word's largest steel exporter in 2011, and there were fears that any slowdown in domestic demand would lead to a surge into international markets. The Chinese companies Herbei and Baosteel are ranked number two and number three in the world.

Substitutes

Steel is a nineteenth-century technology, increasingly substituted for by other materials such as aluminium in cars, plastics and aluminium in packaging and ceramics and composites in many high-tech applications. Steel's own technological advances sometimes work to reduce need: thus steel cans have become about one third thinner over the last few decades.

Buyer power

The major buyers of steel are the global car manufacturers. Car manufacturers are sophisticated users, often leading in the technological development of their materials. In North America at least, the decline of the once dominant 'Big Three' – General Motors, Ford and Chrysler – has meant many new domestic buyers, with companies such as Toyota, Nissan, Honda and BMW establishing local production plants. Another important user of steel is the metal packaging industry. Leading can producers such as Crown Holdings, which makes one third of all food cans produced in North America and Europe, buy in large volumes, coordinating purchases around the world.

Supplier power

The key raw material for steel producers is iron ore. The big three ore producers – Vale, Rio Tinto and BHP Billiton – control about 70 per cent of the market for internationally traded ore. Iron ore prices had multiplied four times between 2005 and 2008, and, despite the recession, were still twice 2005's level in 2012.

Competitive rivalry

World steel production increased by about 50 per cent between 2000 and 2008, dropped about 10 per cent in 2009, before recovering to reach a record in 2012. Despite acquisitions by companies such as Mittal and Tata, the industry is fragmented. The top five producers still accounted for only 17 per cent of world production in 2012, up only 3 per cent since 2000. The world's largest company, ArcelorMittal, accounted for just 7 per cent of production. Over-capacity in the European steel industry was estimated at 25 per cent in 2012, but when ArcelorMittal tried to close down its Florange plant, the French government threatened to nationalise it. After a cyclical peak in 2008, the world steel price was down 40 per cent by 2012, basically the same as in 2005.

Questions

1 How attractive is the world steel industry? What accounts for this?

2 In the future, what might change to make the steel industry less attractive or more attractive?

associated with price competition and low profitability. The *industry life cycle* influences growth rates, and hence competitive conditions: see section 2.3.2.

- *High fixed costs*. Industries with high fixed costs, perhaps because they require high investments in capital equipment or initial research, tend to be highly rivalrous. Companies will seek to spread their costs (i.e. reduce unit costs) by increasing their volumes: to do so, they typically cut their prices, prompting competitors to do the same and thereby triggering price wars in which everyone in the industry suffers. Similarly, if extra capacity can only be added in large increments (as in many manufacturing sectors, for example a chemical or glass factory), the competitor making such an addition is likely to create short-term over-capacity in the industry, leading to increased competition to use capacity.

- *High exit barriers*. The existence of high barriers to exit – in other words, closure or disinvestment – tends to increase rivalry, especially in declining industries. Excess capacity persists and consequently incumbents fight to maintain market share. Exit barriers might be high for a variety of reasons: for example, high redundancy costs or high investment in specific assets such as plant and equipment which others would not buy.

- *Low differentiation*. In a commodity market, where products or services are poorly differentiated, rivalry is increased because there is little to stop customers switching between competitors and the only way to compete is on price.

The threat of entry

How easy it is to enter the industry influences the degree of competition. The greater the threat of entry, the worse it is for incumbents in an industry. An attractive industry has high barriers to entry in order to reduce the threat of new competitors. *Barriers to entry* are the factors that need to be overcome by new entrants if they are to compete in an industry. Five important entry barriers are:

- *Scale and experience*. In some industries, *economies of scale* are extremely important: for example, in the production of automobiles or the advertising of fast-moving consumer goods. Once incumbents have reached large-scale production, it will be very expensive for new entrants to match them and until they reach a similar volume they will have higher unit costs. This scale effect is increased where there are high *investment requirements* for entry, for example research costs in pharmaceuticals or capital equipment costs in automobiles. Barriers to entry also come from *experience curve* effects that give incumbents a cost advantage because they have learnt how to do things more efficiently than an inexperienced new entrant could possibly do (see section 6.3.1). Until the new entrant has built up equivalent experience over time, it will tend to produce at higher cost.

- *Access to supply or distribution channels*. In many industries manufacturers have had control over supply and/or distribution channels. Sometimes this has been through direct ownership (vertical integration), sometimes just through customer or supplier loyalty. In some industries this barrier has been overcome by new entrants who have bypassed retail distributors and sold directly to consumers through e-commerce (e.g. Dell Computers and Amazon).

- *Expected retaliation*. If an organisation considering entering an industry believes that the retaliation of an existing firm will be so great as to prevent entry, or mean that entry would be too costly, this is also a barrier. Retaliation could take the form of a price war or a marketing blitz. Just the knowledge that incumbents are prepared to retaliate is often sufficiently discouraging to act as a barrier.

● *Legislation or government action*. Legal restraints on new entry vary from patent protection (e.g. pharmaceuticals), to regulation of markets (e.g. pension selling), through to direct government action (e.g. tariffs). Of course, organisations are vulnerable to new entrants if governments remove such protection, as has happened with deregulation of the airline industry.

● *Differentiation*. Differentiation means providing a product or service with higher perceived value than the competition; its importance will be discussed more fully in section 6.3.2. Cars are differentiated, for example, by quality and branding. Steel, by contrast, is by and large a commodity, undifferentiated and therefore sold by the tonne. Steel buyers will simply buy the cheapest. Differentiation reduces the threat of entry because of increasing customer loyalty.

The threat of substitutes

Substitutes are products or services that offer a similar benefit to an industry's products or services, but have a different nature. For example, aluminium is a substitute for steel; a tablet computer is a substitute for a laptop; charities can be substitutes for public services. Managers often focus on their competitors in their own industry, and neglect the threat posed by substitutes. Substitutes can reduce demand for a particular type of product as customers switch to alternatives – even to the extent that this type of product or service becomes obsolete. However, there does not have to be much actual switching for the substitute threat to have an effect. The simple risk of substitution puts a cap on the prices that can be charged in an industry. Thus, although Eurostar has no direct competitors in terms of train services from Paris to London, the prices it can charge are ultimately limited by the cost of flights between the two cities.

There are two important points to bear in mind about substitutes:

● *The price/performance ratio* is critical to substitution threats. A substitute is still an effective threat even if more expensive, so long as it offers performance advantages that customers value. Thus aluminium is more expensive than steel, but its relative lightness and its resistance to corrosion give it an advantage in some automobile manufacturing applications. It is the ratio of price to performance that matters, rather than simple price.

● *Extra-industry effects* are the core of the substitution concept. Substitutes come from outside the incumbents' industry and should not be confused with competitors' threats from within the industry. The value of the substitution concept is to force managers to look outside their own industry to consider more distant threats and constraints. The higher the threat of substitution, the less attractive the industry is likely to be.

The power of buyers

Buyers are the organisation's immediate customers, not necessarily the ultimate consumers. If buyers are powerful, then they can demand cheap prices or product or service improvements liable to reduce profits.

Buyer power is likely to be high when some of the following three conditions prevail:

● *Concentrated buyers*. Where a few large customers account for the majority of sales, buyer power is increased. This is the case on items such as milk in the grocery sector in many European countries, where just a few retailers dominate the market. If a product or service accounts for a high percentage of the buyers' total purchases their power is also likely to increase as they are more likely to 'shop around' to get the best price and therefore 'squeeze' suppliers more than they would for more trivial purchases.

- *Low switching costs.* Where buyers can easily switch between one supplier and another, they have a strong negotiating position and can squeeze suppliers who are desperate for their business. Switching costs are typically low for weakly differentiated commodities such as steel.

- *Buyer competition threat.* If the buyer has the capability to supply itself, or if it has the possibility of acquiring such a capability, it tends to be powerful. In negotiation with its suppliers, it can raise the threat of doing the suppliers' job themselves. This is called *backward vertical integration* (see section 7.5), moving back to sources of supply, and might occur if satisfactory prices or quality from suppliers cannot be obtained. For example, some steel companies have gained power over their iron ore suppliers as they have acquired iron ore sources for themselves.

It is very important that *buyers* are distinguished from *ultimate consumers*. Thus for companies like Procter & Gamble or Unilever (makers of shampoo, washing powders and so on), their buyers are retailers such as Carrefour or Tesco, not ordinary consumers. Carrefour and Tesco have much more negotiating power than an ordinary consumer would have. The high buying power of such supermarkets is a strategic issue for the companies supplying them. It is often useful therefore to distinguish '*strategic customers*', powerful buyers (such as the retailers) towards whom the strategy should be primarily orientated. In the public sector, the strategic customer is typically the provider of funds, rather than the consumer of services: for a pharmaceutical company, the strategic customer is the hospital, not the patient.

The power of suppliers

Suppliers are those who supply the organisation with what it needs to produce the product or service. As well as fuel, raw materials and equipment, this can include labour and sources of finance. The factors increasing supplier power are the converse to those for buyer power. Thus *supplier power* is likely to be high where there are:

- *Concentrated suppliers.* Where just a few producers dominate supply, suppliers have more power over buyers. The iron ore industry is now concentrated in the hands of three main producers, leaving the steel companies, still relatively fragmented, in a weak negotiating position for this essential raw material.

- *High switching costs.* If it is expensive or disruptive to move from one supplier to another, then the buyer becomes relatively dependent and correspondingly weak. Microsoft is a powerful supplier because of the high switching costs of moving from one operating system to another. Buyers are prepared to pay a premium to avoid the trouble, and Microsoft knows it.

- *Supplier competition threat.* Suppliers have increased power where they are able to cut out buyers who are acting as intermediaries. Thus airlines have been able to negotiate tough contracts with travel agencies as the rise of online booking has allowed them to create a direct route to customers. This is called *forward vertical integration*, moving up closer to the ultimate customer.

Most organisations have many suppliers, so it is necessary to concentrate the analysis on the most important ones or types. If their power is high, suppliers can capture all their buyers' own potential profits simply by raising their prices. Star football players have succeeded in raising their rewards to astronomical levels, while even the leading football clubs – their 'buyers' – struggle to make money.

Types of industry

Five forces analysis helps to identify four main types of industry structure. In practice, particular industries are typically not pure representatives of these types, but none the less it is helpful to have these broad categories in mind in order to compare the attractiveness of industries and likely broad patterns of competitive behaviour within them. These four types are:

- *Monopolistic industries*. A monopoly is formally an industry with just one firm and therefore no competitive rivalry. Because of the lack of choice between rivals, there is potentially very great power over buyers and suppliers. This can be very profitable. Firms can still have monopolistic power where they are simply the dominant competitor: for example, Google's 66 per cent share of the American search market gives it price-setting power in the internet advertising market. Some industries are monopolistic because of economies of scale: water utility companies are often monopolies in a particular area because it is uneconomic for smaller players to compete. Other industries are monopolistic because of 'network effects', where a product is more valuable because of the number of other people using it: Facebook and Microsoft Office are so powerful precisely because so many friends and colleagues are already users.[10]

- *Oligopolistic industries*. An oligopoly is where just a few firms dominate an industry, with the potential for limited rivalry and great power over buyers and suppliers. The iron ore market is an oligopoly, dominated by Vale, Rio Tinto and BHP Billiton (see Illustration 2.3). Where there are just two oligopolistic rivals, as for Airbus and Boeing in the civil airline industry, the situation is a duopoly. In theory, oligopoly can be highly profitable, but much depends on the extent of rivalrous behaviour, the threat of entry and substitutes and the growth of final demand in key markets. Oligopolistic firms have a strong interest in minimising rivalry between each other so as to maintain a common front against buyers and suppliers.

- *Hypercompetitive industries*. Hypercompetition occurs where the frequency, boldness and aggression of competitor interactions accelerate to create a condition of constant disequilibrium and change.[11] Under hypercompetition, rivals tend to invest heavily in destabilising innovation, expensive marketing initiatives and aggressive price cuts, with negative impacts on profits. Hypercompetition often breaks out in otherwise oligopolistic industries. Thus the global mobile phone industry has some oligopolistic characteristics, with Nokia holding 27 per cent market share, Samsung 23 per cent and Apple 9 per cent in 2012. However, the industry is very dynamic: Apple only entered the industry in 2007, and Nokia has lost around 8 per cent of the market since then. Competitive moves under conditions of hypercompetition are discussed in section 6.4.2.

- *Perfectly competitive industries*. Perfect competition exists where barriers to entry are low, there are many equal rivals each with very similar products, and information about competitors is freely available. Few markets are absolutely perfectly competitive, but many are highly so. In these conditions, firms are unable to earn more profit than the bare minimum required to survive. Competition focuses heavily on price, because competitors typically cannot fund major innovations or marketing initiatives. Minicab services in large cities often come close to perfect competition. Entrepreneurs should beware entering industries with low barriers to entry, as these are liable to be perfectly or highly competitive and good profits will be very hard to earn.

Implications of Five Forces analysis

The Five Forces Framework provides useful insights into the forces at work in the industry or market environment of an organisation. It is important, however, to use the framework for more than simply listing the forces. The bottom line is an assessment of the *attractiveness* of the industry. The analysis should conclude with a judgement about whether the industry is a good one to compete in or not. Here it is important to note that just one significantly adverse force can be enough to undermine the attractiveness of the industry as a whole. For example, powerful buyers can extract all the potential profits of an otherwise attractive industry structure by forcing down prices.

The analysis should next prompt investigation of the *implications* of these forces, for example:

- *Which industries to enter (or leave)?* The fundamental purpose of the five forces model is to identify the relative attractiveness of different industries: industries are attractive when the forces are weak. Entrepreneurs and managers should invest in industries where the five forces work in their favour and avoid, or disinvest from, markets where they are strongly against. Entrepreneurs sometimes choose markets because entry barriers are low: unless barriers are likely to rise quickly, this is precisely the wrong reason to enter.

- *What influence can be exerted?* Industry structures are not necessarily fixed, but can be influenced by deliberate managerial strategies. For example, organisations can build barriers to entry by increasing advertising spend to improve customer loyalty. They can buy up competitors to reduce rivalry and to increase power over suppliers or buyers. Influencing industry structure involves many issues relating to *competitive strategy* and will be a major concern of Chapter 6.

- *How are competitors differently affected?* Not all competitors will be affected equally by changes in industry structure, deliberate or spontaneous. If barriers are rising because of increased R&D or advertising spending, smaller players in the industry may not be able to keep up with the larger players, and be squeezed out. Similarly, growing buyer power is likely to hurt small competitors most. Strategic group analysis is helpful here (see section 2.4.1).

Although originating in the private sector, five forces analysis can have important implications for organisations in the public sector too. For example, the forces can be used to adjust the service offer or focus on key issues. Thus it might be worth switching managerial initiative from an arena with many crowded and overlapping services (e.g. social work, probation services and education) to one that is less rivalrous and where the organisation can do something more distinctive. Similarly, strategies could be launched to reduce dependence on particularly powerful and expensive suppliers, for example energy sources or high-shortage skills.

Key issues in using the five forces framework

The five forces framework has to be used carefully and is not necessarily complete, even at the industry level. When using this framework, it is important to bear the following three issues in mind:

- *Defining the 'right' industry.* Most industries can be analysed at different levels, for example different markets and even different segments within them (see section 2.4.2 below). For example, the airline industry has different geographical markets (Europe, China and so on) and it also has different segments within each market (e.g. leisure, business and freight). The competitive forces are likely to be different for each of these markets and segments and can be analysed separately. It is sometimes useful to conduct industry analysis at a dis-aggregated level, for each distinct segment or market. The overall picture for the industry as a whole can then be assembled, while particular market or segment opportunities can be highlighted.

- *Converging industries.* Industry definition is often difficult too because industry boundaries are continuously changing. For example, many industries, especially in high-tech arenas, are converging. Convergence is where previously separate industries begin to overlap or merge in terms of activities, technologies, products and customers.[12] Technological change has brought convergence between the telephone and photographic industries, for example, as mobile phones have come to include camera and video functions. The camera company Kodak was driven into bankruptcy by mobile phone producers such as Apple and Samsung.

- *Complementary organisations.* Some analysts argue that industry analyses need to include a 'sixth force', the existence of organisations that are complementors rather than simple competitors. **An organisation is your complementor if it enhances your business attractiveness to customers or suppliers.**[13] Thus McAfee computer security is a complement to Microsoft because its Windows software is more attractive to customers when protected. Even competing airline companies can be complementary to each other because for a supplier like Boeing it is more attractive to invest in particular improvements for two customers rather than one. Complementarity implies a significant shift in perspective. While Porter's Five Forces sees organisations as battling against each other for share of industry value, complementors may *cooperate* to increase the total value available.[14] If Microsoft and McAfee keep each other in touch with their technological developments, they increase the value of both their products. Opportunities for cooperation can be seen through a **value net: a map of organisations in a business environment demonstrating opportunities for value-creating cooperation as well as competition.** In Figure 2.5, (p. 51) Sony is a complementor, supplier and competitor to Apple's iPod. Sony and Apple have an interest in cooperating as well as competing.

2.3.2 The dynamics of industry structure

Industry structure analysis can easily become too static: after all, structure implies stability.[15] However, the previous sections have raised the issue of how competitive forces change *over time*. The key drivers for change are likely to alter industry structures and scenario analyses can be used to understand possible impacts. An illustration of changing industry structure, and the competitive implications of this, is provided by Illustration 2.4 on the UK charity sector. This section examines two additional approaches to understanding change in industry structure: the *industry life-cycle* concept and *comparative five forces analyses*.

The industry life cycle

The power of the five forces typically varies with the stages of the industry life cycle. The industry life-cycle concept proposes that industries start small in their development stage, then go through a period of rapid growth (the equivalent to 'adolescence' in the human life cycle), culminating in a period of 'shake-out'. The final two stages are first a period of slow or even zero growth ('maturity'), and then the final stage of decline ('old age'). Each of these stages has implications for the five forces.[16]

The *development stage* is an experimental one, typically with few players, little direct rivalry and highly differentiated products. The five forces are likely to be weak, therefore, though

ILLUSTRATION

ILLUSTRATION 2.4

Chugging and the structure of the charity sector

Industry structure contributes to inefficiency and aggression in the United Kingdom's charity sector.

The charity sector has become controversial in the United Kingdom. The aggressive fund-raising of some charities is epitomised by workers soliciting donations from shoppers on a commission basis. Such is their perceived aggression that these charity workers are known as 'chuggers', compared with the violent street-crime of 'muggers'.

In 2008, there were 189,000 charities registered in England and Wales, 95 per cent having annual incomes of less than £500,000. However, about 80 per cent of all charity income is raised by the largest 20 charities, headed by Cancer Research UK (2008 income, £355 m (~€390 m; ~$532 m)). According to *Charity Market Monitor*, in 2008, the top 300 charities averaged a 0.9 per cent increase in income, but the largest 10 managed income growth of 2.3 per cent (excluding impact of mergers).

The United Kingdom government introduced the 2006 Charities Act with the specific intention of assisting mergers between independent charities. This had followed a report of the Charity Commission, the regulator for charities in England and Wales, which had commented on the charity sector thus:

'Some people believe that there are too many charities competing for too few funds and that a significant amount of charitable resource could be saved if more charities pooled their resources and worked together . . . The majority of charities are relatively small, local organisations that rely entirely on the unpaid help of their trustees and other volunteers. They may have similar purposes to many other charities but they are all serving different communities. The nature of these charities suggests that there are less likely to be significant areas of overlap . . . It is the much larger, professionally run, charities which, because of their size, tend to face charges of duplication, waste and over-aggressive fund-raising. While there are some clear advantages to be had from a healthy plurality of charities, which are constantly refreshed by new charities pursuing new activities, there are also big benefits of public confidence and support to be had from showing collaborative, as opposed to over-competitive, instincts.'

Local authorities in particular were frustrated by duplication and waste, as they increasingly commission local charities to deliver services. With respect to small charities, local authority budgets are relatively large. One charity sector chief executive, Caroline Shaw, told *Charity Times* as she pursued more cooperation between local charities:

'Without a doubt there is increased competition when it comes to [local authority] commissioning . . . Our driving force has really been to try to create a more effective service for front line organisations; to offer more projects, more diverse services, more effective services. There's a huge amount [of charities] all fighting for funding. I really think that people should be looking at working more closely together.'

During 2008, more than 230 charity mergers were registered with the Charity Commission. As the recession began to put pressure on charitable donations throughout the sector, early 2009 saw the merger of two well-established charities helping the elderly in the United Kingdom, Help the Aged and Age Concern. The new charity, Age UK, has a combined income of around £160 million, including £47 million a year raised through fund-raising, and over 520 charity shops.

Sources: 'RS 4a – Collaborative working and mergers: Summary', http://www.charity-commission.gov.uk/publications/rs4a.asp; *Charity Times*, 'Strength in Numbers', August 2007; *Charity Market Monitor*, 2009.

Questions

1 Which of Porter's five forces are creating problems for the United Kingdom's charity sector?

2 What type of industry structure might the charity industry be moving towards? What would be the benefits and disadvantages of that structure?

Figure 2.5 The value net

```
                        ┌──────────────┐
                        │  Customers   │
                        └──────────────┘

┌──────────────┐      ┌──────────────┐      ┌──────────────┐
│ Competitors  │      │   Company    │      │ Complementors│
│ (Sony Walkman│◄────►│   Product    │◄────►│ (e.g. Sony   │
│ MP3 players) │      │(e.g. Apple   │      │   Music)     │
│              │      │   iPod)      │      │              │
└──────────────┘      └──────────────┘      └──────────────┘

                        ┌──────────────┐
                        │  Suppliers   │
                        │(e.g. Sony    │
                        │ lithium      │
                        │ polymer      │
                        │ battery)     │
                        └──────────────┘
```

* An organisation is your complementor if:
  (i) customers value your product more when they have the other organisation's product than when they have the product alone (e.g. sausage and mustard);
  (ii) it's more attractive for suppliers to provide resources to you when it's also supplying the other organisation than when it's supplying you alone (airlines and Boeing).

Note: Organisations can play more than one role. Thus Sony Music (publisher of AC/DC, Sade etc) is a complementor to Apple's iPod; Sony is also a supplier of batteries to the iPod; Sony also competes with its own MP3 players.

Source: Reprinted by permission of *Harvard Business Review*. From 'The Right Game' by A. Brandenburger and B. Nalebuff, July–August 1996, pp. 57–64. Copyright © 1996 by the Harvard Business School Publishing Corporation. All rights reserved.

profits may actually be scarce because of high investment requirements. The next stage is one of *high growth*, with rivalry low as there is plenty of market opportunity for everybody. Low rivalry and keen buyers of the new product favour profits at this stage, but these are not certain. Barriers to entry may still be low in the growth stage, as existing competitors have not built up much scale, experience or customer loyalty. Suppliers can be powerful too if there is a shortage of components or materials that fast-growing businesses need for expansion. The *shake-out stage* begins as the market becomes increasingly saturated and cluttered with competitors. Profits are variable, as increased rivalry forces the weakest competitors out of the business. In the *maturity stage*, barriers to entry tend to increase, as control over distribution is established and economies of scale and experience curve benefits come into play. Products or

Figure 2.6 The industry life cycle

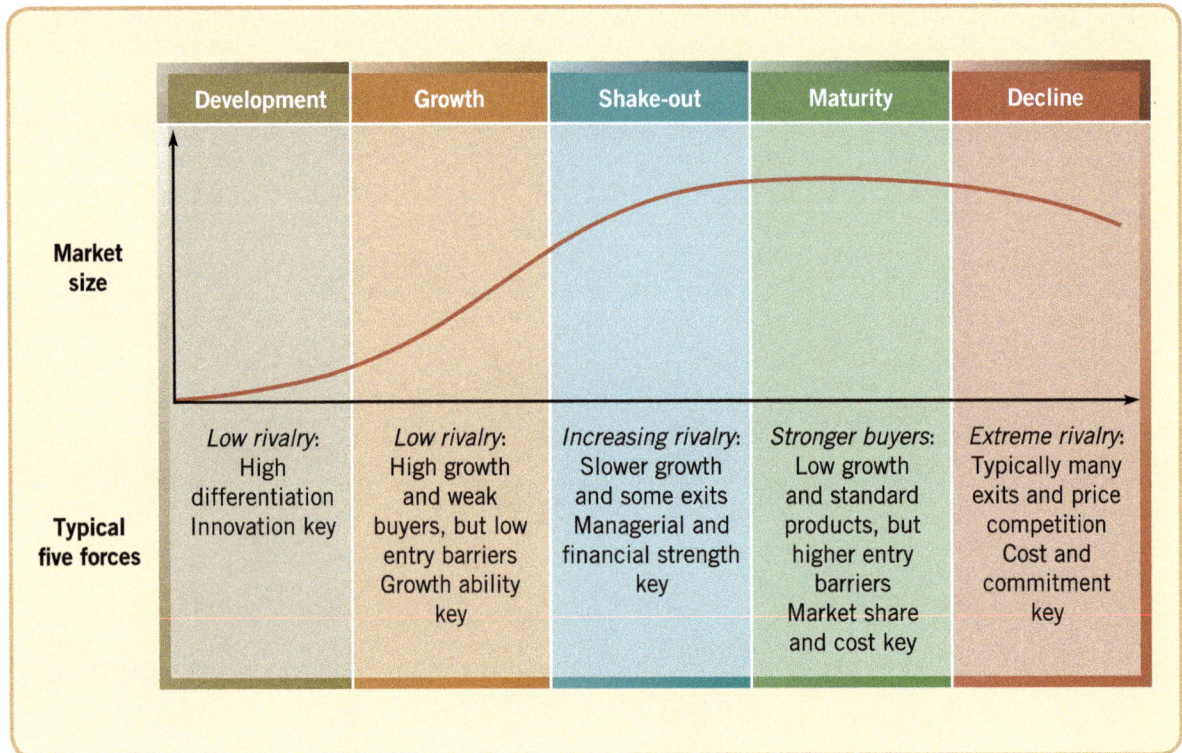

Development	Growth	Shake-out	Maturity	Decline

Market size

Typical five forces

| *Low rivalry*: High differentiation Innovation key | *Low rivalry*: High growth and weak buyers, but low entry barriers Growth ability key | *Increasing rivalry*: Slower growth and some exits Managerial and financial strength key | *Stronger buyers*: Low growth and standard products, but higher entry barriers Market share and cost key | *Extreme rivalry*: Typically many exits and price competition Cost and commitment key |

services tend to standardise, with relative price becoming key. Buyers may become more powerful as they become less avid for the industry's products and more confident in switching between suppliers. Profitability at the maturity stage relies on high market share, providing leverage against buyers and competitive advantage in terms of cost. Finally, the *decline stage* can be a period of extreme rivalry, especially where there are high exit barriers, as falling sales force remaining competitors into dog-eat-dog competition. However, survivors in the decline stage may still be profitable if competitor exit leaves them in a monopolistic position. Figure 2.6 summarises some of the conditions that can be expected at different stages in the life cycle.

It is important to avoid putting too much faith in the inevitability of life-cycle stages. One stage does not follow predictably after another: industries vary widely in the length of their growth stages, and others can rapidly 'de-mature' through radical innovation. Thus the telephony industry, based for nearly a century on fixed-line telephones, rejuvenated rapidly with the introduction of mobile and internet telephony. Anita McGahan of Toronto University warns of the 'maturity mindset', which can leave many managers complacent and slow to respond to new competition.[17] Managing in mature industries is not necessarily just about waiting for decline. However, even if the various stages are not inevitable, the life-cycle concept does remind managers that conditions are likely to change over time. Especially in fast-moving industries, five forces analyses need to be reviewed quite regularly.

Comparative industry structure analyses

The industry life cycle underlines the need to make industry structure analysis dynamic. One effective means of doing this is to compare the five forces over time in a simple 'radar plot'.

Figure 2.7 Comparative industry structure analysis

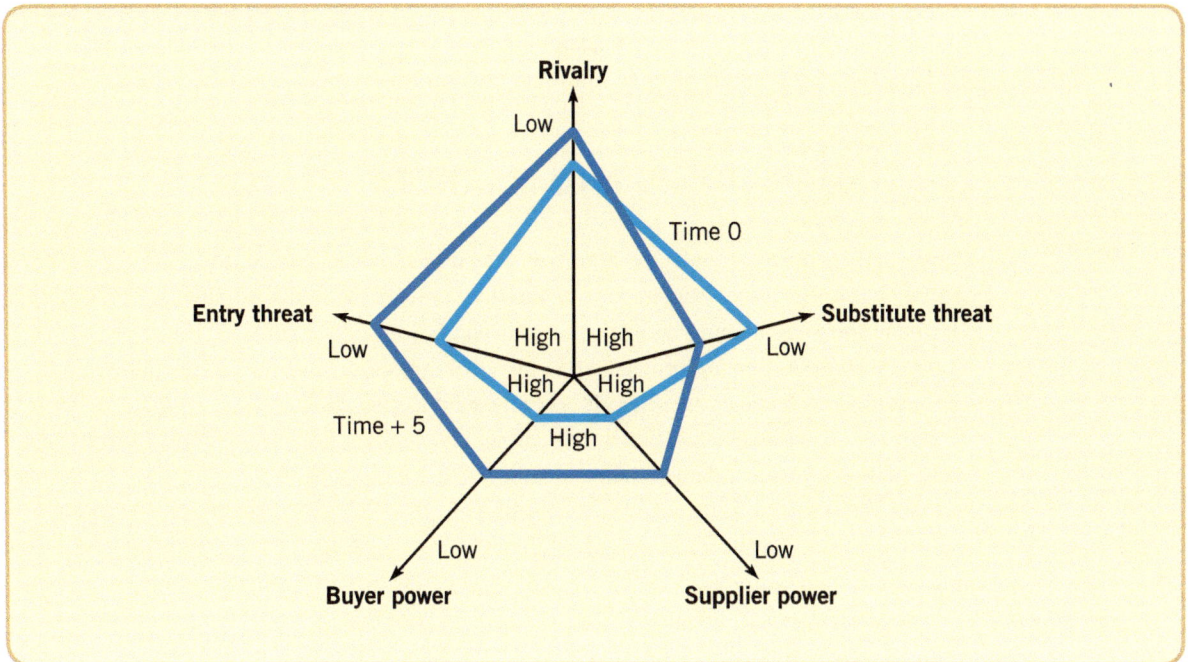

Figure 2.7 provides a framework for summarising the power of each of the five forces on five axes. Power diminishes as the axes go outwards. Where the forces are low, the total area enclosed by the lines between the axes is large; where the forces are high, the total area enclosed by the lines is small. The larger the enclosed area, therefore, the greater is the profit potential. In Figure 2.7, the industry at Time 0 (represented by the light blue lines) has relatively low rivalry (just a few competitors) and faces low substitution threats. The threat of entry is moderate, but both buyer power and supplier power are relatively high. Overall, this looks like only a moderately attractive industry to invest in.

However, given the dynamic nature of industries, managers need to look forward, perhaps using scenario analysis. Figure 2.7 represents five years forward by the dark blue lines. Managers are predicting in this case some rise in the threat of substitutes (perhaps new technologies will be developed). On the other hand, they predict a falling entry threat, while both buyer power and supplier power will be easing. Rivalry will reduce still further. This looks like a classic case of an industry in which a few players emerge with overall dominance. The area enclosed by the blue lines is large, suggesting a relatively attractive industry. For a firm confident of becoming one of the dominant players, this might be an industry well worth investing in.

Comparing the five forces over time on a radar plot thus helps to give industry structure analysis a dynamic aspect. Similar plots can be made to aid diversification decisions (see Chapter 7), where possible new industries to enter can be compared in terms of attractiveness. The lines are only approximate, of course, because they aggregate the many individual elements that make up each of the forces into a simple composite measure. Notice too that if one of the forces is very adverse, then this might nullify positive assessments on the other four axes:

for example, an industry with low rivalry, low substitution, low entry barriers and low supplier power might still be unattractive if powerful buyers were able to demand highly discounted prices. With these warnings in mind, such radar plots can none the less be both a useful device for initial analysis and an effective summary of a final, more refined analysis.

(2.4) COMPETITORS AND MARKETS

An industry or sector may be too high a level to provide for a detailed understanding of competition. The five forces can impact differently on different kinds of players. For example, Hyundai and Porsche may be in the same broad industry (automobiles), but they are positioned differently: they are protected by different barriers to entry and competitive moves by one are unlikely to affect the other. It is often useful to disaggregate. Many industries contain a range of companies, each of which has different capabilities and competes on different bases. Some of these competitor differences are captured by the concept of *strategic groups*. Customers too can differ significantly and these can be captured by distinguishing between different *market segments*. Thinking in terms of different strategic groups and market segments provides opportunities for organisations to develop highly distinctive positionings within broader industries. Competitor differences, both actual and potential, can also be analysed using the strategy canvas and '*Blue Ocean*' thinking, the last topic in this section.

2.4.1 Strategic groups[18]

Strategic groups **are organisations within an industry or sector with similar strategic characteristics, following similar strategies or competing on similar bases.** These characteristics are different from those in other strategic groups in the same industry or sector. For example, in the grocery retailing industry, supermarkets, convenience stores and corner shops each form different strategic groups. There are many different characteristics that distinguish between strategic groups but these can be grouped into two major categories (see Figure 2.8).[19] First, the *scope* of an organisation's activities (such as product range, geographical coverage and range of distribution channels used). Second, the *resource commitment* (such as brands, marketing spend and extent of vertical integration). Which characteristics are relevant differs from industry to industry, but typically important are those characteristics that separate high performers from low performers.

Strategic groups can be mapped onto two-dimensional charts – for example, one axis might be the extent of product range and the other axis the size of marketing spend. One method for choosing key dimensions by which to map strategic groups is to identify top performers (by growth or profitability) in an industry and to compare them with low performers. Characteristics that are shared by top performers, but not by low performers, are likely to be particularly relevant for mapping strategic groups. For example, the most profitable firms in an industry might all be narrow in terms of product range, and lavish in terms of marketing spend, while the less profitable firms might be more widely spread in terms of products and restrained in their marketing. Here the two dimensions for mapping would be product range and marketing spend. A potential recommendation for the less profitable firms would be to cut back their product range and boost their marketing.

Figure 2.9 shows strategic groups among Indian pharmaceutical companies, with research and development intensity (R&D spend as a percentage of sales) and overseas focus (exports

Figure 2.8 Some characteristics for identifying strategic groups

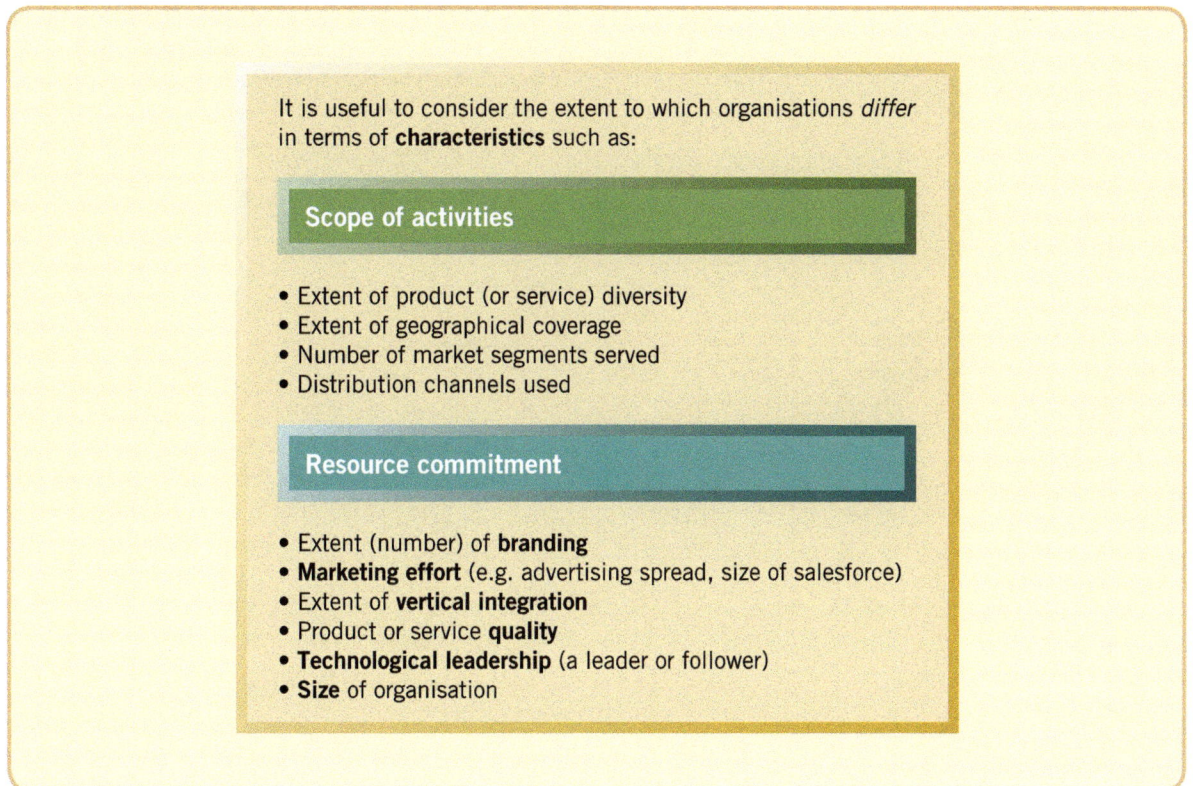

It is useful to consider the extent to which organisations *differ* in terms of **characteristics** such as:

Scope of activities

- Extent of product (or service) diversity
- Extent of geographical coverage
- Number of market segments served
- Distribution channels used

Resource commitment

- Extent (number) of **branding**
- **Marketing effort** (e.g. advertising spread, size of salesforce)
- Extent of **vertical integration**
- Product or service **quality**
- **Technological leadership** (a leader or follower)
- **Size** of organisation

and patents registered overseas) defining the axes of the map. These two axes do explain a good deal of the variation in profitability between groups. The most profitable group is the Emergent globals (11.3 per cent average return on sales), those with high R&D intensity and high overseas focus. On the other hand, the Exploiter group spends little on R&D and is focused on domestic markets, and only enjoys 2.0 per cent average return on sales.

This strategic group concept is useful in at least three ways:

- *Understanding competition.* Managers can focus on their direct competitors within their particular strategic group, rather than the whole industry. They can also establish the dimensions that distinguish them most from other groups, and which might be the basis for relative success or failure. These dimensions can then become the focus of their action.

- *Analysis of strategic opportunities.* Strategic group maps can identify the most attractive 'strategic spaces' within an industry. Some spaces on the map may be 'white spaces', relatively under-occupied. In the Indian pharmaceutical industry, the white space is high R&D investment combined with focus on domestic markets. Such white spaces might be unexploited opportunities. On the other hand, they could turn out to be 'black holes', impossible to exploit and likely to damage any entrant. A strategic group map is only the first stage of the analysis. Strategic spaces need to tested carefully.

- *Analysis of mobility barriers.* Of course, moving across the map to take advantage of opportunities is not costless. Often it will require difficult decisions and rare resources. Strategic groups are therefore characterised by 'mobility barriers', obstacles to movement from one strategic group to another. These are similar to barriers to entry in five forces analysis.

Figure 2.9 Strategic groups in the Indian pharmaceutical industry

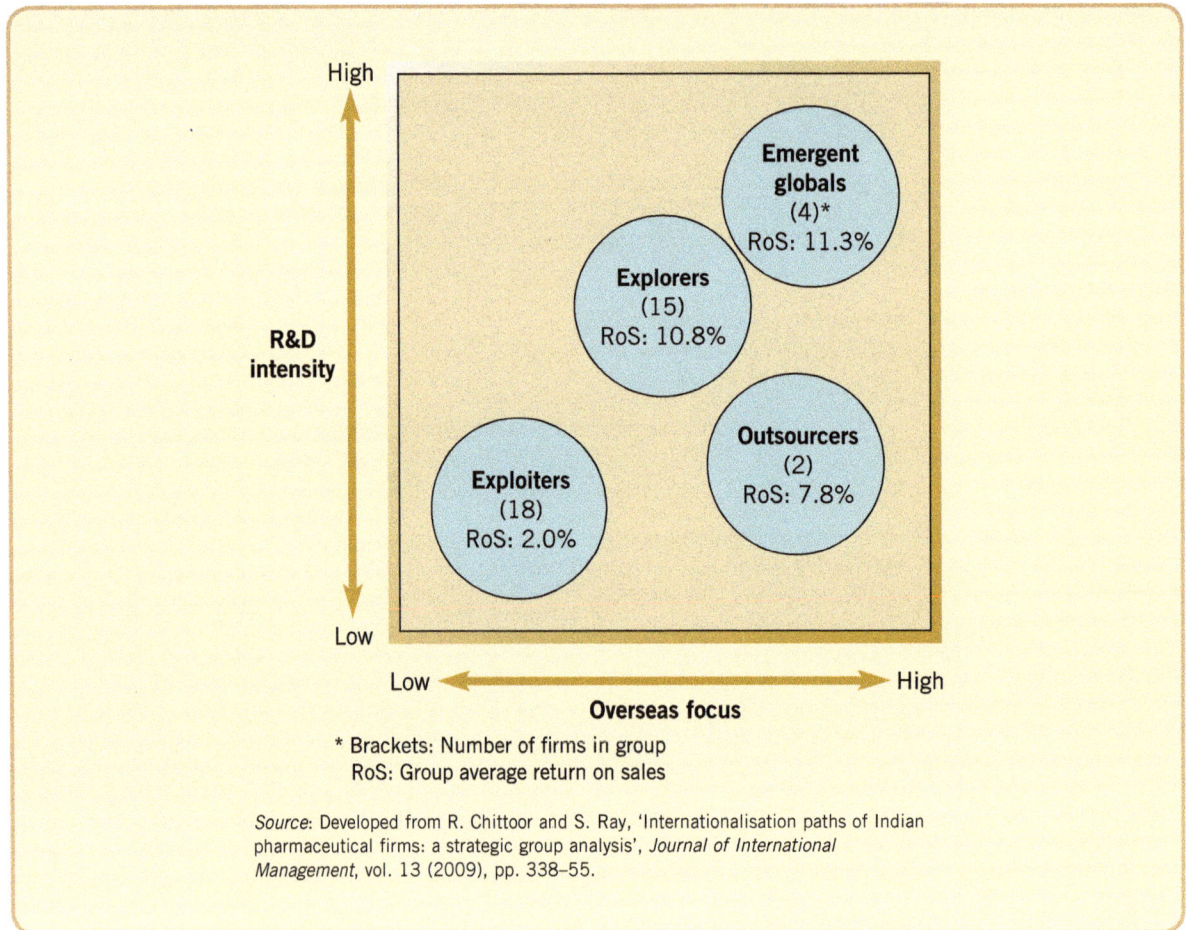

* Brackets: Number of firms in group
RoS: Group average return on sales

Source: Developed from R. Chittoor and S. Ray, 'Internationalisation paths of Indian pharmaceutical firms: a strategic group analysis', *Journal of International Management*, vol. 13 (2009), pp. 338–55.

Although movement from the Exploiter group in Indian pharmaceuticals to the Emergent global group might seem very attractive in terms of profits, it is likely to demand very substantial financial investment and strong managerial skills. Mobility into the Emergent global group will not be easy. As with barriers to entry, it is good to be in a successful strategic group protected by strong mobility barriers, to impede imitation.

2.4.2 Market segments

The concept of strategic groups discussed above helps with understanding the similarities and differences in terms of competitor characteristics. The concept of market segment focuses on differences in *customer* needs. A market segment[20] is a group of customers who have similar needs that are different from customer needs in other parts of the market. Where these customer groups are relatively small, such market segments are often called 'niches'. Dominance of a market segment or niche can be very valuable, for the same reasons that dominance of an industry can be valuable following five forces reasoning.

For long-term success, strategies based on market segments must keep customer needs firmly in mind. Two issues are particularly important in market segment analysis, therefore:

Table 2.1 **Some bases of market segmentation**

Type of factor	Consumer markets	Industrial/organisational markets
Characteristics of people/organisations	Age, gender, ethnicity Income Family size Life-cycle stage Location Lifestyle	Industry Location Size Technology Profitability Management
Purchase/use situation	Size of purchase Brand loyalty Purpose of use Purchasing behaviour Importance of purchase Choice criteria	Application Importance of purchase Volume Frequency of purchase Purchasing procedure Choice criteria Distribution channel
Users' needs and preferences for product characteristics	Product similarity Price preference Brand preferences Desired features Quality	Performance requirements Assistance from suppliers Brand preferences Desired features Quality Service requirements

- *Variation in customer needs*. Focusing on customer needs that are highly distinctive from those typical in the market is one means of building a long-term segment strategy. Customer needs vary for a whole variety of reasons – some of which are identified in Table 2.1. Theoretically, any of these factors could be used to identify distinct market segments. However, the crucial bases of segmentation vary according to market. In industrial markets, segmentation is often thought of in terms of industrial classification of buyers: steel producers might segment by automobile industry, packaging industry and construction industry, for example. On the other hand, segmentation by buyer behaviour (e.g. direct buying versus those users who buy through third parties such as contractors) or purchase value (e.g. high-value bulk purchasers versus frequent low-value purchasers) might be more appropriate. Being able to serve a highly distinctive segment that other organisations find difficult to serve is often the basis for a secure long-term strategy.

- *Specialisation* within a market segment can also be an important basis for a successful segmentation strategy. This is sometimes called a 'niche strategy'. Organisations that have built up most experience in servicing a particular market segment should not only have lower costs in so doing, but also have built relationships which may be difficult for others to break down. Experience and relationships are likely to protect a dominant position in a particular segment. However, precisely because customers value different things in different segments, specialised producers may find it very difficult to compete on a broader basis. For example, a small local brewery competing against the big brands on the basis of its ability to satisfy distinctive local tastes is unlikely to find it easy to serve other segments where tastes are different, scale requirements are larger and distribution channels are more complex.

2.4.3 **Competitor analysis and 'Blue Oceans'**

Any environmental analysis should also include an understanding of competitors. As Michael Porter's five forces framework underlines, reducing industry rivalry involves competitors finding differentiated positions in the marketplace. W. Chan Kim and Renée Mauborgne at INSEAD propose two concepts that help think about the relative positioning of competitors in the environment: the strategy canvas and 'Blue Oceans'.

A strategy canvas **compares competitors according to their performance on key success factors in order to establish the extent of differentiation.** Figure 2.10 shows a strategy canvas for three electrical components companies. The canvas highlights the following three features:

● Critical success factors (*CSFs*) are those factors that either are particularly valued by customers (i.e. strategic customers) or provide a significant advantage in terms of cost. Critical success factors are therefore likely to be an important source of competitive advantage or disadvantage. Figure 2.10 identifies five established critical success factors in this electrical components market (cost, after-sales service, delivery reliability, technical quality and testing facilities). Note there is also a new sixth critical success factor, design advisory services, which will be discussed under the third subhead, value innovation.

● *Value curves* are a graphic depiction of how customers perceive competitors' relative performance across the critical success factors. In Figure 2.10, companies A and B perform well on cost, service, reliability and quality, but less well on testing. They do not offer any design advice. They are poorly differentiated and occupy a space in the market where profits may be hard to get because of excessive rivalry between the two. Company C, on the other hand, has a radically different value curve, characteristic of a 'value innovator'.

Figure 2.10 **Strategy canvas for electrical components companies**

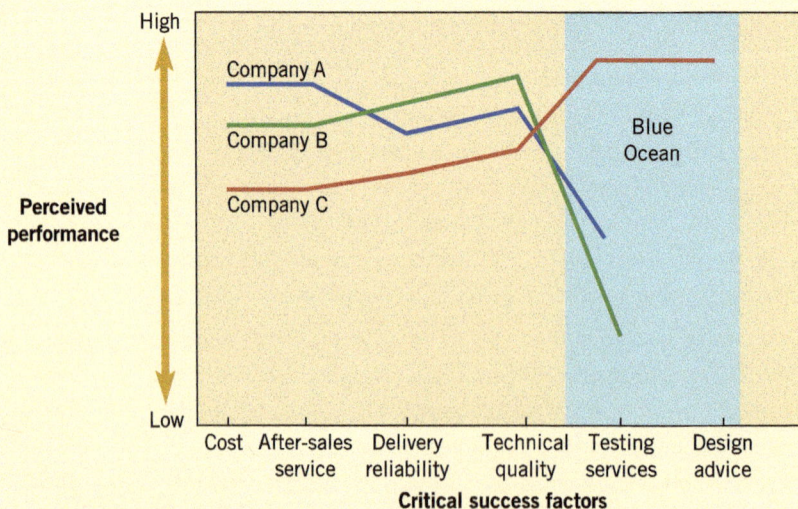

Note: cost is used rather than price for consistency of value curves.

Source: Developed from W.C. Kim and R. Mauborgne, *Blue Ocean Strategy*, Harvard Business School Press, 2005.

- *Value innovation* is the creation of new market space by excelling on established critical success factors on which competitors are performing badly and/or by creating new critical success factors representing previously unrecognised customer wants. Thus in Figure 2.10, company C is a value innovator in both senses. First, it excels on the established customer need of offering testing facilities for customers' products using its components. Second, it offers a new and valued design service advising customers on how to integrate their components in order for them to create better products.

A value innovator is a company that competes in 'Blue Oceans'. Blue Oceans **are new market spaces where competition is minimised.**[21] Blue Oceans contrast with 'Red Oceans', where industries are already well defined and rivalry is intense. Blue Oceans evoke wide empty seas. Red Oceans are associated with bloody competition and 'red ink', in other words financial losses. The Blue Ocean concept is thus useful for identifying potential spaces in the environment with little competition. These Blue Oceans are *strategic gaps* in the marketplace.

In Figure 2.10, company C's strategy exemplifies two critical principles of Blue Ocean thinking: *focus* and *divergence*. First, company C focuses its efforts on just two factors, testing and design services, while maintaining only adequate performance on the other critical success factors where its competitors are already high performers. Second, it has created a value curve that significantly diverges from its competitors' value curves, creating a substantial *strategic gap*, or Blue Ocean, in the areas of testing and design services. This is shrewd. For company C, beating companies A and B in the areas where they are performing well anyway would require major investment and likely provide little advantage given that customers are already highly satisfied. Challenging A and B on cost, after-sales service, delivery or quality would be a Red Ocean strategy, increasing industry rivalry. Far better is to concentrate on where a large gap can be created between competitors. Company C faces little competition for those customers who really value testing and design services, and consequently can charge good prices for them. The task for companies A and B now is to find strategic gaps of their own.

(2.5) OPPORTUNITIES AND THREATS

The concepts and frameworks discussed above should be helpful in understanding the factors in the macro-, industry and competitor/market environments of an organisation (see the Key Debate: just how much do such industry and market factors affect successful strategic outcomes?). However, the critical issue is the *implications* that are drawn from this understanding in guiding strategic decisions and choices. The crucial next stage, therefore, is to draw from the environmental analysis specific strategic opportunities and threats for the organisation. Identifying these opportunities and threats is extremely valuable when thinking about strategic choices for the future (the subject of Chapters 6 to 10). Opportunities and threats form one half of the Strengths, Weaknesses, Opportunities and Threats (SWOT) analyses that shape many companies' strategy formulation (see section 3.4.4). In responding strategically to the environment, the goal is to reduce identified threats and take advantage of the best opportunities.

The techniques and concepts in this chapter should help in identifying environmental threats and opportunities, for instance:

KEY DEBATE

How much does industry matter?

A good start in strategy must be to choose a profitable industry to compete in. But does simply being in the right industry matter more than having the right kinds of skills and resources?

This chapter has focused on the role of the environment in strategy making, with particular regard to industries. But the importance of industries in determining organisational performance has been challenged in recent years. This has led to a debate about whether strategy making should be externally orientated, starting with the environment, or internally orientated, starting with the organisation's own skills and resources (the focus of Chapter 3).

Managers favouring an external approach look primarily *outside* the organisation, for example building market share in their industries through mergers and acquisitions or aggressive marketing. Managers favouring an internal approach concentrate their attention *inside* the organisation, fostering the skills of their people or nurturing technologies, for example. Because managerial time is limited, there is a real trade-off to be made between external and internal approaches.

The chief advocate of the external approach is Michael Porter, Professor at Harvard Business School and founder of the Monitor Consulting Group. An influential sceptic of this approach is Richard Rumelt, a student at Harvard Business School but now at University of California Los Angeles. Porter, Rumelt and others have done a series of empirical studies examining the relative importance of industries in explaining organisations' performance.

Typically, these studies take a large sample of firms and compare the extent to which variance in profitability is due to firms or industries (controlling for other effects such as size). If firms within the same industry tend to bunch together in terms of profitability, it is industry that is accounting for the greater proportion of profitability: an external approach to strategy is supported. If firms within the same industry vary widely in terms of profitability, it is the specific skills and resources of the firms that matter most: an internal approach is most appropriate.

The two most important studies in fact find that more of the variance in profitability is due to firms rather than industries – firms account for 47 per cent in Rumelt's study of manufacturing (see the figure). However, when Porter and McGahan included service industries as well as manufacturing, they found a larger industry effect (19 per cent).

Per cent of variance in profitability due to:

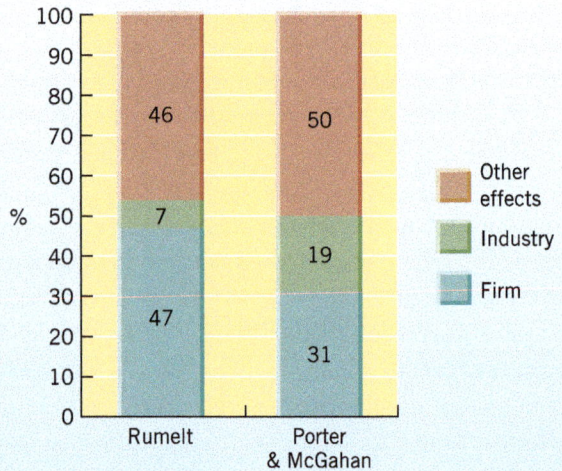

The implication from this work is that firm-specific factors generally influence profitability more than industry factors. Firms need to attend carefully to their own skills and resources. However, the greater industry effect found in Porter and McGahan's study of both manufacturing and services suggests that industry's importance varies strongly by industry. External influences can matter more in some industries than others.

Sources: R.P. Rumelt, 'How much does industry matter?', *Strategic Management Journal*, vol. 12, no. 2 (1991), pp. 167–85; M.E. Porter and A.M. McGahan, 'How much does industry matter really?', *Strategic Management Journal*, vol. 18, Summer Special Issue (1997), pp. 15–30; M.E. Porter and A.M. McGahan, 'The emergence and sustainability of abnormal profits', *Strategic Organisation*, vol. 1, no. 1 (2003), pp. 79–108.

Questions

1 Why might some industries have a larger influence on their members' profitability than others?

2 What other factors might account for business unit profitability?

- *PESTEL analysis* of the macro-environment might reveal threats and opportunities presented by technological change, or shifts in market demographics or such like factors.

- Identification of *key drivers for change* can help generate different scenarios for managerial discussion, some more threatening, others more favourable.

- *Porter's five forces analysis* might, for example, identify a rise or fall in barriers to entry, or opportunities to reduce industry rivalry, perhaps by acquisition of competitors.

- *Blue Ocean* thinking might reveal where companies can create new market spaces; alternatively it could help identify success factors which new entrants might attack in order to turn 'Blue Oceans' into 'Red Oceans'.

While all these techniques and concepts are important tools for understanding environments, it is important to recognise that any analysis is likely to be somewhat subjective. Entrepreneurs and managers often have particular blinkers with regard to what they see and prioritise. Techniques and concepts can be helpful in challenging existing assumptions and encouraging broader perspectives, but they are unlikely to overcome human subjectivity and biases completely.

SUMMARY

- Environmental influences can be thought of as layers around an organisation, with the outer layer making up the *macro-environment*, the middle layer making up the *industry or sector* and the inner layer *strategic groups* and *market segments*.

- The macro-environment can be analysed in terms of *PESTEL factors*, from which *key drivers of change* can be identified. Alternative *scenarios* about the future can be constructed according to how the key drivers develop.

- Industries and sectors can be analysed in terms of *Porter's five forces* – barriers to entry, substitutes, buyer power, supplier power and rivalry. Together, these determine industry or sector attractiveness.

- Industries and sectors are dynamic, and their changes can be analysed in terms of the *industry life cycle* and *comparative five forces radar plots*. In the inner layer of the environment, *strategic group* analysis, *market segment* analysis and the *strategy canvas* can help identify strategic gaps or opportunities.

- *Blue Ocean* strategies are a means of avoiding *Red Oceans* with many similar rivals and low profitability.

VIDEO ASSIGNMENTS

Visit *MyStrategyLab* and watch the Nationwide and Pearson case study for Chapter 2.

1 Using the PESTEL framework as a starting point, discuss the main elements of the external environment that shape strategy at the Nationwide Building Society.

2 How is the nature of Pearson's competitors likely to change with the evolving nature of the textbook industry, and what critical success factors are likely to become important?

WORK ASSIGNMENTS

✱ Denotes more advanced work assignments.

* Refers to a case study in the Text and Cases edition.

2.1 For an organisation of your choice carry out a PESTEL analysis and identify key drivers for change. Use Illustration 2.1 as a model.

2.2✱ For the same organisation as in 2.1, and using Illustration 2.2 as a model, construct four scenarios for the evolution of its environment. What implications are there for the organisation's strategy?

2.3 Drawing on section 2.3, carry out a five forces analysis of the pharmaceutical industry* or Vodafone's position in the mobile phone industry*. What do you conclude about that industry's attractiveness?

2.4✱ Drawing on section 2.3, and particularly using the radar plot technique of Figure 2.7, choose two industries or sectors and compare their attractiveness in terms of the five forces (a) today; (b) in approximately three to five years' time. Justify your assessment of each of the five forces' strengths. Which industry or sector would you invest in?

2.5 With regard to section 2.4.1 and Figure 2.8, identify an industry (e.g. the motor industry or clothing retailers) and, by comparing competitors, map out the main strategic groups in the industry according to key strategic dimensions. Try more than one set of key strategic dimensions to map the industry. Do the resulting maps identify any under-exploited opportunities in the industry?

2.6✱ Drawing on section 2.4.3, and particularly on Figure 2.10, identify critical success factors for an industry with which you and your peers are familiar (e.g. clothing retailers or mobile phone companies). Using your own estimates (or those of your peers), construct a strategy canvas comparing the main competitors, as in Figure 2.10. What implications does your strategy canvas have for the strategies of these competitors?

Integrative assignment

2.7 Carry out a full analysis of an industry or sector of your choice (using for example PESTEL, scenarios, five forces and strategic groups). Consider explicitly how the industry or sector is affected by globalisation (see Chapter 8, particularly Figure 8.2 on drivers) and innovation (see Chapter 9, particularly Figure 9.2 on product and process innovation).

RECOMMENDED KEY READINGS

- The classic book on the analysis of industries is M.E. Porter, *Competitive Strategy*, Free Press, 1980. An updated view is available in M.E. Porter, 'The five competitive forces that shape strategy', *Harvard Business Review*, vol. 86, no. 1 (2008), pp. 58–77. An influential development on Porter's basic ideas is W.C. Kim and R. Mauborgne, *Blue Ocean Strategy: How to Create Uncontested Market Space and Make Competition Irrelevant*, Harvard Business School Press, 2005.

- For approaches to how environments change, see K. van der Heijden, *Scenarios: The Art of Strategic Conversation*, 2nd edn, Wiley, 2005, and the work of Michael Porter's colleague, A. McGahan, *How Industries Evolve*, Harvard Business School Press, 2004.

- A collection of academic articles on PEST, scenarios and similar is in the special issue of *International Studies of Management and Organisation*, vol. 36, no. 3 (2006), edited by Peter McKiernan.

REFERENCES

1. PESTEL is an extension of PEST (Politics, Economics, Social and Technology) analysis, taking more account of ecological and legal issues. PEST is sometimes called STEP analysis. PESTEL is sometimes called PESTLE and is also sometimes extended to STEEPLE in order to include Ethical issues. For an application of PEST analysis to the world of business schools, see H. Thomas, 'An analysis of the environment and competitive dynamics of management education', *Journal of Management Development*, vol. 26, no. 1 (2007), pp. 9–21.

2. D. Bach and D. Allen, 'What every CEO needs to know about nonmarket strategies', *Sloan Management Review*, vol. 51, no. 3 (2010), pp. 41–8; and J. Doh, T. Lawton and T. Rajwani, 'Advancing nonmarket strategy research: institutional perspectives in a changing world', *Academy of Management Perspectives*, August (2012), pp. 22–38.

3. R.A. Slaughter, 'Looking for the real megatrends', *Futures*, October (1993), pp. 823–49.

4. A. Grove, *Only the Paranoid Survive*, Profile Books, 1998.

5. S. Mendonca, G. Caroso and J. Caraca, 'The strategic strength of weak signals', *Futures*, 44 (2012), pp. 218–28; and P. Schoemaker and G. Day, 'How to make sense of weak signals', *Sloan Management Review*, vol. 50, no. 3 (2009), pp. 81–9.

6. For a discussion of scenario planning in practice, see R. Ramirez, R. Osterman and D. Gronquist, 'Scenarios and early warnings as dynamic capabilities to frame managerial attention', *Technological Forecasting and Strategic Change*, vol. 80 (2013), pp. 825–38. For how scenario planning fits with other forms of environmental analysis such as PESTEL, see G. Burt, G. Wright, R. Bradfield and K. van der Heijden, 'The role of scenario planning in exploring the environment in view of the limitations of PEST and its derivatives', *International Studies of Management and Organization*, vol. 36, no. 3 (2006), pp. 50–76.

7. Based on P. Schoemaker, 'Scenario planning: a tool for strategic thinking'. *Sloan Management Review*, vol. 36 (1995), pp. 25–34.

8. See M.E. Porter, *Competitive Strategy: Techniques for Analyzing Industries and Competitors*, Free Press, 1980, p. 5.

9. An updated discussion of the classic framework is M. Porter, 'The five competitive forces that shape strategy', *Harvard Business Review*, vol. 86, no. 1 (2008), pp. 58–77. C. Christensen, 'The past and future of competitive advantage', *Sloan Management Review*, vol. 42, no. 2 (2001), pp. 105–9, provides an interesting critique and update of some of the factors underlying Porter's five forces. A critical overview of Porter's thinking is also provided in R. Huggins and H. Izushi (eds), *Competition, Competitive Advantage, and Clusters: The Ideas of Michael Porter*, Oxford University Press, 2011.

10. D. McIntyre and M. Subramarian, 'Strategy in network industries: a review and research agenda', *Journal of Management*, vol. 35 (2009), pp. 1494–512.

11. This definition is from R. D'Aveni, *Hypercompetition: Managing the Dynamics of Strategic Manoeuvring*, Free Press, 1994, p. 2.

12. See for example A. Malhotra and A. Gupta, 'An investigation of firms' responses to industry convergence', *Academy of Management Proceedings*, 2001, pp. G1–6.

13. A. Brandenburger and B. Nalebuff, 'The right game', *Harvard Business Review*, July–August 1995, pp. 57–64.

14. See K. Walley, 'Coopetition: an introduction to the subject and an agenda for research', *International Studies of Management and Organization*, vol. 37, no. 2 (2007), pp. 11–31. On the dangers of 'complementors', see D. Yoffie and M. Kwak, 'With friends like these', *Harvard Business Review*, vol. 84, no. 9 (2006), pp. 88–98.

15. There is a good discussion of the static nature of the Porter model, and other limitations, in M. Grundy, 'Rethinking and reinventing Michael Porter's five forces model', *Strategic Change*, vol. 15 (2006), pp. 213–29.

16. A classic academic overview of the industry life cycle is S. Klepper, 'Industry life cycles', *Industrial and Corporate Change*, vol. 6, no. 1 (1996), pp. 119–43. See also A. McGahan, 'How industries evolve', *Business Strategy Review*, vol. 11, no. 3 (2000), pp. 1–16.

17. A. McGahan, 'How industries evolve', *Business Strategy Review*, vol. 11, no. 3 (2000), pp. 1–16.

18. For examples of strategic group analysis, see G. Leask and D. Parker, 'Strategic groups, competitive groups and performance in the UK pharmaceutical industry', *Strategic Management Journal*, vol. 28, no. 7 (2007), pp. 723–45; and W. Desarbo, R. Grewal and R. Wang, 'Dynamic strategic groups: deriving spatial evolutionary paths', *Strategic Management Journal*, vol. 30, no. 8 (2009), pp. 1420–39.

19. These characteristics are based on Porter, reference 4 above.

20. A useful discussion of segmentation in relation to competitive strategy is provided in M.E. Porter, *Competitive Advantage*, Free Press, 1985, Chapter 7. See also the discussion on market segmentation in P. Kotler, G. Armstrong, J. Saunders and V. Wong, *Principles of Marketing*, 3rd European edn, Financial Times Prentice Hall, 2002, Chapter 9.

21. W.C. Kim and R. Mauborgne, 'How strategy shapes structure', *Harvard Business Review*, September 2009, pp. 73–80.

Global forces and the advertising industry

Peter Cardwell

*This case is centred on the global advertising industry which faces significant strategic dilemmas driven by the rise of consumer spending in developing economies, technological convergence and pressures from major advertisers for results-based compensation. Strategy in this industry is further explored in **The Strategy Experience** simulation (http://www.mystrategylab.com/strategy-experience).*

In the second decade of the new millennium, advertising agencies faced a number of unanticipated challenges. Traditional markets and industry operating methods, developed largely in North America and Western Europe following the rise of consumer spending power in the twentieth century, were being radically reappraised.

The industry was subject to game-changing forces from the so-called 'digital revolution' with the entry of search companies like Google and Yahoo as rivals for advertising budgets. Changing patterns in global consumer markets have impacted on both industry dynamics and structure. Budgets being spent through traditional advertising agencies were being squeezed as industry rivalry intensified.

Overview of the advertising industry

Traditionally, the business objective of advertising agencies is to target a specific audience on behalf of clients with a message that encourages them to try a product or service and ultimately purchase it. This is done largely through the concept of a brand being communicated via media channels. Brands allow consumers to differentiate between products and services and it is the job of the advertising agency to position the brand so that it is associated with functions and attributes which are valued by target consumers. These brands may be consumer brands (e.g. Coca-Cola, Nike and Mercedes Benz) or business-to-business (B2B) brands (e.g. IBM, Airbus Industrie and KPMG). Some brands target both consumers and businesses (e.g. Microsoft and Apple).

As well as private-sector brand companies, governments spend heavily to advertise public-sector services such as healthcare and education or to influence individual behaviour (such as 'Don't drink and drive'). For example, the UK government had an advertising budget of £285 m (€325) in 2012. Charities, political groups, religious groups and other not-for-profit organisations also use the advertising industry to attract funds into their organisation or to raise awareness of issues. Together these account for approximately 3 per cent of advertising spend.

Advertisements are usually placed in selected media (TV, press, radio, internet, etc.) by an advertising agency acting on behalf of the client brand company: thus they are acting as 'agents'. The client company employs the advertising agency to use its knowledge, skills, creativity and experience to create advertising and marketing to drive consumption of the client's brands. Clients traditionally have been charged according to the time spent on creating the advertisements plus a commission based on the media and services bought on behalf of clients. However, in recent years, larger advertisers such as Coca-Cola and Procter & Gamble have been moving away from this compensation model to a 'value' or results-based model based on a number of metrics, including growth in sales and market share.

Growth in the advertising industry

Money spent on advertising has increased dramatically over the past two decades and is estimated in 2012 at over $165 billion (€127 bn, £102 bn) in the USA and $483 billion worldwide. While there might be a decline in recessionary years, it is predicted that spending on advertising will exceed $560 billion globally by 2015. Over 2011–12, the Dow Jones stock price index for the American media agencies sector (of which the leading advertising agencies are the largest members) rose about 15 per cent ahead of the New York Stock Exchange average (sources: bigcharts.com and dowjones.com).

The industry is shifting its focus as emerging markets drive revenues from geographic sectors that would not have been significant 5 to 10 years ago, such as the

BRIC countries and Middle East and North Africa. This shift has seen the emergence of agencies specialising in Islamic marketing, characterised by a strong ethical responsibility to consumers. Future trends indicate the strong emergence of consumer brands in areas of the world where sophisticated consumers with brand awareness are currently in the minority. (See Table 1.)

In terms of industry sectors, seven of the top 20 global advertisers are car manufacturers. However, the two major fmcg (fast-moving consumer goods) producers Procter & Gamble and Nestlé hold the two top spots for global advertising spend. Healthcare and beauty, telecommunications companies, food and beverage manufacturers, retailers and the entertainment industry are all featured in the top 20 global advertisers. The top 100 advertisers account for nearly 50 per cent of the measured global advertising economy.

Competition in the advertising industry

Agencies come in all sizes and include everything from one- or two-person 'boutique' operations (which rely mostly on freelance outsourced talent to perform most functions), small to medium-sized agencies, large independents to multinational, multi-agency conglomerates employing over 150,000 people. The industry has gone through a period of increasing concentration through acquisition thereby creating multi-agency conglomerates such as those listed in Table 2. While these conglomerates are mainly headquartered in London, New York and Paris, they operate globally.

Large multi-agency conglomerates compete on the basis of the quality of their creative teams (as indicated by industry awards), the ability to buy media more cost-effectively, market knowledge, global reach and breadth and range of services. Some agency groups have integrated vertically into higher-margin marketing services. Omnicom, through its Diversified Agency Services, has acquired printing services and telemarketing/customer care companies. Other agency groups have vertically integrated to lesser or greater degrees.

Mid-sized and smaller boutique advertising agencies compete by delivering value-added services through in-depth knowledge of specific market sectors, specialised services such as digital and by building a reputation for innovative and ground-breaking creative advertising/marketing campaigns. However, they might be more reliant on out sourced creative suppliers than larger agencies.

Many small specialist agencies are founded by former employees of large agencies, such as the breakaway from Young & Rubicam to form the agency Adam + Eve. In turn, smaller specialist agencies are often acquired by the large multi-agency conglomerates in order to acquire specific capabilities to target new sectors or markets or

Table 1 Advertising expenditure by region. Major media (newspapers, magazines, television, radio, cinema, outdoor, internet) (US$ million, currency conversion at 2009 average rates)

	2009	2010	2011	2012	2013
N America	156,556	160,386	164,516	169,277	175,024
W Europe	100,143	104,225	107,520	111,300	114,712
Asia Pacific	99,746	106,021	113,345	122,000	130,711
C & E Europe	25,402	27,095	29,243	32,284	35,514
Latin America	25,711	29,315	31,673	34,082	36,836
Africa/ME/ROW	21,220	22,654	24,150	25,941	28,044
World	**428,778**	**449,696**	**470,447**	**494,884**	**520,841**

Source: ZenithOptimedia, September 2012.

Table 2 Top five multi-agency conglomerates: 2011, by revenue, profit before interest and tax, number of employees and agency brands

Group name	Revenue	PBIT	Employees	Advertising agency brands
WPP (UK)	£10.2 bn	£1.429 bn	158,000	JWT, Grey, Ogilvy, Y&R
Omnicom (US)	$13.9 bn	$952 m	70,600	BBDO, DDB, TBWA
Publicis Groupe (France)	€5.8 bn	€600 m	53,807	Leo Burnett, Saatchi & Saatchi, Publicis, BBH
IPG (US)	$7.0 bn	$520 m	43,500	McCann Erickson, FCB, Lowe & Partners
Havas Worldwide (France)	€1.65 bn	€220 m	15,186	Havas Conseil

Source: Ad Age, Omnicom, WPP, Publicis Groupe, IPG, Havas.

provide additional services to existing clients, like WPP's acquisition of a majority stake in the smaller ideas and innovation agency AKQA for $540 m 'to prepare for a more digital future'.

Recent years have seen new competition in this industry as search companies such as Google, Yahoo and Microsoft Bing begin to exploit their ability to interact with and gain information about millions of potential consumers of branded products.

Sir Martin Sorrell, CEO of WPP, the world's largest advertising and marketing services group, has pointed out that Google will rival his agency's relationships with the biggest traditional media corporations such as TV, newspaper and magazine and possibly even become a rival for the relationships with WPP's clients. WPP group spent more than $2 bn with Google in 2012 (over double the $850 m the group spent on the internet company just four years previously) and $400 m with Facebook. Sorrell calls Google a 'frenemy' – the combination of 'friend' and 'enemy'. Google is a 'friend' where it allows WPP to place targeted advertising based on Google analytics and an 'enemy' where it does not share these analytics with the agency and becomes a potential competitor for the customer insight and advertising traditionally created by WPP.

With the development of the internet and online search advertising, a new breed of interactive digital media agencies, of which AKQA is an example, established themselves in the digital space before traditional advertising agencies fully embraced the internet. These agencies differentiate themselves by offering a mix of web design/development, search engine marketing, internet advertising/marketing, or e-business/e-commerce consulting. They are classified as 'agencies' because they create digital media campaigns and implement media purchases of ads on behalf of clients on social networking and community sites such as MySpace, Facebook, YouTube and other digital media.

Online advertising budgets are increasing faster than other traditional advertising media as search companies like Google generate revenues from paid search as advertisers discover that targeted ads online are highly effective (see Table 3). By mid-2011 Google had a 40 per cent market share of the $31 bn spent on online advertising in the USA, with Facebook also increasing its share.

The disruptive change in the advertising industry at the beginning of the twenty-first century started with the internet. Many industry experts believe that convergence of internet, TV, smart phones, tablets and laptop computers is inevitable, which in turn will have a further

Table 3 Advertising expenditure by medium (US$ million, currency conversion at 2009 average rates)

	2009	2010	2011	2012	2013
Newspapers	97,237	94,199	93,019	92,300	91,908
Magazines	43,844	43,184	42,644	42,372	42,300
Television	165,260	180,280	191,198	202,380	213,878
Radio	31,855	31,979	32,580	33,815	35,054
Cinema	2,104	2,258	2,393	2,538	2,681
Outdoor	28,120	29,319	30,945	32,821	34,554
Internet	54,209	61,884	70,518	80,672	91,516
Total	**422,629**	**443,103**	**463,297**	**486,898**	**511,891**

Note: The totals in Table 3 are lower than in Table 1, since that table includes advertising expenditure for a few countries where it is not itemised by medium.

Source: *ZenithOptimedia*, September 2012.

major impact on the advertising industry. Advertising on mobile devices, such as smart phones and tablets, is still in its infancy but accounted for 8 per cent of all search advertising in the last quarter of 2011 and is forecast to reach 15 per cent by 2016, which has attracted Google to make acquisitions in this sector.

Factors that have driven competitive advantage to date may not be relevant to competitive advantage in the future. Traditionally this industry has embodied the idea of creativity as the vital differentiator between the best and the mediocre. Individuals have often been at the heart of this creativity. With the emergence of Google, Yahoo, Facebook and Bing, influencing and changing the media by which advertising messages are being delivered, a key question is whether creativity will be more or less important in the future, in relation to breadth of services and global reach.

Sources and references

ZenithOptimedia, September 2012; Advertising Age; Omnicom Group http://www.omnicomgroup.com; WPP Group http://www.wpp.com; Publicis http://www.publicisgroupe.com; Interpublic Group of Companies http://www.interpublic.com; Havas Conseils http://www.havas.com/havas-dyn/en/; http://www.financialcontent.com. See also **The Strategy Experience**: the Strategy Simulation designed for *Exploring Strategy*: http://www.mystrategylab.com/strategy-experience.

Questions

1 Carry out a PESTEL analysis of the advertising industry in 2012, with particular attention to megatrends, inflexion points and weak signals.

2 Carry out a five forces analysis of the advertising industry in 2012. Which forces are becoming more negative or positive for the major advertising agencies?

3

STRATEGIC CAPABILITIES

Learning outcomes

After reading this chapter you should be able to:

● Identify *strategic capabilities* in terms of organisational *resources* and *competences* and how these relate to the strategies of organisations.

● Analyse how strategic capabilities might provide sustainable competitive advantage on the basis of their *Value*, *Rarity*, *Inimitability* and *Organisational support (VRIO)*.

● Diagnose strategic capability by means of *VRIO analysis*, *benchmarking*, *value chain analysis*, *activity mapping* and *SWOT analysis*.

● Consider how managers can *develop strategic capabilities* for their organisations.

Key terms

competences p. 70

dynamic capabilities p. 71

inimitable capabilities p. 77

organisational knowledge p. 80

rare capabilities p. 77

resource-based view p. 70

resources p. 70

strategic capabilities p. 71

SWOT p. 91

threshold capabilities p. 73

value p. 76

value chain p. 83

value system p. 83

VRIO p. 76

MyStrategyLab

MyStrategyLab is designed to help you make the most of your studies. Visit **www.pearsoned.co.uk/mystrategylab** to discover a wide range of resources, including:

● A personalised **Study plan** that will help you understand core concepts

● **Audio and video clips** that put the spotlight on strategy in the real world

● **Online glossaries and flashcards** that provide helpful reminders when you're looking for some quick revision.

(3.1) INTRODUCTION

Chapter 2 emphasised the importance of the external environment of an organisation and how it can create both strategic opportunities and threats. However, it is not only the external environment that matters for strategy; there are also differences between organisations that need to be taken into account. For example, manufacturers of saloon cars compete within the same industry and within the same technological environment, but with markedly different success. BMW has been relatively successful consistently; Ford and Chrysler have found it more difficult to maintain their competitive position. And others, such as Rover in the UK and SAAB in Sweden, have gone out of business (even though the brands as such have been acquired by others). It is not so much the characteristics of the environment which explain these differences in performance, but the differences in their company-specific *strategic capabilities* in terms of the *resources and competences* they have. This puts the focus on variations between companies within the same environment and industry and how they vary in their strategic capabilities and arrangements. It is the strategic importance of such capabilities that is the focus of this chapter.

The key issues posed by the chapter are summarised in Figure 3.1. Underlying these are two key concepts. The first is that organisations are not identical, but have different capabilities; they are 'heterogeneous' in this respect. The second is that it can be difficult for one organisation to obtain or copy the capabilities of another. The implication for managers is that they need to understand how their organisations are different from their rivals in ways that may be the basis of achieving competitive advantage and superior performance. These concepts

Figure 3.1 Strategic capabilities: the key issues

What are strategic capabilities?

How do strategic capabilities contribute to competitive advantage and superior performance?

How to diagnose strategic capabilities?

How to manage the development of strategic capabilities?

underlie what has become known as the **resource-based view** (RBV) of strategy[1] (sometimes labelled the 'capabilities view') pioneered by Jay Barney at Ohio State University: **that the competitive advantage and superior performance of an organisation are explained by the distinctiveness of its capabilities.** Resource – or capabilities – views have become very influential, but it should be borne in mind that while the terminology and concepts employed here align with these views, readers will find different terminology used elsewhere.

The chapter has four further sections:

- Section 3.2 discusses the foundations of *strategic capability*; in particular what is meant by *resources, competences* and the related concept of *dynamic capabilities.* It also draws a distinction between *threshold capabilities* required to be able to compete in a market and *distinctive capabilities* that may be a basis for achieving competitive advantage and superior performance.

- Section 3.3 explains the ways in which distinctive capabilities can contribute to the *developing and sustaining of competitive advantage* (in a public-sector context the equivalent concern might be how some organisations sustain relative superior performance over time). In particular, the importance of the *Value, Rarity, Inimitability and Organisational support* (VRIO) of capabilities is explained.

- Section 3.4 moves on to consider different ways strategic capability might be analysed. These include *benchmarking, value chain analysis, VRIO analysis* and *activity system mapping.* The section concludes by explaining the use of *SWOT* analysis as a basis for pulling together the insights from the analyses of the environment (explained in Chapter 2) and of strategic capabilities in this chapter.

- Finally section 3.5 discusses some of the key issues in managing the *development of strategic capabilities* through internal and external development and the management of people.

(3.2) FOUNDATIONS OF STRATEGIC CAPABILITY

Given that different writers, managers and consultants use different terms and concepts, it is important to understand how concepts relating to strategic capabilities are used in this book. Here **strategic capabilities** are **the capabilities of an organisation that contribute to its long-term survival or competitive advantage.** However, to understand and to manage strategic capability it is necessary to explain its components and the characteristics of those components.[2]

3.2.1 Resources and competences

There are two components of strategic capability: resources and competences. Resources are the assets that organisations have or can call upon and competences are the ways those assets are used or deployed effectively. A shorthand way of thinking of this is that resources are 'what we *have*' (nouns) and competences are 'what we *do well*' (verbs). Other terms are common and 'capabilities' and 'competences' are sometimes used interchangeably. For example, Gary Hamel and C.K. Prahalad refer to *core competences* and many writers use the term *intangible assets* as an umbrella term to include competences and capabilities as well as intangible resources such as brands.

Table 3.1 **Components of strategic capabilities**

Strategic capability		
Resources: what we have (nouns), e.g.		**Competences: what we do well (verbs), e.g.**
Machines, buildings, raw materials, products, patents, databases, computer systems	Physical	Ways of achieving utilisation of plant, efficiency, productivity, flexibility, marketing
Balance sheet, cash flow, suppliers of funds	Financial	Ability to raise funds and manage cash flows, debtors, creditors, etc.
Managers, employees, partners, suppliers, customers	Human	How people gain and use experience, skills, knowledge, build relationships, motivate others and innovate
Long-term survival and competitive advantage		

Typically all strategic capabilities have elements of both resources and competences as Table 3.1 shows. Resources are certainly important, but how an organisation employs and deploys its resources matters at least as much. There would be no point in having state-of-the-art equipment if it were not used effectively. The efficiency and effectiveness of physical or financial resources, or the people in an organisation, depend not just on their existence, but on the systems and processes by which they are managed, the relationships and cooperation between people, their adaptability, their innovative capacity, the relationship with customers and suppliers, and the experience and learning about what works well and what does not. Illustration 3.1 shows examples of how executives explain the importance of the resources and capabilities of their different organisations.

3.2.2 **Dynamic capabilities**[3]

If they are to provide a basis for long-term success, strategic capabilities cannot be static; they need to change. University of Berkeley economist David Teece has introduced the concept of **dynamic capabilities**, by which he means **an organisation's ability to renew and recreate its strategic capabilities to meet the needs of changing environments**. He argues that the capabilities that are necessary for efficient operations, like owning certain tangible assets, controlling costs, maintaining quality, optimising inventories, etc., are unlikely to be sufficient for sustaining superior performance.[4] These '*ordinary capabilities*' allow companies to be successful and earn a living now by producing and selling a similar product or service to similar customers over time, but are not likely to provide for long-term survival and competitive advantage in the future.[5]

In other words Teece acknowledges the danger that capabilities that were the basis of competitive success can over time be imitated by competitors, become common practice in an industry or become redundant as its environment changes. So, the important lesson is that if capabilities are to be effective over time they need to change; they cannot be static. Dynamic capabilities are directed towards that strategic change. They are dynamic in the sense that they can create, extend or modify an organisation's existing operational capabilities. Teece suggests the following three generic types of dynamic capabilities:

ILLUSTRATION

ILLUSTRATION 3.1

Strategic capabilities

Executives emphasise different strategic capabilities in different organisations.

The Goddard Space Flight Center

Flight Center NASA's Goddard Space Flight Center manages many aspects of the space agency's missions and lays claim to some unique resources. For example, its 42-foot-tall acoustic test chamber can produce sounds of up to 150 decibels to allow technicians to expose payloads to launch noise. The high bay clean room, which can accommodate two Space Shuttle payloads, circulates 9 million cubic feet of air every minute through its filters to prevent contaminants damaging spacecraft components – essential to space missions since cleaning of such contaminants in space is highly problematic. And its 120-foot-diameter high-capacity centrifuge with two 1250-horsepower motors can accelerate a 2.5-tonne payload up to 30Gs.[1]

Royal Opera House, London

Tony Hall, Chief Executive of the Royal Opera House:

'"World-class" is neither an idle nor boastful claim. In the context of the Royal Opera House the term refers to the quality of our people, the standards of our productions and the diversity of our work and initiatives. Unique? Unashamedly so. We shy away from labels such as "elite", because of the obvious negative connotations of exclusiveness. But I want people to take away from here the fact that we are elite in the sense that we have the best singers, dancers, directors, designers, orchestra, chorus, backstage crew and administrative staff. We are also among the best in our ability to reach out to as wide and diverse a community as possible.'[2]

Infosys

The Indian company Infosys is a global leader in information technology, outsourcing and consulting. It is listed as one of the world's most reputable companies with close to 150,000 employees worldwide. Infosys has developed from providing business process outsourcing services including call centres and back office IT operations to offering IT infrastructure management, system integration services and IT consulting. Today its 'Infosys 3.0 strategy' is taking a further step to provide more advanced IT products and services.

The new strategy emphasises innovation and focuses on higher-value software. Innovation abilities are central for this, as stated on the website: 'The foundation of our innovation capability is our core lab network – Infosys Labs – and the new thinking that our team of over 600 researchers brings to the table.' The new strategy thus requires human resource and training capabilities including the ability to attract, employ, educate and retain new high-quality engineers. As Srikantan Moorthy, Senior Vice President and Group Head explains: 'We are currently hiring and developing talent in the areas of cloud, mobility, sustainability and product development. In addition, a key focus is consultative skills. All of these are in line with our Infosys 3.0 strategy. We place significant value on continuous learning and knowledge sharing.'

Infosys CEO S.D. Shibulal explains Infosys capability build-up: 'We continue to make focused investments in our organisational capabilities.' 'Our Infosys 3.0 strategy requires us to focus on our acquisition strategy to enhance our capabilities. . . .' Accordingly, Infosys acquired the Swiss management and IT consultants Lodestone in September 2012: 'A key plan of our Infosys 3.0 strategy is to expand our consulting and systems integration business. This acquisition fits perfectly into that strategy.'[3]

Sources: (1) Goddard Space Center website. (2) Annual Review, 2005–6, p. 11. (3) *Financial Times*, 13 August 2012; *Financial Times*, 11 September 2012; http://www.infosys.com © Infosys; http://www.skillingindia.com/.

Questions

1 Categorise the range of capabilities highlighted by the executives in terms of section 3.2 and Table 3.1.

2 To what extent and why might these capabilities be the basis of *sustained* competitive advantage?

3 For an organisation of your choice undertake the same exercise as in questions 1 and 2 above.

- *Sensing.* Sensing implies that organisations must constantly scan, search and explore opportunities across various markets and technologies. Research and development and investigating customer needs are typical sensing activities. For example, companies in the PC operating systems industry, like Microsoft, have clearly sensed the opportunities in and threats from tablets and smart phones.

- *Seizing.* Once an opportunity is sensed it must be seized and addressed through new products or services, processes, activities etc. Microsoft, for example, has started to seize opportunities by developing its own tablet device and software and by acquiring the mobile company Nokia.

- *Reconfiguring.* To seize an opportunity may require renewal and reconfiguration of organisational capabilities and investments in technologies, manufacturing, markets, etc. For example, Microsoft's inroad into tablets and smart phones requires major changes in its current strategic capabilities. The company must discard some of its old capabilities, acquire and build new ones and recombine them.

This view of dynamic capabilities above relates directly to the framework for this book: strategic position, strategic choices and strategy in action (see Figure 1.3). Sensing capabilities are to do with understanding an organisation's strategic position; seizing opportunities relate to making strategic choices; and reconfiguration is to do with enacting strategies. Illustration 3.2 provides an example of dynamic capabilities in the context of mobile telephones.

New product development is a typical example of a dynamic capability and strategic planning is another. They both involve activities that can sense and seize opportunities and that are intended to reconfigure capabilities. Outlet proliferation by chain retailers such as Starbucks is another example of a dynamic capability as it extends operational capabilities.[6] Dynamic capabilities may also take the form of relatively formal organisational systems, such as recruitment and management development processes and cooperating with others through alliances or acquisitions, by which new skills are learned and developed.[7]

As Teece acknowledges, however, dynamic capabilities are likely to have 'microfoundations'[8] in people's behaviour of organisations, such as the way in which decisions get taken, personal relationships, and entrepreneurial and intuitive skills. This puts the focus on behaviour and the significance of beliefs, social relationships and experience in capability management, which is discussed in the very last section of this chapter on managing capabilities (see section 3.5).

In brief, strategic capabilities include both operational capabilities and dynamic capabilities that can change operational capabilities in case the environment changes. However, as dynamic capabilities are focused on finding solutions beyond and outside current operational capabilities there is a trade-off and tension between the two that can make it difficult to achieve an optimal balance between them within a single organisation or unit. This is sometimes referred to as exploration/exploitation trade-offs and they are further discussed in Chapter 14.

3.2.3 Threshold and distinctive capabilities

A distinction also needs to be made between strategic capabilities that are at a threshold level and those that might help the organisation achieve competitive advantage and superior performance. Threshold capabilities **are those needed for an organisation to meet the necessary requirements to compete in a given market and achieve parity with competitors in that market.** Without such capabilities the organisation could not survive over time. Indeed many start-up businesses find this to be the case. They simply do not have or cannot obtain the resources or competences needed to compete with established competitors. Identifying

ILLUSTRATION 3.2

Dynamic capabilities (and rigidities) in mobile telephone companies

Dynamic capabilities can help firms sense and seize opportunities and reconfigure operational capabilities in changing environments.

Companies in the mobile telephone industry have built on their dynamic capabilities in their effort to adapt to environmental changes and dominate the market. They have identified and evaluated new opportunities (sensing); addressed these opportunities with new products (seizing) and renewed and redeployed their capabilities accordingly (reconfiguring). This is illustrated in the table.

The pioneers in mobile telephony, Ericsson and Motorola, managed to sense and explore an entirely new mobile telephony market. They satisfied and captured value in that market by recombining and redeploying telecommunication and radio capabilities. However, they got stuck in these early mobile telephone capabilities and were followed by Nokia. Nokia sensed new opportunities as it realised that mobile phones' awkward design and functionality was not suited to what had become a mass consumer and fashion market. The company seized and addressed these new opportunities, offering improved design and functionality, building on design and consumer

behaviour capabilities. Finally, Apple, with a long legacy in consumer products, explored even further opportunities. Apple realised that most phones, even the new smart phones, still maintained a complex and unintuitive interface with limited multimedia functionalities. Apple addressed this by introducing an upgraded multimedia platform smart phone with an intuitive and simple interface combined with complementary services like the App Store and iTunes Music Store. Apple built on a recombination of its prior design, interface and consumer behaviour capabilities and new (for them) mobile phone capabilities.

While the dynamic capabilities of the mobile phone companies helped them adapt, they are no guarantee for keeping ahead permanently as the operating capabilities they developed risk becoming rigidities as markets and technologies change even further. If dynamic capabilities do not manage to detect and alleviate rigidities, competitors may emerge over time with more appropriate dynamic capabilities for the constantly changing environment.

threshold requirements is, however, also important for established businesses. There could be changing *threshold resources* required to meet minimum customer requirements: for example, the increasing demands by modern multiple retailers of their suppliers mean that those suppliers have to possess a quite sophisticated IT infrastructure simply to stand a chance of meeting retailer requirements. Or they could be the *threshold competences* required to deploy resources so as to meet customers' requirements and support particular strategies. Retailers do not simply expect suppliers to have the required IT infrastructure, but to be able to use it effectively so as to guarantee the required level of service.

Identifying and managing threshold capabilities raises a significant challenge because threshold levels of capability will change as critical success factors change (see section 2.4.3) or through the activities of competitors and new entrants. To continue the example above, suppliers to major retailers did not require the same level of IT and logistics support a decade ago. But the retailers' drive to reduce costs, improve efficiency and ensure availability of merchandise to their customers means that their expectations of their suppliers have increased markedly in that time and continue to do so. So there is a need for those suppliers continuously to review and improve their logistics resource and competence base just to stay in business.

Companies	Approximate time period	Product	Sensing	Seizing	Reconfiguring
Ericsson (primarily Europe) **Motorola** (primarily the US)	Mid-1980s– late 1990s	Mobile phones	Need for mobile telephones: Fixed telephony did not offer mobility	Creating the first mobile telephone systems and telephones	Creating a new mobile telephone market Acquiring and building mobile telephone capabilities
Nokia	Late 1990s– early 2000s	Mobile phones with improved design and functionality	Need for well-designed and fashionable mobile phones: Existing mobile phones were close to their car-phone origins and maintained their awkward design and functionality	Upgrading the mobile phone to provide a richer experience in design, fashion and functionality	Entering the mobile telephone market Acquiring and building mobile telephony capabilities Building design and marketing capabilities
Apple	Late 2000s–	Mobile phones with perfected design, functionality and interface	Need for smart phones with multimedia functionality: Existing smart phones maintained a complex and unintuitive interface with limited functionalities	Upgrading the mobile phone to include an intuitive interface and multimedia functionalities containing the App store and iTunes	Entering the mobile telephone market Acquiring mobile telephony capabilities and recombining them with existing design and interface capabilities Cooperating with the music and telephone app industries

Questions

1 What type of dynamic capabilities could help companies avoid becoming stuck in their old capabilities?
2 a What are the possible future opportunities in mobile telephones?
  b How could they be sensed and seized?
  c What type of ordinary capabilities could possibly address them?

While threshold capabilities are important, they do not of themselves create competitive advantage or the basis of superior performance. **Distinctive capabilities are required to achieve competitive advantage.** These are dependent on an organisation having distinctive or unique capabilities that are of value to customers and which competitors find difficult to imitate. This could be because the organisation has *distinctive resources* that critically underpin competitive advantage and that others cannot imitate or obtain – a long-established brand, for example. Or it could be that an organisation achieves competitive advantage because it has *distinctive competences* – ways of doing things that are unique to that organisation and effectively utilised so as to be valuable to customers and difficult for competitors to obtain or imitate. Gary Hamel and C.K. Prahalad argue that distinctive competences typically remain unique because they comprise a *bundle* of constituent skills and technologies rather than a single, discrete skill or technology (they refer to this as a 'core competence').[9] The emphasis is thus on the linked set of skills, activities and resources.

Bringing these concepts together, a supplier that achieves competitive advantage in a retail market might have done so on the basis of a distinctive resource such as a powerful brand, but also by distinctive competences such as the building of excellent relations with retailers. The distinctive competences that are likely to be most difficult for competitors to match and form the basis of competitive advantage will be the multiple and linked ways of providing products, high levels of service and building relationships. Section 3.3 that follows discusses in more depth the role played by distinctive resources and competences in contributing to long-term, sustainable competitive advantage. Section 3.4 then explores further the importance of link-ages between activities.

(3.3) 'VRIO' STRATEGIC CAPABILITIES AS A BASIS OF COMPETITIVE ADVANTAGE

As explained above, distinctive capabilities are necessary for sustainable competitive advant-age and superior economic performance. This section considers four key criteria by which capabilities can be assessed in terms of their providing a basis for achieving such competitive advantage: **v**alue, **r**arity, **i**nimitability and **o**rganisational support – or **VRIO**.[10] Figure 3.2 illustrates these four fundamental criteria and the questions they address.

3.3.1 V – value of strategic capabilities

Strategic capabilities are valuable when they create a product or a service that is of value to customers and if, and only if, they generate higher revenues or lower costs or both. There are three components here:

- *Taking advantage of opportunities and neutralising threats*: the most fundamental issue is that to be valuable capabilities need to provide the potential to address the opportunities and threats that arise in the organisation's environment, which points to an important comple-mentarity with the external environment of an organisation (Chapter 2). Capabilities are valuable if they address opportunities and/or threats and generate higher revenues or lower costs or both compared to if the organisation did not have those capabilities. For example, IKEA's cost-conscious culture, size and its intricate configuration of interlinked activities lower its costs compared to competitors and addresses opportunities of low-priced furniture that competitors do not attend to.

Figure 3.2 VRIO

V	**Value:** Do capabilities exist that are valued by customers and enable the organisation to respond to environmental opportunities or threats?
R	**Rarity:** Do capabilities exist that no (or few) competitors possess?
I	**Inimitability:** Are capabilities difficult and costly for competitors to obtain and imitate?
O	**Organisational support:** Is the organisation appropriately organised to exploit the capabilities?

- *Value to customers*: it may seem an obvious point to make that capabilities need to be of value to customers, but in practice it is often ignored or poorly understood. For example, managers may seek to build on capabilities that *they* may see as valuable but which do not meet customers' critical success factors (see section 2.4.3). Or they may see a distinctive capability as of value simply because it is distinctive, although it may not be valued by customers. Having capabilities that are different from other organisations' is not, of itself, a basis of competitive advantage.

- *Cost*: the product or service needs to be provided at a cost that still allows the organisation to make the returns expected of it. The danger is that the cost of developing or acquiring the capabilities to deliver what customers especially value is such that products or services are not profitable.

Managers should therefore consider carefully which of their organisation's activities are especially important in providing such value and which are of less value. Value chain analysis and activity mapping explained in sections 3.4.2 and 3.4.3 can help here.

3.3.2 R – rarity

Capabilities that are valuable, but common among competitors, are unlikely to be a source of competitive advantage. If competitors have similar capabilities they can respond quickly to the strategic initiative of a rival. This has happened in competition between car manufacturers as they have sought to add more accessories and gadgets to cars. As soon as it becomes evident that these are valued by customers, they are introduced widely by competitors who typically have access to the same technology. **Rare capabilities**, on the other hand, **are those possessed uniquely by one organisation or by a few others**. Here competitive advantage is longer-lasting. For example, a company can have patented products or services that give it advantage. Service organisations may have rare resources in the form of intellectual capital – perhaps particularly talented individuals. Some libraries have unique collections of books unavailable elsewhere; a company can have a powerful brand; or retail stores can have prime locations. In terms of competences, organisations can have unique skills developed over time or have built special relationships with customers or suppliers not widely possessed by competitors. However, it can be dangerous to assume that resources and capabilities that are rare will remain so. So it may be necessary to consider other bases of sustainability.

3.3.3 I – inimitability

It should be clear by now that the search for strategic capability that provides sustainable competitive advantage is not straightforward. Having capabilities that are valuable to customers and relatively rare is important, but this may not be enough. Sustainable competitive advantage also involves identifying **inimitable capabilities** – **those that competitors find difficult and costly to imitate or obtain or substitute**. If an organisation has a competitive advantage because of its particular marketing and sales skills it can only sustain this if competitors cannot imitate, obtain or substitute for them or if the costs to do so would eliminate any gains made. Often the barriers to imitation lie deeply in the organisation in linkages between activities, skills and people.

At the risk of over-generalisation, it is unusual for competitive advantage to be explainable by differences in the tangible resources of organisations, since over time these can usually be

Figure 3.3 Criteria for the inimitability of strategic capabilities

acquired or imitated (key geographic locations, certain raw material resources, brands, etc., can, however, be exceptions). Advantage is more likely to be determined by the way in which resources are deployed and managed in terms of an organisation's activities; in other words on the basis of competences.[11] For example, as indicated above, it is unlikely that an IT system will improve an organisation's competitive standing in itself, not least because competitors can probably buy something very similar on the open market. On the other hand the competences to manage, develop and deploy such a system to the benefit of customers may be much more difficult and costly to imitate. Compared to physical assets and patents, competences, then, tend to involve more intangible imitation barriers. In particular, they often include *linkages* that integrate activities, skills, knowledge and people both inside and outside the organisation in distinct and mutually compatible ways. These linkages can make capabilities particularly difficult for competitors to imitate and there are three primary reasons why this may be so. These are summarised in Figure 3.3 and are now briefly reviewed.

Complexity

The capabilities of an organisation can be difficult to imitate because they are complex and involve interlinkages. This may be for two main reasons:

● *Internal linkages.* There may be linked activities and processes that, together, deliver customer value. The discussion of activity systems in section 3.4.3 below explains this in more detail and shows how such linked sets of activities might be mapped so that they can be better understood. However, even if a competitor possessed such a map, it is unlikely that it would be able to replicate the sort of complexity it represents because of the numerous interactions between tightly knit activities and decisions.[12] This is not only because of the complexity itself but because, very likely, it has developed on the basis of custom and practice built up over years and is specific to the organisation concerned. For example, companies like IKEA and Ryanair still enjoy competitive advantages despite the availability of countless case studies, articles and reports on their successes.

- *External interconnectedness.* Organisations can make it difficult for others to imitate or obtain their bases of competitive advantage by developing activities together with customers or partners such that they become dependent on them. This is sometimes referred to as *co-specialisation.* For example, an industrial lubricants business moved away from just selling its products to customers by coming to an agreement with them to manage the applications of lubricants within the customers' sites against agreed targets on cost savings. The more efficient the use of lubricants, the more both parties benefited.

Causal ambiguity[13]

Another reason why capabilities might be difficult and costly to imitate is that competitors find it difficult to discern the causes and effects underpinning an organisation's advantage. This is called *causal ambiguity.* Causal ambiguity may exist in two different forms:[14]

- *Characteristic ambiguity.* Where the significance of the characteristic itself is difficult to discern or comprehend, perhaps because it is based on tacit knowledge or rooted in the organisation's culture. For example, the know-how of the buyers in a successful fashion retailer may be evident in the sales achieved for the ranges they buy year after year. But it may be very difficult to comprehend just what that know-how is, so competitors will find it difficult to imitate.

- *Linkage ambiguity.* Where competitors cannot discern which activities and processes are dependent on which others to form linkages that create distinctive competences. The expertise of the fashion buyers is unlikely to be lodged in the one individual or even one function. It is likely that there will be a network of suppliers, intelligence networks to understand the market and links with designers. Indeed in some organisations the managers themselves admit that they do not fully comprehend the linkages throughout the organisation that deliver customer value. If this is so it would certainly be difficult for competitors to understand them.

Culture and history

Competences that involve complex social interactions and interpersonal relations within an organisation can be difficult and costly for competitors to imitate systematically and manage. For example, competences can become embedded in an organisation's culture. Coordination between various activities occurs 'naturally' because people know their part in the wider picture or it is simply 'taken for granted' that activities are done in particular ways. We see this in high-performing sports teams, in groups of people that work together to combine specialist skills as in operating theatres; but also, for example, in how some firms integrate different activities in their business to deliver excellent customer service. Linked to this cultural embeddedness is the likelihood that such competences have developed over time and in a particular way. The origins and history by which competences have developed over time are referred to as *path dependency.*[15] This history is specific to the organisation and cannot be imitated (see section 5.2.1). As explained in Chapter 5, there is, however, a danger that culturally embedded competences built up over time become so embedded that they are difficult to change: they become rigidities.

3.3.4 O – organisational support

Providing value to customers and possessing capabilities that are rare and difficult to imitate provides a potential for competitive advantage. However, **the organisation must also be suitably organised to support these capabilities** including appropriate organisational processes and systems. This implies that to fully take advantage of the capabilities an organisation's structure and formal and informal management control systems need to support and facilitate their exploitation (see sections 13.1 and 13.2 for further discussions of organisational structure and systems). The question of organisational support works as an adjustment factor. Some of the potential competitive advantage can be lost if the organisation is not organised in a way that it can fully take advantage of valuable and/or rare and/or inimitable capabilities. The supporting capabilities have been labelled *complementary capabilities* as, by themselves, they are often not enough to provide for competitive advantage, but they are useful and effective in the exploitation of other capabilities that can provide for competitive advantage.[16] In brief, even though an organisation has valuable, rare and inimitable capabilities some of its potential competitive advantage may not be realised if it lacks the organisational arrangements to fully exploit these.

In summary and from a resource-based view of organisations, managers need to consider whether their organisation has strategic capabilities to achieve and sustain competitive advantage. To do so they need to consider how and to what extent it has capabilities which are (i) valuable, (ii) rare, (iii) inimitable and (iv) supported by the organisation. Table 3.2 summarises the VRIO framework of capabilities and shows that there is an additive effect. Strategic capabilities provide sustainable bases of competitive advantage the more they meet all four criteria. Illustration 3.3 gives an example of the challenges in meeting these criteria in the context of an internet-based company. If capabilities for competitive advantage do not exist, then managers need to consider if they can be developed. How this might be done is considered in section 3.5 below.

3.3.5 Organisational knowledge as a basis of competitive advantage

A good example of how both resources and competences may combine to produce competitive advantage for an organisation is in terms of organisational knowledge.[17] Organisational knowledge is organisation-specific, collective intelligence, accumulated through formal systems and people's shared experience.

The reasons why organisational knowledge is seen as especially important illustrate many of the points made above. As organisations become larger and more complex, the need to share what people know becomes more and more important but increasingly challenging.

Table 3.2 The VRIO framework

Is the capability . . .				
valuable?	rare?	inimitable?	supported by the organisation?	Competitive implications
No	–	–	No	Competitive disadvantage
Yes	No	–	↕	Competitive parity
Yes	Yes	No		Temporary competitive advantage
Yes	Yes	Yes	Yes	Sustained competitive advantage

Source: Adapted with the permission of J.B. Barney and W.S. Hesterly, *Strategic Management and Competitive Advantage*, Pearson, 2012.

ILLUSTRATION 3.3

Groupon and the sincerest form of flattery

When a firm identifies a new market niche it must also make sure its strategic capabilities are valuable, rare, inimitable and supported by the organisation.

Chicago-based Groupon was launched in 2008 by Andrew Mason with the idea to email subscribers daily deals of heavily discounted coupons for local restaurants, theatres, spas, etc. Groupon sells a coupon for a product and takes up to half of the proceeds, which represent a big discount on the product's usual price. In return, Groupon aggregates demand from the customers who receive its emails and this provides exposure to and increased business for the local merchants. The venture rapidly became the fastest-growing Internet business ever and grew into a daily deal industry giant. In 2010 Groupon rejected a $6 bn (€4.5 bn) takeover bid by Google and instead went public at $10 bn in November of 2011.

While Groupon's daily deals were valued by customers – the company quickly spread to over 40 countries – they also attracted first hundreds and later thousands of copycats worldwide. Investors started to question Groupon's business model and to what extent it had rare and inimitable strategic capabilities. In 2012 the CEO Andrew Mason denied in *Wall Street Journal* (*WSJ*) that the model was too easy to replicate:

> 'There's proof. There are over 2000 direct clones of the Groupon business model. However, there's an equal amount of proof that the barriers to success are enormous. In spite of all those competitors, only a handful are remotely relevant.'

This, however, did not calm investors and the online coupon seller's shares promptly fell by 80 per cent to its all-time low. The question thus remained – to what extent were Groupon's capabilities rare and inimitable? One significant asset Groupon had that is rare and possibly difficult to imitate is its impressive customer base of more than 50 million customers. The more customers, the better deals and this would make customers come to Groupon rather than the competitors and the cost for competitors to acquire customers would go up. Critics argued, however, that other companies such as Facebook, Google and Amazon had even broader user bases and could possibly

become competitors. Further defending Groupon's competitiveness the CEO emphasised in *WSJ* that it is not as simple as providing daily deals via email, but that a whole series of things have to work together and to imitate Groupon competitors would have to replicate everything in its 'operational complexity':

> 'People overlook the operational complexity. We have 10,000 employees across 46 countries. We have thousands of salespeople talking to tens of thousands of merchants every single day. It's not an easy thing to build.'

Another resource that Andrew Mason stressed was Groupon's advanced technology platform that allowed the company to 'provide better targeting to customers and give them deals that are more relevant to them'. Part of this platform, however, was got via acquisitions – a route competitors possibly could take as well.

If imitation is the highest form of flattery Groupon has been highly complimented. Hundreds of copycats have, however, left the business and Groupon has also beaten back more serious competitors, but the company continues to be under considerable pressure. In February 2013 founder and CEO Andrew Mason was forced to step down, which was a sign that many changes would come at Groupon.

Sources: All Things Digital, 2 November 2012, *Wall Street Journal*: http://allthingsd.com/20121102/groupon-shares-dive-to-new-low-a-year-after-the-ipo/; *Financial Times*, 14 May 2012; *Financial Times*, 2 March 2013; *Wall Street Journal*, 31 January 2012.

Questions

1 Andrew Mason admits that Groupon has thousands of copycats, yet his assessment is that imitating Groupon is difficult. Do you agree?

2 Assess the bases of Groupon's strategic capabilities using the VRIO criteria (Figure 3.2 and Table 3.2).

3 Which is the most important strategic capability that provides, or could provide, Groupon with sustainable competitive advantage?

So organisations that can share knowledge especially well may gain advantage over those that do not. Computerised information systems are available or have been developed by organisations to codify technological, financial and market data that are *valuable* to them; indeed without which they probably could not compete effectively. However, the technology that forms the basis of information systems is hardly *rare*; it is widely available or can be developed. It is therefore less likely that organisations will achieve competitive advantage through such resources and more likely that it will be achieved through the way they manage and develop organisational knowledge more broadly. This may be to do with the competences they employ to utilise and develop information technology. But it is also likely to be about how they draw on and develop the accumulated and dispersed experience-based knowledge in the organisation.

The distinction between e*xplicit* and *tacit organisational knowledge* made by Ikijuro Nonaka and Hiro Takeuchi[18] helps explain why this is important in terms of achieving competitive advantage. Explicit or 'objective' knowledge is transmitted in formal systematic ways. It can take the form of a codified information resource such as a systems manual or files of market research and intelligence. In contrast, tacit knowledge is more personal, context-specific and therefore hard to formalise and communicate. For example, it could be the knowledge of a highly experienced sales force or research and development team; or the experience of a top management team in making many successful acquisitions. It is therefore not only distinctive to the organisation, but likely to be *difficult to imitate* or obtain for the reasons explained in section 3.3.3 above. Such knowledge may have been developed over the years by '*communities of practice*'[19] developing and sharing information because it is mutually beneficial to them. It may also be continually changing as their experience changes. It will also be difficult for competitors to comprehend precisely because it is context specific, experiential and dispersed (and therefore complex and causally ambiguous).

Many organisations that have tried to improve the sharing of knowledge by relying on IT-based systems have come to realise that, while some knowledge can usefully be codified and built into computer-based systems, it can be very difficult to codify the knowledge that truly bestows competitive advantage.

(3.4) DIAGNOSING STRATEGIC CAPABILITIES

So far this chapter has been concerned with explaining concepts associated with the strategic significance of organisations' resources and capabilities. This section now provides some ways in which strategic capabilities can be understood and diagnosed.

3.4.1 Benchmarking[20]

Benchmarking is used as a means of understanding how an organisation compares with others – typically competitors. Many benchmarking exercises focus on outputs such as standards of product or service, but others do attempt to take account of organisational capabilities.

Broadly, there are two approaches to benchmarking:

- *Industry/sector benchmarking.* Insights about performance standards can be gleaned by comparing performance against other organisations in the same industry sector or between similar service providers against a set of performance indicators. Some public-sector organisations have, in effect, acknowledged the existence of strategic groups (see section 2.4.1) by benchmarking against similar organisations rather than against everybody: for example, local government services and police treat 'urban' differently from 'rural' in their bench- marking and league tables. An overriding danger of industry norm comparisons (whether in the private or the public sector) is, however, that the whole industry can be performing badly and losing out competitively to other industries that can satisfy customers' needs in different ways.

● *Best-in-class benchmarking.* Best-in-class benchmarking compares an organisation's performance or capabilities against 'best-in-class' performance – from whichever industry – and therefore seeks to overcome some of the above limitations. It may also help challenge managers' mind-sets that acceptable improvements in performance will result from incre- mental changes in resources or competences. For example, Southwest Airlines improved refuelling time by studying the processes surrounding Formula One Grand Prix motor racing pit stops.[21]

The importance of benchmarking is, then, not so much in the detailed 'mechanics' of comparison but in the impact that these comparisons might have on reviewing capabilities underlying performance. But it has two potential limitations:

● *Surface comparisons.* If benchmarking is limited to comparing outputs, it does not directly identify the reasons for relative performance in terms of underlying capabilities. For example, it may demonstrate that one organisation is poorer at customer service than another, but not show the underlying reasons.

● *Simply achieving competitive parity.* Benchmarking can help an organisation to develop capabilities and create value in the same way as its competitors and those best-in-class. However, the best performance that can be expected out of this exercise is to achieve thresh- old capabilities and/or competitive parity. For organisations with competitive disadvantage this can be highly rewarding, but to achieve competitive advantage an organisation needs to move further and develop its own distinctive capabilities.

3.4.2 The value chain and value system

The value chain describes the categories of activities within an organisation which, together, create a product or service. Most organisations are also part of a wider value system, the set of inter-organisational links and relationships that are necessary to create a product or service. Both are useful in understanding the strategic position of an organisation and where valuable strategic capabilities reside.

The value chain

If organisations are to achieve competitive advantage by delivering value to customers, man- agers need to understand which activities their organisation undertakes that are especially important in creating that value and which are not. This can then be used to model the value generation of an organisation. The important point is that the concept of the value chain invites the strategist to think of an organisation in terms of sets of activities. There are different frameworks for considering these categories: Figure 3.4 is a representation of a value chain as developed by Michael Porter.[22]

Primary activities are directly concerned with the creation or delivery of a product or service. For example, for a manufacturing business:

Figure 3.4 The value chain within an organisation

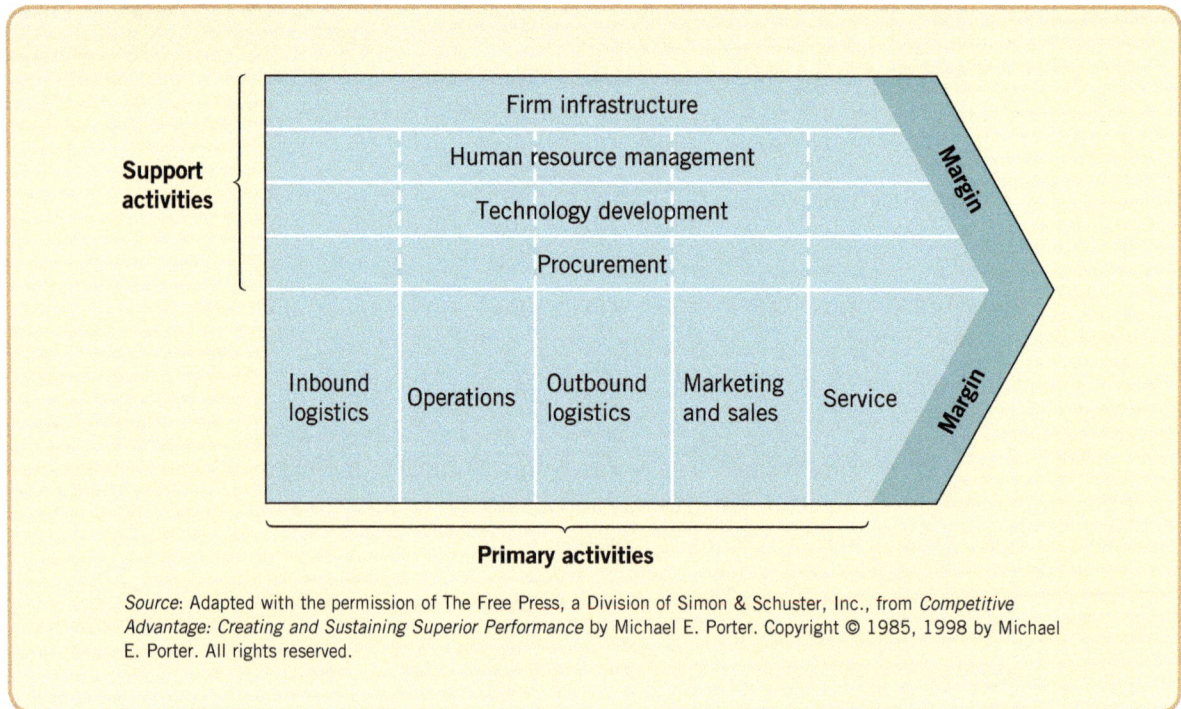

- *Inbound logistics* are activities concerned with receiving, storing and distributing inputs to the product or service including materials handling, stock control, transport, etc.
- *Operations* transform these inputs into the final product or service: machining, packaging, assembly, testing, etc.
- *Outbound logistics* collect, store and distribute the product or service to customers; for example, warehousing, materials handling, distribution, etc.
- *Marketing and sales* provide the means whereby consumers or users are made aware of the product or service and are able to purchase it. This includes sales administration, advertising and selling.
- *Service* includes those activities that enhance or maintain the value of a product or service, such as installation, repair, training and spares.

Each of these groups of primary activities is linked to *support activities* which help to improve the effectiveness or efficiency of primary activities:

- *Procurement.* Processes that occur in many parts of the organisation for acquiring the various resource inputs to the primary activities. These can be vitally important in achieving scale advantages. So, for example, many large consumer goods companies with multiple businesses none the less procure advertising centrally.
- *Technology development.* All value activities have a 'technology', even if it is just know-how. Technologies may be concerned directly with a product (e.g. R&D, product design) or with processes (e.g. process development) or with a particular resource (e.g. raw materials improvements).
- *Human resource management.* This transcends all primary activities and is concerned with recruiting, managing, training, developing and rewarding people within the organisation.

- *Infrastructure.* The formal systems of planning, finance, quality control, information management and the structure of an organisation.

The value chain can be used to understand the strategic position of an organisation and analyse strategic capabilities in three ways:

- As a *generic description of activities* it can help managers understand if there is a cluster of activities providing benefit to customers located within particular areas of the value chain. Perhaps a business is especially good at outbound logistics linked to its marketing and sales operation and supported by its technology development. It might be less good in terms of its operations and its inbound logistics.

- In analysing the competitive position of the organisation using the *VRIO criteria* as follows:

  V Which *value*-creating activities are especially significant for an organisation in meeting customer needs and could they be usefully developed further?

  R To what extent and how does an organisation have bases of value creation that are *rare?* Or conversely are all elements of its value chain common to its competitors?

  I What aspects of value creation are difficult for others to *imitate*, perhaps because they are *embedded* in the activity systems of the organisation (see section 3.4.3 below)?

  O What parts of the value chain support and facilitate value creation activities in other sections of the value chain? For example, firm infrastructure support activities including particular formal and informal management control systems can be necessary to fully exploit value creation in the primary activities.

- To *analyse the cost and value of activities*[23] of an organisation. This could involve the following steps:

  - *Identifying sets of value activities.* Figure 3.4 might be appropriate as a general framework here or a value chain more specific to an organisation can be developed. The important thing is to ask (i) which separate categories of activities best describe the operations of the organisation and (ii) which of these are most significant in delivering the strategy and achieving advantage over competitors? For example, it is likely that in a branded pharmaceutical company research and development and marketing activities will be crucially important.

  - *Relative importance of activity costs internally.* Which activities are most significant in terms of the costs of operations? Does the significance of costs align with the significance of activities? Which activities add most value to the final product or service (and in turn to the customer) and which do not? It can also be important to establish which sets of activities are linked to or are dependent on others and which, in effect, are self-standing. For example, organisations that have undertaken such analyses often find that central services have grown to the extent that they are a disproportionate cost to internal sets of activities and to the customer.

  - *Relative importance of activities externally.* How does value and the cost of a set of activities compare with the similar activities of competitors? For example, although they are both global oil businesses, BP and Shell are different in terms of the significance of their value chain activities. BP has historically outperformed Shell in terms of exploration, but the reverse is the case with regard to refining and marketing.

  - *Where and how can costs be reduced?* Given the picture that emerges from such an analysis it should be possible to ask some important questions about the cost structure of the organisation in terms of the strategy being followed (or that needs to be followed in the

ILLUSTRATION

ILLUSTRATION 3.4

A value system for Ugandan chilled fish fillet exports

Even small enterprises can be part of an international value system. Analysing it can provide strategic benefits.

A fish factory in Uganda barely made any profit. Fish were caught from small motorboats owned by poor fishermen from local villages. Just before they set out they would collect ice and plastic fish boxes from the agents who bought the catch on their return. The boxes were imported, along with tackle and boat parts. All supplies had to be paid for in cash in advance by the agents. Sometimes ice and supplies were not available in time. Fish landed with insufficient ice achieved half of the price of iced fish, and sometimes could not be sold to the agents at all. The fish factory had always processed the fillets in the same way – disposing of the waste back into the lake. Once a week, some foreign traders would come and buy the better fillets; they didn't say who they sold them to, and sometimes they didn't buy very much.

By mapping the value chain it was clear that there were opportunities for capturing more value along the chain and reducing losses. Together with outside specialists, the fish factory and the fishing community developed a strategy to improve their capabilities, as indicated in the figure, until they became a flourishing international business, the Lake Victoria Fish Company, with regular air-freight exports around the world.

You can see more of their current operations at http://www.ufpea.co.ug/.

(The approximate costs and prices given represent the situation before improvements were implemented.)

Questions

1 Draw up a value chain or value system for another business in terms of the activities within its component parts.

2 Estimate the relative costs and/or assets associated with these activities.

3 What are the strategic implications of your analysis?

future). For example, is the balance of cost in line with the strategic significance of the elements of the value chain? Can costs be reduced in some areas without affecting the value created for customers? Can some activities be outsourced (see section 7.5.2), for example those that are relatively free-standing and do not add value significantly? Can cost savings be made by increasing economies of scale or scope; for example, through central procurement or consolidating currently fragmented activities (e.g. manufacturing units)?

The value system

A single organisation rarely undertakes in-house all of the value activities from design through to the delivery of the final product or service to the final consumer. There is usually specialisation of roles so, as Figure 3.5 shows, any one organisation is part of a wider *value system* of different interacting organisations. There are questions that arise here that build on an understanding of the value chain itself:

● *What are the activities and cost/price structures of the value system?* Just as costs can be analysed across the internal value chain, they can also be analysed across the value system: Illustration 3.4 shows this in relation to fish farming. Value system analysis was used by Ugandan fish farmers as a way of identifying what they should focus on in developing a more profitable business model.

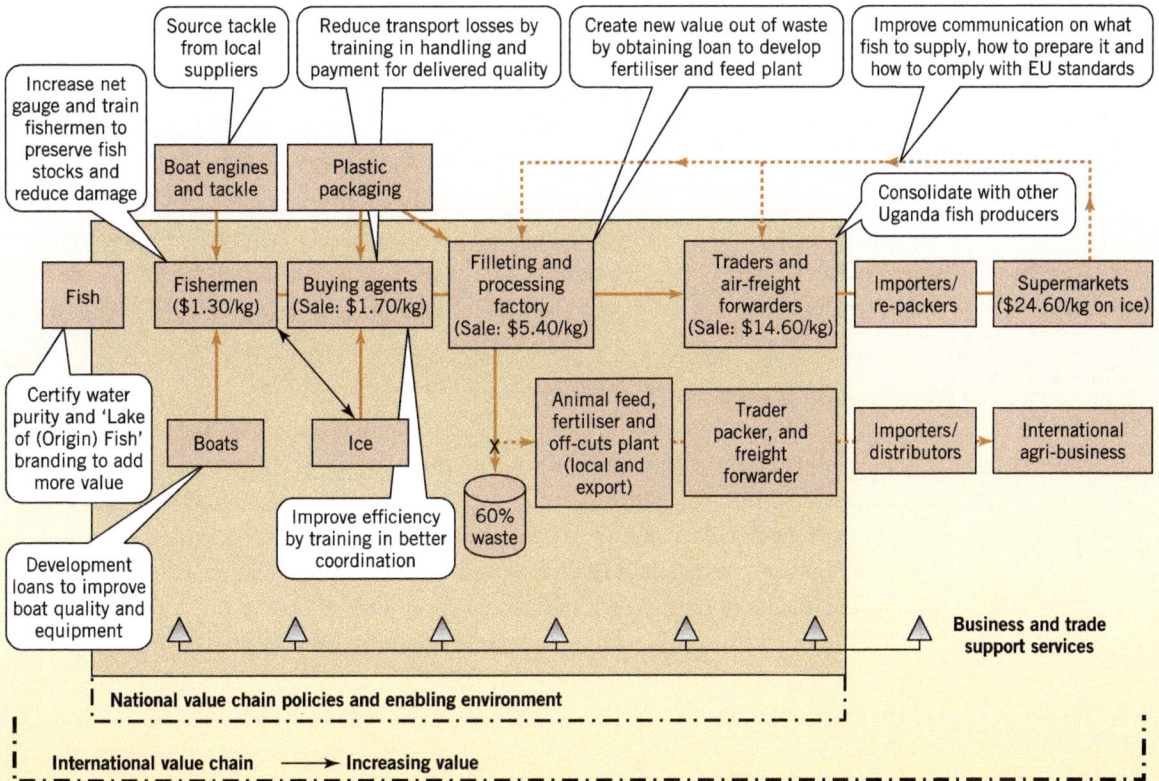

Increase net gauge and train fishermen to preserve fish stocks and reduce damage

Source tackle from local suppliers

Reduce transport losses by training in handling and payment for delivered quality

Create new value out of waste by obtaining loan to develop fertiliser and feed plant

Improve communication on what fish to supply, how to prepare it and how to comply with EU standards

Consolidate with other Uganda fish producers

Fish

Boat engines and tackle

Plastic packaging

Fishermen ($1.30/kg)

Buying agents (Sale: $1.70/kg)

Filleting and processing factory (Sale: $5.40/kg)

Traders and air-freight forwarders (Sale: $14.60/kg)

Importers/ re-packers

Supermarkets ($24.60/kg on ice)

Certify water purity and 'Lake of (Origin) Fish' branding to add more value

Boats

Ice

X

60% waste

Animal feed, fertiliser and off-cuts plant (local and export)

Trader packer, and freight forwarder

Importers/ distributors

International agri-business

Improve efficiency by training in better coordination

Development loans to improve boat quality and equipment

Business and trade support services

I **National value chain policies and enabling environment**

I **International value chain** ⟶ **Increasing value**

Note: $1 is about €0.7.

Source: Ian Sayers, Senior Adviser for the Private Sector, Division of Trade Support Services, International Trade Centre, Geneva. Email: sayers@intracen.org.

Figure 3.5 The value system

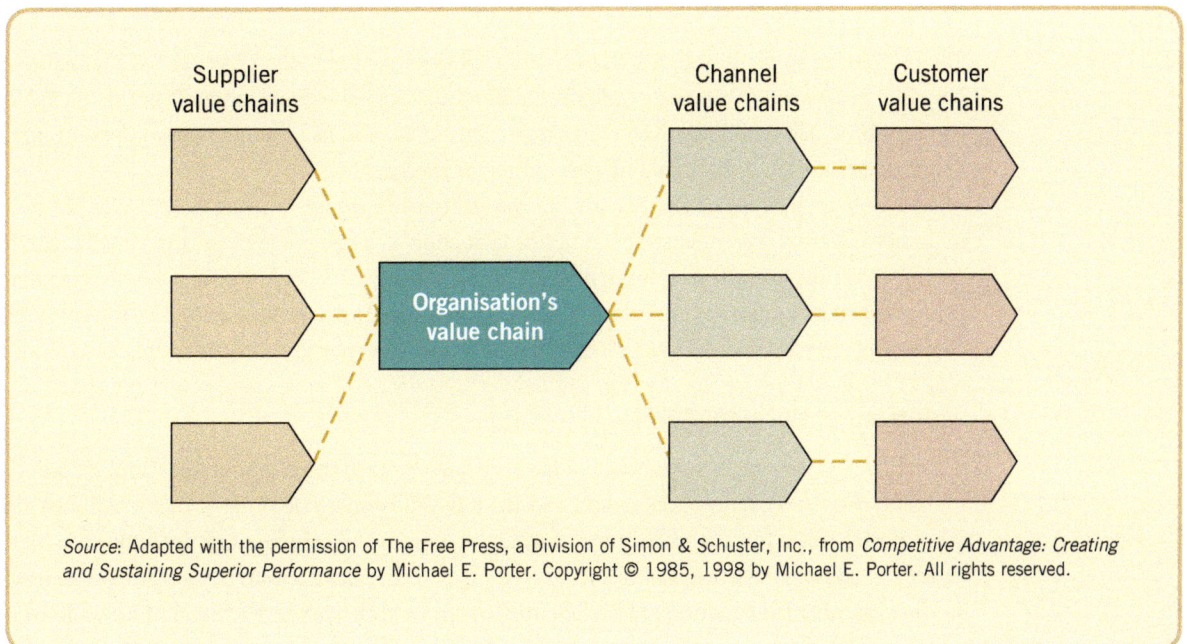

Supplier value chains

Channel value chains

Customer value chains

Organisation's value chain

● *Where are the profit pools?*[24] **Profit pools refer to the different levels of profit available at different parts of the value system.** Some parts of a value system can be inherently more profitable than others because of the differences in competitive intensity (see section 2.3.1). For example, in the computer industry microprocessors and software have historically been more profitable than hardware manufacture. The strategic question becomes whether it is possible to focus on the areas of greatest profit potential. Care has to be exercised here. It is one thing to identify such potential; it is another to be successful in it given the capabilities an organisation has. For example, engineering firms may recognise the greater profit potential in providing engineering consulting services in addition to or instead of manufacturing. None the less many have found it difficult to develop such services successfully either because their staff do not have consultancy capabilities or because their clients do not recognise the firms as having them.

● *The 'make or buy'* decision for a particular activity is critical given some of the above questions. This is the *outsourcing* decision. Increasingly outsourcing is becoming common as a means of lowering costs. Of course, the more an organisation outsources, the more its ability to influence the performance of other organisations in the value system may become a critically important capability in itself and even a source of competitive advantage. For example, the quality of a cooker or a television when it reaches the final purchaser is influenced not only by the activities undertaken within the manufacturing company itself, but also by the quality of components from suppliers and the performance of the distributors. There is, of course, the converse question: which activities most need to be part of the internal value chain because they are central to achieving competitive advantage? There may also be activities that do not generate competitive advantage in themselves, but which the organisation needs to control as they enable the exploitation of competitive advantage in other parts of the value chain, as indicated in section 3.3.4.

● *Partnering.* Who might be the best partners in the various parts of the value system? And what kinds of relationships are important to develop with each partner? For example, should they be regarded as suppliers or should they be regarded as alliance partners (see section 10.4)?

3.4.3 Activity systems

The discussion so far highlights the fact that all organisations comprise sets of capabilities, but that these are likely to be configured differently across organisations. It is this variable configuration of capabilities that makes an organisation and its strategy more or less unique. So for the strategist, understanding this matters a good deal.

Value chain analysis can help with this, but so too can understanding the activity systems of an organisation. As the discussion above in section 3.3 has made clear, the way in which resources are deployed through the organisation actually takes form in the activities pursued by that organisation; so it is important to identify what these activities are, why they are valuable to customers, how the various activities fit together and how they are different from competitors'.

Mapping activity systems

A number of writers,[25] including Michael Porter, have written about the importance of mapping activity systems and shown how this might be done. The starting point is to identify what Porter refers to as 'higher order strategic themes'. In effect these are the ways in which the organisation meets the critical success factors determining them in the industry. The next step is to identify the clusters of activities that underpin each of these themes and how these do or do not fit together. The result is a picture of the organisation represented in terms of activity systems such as that shown in Illustration 3.5. This shows an activity systems map for the Scandinavian strategic communications consultancy, Geelmuyden.Kiese.[26] The core higher-order theme at the heart of its success is its knowledge, built over the years, of how effective communications can influence 'the power dynamics of decision-making processes'. However, as Illustration 3.5 shows, this central theme is related to other higher-order strategic themes, each of which is underpinned by clusters of supporting activities. Three points need to be emphasised here:

- *Relationship to the value chain.* The various activities represented in an activity map can also be seen as parts of a value chain. The in-house methodology is, in effect, part of Geelmuyden.Kiese's operations; its recruitment practices are a component of its human resource management; its stance on integrity and insistence on openness rather than suppression of the information part of its service offering; and so on. However, activity systems mapping encourages a greater understanding of the complexity of strategic capabilities – important if bases of competitive advantage are to be identified and managed.

- *The importance of linkages and fit.* An activity systems map emphasises the importance of different activities that create value to customers pulling in the same direction and supporting rather than opposing each other. So the need is to understand (i) the fit between the various activities and how these reinforce each other and (ii) the fit externally with the needs of clients. There are two implications:

  - The danger of *piecemeal change* or tinkering with such systems which may damage the positive benefits of the linkages that exist.

  - The consequent *challenge of managing change.* When change is needed the implication is that change to one part of the system will almost inevitably affect another; or, put another way, change probably has to be managed to the whole system.

- *Relationship to VRIO.* It is these linkages and this fit that can be the bases of sustainable competitive advantage. In combination they may be *valuable* to clients, truly distinctive and therefore *rare.* Moreover, while individual components of an activity system might be relatively easy to imitate, in combination they may well constitute the complexity and causal ambiguity rooted in culture and history that makes them *inimitable.* Finally, there can be activities in the system that in themselves do not provide for competitive advantage, but that provide *organisational support* for other activities that do.

However, it is not just at the conceptual level that activity maps are important; they can also be directly helpful in the management of strategy:

- *Disaggregation.*[27] Useful as an activity map is, the danger is that, in seeking to explain capabilities underpinning their strategy, managers may identify capabilities at too abstract a level. If the strategic benefits of activity systems are to be understood, greater disaggregation is likely to be needed. For example, managers may talk of 'innovation' or 'putting the customer first' as a basis for 'good service'. These terms are too generic; they are umbrella descriptors of activities that exist at an even more operational level. If an activity map is to be useful for the purposes of managing activities then specific manageable activities need to be identified at an operating level. To take an example from Illustration 3.5, there is the recognition that the mentoring of junior staff by partners is important; but the map itself does not show specifically how this is done. Managers need to delve further and further into explanations of how specific activities support other activities so as to eventually 'deliver' customer benefit.

ILLUSTRATION 3.5

Activity systems at Geelmuyden.Kiese

The strategic capabilities of an organisation can be understood and analysed in terms of linked activities (an activity system).

Geelmuyden.Kiese is the largest Scandinavian strategic communications consultancy – an extension of what has traditionally been known as public relations services (PR). Its clients include organisations in the financial, oil, energy, pharmaceuticals and healthcare sectors. These clients typically approach Geelmuyden.Kiese when they have a problem, the solution of which critically depends on effective external or internal communication. In this context, its services include facilitation of contacts with public agencies, officials and government, investor relations, media relations, communication campaigns for new product launches, crisis management and in-company communication on key strategic issues.

At the heart of the company's success is the knowledge it has built up since its founding in 1989 of the dynamics of decision-making processes, often within influential bodies such as government and, linked to this, 'how effective communication may move power within those decision-making processes'. This knowledge is underpinned by some key aspects in the way in which it does business (see also Figure 3.6 below).

- The company seeks to *work at a strategic level* with its clients, prioritising those clients where such work is especially valued. Here it employs its own in-house methodology, developed on the basis of years of experience, and systematically reviews the assignments it undertakes both internally and on the basis of client surveys.

- The company takes a clear stance on *integrity of communication*. It always advises openness of communication rather than suppression of information and only deals with clients that will accept such principles. It often takes a stance on this approach in controversial and high-profile issues in the public domain.

- Staff are given high degrees of *freedom* but with some absolute criteria of *responsibility*. In this regard there are strict rules for handling clients' confidential information and strict sanctions if such rules are broken.

- *Recruitment* is based on ensuring that such responsibility can be achieved. It is largely on the basis of values of openness and integrity but also humour. The emphasis tends to be on recruiting junior personnel and developing them. Geelmuyden.Kiese has learned that this is a better way of delivering its services than recruiting established 'high-profile' consultants. Combined with its mentoring system for competence development of junior staff, it therefore believes that it offers the *best learning opportunities* in Scandinavia for young communications consultants.

- Geelmuyden.Kiese also offers *strong financial incentives* for top performance within the firm. Such performance includes rewards for the development of junior personnel but is also based on the internal evaluation of leadership qualities and performance.

- *Superfluous activities*. Just as in value chain analysis, but at a more detailed level, the question can be asked: are there activities that are not required in order to pursue a particular strategy? Or how do activities contribute to value creation? If activities do not do this, why are they being pursued by the organisation? Whether Ryanair used activity mapping or not, it has systematically identified and done away with many activities that other airlines commonly have. It is also continually seeking further activities that can be eliminated or outsourced to reduce cost.

Key:

Higher-order themes

Supporting activities

Questions

1 Assuming Geelmuyden.Kiese managers are correct that they have capabilities that provide competitive advantage:

   a What would competitors find difficult to imitate and why?

   b Are there any activities that could be done away with without threatening that advantage?

2 If disaggregation (see section 3.4.3) is important, suggest what even more specific activities underpinning those in the activity map might be important.

3.4.4 SWOT[28]

It can be helpful to summarise the key issues arising from an analysis of strategic capabilities discussed in this chapter and the analysis of the business environment discussed in Chapter 2 to gain an overall picture of an organisation's strategic position. **SWOT** provides a general **summary of the Strengths and Weaknesses explored in an analysis of strategic capabilities (Chapter 3) and the Opportunities and Threats explored in an analysis of the environment**

(Chapter 2). This analysis can also be useful as a basis for generating strategic options and assess future courses of action.

The aim is to identify the extent to which strengths and weaknesses are relevant to, or capable of dealing with, the changes taking place in the business environment. Illustration 3.6 takes the example of a pharmaceuticals firm (Pharmcare).[29] It assumes that key environmental impacts have been identified from analyses explained in Chapter 2 and that major strengths and weaknesses have been identified using the analytic tools explained in this chapter. A scoring mechanism (plus 5 to minus 5) is used as a means of getting managers to assess the interrelationship between the environmental impacts and the strengths and weaknesses of the firm. A positive (+) denotes that the strength of the company would help it take advantage of, or counteract, a problem arising from an environmental change or that a weakness would be offset by that change. A negative (–) score denotes that the strength would be reduced or that a weakness would prevent the organisation from overcoming problems associated with that change.

Pharmcare's share price had been declining because investors were concerned that its strong market position was under threat. This had not been improved by a merger that was proving problematic. The pharmaceutical market was changing with new ways of doing business, driven by new technology, the quest to provide medicines at lower cost and politicians seeking ways to cope with soaring healthcare costs and an evermore informed patient. But was Pharmcare keeping pace? The strategic review of the firm's position (Illustration 3.6a) confirmed its strengths of a flexible sales force, well-known brand name and new healthcare department. However, there were major weaknesses, namely relative failure on low-cost drugs, competence in information and communication technology (ICT) and a failure to get to grips with increasingly well-informed users.

However, in the context of this chapter, if this analysis is to be useful, it must be remembered that the exercise is not absolute but relative to its competitors. So SWOT analysis is most useful when it is comparative – if it examines strengths, weaknesses, opportunities and threats in relation to competitors. When the impact of environmental forces on competitors was analysed (Illustration 3.6b), it showed that Pharmcare was still outperforming its traditional competitor (Company W), but potentially vulnerable to changing dynamics in the general industry structure courtesy of niche players (X and Y).

There are two main dangers in a SWOT exercise:

- *Listing.* A SWOT exercise can generate very long lists of apparent strengths, weaknesses, opportunities and threats, whereas what matters is to be clear about what is really important and what is less important. So prioritisation of issues matters. Three brief rules can be helpful here. First, as indicated above, focus on strengths and weaknesses that differ in *relative* terms compared to competitors and leave out areas where the organisation is at par with competitors. Second, focus on opportunities and threats that are directly *relevant* for the specific organisation and industry and leave out general and broad factors. Third, summarise the *result* and draw concrete conclusions.

- *A summary, not a substitute.* SWOT analysis is an engaging and fairly simple tool. It is also useful in summarising and consolidating other analysis that has been explained in Chapters 2 and 3. It is not, however, a substitute for that analysis. There are two dangers if it is used on its own. The first is that, in the absence of more thorough analysis, managers rely on preconceived, often inherited and biased views. The second is again the danger of a lack of specificity. Identifying very general strengths, for example, does not explain the underlying reasons for those strengths.

ILLUSTRATION

ILLUSTRATION 3.6

SWOT analysis of Pharmcare

A SWOT analysis explores the relationship between the environmental influences and the strategic capabilities of an organisation compared with its competitors.

(a) SWOT analysis for Pharmcare

	Environmental change (opportunities and threats)					
	Healthcare rationing	Complex and changing buying structures	Increased integration of healthcare	Informed patients	+	−
Strengths						
Flexible sales force	+3	+5	+2	+2	12	0
Economies of scale	0	0	+3	+3	+6	0
Strong brand name	+2	+1	0	−1	3	−1
Healthcare education department	+4	+3	+4	+5	16	0
Weaknesses						
Limited competences in biotechnology and genetics	0	0	−4	−3	0	−7
Ever lower R&D productivity	−3	−2	−1	−2	0	−8
Weak ICT competences	−2	−2	−5	−5	0	−14
Over-reliance on leading product	−1	−1	−3	−1	0	−6
Environmental impact scores	+9	+9	+9	+10		
	−6	−5	−13	−12		

(b) Competitor SWOT analyses

	Environmental change (opportunities and threats)				
	Healthcare rationing	Complex and changing buying structures	Increased integration of healthcare	Informed and passionate patients	Overall impact
Pharmcare *Big global player suffering fall in share price, low research productivity and post-mega-merger bureaucracy*	−3 Struggling to prove cost-effectiveness of new drugs to new regulators of healthcare rationing	+6 Well-known brand, a flexible sales force combined with a new healthcare education department creates positive synergy	−3 Weak ICT and lack of integration following mergers means sales, research and admin. are all underperforming	−2 Have yet to get into the groove of patient power fuelled by the internet	−2 Declining performance over time worsened after merger
Company W *Big pharma with patchy response to change, losing ground in new areas of competition*	−4 Focus is on old-style promotional selling rather than helping doctors control costs through drugs	−4 Traditional sales force not helped by marketing which can be unaccommodating of national differences	+0 Alliances with equipment manufacturers but little work done across alliance to show dual use of drugs and new surgical techniques	+4 New recruits in the ICT department have worked cross-functionally to involve patients like never before	−4 Needs to modernise across the whole company
Organisation X *Partnership between a charity managed by people with venture capital experience and top hospital geneticists*	+3 Potentially able to deliver rapid advances in genetics-based illnesses	+2 Able possibly to bypass these with innovative cost-effective drug(s)	+2 Innovative drugs can help integrate healthcare through enabling patients to stay at home	+3 Patients will fight for advances in treatment areas where little recent progress has been made	+10 Could be the basis of a new business model for drug discovery – but all to prove as yet
Company Y *Only develops drugs for less common diseases*	+3 Partnering with big pharma allows the development of drugs discovered by big pharma but not economical for them to develop	0 Focus on small market segments so not as vulnerable to overall market structure, but innovative approach might be risky	+2 Innovative use of web to show why products still worthwhile developing even for less common illnesses	+1 Freephone call centres for sufferers of less common illnesses Company, like patients, is passionate about its mission	+6 Novel approach can be considered either risky or a winner, or both!

Questions

1 What does the SWOT analysis tell us about the competitive position of Pharmcare with the industry as a whole?

2 How readily do you think executives of Pharmcare identify the strengths and weaknesses of competitors?

3 Identify the benefits and dangers (other than those identified in the text) of a SWOT analysis such as that in the illustration.

Prepared by Jill Shepherd, Segal Graduate School of Business, Simon Fraser University, Vancouver, Canada.

Figure 3.6 The TOWS matrix

	Internal factors	
	Strengths (S)	**Weaknesses (W)**
Opportunities (O)	**SO Strategic options** Generate options here that use strengths to take advantage of opportunities	**WO Strategic options** Generate options here that take advantage of opportunities by overcoming weaknesses
Threats (T)	**ST Strategic options** Generate options here that use strengths to avoid threats	**WT Strategic options** Generate options here that minimise weaknesses and avoid threats

(External factors)

SWOT can also help focus discussion on future choices and the extent to which an organisation is capable of supporting these strategies. A useful way of doing this is to use a TOWS matrix[30] as shown in Figure 3.6. This builds directly on the information in a SWOT exercise. Each box of the TOWS matrix can be used to identify options that address a different combination of the internal factors (strengths and weaknesses) and the external factors (opportunities and threats). For example, the top left-hand box prompts a consideration of options that use the strengths of the organisation to take advantage of opportunities in the business environment. An example for Pharmcare might be the re-training of the sales force to deal with changes in pharmaceuticals buying. The bottom right-hand box prompts options that minimise weaknesses and also avoid threats; for Pharmcare this might include the need to develop its ICT systems to better service more informed patients. Quite likely this would also help take advantage of opportunities arising from changes in the buying structure of the industry (top right). The bottom left box suggests the need to use strengths to avoid threats, perhaps by building on the success of the healthcare education department to also better service informed patients.

(3.5) MANAGING STRATEGIC CAPABILITY

The previous section was concerned with diagnosing strategic capability. This section considers what managers might do to manage and improve resources and capabilities to the strategic benefit of their organisation.

One lesson that emerges from an understanding of the strategic importance of capabilities is that it can be difficult to discern where the basis of competitive advantage lies. Hence, if managers are to manage the resources and capabilities of their organisation, the sort of analyses explained here, especially VRIO, value chain analysis and activity systems mapping, are centrally important. If capabilities are not understood at these levels, there are dangers that managers can take the wrong course of action. For example, managers in an industrial cleaning company undertook an activity mapping exercise. It revealed that the way their van drivers dealt with collecting often filthy garments from industrial premises was especially valued by customers. This had developed through custom and practice, competitors did not do it and the managers themselves were not aware of it explicitly until they did the exercise. The irony was that they were just about to outsource the van delivery service! They were about to lose control of one of their potential bases of competitive advantage for the sake of cost reduction. This demonstrates the significance of diagnosing strategic capabilities. However, developing strategic capabilities that provide for competitive advantage can be extremely challenging as indicated by the strict criteria they need to fulfil in section 3.3 above. The question, then, is what can managers do to create, extend or upgrade an organisation's strategic capabilities after having diagnosed them?[31]

There are several different ways in which managers might develop strategic capabilities:

- *Internal capability development.* Could capabilities be added or upgraded so that they become more reinforcing of outcomes that deliver against critical success factors? This might be done, for example, by:

    - *Building and recombining capabilities.* Creating entirely new capabilities that provide for competitive advantage requires entrepreneurship and intrapreneurship skills. Managers can build managerial systems and a culture that promote capability innovation or form new venture units outside the rules of ordinary R&D and product development.[32]

    - *Leveraging capabilities.* Managers might identify strategic capabilities in one area of their organisation, perhaps customer service in one geographic business unit of a multinational, that are not present in other business units. They might then seek to extend this throughout all the business units. While this may seem straightforward, research has demonstrated that it can be rather difficult.[33] The capabilities of one part of an organisation might not be easily transferred to another because of the problems of managing change (see Chapter 14).

    - *Stretching capabilities.* Managers may see the opportunity to build new products or services out of existing capabilities. Indeed, building new businesses in this way is the basis of related diversification, as explained in Chapter 7.

- *External capability development.* Similarly, there may be ways of developing capabilities by looking externally. For example, this could be by developing new capabilities by acquisition or entering into alliances and joint ventures (see Chapter 10).

- *Ceasing activities.* Could current activities, not central to the delivery of value to customers, be done away with, outsourced or reduced in cost? If managers are aware of the capabilities central to bases of competitive advantage, they can retain these and focus on areas of cost reduction that are less significant.

KEY DEBATE

How useful is the resource-based view?

Although the resource-based view (RBV) of strategy has been highly influential during the last couple of decades it has been questioned by some academics.

Three recurring critiques have been considered as particularly damaging:

1 *The risk of tautology.* The underlying explanation of RBV is that the resource or capability characteristics that lead to competitive advantage are those that are valuable and rare. Richard Priem and John Butler argue that since competitive advantage is defined in terms of value and rarity this verges on tautology. To say that a business performs better than another because it has superior resources or is better at some things than other businesses is not helpful unless it is possible to be specific about what resources are important, why and how they can be managed.

2 *The lack of specificity.* A second and related critique centres on RBV's axiomatic definitions and that resources are not specified. The definitions of resources have been overly inclusive and can include virtually every asset of a firm. However, if everything can be a resource, nothing strategically useful can be associated with the firm that is not a resource. The specifics of resources and capabilities have, however, rarely been defined in RBV. Priem and Butler suggest this is particularly so with regard to the argued importance of tacit knowledge in bestowing competitive advantage: 'This may be descriptively correct, but it is likely to be quite difficult for practitioners to effectively manipulate that which is inherently unknowable.' Others agree that RBV has to come to grips with this as 'the practical assessment and valuation of resources involve subjectivism, knowledge creation and entrepreneurial judgement' (Kraaijenbrink et al.), something RBV largely ignores.

3 *The lack of dynamics.* Critics argue that RBV may only hold in relatively stable conditions where 'the rules of the game' in an industry remain relatively fixed. In more unpredictable environments the value of resources can easily and quickly diminish. Also, to keep up with dynamic environments resources must change, but RBV does not explain the origins of resources that provide for competitive advantage.

Jay Barney, one of the main proponents of the RBV, rejects most of the critique above even if he admits that we need to know more about how resources provide for sustainable competitive advantage:

1 Barney defends the view's practical value as it emphasises that managers must identify, evaluate and develop critical resources even if RBV does not specify exactly how. According to him, many strategy theories becomes tautological if restated in the way the RBV critics do and many of them are of a descriptive rather than prescriptive type in their early stages. Although he does not agree with the tautology critique, he concurs that the value of resources has to be exogenously determined on a market.

2 Barney admits that resources are defined to be all-inclusive, but he rejects that this lowers RBV's managerial relevance. On the contrary, he argues, this enhances its applicability. According to him, it is not possible to provide a comprehensive list of all resources that provides sustained competitive advantages. What RBV does is to clearly define the specific attributes required and then managers can apply this logic when evaluating and developing resources.

3 RBV proponents argue that, contrary to the dynamics critique, the view explicitly acknowledges that changes in environmental conditions might undermine the competitive advantage of a particular resource. Barney admits, however, that dynamic issues of resource change and creation are not covered by RBV and that it needs to be integrated with the dynamic capabilities approach.

Sources: R. Priem and J.E. Butler, 'Is the resource-based view a useful perspective for strategic management research?', *Academy of Management Review*, vol. 26, no. 1 (2001), pp. 22–40; J. Kraaijenbrink, J.-C. Spender and A.J. Groen, 'The resource-based view: a review and assessment of its critiques', *Journal of Management*, vol. 36, no. 1 (2010), pp. 349–72; J.B. Barney, 'Is the resource based view a useful perspective for strategic management research? Yes', *Academy of Management Review*, vol. 26, no. 1 (2001), pp. 41–56.

Questions

1 How easy do you think it would be to identify and imitate the strategic capabilities that give firm competitive advantage?

2 What roles do you think imagination and creativity play in identifying new and valuable strategic capabilities and combinations?

3 Is RBV useful?

- *Monitor outputs and benefits when it is not possible to fully understand capabilities.* There are organisations where managers may know that there are activities that have a positive impact on competitive advantage, but may not fully understand just how such positive impact arises. For example, the delivery of value can be dependent on highly specialised skills as in a cutting-edge hi-tech firm, or on complex linkages far down in the organisation. Here managers may have to be careful about disturbing the bases of such capabilities while, at the same time, ensuring that they monitor the outputs and benefits created for customers.[34]

- *Awareness development.* One of the lessons of this chapter is that the bases of competitive advantage often lie in the day-to-day activities that people undertake in organisations, so developing the ability of people to recognise the relevance of what they do in terms of how that contributes to the strategy of the organisation is important. This suggests that staffing policies, training and development including developing employee's awareness of how they contribute to competitive advantage are all central to capability deployment and development. Together with organisational learning these issues are discussed in later chapters on organising for success and leading strategic change (Chapters 13 and 14).

Much of the discussion in this chapter builds on research and the writing of scholars who take a resource-based view of strategy. They therefore emphasise the central importance of managing resources and capabilities for competitive advantage. The Key Debate summarises the arguments for and against the practical value of such an approach.

SUMMARY

- *The competitive advantage* of an organisation is likely to be based on the strategic *capabilities* it has that are valuable to customers and that its rivals do not have or have difficulty in obtaining. Strategic capabilities comprise both *resources and competences*.

- The concept of *dynamic capabilities* highlights that strategic capabilities need to change as the market and environmental context of an organisation changes.

- Sustainability of competitive advantage is likely to depend on an organisation's capabilities being of at least *threshold value* in a market, but also being *valuable*, relatively *rare*, *inimitable* and *supported by the organisation* and consequently fulfilling the *VRIO* criteria.

- Ways of diagnosing organisational capabilities include:
  - *VRIO analysis* of strategic capabilities as a tool to evaluate if they contribute to competitive advantage.
  - *Benchmarking* as a means of understanding the relative performance of organisations.
  - Analysing an organisation's *value chain* and *value system* as a basis for understanding how value to a customer is created and can be developed.
  - *Activity mapping* as a means of identifying more detailed activities which underpin strategic capabilities.
  - *SWOT analysis* as a way of drawing together an understanding of the strengths, weaknesses, opportunities and threats an organisation faces.

- Managers need to think about how and to what extent they can manage the *development of strategic capabilities* of their organisation by internal and external capability development and by the way they manage people in their organisation.

VIDEO ASSIGNMENTS

Visit **MyStrategyLab** and watch the CISCO case study for Chapter 3.

1 Using the video, identify the distinctive strengths and capabilities that give CISCO a competitive advantage.

2 Using Figure 3.2 and Table 3.2 from the text and referring to the VRIO criteria, explain how CISCO may be able to sustain its competitive advantage over time.

WORK ASSIGNMENTS

✱ *Denotes more advanced work assignments.*
* *Refers to a case study in the Text and Cases edition.*

3.1 Using Table 3.1 identify the resources and competences of an organisation with which you are familiar, your university or school for example. Alternatively, you can answer this in relation to, H&M* or Formula One* if you wish.

3.2✱ Undertake an analysis of the strategic capabilities of an organisation with which you are familiar in order to identify which capabilities, if any, meet the criteria of (a) value, (b) rarity, (c) inimitability and (d) organisational support (see section 3.3; Figure 3.2 and Table 3.2). You can answer this in relation to H&M* or Formula One* or the end case, Rocket Internet, if you so wish.

3.3✱ For an industry or public service of your choice consider how the strategic capabilities that have been the basis of competitive advantage (or best value in the public sector) have changed over time. Why have these changes occurred? How did the relative strengths of different companies or service providers change over this period? Why? Did dynamic capabilities play any role? Which?

3.4 Undertake a value chain or system analysis for an organisation of your choice (referring to Illustration 3.4 could be helpful). You can answer this in relation to a case study in the book such as Ryanair* or the end case, Rocket Internet, if you wish.

3.5✱ For a benchmarking exercise to which you have access, make a critical assessment of the benefits and dangers of the approach that was taken.

Integrative assignment

3.6 Prepare a SWOT analysis for an organisation of your choice (see Illustration 3.6). Explain why you have chosen each of the factors you have included in the analysis, in particular their relationship to other analyses you have undertaken in Chapters 2 and 3. What are the conclusions you arrive at from your analysis and how would these inform an evaluation of strategy (see Chapter 11)?

RECOMMENDED KEY READINGS

- For an understanding of the resource-based view of the firm, an early and much cited paper is by Jay Barney: 'Firm resources and sustained competitive advantage', *Journal of Management*, vol. 17 (1991), pp. 99–120. An overview of RBV research is written by Jay B. Barney, David J. Ketchen Jr and Mike Wright; 'The future of resource-based theory: revitalization or decline?', *Journal of Management*, vol. 37, no. 5 (2011), pp. 1299–315.

- A comprehensive book on dynamic capabilities is written by C. Helfat, S. Finkelstein, W. Mitchell, M. Peteraf, H. Singh, D. Teece and S. Winter, *Dynamic Capabilities: Understanding Strategic Change in Organisations*, Blackwell Publishing, 2007. The concept of dynamic capabilities is reviewed in Barreto, I., 'Dynamic capabilities: a review of past research and an agenda for the future', *Journal of Management*, vol. 36, no. 1 (2010), pp. 256–80.

- For a discussion of micro-foundations and dynamic capabilities see D.J. Teece, 'Explicating dynamic capabilities: the nature and microfoundations of (sustainable) enterprise performance', *Strategic Management Journal*, vol. 28, pp. 1319–50 (2007) and his book *Dynamic capabilities and strategic management – organising for innovation and growth*, Oxford University Press, 2009.

- Michael Porter explains how mapping activity systems can be important in considering competitive strategy in his article 'What is strategy?', *Harvard Business Review*, November–December 1996, pp. 61–78.

- For a critical discussion of the use and misuse of SWOT analysis see T. Hill and R. Westbrook, 'SWOT analysis: it's time for a product recall', *Long Range Planning*, vol. 30, no. 1 (1997), pp. 46–52.

REFERENCES

1. The concept of resource-based strategies was introduced by B. Wernerfelt, 'A resource-based view of the firm', *Strategic Management Journal*, vol. 5, no. 2 (1984), pp. 171–80. The seminal and most cited paper is by Jay Barney, 'Firm resources and sustained competitive advantage', *Journal of Management*, vol. 17, no. 1 (1991), pp. 99–120. There are now many books and papers that explain and summarise the approach: for example, D. Hoopes, T. Madsen and G. Walker in the special issue of the *Strategic Management Journal*, 'Why is there a resource based view?', vol. 24, no. 10 (2003), pp. 889–902; and J. Barney and D. Clark, *Resource-Based Theory: Creating and Sustaining Competitive Advantage*, Oxford University Press, 2007.

2. The literature most commonly differentiates between 'resources' and 'capabilities'. See, for example, an early article by Raphael Amit and Paul Schoemaker: Amit, R. and Schoemaker, P.J.H. 'Strategic assets and organizational rent', *Strategic Management Journal*, vol. 14 (1993), pp. 33–46; and Jay Barney's book: J.B. Barney, *Gaining and sustaining competitive advantage*, Addison-Wesley, 1997. The term 'core competences' was promoted by Gary Hamel and C.K. Prahalad in the early 1990s: G. Hamel and C.K. Prahalad, 'The core competence of the corporation', *Harvard Business Review*, vol. 68, no. 3 (1990), pp. 79–91. 'Capabilities' is, however, a more common term today, but it is sometimes used interchangeably with 'competences' in the literature. Later 'capabilities' has been distinguished into 'operational capabilities' and 'dynamic capabilities. David Teece and his co-authors were first to introduce 'dynamic capabilities': D.J. Teece, G. Pisano and A. Shuen, 'Dynamic Capabilities and strategic management', *Strategic Management Journal*, vol. 18, no.7 (1997), pp. 509–533. Sid Winter later explained the differences between 'ordinary' and 'dynamic capabilities': S.G. Winter, 'Understanding dynamic capabilities', *Strategic Management Journal*, vol. 24 (2003), no. 10, pp. 991–5.

3. For summary papers on dynamic capabilities see I. Barreto, 'Dynamic capabilities: a review of past research and an agenda for the future', *Journal of Management*, vol. 36, no. 1 (2010), pp. 256–80; C.L. Wang and P.K. Ahmed, 'Dynamic capabilities: a review and research agenda', *International Journal of Management Reviews*, vol. 9, no. 1 (2007), pp. 31–52; and V. Ambrosini and C. Bowman, 'What are dynamic capabilities and are they a useful construct in strategic management?', *International Journal of Management Reviews*, vol. 11, no. 1 (2009), pp. 29–49. The most comprehensive book on dynamic capabilities is written by C. Helfat, S. Finkelstein, W. Mitchell, M. Peteraf, H. Singh, D. Teece and S. Winter, *Dynamic Capabilities: Understanding Strategic Change in Organizations*, Blackwell Publishing, 2007.

4. David Teece has written about dynamic capabilities originally in D.J. Teece, G. Pisano and A. Shuen: 'Dynamic capabilities and strategic management', *Strategic Management Journal*, vol. 18, no. 7 (1997), pp. 509–34. More recently he has expanded his explanation in D.J. Teece, 'Explicating dynamic capabilities: the nature and microfoundations of (sustainable) enterprise performance', *Strategic Management Journal*, vol. 28, vol. 1 (2007), pp. 1319–50; and in the book *Dynamic capabilities and strategic management – organizing for innovation and growth*, Oxford University Press, 2009.

5. Sid Winter has explained the differences between ordinary and dynamic capabilities in S.G. Winter, 'Understanding dynamic capabilities', *Strategic Management Journal*, vol. 24, no. 10 (2003), pp. 991–5.

6. For a discussion of outlet proliferation as dynamic capability see S.G. Winter, 'Understanding dynamic capabilities', *Strategic Management Journal*, vol. 24, no. 10 (2003), pp. 991–5.

7. For a list of examples of dynamic capabilities see K.M. Eisenhardt and J.A. Martin, 'Dynamic capabilities: what are they?', *Strategic Management Journal*, vol. 21, no. 10/11 (2000), pp. 1105–21.

8. For a discussion of microfoundations of capabilities and managerial beliefs see G. Gavetti, 'Cognition and hierarchy: rethinking microfoundations of capabilities development', *Organization Science*, vol. 16 (2005) pp. 599–617.

9. Gary Hamel and C.K. Prahalad were the academics who promoted the idea of core competences. For example, G. Hamel and C.K. Prahalad, 'The core competence of the corporation', *Harvard Business Review*, vol. 68, no. 3 (1990), pp. 79–91. This idea of driving strategy development from the resources and competences of an organisation is discussed in G. Hamel and C.K. Prahalad, 'Strategic intent', *Harvard Business Review*, vol. 67, no. 3 (1989), pp. 63–76; and G. Hamel and C.K. Prahalad, 'Strategy as stretch and leverage', *Harvard Business Review*, vol. 71, no. 2 (1993), pp. 75–84.

10. The VRIO criteria were introduced by Jay Barney in J.B. Barney, *Gaining and sustaining competitive advantage*, Addison-Wesley, 1997. Originally the acronym *VRIN* was used to also emphasise Non-substitutability and how competitors must not be able to substitute a valuable, rare and inimitable capability for another, but this is now encompassed in the inimitability criterion (see 1 above; Barney, 1991).

11. This is borne out in a meta-study of research on RBV by S.L. Newbert, 'Empirical research on the Resource Based View of the firm: an assessment and suggestions for future research, *Strategic Management Journal*, vol. 28 (2007), pp. 121–46.

12. For an explanation of how complex capabilities and strategies contribute to inimitability see J.W. Rivkin, 'Imitation of complex strategies', *Management Science*, vol. 46, no. 6 (2000), pp. 824–44.

13. The seminal paper on causal ambiguity is S. Lippman and R. Rumelt, 'Uncertain imitability: an analysis of interfirm differences in efficiency under competition', *Bell Journal of Economics*, vol. 13 (1982), pp. 418–38. For a summary and review of research on causal ambiguity see A.W. King, 'Disentangling interfirm and intrafirm causal ambiguity: a conceptual model of causal ambiguity and sustainable competitive advantage, *Academy of Management Review*, vol. 32, no. 1 (2007), pp. 156–78.

14. The distinction between and importance of characteristic and linkage ambiguity is explained by A.W. King and C.P. Zeithaml, 'Competencies and firm performance: examining the causal ambiguity paradox', *Strategic Management Journal*, vol. 22, no. 1 (2001), pp. 75–99.

15. For a fuller discussion of path dependency in the context of strategic capabilities, see D. Holbrook, W. Cohen, D. Hounshell and S. Klepper, 'The nature, sources and consequences of firm differences in the early history of the semiconductor industry', *Strategic Management Journal*, vol. 21, nos 10–11 (2000), pp. 1017–42.

16. For an extensive discussion about complementary assets and capabilities see D. Teece, 'Profiting from technological innovation', *Research Policy*, vol. 15, no. 6 (1986), pp. 285–305.

17. The knowledge-based view was pioneered by B. Kogut, and U. Zander, 'Knowledge of the firm, combinative capabilities, and the replication of technology', *Organization Science*, vol. 3, no. 3 (1992), pp. 383–97. The importance of analysing and understanding knowledge is discussed in I. Nonaka and H. Takeuchi, *The Knowledge-creating Company*, Oxford University Press, 1995. There are also collections of articles on organisational knowledge: e.g. the Special Issue of the *Strategic Management Journal* edited by R. Grant and J.-C. Spender, vol. 17 (1996) and the *Harvard Business Review on Knowledge Management*, HBR Press, 1998. More recently Mark Easterby-Smith and Isabel Prieto have explored the relationships in: 'Dynamic capabilities and knowledge management: an integrative role for learning', *British Journal of Management*, vol. 19 (2008), pp. 235–49.

18. See I. Nonaka and H. Takeuchi, reference 17 above.

19. E.C. Wenger and W.M. Snyder, 'Communities of practice: the organisational frontier', *Harvard Business Review*, vol. 73, no. 3 (2000), pp. 201–7; and E. Wenger, *Communities of Practice: Learning, Meaning and Identity*, Cambridge University Press, 1999.

20. See R. Camp, *Benchmarking: the Search for Industry Best Practices that Lead to Superior Performance*, Quality Press, 2006.

21. See A. Murdoch, 'Lateral benchmarking, or what Formula One taught an airline', *Management Today* (November 1997), pp. 64–7. See also the Formula One case study in the case study section of this book (Text and Cases version only).

22. An extensive discussion of the value chain concept and its application can be found in M.E. Porter, *Competitive Advantage*, Free Press, 1985.

23. For an extended example of value chain analysis see 'Understanding and using value chain analysis' by Andrew Shepherd in *Exploring Techniques of Analysis and Evaluation in Strategic Management*, edited by Veronique Ambrosini, Prentice Hall, 1998.

24. The importance of profit pools is discussed by O. Gadiesh and J.L. Gilbert, 'Profit pools: a fresh look at strategy', *Harvard Business Review*, vol. 76, no. 3 (1998), pp. 139–47.

25. See M. Porter, 'What is strategy?', *Harvard Business Review*, Nov.–Dec. (1996), pp. 61–78; and N. Siggelkow, 'Evolution towards fit', *Administrative Science Quarterly*, vol. 47, no. 1 (2002), pp. 125–59.

26. We are grateful for this example based on the doctoral dissertation of Bjorn Haugstad, *Strategy as the Intentional Structuration of Practice: Translation of Formal Strategies into Strategies in Practice*, submitted to the Saïd Business School, University of Oxford, 2009.

27. 'Disaggregation' is a term used by D. Collis and C. Montgomery, 'Competing on resources', *Harvard Business Review*, July–August (2008), pp. 140–50.

28. The idea of SWOT as a common-sense checklist has been used for many years: for example, S. Tilles, 'Making strategy explicit', in I. Ansoff (ed.), *Business Strategy*,

Penguin, 1968. See also T. Jacobs, J. Shepherd and G. Johnson's chapter on SWOT analysis in V. Ambrosini (ed.), *Exploring Techniques of Strategy Analysis and Evaluation*, Prentice Hall, 1998. For a critical discussion of the (mis)use of SWOT, see T. Hill and R. Westbrook, 'SWOT analysis: it's time for a product recall', *Long Range Planning*, vol. 30, no. 1 (1997), pp. 46–52.

29. For background reading on the pharmaceutical industry see, for example, 'From vision to decision Pharma 2020', PWC, www.pwc.com/pharma, 2012; 'The pharmaceutical industry', Scherer, F.M., *Handbook of health economics*, vol. 1 (2000), part B, pp. 1297–336; 'A wake-up call for Big Pharma', *McKinsey Quarterly*, December 2011; and Gary Pisano, *Science Business*, Harvard Business School Press, 2006.

30. See H. Weihrich, 'The TOWS matrix – a tool for situational analysis', *Long Range Planning* (April 1982), pp. 54–66.

31. For a fuller discussion of how managers may manage strategic capabilities, see C. Bowman and N. Collier, 'A contingency approach to resource-creation processes', *International Journal of Management Reviews*, vol. 8, no. 4 (2006), pp. 191–211.

32. For a discussion of how the periphery in organisations can build radically new capabilities see P, Regnér, 'Strategy creation in the periphery: inductive versus deductive strategy making', *Journal of Management Studies*, vol. 40, no. 1 (2003), pp. 57–82.

33. See C.A. Maritan and T.H. Brush, 'Heterogeneity and transferring practices: implementing flow practices in multiple plants', *Strategic Management Journal*, vol. 24, no. 10 (2003), pp. 945–60.

34. This observation is made by Veronique Ambrosini in her book (see reference 23 above).

Rocket Internet – will the copycat be imitated?

Introduction

Rocket Internet is a very successful Berlin-based start-up incubator and venture capital firm. It starts, develops and funds e-commerce and other online consumer businesses. It has 25 offices around the world with over 700 employees and an additional 15,000 in its portfolio companies. It has helped create and launch over 100 start-ups and is currently active in more than 50 portfolio companies across more than 40 countries.

The company was founded by the Samwer brothers, Alexander, Oliver and Marc. After going to Silicon Valley in the late 1990s they became inspired by the Californian entrepreneurial culture and especially eBay. The brothers offered eBay to create a German version of the online auction house, but they received no reply from eBay. Instead they launched their own eBay clone, Alando, and adapted it to German conditions. A month later they were acquired by eBay for $50 m. This was to be their first great online success, but far from the last.

Next the brothers created Jamba, a mobile phone content platform. It was sold to VeriSign, a network infrastructure company, for $273 m in 2004. Since then they have become experts in spotting promising business models, especially in the USA, and imitating and scaling them internationally quicker than the originals. This model is the basis of Rocket Internet, which was founded in 2007. Several of their ventures have been acquired by the company with the original idea (see table). Two of their most high-profile ventures after

Source: Dieter Mayr Photography

The Samwer brothers

Alando were CityDeal, which was sold off to American Groupon, and eDarling sold to American eHarmony.

The company's has frequently been criticised for simply being a copycat machine without any original ideas and some have even claimed it is a scam that rips off the originals. However, the question remains: if Rocket Internet has been so incredibly successful and what it does is simply copying, why has no one successfully imitated Rocket Internet yet? The brothers, through Oliver Samwer, defend their model in *Wired*:

'But look at the reality. How many car manufacturers are out there? How many washing-machine manufacturers are there? How many Best Buys? Did someone write that Dixons copied Best Buy, or did anyone ever write that Best Buy copied Dixons, or that [German electronics retailer] Media Markt copied Dixons? No, they talk about Media Markt. They talk about Dixons.

Company	Founded	Business	Buyer	Founded	Price, $m	Transaction date
Alando	1999	Online marketplace	eBay	1995	50	1999
cember.net	2005	Online business network	Xing	2003	6.4	2008
eDarling	2009	Online dating	eHarmony	1998	30% stake*	2010
GratisPay	2009	Virtual currency for online games	SponsorPay	2009	na	2010
CityDeal	2009	Discount deals for consumers	Groupon	2008	126†	2010
viversum	2003	Online astrology	Questico	2000	na	2010

*With option to buy more   † Including a stake in Groupon
Source: Gründerszene.de

They talk about Best Buy. What is the difference? Isn't it all the same thing?'

Source: http://www.economist.com/node/21525394#

Finance and expert teams

Rocket Internet has strong financial backup from its main investor globally, Kinnevik, a Swedish investment company. Kinnevik also contributes with its long-time experience from investing in new businesses and its global network of contacts. Many other investors invest directly in the start-ups and in the later growth stages, among them the American investment bank J.P. Morgan. To work with the investors and structure the financial solutions Rocket Internet has a team of about 35 experts in finance at the Berlin headquarters.

While Rocket Internet has the financial skills needed for an incubator and venture capital firm, it also develops the concepts of new ventures, provides the technology platforms and combines various skills necessary for setting up new ventures. It has about 250 specialists working at the Berlin head office. These specialists are part of diverse expert teams. Engineering including IT software, programming and web design skills are of course essential for product development. At head office there are around 200 engineers who have access to state-of-the art technologies and tools.

There are several other expert teams as well, not least in marketing, including experts in customer management, customer relationship marketing and online marketing. Other teams include Operations, Business Intelligence and HR. Apart from this expertise Rocket Internet has a Global Venture Development programme that includes a global mobile task force of entrepreneurial talents that can bring further know-how to all international markets. This task force includes venture developers with functional skills in product development, supply management, operations and online marketing. They rotate every 4–6 months to a new venture in another part of the world.

Human resource management and culture

The HR team recruit not only regular staff support for Rocket Internet, but specialists for the expert teams and Global Venture Development programme and, not least, the founders of the ventures. Based on their Silicon Valley entrepreneurial spirit they emphasise personal drive rather than good school grades. Head of HR, Vera Termuhlen, explains to VentureVillage.com:

'All in all, it doesn't matter if an applicant is from an elite university. For the area of global venture development, we look for applicants that are hands-on, first-class, have analytical skills, describe themselves as entrepreneurs, have a passion for the online start-up scene along and a willingness to work internationally, often in exotic locations like the Philippines or Nigeria.'

The co-founders and managing directors of the individual ventures establish all operations, build the team around a venture, and develop the business. They act as entrepreneurs and hold personal stakes in a venture's equity. Recruiting them is central and Rocket Internet normally recruits extraordinary, ambitious MBA-level graduates with high analytic skills from within the local regions where the venture is set up. As Alexander Kudlich, Managing Director of Rocket Internet, says:

'We are looking for those who from an analytical point of view understand the beauty of the business model, understand the rationale and understand what a huge opportunity is. Sometimes we say we are looking for analytical entrepreneurs rather than accidental billionaires.'

The company emphasises not only strong expertise, but 'a close cultural connection to Rocket Internet'. Rocket Internet has an intense entrepreneurial working culture that is highly performance driven including high pressure, long working hours, often from 09.00 to 23.00, and little job security. While this is attractive to some, the culture has also been criticised for being too tough and aggressive. Rocket Internet's Managing Director Alexander Kudlich comments on the culture:

'I would describe our culture as very focused, we have young teams – the average age is below 30. There is no place where you get more freedom and where you can take as much responsibility as you want. The only thing we want back is accountability.'

Identification of business models and execution

While some of Rocket Internet's skills are common among other Berlin incubators and indeed incubators throughout Europe, the company is more of an international venture builder compared to most. Expertise is shared throughout the portfolio of ventures globally and its best practice can be applied across the diverse business models (ranging from online fashion to payments to deals to social networking). Compared to many other incubators, the function of the headquarters is central. While entrepreneurs are hired to oversee individual ventures, overall strategy for Rocket Internet is largely shaped at the head office. In particular, this is the case in the identification of new ideas, concepts and business models. The four managing directors at head office lead the scanning for and identification of novel and proven online and mobile transaction-based business models that are internationally scalable. Former Managing Director Florian Heinemann explains in *Wired*: 'We take a pretty systematic look at business models that are already out there and we basically try to define whether a model suits our competence and is large enough that it's worth it for us to go in there.'

Another significant aspect of Rocket Internet's centralised model is the speed at which it can launch novel business models internationally. This is different compared to many US counterparts, but also European ones. Rocket Internet has an international infrastructure and distribution network that build ventures on an international scale in just a few months. The capacity for multiplying business models has been demonstrated repeatedly for diverse types of online business models. As Managing Director Kudlich explains in *Wall Street Journal*:

> 'When we identify a business model we can, within a few weeks, build a platform out of our central teams. In the meantime the local Rocket offices will have hired or allocated the people who will execute on the ground . . . That gives us the speed. The combination of access to the best talent in each country combined with highly standardised or modular approach in terms of platform and systems which are rolled out by our headquarters.'

In brief, Rocket Internet specialises in execution rather than innovation. This is also how the management defend their model when they are blamed for simply being a clone machine. Oliver Samwer says that they are 'execution entrepreneurs' rather than 'pioneering entrepreneurs'. Managing Director Kudlich explains to *Inc. Magazine*: 'Which is harder: to have the idea of selling shoes online or to build a supply chain and warehouse in Indonesia? Ideas are important. But other things are more important.'

Paradoxically, even though Rocket Internet often builds on others' ideas it prefers to keep its own ideas for itself as explained by Marc Samwer in the *New York Times*: 'We really don't like to speak about our investments since our track record encourages people to set up competing sites . . . Ideas travel much faster these days.'

The future

Rocket Internet's success has continued. Zalando, which initially mimicked the online shoe retailing business in the USA by Zappos, now part of Amazon, has expanded into clothing and jewellery. Sales are rising rapidly; annual revenues for 2011 were $650 m and Rocket Internet claim $130 m in revenue per month. Recently it has also launched an Amazon clone, Lazada in South East Asia and a mobile payments company, Payleven, inspired by American Square.

Rocket Internet has, however, started to attract imitators of its own. One of the operations is Wimdu, a copy of the American Airbnb, which allows individual home and apartment owners to list their properties as holiday accommodation. However, Airbnb quickly formed a partnership with another Berlin incubator, Springstar, and they have since been rolling out Airbnb globally. Similarly, the original company responded swiftly when Rocket Internet imitated Fab.com, a designer deal site, with its Bamarang. Fab acquired Casacanda, a parallel European site, and quickly relaunched it as a Fab internationally and Rocket Internet had to close down Bamarang. Rocket Internet is even facing imitators from within. Two of its managing directors have together with other former employees left to set up the Berlin incubator 'Project A Ventures'. There are thus signs that Rocket Internet may eventually be imitated itself.

Questions

1 Based on the data from the case (and any other sources available) use the frameworks from the chapter and analyse the strategic capabilities of Rocket Internet:

 a What are its resources and competences?

 b What are its threshold, distinctive and dynamic capabilities?

2 Based on your initial analysis and answers to question 1, carry out a VRIO analysis for Rocket Internet. What do you conclude? To what extent does Rocket Internet have strategic capabilities with sustained competitive advantage?

3 What is the importance of the Samwers brothers? What would happen if they left or sold the company?

References

1. Joel Kaczmarek, 'An inside look at Rocket Internet', *VentureVillage.com*, 18 November 2012.
2. Max Chafkin, 'Lessons from the world's most ruthless competitor', *Inc. Magazine*, 29 May 2012.
3. Ben Rooney, 'Rocket Internet leads the clone war', *The Wall Street Journal*, 14 May 2012.
4. Gerrit Wiesmann, 'Zalando to set foot in seven new countries', *Financial Times*, 26 March 2012.
5. Tim Bradshaw, 'Facebook backers to take stake in Zalando', *Financial Times*, 2 February 2012.
6. Matt Cowan, 'Inside the clone factory', *Wired UK*, 2 March 2012.
7. Robert Levine, 'The kopy kat kids', *Cnnmoney.com*, 2 October 2007.
8. *New York Times*, 3 December 2006.
9. *The Economist*, 'Attack of the clones', 6 August 2011.

Suggested video clip

http://www.youtube.com/watch?v=Tq7WnzY89KE

4

STRATEGIC PURPOSE

Learning outcomes

After reading this chapter you should be able to:

● Assess the *strategic purpose* of an organisation in terms of *mission*, *vision*, *values* and *objectives*.

● Analyse the strategic significance of different *ownership models* for an organisation's purpose.

● Evaluate the implications for strategic purpose of the *shareholder* and *stakeholder models* of corporate governance.

● Undertake *stakeholder analysis* as a means of identifying the influence of different stakeholder groups in terms of their power and interest.

● Relate *corporate responsibility* and *personal ethics* to purpose and strategy.

MyStrategyLab

MyStrategyLab is designed to help you make the most of your studies. Visit **www.pearsoned.co.uk/mystrategylab** to discover a wide range of resources, including:

● A personalised **Study plan** that will help you understand core concepts

● **Audio and video clips** that put the spotlight on strategy in the real world

● **Online glossaries and flashcards** that provide helpful reminders when you're looking for some quick revision.

(4.1) INTRODUCTION

In Spring 2012, Sir Stelios Haji-Ioannou, founder of the easyJet airline, took his former company to court as part of his campaign to curb what he saw as its excessive growth. Although he had retired from a management role, Sir Stelios and his family were still major shareholders in easyJet, with 38 per cent ownership, and they had become fierce critics of the company's growth strategy. According to Sir Stelios, easyJet's current management were investing in growth at the expense of dividends for shareholders. At stake in the clash between founder and managers were crucial issues about the purpose of business – long-term growth or immediate dividends – and who has the right to control strategy – owners or management.

The previous two chapters have looked at the importance of the external environment and internal capabilities for an organisation's strategic position. This chapter examines how external pressures and internal aspirations interact in the setting of organisational purpose. The chapter warns that organisational purpose can rarely be reduced to a simple formula such as 'profit maximisation'. Organisational purposes are typically complex and diverse. It is important to be clear about what purposes drive strategy, who influences such purposes and who monitors performance against them. These are the concerns of this chapter.

An important concept here is that of **stakeholders**, **those individuals or groups that depend on an organisation to fulfil their own goals and on whom, in turn, the organisation depends**. An underlying question is whether the strategic purpose of the organisation should reflect the expectations of a particular stakeholder, for example shareholders, or incorporate broader stakeholder interests, such as employees, customers and the local community. Figure 4.1 summarises the different influences on strategic purpose discussed in the chapter:

- The chapter begins in section 4.2 by developing the discussion in Chapter 1 about different ways in which organisations express *strategic purpose*, including statements of *mission*, *vision*, *values* and *objectives*.

- Section 4.3 considers the *ownership* structures and the *corporate governance* framework within which organisations operate. The concern is with the way in which formally constituted bodies such as investors or boards influence strategic purpose through the formalised processes for supervising executive decisions and actions.

Figure 4.1 Influences on strategic purpose

- In determining purpose, it is important to understand how different *stakeholders* may be involved in strategy. Section 4.4 addresses the different power and interest of various stakeholders through *stakeholder analysis*.

- Section 4.5 is concerned with issues of *social responsibility* and *ethics*. Here the question is which purposes an organisation *should* fulfil. How should managers respond to the expectations society has of their organisations, both in terms of *corporate responsibility* and in terms of the *behaviour of individuals* within organisations, not least themselves?

(4.2) MISSION, VISION, VALUES AND OBJECTIVES

Harvard University's Cynthia Montgomery[1] argues that defining and expressing a clear and motivating purpose for the organisation is the core of a strategist's job. Even for private-sector organisations, this purpose is typically more than simple profit maximisation. Long-term prosperity and employee motivation usually require expressions of purpose that go beyond just profits. According to Montgomery, the stated purpose of the organisation should address two related questions: *how* does the organisation make a difference; and *for whom* does the organisation make that difference? If the stakeholders of an organisation can relate to such a purpose it can be highly motivating. Indeed, research by Jim Collins and Jerry Porras suggests that the long-run success of many US corporations – such as Disney, General Electric or 3M – can be attributed (at least in part) to the clear guidance and motivation offered by such statements of purpose.[2]

There are four ways in which organisations typically define their purpose:

- A **mission statement** aims to provide employees and stakeholders with clarity about what the organisation is fundamentally there to do. This is often expressed in the apparently simple but challenging question: 'What business are we in?' Two linked questions that can clarify an organisation's 'business' are: 'What would be lost if the organisation did not exist?'; and 'How do we make a difference?' Though they do not use the term 'mission statement', Collins and Porras[3] suggest that understanding the fundamental mission can be done by starting with a descriptive statement of what the organisation actually does, then repeatedly delving deeper into the organisation's purpose by asking 'why do we do this?' They use the example of managers in a gravel-and-asphalt company arriving at the conclusion that its mission is to make people's lives better by improving the quality of built structures. At the University of Utrecht (see Illustration 1.2), the mission includes educating students, training the next generation of researchers and addressing social issues.

- A **vision statement** is concerned with the future the organisation seeks to create. The vision typically expresses an aspiration that will enthuse, gain commitment and stretch performance. So here the question is: 'What do we want to achieve?' Porras and Collins suggest managers can identify this by asking: 'If we were sitting here in twenty years what do we want to have created or achieved?' They cite the example of Henry Ford's original vision in the very early days of automobile production that the ownership of a car should be within the reach of everyone. For the Swedish music site Spotify, the vision is to become 'the Operating System of music', a universal platform for listening just as Microsoft is for office software.

- **Statements of corporate values** communicate the underlying and enduring core 'principles' that guide an organisation's strategy and define the way that the organisation should operate. For example, Google famously includes in its values 'you can be serious without a suit', 'fast is better than slow' and 'don't be evil'. It is important that these values be enduring, so a question to ask is: 'Would these values change with circumstances?' If the answer is 'yes', then they are not 'core' and not 'enduring'. An example is the importance of leading-edge research in some universities. Whatever the constraints on funding, such universities hold to the enduring centrality of research. On the other hand, as Google has grown and diversified, some critics wonder whether the company still abides by its principle of 'don't be evil' (see Chapter 12 end case).

- **Objectives** **are statements of specific outcomes that are to be achieved.** These are often expressed in precise financial terms, for instance the level of sales, profits or share valuation in one, two or three years' time.[4] Organisations may also have quantifiable market-based objectives, such as market share, customer service, repeat business and so on. Sometimes objectives focus on the basis of competitive advantage: for example, low-cost airlines such as Ryanair set objectives on turnaround time for their aircraft because this is at the core of their distinctive low-cost advantage. Increasingly organisations are also setting objectives referred to as 'the triple bottom line', by which is meant not only economic objectives such as those above, but also environmental and social objectives to do with their corporate responsibility to wider society (see section 4.4.1 below).

Some critics regard vision, mission and values statements as liable to become bland and too wide-ranging.[5] Objectives can seem attractively precise by contrast. However, vision, mission and values statements provide a longer-term view of the organisation and its underlying strategy. While objectives are useful for guiding and monitoring performance in the short term, visions, missions and values can offer more enduring sources of direction and motivation. But it remains crucial to make vision, mission and values statements meaningful.

Three principles are helpful in creating meaningful vision, mission and values statements:[6]

- *Focus*: statements should focus attention and help guide real decisions. Effective vision, mission and values statements should define what is excluded from the organisation's strategy as much as what is included. At Apple, the visionary founder Steve Jobs regarded as crucial the ability to say 'no' to non-core activities. Statements should also be practical decision-making tools. Google's value of 'fast' can guide choices between strategic options with different levels of complexity: Google's product development managers will cut product features which slow down its essential search and advertising functions, even if they might be nice to have.

- *Motivational*: statements should motivate employees to do their best. Here it is important that they not be so bland as to be applicable to nearly all organisations, but rather be distinctive and authentic to the particular organisation in question. To motivate, they should stretch organisational performance to higher levels, but at the same time the targets must be credible. Thus Apple's vision of making computers available to everybody inspired Steve Jobs' employees in the early years of the company.

- *Clear*: the third important principle in such statements is clarity. In order to motivate employees in their day-to-day work, visions, missions and values should be easy to communicate, understand and remember. Here it is often useful to be crisp and simple. Thus founder Mark Zuckerberg identified three of Facebook's values as 'move fast', 'be bold' and 'be open': these are clear, memorable and actionable.

ILLUSTRATION 4.1

Mozilla's mission: beyond Firefox

Can the Mozilla Foundation's mission and principles guide and motivate it into a new generation of products beyond its Firefox browser?

The Mozilla Foundation is a non-profit organisation that originated in the late 1990s from the old web-browser company Netscape. Mozilla's best known product is the Firefox open source web-browser, produced largely for free by a community of volunteer software developers. In 2012, Firefox had about 25 per cent share of the world's browser market, recently over taken by Google's Chrome. About 85 per cent of Mozilla's revenue is a contract with Google, renewed for three years in 2011, which pays the Foundation in return for using Google as Firefox's default search engine.

Mozilla says the following about itself:

'Mozilla's mission is to promote openness, innovation and opportunity on the web.

What we do

We do this by creating great software, like the Firefox browser, and building movements, like Drumbeat [the community of software developers], that give people tools to take control of their online lives.

What we strive for

As a non-profit organisation, we define success in terms of building communities and enriching people's lives instead of benefiting shareholders. We believe in the power and potential of the Internet and want to see it thrive for everyone, everywhere.'

Mozilla also publishes what it calls a 'Manifesto', containing a set of principles intended 'to make Mozilla contributors proud of what we're doing and motivate us to continue'. Principles of the Manifesto include:

● The internet is a global public resource that must remain open and accessible.
● The internet should enrich the lives of individual human beings.
● Individuals' security on the internet is fundamental and cannot be treated as optional.

● Individuals must have the ability to shape their own experiences on the internet.
● Free and open-source software promotes the development of the internet as a public resource.

In 2012, Mozilla was developing a range of new initiatives. The most notable is 'Pancake', a cloud-based framework that allows users to carry and manage their personal data wherever they go. One objective of Pancake is to counter the way mobile apps are fragmenting the internet. Mozilla's President, Mitchell Baker, explained to the BBC: 'The internet was meant to be connected – not siloed. We really do want to encourage developers to develop across devices, using the same kind of power and explosive innovation and freedoms that the web has given us over the last 15 years.'

For Mitchell Baker, 'the reason for [these] initiatives is not driven by revenue. It is driven because we cannot fulfil the Mozilla mission unless we have a presence in these other spaces.' She continued, referring particularly to Mozilla's users and developers: 'Our stakeholders – we don't have shareholders – are not looking for a financial return on investment. The return on their time and energy and goodwill that they're looking for is the product that they like, and an internet that has a layer of user sovereignty in it.'

Sources: Mozilla website, 2012; and www.bbc.co.uk, 'Life after Firefox', 10 April 2012.

Questions

1 Mozilla does not produce a formal vision statement. Based on the materials here, what do you think Mozilla's vision would be?

2 How do Mozilla's mission and principles influence its approach to new initiatives? Is there any danger in its apparent priorities?

Whatever statements of mission, vision and values are employed, or whatever the objectives which are set, it is important to understand who influences what they are. The following sections examine key influencers.

(4.3) OWNERS AND MANAGERS

Purpose is typically set by the organisation's owners and managers. Owners and managers are not always the same and their interests can diverge. This section explores different kinds of ownership models and the governance issues involved in reconciling owners and managers.

4.3.1 Ownership models

There are many types of ownership, and the boundaries between them often blur.[7] However, it is useful to distinguish four main ownership models, each with different implications for strategic purpose. Figure 4.2 ranges these four models along two axes. The horizontal axis describes the dominant modes of management, ranging from wholly *professional* (with managers employed for their professional expertise) to wholly *personal* (with management determined by personal connections to ownership). The vertical axis describes the extent to which purpose is focused on profit as an exclusive goal or on profit as just one of a mix of motives. In each case, there is a range along the axes: organisations vary in their relative positioning and sometimes organisations do not conform to the typical behaviour of their ownership model. None the less organisations with different ownership models do tend to bunch together in distinctive ways.

Figure 4.2 Ownership, management and purpose

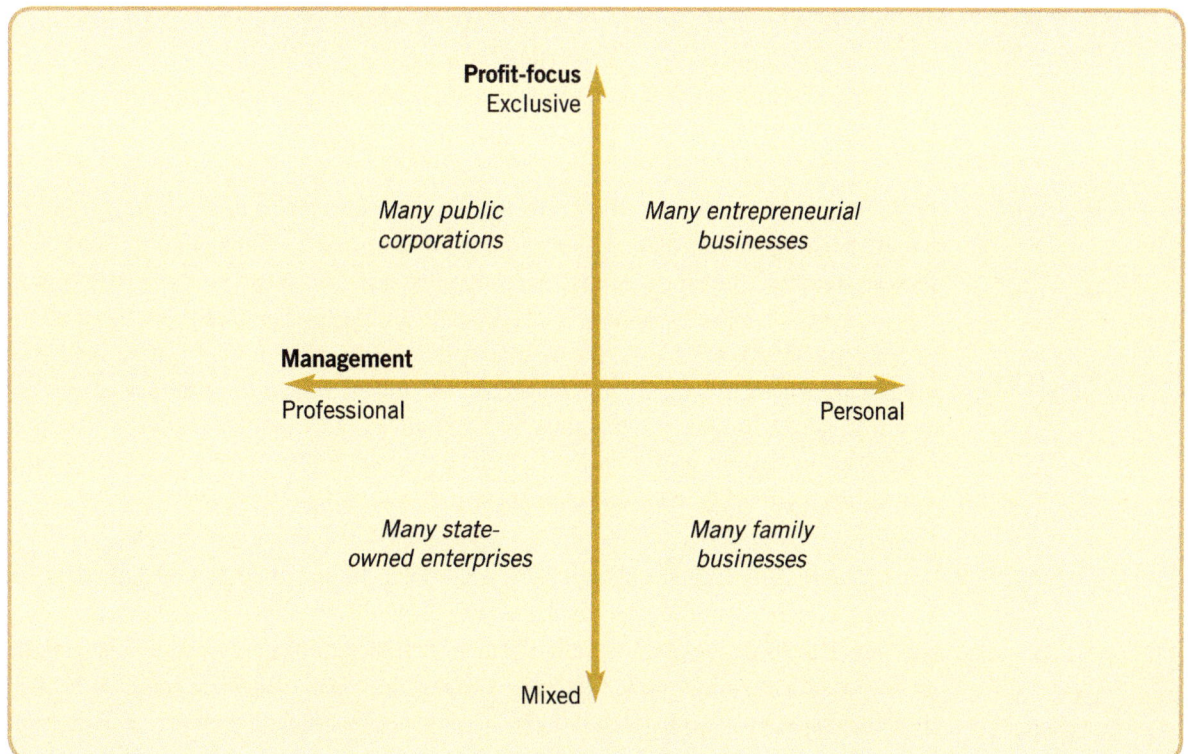

The four main ownership models are as follows:

● *Public companies* (often called publicly traded companies or public limited companies) are the most important ownership model in economies such as these of the USA, northern Europe, Japan and many others. These companies sell their shares to the public, with ownership typically in the hands of individual investors or, frequently, institutions such as pension funds, banks or insurance companies.[8] Usually owners do not manage public companies themselves, but delegate that function to professional managers. In principle, company managers work to make a financial return for their owners – that is why the public usually buy the shares in the first place. If shareholders are not satisfied financially, they can either sell the shares or seek the removal of the managers. In terms of Figure 4.2 therefore, most public companies focus strongly on profit. However, profit maximisation is rarely a simple goal for companies. There is often a delicate balance to be struck between the short-run profits and long-term survival, for example. Short-term profits might be improved by cutting research budgets or taking advantage of loyal customers, but such action may well be at the expense of the long run. In relation to the vertical axis in Figure 4.2, public companies may therefore vary in how extremely they focus on profit objectives.

● *State-owned enterprises* are wholly or majority owned by national or sometimes regional governments. They are very important in many developing economies: about 80 per cent of stock market value is accounted for by state-owned companies in China, 60 per cent in Russia and 40 per cent in Brazil.[9] Privatisation has reduced the role of state-owned enterprises in many developed economies, but quasi-privatised agencies such as hospital trusts and school academies in the United Kingdom operate in a similar way. In state-owned enterprises, politicians typically delegate day-to-day control to professional managers, though they may intervene on major strategic issues. State-owned enterprises usually have to earn some kind of profit or surplus in order to fund investment and build financial reserves, but they are also likely to pursue a range of other objectives that are in keeping with government policy. For Chinese state-owned enterprises, for example, securing access to overseas resources such as minerals and energy is an important objective.

● *Entrepreneurial businesses* are businesses that are substantially owned and controlled by their founders. Lakshmi Mittal remains chairman and chief executive of his creation, Arcelor Mittal, the largest steel company in the world. Sir Richard Branson is chairman of the Virgin Group, founded as a record store in 1972 and now including airline, train and sports businesses. None the less, as they grow, entrepreneurial businesses are likely both to rely more on professional managers to cope with increasing complexity and to draw in external investors in order to fund new opportunities. Typically entrepreneurial companies need to focus heavily on profit in order to survive and grow, and the presence of external investors is likely to increase the pressure for financial performance. However, entrepreneurial businesses may also be partly directed by personal missions, for instance developing a particular technology to its full potential.[10]

● *Family businesses* are typically businesses where ownership by the founding entrepreneur has passed on to his or her family, on account of the founder's death or retirement for instance. Typically family businesses are small to medium-sized enterprises, but can be very big: Ford, Fiat, Samsung and Walmart, the largest retailer in the world, are all under family ownership and retain significant family involvement in top management roles. Quite often the family retains a majority of the voting shares, while releasing the remainder to the public on the stock market: thus half of stock market-listed companies in the 10 largest Asian markets are effectively family-controlled.[11] Also, management may be partly profession-alised, even though top management remains ultimately under family control: thus the Chief Executive of Ford is a non-family member, but the Executive Chairman is still William Ford Jr. For family businesses, retaining control over the company, passing on management to the next generation and ensuring the company's long-term survival are often very important objectives, and these might rule out profit-maximising strategies that involve high risk or require external finance. Thus a family business might diversify into lots of small businesses rather than engage in one large one, because that would minimise risk and give a chance to younger family members to work in distinct areas of activity.[12]

As well as these four main types of ownership model, there are several other variants which play smaller but still significant roles in the economy.[13] *Not-for-profit* organisations, such as Mozilla (Illustration 4.1), are typically owned by a charitable foundation: they may need to make some kind of surplus to fund investment and protect against hard times, but they fundamentally exist to pursue social missions. The *partnership* model, in which the organisation is owned and controlled by senior employees (its partners), is important in many professional services such as law and accounting. There are also *employee-owned* firms, which spread ownership among employees as a whole. The most famous example of this in the United Kingdom is the retailer John Lewis, but this model is also being promoted for hospitals in the British National Health Service. Typically these not-for-profits, partnerships and employee-owned firms are restricted in their ability to raise external finance, making them more conservative in their strategies.

Clearly everybody should know how the ownership of their own organisation relates to its strategic purpose: as above, strategy for a state-owned business is likely to be very different to that of a public company. However, it is also important for managers to understand the owner-ship of other organisations with which they engage, for example competitors and partners. Different ownership models will shape their purpose and drive their strategic decisions as well. Without understanding the relationship between ownership and purpose, it is easy to be sur-prised by competitors and partners with different priorities to your own. For example, Western public mining companies have often found themselves outbid for overseas mining opportuni-ties by Chinese state-owned companies keen to secure supplies.

4.3.2 Corporate governance

The varying roles of owners and professional managers raise issues of corporate governance.[14] **Corporate governance is concerned with the structures and systems of control by which man-agers are held accountable to those who have a legitimate stake in an organisation.**[15] Key stakeholders in corporate governance are typically the owners, but may include other groups such as employee representatives. Connecting stakeholder interests with management action is a vital part of strategy. Failures in corporate governance have contributed to calamitous strategic choices in many leading companies, even resulting in the complete destruction of global companies such as the energy giant Enron in 2001 and the leading investment bank Lehman Brothers in 2008. With the survival of whole organsations at stake, governance is increasingly recognised as a key strategic issue.

Managers and stakeholders are linked together via the governance chain. **The governance chain shows the roles and relationships of different groups involved in the governance of an organisation.** In a small family business, the governance chain is simple: there are family share-holders, a board with some family members and there are managers, some of whom may be family too. Here there are just three layers in the chain. In large public corporations, however, influences on governance can be complex. Figure 4.3 shows a governance chain for a typical large, public corporation. Here the size of the organisation means there are extra layers of management internally, while being publicly quoted introduces more investor layers too. Individual investors (the ultimate beneficiaries) often invest in public corporations through investment funds, i.e. institutional investors such as unit trusts or pension funds, which then invest in a range of companies on their behalf. Funds are typically controlled by trustees, with day-to-day investment activity undertaken by investment managers. So the ultimate beneficiaries may not even know in which companies they have a financial stake and have little power to influence the companies' boards directly.

Economists analyse the relationships in such governance chains in terms of the *principal–agent model*.[16] Here 'principals' pay 'agents' to act on their behalf, just as homeowners employ estate agents to sell their homes. Classically, the principal is simply the owner and the agent is the manager. However, the reality for large public corporations is usually more complex, with principals and agents at every level. In Figure 4.3, the beneficiaries are the ultimate principals

Figure 4.3 The chain of corporate governance: typical reporting structures

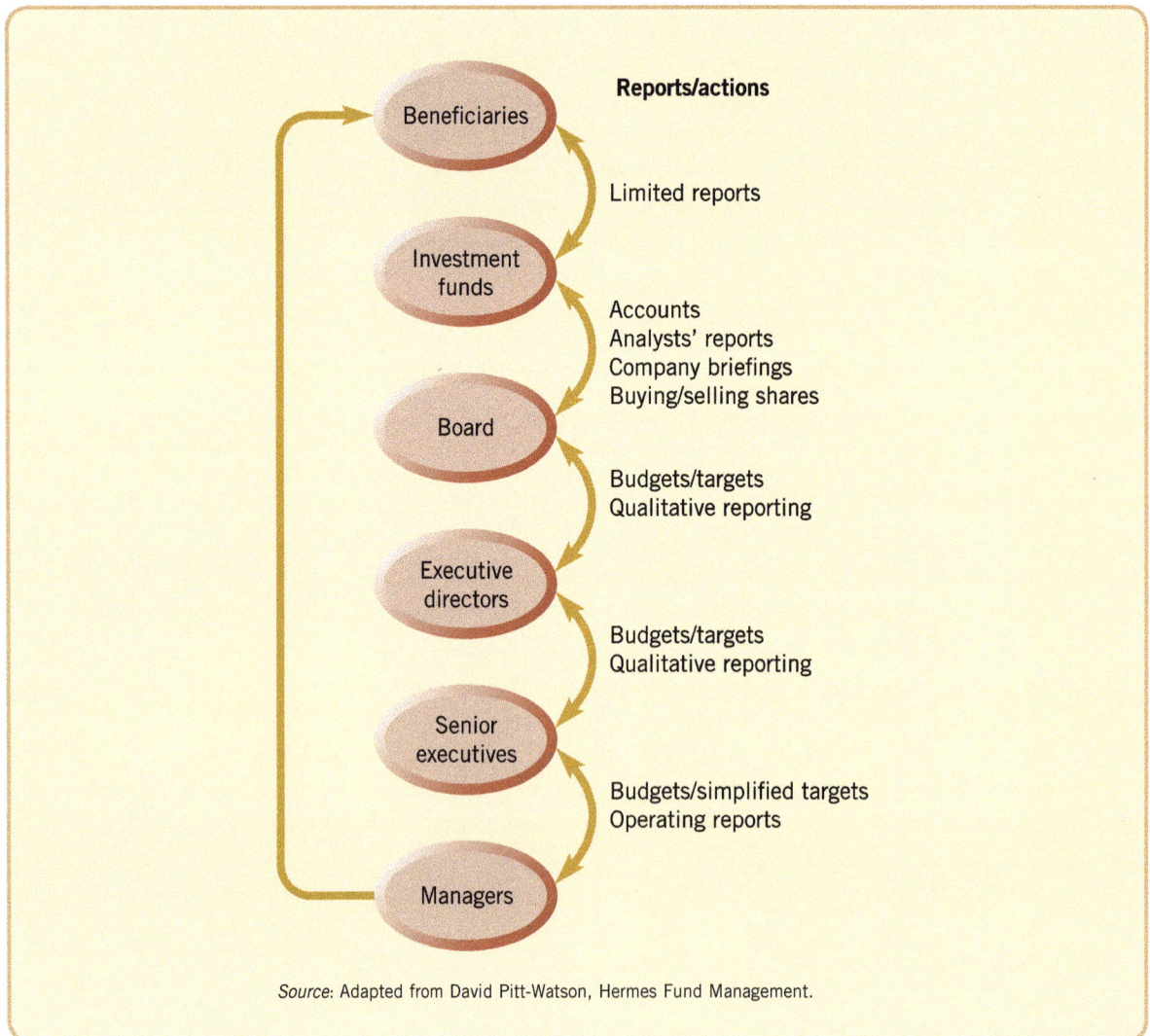

Reports/actions

Beneficiaries

Limited reports

Investment funds

Accounts
Analysts' reports
Company briefings
Buying/selling shares

Board

Budgets/targets
Qualitative reporting

Executive directors

Budgets/targets
Qualitative reporting

Senior executives

Budgets/simplified targets
Operating reports

Managers

Source: Adapted from David Pitt-Watson, Hermes Fund Management.

and fund trustees and investment managers are their immediate agents in terms of achieving good returns on their investments. Further down the chain, company boards can be considered as principals too, with senior executives their agents in managing the company. Thus there are many layers of agents between ultimate principals and the managers at the bottom, with the reporting mechanisms between each layer liable to be imperfect. Weak links in the governance chain at several levels is what led to the scandals at News Corporation for example (see Illustration 4.2).

The governance issues in principal–agent theory arise from three problems:

- *Knowledge imbalances*: agents typically know more than principals about what can and should be done. After all, it is they who are actually doing the job and they have presumably been hired for their expertise.

- *Monitoring limits*: it is very difficult for principals to monitor closely the performance of their agents. This limit is made worse because principals usually have many investments, so their attention is likely to be split several ways.

- *Misaligned incentives*: unless their incentives are closely aligned to principals' interests, agents are liable to pursue other objectives that reward them better. Principals might introduce bonus schemes in order to incentivise desired performance, but then agents may game the system: for example, they might use their superior knowledge to negotiate bonus targets that are in reality easy to meet.

Principal–agent theory therefore stresses the importance of knowledgeable principals, effective monitoring systems and well-designed incentives in order to make sure that large organisations actually pursue the purposes that their owners set for them.

4.3.3 Different governance models

The governing body of an organisation is typically a board of directors. Although the legal requirements vary in detail around the world, the primary responsibility of a board is typically to ensure that an organisation fulfils the wishes and purposes of those whom it represents. However, who the board represents varies. In the private sector in some parts of the world it is primarily shareholders, but in other parts of the world it is a broader or different stakeholder base. In the public sector, the governing body is accountable to the political arm of government – possibly through some intermediary such as a funding body. These differences have implications for organisational purpose and strategy as well as the role and composition of boards.

At the most general level there are two governance models: the shareholder model, prioritising shareholder interests; and the stakeholder model, recognising the wider set of interests that have a stake in an organisation's success.[17] These two models are pure types, and there are many variants on each. The question for managers, therefore, is where their organisation is positioned on the range between the pure shareholder and pure stakeholder models of governance.

A shareholder model of governance

The shareholder model is dominant in public companies, especially in the USA and UK. Shareholders have priority in regard to the wealth generated by the company, as opposed to employees for example. The shareholder interest in a company is assumed to be largely financial. Shareholders can vote for the board of directors according to the number of their shares and, in the

ILLUSTRATION

ILLUSTRATION 4.2

A family affair? News Corporation's governance crisis

The governance chain at News Corporation seems to have failed at several levels, putting at risk family control.

In 2012, Rupert Murdoch was 81 years old and still Chairman and Chief Executive of News Corporation, the international media conglomerate that he had launched in Australia in the 1950s. News Corporation's assets included Fox News, the *Wall Street Journal* and the movie studio 20th Century Fox. The company also owned several leading British newspapers, including the *Sun*, *The Times* and the *Sunday Times*, and a 39 per cent holding in the dominant United Kingdom pay-TV broadcaster, BSkyB. The Murdoch family owned 39 per cent of the corporation's voting shares and a family friend, Prince Al Waleed bin Talal, held a further 7 per cent. Other important shareholders included the Bank of New York, the investment management company Invesco, and Calpers, the Californian teachers' pension fund.

News Corporation was run as something of a family fiefdom. Rupert Murdoch's son Lachlan had been Deputy Chief Operating Officer until 2005, when he resigned abruptly for unexplained reasons. Murdoch's daughter Elisabeth had been Managing Director of BSkyB before setting up her own television production company, Shine, with backing from BSkyB itself. In 2011, Shine was bought by News Corporation for £290 m (€350 m; $440 m): Elisabeth personally received more than half this sum, at the same time as retaining her role as Shine's Chairman and Chief Executive and joining the News Corporation main board. Some News Corporation shareholders accused the company of paying too much for Shine. Another of Rupert's sons was James, who was News Corporation's Deputy Chief Operating Officer. At the start of 2012, James was also Chairman of BSkyB and Chairman and Chief Executive of News Corporation Europe and Asia, overseeing a range of international assets including the group's British newspapers.

This last position placed James Murdoch in the front line of the telephone hacking scandal that engulfed News Corporation's British newspapers during 2011–12. In a fiercely competitive market, News Corporation's tabloid newspaper editors had encouraged journalists to get the most sensational stories they could, and this often led them to break into people's mobile phone and email accounts. It was unclear when James Murdoch became aware of these practices: he claimed in a British Parliamentary inquiry that he did not know of them until much later. If James was unaware, he appeared not to be in close control of his own newspapers and to be very lax in investigating accusations of lawless behaviour by his employees.

In early 2012, James Murdoch resigned all his British responsibilities. But James continued as Deputy Chief Operating Officer of News Corporation globally, while retaining responsibilities for the company's Continental European interests. Shareholders were deeply unhappy with the Murdoch family's management, despite the strong performance of News Corporation's shares relative to competitors' since 2009. In October 2011, more than half the independent shareholders had either voted against or abstained on the re-appointment of Rupert Murdoch as Chairman and a similar proportion had voted against the reappointment to the board of James. Of course, the family controlled enough shares to win the overall majority. However, Anne Simpson, Head of Corporate Governance for Calpers, said of the hostile votes: 'This sends a strong signal to the News Corp board that investors are looking for robust independence. It's a vote in favour of board rejuvenation.'

Main sources: *Financial Times*, 25 October 2011 and 3 April 2012.

Questions

1 Referring to Figure 4.3, at what levels did the governance chain at News Corporation seem to fail?

2 Given that News Corporation's share price was outperforming competitors', why would shareholders vote against the Murdochs' management at News Corporation? What else could they do?

pure model at least, there are many shareholders so that no single shareholder dominates. Shareholders can also exert control indirectly through the trading of shares. Dissatisfied shareholders may sell their shares, leading to a drop in the company's share price and an increased threat to directors of takeover by other firms.

There are arguments for and against the shareholder model. The argued advantages include:

- *Higher rates of return.* The unambiguous focus on shareholder interests means that investors typically get a higher rate of return than in the stakeholder model. Managers are not distracted by the interests of other stakeholders.

- *Reduced risk.* Shareholders face less risk in the shareholder model, especially if operating within an economy with an efficient stock market. Shareholders can diversify their risk by using the stock market to buy shares in many different companies. They can also use the stock market to sell the shares of companies that look in danger.

- *Increased innovation and entrepreneurship.* Since the system facilitates higher risk-taking by investors, the shareholder model should promote entrepreneurship, innovation and higher growth. It is easier to attract capital investment where investors know that they can easily diversify their shareholdings and trade their shares.

- *Better decision making.* Arguably the separation of ownership and management makes strategic decisions more objective in relation to the potentially different demands and constraints of financial, labour and customer markets. If the shareholders are well spread, no one shareholder is likely to exercise undue control of management decisions.

Potential disadvantages of the shareholder model include:

- *Diluted monitoring.* Where there are many shareholders, each with small stakes and often with many other investments, the principal–agent problem is exacerbated. Any single shareholder may not think it worthwhile monitoring performance closely, and simply hope that other shareholders are doing so. This may allow managers to sacrifice shareholder value to pursue their own agendas. For example, CEOs may further their own egos and empires with mergers that add no value to shareholders.

- *Vulnerable minority shareholders.* On the other hand, especially where corporate governance regulation is weak, the shareholder model can be abused to allow the emergence of dominant shareholders. Such dominant shareholders may exploit their voting power to the disadvantage of minority shareholders. This is the *principal–principal problem*: the dominant shareholder (principal) may appoint managers, make acquisitions, guarantee debts or sell assets contrary to the interests of the other shareholders (also principals).[18] Minority shareholders do not have enough votes to control abusive majority shareholders.

- *Short-termism.* The need to make profits for shareholders may encourage managers to focus on short-term gains at the expense of long-term projects, such as research and development. Some high-technology public companies such as Google and Facebook have deliberately adopted a dual-class shareholder structure, where the original founders and their associates have larger voting rights in order to protect these companies' commitment to long-term innovation.

The stakeholder model of governance

An alternative model of governance is the stakeholder model. This is founded on the principle that wealth is created, captured and distributed by a variety of stakeholders. It is not just shareholders who have a stake in the future of a business. Important stakeholders may include employees, local communities, local governments, major suppliers and customers, and banks. Shareholders are also stakeholders, of course, but in the stakeholder model they are likely to take larger stakes in their companies than in the pure shareholder model and to hold these stakes longer term. Thus in the stakeholder governance model, management need to be responsive to multiple stakeholders. In some governance systems, some of these stakeholders, for example banks and employees, may be formally represented on boards.

The argued advantages for the stakeholder model of governance include:

- *Long-term horizons.* It is argued that when shareholders hold large blocks of shares, they are likely to regard their investments as long term. It is harder to dispose of large shareholdings when business is going wrong, and the incentive to get involved in order to maintain the value of the stake is proportionately greater. Thus the predominance of large investors in the stakeholder model reduces the pressure for short-term results as against longer-term performance.

- *Less reckless risk-taking.* Many stakeholders are more risk-averse than diversified shareholders. Employees fear for their livelihoods. Large-scale shareholders have more to lose, and find it harder to exit in the case of difficulty. Local government bodies may face the loss of major employers in their regions. The stakeholder model therefore discourages excessive risk-taking.

- *Better management.* Given stakeholders' concern for the long-term prosperity of the company, there may be a closer level of monitoring of management and greater demands for information from within the firm. Management are under greater pressure to perform. Further, because power may reside with a limited number of large shareholders, it is easier to intervene in the case of management failure.

There are also possible disadvantages to the stakeholder model of governance:

- *Weaker decision making.* Close monitoring by powerful stakeholders could lead to interference, slowing down of decision processes and the loss of management objectivity when critical decisions have to be made.

- *Uneconomic investments.* Due to lack of financial pressure from shareholders, long-term investments may also be made in projects where the returns may be below market expectations.

- *Reduced innovation and entrepreneurship.* Because investors fear conflicts with the interests of other stakeholders, and because selling shares may be harder, they are less likely to provide capital for risky new opportunities.

The stakeholder model recognises that organisations typically operate within a complex set of relationships, going beyond simple economic ones. As discussed in section 5.3, organisations participate in *organisational fields* in which *legitimacy* matters, not just profits.[19] Legitimacy typically means more than sticking to the letter of the law; it involves following norms of appropriate conduct in the eyes of key members of an organisation's institutional field (e.g. governments, regulators, trade unions and customers, as well as shareholders). Legitimacy is an overarching concept of purpose, where profits, ethical conduct and fairness to stakeholders all play a role. Even if an organisation does not operate explicitly according to a stakeholder model, it is typically important that strategies be legitimate in this wider sense of satisfying all key stakeholders' expectations of appropriate conduct. Firms operating on a shareholder model also need to maintain legitimacy in their field if they are to avoid interference by regulators, consumer boycotts and demoralised employees.

4.3.4 **How boards of directors influence strategy**

A central governance issue is the role of boards of directors and of directors themselves. Since boards have the ultimate responsibility for the success or failure of an organisation as well as the benefits received by shareholders or wider stakeholders, they must be concerned with strategy.

Under the shareholder model there is typically a single-tier board structure, with a majority of 'non-executive' directors, outsiders who do not have day-to-day managerial responsibilities but provide oversight on behalf of shareholders. The emphasis on outside directors is intended to bring greater independence to the primary role of the board, protecting shareholders' interests. However, as explained above, this is not without its problems since the choice of non-executives is often influenced by the executive directors themselves.

The stakeholder model can involve a two-tier board structure. For example, in Germany for firms of more than 500 employees there is a supervisory board (*Aufsichtsrat*) and a management board (*Vorstand*). The supervisory board is a forum where the interests of various stakeholder groups are represented, including shareholders and employees but also banks with a long-term involvement in the company. Strategic planning and operational control are vested with the management board, but major decisions like mergers and acquisitions require approval of the supervisory board. Two-tier boards also exist in other European countries, notably the Netherlands and France.

Two issues are especially significant here:

- *Delegation.* Strategic management can be entirely delegated to management, with the board receiving and approving plans and decisions. Here it is important that an organisation's strategy is not 'captured' by management at the expense of other stakeholders. The two-tier board system seeks to prevent this. It is less clear how this occurs in the single-board structure typical of the shareholder model.

- *Engagement.* The board can engage in the strategic management process. This has practical problems concerning the time and knowledge level of non-executive directors in particular to perform their role this way. This problem can be especially pronounced in organisations such as charities or public bodies with governing boards or trustees of people committed to the mission of the organisation, keen to become involved but with limited operational understanding of it.

In the guidelines increasingly issued by governments[20] or advocated by commentators there are some common themes:

- Boards must be seen to *operate 'independently' of the management* of the company. So the role of non-executive directors is heightened.

- Boards must be *competent to scrutinise the activities of managers.* So the collective experience of the board, its training and the information available to it are crucially important.

- Directors must have the *time* to do their job properly. So limitations on the number of directorships that an individual can hold are also an important consideration.

However, it is the *behaviour of boards* and their members that are likely to be most significant whatever structural arrangements are put in place.[21] Important, therefore, are respect, trust, 'constructive friction' between board members, fluidity of roles, individual as well as collective responsibility, and the evaluation of individual director and collective board performance. Board behaviour was a problem at ENRC (see Illustration 4.3).

ILLUSTRATION 4.3

ENRC's boardroom – City or Soviet?

After spectacular dismissals, this Kazakhstan multinational seeks to shake off doubts about the operations of its board.

The Eurasian Natural Resources Company (ENRC) originated in the 1990s, with the bulk of the assets acquired by three entrepreneurs – Patokh Chodiev, Alijan Ibragimov and Alexander Machkevitch – during the privatisation of Kazakhstan's heavy industries from 1994 to 1996. All three men are now billionaires, owning between them 35 per cent of what has become a multinational company headquartered and listed in the City of London. With 70,000 employees, ENRC is one of the world's largest producers of ferrochrome, one of the world's biggest exporters of iron ore and the world's ninth largest producer of traded alumina. It has substantial interests in Brazil and Africa as well as back home in Kazakhstan. The Kazak state owns 12 per cent of the company, and another Kazak entrepreneur controls a further 26 per cent through his company, Kazakhmys.

However, since 2008, when ENRC listed on the London Stock Exchange, the company has had a significant proportion of ownership by ordinary external investors. The listing had raised £1.4 bn (€1.7 bn or $2.1 bn) in additional capital, intended to fund international expansion: the Kazakh government was keen on creating a 'national champion'. The listing had also provided an opportunity to tidy up the company's corporate governance arrangements in order both to meet Stock Exchange requirements and to improve acceptability as an acquirer of businesses internationally. It also offered Chodiev, Ibragimov and Machkevitch a convenient means of realising the value of their shareholdings, which could now be easily traded in the market should they want to.

The three entrepreneurs were not, however, allowed to sit on the main board of ENRC, because of an ongoing prosecution by the Belgian authorities regarding alleged money-laundering. Nevertheless, the company recruited some highly respected non-executive directors to its board, including Ken Olisa and Sir Richard Sykes. Olisa had had a distinguished career at IBM and Wang Laboratories, before entering investment banking in the City of London. Sykes is a former chairman of pharmaceuticals giant GlaxoSmithKline and former rector (head) of Imperial College, London.

The board chairman was Dr Johannes Sittard, a German executive who had formerly worked for the Mittal international steel group.

Not all went well for the non-executives. After long-standing rumours about disagreements over governance and international strategy, Sir Richard Sykes and Ken Olisa were voted off the board in 2011 by the three founding entrepreneurs and allied shareholders. Ken Olisa wrote to *The Times* newspaper immediately afterwards: 'Although the founding shareholders had signed Representation Agreements committing them to support an independent board, it soon became obvious that the original owners' informal historical links with Directors and senior management meant that their influence would be ever-present . . . The chairman frequently played the part of founders' messenger – not always accurately – rather than as leader of an independent board.' Olisa went on to describe his dismissal as 'more Soviet than City'.

ENRC responded by reviewing its corporate governance. In February 2012, a new chairman was appointed: Mehmet Dalman, formerly with the leading German company Commerzbank. In his first official meeting with investors, Dalman commented on the ENRC board: 'We have continued to review board composition, mindful of the need to progressively refresh the board, with a view to affording it with talented and dedicated directors exhibiting, among other qualifications, domain knowledge, long experience of best-in-class corporate governance practices, as well as corporate finance and strategy.'

Sources: Financial Times, 8 June 2011; 3 February 2012; Daily Telegraph, 21 March 2012.

Questions

1 Ideally, what sort of companies and roles might Dalman's new non-executive directors have worked in previously?

2 Should ENRC's governance not improve, what could (i) independent investors and (ii) the London Stock Exchange do?

(4.4) **STAKEHOLDER EXPECTATIONS**[22]

It should be clear by now that managers' decisions about the purpose and strategy of their organisation are influenced by the expectations of stakeholders. Even in a shareholder model, managers cannot entirely ignore stakeholders such as employees or local communities: whether or not they are represented on the organisational board, their support is important for long-term success. This poses a challenge because there are likely to be many stakeholders, especially for a large organisation (see Figure 4.4), with different, perhaps conflicting, expectations. This means that managers need to take a view on: (i) which stakeholders will have the greatest influence; (ii) which expectations they need to pay most attention to; (iii) the extent to which the expectations of different stakeholders vary.

4.4.1 Stakeholder groups

External stakeholders can be usefully divided into four types in terms of the nature of their relationship with the organisation and how they might affect the success or failure of a strategy:

Figure 4.4 Stakeholders of a large organisation

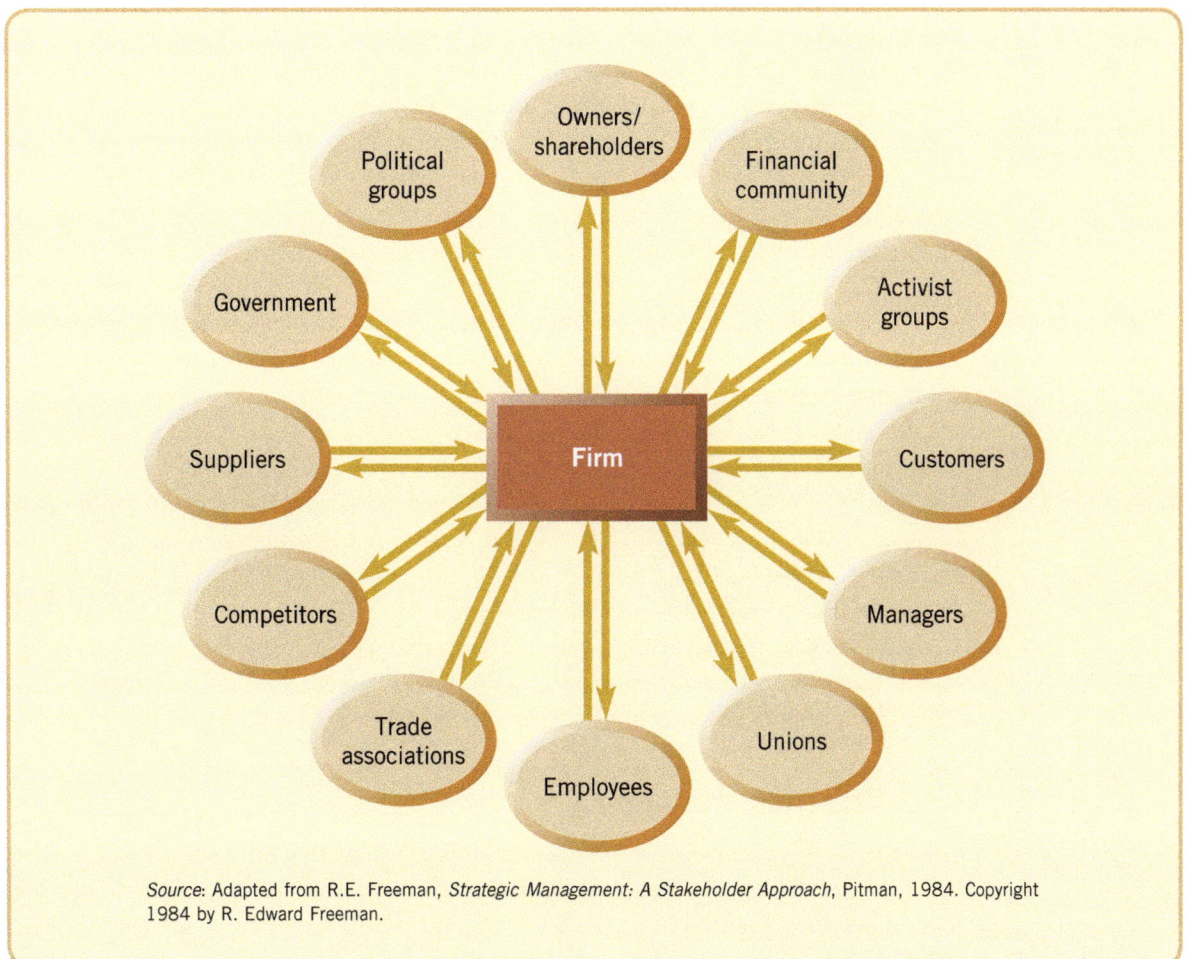

Source: Adapted from R.E. Freeman, *Strategic Management: A Stakeholder Approach*, Pitman, 1984. Copyright 1984 by R. Edward Freeman.

- *Economic stakeholders*, including suppliers, customers, distributors, banks and shareholders.

- *Social/political stakeholders*, such as policy-makers, regulators and government agencies that may influence the strategy directly or via the context in which strategy is developed.

- *Technological stakeholders*, such as key adopters, standards agencies and ecosystem members supplying complementary products or services (e.g. applications for particular mobile phones).

- *Community stakeholders*, who are affected by what an organisation does; for example, those who live close to a factory or, indeed, the wider society. These stakeholders typically have no formal relationship with the organisation but may, of course, take action (e.g. through lobbying or activism) to influence the organisation.

The influence of these different types of stakeholders is likely to vary in different situations. For example, the 'technological group' will be crucial for strategies of new product development, while the 'social/political' group is usually particularly influential in the public-sector context or for companies operating in different countries with different political and legal systems.

There are also stakeholder groups internal to an organisation, which may be departments, geographical locations or different levels in the hierarchy. Individuals may belong to more than one stakeholder group and such groups may 'line up' differently depending on the issue or strategy in hand. Of course, external stakeholders may seek to influence an organisation's strategy through their links with internal stakeholders. For example, customers may exert pressure on sales managers to represent their interests within the company.

Since the expectations of stakeholder groups will differ, it is normal for conflict to exist regarding the importance or desirability of aspects of strategy. In most situations, a compromise will need to be reached. The more companies globalise, the more they add further complications as they operate in multiple arenas. For example, an overseas division is part of the parent company, which will likely have expectations about consistent global behaviour and performance, but is also part of a local community, which may well have different expectations. Table 4.1 shows some typical situations which give rise to conflicting stakeholder expectations. It may, however, also be possible in developing a strategy to look for compatible stakeholder expectations. For example, managers of the English conservation tourist attraction, the Eden Project, looked for 'synergies around purpose' among different stakeholders to obtain support and funding for it. Both the European Union and the local economic development agency were interested in developing the economy of Cornwall, one of the poorest areas in the UK, while the Millennium Commission, a government-sponsored funding body, was interested in developing iconic architecture in the area. The synergies between the three led to the success that the Eden Project has since become.

The stakeholder concept is, then, valuable when trying to understand the political context within which strategy develops. Indeed, taking stakeholder expectations and influence into account is an important aspect of strategic choice, as will be seen in Chapter 11.

4.4.2 Stakeholder mapping[23]

In defining strategic purpose, it is useful to identify and categorise all the various stakeholders. Stakeholder mapping identifies stakeholder interest and power and helps in understanding political priorities. The focus is on the *power* different stakeholders have to influence strategy and the *interest* each stakeholder has in particular issues.

Table 4.1 **Some common conflicts of expectations**

- In order to grow, short-term profitability, cash flow and pay levels may need to be sacrificed.

- 'Short-termism' may suit managerial career aspirations but preclude investment in long-term projects.

- When family businesses grow, the owners may lose control if they need to appoint professional managers.

- New developments may require additional funding through share issue or loans. In either case, financial independence may be sacrificed.

- Public ownership of shares will require more openness and accountability from the management.

- Cost efficiency through capital investment can mean job losses.

- Extending into mass markets may require a reduction in quality standards.

- In public services, a common conflict is between mass provision and specialist services (e.g. preventative dentistry or heart transplants).

- In large multinational organisations, conflict can result because of a division's responsibilities to the company and also to its host country.

These two dimensions form the basis of the power/interest matrix shown as Figure 4.5. The matrix classifies stakeholders in relation to the power they hold and the extent to which they are likely to show interest in supporting or opposing a particular strategy. The matrix allows different stakeholders to be plotted either according to the simple either – or dichotomy of low or high, or more subtly according to their relative positions along the continuous axes from low to high. The positions of different stakeholders on the matrix are likely to vary according to each issue, especially to the amount interest they have. Stakeholder groups are also likely to vary in their power according to the governance structures under which they operate (see section 4.3) and the stance taken on corporate responsibility (section 4.5.1). For example, in some countries unions may be weak but in others they may be represented on supervisory boards; banks may take a 'semi-detached' view of strategy in some countries, but be part of the governance structures in others.

In order to show the way in which the matrix may be used, take the example of a business where managers see themselves as formulating strategy by trying to ensure the compliance of stakeholders with their own assessment of strategic imperatives. In this context the matrix indicates the type of relationship that managers might typically establish with stakeholder groups in the different quadrants. Clearly, the acceptability of strategies to *key players* (segment D) is of major importance. It could be that these are major investors or particular agencies with a lot of power – for example, a major shareholder in a family firm or a government funding agency in a public-sector organisation. Often the most difficult issues relate to stakeholders in segment C. Although these might, in general, be relatively passive, a disastrous situation can arise when their level of interest is underrated and they reposition to segment D and frustrate the adoption

Figure 4.5 Stakeholder mapping: the power/interest matrix

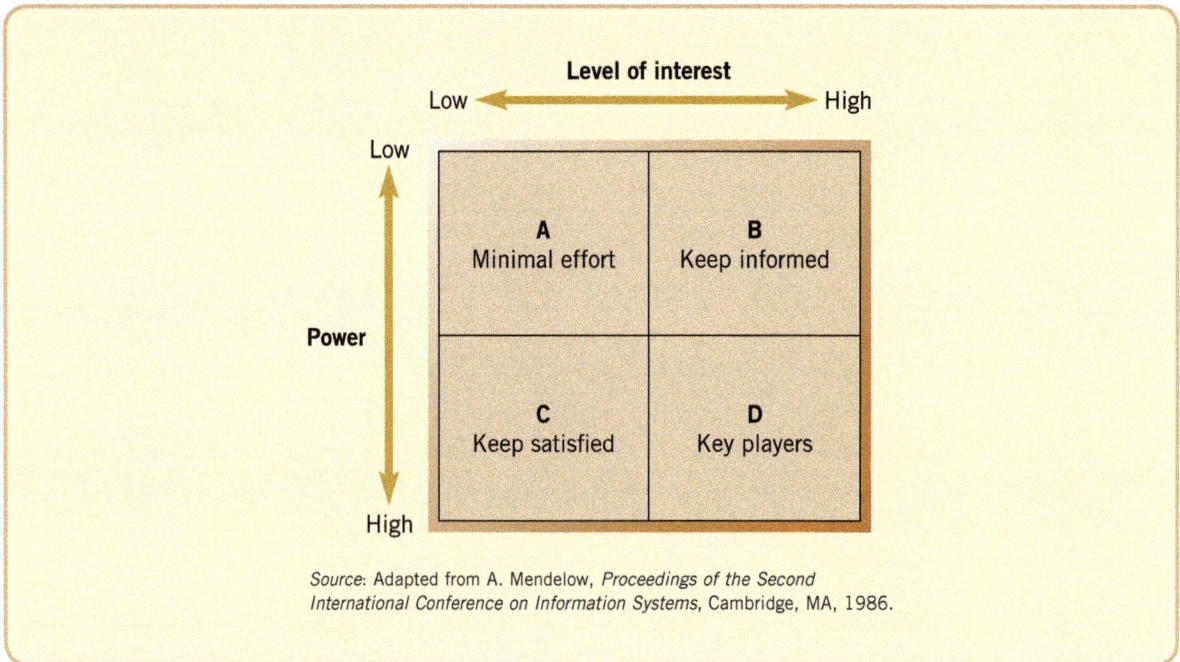

Source: Adapted from A. Mendelow, *Proceedings of the Second International Conference on Information Systems*, Cambridge, MA, 1986.

of a new strategy. Institutional shareholders such as pension funds or insurance firms can fall into this category. They may show little interest unless share prices start to dip, but may then demand to be heard by senior management. Managers might choose to address the expectations of stakeholders in segment B, for example community groups, through information provision. It may be important not to alienate such stakeholders because they can be crucially important 'allies' in influencing the attitudes of more powerful stakeholders: for example, through lobbying.

Stakeholder mapping can also help in understanding the following three issues:

● Who the key *blockers* and *facilitators* of a strategy are likely to be and the appropriate response.

● Whether *repositioning* of certain stakeholders is desirable and/or feasible: for example, to lessen the influence of a key player or, in certain instances, to ensure that there are more key players who will champion the strategy (this is often critical in the public-sector context).

● *Maintaining* the level of interest or power of some key stakeholders: for example, public 'endorsement' by powerful suppliers or customers may be critical to the success of a strategy. It may also be necessary to discourage some stakeholders from repositioning themselves. This is what is meant by *keep satisfied* in relation to stakeholders in segment C, and to a lesser extent *keep informed* for those in segment B.

All this can raise difficult ethical issues for managers in deciding the role they should play in the political activity surrounding stakeholder management: see Illustration 4.4 on EADS for an example of conflict among stakeholders. For example, should managers be simple, honest brokers balancing the conflicting expectations of all stakeholder groups? Or should they be answerable to one stakeholder – such as shareholders – and hence is their role to ensure the

ILLUSTRATION 4.4

Conflict at the European Aeronautic Defence and Space Company

Strains are emerging between stakeholders in this complex consortium, with political repercussions.

The European Aeronautic Defence and Space Company (EADS) was established in 2000 as a means to group some of Europe's most important aeronautics and related activities. In particular, EADS brought together Aérospatiale-Matra of France, DaimlerChrysler Aerospace AG (DASA) of Germany, and Construcciones Aeronáuticas SA (CASA) of Spain. By 2013, EADS included Airbus, the world's leading manufacturer of commercial aircraft; Airbus Military covering tanker, transport and mission aircraft; Eurocopter, the world's largest helicopter supplier; Astrium, the European leader in space programmes such as Ariane and Galileo; and Cassidian, a major provider of defence and security systems for missiles and fighter jets. With revenues of €50 bn (about £40 bn or $65 bn) and 120,000 employees, EADS was one of Europe's largest manufacturers, exporters and investors in R&D, besides spending €31 bn annually with suppliers, mostly in Europe.

The ownership of EADS is complex, with 50.66 per cent owned by a three-way international partnership. The partners are SOGEADE (22.36 per cent), two-thirds owned by the French state and one third owned by the French media company Lagardère; the German car manufacturer Daimler AG (22.36 per cent), representing the German government and some major German banks as well; and SEPI (5.44 per cent), a Spanish state holding company. The remainder of the stock is traded publicly, though the French state owns a further 0.06 per cent this stock. EADS had made substantial losses in 2009, but returned to profitability in the following two years.

During 2011–12, the chief executive, Frenchman Louis Gallois, was promoting a strategy of greater internationalisation. This internationalisation, he argued, required a reduction in French and German state ownership. State ownership restricted EADS's ability to make major acquisitions in the US and emerging markets. Overseas acquisitions could access valuable technologies and manufacturing bases, and help win orders in markets where a local presence was seen as critical. Gallois also believed that the ownership structure gave the 'controlling shareholders a feeling of being trapped and always creating the risk of inequalities between different categories of shareholders'.

Early 2012 saw furious arguments between German and French partners. The immediate cause was the decision to move EADS's overall headquarters from Munich to Toulouse, the location of the subsidiary Airbus headquarters and with more than 16,000 staff already. Although there were only 300 staff involved in the EADS headquarters move, the German deputy economics minister wrote a letter to EADS alleging an 'unacceptable' bias towards French management and production in France. He particularly complained that €500 m aid supplied by the German government for the development of the A350 aircraft had not led to the promised strengthening of Airbus's north German sites in Hamburg (with 13,000 employees) and Bremen (with more than 3,000 employees). He demanded that the company put more Germans in top posts at Airbus or risk losing German development aid and export-credit guarantees. German anxiety was increased by the fact that two thirds of EADS's revenues came from civil Airbus sales, while Germany was home to the Cassidian military division, whose revenues were falling because of government spending cuts. CEO Gallois responded that the German minister's letter was not in 'accordance with the governance of a listed company. We will choose the best industrial set-up in the company's interests – without external interference.'

Main sources: Financial Times, 19 June 2011, 2 March 2012, 8 March 2012.

Questions

1 With reference to the power/interest matrix (Figure 4.5), how would powerful stakeholders' level of interest vary with regard to the location of the EADS headquarters and internationalisation?

2 Given the ownership structure, is CEO Gallois right to assert the primacy of company interests and reject German ministerial 'interference'?

acceptability of their strategies to other stakeholders? Or are they, as many authors suggest, the real power themselves, constructing strategies to suit their own purposes and managing stakeholder expectations to ensure acceptance of these strategies?

4.4.3 Power[24]

In considering stakeholder expectations the previous section highlighted the importance of power and how it is shared unequally between various stakeholders. For the purposes of this discussion, power **is the ability of individuals or groups to persuade, induce or coerce others into following certain courses of action**. As Table 4.2 shows, there are different sources of power. It is not only derived from people's hierarchical position within an organisation or formal corporate governance arrangements. It could be a function of the resources or know-how they control or the networks they have built up, for example.

The relative importance of these sources of power will vary over time. Indeed changes in the business environment can significantly shift the power balance between organisations and their stakeholders. For example, consumers' knowledge of different companies' offerings through internet browsing has increased their power as they compare different offerings and reduce their traditional loyalty to a particular supplier. The distribution of power will also vary in relation to the strategy under consideration. For example, a corporate finance function will

Table 4.2 Sources and indicators of power

Sources of power	
Within organisations	**For external stakeholders**
• Hierarchy (formal power), e.g. autocratic decision making	• Control of strategic resources, e.g. materials, labour, money
• Influence (informal power), e.g. charismatic leadership	• Involvement in strategy implementation, e.g. distribution outlets, agents
• Control of strategic resources, e.g. strategic products	• Possession of knowledge or skills, e.g. subcontractors, partners
• Possession of knowledge and skills, e.g. computer specialists	• Through internal links, e.g. informal influence
• Control of the human environment, e.g. negotiating skills	
• Involvement in strategy implementation, e.g. by exercising discretion	
Indicators of power	
Within organisations	**For external stakeholders**
• Status	• Status
• Claim on resources	• Resource dependence
• Representation	• Negotiating arrangements
• Symbols	• Symbols

be more powerful in relation to developments requiring new capital or revenue commitments than in relation to ones which are largely self-financing or within the financial authority of separate divisions or subsidiaries.

Since there are a variety of different sources of power, it is useful to look for *indicators of power*, the visible signs that stakeholders have been able to exploit sources of power. These include: the *status* of the individual or group (such as job grade or reputation); the *claim on resources* (such as budget size); *representation* in powerful positions; and *symbols* of power (such as office size or use of titles and names). For external stakeholders, a key indicator is the organisation's *resource dependence*, in other words its dependence on particularly large shareholders, lenders, customers or suppliers. One way of assessing resource dependence is to consider the ease with which a supplier, financier or customer could switch or be switched at short notice.

An underlying theme in this chapter has been that strategists have to consider the overall strategic purpose of their organisations. However, a central question that arises is what stakeholder expectations they should respond to in so doing. The Key Debate at the end of this chapter provides three views on this in the context of publicly quoted large commercial organisations.

(4.5) SOCIAL RESPONSIBILITY AND ETHICS[25]

Underlying the discussion of corporate governance is an issue highlighted in the introduction to this chapter. Is the purpose of an organisation and its strategy for the benefit of a primary stakeholder such as the shareholders of a company, or is it there for the benefit of a wider group of stakeholders? In turn this raises the question of societal expectations placed on organisations, how these impact on an organisation's purposes and, in turn, on its strategy. This section considers, first, *corporate social responsibility*: the role businesses and other organisations might take in society. Second, it considers the *ethics* of the behaviour and actions of people in relation to the strategy of their organisations.

4.5.1 Corporate social responsibility

The sheer size and global reach of many companies means that they are bound to have significant influence on society. Further, the widely publicised corporate scandals and failures of the last two decades have fuelled a concern about the role they play. The regulatory environment and the corporate governance arrangements for an organisation determine its minimum obligations towards its stakeholders. However, such legal and regulatory frameworks set minimum obligations and stakeholders typically expect greater responsibility on the part of organisations. Corporate social responsibility (CSR) **is the commitment by organisations to behave ethically and contribute to economic development while improving the quality of life of the workforce and their families as well as the local community and society at large.**[26] CSR is therefore concerned with the ways in which an organisation exceeds its minimum legal obligations.

Different organisations take different stances on CSR. Table 4.3 outlines four basic types to illustrate these differences. They represent a progressively more inclusive 'list' of stakeholder interests and a greater breadth of criteria against which strategies and performance will be judged. The discussion that follows also explains what such stances typically involve

Table 4.3 **Corporate social responsibility stances**

	Laissez-faire	Enlightened self-interest	Forum for stakeholder interaction	Shaper of society
Rationale	Legal compliance: make a profit, pay taxes and provide jobs	Sound business sense	Sustainability or triple bottom line	Social and market change
Leadership	Peripheral	Supportive	Champion	Visionary
Management	Middle-management responsibility	Systems to ensure good practice	Board-level issue; organisation-wide monitoring	Individual responsibility throughout the organisation
Mode	Defensive to outside pressures	Reactive to outside pressures	Proactive	Defining
Stakeholder relationships	Unilateral	Interactive	Partnership	Multi-organisation alliances

in terms of the ways companies act.[27] Illustration 4.5 discusses how leading clothing retailer H&M pursues social responsibility in order to give it a more ethical profile than some of its rivals and pre-empt protests against the clothing industry's traditionally wasteful and exploitative practices.

The *laissez-faire* view (literally 'let do' in French) represents an extreme stance. In this view, organisations should be let alone to get on with things on their own account. Proponents argue that the only responsibility of business is to make a profit and provide for the interests of shareholders.[28] It is for government to protect society through legislation and regulation; organisations need do no more than meet these minimum obligations. Expecting companies to exercise social duties beyond this only confuses decision making and undermines the accountability of managers to their shareholders. In this view, society benefits anyway from the profits: after all, these can either be used for further investment in the business or be paid out to shareholders, who may be pensioners relying on the income or similar. This laissez-faire stance may be taken by executives who are persuaded of it ideologically or by smaller businesses that do not have the resources to do other than minimally comply with regulations.

Enlightened self-interest is guided by recognition of the potential long-term financial benefit to the shareholder of well-managed relationships with other stakeholders. Here the justification for social responsibility is that it makes good business sense. For most organisations a good reputation in the eyes of customers and suppliers is important to long-term financial success. Working constructively with suppliers or local communities can actually increase the 'value' available for all stakeholders to share: for example, helping improve the quality of marginal suppliers in the developing world is likely to create a stronger over all supply chain; supporting education in the local workforce will increase the availability of skilled labour. Indeed, there is mounting evidence that responsible strategies can also reward shareholders.[29] Thus, like any other form of investment or promotion expenditure, corporate philanthropy or welfare provision might be regarded as sensible expenditure.

Managers with this enlightened self-interest stance take the view that organisations have not only *responsibilities to* society, but also *relationships with* other stakeholders. So communication with stakeholder groups is likely to be more interactive than for laissez-faire-type organisations. They may well also set up systems and policies to ensure compliance with best practice (e.g. ISO 14000 certification, the protection of human rights in overseas operations, etc.) and begin to monitor their social responsibility performance. Top management may also play more of a part, at least insofar as they support the firm taking a more proactive social role.

A *forum for stakeholder interaction*[30] explicitly incorporates multiple stakeholder interests and expectations rather than just shareholders as influences on organisational purposes and strategies. Here the argument is that the performance of an organisation should be measured in a more pluralistic way than just through the financial bottom line. Such organisations adopt the principle of *sustainability* in strategy, one that ensures a better quality of life by attending to all three dimensions of environmental protection, social responsibility and economic welfare. Social responsibility here can be measured in terms of *the triple bottom line* – social and environmental benefits as well as profits (see section 11.2.1). Companies in this category might retain uneconomic units to preserve jobs, avoid manufacturing or selling 'anti-social' products and be prepared to bear reductions in profitability for the social good. Sustainability will typically have board-level champions in these kinds of organisations.

Shapers of society regard financial considerations as of secondary importance or a constraint. These are visionary organisations seeking to change society and social norms. Public-sector organisations and charities are typically committed to this kind of stance. There are also *social entrepreneurs* who found new organisations that earn revenues but pursue a specific social purpose (see Chapter 9). For example, Traidcraft UK is a public limited company with a chain of retail shops that fights developing world poverty by promoting 'fair trade'. For shapers of society, the social role is the *raison d'être* of the business, not profits. Financial viability is important only as providing the means for continuing the social mission.

Table 4.4 provides some questions against which an organisation's actions on CSR can be assessed.

4.5.2 The ethics of individuals and managers

Ethical issues have to be faced at the individual as well as corporate level and can pose difficult dilemmas for individuals and managers. For example, what is the responsibility of an individual who believes that the strategy of his or her organisation is unethical (e.g. its trading practices) or is not adequately representing the legitimate interests of one or more stakeholder groups? Should that person leave the company on the grounds of a mismatch of values; or is *whistle-blowing* appropriate, such as divulging information to outside bodies, for example regulatory bodies or the press?

Given that strategy development can be an intensely political process with implications for the personal careers of those concerned, managers can find difficulties establishing and maintaining a position of integrity. There is also potential conflict between what strategies are in managers' own best interests and what strategies are in the longer-term interests of their organisation and the shareholders. Some organisations set down explicit guidelines they expect their employees to follow. Texas Instruments posed these questions:[31]

Is the action legal? . . . If not, stop immediately.

Does it comply with our values? . . . If it does not, stop.

If you do it would you feel bad? . . . Ask your own conscience if you can live with it.

How would this look in the newspaper? . . . Ask if this goes public tomorrow would you do it today?

If you know it's wrong . . . don't do it.

If you are not sure . . . ask; and keep asking until you get an answer.

Table 4.4 Some questions of corporate social responsibility

Should organisations be responsible for . . .

INTERNAL ASPECTS

Exployee welfare
. . . providing medical care, assistance with housing finance, extended sick leave, assistance for dependants, etc.?

Working conditions
. . . job security, enhancing working surroundings, social and sporting clubs, above-minimum safety standards, training and development, etc.?

Job design
. . . designing jobs to the increased satisfaction of workers rather than just for economic efficiency? This would include issues of work/life balance?

Intellectual property
. . . respecting the private knowledge of individuals and not claiming corporate ownership?

EXTERNAL ASPECTS

Environmental issues
. . . reducing pollution to below legal standards if competitors are not doing so?
. . . energy conservation?

Products
. . . dangers arising from the careless use of products by consumers?

Markets and marketing
. . . deciding not to sell in some markets?
. . . advertising standards?

Suppliers
. . . 'fair' terms of trade?
. . . blacklisting suppliers?

Employment
. . . positive discrimination in favour of minorities?
. . . maintaining jobs?

Community activity
. . . sponsoring local events and supporting local good works?

Human rights
. . . respecting human rights in relation to: child labour, workers' and union rights, oppressive political regimes? Both directly and in the choice of markets, suppliers and partners?

ILLUSTRATION

ILLUSTRATION 4.5

H&M's sustainability strategy

Swedish clothing retailer H&M claims to be pursuing a strategy that delivers profits, environmental gains and worker benefits.

H&M is the world's second-largest clothing retailer, just behind Inditex, owner of Zara. It has 2,500 stores worldwide, operating in 44 countries. It sells about 550 million items of clothing per year. As such, it has traditionally been a leader in so-called 'fast-fashion', the retailing of cheap fashion items which are designed to be worn only a few times before disposal.

Fast-fashion is a voracious industry. There are now 30–50 trend-driven fashion seasons a year. Eighty billion garments are made annually worldwide, from virgin resources. There are 40 million garment workers in the world, predominantly making fast-fashion. A garment worker in Bangladesh, a major supplier, earns an average monthly wage of $40. A pair of underpants costs about one pence (or roughly a Euro cent) to make in a Third World sweat shop. Fast-fashion is a target of international campaign groups such as the 'Clean Clothes Campaign'.

During 2012, the Clean Clothes Campaign organised mass 'faint-ins' in prominent stores such as Gap, Zara and H&M across Europe, drawing attention to how under-nourished women workers frequently faint at work in Third World garment factories. A Clean Clothes spokesperson says: 'The human cost of brands like H&M or Zara paying poverty wages is seen when hundreds of workers pass out due to exhaustion and malnutrition . . . For decades, global fashion brands have made excuses about why they shouldn't pay a living wage. It's not a choice, it's a pressing necessity. Hiding behind . . . company codes of conduct is no longer acceptable.'

In 2012, H&M launched its new 'Conscious' range of clothing, making use of a large proportion of recycled materials and more environmentally-friendly virgin materials such as hemp. The company's website explained the motivation: 'Our vision is that all business operations shall be run in a way that is economically, socially and environmentally sustainable.' This was accompanied by a Sustainability Report with some impressive statistics: for example, 2.5 million shoes were made during 2011 using lower-impact water-based solvents and H&M was the biggest user of organic cotton in the world.

Guardian journalist Lucy Singh asked H&M's Head of Sustainability, Helena Helmersson, whether she could offer guarantees for the sustainability of the company's products across its ranges. Helmersson responded:

'I don't think guarantee is the right word. A lot of people ask for guarantees: "Can you guarantee labour conditions? Can you guarantee zero chemicals?" Of course we cannot when we're such a huge company operating in very challenging conditions. What I can say is that we do the very best we can with a lot of resources and a clear direction of what we're supposed to do. We're working really hard . . . Remember that H&M does not own any factories itself. We are to some extent dependent on the suppliers – it is impossible to be in full control.'

Between 2006 and 2012, H&M's share price has increased by more than a third, well ahead of the local Stockholm market index. Sales too have increased by a third and total operating profit after tax in this period has been nearly SEK98 billion (€11 billion). H&M's return on capital employed for year-end 2011 is 47.1 per cent.

Main sources: *Guardian*, 7 April 2012; *Ecouterre*, 21 September 2012; www.hm.com; H&M Concsious Actions and Sustainability Report, 2011.

Questions

1 Where would you place H&M in terms of the four stances on social responsibility in Table 4.2?

2 What are the kinds of triple-bottom-line measures that would be appropriate for a sustainable strategy in clothing retail (see also section 11.2.1)?

KEY DEBATE

Three views on the purpose of a business

Since there is no one categoric view of the overarching purpose of a business, stakeholders, including managers, have to decide.

Milton Friedman and profit maximisation

Milton Friedman, the renowned economist, wrote:

'In a free enterprise, private property system, a corporate executive is an employee of the owners of the business. He has direct responsibility to his employers. That responsibility is to conduct the business in accordance with their desires, which generally will be to make as much money as possible while conforming to the basic rules of society . . . What does it mean to say that the corporate executive has a "social responsibility"? . . . If the statement is not pure rhetoric, it must mean that he is to act in some way that is not in the interests of his employers . . . Insofar as his actions in accord with his "social responsibility" reduce returns to stockholders, he is spending their money. Insofar as his actions raise the price to customers, he is spending the customers' money. Insofar as his actions lower the wages of some employees he is spending their money.'

Charles Handy's stakeholder view

Charles Handy has a less respectful view of owners:

'There is, first, a clear and important need to meet the expectations of a company's theoretical owners: the shareholders. It would, however, be more accurate to call them investors, perhaps even gamblers. They have none of the pride or responsibility of ownership and are . . . only there for the money . . . But to turn shareholders' needs into a purpose is to be guilty of a logical confusion. To mistake a necessary condition for a sufficient one. We need to eat to live; food is a necessary condition of life. But if we lived mainly to eat, making food a sufficient or sole purpose of life, we would become gross. The purpose of a business, in other words, is not to make a profit. It is to make a profit so that the business can do something more or better. That "something" becomes the real justification for the business.'

The 'new capitalists' argument

In their book *The New Capitalists*, Davis, Lukommik and Pitt-Watson point out that major corporations are often owned by millions of savers – the 'new capitalists' – through pension and other investment funds. Each of these funds holds shares in many companies. Davis and colleagues then argue:

'Imagine that all your savings were invested in one company. The success of that company alone would be your only interest. You would want it to survive, prosper and grow, even if that did damage to the economic system as a whole. But your perspective would change if you had investments in lots of companies. [Then] it is to your disadvantage that any business should seek to behave socially irresponsibly towards other businesses, the customers, employees or society generally. By so doing they will damage the interests of other firms in which you have an interest. The new capitalist has an interest in all the firms in which he or she is investing behaving responsibly.'

Sources: M. Friedman, 'The social responsibility of business is to increase its profits', *New York Times Magazine*, 13 September 1970; C. Handy, 'What's a business for?', *Harvard Business Review*, vol. 80, no. 12 (2002), pp. 49–55; S. Davis, J. Lukommik and D. Pitt-Watson, *The New Capitalists*, Harvard Business School Press, 2006.

Questions

1 Which view would you be more likely to hold:
   a as a manager?
   b as a shareholder?
   c as a pensioner?
2 What are the implications of the different views for how managers go about developing organisational strategy?

Perhaps the biggest challenge for managers is to develop a high level of self-awareness of their own behaviour in relation to the issues raised above.[32] This can be difficult because it requires them to stand apart from often deep-rooted and taken-for-granted assumptions that are part of the culture of their organisation – a key theme of the next chapter.

SUMMARY

- An important managerial task is to decide how the organisation should express its strategic purpose through statements of *mission*, *vision*, *values* and *objectives*.

- The purpose of an organisation will be influenced by the expectations of its *stakeholders*.

- The influence of some key stakeholders will be represented formally within the *governance structure* of an organisation. This can be represented in terms of a *governance chain*, showing the links between ultimate beneficiaries and the managers of an organisation.

- There are two generic governance structure systems: the *shareholder model* and the *stakeholder model*, though there are variations of these internationally.

- Different stakeholders exercise different influence on organisational purpose and strategy, dependent on the extent of their power and interest. Managers can assess the influence of different stakeholder groups through *stakeholder analysis*.

- Organisations adopt different stances on *corporate social responsibility* depending on how they perceive their role in society. Individual managers may also be faced with ethical dilemmas relating to the purpose of their organisation or the actions it takes.

VIDEO ASSIGNMENTS

Visit **MyStrategyLab** and watch the case study for Chapter 4 (which features various companies).

1 Using the video interviews and section 4.5 of the text, discuss the importance of corporate social responsibility to the companies featured in the video.

2 How does corporate social responsibility relate to stakeholder expectations and governance in determining the purpose of an organisation? Use the companies featured in the video as examples.

WORK ASSIGNMENTS

✱ *Denotes more advanced work assignments.*

* *Refers to a case study in the Text and Cases edition.*

4.1 Write mission and vision statements for any of Manchester United FC*, Sustainability*, HomeCo* or an organisation of your choice and suggest what strategic objectives managers might set. Explain why you think these are appropriate.

4.2 For Drinking Partners (end chapter case) or Adnams* or an organisation of your choice, map out a governance chain that identifies the key players through to the beneficiaries of the organisation's good (or poor) performance. To what extent do you think managers are:

    a knowledgeable about the expectations of beneficiaries;

    b actively pursuing their interests;

    c keeping them informed?

4.3 What are your own views of the strengths and weaknesses of the stakeholder and shareholder models of governance?

4.4✱ Identify organisations that correspond to the overall stances on corporate social responsibility described in Table 4.3.

4.5 Identify the key corporate social responsibility issues which are of major concern in the Brewing* or Advertising (Chapter 2 end case) industries or an industry or public service of your choice (refer to Table 4.4). Compare the approach of two or more organisations in that industry, and explain how this relates to their competitive standing.

4.6✱ Using the stakeholder mapping power/interests matrix, identify and map out the stakeholders for International AIDS Alliance*, Manchester United*, QR National (Anrizon)* or an organisation of your choice in relation to:

    a current strategies;

    b different future strategies of your choice.

What are the implications of your analysis for the strategy of the organisation?

Integrative assignment

4.7 Using specific examples suggest how changes in corporate governance and in expectations about corporate social responsibility may require organisations to deal differently with environmental opportunities and threats (Chapter 2) or develop new capabilities (Chapter 3).

RECOMMENDED KEY READINGS

- The case for the importance of clarity of strategic values and vision is especially strongly made by J. Collins and J. Porras, *Built to Last: Successful Habits of Visionary Companies*, Harper Business, 2002 (in particular see Chapter 11).

- A good review of important ideas in both corporate governance and corporate social responsibility is S. Benn and D. Bolton, *Key Concepts in Corporate Responsibility*, Sage, 2011. Specifically on corporate governance, a leading guide is B. Tricker, *Corporate Governance: Principles, Policies and Practices*, 2nd edn, Oxford University Press, 2012. For a comprehensive review of corporate social responsibility, see A. Crane, A. McWilliams, D. Matten and D. Siegel, *The Oxford Handbook of Corporate Social Responsibility*, Oxford University Press, 2009.

REFERENCES

1. Cynthia A. Montgomery, 'Putting leadership back into strategy', *Harvard Business Review* (January 2008), pp. 54–60.
2. See J. Collins and J. Porras, *Built to Last: Successful Habits of Visionary Companies*, Harper Business, 2002.
3. J. Collins and J. Porras, 'Building your company's vision', *Harvard Business Review* (September–October 1996), pp. 65–77.
4. See Sayan Chatterjee, 'Core objectives: clarity in designing strategy', *California Management Review*, vol. 47, no. 2 (2005), pp. 33–49. For some advantages of ambiguity, see J. Sillince, P. Jarzabkowski and D. Shaw, 'Shaping strategic action through the rhetorical construction and exploitation of ambiguity', *Organization Science*, vol. 22, no. 2 (2011), pp. 1–21.
5. For example, see B. Bartkus, M. Glassman and B. McAfee, 'Mission statements: are they smoke and mirrors?', *Business Horizons*, vol. 43, no. 6 (2000), pp. 23–8.
6. See P. Lencioni, 'Make your values mean something', *Harvard Business Review*, vol. 80, no. 7 (2002), pp. 113–17; and S. Kantabutra and G. Avery, 'The power of vision: statements that resonate', *Journal of Business Strategy*, vol. 31, no. 1 (2009), pp. 37–45.
7. See for instance M. Nordqvist and L. Melin, 'Entrepreneurial families and family firms', *Entrepreneurship and Regional Development*, vol. 22, no. 3–4 (2010), pp. 211–39.
8. In the United Kingdom and associated countries, this kind of corporation is called a public limited company (plc); in Francophone countries, it is the Société Anonyme (SA); in Germany, it is the Aktiengesellschaft (AG).
9. *The Economist*, 'The rise of state capitalism' (21 January 2012).
10. For a discussion, see R. Rumelt (2005), 'Theory, strategy and entrepreneurship', *Handbook of Entrepreneurship Research*, vol. 2 (2005), pp. 11–32.
11. Credit Suisse, *Asian Family Businesses Report 2011: Key Trends, Economic Contribution and Performance*, Singapore, 2011.
12. I. Le Bretton-Miller, D. Miller and R.H. Lester, 'Stewardship or agency? A social embeddedness reconciliation of conduct and performance in public family businesses', *Organization Science*, vol. 22, no. 3 (2011), pp. 704–21.
13. The Ownership Commission, *Plurality, stewardship and engagement*, London, 2012.
14. Useful general references on corporate governance are: R. Monks and N. Minow (eds), *Corporate Governance*, 4th edn, Blackwell, 2008. Also see Ruth Aguilera and Gregory Jackson, 'The cross-national diversity of corporate governance: dimensions and determinants', *Academy of Management Review*, vol. 28, no. 3 (2003), pp. 447–65.
15. This definition is adapted from S. Jacoby, 'Corporate governance and society', *Challenge*, vol. 48, no. 4 (2005), pp. 69–87.
16. A recent debate on principal–agent theory is: D. Miller and C. Sardais, 'Angel agents: agency theory reconsidered', *Academy of Management Perspectives*, vol. 25, no. 2 (2011), pp. 6–13; and V. Mehrotra, 'Angel agents: what we can (and cannot) learn from Pierre Lefaucheux's stewardship of Régie Renault', *Academy of Management Perspectives*, vol. 25, no. 2 (2011), pp. 14–20.
17. S. Letza, X. Sun and J. Kirkbride, 'Shareholding versus stakeholding: a critical review of corporate governance', *Corporate Governance*, vol. 12 no. 3 (2005), pp. 242–62. Within this broad classification, there are other models: see, for example, A. Murphy and K. Topyan, 'Corporate governance: a critical survey of key concepts, issues, and recent reforms in the US', *Employee Responsibility and Rights Journal*, vol. 17, no. 2 (2005), pp. 75–89.
18. M.N. Young, M.W. Peng, D. Ahlstrom, G.D. Bruton and Y. Jiang, 'Corporate governance in emerging economies: a review of the principal–principal perspective', *Journal of Management Studies*, vol. 45, no. 1 (2008), pp. 1467–86.
19. R. Greenwood, M. Raynard, F. Kodeih, E. Micelotta and M. Lounsbury, 'Institutional complexity and organisational responses', *Academy of Management Annals*, vol. 5, no. 1 (2011), pp. 317–71.
20. In the USA: the Sarbanes–Oxley Act (2002). In the UK: D. Higgs, 'Review of the role and effectiveness of non-executive directors', UK Department of Trade and Industry, 2003.
21. J. Sonnenfeld, 'What makes great boards great', *Harvard Business Review*, vol. 80, no. 9 (2002), pp. 106–13.

22. R.E. Freeman, *Strategic Management: A Stakeholder Approach*, Pitman, 1984. Also see L. Bidhan, A. Parmar and R.E. Freeman, 'Stakeholder theory: the state of the art', *Academy of Management Annals*, vol. 4, no. 1 (2010), pp. 403–45. Our approach to stakeholder mapping has been adapted from A. Mendelow, *Proceedings of the 2nd International Conference on Information Systems*, Cambridge, MA, 1991. See also Graham Kenny, 'From the stakeholder viewpoint: designing measurable objectives', *Journal of Business Strategy*, vol. 33, no. 6 (2012), pp. 40–6.

23. D. Walker, L. Bourne and A. Shelley, 'Influence, stakeholder mapping and visualization', *Construction Management and Economics* [serial online], vol. 26, no. 6 (2008), pp. 645–58.

24. D. Buchanan and R. Badham, *Power, Politics and Organisational Change: Winning the Turf Game*, Sage, 1999, provide a useful analysis of the relationship between power and strategy.

25. B. Kelley, *Ethics at Work*, Gower, 1999, covers many of the issues in this section and includes the Institute of Management guidelines on ethical management. Also see M.T. Brown, *Corporate Integrity: Rethinking Organisational Ethics and Leadership*, Cambridge University Press, 2005.

26. This definition is based on that by the World Business Council for Sustainable Development.

27. P. Mirvis and B. Googins, 'Stages of corporate citizenship', *California Management Review*, vol. 48, no. 2 (2006), pp. 104–26.

28. Often quoted as a summary of Milton Friedman's argument is M. Friedman: 'The social responsibility of business is to increase its profits', *New York Times Magazine* (13 September 1970). See also A. McWilliams and D. Seigel, 'Corporate social responsibility: a theory of the firm perspective', *Academy of Management Review*, vol. 26 (2001), pp. 117–27.

29. See M. Porter and M. Kramer, 'Creating shared value', *Harvard Business Review*, vol. 89, no. 1/2 (2011), pp. 62–77; and D. Vogel, 'Is there a market for virtue? The business case for corporate social responsibility', *California Management Review*, vol. 47, no. 4 (2005), pp. 19–45. For a sceptical view: A. Karnani, 'Doing well by doing good: the grand illusion', *California Management Review*, vol. 53, no. 2 (2011), pp. 69–86. For some evidence, see C. E. Hull and S. Rothenberg, 'Firm performance: the interactions of corporate social performance with innovation and industry differentiation', *Strategic Management Journal*, vol. 29 (2008), pp. 781–9.

30. H. Hummels, 'Organizing ethics: a stakeholder debate', *Journal of Business Ethics*, vol. 17, no. 13 (1998), pp. 1403–19.

31. We are grateful to Angela Sutherland of Glasgow Caledonian University for this example.

32. M.R. Banaji, M.H. Bazerman and D. Chugh, 'How (UN) ethical are you?', *Harvard Business Review*, vol. 81, no. 12 (2003), pp. 56–64.

Drinking partners: India's United Breweries Holdings Ltd

In 2012, United Breweries Holdings Ltd (UBHL) was one of India's most powerful and dynamic conglomerates. Under the leadership of its colourful chairman Vijay Mallya, it controlled India's largest brewery, India's largest spirits company, a leading domestic and international airline, a Formula One racing team, and substantial chemicals and fertiliser interests. But the UBHL empire was tottering under heavy debts and Vijay Mallya himself faced an arrest warrant for bouncing cheques. Partnership with the London-based Diageo drinks business offered one route to survival. But how far could anyone rely on a partner with Mallya's record?

King of the Good Times

Vijay Mallya had inherited control of UBHL at the age of 28, upon the death of his father in 1983. His father had himself taken over the original core business of United Breweries from its British management in the period around Indian Independence in 1947, and built from this a diverse and complex conglomerate of subsidiary companies. Vijay Mallya spent the early years of his leadership of UBHL by divesting non-core businesses and reorganising the tangle of subsidiaries into a clearer divisional structure based on coherent business areas. UBHL grew rapidly and by 2007 Vijay Mallya ranked 664 on the *Forbes* global list of billionaires, with an estimated fortune of $1.5 bn (about £950 m or €1.2 bn).

As it entered the second decade of the century, UBHL was selling about 60 per cent of India's spirits and 50 per cent of its beer. The group was organised into four main businesses, each with substantial external shareholders: for example, the Dutch brewer Heineken was a substantial minority shareholder in the brewing business. However, Mallya's effective control of each business was guaranteed by UBHL's position as the largest shareholder, if not the majority owner (see Figure 1). These arrangements maximised control while reducing capital obligations. Mallya's overall control of the parent UBHL was assured by dominance of the voting A class shares, while Indian and foreign institutional shareholders held the overwhelming majority of non-voting B class shares.

Though clearly a shrewd businessman, Mallya has his extravagant side. Playing on the name of his most prominent beer brand, Kingfisher, he often describes himself as 'King of the Good Times'. He likes to surround himself with beautiful models and actresses, and the annual Kingfisher Calendar is famed in India for its photographs of scantily-clad women. He owns several expensive yachts and a fleet of luxury vintage cars. In 2008, Mallya and a business partner bought a Formula One racing team, renamed Force India. A similar patriotic theme underpinned his acquisition of the sword of the great Indian leader, Tipu Sultan, captured by the British in the eighteenth century, and his generous assistance

Figure 1 United Breweries Holdings Ltd, principal businesses, 2011

As of 2011, Vijay Mallya and associates controlled 51.5 per cent of UBHL. Shares in each of the principal businesses controlled directly by UBHL or by Mallya and associates are indicated in brackets

with the repatriation of some of the few surviving arte-facts owned by Mahatma Gandhi, India's campaigner for Independence. Mallya's personal popularity was reflected in his election to the Upper House of India's federal parliament.

But it was Mallya's extravagance in the business realm that was pushing UBHL to the brink in 2012.

Internationalisation and diversification

The first of two fatally extravagant moves was Mallya's diversification into airlines. To celebrate his son's 18th birthday, Mallya launched Kingfisher Airlines in 2005, with 50.2 per cent of the ownership in his hands. It might have been a good opportunity: the Indian air market was growing and deregulated. Mallya gave the new airline a glitzy launch. Promoting its superior food and pretty female staff, Mallya declared that the Kingfisher Airline would have neither business class nor economy class, but its own 'K class' – a rather pricey compromise. In 2008, Kingfisher paid over the odds to buy India's pioneering low-cost carrier, Deccan Airlines. The merged airline boasted 100-plus aircraft, 300 daily flights, over 7,000 employees and a domestic market share of about 30 per cent. With Deccan's track-record, Kingfisher was able to launch international services as well, with an order for the new Airbus A380 superjumbo jet. Mallya, sporting long hair and a beard, did not dis-courage comparisons with another flamboyant airline boss, Sir Richard Branson of Virgin.

Unfortunately, domestic deregulation also brought a surfeit of competition to the Indian airline market. At the same time, fuel prices were rising and crowded airports were demanding higher landing fees. By 2011, all but one Indian airline was making losses. Kingfisher had never made a profit in its entire existence. By 2012, Kingfisher had been forced to ground all but 15 of its aircraft, airports and fuel suppliers had not been paid, and most of its employees, including pilots, had received no salary for seven months. Kingfisher's total debts and losses stood at about $4.5 bn. Although Kingfisher had by now been transferred formally outside the group and UBHL had been forced to dilute its ownership to about 30 per cent, the holding company still guaranteed $2.2 bn of the airline's debt. Canadian research firm Veritas warned that Kingfisher would drag down UBHL. The holding company was 'staring into a black hole. We believe that the ill-conceived foray into the airline business has already cost UBHL shareholders dearly, and that their ownership of India's premier liquor and

beer assets has been sacrificed at the altar of egoistic ambitions.'

The second extravagant move was into international markets, with the 2007 acquisition of the leading Scottish whisky company Whyte & Mackay. UBHL's United Spirits business needed access to genuine Scotch whisky brands as its increasingly sophisticated Indian customers sought higher-quality spirits than those tradi-tionally made in India. Rivals such as Diageo, with about one third of the world's whisky market and owner of the world's leading Johnnie Walker brand, were suspected of deliberately squeezing their supplies to United Spirits in order to build their own position in India. Acquisition of Whyte & Mackay gave United Spirits control over more than 140 venerable whisky brands, all genuine Scotch. United Spirits became the third-largest spirits producer in the world, behind Diageo and Pernod Ricard.

But Mallya had paid more for Whyte & Mackay than he could really afford: the United Spirits business was left with debts of $1.1 bn. In 2009, Whyte & Mackay was forced to cut about 15 per cent of its jobs. That year, UBHL entered talks with Diageo about selling a stake in the United Spirits business in order to secure a cash injection. The talks failed amid concerns about price, managerial control and a possible intervention by competition authorities. With the holding company stock price crashing to about 10 per cent of its former high (Figure 2), UBHL staggered on until the crisis of 2012.

Foreign rescue?

The year 2012 had not started well for UBHL. As well as continuing losses in Kingfisher, both United Spirits and United Breweries saw net profits fall by more than 80 per cent in the first three months. Mallya desperately needed partners in order to keep UBHL afloat. Diageo, the world's largest spirits producer, was again a prime candidate.

Price had been an issue in the 2009 discussions with Diageo, but Mallya was in a much weaker negotiating position now. There remained monopoly concerns, given the combined power of Diageo and UBHL in the whisky market, but these could probably be satisfied by some selective divestments. Moreover, Diageo was still inter-ested, as rival Pernod Ricard was now making rapid progress in India, one of the largest spirits markets in the world. UBHL was not discouraging rumours that there were possibly three other candidates for a United Spirits stake. For Diageo, though, the deal-breaker could be managerial control.

Figure 2 UBHL stock price performance, 2007–12 (rupees)

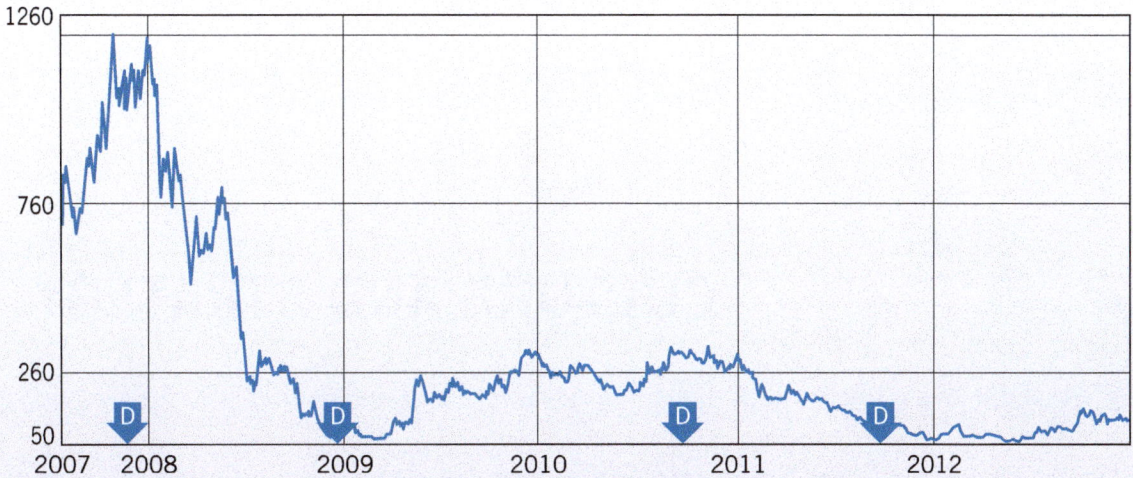

Source: www.moneycontrol.com, 28 December 2012 ('D' refers to dividend payments).

Diageo's chief worry as a large multinational was its exposure to the somewhat idiosyncratic Vijay Mallya. In 2011, Diageo itself had been fined $15 m by the American Securities and Exchange Commission for bribing government officials in India, Thailand and South Korea. The company had given a pledge to 'cease and desist' from such corrupt practices, and risked much larger penalties for any repeat offences. Even as a minority partner, Diageo would be liable for any corruption at United Spirits. However, Mallya was set upon maintaining control. He told the Indian *Business Standard* newspaper: 'One must also understand that running an alcohol beverages business in India across 28 cities is not an easy task for a relatively new player (like Diageo). They will require me to run their business effectively and control of the business is one aspect of that.'

In November 2012, Diageo and UBHL reached a deal. The terms were complex. Diageo would buy 19.3 per cent of United Spirits' existing shares from Mallya's personal and related holdings, while United Spirits would issue new equity, amounting to 10 per cent of the expanded capital base, to Diageo. Together, these steps would give Diageo an initial 27 per cent of the voting shares in United Spirits. Diageo would also launch an open offer to external shareholders in United Spirits, in order to take its total holding up to 53.4 per cent. The deal would cost Diageo up to $1.9 bn. The price valued United Spirits at 20 times annual earnings (before interest, tax, depreciation and amortisation), about a third more than usual for acquisitions in the international drinks business.

Mallya described the deal as a 'win–win'. Diageo would be able to use United Spirits' unparalleled Indian distribution channels for its high-profile brands, and UBHL would be able to ease its various debts. Mallya himself would be left in control of 13.5 per cent of United Spirits' expanded equity and was allowed to continue his position as United Spirits chairman. Mallya insisted to the media: 'I have not sold the family silver, or family jewels; I have only embellished them . . . If you have the impression that I have passed on control, and moved out, that is not the correct impression.'

Principal sources: The Times, 26 September 2012; *Business Standard*, 27 September 2012; *India Business Journal*, 6 November 2012; *Financial Times*, 9 November 2012; *Times of India*, 11 November 2012.

Questions

1 Consider the governance chain leading from the various shareholders of UBHL to the managers in the main businesses, with particular reference to United Spirits. Why might there be breakdowns in accountability and control in this chain?

2 Group the various key stakeholders discussed in this case (economic, social/political, community and technological). What risks do key stakeholder groups face (including Diageo)?

5

CULTURE AND STRATEGY

Learning outcomes

After reading this chapter you should be able to:

● Analyse how *history* influences the strategic position of an organisation.

● Analyse the influence of an *organisation's culture* on its strategy using the *cultural web*.

● Recognise the importance of strategists questioning the *taken-for-granted aspects of a culture*.

● Identify organisations which may be experiencing the symptoms of *strategic drift*.

Key terms

cultural web p. 155

legitimacy p. 150

organisational culture p. 147

organisational field p. 150

paradigm p. 153

path dependency p. 143

recipe p. 150

strategic drift p. 162

MyStrategyLab

MyStrategyLab is designed to help you make the most of your studies. Visit **www.pearsoned.co.uk/mystrategylab** to discover a wide range of resources, including:

• A personalised **Study plan** that will help you understand core concepts

• **Audio and video clips** that put the spotlight on strategy in the real world

• **Online glossaries and flashcards** that provide helpful reminders when you're looking for some quick revision.

(5.1) **INTRODUCTION**

Chapters 2, 3 and 4 have considered the important influences of the environment, organisational capabilities and stakeholder expectations on the development of strategy. Vital as these are to understand, there is a danger that managers fail to take into account other significant issues. Many organisations have long histories. The large Japanese Mitsui Group was founded in the seventeenth century; Daimler was founded in the nineteenth century; managers in the UK retailer Sainsbury's still refer to the founding principles of the Sainsbury family in the nineteenth century. All these and many public-sector organisations – government departments, the police, universities, for example – are strongly influenced by their historical legacies that have become embedded in their cultures. The cultural heritage of an organisation may work to its advantage because it cannot be readily replicated by its competitors. Culture may, however, also be problematic since it can be a significant barrier to change. Either way, if an organisation's strategy is to be understood, so must the history and culture that influenced it. This is the focus of this chapter.

After summarising this chapter (see Figure 5.1), the next section, 5.2, examines the influence of the history of an organisation on its current and future strategy and goes on to consider how that history can be analysed. Section 5.3 then explains what is meant by culture and how cultural influences at the regional, national, institutional and organisational levels influence current and future strategy. It then suggests how a culture can be analysed and its influence on strategy understood. The chapter concludes in section 5.4 by explaining the phenomenon of *strategic drift* that highlights the importance of history and culture in relation to strategy development and identifies important challenges managers face in managing that development.

Figure 5.1 The influence of history and culture

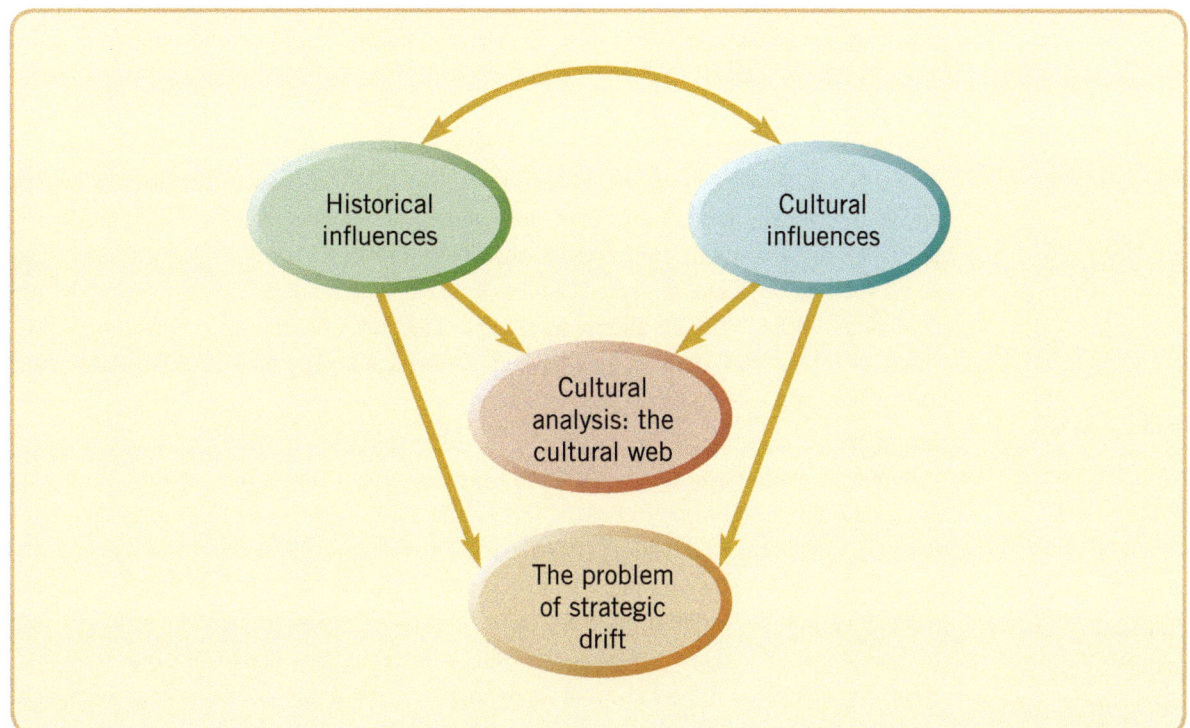

The theme of this chapter is, then, that an understanding of the history and culture of an organisation is important because they can be a major influence on its strategy. It should, however, be borne in mind that historical and cultural perspectives can also help an understanding of both the opportunities and constraints that organisations face. The business environment (Chapter 2) cannot be understood without considering how it has developed over time. The capabilities of an organisation (Chapter 3), especially those that provide organisations with competitive advantage, may have built up over time in ways unique to that organisation. In so doing such capabilities may become part of the culture of an organisation – the taken-for-granted way of doing things – and therefore difficult for other organisations to copy. However, they may also be difficult to change. The power and influence of different stakeholders (Chapter 4) are also likely to have historical origins. An understanding of an organisation's history and culture also informs the evaluation of the feasibility of a strategy (Chapter 11), helps explain how strategies develop (Chapter 12) and informs the challenges of strategic change (Chapter 14).

(5.2) WHY IS HISTORY IMPORTANT?

Taking history's influence on strategy development seriously can have at least four benefits:[1]

- *History and managers' experience.* Managers' own experience is an important influence on strategy development (see the discussion on the 'experience lens' in the Commentary at the end of this part of the book). Managers may have spent many years in an organisation or in an industry such that the experience on which they base their decisions may be heavily influenced by the past. It is helpful if managers can 'stand apart' from that history so as to understand the influence it has on them, the extent to which it constrains them and the opportunities it may offer them.

- *Learning from the past.* Understanding the current strategic position of an organisation in terms of the past can provide useful lessons. For example, have there been historical trends or cycles that may repeat themselves as is the case in the construction and paper industries? How have competitors responded to strategic moves in the past? A historical perspective may also help managers see what gave rise to events that were seen as surprises in the past and learn from how their organisation dealt with them. They might also ask 'what if' questions. Asking what might have happened had there been other influences in the environment, different responses to strategic moves from competitors or different leadership within their organisation all make the present more evidently a product of circumstances. The current strategic position may then be seen as less fixed and possibilities for change in the future more possible.

- *Innovation based on historic capabilities.* In the BMW museum in Munich there is a quote: 'Anyone who wants to design for the future has to leaf through the past.'[2] While the museum is about the history of BMW, it is also about how the lessons of the past can give rise to new ideas and innovation. Indeed the Innovation and Technology Division of BMW is sited next to the museum and the archives of BMW. Innovation may build on historic capabilities in at least two ways. First, as technologies change, firms with experience and skills built over time that are most appropriate to those changes tend to innovate more than those that do not.[3] Or it could be that there are new combinations of knowledge as capabilities built up in adjacent technologies are adapted in innovative ways to new technological opportunities. For example, successful firms that created the TV industry were previously radio manufacturers. They exhibited greater innovation as the industry developed than the non-radio producers by building on their historic capabilities in assembling small components and in mass distribution.[4] If managers seek to build future strategy on historic capabilities they do, however, need to ask if changes in markets, technologies and other aspects of the environment discussed in Chapter 2 are potentially consistent with those capabilities. They need to develop a sensitivity, not only to the historic capabilities that matter but also to the relationship of these to an evolving environment.

- *History as legitimisation*. History can be used as a resource to legitimise strategies or strategic change. For example, in the Swedish bank Handelsbanken, there were frequent stories about the successful turnaround strategy of a highly respected managing director, Jan Wallender, appointed in 1970 following a crisis in the bank.[5] Such stories served to emphasise the continuity of current strategy and structure with the success of that era. Past successes effecting strategic change in innovation or product development may also be used as evidence of the organisational potential in managing change and innovation or to encourage commitment to future changes. Managers may also deliberately draw on the past to legitimise the strategy of an organisation in its market, as has been the case with businesses as varied as bankers Rothschilds, US whisky distillers Jack Daniels, jeans manufacturer Levis Strauss and, of course, many eminent universities.

5.2.1 Path dependency

A useful way of thinking of the role and influence of history is through the concept of **path dependency where early events and decisions establish 'policy paths' that have lasting effects on subsequent events and decisions**.[6] This suggests that organisational decisions may be historically conditioned.

Examples often relate to technology. There are many instances where the technology we employ is better explained by path dependency than by the optimisation of such technology. A famous one is the system used for organising characters on typewriter keyboards in most English-speaking countries: QWERTY. This originated in the nineteenth century as a way of reducing the problem of the keys on mechanical typewriters getting tangled when sales people demonstrated the machine at maximum speed by typing the word 'typewriter'. There are more optimal layouts, but QWERTY has remained with us for over 150 years despite changes in typewriter technology and the eventual development of personal computers.[7] There are countless other examples ranging from technologies in nuclear power stations through to vehicle engines.

Path dependency is, however, not just about technology. It also relates to any form of behaviour that has its origins in the past and becomes entrenched such that 'lock-in' occurs. This could begin with a decision which, of itself, may or may not be especially significant and where consequential succeeding events are unforeseeable. For example, Hollywood was originally chosen by the few silent film makers of the early nineteenth century because what was then a quiet backwater had a reliable climate for filming. This initial decision led to more and more film makers joining those already there. Eventually the build-up of film-making services and skills and the availability of actors meant that Hollywood became *the* place to make films. So an initial, maybe fortuitous decision achieves 'positive feedback' (the attraction of many film makers and actors) and leads to the development of self-reinforcing mechanisms. Such self-reinforcing mechanisms could include the development of logistics, technology and training that make up systems of production, selling, marketing and recruiting,[8] externally reinforced by repeated usage of a product or service by networks of customers and suppliers. The result could be '*lock-in*' where the infrastructure of an industry comes to be based around a product or service such that there are costs of switching from the standard offering.

Similar patterns of path dependency and lock-in gave rise to the concentration of automobile production in Detroit (USA), Formula One constructors in mid-England and industry clusters more generally. A further example is that of accounting systems. Lock-in here has occurred at multiple levels involving networks comprising what accountants do, those with whom they interact within and outside their organisation, the skills, standards and systems in which they are trained and objects and technologies they generate or use. All these have developed over time and mutually reinforce each other, as Figure 5.2 shows. They also persist despite increasing numbers of experts, both in the accountancy profession and elsewhere,[9] who point to fundamental weaknesses in such systems, not least the failure of accounting systems to provide measures for many of the factors that account for the market value of firms.

Path dependency is, then, a way of thinking about how historical events and decisions, within and around an organisation, have an effect on that organisation for good or ill in at least three ways:

● *Building strategy around the path-dependent capabilities* that may have developed within an organisation. This is at the root of much of the argument put forward for the building of competitive advantage discussed in Chapter 3 and further developed in Chapter 6. Path dependency has been shown to explain organisational strategies.[10] Firms tend to enter

Figure 5.2 Path dependency and lock-in

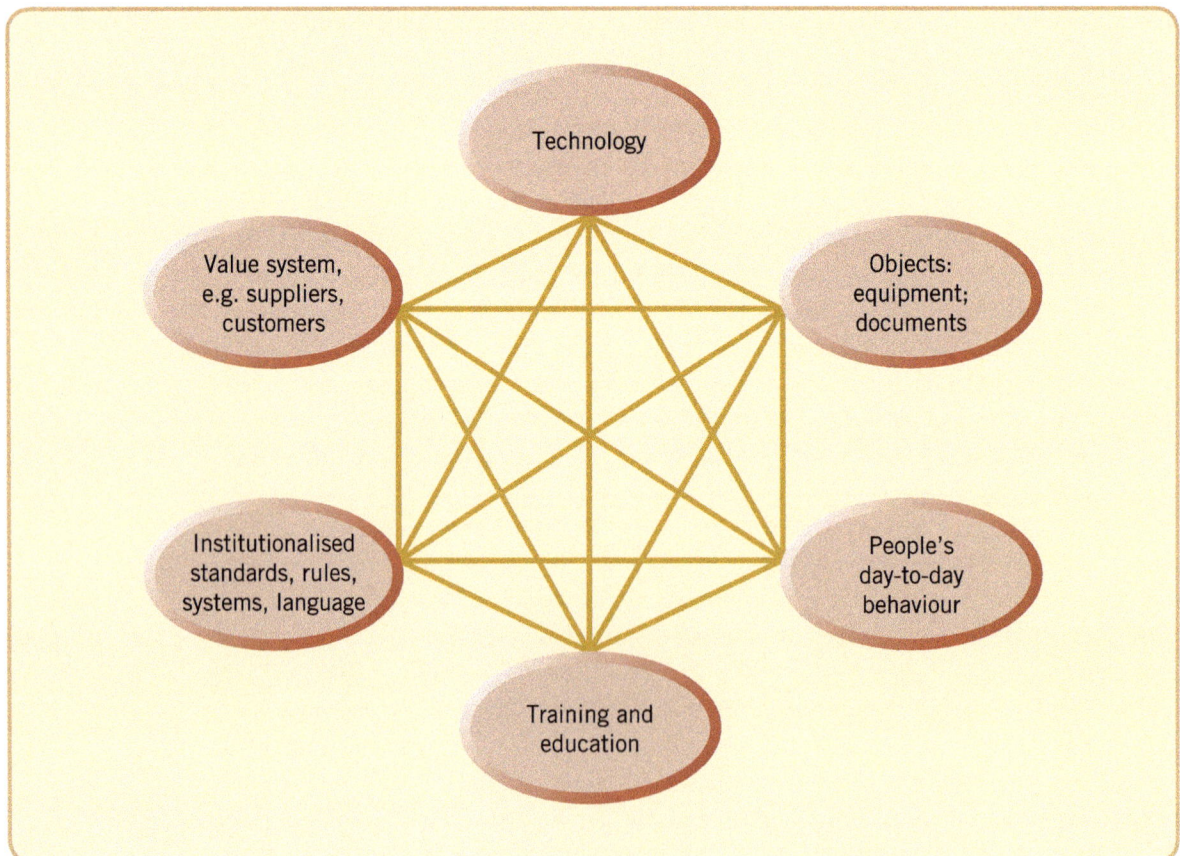

markets, focus on market segments and diversify in line with the previous path-dependent capabilities they have developed. In so doing they tend to focus on types of customers that they have serviced or capabilities on which their success has been based. This may be a basis for success but can also have negative influences as Illustration 5.1 shows. Path dependency has been described as like the 'furrows in a road' that become deeper and deeper as more and more traffic goes along. Once that happens the traffic has no option but to go along those furrows. Hence capabilities, once the bases of competitive advantage and success, become difficult to change leading to the phenomenon of strategic drift explained in section 5.4 later in the chapter.

- *Path creation* suggests that some managers, while acknowledging the relevance and potential benefits of history, may actively seek to amend and deviate from path-dependent ways of doing things. In so doing, they may be sensitive enough to history to recognise what they can and cannot change. Going too far may be risky (see the discussion on 'legitimacy' in section 5.3.2 below), but setting in motion changes that are accepted as appropriate and beneficial by others in the network may be a way of achieving advantage. Arguably this is what new players such as online providers or retailers such as Tesco and Marks & Spencer have done in the insurance market and banking. They have not tried to change basic principles of insurance and banking provision, but they have significantly changed the way in which insurance and banking are sold and distributed. In such circumstances managers need to see the past in relation to the future and ask what is relevant from the past that can help with the future and what the future demands that is not required from the past.

- *Management style* may also have its roots in history. This may be not only in terms of the values of the founder, which indeed may have a strong influence, but also in the interplay between past ways of doing things and the lessons learned from the organisation's evolving environment. Take Tesco as an example again. It became one of the most successful international retailers. In its early days it was a family firm run by founder Jack Cohen, renowned for his authoritative and confrontational style. This gave rise to internal conflicts within the firm, within the Cohen family and between suppliers and Tesco. As Tesco developed, the historic conflict evolved into productive challenge and contestation between managers that, arguably, substantially contributed to its success, especially from the 1990s to 2010.[11] Again, however, there is another side to these potential benefits. Just as capabilities that are path dependent and rooted in history may become entrenched, so might management style and this too may not be in line with the needs of a changing environment, giving rise to problems of change (see Chapter 14).

5.2.2 Historical analysis

How then might managers undertake an historical strategic analysis of their organisation? There are four ways this may be done:[12]

- *Chronological analysis.* At the most basic level this involves setting down a chronology of key events showing changes in the organisation's environment – especially its markets – how the organisation's strategy itself has changed and with what consequences – not least financial. Some firms have done this much more extensively by commissioning corporate histories. These may sometimes be little more than public relations exercises, but the better ones are serious exercises in documenting history[13] and can help sensitise managers to the sort of questions raised above.

ILLUSTRATION 5.1

History and strategy at Unilever[1]

The historical legacy of an organisation can be at the root of major strategic issues.

In 1927 Dutch companies Jurgens and Van den Bergh merged to form Margarine Unie. Then in 1929 British Lever Brothers merged with Margarine Unie to form Unilever. Inherited from the Dutch side was the desire to achieve consensus within the business. The Lever legacy was the pursuit of market leadership through product development and geographical expansion.[2]

The governance structure reflected the merger. In 1930 the boards of Unilever NV, the Dutch company, and Unilever Ltd, the British company, delegated corporate authority to a 'special committee' headed by the chairmen of NV and Ltd, and a third member, the chairman-in-waiting for either NV or Ltd. This was to have a long-lasting effect. As one former Unilever director put it, 'From the merger in 1929, our strategy has suffered from the need to manage the balance between the Dutch and English sides of the business.'

However, there was synergy. The Dutch, strong in Continental Europe, specialised in edible fats; the British, strong in the then Commonwealth countries, specialised in soap. Unilever sought to build on this to make itself too large and diversified to fail through product and geographical leadership, together with a respect for local market needs and the virtues of local initiative and control.

In terms of products, by the 1970s, Unilever had diversified into fishing, shipping, retailing, packaging and plastics, convenience foods, ice cream, tea, personal care products, speciality chemicals, animal feeds as well as the original oils, fats and detergents.

Unilever's decentralisation gave rise to long-standing superiority in many emerging markets, where adaptation in line with local needs was encouraged. This contrasted to the standardised approach of Procter & Gamble who, without the multicompany heritage, developed a more 'mass marketing' approach as early as 1931.

Autonomy also resulted in the power of local 'barons' who resisted Unilever's attempts to become more globally coordinated in the 1960s and 1970s. For example, 'coordinators', introduced in 1959 to create a greater uniformity for international brands, were seen as threatening the company's devolved power. The US business went to the lengths of anti-trust claims to resist more central control.

It was not until the 1990s that attempts to achieve a global strategy began to take shape. In response to investor concern the company decided to focus on seven business areas and scrap the special committee.

By the beginning of this century investors were still critical of a portfolio they believed lacked coherence and a management unwilling to deal with it. Indicative was the demise of the frozen food business Birds Eye, once a 'star' of the portfolio, whose failure to change to address changing market conditions showed how Unilever's 'steady-as-she-goes' approach resulted in a failure to act on long-evident problems.

In 2008 Unilever appointed its first ever chief executive from outside, Paul Polman, whose career had been with rivals Procter & Gamble and Nestlé. His appointment was applauded by the financial markets. He quickly announced a focus on emerging markets and on sustainability. In 2011 he restructured the company to decentralise operations but to have product categories under global heads reporting to him.

Sources
1. This illustration is based on the account of Unilever's history in *Strategic Transformation: Changing while Winning*, by M. Hensmans, G. Johnson and G. Yip, Palgrave, 2013.
2. Wilson, C. *The History of Unilever: A Study in Economic Growth and Social Change*, vol. 2, p. 38, Cassell, 1954.

Questions

1 What symptoms of path dependency are evident in the Unilever story?

2 Extend the examples of organisations given on page 145 that have deliberately employed their history to legitimise their strategies.

- *Cyclical influences.* Is there evidence of cyclical influences? These include economic cycles, but perhaps also cycles of industry activity, such as periods of high levels of mergers and acquisitions. Understanding when these cycles might occur and how industry and market forces can change during such cycles can inform decisions on whether to build strategy in line with those cycles or in a counter-cyclical fashion.

- *Key events and decisions.* History may be regarded as continuous but historical events can also be significant for an organisation at particular points in time. These could be particularly significant events, in terms of either industry change or an organisation's strategic decisions. Or they might be policies laid down by a founder or by powerful senior executives; or major successes or failures; or defining periods of time that managers have come to see as especially important; for example, the Wallander era at Handelsbanken. This could, of course, be for the good: it may help provide a clear overall direction strategically that contributes to the sort of vision discussed in the previous chapter. It could, on the other hand, be a major barrier to challenging existing strategies or changing strategic direction. A famous example is Henry Ford's maxim 'You can have any colour provided it's black', which set a trajectory for mass production and low variety in the car industry for decades.

- *Historical narratives.* How do people in an organisation talk about and explain its history? In trying to understand the foundations of the strategy of an organisation a new chief executive or an external consultant will typically spend a good deal of time talking with people to try and understand the meaning and gain insights from their personal accounts of history. What do they have to say about the way they see their organisation and its past, not least in terms of the origins of success? In turn, what are the implications for future strategy development? Does what people say suggest an organisation with the historic capabilities of relevance to current markets and customers; one capable of innovation and change or one so rooted in past ways of doing things that will be difficult to change?

History, then, is important in terms of how it influences current strategy for better or worse. It is not always easy, however, to trace the links to the organisation as it currently exists. It is here that understanding the organisation's culture becomes important. The current culture of an organisation is, to a great extent, the legacy of its history; history becomes 'encapsulated in culture'.[14] So understanding an organisation's culture is one way of understanding the historical influences, which, as we have seen, can be very powerful. The next section goes on to explain what culture is and how it can be analysed.

(5.3) WHAT IS CULTURE AND WHY IS IT IMPORTANT?

Edgar Schein defines *organisational culture* as the 'basic *assumptions and beliefs* that are shared by members of an organisation, that operate unconsciously and define in a basic taken-for-granted fashion an organisation's view of itself and its environment'.[15] Related to this are taken-for-granted *ways* '*we do things around here*'[16] that accumulate over time. So **organisational culture is the taken-for-granted assumptions and behaviours that make sense of people's organisational context** and therefore contributes to how groups of people respond and behave in relation to issues they face. It therefore has important influences on the development and change of organisational strategy.

Figure 5.3 Cultural frames of reference

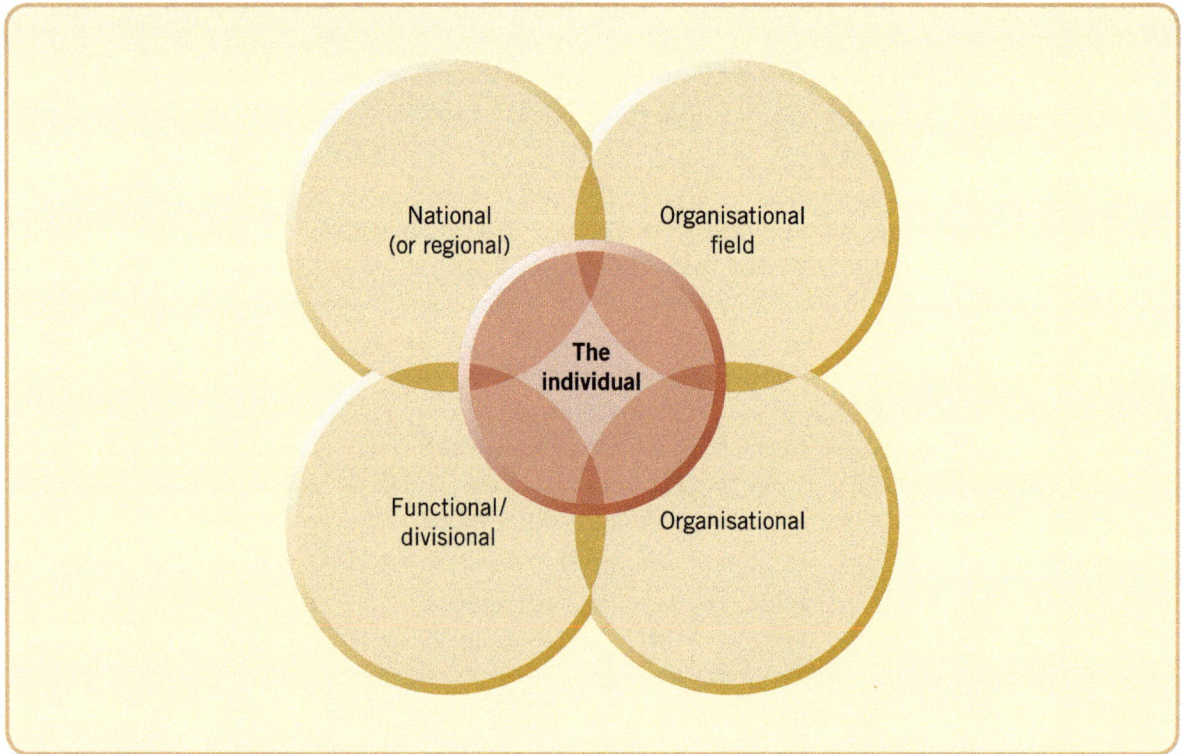

Different cultural contexts are likely to influence individuals, as Figure 5.3 shows. The sections that follow explain these different cultural frames of reference and then show how culture can be analysed and characterised as a means of understanding its influences on both current and future organisational purposes and strategies. The Key Debate at the end of the chapter then raises some questions about undertaking such analysis.

5.3.1 Geographically based cultures

Many writers, perhaps the most well known of whom is Geert Hofstede,[17] have shown how attitudes to work, authority, equality and other important factors differ from one country to another. Such differences have been shaped by powerful cultural forces concerned with history, religion and even climate over many centuries. Organisations that operate internationally need to understand and cope with such differences, which can manifest themselves in terms of different standards, values and expectations in the various countries in which they operate.[18] For example, Wal mart failed to develop its retail presence in Germany and China because it did not understand how local shopping behaviour differed from that in the USA. Indeed many Western firms that seek to build a presence in China have had to adjust to different cultural norms in terms of buyer and supplier behaviour as well as employee relations. Illustration 5.2 also shows how cultural differences underpin different conceptions of management between Chinese and Western managers.

Although they are not shown separately in Figure 5.3 (for reasons of simplification), it may also be important to understand *subnational* (usually regional) cultures. For example, attitudes

ILLUSTRATION 5.2

Project management: Chinese and UK perspectives

A study of how project management is viewed in China and the UK brought to the surface significant different perspectives on management.

Project management can be important in the implementation of strategy and since the 1980s has become increasingly recognised in China as a useful management tool. Researchers have, however, found different conceptions of project management between managers in China and managers in the UK. These findings, in turn, inform an understanding of some underlying differences of the wider conception of management itself.

Relationship with the company

Chinese managers saw their personal career development as strongly linked to the company's development: none of those studied had changed their company since the start of their career in the construction industry. UK managers, on the other hand, were more individualistic and most had changed companies several times.

Teamwork

Both Chinese and UK managers placed a high value on teamwork, relationships with clients and with subcontractors, but interpreted these differently. Chinese managers saw the team like a family where the team leader was like the father of the family and team members should support each other. So Chinese managers preferred to stay with their established teams and select new team members introduced to them by other members of the team. UK managers placed an emphasis on respect and trust but much more within the work context and with much less concern for how long people had worked in the team.

Relationship with clients

Chinese managers saw the client as: 'like your parents; you need to do whatever they instruct you . . . you need to do all you can to make them happy'. It was also important to build strong personal relationships with the client. UK managers saw the client as the provider of project funds, with a greater emphasis on contractual relationships: 'we deliver what the client wants, based on the contract'.

Relationship with subcontractors

For Chinese managers, subcontractors were like brothers and sisters of their project team family. They recognised that there could be competition with subcontractors but saw the answer to this as the building of long-term relationships. UK managers also saw subcontractors as members of the project team but with an emphasis on their specialised techniques and skills. Again they preferred to keep a more impersonal, contractual distance.

Conflict resolution

Both groups of managers acknowledged that conflict with clients or subcontractors could be a possibility. For Chinese managers negotiation was the basis of conflict resolution. Failure to resolve problems which might end with a claim against a subcontractor was regarded as a loss of 'face' and reputation. Conflicts needed to be resolved amicably. Though they also preferred to settle things amicably, UK managers again emphasised contractual conditions. Claims on clients or contractual penalties on subcontractors were normal project management practice.

Attitudes to uncertainty

Both Chinese and UK managers accepted uncertainty as inherent in project management. However, Chinese managers found this more stressful and problematic than UK managers, who, rather, enjoyed the challenges that arose: 'I am very lucky in my job in that I have numerous different challenges every day and it's full of change.'

Source: Ping Chen and David Partington, 'An interpretive comparison of Chinese and Western conceptions of relationships in construction project management work', *International Journal of Project Management*, vol. 22, no. 5 (2004), pp. 397–406.

Questions

1 In what other aspects of managing strategy might the differences identified here be important?

2 If you are seeking to operate in a country with a very different culture, how would you set about trying to understand that culture and its underlying assumptions?

to some aspects of employment and supplier relationships may differ at a regional level even in a relatively small and cohesive country like the UK, and quite markedly elsewhere in Europe (e.g. between northern and southern Italy). Such differences can affect the success of a strategy. For example, even within a country the integration of mergers between similar businesses can be problematic given regional differences of customer behaviour or employee attitudes and experience.[19]

5.3.2 Organisational fields[20]

The culture of an organisation is also shaped by 'work-based' groupings such as an industry (or sector), a profession or what is sometimes known as 'an organisational field'. An **organisational field** **is a community of organisations that interact more frequently with one another than with those outside the field and that have developed a shared meaning system.**[21] Such organisations may share a common technology, set of regulations or education and training. In turn this can mean that they tend to cohere around a **recipe:**[22] **a set of assumptions, norms and routines held in common within an organisational field about the appropriate purposes and strategies of field members**; in effect a 'shared wisdom'. For example, there are many organisations in the organisational field of 'justice', such as lawyers, police, courts, prisons and probation services. The roles of each are different and their detailed prescriptions as to how justice should be achieved differ. However, they are all committed to the principle that justice is a good thing which is worth striving for, they interact frequently on this issue, have developed shared ways of understanding and debating issues that arise and operate common routines or readily accommodate the routines of others in the field. Similar coherence around a recipe is common in other organisational fields: for example, professional services such as accountancy (see Illustration 5.3), medicine and industrial sectors such as engineering.

This links to the concept of path dependency discussed above. The different parties in an organisational field form a self-reinforcing network built on such assumptions and behaviours that, quite likely, will lead to behavioural lock-in. Indeed professions, or trade associations, often attempt to formalise an organisational field where the membership is exclusive and the behaviour of members is regulated. Such cultural influences can be advantageous in maintaining standards and consistency between individual providers. Managers can, however, become 'institutionalised' such that they do not see the opportunities or indeed threats from outside their organisational field and the recipes they inherit become difficult to change.

Institutionalisation in turn leads to the idea of legitimacy. **Legitimacy** **is concerned with meeting the expectations within an organisational field in terms of assumptions, behaviours and strategies.** Just as previous chapters have shown the important influence of environmental forces (Chapter 2), strategic capabilities (Chapter 3) and stakeholder expectations (Chapter 4), strategies can be shaped by the need for legitimacy in several ways. For example, this may occur through *regulation* (e.g. standards and codes of behaviour specified, perhaps by a professional body), *normative expectations* (what is socially expected), or simply that which is taken for granted as being appropriate (e.g. the *recipe*). Over time, there tends to develop a consensus within an organisational field about strategies that will be successful or acceptable – so strategies themselves become legitimised. By conforming to such norms, organisations may secure approval, support and public endorsement, thus increasing their legitimacy. Stepping outside that strategy may be risky because important stakeholders (such as customers or bankers) may not see such a move as legitimate. Therefore, organisations tend to mimic each other's strategies. There may be differences in strategies between organisations but within bounds of legitimacy.[23] This is shown in the discussion of strategy in Illustration 5.3. Of course,

ILLUSTRATION 5.3

Strategy debate in an accounting firm

The perceived legitimacy of a strategy may have different roots.

Edward Grey, the Managing Partner of QDG, one of the larger accountancy firms in the world, was discussing its global development with two of his senior partners. Global development had been the main issue at the firm's international committee in the USA the previous week. Like most accountancy firms, QDG was organised along national lines. Its origins were in auditing but it now offered tax and financial advice, corporate recovery and information systems services. International cooperation was based on personal contacts of partners across the world. However, large clients were beginning to demand a 'seamless global service'. At the meeting was Alan Clark, with 20 years' experience as a partner and high reputation in the accountancy profession, and Michael Jones, new to QDG and unlike the others not an accountant, who headed up the information systems arm of QDG, having been recruited from a consultancy firm.

Grey: 'Unless we move towards a more global form of business, QDG could lose its position as one of the leading accountancy firms in the world. Our competitors are moving this way, so we have to. The issue is how?'

Clark was sympathetic but cautionary. He pointed out that clients were entering growing economies such as China. 'Governments there will insist on international standards of practice, but they have difficulties. For example, in China historically there has been no real concept of profit, let alone how to measure it. If there is to be a market economy, the need for the services we provide is high. There are however major problems, not least, the enormous number of people required. It is not possible to churn out experienced accountants overnight. Our professional standards would be compromised. The firm cannot be driven by market opportunity at the expense of standards. There is another issue. Our business is based on personal relationships and trust; this must not be compromised in the name of "global integration".'

Michael Jones suggested that the problem was more challenging: 'All our competitors are going global. They will be pitching for the same clients, offering the same services and the same standard of service. Where is the difference? To achieve any competitive advantage we need to do things differently and think beyond the obvious. For example, why not a two-tier partnership, where smaller countries are non-equity partners. That would allow us to make decisions more quickly, allow us to enforce standards and give formal authority to senior partners looking after our major international clients.'

Alan Clark had expected this: 'This is not an opportunity to make money; it's about the development of proper systems for the economies of previously closed countries. We need to cooperate with other firms to make sure that there are compatible standards. This cannot be helped by changing a partnership structure that has served well for a hundred years.'

Grey: 'The view at last week's meeting was certainly that there is a need for a more internationally coordinated firm, with a more effective client management system, less reliance on who knows whom and more on drawing on the best of our people when we need them.'

Clark: 'I could equally argue that we have an unparalleled network of personal relationships throughout the world which we have been building for decades. That what we have to do is strengthen this using modern technology and modern communications.'

Edward Grey reconciled himself to a lengthy discussion.

Source: Adapted from the case study in G. Johnson and R. Greenwood, 'Institutional theory and strategic management', in *Strategic Management: A Multiple-Perspective Approach*, edited by Mark Jenkins and V. Ambrosini, Palgrave, 2007.

Questions

1 What are the underlying assumptions of the arguments being advanced by the three partners?

2 What may be the origins of these assumptions?

3 How do the different views correspond to the discussions of strategic capabilities (Chapter 3) and competitive strategy (Chapter 6)?

some businesses that begin as fringe players may actually be the foundation of successful future strategies (e.g. internet providers of downloadable music), but *initially* this may not be seen – customers may remain loyal to established companies; investors and bankers may be reluctant to fund such ventures; and existing players in the market may dismiss what they see as aberrations.

Because recipes vary from one field to another, the transition of managers between sectors can prove difficult. For example, private-sector managers have been encouraged to join public services in an attempt to inject new ways of doing things into the public sector. Many have found difficulties in gaining acceptance of their ways of working and in adjusting their management style to the different traditions and expectations of their new organisation, for example in issues like consensus building as part of the decision-making process. Or, to take the example in Illustration 5.3, Michael Jones's different career background means he has some quite different views on strategy from his accountant colleagues.

5.3.3 Organisational culture

As the different definitions of culture provided at the beginning of this section suggest, culture can be conceived as consisting of different layers. The four proposed by Edgar Schein[24] are (see Figure 5.4):

- *Values* may be easy to identify in terms of those formally stated by an organisation since they are often explicit, perhaps written down (see section 4.2). The values driving a strategy may, however, be different from those in formal statements. For example, in the last decade, many banks espoused values of shareholder value creation, careful risk management and, of course, high levels of customer service. But they indulged in highly risky lending, resulting in the need for huge government financial support in 2009. It is therefore important to delve beneath espoused values to uncover underlying, perhaps taken-for-granted, values that can help explain the strategy actually being pursued by an organisation (see section 5.3.7 below).

- *Beliefs* are more specific. They can typically be discerned in how people talk about issues the organisation faces; for example, a belief that the company should not trade with particular countries or, as with Alan Clark in Illustration 5.3, a belief in the rightness of accountancy systems and standards.

With regard to both values and beliefs it is important to remember that, in relation to culture, the concern is with the collective rather than individuals' values and beliefs. Indeed it may be that individuals in organisations have values and beliefs that at times run counter to their organisation's, which can give rise to the sort of ethical tensions and problems discussed in section 4.4.2.

- *Behaviours* are the day-to-day way in which an organisation operates and that be seen by people both inside and often outside the organisation. This includes the work routines, how the organisation is structured and controlled and 'softer' issues around symbolic behaviours (see section 5.3.6 below). These behaviours may become the taken-for-granted 'ways we do things around here' that are potentially the bases for inimitable strategic capabilities (see section 3.3.3) but also significant barriers to achieving strategic change if that becomes necessary (see Chapter 14).

Figure 5.4 Culture in four layers

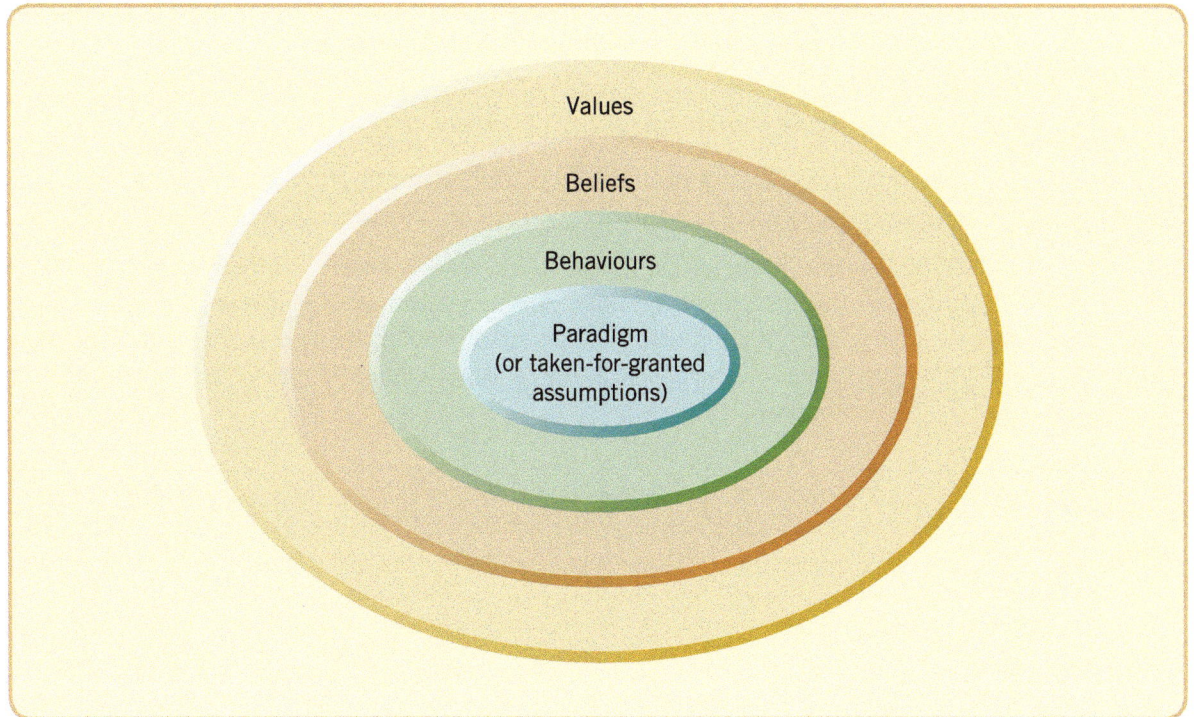

- *Taken-for-granted assumptions* are the core of an organisation's culture which, in this book, we refer to as the organisational *paradigm*. The **paradigm is the set of assumptions held in common and taken for granted in an organisation**. In effect these shared assumptions represent *collective experience* about fundamental aspects of the organisation that, in turn, guide people in that organisation about how to view and respond to different circumstances that they face. The paradigm can underpin successful strategies by providing a basis of common understanding in an organisation but, again, can be a major problem when major strategic change is needed (see Chapter 14). The importance of the paradigm is discussed further in section 5.3.6.

5.3.4 Organisational subcultures

In seeking to understand the relationship between culture and an organisation's strategies, it may be possible to identify some aspects of culture that pervade the whole organisation. However, there may also be important *subcultures*. These may relate to the structure of the organisation: for example, the differences between geographical divisions in a multinational company, or between functional groups such as finance, marketing and operations. Differences between divisions may be particularly evident in organisations that have grown through acquisition. Also different divisions may be pursuing different types of strategy that require or foster different cultures. Indeed, aligning strategic positioning and organisational culture is a critical feature of successful organisations. Differences between business functions can also relate to the different nature of work in different functions. For example, in a major oil company differences are likely between those functions engaged in 'upstream' exploration, where time horizons may be in decades, and those concerned with 'downstream' retailing, with much shorter market-driven time horizons. Arguably, this is one reason why Shell took the decision to sell its retail outlets and other downstream activities.

5.3.5 Culture's influence on strategy

The taken-for-granted nature of culture is what makes it centrally important in relation to strategy and the management of strategy. There are three primary reasons for this:

- *Cultural 'glue'*. There are benefits in the taken-for-granted nature of culture. Josephine Rydberg-Dumont, president of IKEA, argues that, because all employees cohere around the founding principles and values of the firm, it reduces the need for constant supervision. Moreover, since one such value is the benefit of constantly questioning the status quo, it 'fuels' innovation.

- *Captured by culture*. Organisations can, however, be 'captured' by their culture. Managers, faced with a changing business environment, are more likely to attempt to deal with the situation by searching for what they can understand and cope with in terms of the existing culture. The result is likely to be the incremental strategic change with the risk of eventual strategic drift explained in section 5.4. Culture is, in effect, an unintended driver of strategy.

- *Managing culture*. Because it is difficult to observe, identify and control that which is taken for granted, it is also difficult to manage. This is why having a way to analyse culture so as to make it more evident is important – the subject of the next section. (However, see the Key Debate at the end of the chapter.)

Mark Fields, President of Ford Motor Company in 2006, famously argued that 'culture eats strategy for breakfast', by which he meant to emphasise the dominant influence of culture on the strategy of the business. The likely effect of culture on strategy is shown in Figure 5.5.[25] Faced with a stimulus for action, such as declining performance, managers first try to improve the implementation of existing strategy (step 1). This might be through trying to lower cost, improve efficiency, tighten controls or improve accepted ways of doing things. If this is not effective, a change of strategy may occur, but a change in line with the existing culture (step 2). For example, managers may seek to extend the market for their business, but assume that it will be similar to their existing market, and therefore set about managing the new venture in much the same way as they have been used to. Alternatively, even where managers know intellectually that they need to change strategy, indeed know technologically how to do so, they find themselves constrained by path-dependent organisational routines and assumptions or political processes, as seems likely in the case of Kodak (see Illustration 5.5). This often happens, for example, when there are attempts to change highly bureaucratic organisations to be customer-orientated. Even if people accept the need to change a culture's emphasis on the importance of conforming to established rules, routines and reporting relationships, they do not readily do so. It is a fallacy to assume that reasoned argument necessarily changes deeply embedded assumptions rooted in collective experience built up over long periods of time. Readers need only think of their own experience in trying to persuade others to rethink their religious beliefs, or, indeed, allegiances to sports teams, to realise this. Changes in strategy which entail a fundamental change to an organisation's culture (step 3) are likely to be rare and triggered by dramatic evidence of the redundancy of that culture such as a financial crisis or major loss of market share.

Figure 5.5 Culture's influence on strategy development

Source: Adapted from P. Gringer and J.-C. Spender, *Turnaround: Managerial Recipes for Strategic Success*, Associated Business Press, 1979, p. 203.

5.3.6 Analysing culture: the cultural web

In order to understand the existing culture and its effects it is important to be able to analyse an organisation's culture. The cultural web[26] is a means of doing this (see Figure 5.6). The **cultural web shows the behavioural, physical and symbolic manifestations of a culture** that inform and are informed by the taken-for-granted assumptions, or paradigm, of an organisation. It is in effect the inner two ovals in Figure 5.4. The cultural web can be used to understand culture in any of the frames of reference discussed above but is most often used at the organisational and/or functional levels in Figure 5.3.[27] The elements of the cultural web are as follows:

- The *paradigm* is at the core of Figure 5.6. As previously defined it is the set of assumptions held in common and taken for granted in an organisation. The assumptions of the paradigm are, quite likely, very basic. For example, a common problem in technology and engineering firms is the propensity of people to focus on the technical excellence of products rather than customer-perceived needs. Or the paradigm of practitioners in the National Health Service in the UK is about curing illnesses. It is quite likely that, even if the rational view is to build a strategy around the engineering business's customer needs or the need for prevention (as distinct from curing) of illnesses, people in those organisations may still interpret issues and behave in line with its paradigm. So understanding what the paradigm is and how it informs debate on strategy matters. The problem is that, since it is unlikely to be talked

Figure 5.6 The cultural web of an organisation

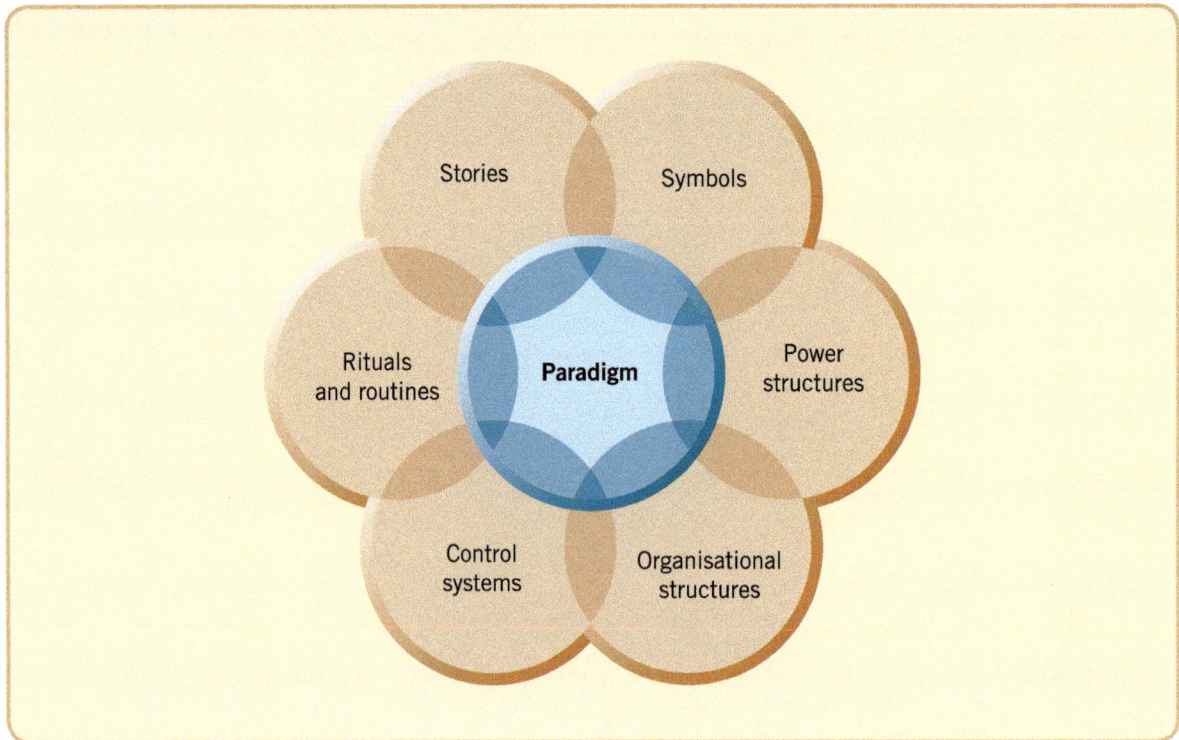

about, or even be something that people are conscious of, trying to identify it can be difficult, especially if you are part of that organisation. Outside observers may find it easier to identify simply by listening to what people say and emphasise. One way of 'insiders' getting to see the assumptions they take for granted is to focus initially on other aspects of the cultural web because these are to do with more visible manifestations of culture. Moreover these other aspects are likely to act to reinforce the assumptions of the paradigm.

- *Routines* are 'the way we do things around here' on a day-to-day basis. These may have a long history and may well be common across organisations. At their best, routines lubricate the working of the organisation, and may provide a basis for distinctive organisational capabilities. However, they can also represent a taken-for-grantedness about how things should happen which, again, can guide how people deal with situations and be difficult to change. For example, managers trying to achieve greater customer focus in engineering firms often report that customer-facing sales engineers routinely tend to tell customers what they need rather than listening to their needs.

- The *rituals*[28] of organisational life are particular activities or special events that emphasise, highlight or reinforce what is important in the culture. Examples include training programmes, interview panels, promotion and assessment procedures, sales conferences and so on. An extreme example, of course, is the ritualistic training of army recruits to prepare them for the discipline required in conflict. However, rituals can also be informal activities such as drinks in the pub after work or gossiping around photocopying machines. A checklist of rituals is provided in Chapter 14 (see Table 14.2).

- The *stories* told by members of an organisation to each other, to outsiders, to new recruits, and so on, may act to embed the present in its organisational history and also flag up important events and personalities. They typically have to do with successes, disasters, heroes, villains and mavericks (who deviate from the norm). They can be a way of letting people know what is conventionally important in an organisation.

- *Symbols* are objects, events, acts or people that convey, maintain or create meaning over and above their functional purpose. For example, offices and office layout, cars and job titles have a functional purpose, but are also typically signals about status and hierarchy. Particular people may come to represent especially important aspects of an organisation or historic turning points. The form of language used in an organisation can also be particularly revealing, especially with regard to customers or clients. For example, in a major teaching hospital in the UK, consultants described patients as 'clinical material'. While this might be amusing, it reveals something of the underlying assumptions of the paradigm that might play a significant role in influencing strategy. Although symbols are shown separately in the cultural web, it should be remembered that many elements of the web are symbolic. So, routines, control and reward systems and structures are not only functional but also symbolic.

- *Power* was defined in Chapter 4 as the ability of individuals or groups to persuade, induce or coerce others into following certain courses of action. So *power structures* are distributions of power to groups of people in an organisation. The most powerful individuals or groups are likely to be closely associated with the paradigm and long-established ways of doing things. In analysing power the guidance given in Chapter 4 (section 4.5.2) is useful.

- *Organisational structures* are the roles, responsibilities and reporting relationships in organisations. These are likely to reflect power structures and how they manifest themselves. Formal hierarchical, mechanistic structures may emphasise that strategy is the province of top managers and everyone else is 'working to orders'. Structures with less emphasis on formal reporting relationships might indicate more participative strategy making. Highly devolved structures (as discussed in Chapter 13) may signify that collaboration is less important than competition and so on.

- *Control systems* are the formal and informal ways of monitoring and supporting people within and around an organisation and tend to emphasise what is seen to be important in the organisation. They include measurements and reward systems. For example, public-service organisations have often been accused of being concerned more with stewardship of funds than with quality of service. This is reflected in their control systems, which are more about accounting for spending rather than with quality of service. Remuneration schemes are a significant control mechanism. Individually based bonus schemes related to volume are likely to signal a culture of individuality, internal competition and an emphasis on sales volume rather than teamwork and an emphasis on quality.

As the banking crisis of 2009 onwards developed, many familiar with the banking industry blamed the problems on 'the banking culture', which needed to change. Notably missing, however, were specifics as to what that culture was, so it was difficult to be clear about just what needed to change. Illustration 5.4 shows two cultural webs drawn up on the basis of interviews with longstanding employees of the retail side of Barclays Bank. They show some of the differences between the culture of Barclays prior to the 1990s and at the time of the crisis. In the past it was a paternalistic culture, in terms of both assumptions about customers and the way in which staff were treated, with an emphasis on avoiding risk. The branch manager,

ILLUSTRATION 5.4

Cultural webs of Barclays Retail

The cultural web can be used to identify the taken-for-granted behaviours and assumptions of an organisation.

The cultural web of Barclays Retail pre-1990s

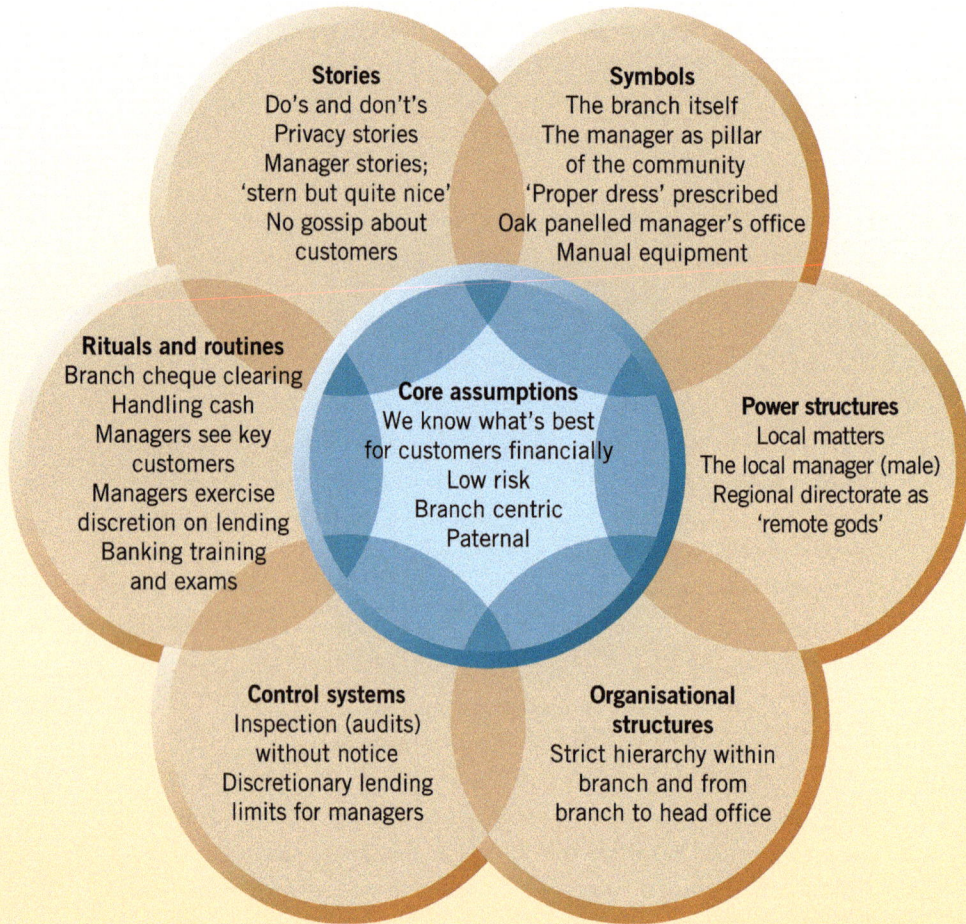

Stories
Do's and don't's
Privacy stories
Manager stories;
'stern but quite nice'
No gossip about
customers

Symbols
The branch itself
The manager as pillar
of the community
'Proper dress' prescribed
Oak panelled manager's office
Manual equipment

Rituals and routines
Branch cheque clearing
Handling cash
Managers see key
customers
Managers exercise
discretion on lending
Banking training
and exams

Core assumptions
We know what's best
for customers financially
Low risk
Branch centric
Paternal

Power structures
Local matters
The local manager (male)
Regional directorate as
'remote gods'

Control systems
Inspection (audits)
without notice
Discretionary lending
limits for managers

**Organisational
structures**
Strict hierarchy within
branch and from
branch to head office

often a 'pillar of the community', was a dominant influence on the service provided as well as a symbol of what Barclays stood for. The branches themselves were where bank staff 'looked after' customers and processed their cash and cheques and where the manager interviewed important customers and made decisions, for example about loans and credit limits. Propriety in matters financial was ensured by periodic unannounced audits by otherwise remote head office staff. This culture changed with the centralisation of bank services and operations and with the growing importance of investment banking on the profits of Barclays (together with other banks). Retail banking had become secondary to investment banking; the branches

The cultural web of Barclays Retail in the 2000s

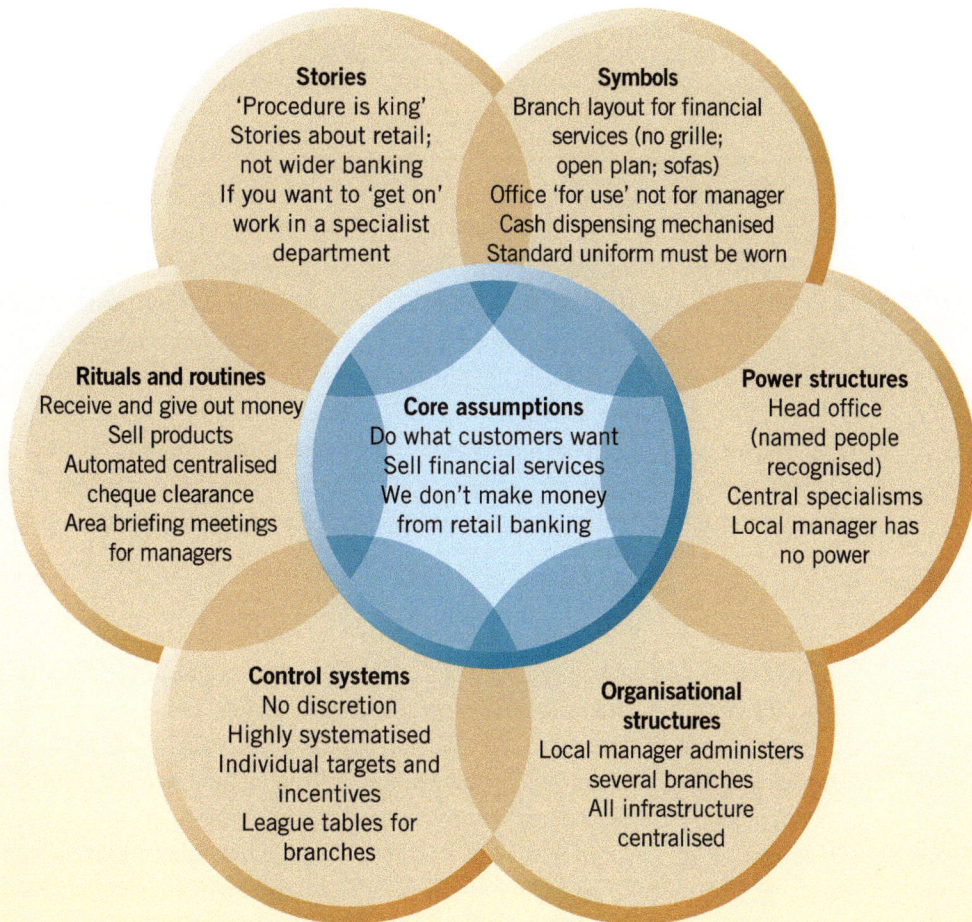

Stories
'Procedure is king'
Stories about retail;
not wider banking
If you want to 'get on'
work in a specialist
department

Symbols
Branch layout for financial
services (no grille;
open plan; sofas)
Office 'for use' not for manager
Cash dispensing mechanised
Standard uniform must be worn

Rituals and routines
Receive and give out money
Sell products
Automated centralised
cheque clearance
Area briefing meetings
for managers

Core assumptions
Do what customers want
Sell financial services
We don't make money
from retail banking

Power structures
Head office
(named people
recognised)
Central specialisms
Local manager has
no power

Control systems
No discretion
Highly systematised
Individual targets and
incentives
League tables for
branches

**Organisational
structures**
Local manager administers
several branches
All infrastructure
centralised

Questions

1 How might the webs help those seeking to address the problems of 'the banking culture'?
2 How do the various elements of the web interrelate?
3 Draw up a cultural web for an organisation of your choice.

had become vehicles for selling financial services; staff were incentivised to do so; the local branch manager was no more and local discretion was removed. Cash was increasingly automatically dispensed, cheques were cleared centrally and staff operated to standardised procedures. The layout of the branch itself de-emphasised financial security or the role of a branch manager; it was more open plan facilitating contact between staff and customers.

It was this sales culture, also common in other banks, which led to the huge fines imposed for the mis-selling of payment protection insurance policies by Barclays as well as other banks.

5.3.7 **Undertaking cultural analysis**

If an analysis of the culture of an organisation is to be undertaken, there are some important issues to bear in mind:

● *Questions to ask.* Figure 5.7 outlines some of the questions that might help build up an understanding of culture using the cultural web.

● *Statements of cultural values.* As section 4.2 and section 5.4.3 above explained, organisations may make public statements of their values, beliefs and purposes, for example in annual reports, mission or values statements and business plans. There is a danger that these are seen as useful descriptions of the organisational culture. But this is likely to be at best only partially true, and at worst misleading. This is not to suggest that there is any organised deception. It is simply that the statements of values and beliefs are often carefully considered and carefully crafted statements of the aspirations of a particular stakeholder (such as the CEO) rather than descriptions of the actual culture. For example, an outside observer of a police force might conclude from its public statements of purpose and priorities that it had a balanced approach to the various aspects of police work – catching criminals, crime preven- tion, community relations. However, a deeper probing might reveal that (in cultural terms) there is the 'real' police work (catching criminals) and the 'lesser work' (crime prevention, community relations).

● *Pulling it together.* The detailed 'map' produced by the cultural web can be a rich source of information about an organisation's culture, but it is useful to be able to characterise the culture that the information conveys. Sometimes this is possible by means of graphic descriptors. For example, managers who undertook a cultural analysis in the UK National Health Service (NHS) summed up their culture as 'The National Sickness Service'. Although this approach is rather crude and unscientific, it can be powerful in terms of organisational members seeing the organisation as it really is – which may not be immediately apparent from all of the detailed points in the cultural web. It can also help people to understand that culture may drive strategy; for example, a 'national sickness service' will prioritise strategies that are about developments in curing sick people above strategies of health promotion and prevention. So those favouring health promotion strategies need to understand that they are facing the need to change a culture.

If managers are to develop strategies that are different from those of the past, they need to be able to challenge, question and potentially change the organisational culture that underpins the current strategy. In this context, the cultural analysis suggested in this chapter can inform aspects of strategic management discussed in other parts of this book. These include the following:

● *Strategic capabilities.* As Chapter 3 makes clear, historically embedded capabilities are, very likely, part of the culture of the organisation. The cultural analysis of the organisation therefore provides a complementary basis of analysis to an examination of strategic capab- ilities (see Chapter 3). In effect, such an analysis of capabilities should end up digging into the culture of the organisation, especially in terms of its routines, control systems and the everyday way in which the organisation runs.

● *Strategy development.* An understanding of organisational culture sensitises managers to the way in which historical and cultural influences will likely affect future strategy for good or ill. It therefore relates to the discussion on strategy development in Chapter 12.

Figure 5.7 The cultural web: some useful questions

Stories
- What core beliefs do stories reflect?
- What stories are commonly told, e.g. to newcomers?
- How do these reflect core assumptions and beliefs?
- What norms do the mavericks deviate from?

Symbols
- What objects, events or people do people in the organisation particularly identify with?
- What are these related to in the history of the organisation?
- What aspects of strategy are highlighted in publicity?

Routines and rituals
- Which routines are emphasised?
- Which are embedded in history?
- What behaviour do routines encourage?
- What are the key rituals?
- What assumptions and core beliefs do they reflect?
- What do training programmes emphasise?
- How easy are rituals/routines to change?

Power structures
- Where does power reside? Indicators include:
  (a) status
  (b) claim on resources
  (c) symbols of power
- Who 'makes things happen'?
- Who stops things happening?

Stories   Symbols

Routines and rituals   **Paradigm**   Power structures

Control systems   Organisational structures

Control systems
- What is most closely monitored/controlled?
- Is emphasis on reward or punishment?
- Are controls rooted in history or current strategies?
- Are there many/few controls?

Organisational structures
- What are the formal *and* informal structures?
- How rigid are the structures?
- Do structures encourage collaboration or competition?
- What types of power structure do they support?

Overall
- What do the answers to these questions suggest are the (few) fundamental assumptions that are the paradigm?
- How would you characterise the dominant culture?
- How easy is this to change?
- How and to what extent do aspects of the web inter relate and re-enforce each other?

- *Managing strategic change.* An analysis of the culture also provides a basis for the management of strategic change, since it provides a picture of the existing culture that can be set against a desired strategy so as to give insights as to what may constrain the development of that strategy or what needs to be changed in order to achieve it. This is discussed more extensively in Chapter 14 on managing strategic change.

- *Leadership and management style.* Chapter 14 also raises questions about leadership and management style. If one of the major requirements of a strategist is to be able to encourage the questioning of that which is taken for granted, it is likely to require a management style – indeed a culture – that allows and encourages such questioning. If the leadership style is such as to discourage such questioning, it is unlikely that the lessons of history will be learned and more likely that the dictates of history will be followed.

● *Culture and experience.* There have been repeated references in this section to the role culture plays as a vehicle by which meaning is created in organisations. This is discussed more fully in the Commentary on the experience lens and provides a useful way in which many aspects of strategy can be considered (see the Commentaries throughout the book).

(5.4) STRATEGIC DRIFT

The influence of an organisation's history and culture on its strategic direction is evident in the pattern of strategy development depicted in Figure 5.8. **Strategic drift**[29] **is the tendency for strategies to develop incrementally on the basis of historical and cultural influences, but fail to keep pace with a changing environment.** An example of strategic drift in Kodak is given in Illustration 5.5. The reasons and consequences of strategic drift are important to understand, not only because it is common, but also because it helps explain why organisations often seem to stagnate in their strategy development and their performance. Strategic drift also highlights some significant challenges for managers that, in turn, point to some important lessons.

5.4.1 Incremental strategic change

Strategies of organisations most often change gradually. There is a tendency for strategies to develop on the basis of what the organisation has done in the past – especially if that has been

Figure 5.8 Strategic drift

ILLUSTRATION 5.5

Kodak: the decline and fall of a market leader

Knowledge of technological and market changes may not be enough to avoid strategic drift.

In the twentieth century Kodak, the manufacturer of photographic film and cameras, was one of the world's most valuable brands. Based in Rochester in New York State, by 1976 Kodak had 90 per cent of film and 85 per cent share of camera sales in the USA, by 1996 turnover was $16 billion and in 1999 profits nearly $2.5 billion. Initially, known for its innovative technology and marketing, it had developed digital camera technology by 1975, but did not launch digital cameras until the late 1990s by when it was too late.

By 2011 its traditional photography business had been almost entirely eroded by, first, digital cameras and then by smart phones. Turnover was only $6 billion, it was loss making, the share price had plummeted and in 2012 it filed for bankruptcy protection. How did Kodak miss such a fundamental shift in the market?

According to Steve Sasson, the engineer who invented the first digital camera, the response to his invention in Kodak was dismissive because it was filmless photography. There were similar responses to early internal intelligence reports on digital technology: 'Larry Matteson, a former Kodak executive . . . recalls writing a report in 1979 detailing fairly accurately how different parts of the market would switch from film to digital, starting with government reconnaissance, then professional photography and finally the mass market, all by 2010.'[1] Another internal report in the early 1980s concluded that digital technology would take over the camera industry in about 10 years; 10 years in which Kodak could work out its response.

The Kodak response was to use digital to enhance the film business. For example, in 1996 Kodak launched a film system using digital technology to provide users with a preview of shots taken and indicate the number of prints required. It flopped.

It was executives in the film division who carried most weight and they were over-confident about Kodak's brand strength. They also misjudged the speed of the change in customer buying preferences. For example, they believed that people in fast-developing markets such as China would buy lots of film, but many moved from no camera at all to digital. The profit margin on digital was also tiny compared with film and there was a real fear of product cannibalisation. Rosabeth Moss Kanter of Harvard Business School also pointed to the Kodak culture: 'Working in a one company town did not help . . . Kodak's bosses in Rochester seldom heard much criticism . . .'. Moreover, 'executives suffered from a mentality of perfect products, rather than the hi-tech mindset of make it, launch it, fix it.'[1] They also moved slowly: 'Even when Kodak decided to diversify, it took years to make its first acquisition.'[1] Kodak's attempts to diversify by developing the thousands of chemicals its researchers had created for use in film for the drug market also failed.

In 1989, the Kodak board needed to choose a new CEO. The choice was between Kay R. Whitmore, a long-serving executive in the traditional film business, and Phil Samper, who was more associated with digital technology. The board chose Whitmore, who insisted that he would make sure Kodak stayed closer to its core businesses in film and photographic chemicals.[2]

As late as 2007, a Kodak marketing video announced that 'Kodak is back' and 'wasn't going to play grab ass anymore' with digital.[3]

Sources
1. *The Economist*, 'The last Kodak moment?', 14 January 2012.
2. *New York Times*, 9 December 1989.
3. Chunka Mui, 'How Kodak failed', *Forbes*, 18 January 2012.

Questions

1 Which of the reasons for strategic drift are evident in the Kodak story?

2 Drawing on the lessons from Part I of the book, how might Kodak's problems have been avoided?

successful.[30] This is discussed more fully in Chapter 12. This was the case for Kodak, which dominated the market for camera film throughout most of the twentieth century. To take another example, for many years UK retailer HMV had successfully developed its business by adapting to changing technology and tastes in the entertainment market. HMV had made huge profits as music lovers replaced their vinyl records with CDs; it introduced DVDs and computer games when they arrived on the market, and increased the space allocation to them as demand increased. This is shown in phase 1 of Figure 5.8. In most successful businesses there are usually long periods of relative *continuity* during which established strategy remains largely unchanged or changes very *incrementally*. There are three main reasons for this:

- *Alignment with environmental change*. It could be that the environment, particularly the market, is changing gradually and the organisation is keeping in line with those changes by such incremental change. It would make no sense for the strategy to change dramatically when the market is not doing so.

- *The success of the past*. There may be a natural unwillingness by managers to change a strategy significantly if it has been successful in the past. This will especially be so if that strategy is built on capabilities that have been shown to be the basis of competitive advantage (see Chapters 3 and 6) or of innovation (see Chapter 9). Managers quite understandably will argue that they should stick to what they know and do best.

- *Experimentation around a theme*. Managers may have learned how to build variations around their successful formula, in effect experimenting without moving too far from their capability base. (This is akin to what some writers have referred to as 'logical incrementalism'; see section 12.3.1.)

This poses challenges for managers, however. For how long and to what extent can they rely on incremental change being sufficient? When should they make more fundamental strategic changes? And how can they detect when this is necessary?

5.4.2 The tendency towards strategic drift

For many years HMV persisted in the conviction that there was a market for the sale of music and DVDs through specialist retail outlets. HMV continued to adjust its retail formats and extended product ranges in the search for a sustainable competitive position. Senior management in particular had difficulty, however, reconciling themselves to the need for more fundamental change to their business model given the shifts in the first decade of this century to the way in which people accessed music, films and games through the internet. A similar persistence with established strategy was evident in Kodak.

Given that an organisation's strategy may continue to change incrementally, there does not need to be sudden or dramatic environmental changes for the strategy to become less aligned with the environment. Phase 2 of Figure 5.8 shows environmental change accelerating, but it is not sudden. For HMV it was not as if changes in buyer behaviour or the growth in supermarket sales of CDs and DVDs happened overnight. These changes took place over years. The problem that gives rise to strategic drift is that, as with many organisations, HMV's strategy was not keeping pace with these changes. There are at least five reasons for this:

- *Steady as you go*. Chapter 2 has provided ways to analyse the environment and such analyses may yield insights. But how are managers to be sure of the direction and significance of such changes? Or changes may be seen as temporary. Managers may be understandably wary of changing what they are likely to see as a winning strategy, on the basis of what might only be a fad in the market, or a temporary downturn in demand. It may be easy to see major changes with hindsight, but it may not be so easy to see their significance as they are happening. Rebecca Henderson of MIT suggested how a Kodak executive might have responded to reports on the threat of digital technology (see Illustration 5.5): '. . . you are suggesting that we invest millions of dollars in a market that may, or may not exist but that is certainly smaller than our existing market, to develop a product that customers may or may not want using a business model that will almost certainly give us lower margins than our existing product lines . . . Tell me again just why we should make this investment?'[31]

- *Building on the familiar*. Managers may see changes in the environment about which they are uncertain or which they do not entirely understand. In these circumstances they may try to minimise the extent to which they are faced with such uncertainty by looking for answers that are familiar, which they understand and which have served them well in the past. This will lead to a bias towards continued incremental strategic change.

- *Core rigidities*. Capabilities that have been bases of competitive advantage can become difficult to change; in effect *core rigidities*.[32] This occurs because ways of doing things develop over time and become more and more embedded in organisational routines that reinforce, rely on each other and are difficult to unravel. Such routines may also become taken for granted. As the discussion in section 3.3.3 explains, this may be an advantage because it is difficult for competitors to imitate strategic capabilities based on routines that are interconnected and taken for granted. Taken-for-granted capabilities rarely get questioned, however, and therefore tend to persist beyond their usefulness.

- *Relationships become shackles*.[33] Success may have been built on excellent relationships with customers, suppliers and employees. Maintaining these may quite rightly be seen as fundamental to the long-term health of the organisation. Yet these relationships may make it difficult to make significant changes to strategy that could entail changing routes to market or the customer base, developing products requiring different suppliers or changing the skill base of the organisation with the risk of disrupting relationships with the workforce.

- *Lagged performance effects*. The effects of such drift may not be easy to see in terms of the performance of the organisation. Financial performance may continue to hold up in the early stages of strategic drift. Customers may be loyal and the organisation, by becoming more efficient, cutting costs or simply trying harder, may continue to exhibit high levels of performance. So there may not be internal signals of the need for change, or indeed pressure from external observers, to make major changes.

For all these reasons, as the consultants McKinsey point out, the tendency is for 'most companies to allocate the same resources to the same business units year after year'.[34]

However, over time, if strategic drift continues, there will be symptoms that become evident: a downturn in financial performance, a loss in market share to competitors or a decline in the share price. Indeed such a downturn may happen quite rapidly once external observers, not least competitors and financial analysts, have identified that such drift has occurred. Even the most successful companies may drift in this way. Indeed, there is a tendency – which Danny Miller has called the Icarus Paradox[35] – for businesses to become victims of the very success of their past. They become captured by the formula that has delivered that success.

5.4.3 **A period of flux**

The next phase (phase 3) may be a period of *flux* triggered by the downturn in performance. Strategies may change but in no very clear direction. There may also be management changes, often at the very top as the organisation comes under pressure from its stakeholders to make changes, not least shareholders in the case of a public company. There may be internal rivalry as to which strategy to follow, quite likely based on differences of opinion as to whether future strategy should be based on historic capabilities or whether those capabilities are becoming redundant. Indeed, there have been highly publicised boardroom rows when this has happened. All this may result in a further deterioration of confidence in the organisation: perhaps a further drop in performance or share price, a difficulty in recruiting high-quality management, or a further loss of customers' loyalty. By 2012 HMV had closed many of its stores and shoppers would find its product offering skewed towards video games and DVDs but also merchandise such as T-shirts and posters in an attempt to ramp up sales.

5.4.4 **Transformational change or death**

As things get worse it is likely that the outcome (phase 4) will be one of three possibilities. (a) The organisation may die; in the case of a commercial organisation it may go into receivership for example, as Kodak did in 2012 and HMV did in 2013. Some private companies can, however, experience a lingering death as their, often, owner managers persist in following the strategy of the past. (b) It may get taken over by another organisation. (c) Or it may go through a period of *transformational change*. Such change could take form in multiple changes related to the organisation's strategy; perhaps a change to its whole business model (see section 9.2.4) as well as changes in the top management of the organisation and perhaps the way the organisation is structured.

Transformational change does not take place frequently in organisations and usually follows a major downturn in performance. Often it is transformational changes that are heralded as the success stories of top executives; this is where they most visibly make a difference. The problem is that, from the point of view of market position, shareholder wealth and jobs, it may be rather late. Competitive position may have been lost, shareholder value has probably already been destroyed and, very likely, many jobs will have been lost too. The time when 'making a difference' really matters most is in phases 1 or 2 in Figure 5.8, before an organisation suffers performance decline. However, a study of 215 major UK firms over the 20-year period 1983–2003 identified only four that could be said to have *both* maintained consistently high levels of performance and effected major transformational change over that period.[36] The problem is that, very likely, strategic drift is not easy to see before performance suffers. So, to avoid the damaging effects of strategic drift, it is vital to take seriously the extent to which historical tendencies in strategy development tend to persist in the cultural fabric of organisations. There is also emerging evidence that firms that are able to enact change regularly before pressured to do so benefit in terms of financial performance.[37]

KEY DEBATE

Understanding organisational culture

If organisational culture is so important an influence on strategy, then understanding what it is and its influences are of key importance. But is this possible?

There are many tools and techniques for analysing organisational cultures. Denison Consulting,[1] based in Ann Arbour, Michigan, employs the Denison model to help clients diagnose their cultures.

Denison argues that there are four key cultural traits that affect performance measures such as profitability, sales growth, quality, and market value. Founder Dan Denison explained:[2]

'Generally speaking, an organisation's sense of *Mission* and its *Adaptability* can forecast its growth rate fairly well. A growth company sets its vision on external markets, and is sensitive to the changes in the market. Its actions are informed by the market and it clearly understands the significance of its existence in the market. If a corporation has strong *Involvement* and *Consistency*, and the company culture is very "internal," the company may not grow quickly, but performance indicators such as quality and efficiency are typically pretty good. Innovative companies always get high scores in aspects of *Adaptability* and *Involvement*. A company with a strong *Mission* and *Consistency* will have steady performance over a long time period.'

These traits are further broken down into 60 items, measured via a five-point Likert scale in a survey that managers can complete. The results produce a picture of the culture. Denison argues that the highest-performing firms are those that score high on all four of the key traits. It also suggests that survey results can be used to identify the weaknesses in an organisation's culture, track changes in the culture and benchmark against other companies.

However, Mats Alvesson[3] suggests that there is a tendency to simplify and trivialise what organisational culture means. Managers often fall victim to 'sins' that include:

Reifying culture: Seeing culture as something 'thing-like' that, for example, directly links to performance or can be readily managed. What really matters is the meaning shared by a collective and that is a more complex idea.

Essentialising culture: Describing culture in terms of a few essential traits. The danger is a 'too

strongly ordered and superficial view on culture'. The need is for a more careful interpretation and a recognition of variations within a culture.

Consensualising culture: 'Shared meanings do not necessarily imply consensus and harmony ... an organisation may be characterised by shared ideas and beliefs about the significance of self interest, fierce internal competition and a view of corporate life as fairly harsh and jungle-like.'

Totalising culture: Assuming that a culture can be captured 'once and for all' when 'it is the shared meanings on a specific topic that is of interest to pay attention to' such as core competences or the future of an industry.

Unifying culture: 'Equating cultural boundaries with formal or legal ones, as implied by terms such as corporate culture or national culture.'

Alvesson grants, however, that there are 'sometimes pragmatic reasons ... for simplifications and the expression of something accessible – which often leads to some of the sins above ... My point is, however, that the traps and temptations should be handled with great care and care taken that they are not "privileged".'

Sources
1. www.denisonconsulting.com.
2. Xuejun Yi, 'The yin and yang of corporate culture', *Harvard Business Review*, China, January 2008, pp. 70–82.
3. M. Alvesson, *Understanding Organisational Culture*, Sage, 2002, pp. 186–9.

Questions

1 Which of Alvesson's 'sins' apply to the Denison model?

2 To what extent do Alvesson's sins apply to the cultural web?

3 If, as Alvesson suggests, pragmatically some of the sins are difficult to avoid, how can managers avoid 'privileging' them?

4 Undertake a cultural analysis of an organisation. To what extent did you find yourself committing any of the 'sins'?

SUMMARY

- The *history and culture* of an organisation may contribute to the distinct and unique nature of an organisation's strategic capabilities.

- Historical, *path-dependent processes* may play a significant part in the success or failure of an organisation and need to be understood by managers. There are historical analyses that can be conducted to help uncover these influences.

- *Cultural and institutional influences* both inform and constrain the strategic development of organisations.

- *Organisational culture* is the basic taken-for-granted assumptions, beliefs and behaviours shared by members of an organisation.

- An understanding of the culture of an organisation and its relationship to organisational strategy can be gained by using the *cultural web*.

- Historic and cultural influences may give rise to *strategic drift* as strategy develops incrementally on the basis of such influences and fails to keep pace with a changing environment.

WORK ASSIGNMENTS

✱ *Denotes more advanced work assignments.*
* *Refers to a case study in the Text and Cases edition.*

5.1✱ In the context of section 5.2, undertake a historical analysis of the strategy development of an organisation of your choice and consider the question: 'Does history matter in managing strategy?'

5.2 Map out an organisational field (see section 5.4.2) within which an organisation of your choice operates. (As a basis for this you could, for example, use accountancy, an organisation operating in the public sector such as a university or Formula One*.)

5.3 Identify (a) an organisation where its publicly stated values correspond with your experience of it and (b) one where they do not. Explain why (a) and (b) might be so.

5.4 Use the questions in Figure 5.8 to plot a cultural web for Barclays Investment Bank, Adnams* or an organisation of your choice.

5.5 Identify four organisations that, in your view, are in the different phases of strategic drift (see the explanation of the phases in section 5.4). Justify your selection.

5.6✱ By using a number of the examples from above and taking into account the issues raised in the Key Debate, critically appraise the assertion that 'culture can only really be usefully analysed by the symptoms displayed in the way the organisation operates'. (You may wish to refer to Schein's book in the recommended key readings to assist you with this task.)

Integrative assignment

5.7✱ Choose an example of a major change in strategy of an organisation. Explain to what extent and how its strategic capabilities and its organisation culture changed. (Refer to Chapters 3, 5, 6, and 14.)

VIDEO ASSIGNMENTS

Visit **MyStrategyLab** and watch the case study for Chapter 5 (which features various companies).

1 Give examples from the video clips of what is meant by 'organisational culture'.

2 Use the video clips to explain how an organisation's culture can be a valuable asset in implementing a strategy.

RECOMMENDED KEY READINGS

- For a historical perspective on strategy see: Manuel Hensmans, Gerry Johnson and George Yip, *Strategic Transformation: Changing while Winning*, Palgrave Macmillan, 2013 (summarised in G. Johnson, G. Yip and M. Hensmans, 'Achieving successful strategic transformation', *MIT Sloan Management Review*, vol. 53, no. 3 (2012), pp. 25–32); and John T. Seaman Jr and George David Smith, 'Your company's history as a leadership tool', *Harvard Business Review* (December 2012), 1–10.

- For a summary and illustrated explanation of institutional theory see Gerry Johnson and Royston Greenwood, 'Institutional theory and strategy', in *Strategic Management: A Multiple-Perspective Approach*, edited by Mark Jenkins and V. Ambrosini, Palgrave, 2007.

- For a comprehensive and critical explanation of organisational culture see Mats Alvesson, *Understanding Organisational Culture*, Sage, 2002.

- For a more thorough explanation of the phenomenon of strategic drift and the cultural web see Gerry Johnson, 'Rethinking incrementalism', *Strategic Management Journal*, vol. 9 (1988), pp. 75–91, and 'Managing strategic change – strategy, culture and action', *Long Range Planning*, vol. 25, no. 1 (1992), pp. 28–36.

REFERENCES

1. See J.T. Seaman Jr and G.D. Smith, 'Your company's history as a leadership tool', *Harvard Business Review* (December 2012), pp. 1–10.

2. This quote by André Malroux and the story of the BMW museum was provided by the business historian Mary Rose.

3. See D. Holbrook, W. Cohen, D. Hounshell and S. Klepper, 'The nature, sources and consequences of firm differences in the early history of the semiconductor industry', *Strategic Management Journal*, vol. 21, no. 10–11 (2000), pp. 107–42.

4. S. Klepper and K.L. Simons, 'Dominance by birthright: entry of prior radio producers and competitive ramifications in the US television receiver industry', *Strategic Management Journal*, vol. 21, no. 10–11 (2000), pp. 987–1016.

5. O. Brunninge, 'Using history in organization: how managers make purposeful reference to history in strategy processes', *Journal of Organizational Change Management*, vol. 22, no. 1 (2009), pp. 8–26.

6. W.B. Arthur, 'Competing technologies, increasing returns and lock in by historical events', *Economic Journal*, vol. 99 (1989), pp. 116–31.

7. P.A. David, 'Clio and the economics of QWERTY', *American Economic Review*, vol. 75, no. 2 (1985), pp. 332–7, but also for a challenge to David's argument see S.J. Liebowitz, and S.E. Margolis, 'The fable of the keys'. *Journal of Law & Economics*, vol. 30, April 1990, pp. 1–26.

8. For discussions of path dependency in an organisational context see: Jorg Sydow, George Schraeyogg and Jochen Koch, 'Organisational path dependance: opening the black box', *Academy of Management Review*, vol. 34, no. 4 (2009), pp. 689–708. The same authors provide a case example of the German book club Bertelsmann AG in G. Schreyögg, J. Sydow and P. Holtman, 'How history matters in organisations: the case of path dependence.' *Management & Organizational History*, vol. 6, no. 1 (2011), pp. 81–100.

9. The world's biggest accounting firms have called for radical reform; 'Big four in call for real time accounts', *Financial Times* (8 November 2006), p. 1.

10. Holbrook et al. (reference 3 above).

11. See M. Hensmans, G. Johnson and G. Yip, *Strategic Transformation: Changing while Winning*, Palgrave Macmillan, 2013.

12. Also see D.J. Jeremy, 'Business history and strategy', in *The Handbook of Strategy and Management*, pp. 436–60, edited by A. Pettigrew, H. Thomas and R. Whittington, Sage, 2002.

13. For good examples of corporate histories see G. Jones, *Renewing Unilever: Transformation and Tradition*, Oxford University Press, 2005; R. Fitzgerald, *Rowntrees and the Marketing Revolution, 1862–1969*, Cambridge University Press, 1995; T.R. Gourvish, *British Railways 1948–73*, Cambridge University Press, 1986.

14. This quote is from S. Finkelstein, 'Why smart executives fail: four case histories of how people learn the wrong lessons from history', *Business History*, vol. 48, no. 2 (2006), pp. 153–70.

15. This definition of culture is taken from E. Schein, *Organisational Culture and Leadership*, 3rd edn, Jossey-Bass, 2004, p. 6.

16. This is how Terrence Deal and Alan Kennedy define organisational culture in *Corporate Cultures: the Rites and Rituals of Corporate Life*, Addison-Wesley, 1982.

17. See G. Hofstede, *Culture's Consequences*, Sage, 2nd edn, 2001. For critiques of Hofstede's work, see B. McSweeney, 'Hofstede's model of national cultural differences and their consequences: a triumph of faith – a failure of analysis', *Human Relations*, vol. 55, no. 1 (2002), pp. 89–118 and A.M. Soares, M. Farhangmeher and A.S. Shoham, 'Hofstede's dimensions of culture in international marketing studies', *Journal of Business Research*, vol. 60, no. 3 (2007), pp. 277–84.

18. On cross-cultural managerment also see R. Lewis, *When Cultures Collide: Managing Successfully across Cultures*, 2nd edn, Brealey, 2000, a practical guide for managers. It offers an insight into different national cultures, business conventions and leadership styles. Also S. Schneider and J.-L. Barsoux, *Managing across Cultures*, 2nd edn, Financial Times Prentice Hall, 2003.

19. For example, differences in regional cultures impacted on the integration of banking mergers in Nigeria, as shown by 'E. Gomes, D. Angwin and K. Melahi, HRM practices throughout the mergers and acquisition (M&A) process: a study of domestic deals in the Nigerian banking industry', *International Journal of Human Resource Management*, vol. 23, no. 14 (2012), pp. 2874–900.

20. A useful review of research on this topic is: T. Dacin, J. Goodstein and R. Scott, 'Institutional theory and institutional change: introduction to the special research forum', *Academy of Management Journal*, vol. 45, no. 1 (2002), pp. 45–57. For a more general review see G. Johnson and R. Greenwood, 'Institutional theory and strategy', in *Strategic Management: a Multiple-Perspective Approach*, edited by Mark Jenkins and V. Ambrosini, Palgrave, 2007.

21. This definition is taken from W. Scott, *Institutions and Organizations*, Sage, 1995.

22. The term 'recipe' was introduced to refer to industries by J.-C. Spender, *Industry Recipes: the Nature and Sources of Management Judgement*, Blackwell, 1989. We have broadened its use by applying it to *organisational fields*. The fundamental idea that behaviours are driven by a collective set of norms and values remains unchanged.

23. D. Deephouse, 'To be different or to be the same? It's a question (and theory) of strategic balance', *Strategic Management Journal*, vol. 20, no. 2 (1999), pp. 147–66.

24. E. Schein (see reference 15) and A. Brown, *Organisational Culture*, Financial Times Prentice Hall, 1998, are useful in understanding the relationship between organisational culture and strategy. For a useful critique of the concept of organisational culture see M. Alvesson, *Understanding Organizational Culture*, Sage, 2002.

25. Figure 5.4 is adapted from the original in P. Grinyer and J.-C. Spender, *Turnaround: Managerial Recipes for Strategic Success*, Associated British Press, 1979, p. 203.

26. A fuller explanation of the cultural web can be found in G. Johnson, *Strategic Change and the Management Process*, Blackwell, 1987, and G. Johnson, 'Managing strategic change: strategy, culture and action', *Long Range Planning*, vol. 25, no. 1 (1992), pp. 28–36.

27. A practical explanation of cultural web mapping is a 'white paper' by Gerry Johnson, 'Mapping and Re-mapping Organisational Culture: a Local Government Example', www.strategyexplorers.com.

28. See A.C.T. Smith and B. Stewart, 'Organizational rituals: features, functions and mechanisms', *International Journal of Management Reviews*, vol. 13, no. 2 (2011), pp. 113–33; and G. Islam and M.J. Zyphur 'Rituals in organizations: a review and expansion of current theory', *Group & Organization Management*, vol. 34 (2009), pp. 114–39.

29. For an explanation of strategic drift see G. Johnson, 'Rethinking incrementalism', *Strategic Management Journal*, vol. 9 (1988), pp. 75–91; and 'Managing strategic change – strategy, culture and action', *Long Range Planning*, vol. 25, no. 1 (1992), pp. 28–36. Also see E. Romanelli and M.T. Tushman, 'Organizational transformation as punctuated equilibrium: an empirical test', *Academy of Management Journal*, vol. 7, no. 5 (1994), pp. 1141–66. They explain the tendency of strategies to develop incrementally with periodic transformational change.

30. See D. Miller and P. Friesen, 'Momentum and revolution in organisational adaptation', *Academy of Management Journal*, vol. 23, no. 4 (1980), pp. 591–614.

31. John Naughton, 'The lessons we can learn from the rise and fall of Kodak', *Observer Discover*, 22 January 2012.

32. See D. Leonard-Barton, 'Core capabilities and core rigidities: a paradox in managing new product development', *Strategic Management Journal*, vol. 13 (1992), pp. 111–25.

33. This is a term used by Donald S. Sull in accounting for the decline of high-performing firms (see 'Why good companies go bad', *Harvard Business Review*, July/August (1999), pp. 42–52).

34. S. Hall, D. Lovallo and R. Musters, 'How to put your money where your strategy is', *McKinsey Quarterley* (March 2012).

35. In *The Icarus Paradox* (Harper-Collins, 1990) Danny Miller makes a convincing case that organisations' success leads to a number of potentially pathological tendencies, not least of which are the tendencies to inflate the durability of bases of success and to build future strategies relatively uncritically. Hence the idea of the Icarus paradox, building on the Greek mythological character, Icarus, who successfully built himself wings to fly but then flew too close to the sun such that they melted.

36. See G. Yip, T. Devinney and G. Johnson, 'Measuring long-term superior performance: the UK's long term superior performers 1984–2003', *Long Range Planning*, vol. 43, no. 3 (2009), pp. 390–413.

37. P. Klarner and S. Raisch, 'Move to the beat – rhythms of change and firm performance', *Academy of Management Journal*, vol. 56, no. 1 (2013), pp. 160–84.

Bonuses and 'gaming' at Barclays Bank

In 2012 Bob Diamond, the CEO of Barclays Bank, resigned in the wake of government, shareholder and media criticism of the bank's manipulation of the interbank lending rate, Libor. That criticism was often linked to a condemnation of the culture at Barclays, in particular the investment arm of the bank, which the UK Financial Services Authority called 'a culture of gaming' and BBC's *Panorama* programme dubbed a 'bonus culture'.

Quaker origins

What was so widely condemned as malpractice at Barclays seemed alien to a bank with its origins. The founding families were from the Quaker religious movement, with their emphasis on sobriety, pacificism and high ethical standards, and their descendants were still in important executive positions in the mid-twentieth century. As the *Financial Times* observed:

> 'In many ways the bank resembled a club and, as so often with British clubs, the thing worked surprisingly well despite its flaws ... It was, in fact, the most innovative of the British clearing banks in the post-war period. In 1967 it installed the world's first automated cash teller machine ... Barclays also came up with the first plastic payment device, Barclaycard, still outstandingly successful.'

The success did not continue: 1986 brought 'Big Bang', the deregulation of financial markets in the UK. One effect was the entry of US investment banks, so increasing competition and doing away with the 'clubby' culture of the past. Barclays responded by attempting a rapid growth strategy with disastrous results; by the early 1990s it needed to raise additional funds through two rights issues.

The development of investment banking

Barclays began in 1809 and, as Overend, Gurney & Co. built a reputation for accepting bills from other banks to reinvest in businesses – an early form of investment banking. However, poor investments led to bankruptcy in

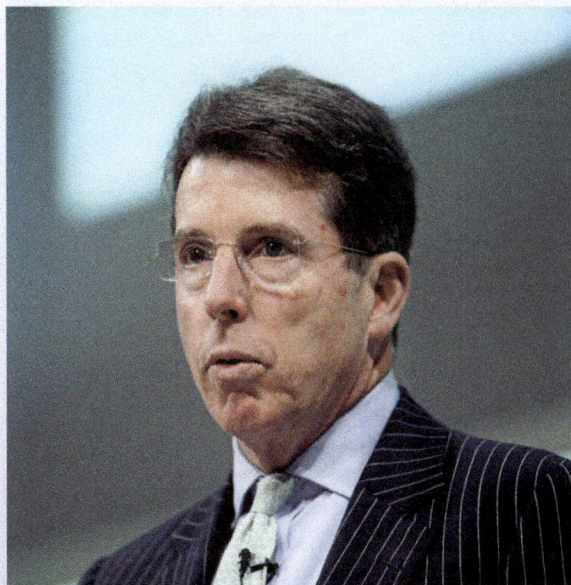

Bob Diamond

the 1890s contributing to the merger of several Quaker banks in 1896 to form Barclays. Barclays therefore inherited investment banking, risk aversion and a conservative approach to growth until the late 1980s.

The interest in investment banking received a huge impetus after Big Bang. Barclays embarked on acquisitions including a stock broker. The outcome was the formation of an investment bank – Barclays de Zoete Wedd (BZW). In common with other investment banks who got involved in equities trading, however, Barclays had great difficulty combining conventional and investment banking in a coherent model. As the *Financial Times* put it:

> 'The chief problem was culture. As Michael Lewis, author of Liar's Poker, a commentary on Wall Street in the 1980s, memorably put it, a commercial banker was someone who had a wife, a station wagon, 2.2 children and a dog that brought him his slippers when he returned home from work at 6 pm. An investment banker, by contrast, was a breed apart, a member of a master race of dealmakers. He possessed vast, almost unimaginable talent and ambition. If he had a

dog it snarled. He had two little red sports cars yet wanted four. To get them, he was, for a man in a suit, surprisingly willing to cause trouble.'

Investment banking was notorious for its hard work and 'hard play'. It was common for investment bankers to work through the night or to be seen to be doing so – stories had it that they would own two suit jackets so they could leave one on the back of the chair to pretend they were still in the office working. It was also a 'can-do' mentality which legitimated, for example, a day trip to Australia for a one-hour meeting. No expense was spared on flights, entertainment or accommodation provided a big deal was signed. There was also much visible excess with traders spending thousands of pounds a night at champagne bars.

The development of investment banking

In 1994 Martin Taylor, a former *Financial Times* journalist who had been chairman of Courtaulds Textiles, was appointed as chief executive of Barclays. His initial assessment was that BZW was underperforming in a highly competitive and overcrowded market. He decided to bring in new personnel and this included Bob Diamond, who had established a reputation as a trader in investment banking at CS First Boston in New York.

Martin Taylor's concerns continued. In 1997 he presented a paper to the board arguing that the various activities of BZW lacked scale in an increasingly global market and that Barclays should exit investment banking. The board did not accept the argument, believing that Barclays needed to further develop its investment banking. They did, however, succumb to investor pressure on the relatively low returns being generated from BZW and decided to dispose of its corporate finance business, leaving an emphasis on trading, Bob Diamond's area of expertise. Martin Taylor resigned in 1998.

Throughout the first decade of the new century, Bob Diamond's influence grew. A past employee of Barclays investment arm, interviewed in a BBC *Panorama* programme, claimed that Bob Diamond 'installed Wall Street values into Barclays; it was every man for himself . . . It was all about doing ever bigger deals' and being willing to take 'extreme risks' to make 'super profits' and generate huge bonuses for the traders involved. Diamond also grew the much criticised Structured Capital Markets 'tax planning' business, which many saw as Barclays 'tax avoidance' business. Employing only a hundred people by 2010 this business was generating £1 (1.2 euros;

$1.5) billion a year in profits. This was where the highest bonuses were paid.

Bob Diamond succeeded in growing the trading arm of the bank into a major profit contributor accounting for 58 per cent of Barclays overall pre-tax earnings by 2011. He also succeeded in achieving a powerful position on Wall Street for Barclays with what the *Financial Times* described as the 'opportunistic grab for Lehman Brothers' US business after its collapse in 2008'. His reward was to become chief executive of the whole bank early in 2011. Yet, there were already signs of future problems. There were investigations into the mis-selling of payment protection insurance by the retail banks and for the manipulation of the inter-bank lending rate, Libor, to generate unfair profits, in both of which Barclays was heavily involved. Traders at Barclays were under investigation for allegedly manipulating Californian electricity prices. There was widespread criticism of the bank's tax avoidance activities and public criticism of Bob Diamond's huge remuneration package, estimated by the BBC *Panorama* programme to be around £120 million between 2007 and 2012. While Barclays publicity still made reference to its Quaker heritage, its reputation was 'in tatters'. Bob Diamond resigned in 2012.

Bonuses and tribal bonding

Many attributed Barclays' problems to the 'bonus culture' so evident in the investment bank. The *Financial Times* quoted Philip Augar, who ran NatWest's global equities business between 1992 and 1995:

'The battleground between conventional bankers and investment bankers usually concerned pay and resources . . . the bonus round in an investment bank is the most important time of year. Get it wrong and the business unravels; pay too much and profitability is shot to ribbons. In a universal institution, the retail and commercial bankers often, maybe always, feel that too many of the investment profits are being paid to staff and inevitably resent the fact that investment bankers' bonuses are bigger than their own. For their part, the investment bankers always fear that the management wants to build the investment side on the cheap.'

Barclays was criticised for continuing to pay high bonuses to staff even after the financial crisis of 2008–9. BBC's *Panorama* calculated that in 2010–11 payments to shareholders had amounted to £1.4 billion while payment of bonuses for staff amounted to £6 billion. Martin Taylor, interviewed on the *Panorama* programme, argued that, in effect, shareholders were subsidising the payment of bonuses and that the bonus levels were unjustified.

However the *Guardian* newspaper argued that the roots of the problem were not just a matter of remuneration. It asked why people inside Barclays who knew what was happening with regard to Libor did nothing and suggested it was because of a culture 'of fierce tribal bonding':

'. . . it is clear that at least some people in finance are not primarily driven by money. But they are afraid, powerless, or both. Indeed, if you had to design a working environment that encouraged short-termist conformism and discouraged whistle blowing, then the finance sector would be your blueprint.

Take job security. In most big banks you can receive notice and find yourself being marched out of the building by security five minutes later. Some banks have annual "cullings", but even those who have avoided this have been going through redundancy rounds because of the harsh economic climate . . . If this creates a climate of fear, consider the average career pattern. Most people try to switch banks or roles every few years. Imagine when you know there is a huge problem in your bank – you also know it's time to move on to the next job.

Add to this the fact that people in finance are generally overpaid, so if they move to another industry they have to take a cut – which affects their ability to pay school fees and mortgages. That is assuming they can find a job – because (in 2012) the economy isn't exactly booming and skills that are highly valued in finance are next to worthless elsewhere.

Finally, there's the psychological dynamic, perhaps the strongest of all. Most high-flyers in investment banks describe their job not as work, but as a life. . . . Bankers work in teams, and the ethic there is: you are with us or you're against us. Speaking out makes you vulnerable. If you have a guilty secret hidden somewhere, they'll find it and expose you . . . If you go public about something in the bank you believe to be wrong, in one stroke you place yourself outside of that world. It's not just your job – it's your identity.'

The future

By 2012 and following the similarly questionable behaviour of UK banks such as RBS and Lloyds, as well as other European banks such as UBS and US banks such as J.P. Morgan, the whole business model of UK banks was being questioned. The Vickers Commission, established by the UK government to review the future of banking, was considering the separation of retail from investment banking. Early in 2013 there was a European Union directive that bankers' bonuses could be no more than one year's salary unless approved by shareholders. The new Barclays CEO Antony Jenkins also undertook a strategic review of the firm, examining the performance and reputation of 75 business units. In February 2013 this concluded that 39 business units were in good shape, 15 needed some attention, 17 needed serious attention to avoid closure or sale and 4 would definitely be sold or closed, 1 of which was its Structured Capital Markets business unit. Investment banking would remain with only modest proposed changes.

An internal memo from Jenkins to all Barclays staff also stated:

'Over a period of almost 20 years, banking became too aggressive, too focused on the short term, too disconnected from the needs of our customers and clients, and wider society. We were not immune at Barclays from these mistakes . . . Performance assessment will be based not just on what we deliver but on how we deliver it. We must never again be in a position of rewarding people for making the bank money in a way which is unethical or inconsistent with our values.'

Going forwards, Barclays staff would receive training on the central importance of five core values: respect, integrity, service, excellence and stewardship.

Sources: John Plender, 'How traders trumped Quakers', *Financial Times*, 6 July 2012.
Panorama: Inside Barclays: Banking on Bonuses, 11 February 2013. http://www.youtube.com/watch?v=FejXTeLAQ0Y.
Joris Luyendijk, 'Barclays emails reveal a climate of fear and fierce tribal bonding among traders', *Guardian*, 28 June 2012.
P. Jenkins, D. Schäfer and J. Thompson, 'Evangelism belies change at Barclays', *Financial Times*, 12 February 2013.

Questions

1 Undertake a cultural web analysis of Barclays Bank's investment arm.

2 How might your cultural web from 1 above and the cultural webs for Barclay's retail (Illustration 5.4) be of help to Antony Jenkins?

3 If you were Antony Jenkins, how might you draw on Barclay's history in order to redefine the company's strategy and culture?

COMMENTARY ON PART I
THE STRATEGY LENSES AND
THE STRATEGIC POSITION

The last five chapters have introduced a wide range of strategy concepts and frameworks. Some of these adopt an economic focus on market structures, for instance Chapter 2's five forces analysis. Others are more sociological, such as the highlighting of legitimacy in Chapters 4 and 5. Some concepts and frameworks emphasise opportunities for innovation, as in the strategy canvas of Chapter 2. Others stress conservatism in organisations, for example strategic drift and organisational culture in Chapter 5. Generally, the chapters assume objectivity in analysis, but issues such as the principal–agent problem in Chapter 4 warn of the scope for divergent political interests in organisations, while organisational culture can be a source of bias too. What should be clear from these chapters, therefore, is that there are many different ways of seeing strategy. The strategy lenses offer four basic approaches to exploring strategic issues, each emphasising their particular sets of concepts and frameworks, and each with distinct implications for practice.

The four strategy lenses are as follows:

- **The design lens views strategy development as a logical process of analysis and evaluation.** This is the most commonly held view about how strategy is developed and what managing strategy is about. It encourages objective analysis through the use of formal concepts and frameworks.

- **The experience lens views strategy development as the outcome of people's taken-for-granted assumptions and ways of doing things.** Given that strategies are chosen and implemented by people, then their experience is going to matter. Strategy through the experience lens puts people, culture and history centre stage in strategy development.

- **The variety lens* views strategy as the bubbling up of new ideas from the variety of people in and around organisations.** Top managers cannot know everything about their organisations and markets. According to the variety lens, therefore, strategy can emerge not just from the top, but also from the periphery and bottom of the organisation.

- **The discourse lens views language as important both for understanding and changing strategy and for managerial power and identity.** Managers are always using language to pursue their objectives. Through this lens, unpicking managers' discourse can uncover hidden meanings and political interests.

Exploring strategy through these four lenses is useful because they all raise different questions and suggest different insights. Think of everyday discussions you have. It is not unusual for people to say: 'But what if you looked at it this way instead?' Taking just one view can lead to a partial and perhaps biased understanding. Looking at an issue another way can give a much fuller picture, generating new and different insights. For example, is a proposed strategy the result of objective analysis or is it rather the reflection of the proposer's personal experience or political self-interest? The lenses can also prompt different options or solutions to strategic problems. For example, again, should organisations rely just on top managers to create new strategies, or rather expect future strategy to emerge from initiatives and experiments occurring at the bottom of the organisation? Thus taking a multi-perspective approach to strategy can help managers and students consider a wider range of issues and responses.

---

* In previous editions, the variety lens was known as the ideas lens.

The rest of this Commentary explains the four lenses in more detail. In particular, it will compare how each relates to the following three key dimensions of managing strategy:

- *Rationality*: the extent to which the development of strategy is rationally managed. The design lens assumes high rationality, but the other lenses question this.

- *Innovation*: the extent to which strategy is likely to develop innovative, change-oriented organisations, or alternatively consolidate past experience and existing power structures.

- *Legitimacy*: the extent to which strategy analysis and discourse fits with the expectations of key stakeholders, thereby reinforcing managers' power and identities in organisations.

This Commentary concludes with a short case on Nokia, illustrating how the four lenses can be used to explore a real company's strategy. There will be shorter Commentaries later in the book helping readers to reflect on the concepts and frameworks highlighted in Parts II and III. Meanwhile, this Commentary relates mostly to the material in the first five chapters of this book.

The design lens

The design lens evokes an image of the strategist as detached designer, drawing up precise blueprints distant from the messy realities of action. In terms of the three key dimensions, the design lens therefore puts a strong premium on rational analysis and decision-making (see Figure C.i).[1] Because of its overt commitment to optimising the performance of organisations, the design lens tends also to be highly legitimate, especially to owners and regulators. Rational analysis is what counts, not passion or intuition. However, this commitment to dry analysis can sometimes work against innovation.

The design lens is associated broadly with strategy theorists such as the former Lockheed Corporation strategic planner Igor Ansoff or the economics-trained Harvard Business School Professor Michael Porter.[2] It has its origins in traditional economists' expectations about perfect information and 'rational economic man', and is further informed by management science techniques for resource optimisation. The design lens is also how strategy is often explained in textbooks, by teachers and indeed by managers. The design lens makes the following three assumptions about how strategic decisions are made:

- *Systematic analysis is key*. Although there are many influences on an organisation's performance, careful analysis can identify those that are most significant. In this view, calculating

Figure C.i Design lens

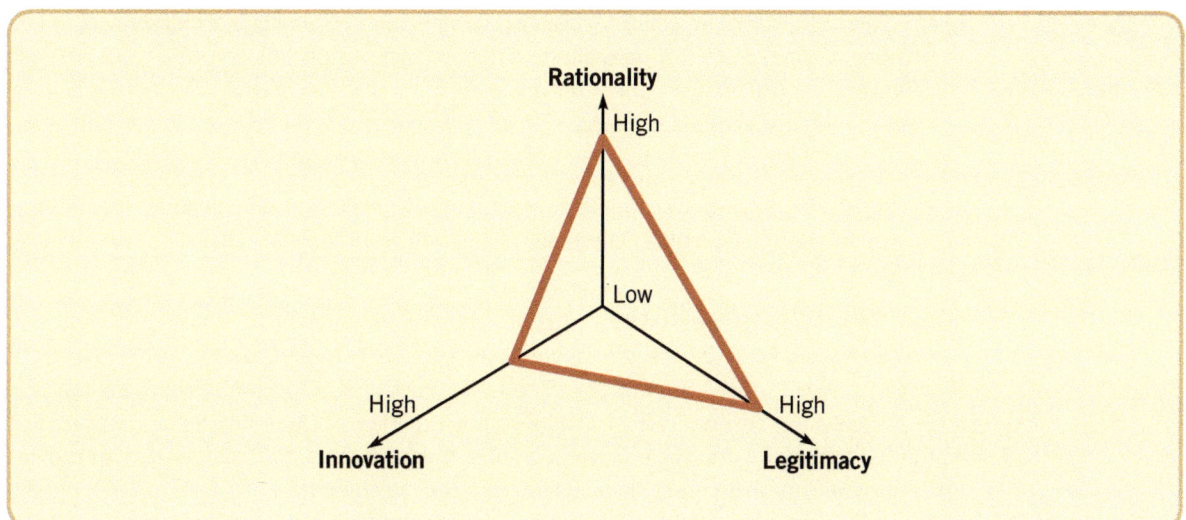

the attractiveness of an industry using Porter's five forces (Chapter 2), and identifying strategic capabilities using Valuable, Rare, Inimitable and Non-Substitutable criteria (Chapter 3), would be standard processes for estimating future performance.

- *Analysis precedes action.* In the design lens, strategy is generally seen as a linear process. Decisions about strategy are separate from and precede implementation. From this point of view, therefore, environmental analysis – for example, forecasting industry life cycles or projecting scenarios (Chapter 2) – is the crucial first step in strategy making.

- *Objectives should be clear.* Rational analysis and decision making need unambiguous criteria by which to evaluate options. Missions and visions (Chapter 4) should be set in advance as precisely as possible, with little scope for adjustment as new opportunities or constraints are discovered in action.

These design lens assumptions about how decisions should be made are in turn associated with two key views about the nature of organisations:

- *Organisations are hierarchies.* It is the responsibility of top management to plan the destiny of the organisation. The responsibility of the rest of the organisation is simply to implement the strategy decided at the top.

- *Organisations work mechanically.* This hierarchical approach implies a view of organisations as engineered systems or even machines. Pulling the right organisational levers should produce predictable results. Principal–agent problems can be controlled by the appropriate gearing of incentives (Chapter 4). Even organisational cultures (Chapter 5) can be designed from above.

Implications

The design lens has practical implications for both managers and students. From the design point of view, it is worth investing extensive time in formal analysis, especially economic forms of analysis. Formal strategic planning and financial calculations are crucial parts of the design lens approach. But even if strategic plans do not always produce the expected results, there are two further reasons for taking a design lens approach:

- *Dealing with complexity and uncertainty.* The design lens provides a means of talking about complex and uncertain issues in a rational, logical and structured way. Even if rational analysis can sometimes over-simplify or convey undue precision, it is usually better than just concluding that everything is all just too complicated for any kind of plan or calculation. Strategy is more than guesswork.

- *Meeting stakeholder expectations.* As well as the sheer analytical value of a design approach, adopting rational procedures is something that important stakeholders (see Chapter 4) such as banks, financial analysts, investors and employees typically expect. For these audiences, analysis is highly legitimate. Taking a design lens approach is therefore an important means of gaining the support and confidence of significant internal and external actors.

Employing the techniques of rational strategy analysis can also have implications for managerial power and personal identity. These side-effects will be discussed further with the discourse lens later.

In summary, the design lens is useful in highlighting the potential value of systematic analysis, step-by-step sequences and the careful engineering of organisational objectives and systems. However, the design lens does have its limits. In particular, a narrow design lens tends to underestimate the positive role of intuition and experience, the scope for unplanned and bottom-up initiatives, and the power effects of strategy analysis. Different lenses can provide useful insights into these other elements of strategy development.

Strategy as experience

The experience lens sees strategy as coming less from objective analysis on a clean sheet of paper and more from the prior experience of the organisation's managers. History and culture matter. Strategy is shaped by people's individual and collective taken-for-granted assumptions and ways of doing things. As indicated in Figure C.ii, the experience lens therefore places less emphasis than the design lens on rationality. It also sets low expectations in terms of innovation and change. Legitimacy is important, but this is defined in terms of personal experience or organisational routines and culture rather than simple appeal to analysis and 'the facts'.

The experience lens is based on a good deal of research about how strategies actually develop in the real world. As early as the 1950s, Nobel prize winner Herbert Simon was developing the Behavioral Theory of the Firm, based on how managers really behave.[3] The Behavioral Theory of the Firm underlines two kinds of problem for rational analysis in practice:

- *External constraints*: Behavioral theory points to real-world barriers to rationality: for example, it is practically impossible to obtain all the information required for comprehensive analysis; it is hard to forecast accurately in an uncertain future; and there are cost and time limits to undertaking complete analyses. In these conditions, managers often 'satisfice' when analysing strategic options: in other words, they settle for adequate solutions rather than the rational optimum.

- *Internal psychological limitations*: Behavioral theory underlines how managers suffer from 'bounded rationality', human limitations on the intellectual ability to process information and carry out analysis. They are also liable to 'cognitive bias': in other words, managers tend to be selective in the attention they give to issues and often automatically favour some types of solutions rather than others.

Cognitive bias is often based on managers' experience, both individual and collective:

- *Individual experience* can particularly shape managers' taken-for-granted assumptions about what is important and what kinds of actions work best. Influential sources of experience can be education and training. For example, accountants tend to see things differently to engineers; managers with MBAs are often accused of favouring excessively analytical approaches to solving problems. Other kinds of influential individual experience are personal careers.

Figure C.ii Experience lens

Thus a manager who had spent his or her career in the traditional television industry (for instance, the British BBC or the German ARD) might have found it difficult to recognise new internet media channels (for instance, YouTube) as true competitors. Differences in individual experience within an organisation can lead to debate and negotiation between managers with divergent views about what is important and what should be done. Stakeholder mapping (Chapter 4) of different managers' power and interest can be useful in resolving divergent views.

- *Collective experience* tends to form habitual patterns of thinking and acting, which can translate into standard responses to strategic issues. One kind of collective experience is encapsulated in organisational culture, as discussed in Chapter 5. Another kind of collective experience is reflected by national culture: so for instance Chinese and American managers may see the world differently (Chapter 5). A third kind of collective experience is embodied in industry 'recipes' (Chapter 5), based on years of regular interaction between existing competitors: for example, managers in the clothing industry come to believe over time that style is important to success, even though new ideas from outside the industry imply that new technologies may be the source of competitive advantage in the future. By contrast with individual experience, collective experience tends to suppress debate in management teams, and it becomes hard to challenge the consensus. A consequence can be 'strategic drift' (section 5.2), with everybody agreeing to continue as before, even in the face of environmental change.

Implications

The experience lens has significant implications for strategy. First there are two important warnings:

- *Analysis is typically biased to some extent*: all managers – and even students – bring their own particular experience to any set of strategic issues. It is very hard to analyse a situation as if from a clean sheet of paper. You should distrust claims to complete objectivity. Ask where people are coming from.

- *Watch out for undue conservatism*: experience is likely to lead to routinised responses, even to new problems. Tried-and-tested solutions become too legitimate; managers become powerful because of successes experienced in the past. 'Path dependency' and 'lock-in' are enduring risks (Chapter 5). Organisations can end up like old-fashioned generals, always fighting the last war.

On the other hand, the experience lens has some positive practical advice:

- *Analysis can cost more than it's worth*: because good information is hard and expensive to get, and because analysis can consume too much time, sometimes it is sensible simply to cut short information search and analysis. Depending on the availability of information and the ability to analyse it, beyond a certain point it might be sensible just to drop the analysis.

- *Experience may provide a good enough guide*: if analysis is not going to produce perfect answers, then relying on the rules-of-thumb and instincts of experienced managers may be at least as effective. Sometimes a quick response that is half right is better than an analytical response that is only slightly better but much slower.

- *Challenge the consensus*: while established rules-of-thumb can be effective, sometimes it is necessary to challenge the consensus in an organisation. As in Chapter 12, 'groupthink' is a risk. It is useful to encourage a diversity of views within an organisation, for instance via non-executive directors (Chapter 4), or by bringing in new leaders from outside the organisation (Chapter 11), or by encouraging more participation from all employees, for instance by 'jamming' (Chapter 15).

Strategy as variety

The extent to which the design and experience lenses help explain innovation is rather limited. The variety lens, on the other hand, emphasises innovation and change. However, as indicated in Figure C.iii, the variety lens puts low value on rational analysis and tends to give little weight to what is simply legitimate in an organisation. Viewed through the variety lens, strategies are seen as emerging from the different ideas that bubble up from the variety in and around organisations.

The variety lens builds on two theoretical perspectives from the natural sciences, both emphasising spontaneity. First there is *evolutionary theory*, in which natural phenomena evolve through a Darwinian process of variety, selection and retention.[4] Various genetic mutations emerge as more or less random experiments; some variations are selected for success by their environments; and these successful variations may be retained over the long term because of continuing good environmental fit. Second, there is *complexity theory*, where phenomena are characterised by complex, dynamic sets of interactions, from which surprisingly stable patterns of order may emerge.[5] An example is how hundreds of birds can move as a cohesive flock, without any bird apparently in command. In both evolutionary and complexity theories, variety in the form of many experiments or interactions leads to coherent and effective outcomes. These outcomes are generated spontaneously, with very little top-down direction.

Moving from nature to strategy, the variety lens de-emphasises the deliberate decision making of the design lens. Likewise, the emphasis on spontaneity contrasts with the conservatism of the experience lens. For human organisations, the three elements of evolutionary theory work as follows:

- *Variety*: organisations and their environments potentially offer a rich 'ecology' for the generation of different ideas and initiatives. There are many kinds of people and many kinds of circumstance. Sales people working closely with customers may be able to sense new opportunities at least as well as top managers at headquarters. Since people interact with their environment throughout the organisation, new ideas often come from low down in the hierarchy, not just from the top.[6] Complexity theorist Bill McKelvey refers to this as the 'distributed intelligence' of an organisation.[7] Variety can even come from apparent mistakes, just as genetic mutations come from imperfect genes. A famous example is Post-it notes, which originated from an 'imperfect' glue being applied to paper, but resulted in a semi-adhesive for which the researcher saw market potential.

Figure C.iii Variety lens

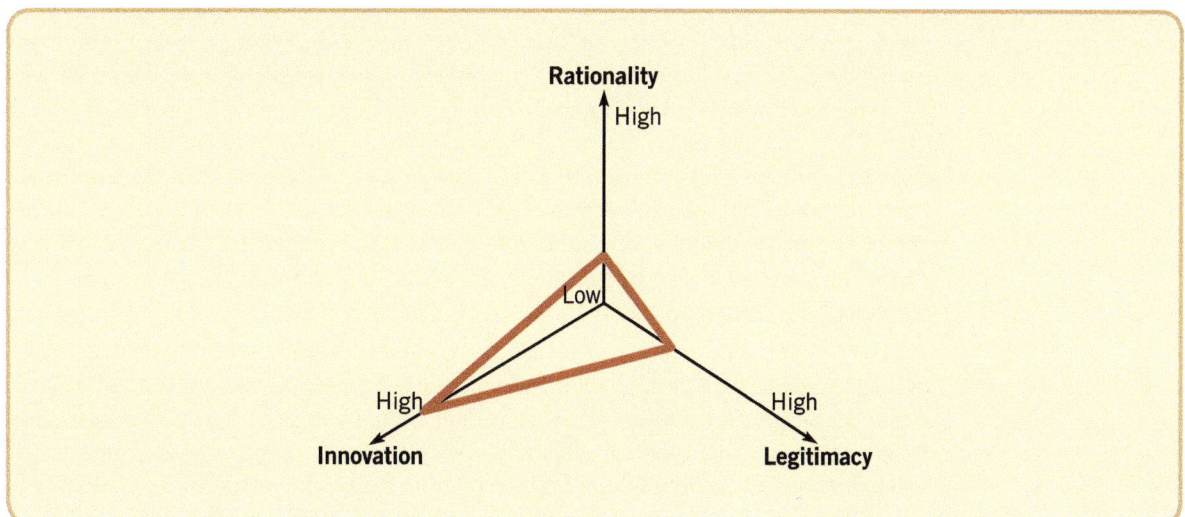

- *Selection*: in nature, selection is 'blind', determined by environmental fit rather than deliberate intervention. In organisations, selection can be nearly as blind, with strategies selected according to how well they match prevailing cultures or standard investment criteria. In this view, there is an 'internal ecology' within organisations, with ideas and initiatives winning out against competing ideas and initiatives according to their internal fit.[8] A good idea may fail simply because it does not meet existing selection rules, regardless of its overall merits: for example, a company may apply standard return on capital criteria that are outdated on the basis of the current real cost of capital (see Chapter 11 on strategy evaluation). On the other hand, as in complexity theory, ideas can gain rapid momentum as they attract 'positive feedback': the support of one important set of actors can attract the support of another, and the support of that set of actors attracts the support of still others, and so on in an escalating process. Thus selection mechanisms can be self-reinforcing, speeding the passage of both good and bad ideas.

- *Retention*: as well as processes of selection, there are processes of retention. Retention refers to the preservation and reproduction over time of selected variations.[9] Retention may happen as particular policies or preferences become embedded in the organisation. Retention may be achieved by instituting formal procedures: for example, job descriptions, accounting and control systems, management information systems, training and organisation structure. Often it is done through more informal processes of routinisation, in which simple repetition of certain routine behaviours leads to the eventual imprinting of such routines in the culture and capabilities of the organisation.

Implications

A key insight from the variety lens is that managers need to be wary of assuming they can wholly control the generation and adoption of new ideas. However, there are a number of things managers can do to foster initiatives and prevent the undue suppression of good ideas. At the same time, the variety lens points both managers and students to distinctive sources of innovation in organisations. We highlight three key implications:

- *Allow for emergence*: rather than being deliberately designed, strategies often emerge from the bottom and the periphery of organisations, accumulating coherence over time. As in Chapter 1, Henry Mintzberg's definition of strategy as an emergent 'pattern' rather than an explicit statement is widely relevant. Managers and students should not necessarily trust in the stated strategic vision and mission (Chapter 4), but rather look to what is actually happening, especially on the ground. The future of an organisation may well be emerging from somewhere far outside headquarters' formal initiatives.

- *Encourage interaction, experiment and change*: from a variety lens point of view, organisations can be too stable and ordered. To generate variety, managers should promote potentially disruptive interactions across internal and external organisational boundaries: cross-departmental initiatives are important internally and communication with customers, suppliers, partners and innovators should be extensive externally. Google encourages experiments by giving staff 20 per cent of their time to pursue their own projects. Complexity theorists prescribe regular change in order to stay at the dynamic 'edge of chaos', the delicate balancing point where organisations neither settle down into excessive stability nor topple over into destructive chaos.[10]

- *Attend to the rules*: if strategies tend get adopted according to their fit with established organisational cultures or investment criteria, then managers need to attend at least as much to setting the context for strategy as to individual strategic decisions. As above, managers should create a context conducive to interaction, experiment and change. But they should particularly attend to the selection and retention rules by which strategies are allowed to emerge. Drawing on complexity theory, Kathy Eisenhardt encourages the design of 'simple rules', clear guidelines for strategy selection and retention.[11] For example, the movie studio Miramax only selects movies that revolve round a central human condition (e.g. love), feature an appealing but flawed central character, and have a clear story-line. The Danish hearing aid company Oticon does not retain projects where any key team member chooses to switch from that project to another.

Strategy as discourse

In many ways management is about discourse. Managers spend 75 per cent of their time communicating: for example, gathering information, persuading others or following up decisions.[12] In particular, strategy has a high discursive component, involving both talk and text. Strategy is debated in meetings, written as formal plans, explained in annual reports and media releases, presented on PowerPoints, and communicated to employees.[13] The discourse lens recognises this discursive component as central to strategy. Here, as indicated in Figure C.iv, the legitimacy of discourse is particularly important. The importance of legitimacy, however, can work against both objective rationality and organisational innovation.

An important influence on the discourse lens is the work of the French philosopher Michel Foucault. Foucault stresses the subtle effects that language can have on understanding, power and personal identities. For example, he shows how changing scientific discourses in the seventeenth and eighteenth centuries redefined insanity as an illness rather than a natural foolishness.[14] The insane now had a new identity, medically ill, and became subject to a new power, the medical doctors with the task of curing them. Those taking a discourse lens are similarly sensitive to how strategy discourse can shape understanding, change personal identities and disseminate power.

These three effects of strategy discourse are explored as follows:

● *Shaping understanding*: the language of strategy has characteristics that make it convincing to others.[15] Its concepts and jargon have high legitimacy in many organisations. Here the discourse lens reveals the design lens in another light. The legitimacy of strategy discourse gives the analytic apparatus of the design lens a persuasiveness that often goes beyond the technical effectiveness of the analysis itself. Drawing on established techniques such as Porter' five forces (section 2.3.1) or fashionable concepts such as Blue Ocean strategy (section 2.4.3) can add to the authority of strategic recommendations. The ability to write

Figure C.iv Discourse lens

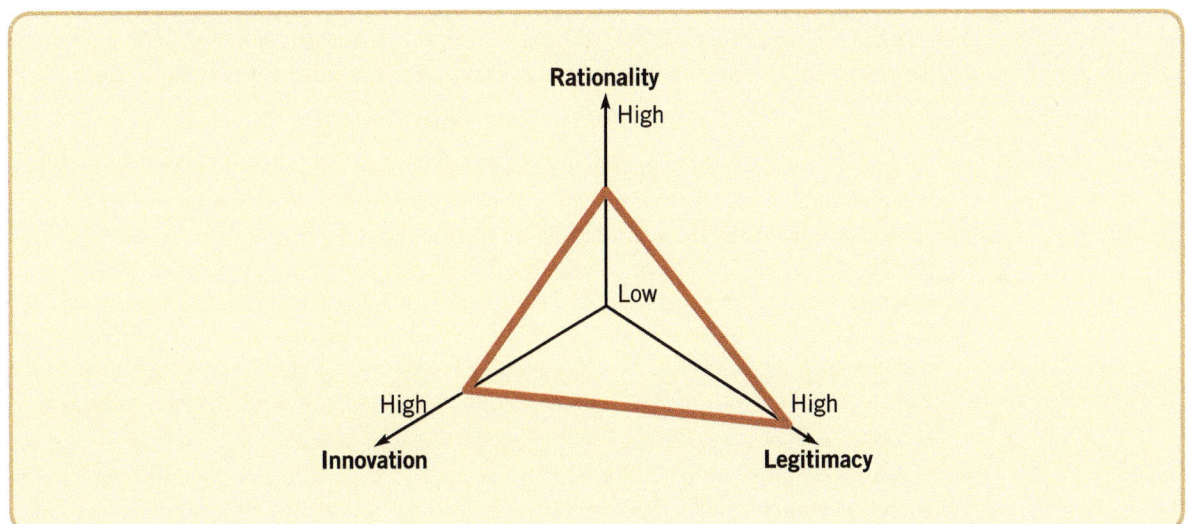

inspiring vision and mission statements (Chapter 4) can help motivate a whole organisation. The justification of strategic change by the radical rhetoric of hypercompetition (Chapter 2) or disruptive innovation (Chapter 8) may give legitimacy to radical actions that might otherwise be rejected as excessive. In other words, managers draw on the rhetoric of strategy and the apparent 'rightness' of strategy concepts to convince others they should comply.

- *Defining identities*: how managers talk about strategy also positions them in relation to others, either by their own deliberate choice or as a result of how they are perceived.[16] Discourse therefore influences the identity and legitimacy of managers as 'strategists'. The ability to use the rational analytical language of the design lens helps define managers as legitimate participants in the strategy process. Of course, sometimes other kinds of discursive identity may be appropriate. For example, in some contexts the language of the heroic leader (Chapter 14) or the innovative entrepreneur (Chapter 9) might offer more support for the decision-maker's identity than simple rational analyst. Whatever the precise identity, the assumptions built into strategy discourse are liable to affect behaviour. For example, lower-level managers and professionals who internalise the strategy discourse of competitiveness and performance as part of their identities come to prioritise those values in their everyday work, subordinating to some degree the administrative or professional values (such as equity or care) that might otherwise be important in their roles.

- *Instrument of power*: here strategy discourse is linked to power and control.[17] By understanding the concepts of strategy, or being seen to do so, top managers or strategy specialists are positioned as having the knowledge about how to deal with the really difficult problems the organisation faces. The possession of such knowledge gives them power over others who do not have it. Design lens discourse, with its commitment to demanding forms of technical analysis, can be particularly elitist and exclusive. Thus mastering the discursive language of the design lens offers a political advantage as well as an analytical one. At the same time, the internalisation of strategy discourse by employees renders them more compliant to the strategy: they see pursuing the strategy as a natural part of their role. In this sense discourse is associated with power when it attracts followers and is self-reproducing and self-reinforcing. Insofar as strategy discourse serves the interests of the powerful, it may suppress innovation and change and distort objective rational analysis from the point of view of the organisation as a whole.

Implications

The discourse lens suggests the importance of the appearance, as well as the reality, of rational argument. Through the discourse lens, strategies need to be legitimate, not simply correct. Strategy discourse, moreover, helps define who holds the identity of legitimate participant in strategic decision making and gives power to the decisions that are ultimately made. The fundamental lesson for managers and students is that the language of strategy matters.

The implications of the discourse lens have both instrumental and critical aspects:

- *Use strategy discourse skilfully*: the right discourse can add legitimacy to particular strategies or individuals in an organisation. This discourse needs to match particular contexts and circumstances. Justifying a strategy to a potential investor may call for a logical, highly quantitative financial case; explaining the same strategy to employees may involve emphasising implications for job security and career growth. For some organisations, the analytic discourse of the design lens will be a legitimate mode of justification; in other organisations, appeal to technical or professional values may be more effective. The instrumental value of the discourse lens lies in this: using the right language matters both for justifying and imposing strategies and for participating in strategy discussions in the first place.

- *Treat strategy discourse sceptically*: just as strategy discourse can be used instrumentally, so should managers and students be ready to take a critical perspective towards such discourse. Are concepts and frameworks being used as a smokescreen for some particular individuals or groups in an organisation to advance their sectional power and interests? Are strengths and weaknesses, threats and opportunities (section 3.4.4) being mystified or exaggerated? Are the grandiose ambitions of vision and mission statements just empty rhetoric (section 4.2)? Seeing strategy as discourse can prompt the healthy questioning of concepts, ideas and rhetorics that might otherwise be taken for granted. The discourse lens encourages managers and students to see through the surface language of strategy to uncover the deeper interests and motives behind it. Adopters of the discourse lens are naturally sceptical.

Conclusion

The core assumptions and the key implications of the four lenses of design, experience, variety and discourse are summarised in Table C.i. They are not offered here as an exhaustive list, but to crystalise the distinctive perspectives of each lens. Indeed, this Commentary as a whole is merely an introduction and you may usefully explore each of the lenses further yourself. After all, each of the lenses presented here actually includes several perspectives itself. For example, the variety lens builds on both evolutionary theory and complexity theory, each of which offers distinctive points of their own. So, within these lenses there are finer-grained insights to discover. The references at the end of this Commentary should help with deeper exploration of the lenses. In addition there are whole books written that provide multiple perspectives on strategy, from the four different ones that Richard Whittington offers, to the ten of Henry Mintzberg and his co-authors, or even the thirteen 'images' provided in the collection by Stephen Cummings and David Wilson.[18]

However, the overarching message that comes from all four lenses is this: in considering a topic like strategy, it is often valuable to take more than one perspective. The rational analysis of the design lens may not be enough. Use the experience lens to consider sources of

Table C.i A summary of the strategy lenses

	Strategy as:			
	Design	**Experience**	**Variety**	**Discourse**
Strategy develops through . . .	A logical process of analysis and evaluation	People's experience, assumptions and taken-for-granted ways of doing things	Ideas bubbling up from the variety of people in and around organisations	Managers seeking influence, power and legitimacy through the language they use
Assumptions about organisations	Mechanistic, hierarchical, rational systems	Cultures based on experience, legitimacy and past success	Complex, diverse and spontaneous systems	Arenas of power and influence shaped by discourse
Role of top management	Strategic decision-makers	Enactors of their experience	Creators of context	Manipulators of language
Key implications	Undertake careful and thorough analysis of strategic issues	Recognise that people's experience is central but also needs challenging	Look for ideas from the bottom and periphery of the organisation	See through strategy language to uncover hidden assumptions and interests

unconscious bias; take a variety lens approach to be sensitive to spontaneous initiatives from the bottom or periphery; stay sceptical by interpreting strategy talk through the discourse lens. It is because different perspectives are important that we shall return to the four lenses in the Commentaries at the ends of Parts II and III of this book. Throughout your course, we encourage you to approach the topics of strategy with eyes open to different points of view. To get into the habit, you might now want to consider the short Nokia case through the four strategy lenses.

REFERENCES

1. A useful review of the principles of rational decision making can be found in J.G. March, *A Primer on Decision Making: How Decisions Happen*, Simon & Schuster, 1994, Chapter 1, Limited liability, pp. 1–35.
2. An introduction to Ansoff's thought is Moussetis, 'Ansoff revisited', *Journal of Management History*, vol. 17, no. 1 (2011), pp. 102–25. R. Porter discusses his thinking in N. Argyres and A. McGahan, 'An interview with Michael Porter', *Academy of Management Executive*, vol. 16, no. 2, (2002), pp. 43–52.
3. An updated view of the Behavioral Theory of the Firm is in G. Gavetti, D. Levinthal and W. Ocasio, 'The Behavioral Theory of the Firm: assessment and prospects', *Academy of Management Annals*, vol. 6, no.1 (2012) pp. 1–40. A contrast with traditional economics is provided in M. Augier, 'The early evolution of the foundations for behavioral organization theory and strategy', *European Management Journal*, vol. 28, (2012), 84–102.
4. W.P. Barnett, and R. Burgelman, 'Evolutionary perspectives on strategy', *Strategic Management Journal*, vol. 17, S1 (2007), pp. 5–19.
5. P. Anderson, A. Meyer, K.M. Eisenhardt, K. Carley and A. Pettigrew, 'Introduction to the special issue: applications of complexity theory to organization science', *Organization Science*, vol. 10, no. 3 (1999), pp. 233–6.
6. See G. Johnson and A.S. Huff, 'Everyday innovation/everyday strategy', in G. Hamel, G.K. Prahalad, H. Thomas and D. O'Neal (eds), *Strategic Flexibility – Managing in a Turbulent Environment*, Wiley, 1998, pp. 13–27. Patrick Regnér also shows how new strategic directions can grow from the periphery of organisations in the face of opposition from the centre, see 'Strategy creation in the periphery: inductive versus deductive strategy making', *Journal of Management Studies*, vol. 40, no. 1 (2003), pp. 57–82.
7. Bill McKelvey, a complexity theorist, argues that the variety within this distributed intelligence is increased because individual managers seek to become better informed about their environment: see B. McKelvey, 'Simple rules for improving corporate IQ: basic lessons from complexity science', in P. Andriani and G. Passiante (eds), *Complexity, Theory and the Management of Networks*, Imperial College Press, 2004.
8. R. Burgelman and A. Grove, 'Let chaos reign, then rein in chaos – repeatedly: managing strategic dynamics for corporate longevity', *Strategic Management Journal*, vol. 28, no. 10 (2007), pp. 965–9.
9. B. McKelvey and H. Aldrich, 'Populations, natural selection, and applied organizational science', *Administrative Science Quarterly*, vol. 28, no. 1 (1983), pp. 101–28.
10. K.M. Eisenhardt and S. Brown, 'Competing on the edge: strategy as structured chaos', *Long Range Planning*, vol. 31, no. 5 (1998), pp. 786–9.
11. C B. Bingham, and K.M. Eisenhardt, 'Rational heuristics: the 'simple rules' that strategists learn from process experience.' *Strategic Management Journal*, vol. 32, no. 13 (2011) pp. 1437–64.
12. H. Mintzberg, *The Nature of Managerial Work*, Harper & Row, 1973.
13. See A. Spee and P. Jarzabkowski, 'Strategic planning as communicative process', *Organization Studies*, vol. 32, no. 9 (2011), pp. 1217–45. Also W. Küpers, S. Mantere and M. Statler, 'Strategy as storytelling: a phenomenological collaboration', *Journal of Management Inquiry*, vol. 22, no. 1 (2013), pp. 83–100.
14. M. Foucault, *Discipline and Punish*, Vintage, 1995.
15. D. Barry and M. Elmes, 'Strategy retold: toward a narrative view of strategic discourse', *Academy of Management Review*, vol. 22, no. 2 (1997).
16. S. Mantere and E. Vaara, 'On the problem of participation in strategy: a critical discursive perspective', *Organization Science*, vol. 19, no. 2 (2008), pp. 341–58.
17. C. Hardy and R. Thomas, 'Strategy, discourse and practice: the intensification of power', *Journal of Management Studies*, forthcoming (2013).
18. R. Whittington, *What is Strategy – and Does it Matter?*, Thompson, 2000; H. Mintzberg, B. Ahlstrand and J. Lampel, *Strategy Safari*, Prentice Hall, 1998; S. Cummings and D. Wilson, *Images of Strategy*, Sage, 2003.

Nokia through the lenses

In 2012, Nokia was in crisis. It had ceded leadership of the global mobile phone market to Samsung and its share price was less than 10 per cent of its peak just five years earlier. But the company's CEO Stephen Elop reminded employees and investors of the company's history. Nokia had been through crisis and transition before. Elop insisted it would do so again.

Nokia had started out in 1865 as a Finnish paper pulp mill. The company only began to take its modern form in 1966 when it had merged with the Finnish Rubber Works and the Finnish Cable Company to form a conglomerate with businesses ranging from rubber boots to aluminium parts. The Finnish Cable Works had established a small electronics department in 1960 in one corner of its main factory. This electronics department in turn spawned several businesses, including a mobile phone unit launched in 1979 through a joint venture with another Finnish company, Salora.

During the 1980s, Nokia became committed to an active diversification strategy, especially internationally. Businesses were acquired in the television and computer industries, and Salora itself was taken over in 1984. By 1987, an internal strategic planning document identified over 30 strategic business units in a Boston Consulting Group portfolio matrix (see Chapter 7), with mobile phone labelled one of several 'star' businesses ripe for investment.

But Nokia then hit a very rough patch. Its chairman and CEO committed suicide in 1988, and many of its industrial markets were hit hard by the collapse of the then Soviet Union. There was a period of losses and top management turmoil, from which finally emerged a new CEO, Jorma Ollila. Ollila had only arrived at Nokia in 1985, after an early career in the American investment bank Citibank. Since 1990, he had been head of the mobile phone business, then accounting for only 10 per cent of Nokia's total sales.

On appointment as CEO, Ollila had promised continuity. In fact, the company rapidly focused on mobile phones. By 1996, mobile phones accounted for 60 per cent of Nokia sales and two years later Nokia became the

Stephen Elop and Steve Ballmer

Source: Simon Dawson/Bloomberg via Getty Images

world's largest mobile phone company. Other businesses were divested, so that soon the only other substantial business was Nokia's telecommunications networks and infrastructure business (merged with Siemens in 2007).

Nokia's phone business flourished for more than a decade, until two cataclysmic events: first, Apple's launch of the iPhone in 2007 and then the 2009 launch of Google's Android operating system supported by companies such as HTC and Samsung. At the same time, Chinese manufacturers began to attack Nokia's position in low-cost phones, especially in developing markets. In 2010, Nokia responded to the growing pressure by appointing its first non-Finnish CEO, the Canadian Stephen Elop.

Elop joined from Microsoft, another company struggling in the phone market, though he himself had been responsible for Microsoft's Office products business. The new CEO launched a wide-ranging strategic review: 'The very first day I began, I sent out an email to all of the employees and I asked them:[17] what do you think I need to change? What do you think I need not or should not change? What are you afraid I'm going to miss?' A key issue that he and his management team struggled with during the first year was whether Nokia should continue with its own operating system. Operating systems are highly expensive to develop and sustain and need to be attractive to external software developers in order to secure a competitive range of apps. Within a few months, Elop and his team had decided to abandon Nokia's own operating system. There were two alternative operating systems available: Google's or Microsoft's. Elop inclined towards Microsoft. His reasoning was that Microsoft was the weaker of the two, and therefore needed Nokia more than Google did. Nokia also feared being just another Android phone manufacturer competing on the same basis as HTC or Samsung.

In February 2011, Elop released what would become his famous 'burning platform' memo to all employees. Nokia was compared to a man on a burning oil platform, who could only survive by leaping into the sea. Nokia had been too slow, and must now make a dramatic move. Elop told his employees: 'We poured gasoline on our own burning platform. I believe we have lacked accountability and leadership to align and direct the company through these disruptive times. We had a series of misses. We haven't been delivering innovation fast enough. We're not collaborating internally. Nokia, our platform is burning.' Several days later, he announced to the world that he was abandoning Nokia's own operating system in favour of Microsoft's, sealed by a public handshake with his old boss, Steve Ballmer, CEO of Microsoft. A senior Google executive commented on the Nokia–Microsoft alliance: 'two turkeys do not make an eagle'.

Nokia's first phones with the new operating system were not an immediate success and Nokia's losses deepened. By spring 2012, Stephen Elop was describing Nokia in terms of a famous Finnish long-distance runner, Lasse Virén, who had tripped during a race in 1972 but still won in the end: 'like Virén we are off the grass, on the track and running again'. But Nokia's share price was still only one fifth of what it had been at the time when the alliance had been announced. Many speculated that Nokia would not survive as an independent company at all. Indeed, in the summer of 2013, Nokia announced that its mobile phone business would be sold to Microsoft, with Stephen Elop returning to his original employer as well. Elop was now a leading candidate to succeed Steve Ballmer as CEO of Microsoft as a whole.

Key sources: J. Aspara, J.A. Lamberg, A. Laukia and H. Tikkanen, 'Strategic management of business model transformation: lessons from Nokia', *Management Decision*, vol. 49, no. 4 (2011), pp. 622–47; *Financial Times*, 9 February 2011, 11 April 2011 and 3 May 2012.

Questions

1 How could you use the design lens, the experience lens and the variety lens to account for the development of the mobile phone business within Nokia?

2 How could you use the design lens and the experience lens to explain Stephen Elop's adoption of the Microsoft operating system?

3 Comment on Stephen Elop's changing language from a discourse lens perspective.

PART II

STRATEGIC CHOICES

This part explains strategic choices in terms of:

- How organisations relate to competitors in terms of their competitive business strategies.

- How broad and diverse organisations should be in terms of their corporate portfolios.

- How far organisations should extend themselves internationally.

- How organisations are created and innovate.

- How organisations pursue strategies through organic development, acquisitions or strategic alliances.

Strategic
Position

Business

Corporate   **Strategic Choices**   International

Strategy
in Action

Innovation   Acquisitions
& Alliances

INTRODUCTION TO PART II

This part is concerned with the strategic choices, or options, potentially available to an organisation for responding to the positioning issues discussed in Part I of the book. There are three overarching choices to be made as shown in Figure II.2. These are:

- Choices as to *how an organisation at a business level positions itself in relation to competitors.* This is a matter of deciding how to compete in a market. For example, should the business compete on the basis of cost or differentiation? Or is competitive advantage possible through being more flexible and fleet-of-foot than competitors? Or is a more cooperative approach to competitors appropriate? These *business strategy* questions are addressed in Chapter 6.

- Choices of *strategic direction*: in other words, which products, industries and markets to pursue. Should the organisation be very focused on just a few products and markets? Or should it be much broader in scope, perhaps very diversified in terms of both products (or services) and markets? Should it create new products or should it enter new territories? These questions relate to corporate strategy, addressed in Chapter 7, international strategy in Chapter 8 and innovation and entrepreneurial strategy, as discussed in Chapter 9.

- Choices about *methods by which to pursue strategies.* For any of these choices, should they be pursued independently by organic development, by acquisitions or by strategic alliances with other organisations? This is the theme of Chapter 10.

The discussion in these chapters provides frameworks and rationales for a wide range of strategic choices. But some words of warning are important here:

- *Strategic choices relate back to analysis of strategic position.* Part I of the book has provided ways in which strategists can identify forces at work in the business environment (Chapter 2), identify and build on strategic capabilities (Chapter 3), meet stakeholder expectations (Chapter 4) and build on the benefits, as well as be aware of the constraints, of their organisation's historical and cultural context (Chapter 5). Exploring these issues will provide the

Figure II.2 Strategic choices

Strategic choices

Business strategy	Strategic directions	Strategy methods
Choices about business positioning relative to competitors	Choices of products, industries and markets to pursue	How to pursue strategies: organic, acquisition or alliance

foundation for considering strategic options. However, the *Exploring Strategy* Model (Figure 1.2) implies that issues of position, choice and action overlap. Thus working through the choices of Part II is also likely to feed back into the initial analysis of strategic position. Similarly, the potential of some strategic choices will only be revealed in action, the theme of Part III.

- *Key strategic issues*. Choices have to be made in the context of an organisation's strategic position, of course. But here it is important that the analysis of strategic position distinguishes the *key strategic issues* from all the many positioning issues that are likely to arise. Analysis needs to avoid producing a very long list of observations without any clarity of what such key issues are. There is no single 'strategy tool' for this. Identifying key strategic issues is a matter of informed judgement and, because managers usually work in groups, of debate. The analytic tools provided can help, but are not a substitute for judgement.

6

BUSINESS STRATEGY

Learning outcomes

After reading this chapter you should be able to:

- Identify *strategic business units* (SBUs) in organisations.

- Assess business strategy in terms of the generic strategies of *cost leadership*, *differentiation* and *focus*.

- Identify business strategies suited to *hypercompetitive* conditions.

- Assess the benefits of *cooperation* in business strategy.

- Apply principles of *game theory* to business strategy.

Key terms

competitive advantage p. 193

competitive strategy p. 193

cost-leadership strategy p. 194

differentiation p. 197

focus strategy p. 199

game theory p. 212

strategic business unit p. 192

strategic lock-in p. 204

MyStrategyLab

MyStrategyLab is designed to help you make the most of your studies. Visit **www.pearsoned.co.uk/mystrategylab** to discover a wide range of resources, including:

- A personalised **Study plan** that will help you understand core concepts

- **Audio and video clips** that put the spotlight on strategy in the real world

- **Online glossaries and flashcards** that provide helpful reminders when you're looking for some quick revision.

(6.1) INTRODUCTION

This chapter is about a fundamental strategic choice: what strategy should a business unit (or other organisational subunit) adopt in its market? Business strategy questions are fundamental both to standalone small businesses and to all the many business units that typically make up large diversified organisations. Thus a restaurant business has to decide a range of issues such as menus, décor and prices in the light of competition from other restaurants locally. Similarly, in a large diversified corporation such as Unilever or Nestlé, every business unit must decide how it should operate in its own particular market. For example, Unilever's ice-cream business has to decide how it will compete against Nestlé's ice-cream business on a range of dimensions including product features, pricing, branding and distribution channels. These kinds of *business* strategy issues are distinct from the question as to whether Unilever should own an ice-cream business in the first place: this is a matter of *corporate* strategy, the subject of Chapter 7.

Figure 6.1 shows the main themes that provide the structure for the rest of the chapter. Starting from a definition of *strategic business units* (SBUs), the chapter has two main themes:

- *Generic competitive strategies*, including *cost leadership*, *differentiation*, *focus* and *hybrid* strategies. An important theme here will be how far these strategies are sustainable over time and here *strategic lock-in* is often important.

- *Interactive strategies*, building on the notion of generic strategies to consider interaction with competitors, especially in *hypercompetitive environments*, and including both *cooperative strategies* and *game theory*.

Business strategy is not just relevant to the private business sector. Charities and public-sector organisations both cooperate and compete. Thus charities compete between each other for support from donors. Public-sector organisations also need to be 'competitive' against comparable organisations in order to satisfy their stakeholders, secure their funding and protect themselves from alternative suppliers from the private sector. Schools compete in terms of examination results, while hospitals compete in terms of waiting times, treatment survival

Figure 6.1 Business strategy

rates and so on. Although some of the detailed implications may vary between sectors, wherever comparison is possible with other similar organisations, basic principles of business strategy are likely to be relevant. Very few organisations can afford to be demonstrably inferior to peers, and almost all have to make choices on key competitive variables such as costs, prices and quality.

(6.2) IDENTIFYING STRATEGIC BUSINESS UNITS

The starting point for business strategy is identifying the relevant business unit. A **strategic business unit** (SBU) **supplies goods or services for a distinct domain of activity**. A small business focused on a single market, such as a restaurant or specialist retailer, would count as a strategic business unit. More commonly, though, SBUs refer to the distinct businesses within a large diversified corporation (sometimes these SBUs are called 'divisions' or 'profit centres'). For example, Nestlé has SBUs focused on Confectionery products, Beverage products and Dairy products, among others. Typically within a large diversified corporation, each SBU will have responsibility for its own business strategy and profit performance. In a large public-sector organisation, such as a local authority, individual schools might be considered as SBUs, with their domain of activity being education in a geographical area.

Thus the SBU concept has three effects within large organisations. First, SBUs decentralise initiative to smaller units within the corporation as a whole. In Nestlé, Beverages can pursue its business strategy without continuously seeking permission from central headquarters for minor adjustments (see also section 7.6 on the role of the centre). Second, SBUs allow large corporations to vary their business strategies according to the different needs of the various external markets they serve. Nestlé does not have to impose the same business strategy (e.g. a focus on supermarket distribution) across all its SBUs. Finally, the SBU concept encourages accountability. If managers determine the business strategy for their own SBU, then they can be held accountable for the success or failure of that strategy.

Identifying the right boundaries for SBUs is often complex.[1] Distinct markets can be defined at different levels of analysis: for example, Nestlé's Confectionery business could be further segmented by target market (the mass market KitKat, or the sophisticated Cailler brand), distribution channel (supermarket or small retailer) or geography (Europe or Asia). In many corporations, SBU boundaries change frequently as well: the computer company Dell is well known for reorganising its SBUs continuously, as market conditions change and units get too big. There are two basic criteria that can help in identifying appropriate SBUs:

● *Market-based criteria.* Different parts of an organisation might be regarded as the same SBU if they are targeting the same *customer types*, through the same sorts of *channels* and facing similar *competitors*. On the other hand, it would usually be sensible to distinguish a unit tailoring products or services to specific local needs from one that offers standardised products or services globally.

● *Capabilities-based criteria.* Parts of an organisation should only be regarded as the same SBU if they have similar strategic capabilities. Many traditional retailers or financial services companies operate their internet services as distinct SBUs. Even though they may be targeting very similar customers, the capabilities involved in the internet-based businesses are typically too different to the original physical stores or outlets to manage within the same unit.

(6.3) GENERIC COMPETITIVE STRATEGIES

This section introduces the competitive element of business strategy, with cooperation addressed particularly in section 6.4. **Competitive strategy is concerned with how an SBU strategic achieves competitive advantage in its domain of activity.** Competitive strategy therefore involves issues such as costs, product features and branding. In turn, **competitive advantage is about how an SBU creates value for its users both greater than the costs of supplying them and superior to that of rival SBUs.** Competitive advantages should underpin competitive strategies. There are two important features of competitive advantage. To be *competitive* at all, the SBU must ensure that customers see sufficient value that they are prepared to pay more than the costs of supply. To have an *advantage*, the SBU must be able to create greater value than competitors. In the absence of a competitive advantage, an SBU's competitive strategy is always vulnerable to competitors with better products or offering lower prices.

Michael Porter[2] argues that there are two fundamental means of achieving competitive advantage. An SBU can have structurally lower costs than its competitors. Or it can have products or services that are 'differentiated' from competitors' products in ways that are so valued by customers that it can charge higher prices. In defining competitive strategies, Porter adds a further dimension based on the scope of customers that the business chooses to serve. Businesses can choose to focus on narrow customer segments, for example a particular demographic group such as the youth market. Alternatively they can adopt a broad scope, targeting customers across a range of characteristics such as age, wealth or geography.

Porter's distinctions between cost, differentiation and scope define a set of 'generic' strategies: in other words, basic types of strategy that hold across many kinds of business situations. These three generic strategies are illustrated in Figure 6.2. In the top left-hand corner is a strategy of *cost leadership*, as exemplified in the British women's clothing market by retailers such as Primark. Primark seeks to use large economies of scale and tight cost discipline to serve a wide

Figure 6.2 Three generic strategies

range of women with reasonably fashionable clothing at a good price. Monsoon's shops pursue a strategy of *differentiation*, offering arty styles ('boho chic') to women across a range of ages at significantly higher prices. The third generic strategy is *focus*, involving a narrow competitive scope. Porter distinguishes between cost focus and differentiation focus, but for him narrow scope is such a distinctive fundamental principle that these two are merely variations on the same basic theme of narrowness. For example, Evans targets only women needing larger-sized clothing, achieving a higher price for its distinctive products (promoted by Beth Ditto) through a *differentiation focus* strategy. On the other hand, the clothing lines of the major supermarkets target shoppers who are simply looking for good-value standard clothing for their families, a *cost focus* strategy. The rest of this section discusses these three generic strategies in more detail.

6.3.1 Cost leadership

Cost-leadership strategy involves becoming the lowest-cost organisation in a domain of activity. There are four key *cost drivers* that can help deliver cost leadership, as follows:

- *Input costs* are often very important, for example labour or raw materials. Many companies seek competitive advantage through locating their labour-intensive operations in countries with low labour costs. Examples might be service call centres in India or manufacturing in China. Location close to raw material sources can also be advantageous, as for example the Brazilian steel producer CSN which benefits from its own local iron-ore facilities.

- *Economies of scale* refer to how increasing scale usually reduces the average costs of operation over a particular time period, perhaps a month or a year. Economies of scale are important wherever there are high fixed costs. Fixed costs are those costs necessary for a level of output: for example, a pharmaceutical manufacturer typically needs to do extensive R&D before it produces a single pill. Economies of scale come from spreading these fixed costs over high levels of output: the average cost due to an expensive R&D project halves when output increases from one million to two million units. Economies of scale in purchasing can also reduce input costs. The large airlines, for example, are able to negotiate steep discounts from aircraft manufacturers. For the cost-leader, it is important to reach the output level equivalent to the *minimum efficient scale*. Note, though, that *diseconomies of scale* are possible. Large volumes of output that require special overtime payments to workers or involve the neglect of equipment maintenance can soon become very expensive. As in Figure 6.3, therefore, the economies of scale curve is typically somewhat U-shaped, with the average cost per unit actually increasing beyond a certain point.

- *Experience*[3] can be a key source of cost efficiency. The *experience curve* implies that the cumulative experience gained by an organisation with each unit of output leads to reductions in unit costs (see Figure 6.3). For example, for many electronic components per unit costs can drop as much as 95 per cent every time the accumulated volume doubles. There is no time limit: simply the more experience an organisation has in an activity, the more efficient it gets at doing it. The efficiencies are basically of two sorts. First, there are gains in labour productivity as staff simply learn to do things more cheaply over time (this is the specific *learning curve* effect). Second, costs are saved through more efficient designs or equipment as experience shows what works best. The experience curve has three important implications for business strategy. First, entry timing into a market is important: early entrants into a market will have experience that late entrants do not yet have and so will gain a cost advantage. Second, it is important to gain and hold market share, as companies with higher market

Figure 6.3 Economies of scale and the experience curve

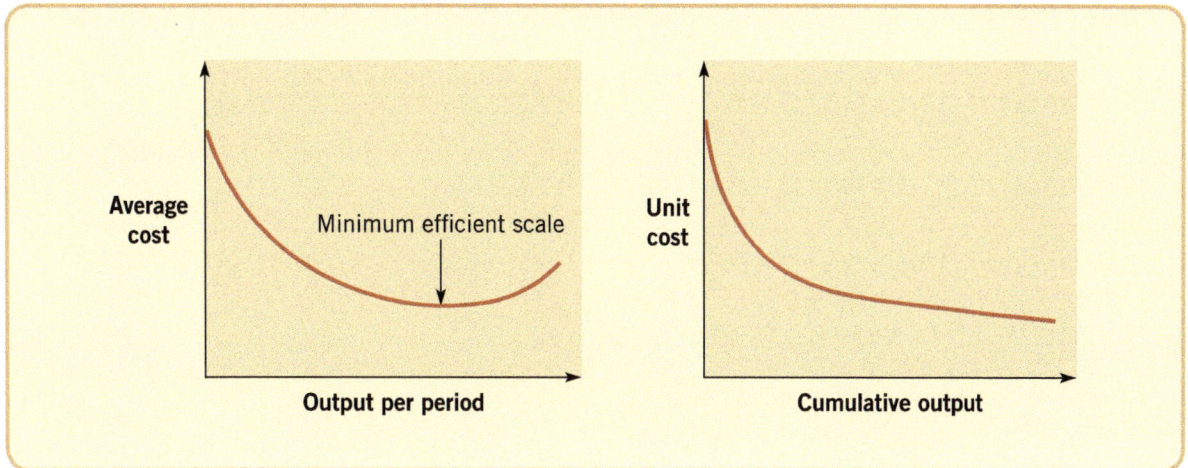

share have more 'cumulative experience' simply because of their greater volumes. Finally, although the gains from experience are typically greatest at the start, as indicated by the steep initial curve in Figure 6.3, improvements normally continue over time. Opportunities for cost reduction are theoretically endless. Figure 6.3 compares the experience curve and economies of scale in order to underline the contrast here. Unlike scale, where diseconomies appear beyond a certain point, the experience curve implies at worst a flattening of the rate of cost reduction. Cost savings due to accumulated experience are continuously available.

- *Product/process design* also influences cost. Efficiency can be 'designed in' at the outset. For example, engineers can choose to build a product from cheap standard components rather than expensive specialised components. Organisations can choose to interact with customers exclusively through cheap web-based methods, rather than via telephone or stores. Organisations can also tailor their offerings in order to meet the most important customer needs, saving money by ignoring others: this, arguably, is the strategy of Barnet, the 'easy-Council' (Illustration 6.1). In designing a product or service, it is important to recognise *whole-life costs*: in other words, the costs to the customer not just of purchase but of subsequent use and maintenance. In the photocopier market, for example, Canon eroded Xerox's advantage (which was built on service and a support network) by designing a copier that needed far less servicing.

Porter underlines two tough requirements for cost-based strategies. First of all, the principle of competitive advantage indicates that a business's cost structure needs to be *lowest* cost (i.e. lower than all competitors'). Having the second-lowest cost structure implies a competitive disadvantage against somebody. Competitors with higher costs than the cost-leader are always at risk of being undercut on price, especially in market downturns. For businesses competing on a cost basis, cost leadership is always more secure than being second or third in terms of costs.

Porter's second requirement is that low cost should not be pursued in total disregard for quality. To sell its products or services, the cost-leader has to be able to meet market standards. For example, low-cost Chinese car producers seeking to export into Western markets need to offer not only cars that are cheap, but cars that meet acceptable norms in terms of style, service network, reliability, resale value and other important characteristics. Cost-leaders have two options here:

ILLUSTRATION 6.1

easyCouncils: a not so easy low-cost strategy

The London Borough of Barnet has chosen a budget airline model for its services, on the lines of easyJet.

In 2008–9, with pressures on budgets increasing, Conservative-Party-controlled councils in the United Kingdom were looking to save costs by adopting the low-cost model pioneered by airlines such as Ryanair and easyJet. Barnet, a borough council in North London with a population of over 300,000, is one of the pioneers.

The Conservative borough council was led at the time by a former PwC management consultant, Mike Freer. In a context of falling central government subsidies, and wanting to save local taxes, the council was looking to cut costs by £15 m (~€16.5 m; ~$22.5 m) a year. In 2008, the council launched a consultation process on radical reform called 'Future Shape'. In 2009, it declared its intention to adopt a budget airline model, which council officials dubbed 'easyCouncil'.

Mike Freer gave some examples. Just as budget airlines allow passengers to pay extra for priority boarding, in future householders will be able to pay extra to jump the queue in order to get faster responses on planning applications for new buildings or house extensions. Similarly, as airline passengers can choose whether to have a meal or not (and pay accordingly), users of adult social care will be allowed to choose their own options. Freer explained to the *Guardian*:

'In the past we would do things for our residents rather than letting them choose for themselves. We would tell them they need one hour help shopping, or one hour cleaning, meals-on-wheels, and they would get it, like it or not. Instead, we will assess what level of personal care they need, place a value on it and give them the budget. If they say, "Frankly, I'd like a weekend in Eastbourne [a holiday resort]", they can have it.'

Opposition Labour leader Alison Moore warned in the *Guardian*:

'There is a real danger of problems in the local community and that vulnerable people will lose out. People who are dependent on care services may find that they aren't there at the same quality as before.'

None the less, the new low-cost strategy was launched in 2009. Unfortunately, the costs of retraining staff, building an in-house delivery team, hiring consultants and closing facilities were higher than originally projected. The council estimated it spent £1.5 m on delivering the first year of the reform programme. On the other hand, savings were slower to come through than expected, with a series of strikes by council workers resisting job cuts and the transfer of many employees to private-sector subcontractors. Savings in the first year were just £1.4 m, less than half of what had been projected. Alison Moore, leader of the Opposition, commented: 'Barnet claim that easy-Council is all about a relentless drive for efficiency, so it is absurd that in the first year, they've spent more money than they've saved.' By this time, Mike Freer had moved on to become a Member of Parliament. However, Lynne Hillan, the new council leader, said it was too soon to judge. Big savings would come soon: 'The programme took longer to establish than planned because we took the decision to develop an in-house team of officers. I've no doubt this will give us the most efficient process and the greatest long-term savings.'

Sources: Guardian, 27 August 2009; *Guardian*, 26 October 2010; *The Economist*, 22 September 2012.

Questions

1 What are the advantages and disadvantages of this approach to low-cost council services?

2 In what sense do borough councils 'compete'?

Figure 6.4 Costs, prices and profits for generic strategies

- *Parity* (in other words, equivalence) with competitors in product or service features valued by customers. Parity allows the cost-leader to charge the same prices as the average competitor in the marketplace, while translating its cost advantage wholly into extra profit (as in the second column of Figure 6.4). The Brazilian steel producer CSN, with its cheap iron-ore sources, is able to charge the average price for its steel, and take the cost difference in greater profit.

- *Proximity* (closeness) to competitors in terms of features. Where a competitor is sufficiently close to competitors in terms of product or service features, customers may only require small cuts in prices to compensate for the slightly lower quality. As in the third column in Figure 6.4, the proximate cost-leader still earns better profits than the average competitor because its lower price eats up only a part of its cost advantage. This proximate cost-leadership strategy might be the option chosen initially by Chinese car manufacturers in export markets, for example.

6.3.2 Differentiation strategies

For Porter, the principal alternative to cost leadership is differentiation.[4] **Differentiation involves uniqueness along some dimension that is sufficiently valued by customers to allow a price premium.** Relevant points of differentiation vary between markets. Within each market too, businesses may differentiate along different dimensions. Thus in clothing retail, competitors may differentiate by store size, locations or fashion. In cars, competitors may differentiate by safety, style or fuel efficiency. Where there are many alternative dimensions that are valued by customers, it is possible to have many different types of differentiation strategy in a market. Thus, even at the same top end of the car market, BMW and Mercedes differentiate in different ways, the first typically with a sportier image, the second with more conservative values.

Figure 6.5 Mapping differentiation in the US airline industry

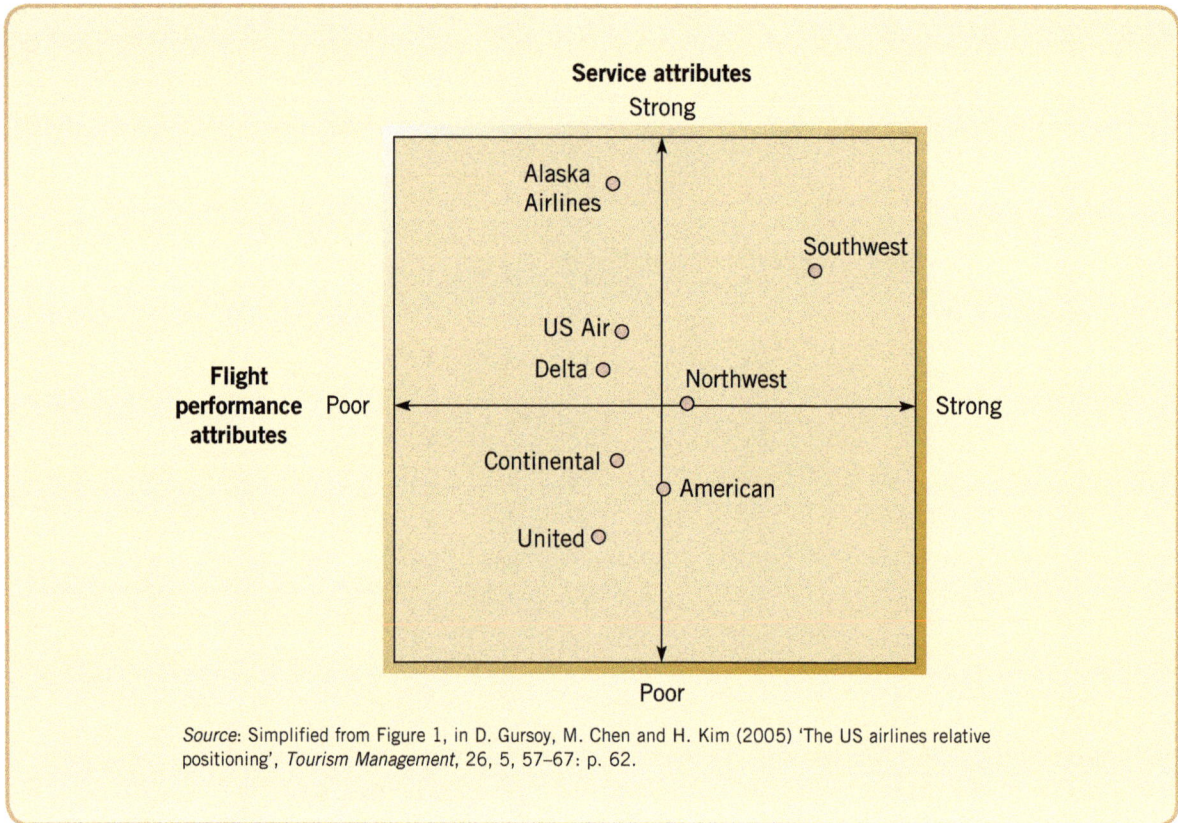

Source: Simplified from Figure 1, in D. Gursoy, M. Chen and H. Kim (2005) 'The US airlines relative positioning', *Tourism Management*, 26, 5, 57–67: p. 62.

The strategy canvas provides one means of mapping these various kinds of differentiation (see section 2.4.3).

Managers can identify potential for differentiation by using perceptual mapping of their products or services against those of competitors. For example, Figure 6.5 maps customer perceptions of American airline companies in the 2000s along two bundles of attributes: flight performance attributes such as delays, and service attributes such as baggage problems or boarding complaints. Most of the larger airlines are quite closely bunched together. For example, US Air and Delta are not significantly differentiated from each other in terms of on-time flights, and they are perceived similarly in terms of service elements such as boarding, ticketing and reservations. One airline that does stand out as a differentiator is Southwest, which does well in terms of both flight delays and service. In the period studied, Southwest was also the most profitable of these airlines. It seems that Southwest was able to differentiate on attributes that were highly valued by its customers.

However, the attributes on which to differentiate need to be chosen carefully. Differentiation strategies require clarity about two key factors:

● *The strategic customer.* It is vital to identify clearly the strategic customer on whose needs the differentiation is based. This is not always straightforward, as discussed in section 2.4.2. For example, for a newspaper business, the strategic customers could be readers (who pay a purchase price), advertisers (who pay for advertising), or both. Finding a distinctive means of prioritising customers can be a valuable source of differentiation.

- *Key competitors.* It is very easy for a differentiator to draw the boundaries for comparison too tightly, concentrating on a particular niche. Thus specialist Italian clothing company Benetton originally had a strong position with its specialist knitwear shops. However, it lost ground because it did not recognise early enough that general retailers such as Marks & Spencer could also compete in the same product space of colourful pullovers and similar products.

There is an important condition for a successful differentiation strategy. Differentiation allows higher prices, but usually comes at a cost. To create a point of valuable differentiation typically involves additional investments, for example in R&D, branding or staff quality. The differentiator can expect that its costs will be higher than those of the average competitor. But, as in the fourth column of Figure 6.4, the differentiator needs to ensure that the additional costs of differentiation do not exceed the gains in price. It is easy to pile on additional costs in ways that are not valued sufficiently by customers. The historic failures under British ownership of the luxury car companies Rolls-Royce and Bentley against top-end Mercedes cars are partly attributable to the expensive crafting of wood and leather interiors, the full cost of which even wealthy customers were not prepared to pay for. Just as cost-leaders should not neglect quality, so should differentiators attend closely to costs, especially in areas irrelevant to their sources of differentiation. As in Illustration 6.2, Volvo's differentiation strategy in the Indian bus market seems to have involved keeping an eye on costs as well.

6.3.3 Focus strategies

Porter distinguishes focus as the third generic strategy, based on competitive scope. A **focus strategy targets a narrow segment or domain of activity and tailors its products or services to the needs of that specific segment to the exclusion of others**. Focus strategies come in two variants, according to the underlying sources of competitive advantage, cost or differentiation. In air travel, Ryanair follows a *cost focus strategy*, targeting price-conscious holiday travellers with no need for connecting flights. In the domestic detergent market, the Belgian company Ecover follows a *differentiation focus* strategy, gaining a price premium over rivals on account of its ecological cleaning products.

The focuser achieves competitive advantage by dedicating itself to serving its target segments better than others which are trying to cover a wider range of segments. Serving a broad range of segments can bring disadvantages in terms of coordination, compromise or inflexibility. Focus strategies are able to seek out the weak spots of broad cost-leaders and differentiators:

- *Cost focusers* identify areas where broader cost-based strategies fail because of the added costs of trying to satisfy a wide range of needs. For instance, in the United Kingdom food retail market, Iceland Foods has a cost-focused strategy concentrated on frozen and chilled foods, reducing costs against generalist discount food retailers such as Aldi which have all the complexity of fresh foods and groceries as well as their own frozen and chilled food ranges.

- *Differentiation focusers* look for specific needs that broader differentiators do not serve so well. Focus on one particular need helps to build specialist knowledge and technology, increases commitment to service and can improve brand recognition and customer loyalty. For example, ARM Holdings dominates the world market for mobile phone chips, despite being only a fraction of the size of the leading microprocessor manufacturers, AMD and Intel, which also make chips for a wide range of computers.

ILLUSTRATION 6.2

Volvo's different Indian buses

Volvo has a strategy to sell buses at nearly four times the prevailing market price.

The Indian bus market has long been dominated by two home players, subsidiaries of major Indian conglomerates: Tata Motors and Ashok Leyland. The two companies made simple coaches on a design that had hardly changed for decades. On top of a basic truck chassis, the two companies bolted a rudimentary coach body. Engines were a meagre 110–120 horse-power, and roared heartily as they hauled their loads up the steep mountain roads of India. Mounted at the front, the heat from the over-strained engines would pervade the whole bus. Air conditioning was a matter of open windows, through which the dust and noise of the Indian roads would pour. Suspension was old-fashioned, guaranteeing a shaky ride on pot-holed roads. Bags were typically slung on the top of the bus, where they were easily soiled and at high risk of theft. But at least the buses were cheap, selling to local bus companies at around Rs 1.2 m (€15,000; $21,000).

In 1997, Swedish bus company Volvo decided to enter the market, with buses priced at Rs 4 m, nearly four times as much as local products. Akash Passey, Volvo's first Indian employee, commissioned a consultancy company to evaluate prospects. The consultancy company recommended that Volvo should not even try. Passey told the *Financial Times*: 'My response was simple – I took the report and went to the nearest dustbin and threw it in.' Passey entered the market in 2001 with the high-priced luxury buses.

Passey used the time to develop a distinctive strategy. His basic product had superior features. Volvo's standard engines were 240–250 hp and mounted at the back, ensuring a faster and quieter ride. Air conditioning was standard of course. The positioning of the engine and the specific bus design of the chassis meant a more roomy interior, plus storage for bags internally. But Passey realised this would not be enough. He commented to the *Financial Times*: 'You had to do a lot of things to break the way business is done normally.'

Volvo offered post-sale maintenance services, increasing life expectancy of buses from three to ten years, and allowing bus operating companies to dispense with their own expensive maintenance workshops. Free training was given to drivers, so they drove more safely and took more care of their buses. The company advertised the benefits of the buses direct to customers in cinemas, rather than simply promoting them to the bus operators. To kick-start the market, Volvo supplied about 20 subsidised trial units to selected operators. Volvo trainees rode these buses, alerting the company immediately when something went wrong so Volvo could immediately send its engineers. Faster, smoother and more reliable travel allowed the bus operators to increase their ticket prices for the luxury Volvo buses by 35 per cent.

Business people and the middle classes were delighted with the new Volvo services. Speedier, more comfortable journeys allowed them to arrive fresh for meetings and potentially to save the costs of overnight stays. Tata and Ashok Leyland both now produce their own luxury buses, with Mercedes and Isuzu following Volvo into the market. None the less, the phrase 'taking a Volvo' has become synonymous with choosing a luxury bus service in India, rather as 'hoover' came to refer to any kind of vacuum cleaner.

In 2008, Volvo opened a new state-of-the-art bus factory in Bangalore. It is Volvo's most efficient bus factory worldwide, producing a fully built bus in 20–25 days. Annual capacity is 1,000 buses per year.

Source: Adapted from J. Leahy, 'Volvo takes a lead in India', *Financial Times*, 31 August 2009.

Questions

1 Rank the elements of Passey's strategy for Volvo in order of importance. Could any have been dispensed with?

2 How sustainable is Volvo's luxury bus strategy?

Successful focus strategies depend on at least one of three key factors:

- *Distinct segment needs.* Focus strategies depend on the distinctiveness of segment needs. If segment distinctiveness erodes, it becomes harder to defend the segment against broader competitors. For example, when the boundaries blurred between smart phones used by general consumers and smart phones used by business people, it has become easier for Apple to attack the distinctive niche once dominated by BlackBerry's business phones.

- *Distinct segment value chains.* Focus strategies are strengthened if they have distinctive value chains that will be difficult or costly for rivals to construct. If the production processes and distribution channels are very similar, it is easy for a broad-based differentiator to push a specialised product through its own standardised value chain at a lower cost than a rival focuser. In detergents, Procter & Gamble cannot easily respond to Ecover because achieving the same ecological friendliness would involve transforming its purchasing and production processes.

- *Viable segment economics.* Segments can easily become too small to serve economically as demand or supply conditions change. For example, changing economies of scale and greater competition have eliminated from many smaller cities the traditional town-centre department stores, with their wider ranges of different kinds of goods from hardware to clothing.

6.3.4 'Stuck in the middle'?

Porter claims that managers face a crucial choice between the generic strategies of cost leadership, differentiation and focus. According to him, it is unwise to blur this choice. As earlier, the lowest-cost competitor can always undercut the second lowest-cost competitor. For a company seeking advantage through low costs, therefore, it makes no sense to add extra costs by half-hearted efforts at differentiation. For a differentiator, it is self-defeating to make economies that jeopardise the basis for differentiation. For a focuser, it is dangerous to move outside the original specialised segment, because products or services tailored to one set of customers are likely to have inappropriate costs or features for the new target customers. This was a problem for BlackBerry as it tried to move its secure business phones into the broader consumer market, for which the availability of apps was more important than the business need of email encryption. Porter's argument is that managers are generally best to choose which generic strategy they are pursuing and then stick rigorously to it. Otherwise there is a danger of being *stuck in the middle*, doing no strategy well.

Porter's warning about the danger of being stuck in the middle provides a useful discipline for managers. It is very easy for them to make incremental decisions that compromise the basic generic strategy. As profits accumulate, the successful cost-leader will be tempted to stop scrimping and saving. In hard times, a differentiator might easily cut back the R&D or advertising investments essential to its long-term differentiation advantage. Consistency with generic strategy provides a valuable check for managerial decision making.

However, Porter's argument for pure generic strategies is controversial.[5] For example, it has been suggested that the criticisms against combining generic strategie reflect a Western cultural preference for binary oppositions, as against an Eastern willingness to seek balance and synthesis. Thus Singapore Airlines has been able to combine strategies of service differentiation and low cost in a way that Western airlines have found difficult. Porter himself acknowledges there are circumstances in which the strategies can be combined:[6]

- *Organisational separation.* It is possible for a company to create separate SBUs, each pursuing different generic strategies and with different cost structures. The challenge, however, is to prevent negative spill-overs from one SBU to another. For example, a company mostly pursuing differentiated strategies is liable to have high head office costs that the low-cost SBUs will also have to bear. On the other hand, a cheap cost-leader might damage the brand value of a sister SBU seeking differentiation. Because of these kinds of trade offs, it can be very difficult to pursue different generic strategies within a single set of related businesses. Despite the success of Singapore Airlines, Europe's leading airline Lufthansa has struggled to combine its low-cost subsidiaries, Germanwings and BMI (now sold), with its traditional higher-service core business.

- *Technological or managerial innovation.* Sometimes technological innovations allow radical improvements in both cost and quality. Internet retailing reduces the costs of bookselling, at the same time as increasing differentiation by greater product range and, through online book reviews, better advice. Managerial innovations are capable of such simultaneous improvements too. The Japanese car manufacturers' introduction of Total Quality Management led to reductions in production line mistakes that both cut manufacturing costs and improved car reliability, a point of successful differentiation.

- *Competitive failures.* Where competitors are also stuck in the middle, there is less competitive pressure to remove competitive disadvantage. Equally, where a company dominates a particular market, competitive pressures for consistency with a single competitive strategy are reduced.

6.3.5 **The Strategy Clock**

The **Strategy Clock** provides another way of approaching the generic strategies (see Figure 6.6), one which gives more scope for *hybrid* strategies.[7] The Strategy Clock has two distinctive features. First, it is focused on prices to customers rather than costs to the organisation: because prices are more visible than costs, the Strategy Clock can be easier to use in comparing competitors. Second, the circular design of the clock allows for more continuous choices than Michael Porter's sharp contrast between cost leadership and differentiation: there is a full range of incremental adjustments that can be made between the 7 o'clock position at the bottom of the low-price strategy and the 2 o'clock position at the bottom of the differentiation strategy. Organisations often travel around the clock, as they adjust their pricing and benefits over time.

The Strategy Clock identifies three zones of feasible strategies, and one zone likely to lead to ultimate failure:

- *Differentiation (zone 1).* This zone contains a range of feasible strategies for building on high perceptions of product or service benefits among customers. Close to the 12 o'clock position is a strategy of *differentiation without price premium.* Differentiation without a price premium combines high perceived benefits and moderate prices, typically used to gain market share. If high benefits also entail relatively high costs, this moderate pricing strategy would only be sustainable in the short term. Once increased market share has been achieved, it might be logical to move to *differentiation with price premium* closer to a 1 or 2 o'clock position. Movement all the way towards the 2 o'clock position is likely to involve a focus strategy, in Michael Porter's terms. Such a *focused differentiation* strategy targets a

Figure 6.6 The Strategy Clock

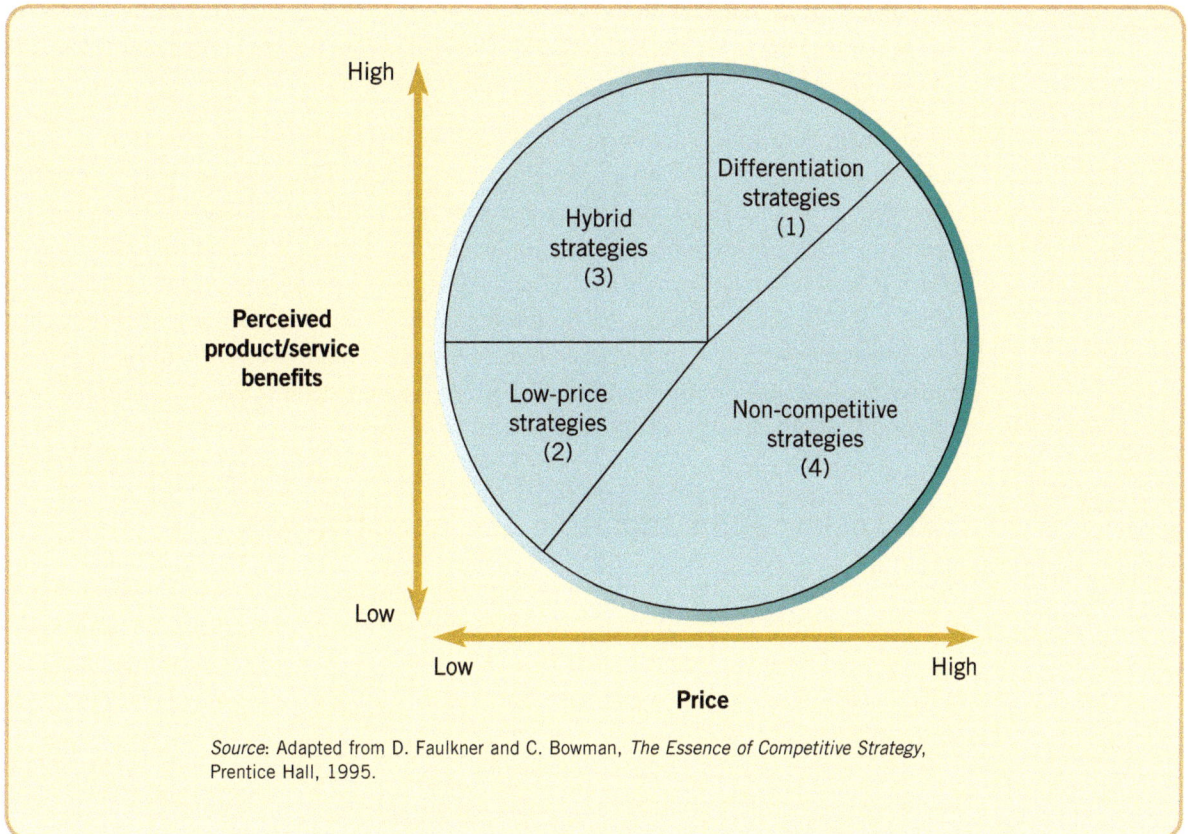

Source: Adapted from D. Faulkner and C. Bowman, *The Essence of Competitive Strategy*, Prentice Hall, 1995.

niche where the higher prices and reduced benefits are sustainable, for instance because of a lack of competition in a particular geographical area.

- *Low-price (zone 2).* This zone allows for different combinations of low prices and low perceived value. Close to the 9 o'clock position, a standard *low-price* strategy would gain market share, by combining low prices with reasonable value (at parity with competitors). To be sustainable, this strategy needs to be underpinned by some cost advantage, such as economies of scale gained through increased market share. Without such a cost advantage, cuts in benefits or increases in prices become necessary eventually. A variation on the standard low-price strategy is the *no-frills* strategy, close to the 7 o'clock position. No-frills strategies involve both low benefits and low prices, similar to low-cost airlines such as Ryanair (which even proposed to charge for use of its on-board toilets).

- *Hybrid strategy (zone 3).* A distinctive feature of the Strategy Clock is the space it allows between low-price and differentiation strategies.[8] Hybrid strategies involve both lower prices than differentiation strategies, and higher benefits than low-price strategies. Hybrid strategies are often used to make aggressive bids for increased market share. They can also be an effective way of entering a new market, for instance overseas. Even in the case of innovations with high benefits, it can make sense to price low initially in order to gain experience curve efficiencies or lock-in through network effects (see section 6.3.6). Some companies sustain hybrid strategies over long periods of time: for example, furniture store IKEA, which uses scale advantages to combine relatively low prices with differentiated Swedish design (see Chapter end case).

- *Non-competitive strategies (zone 4).* The final set of strategies occupies a zone of unfeasible economics, with low benefits and high prices. Unless businesses have exceptional strategic lock-in, customers will quickly reject these combinations. Typically these strategies lead to failure.

The Strategy Clock's focus on price, and its scope for incremental adjustments in strategy, provide a more dynamic view on strategy than Porter's generic strategies. Instead of organisations being fairly fixed in terms of either a cost or a differentiation strategy, they can move around the clock. For example, an organisation might start with a *low-price* strategy to gain market share, later shift to a higher-priced *differentiation with premium* strategy in order to reap profits, and then move back to a *hybrid strategy* in order to defend itself from new entrants. However, Porter's generic strategies do remind managers that costs are critical. Unless an organisation has some secure cost advantage (such as economies of scale), a hybrid strategy of high perceived benefits and low prices is unlikely to be sustainable for long.

6.3.6 Lock-in and sustainable business strategies

Business strategies should ideally be sustainable over time. This may involve having competitive advantages that rivals cannot match. Thus, as in section 3.3, strategies are more likely to be sustained if underpinned by capabilities that combine all the VRIO characteristics of value, rarity, inimitability and non-substitutability. Another approach to sustaining business strategies is creating 'lock-in'.

Strategic lock-in **is where users become dependent on a supplier and are unable to use another supplier without substantial switching costs.**[9] Strategic lock-in is related to the concept of path dependency (see section 5.2.1) and essentially extends the principles of inimitability and non-substitutability. Under conditions of lock-in, imitators and substitutes are unable to attract customers. This is particularly valuable to differentiators. With customers securely locked in, it becomes possible to keep prices well above costs.

Lock-in can be achieved in two main ways:

- *Controlling complementary products or services.* Opportunities for lock-in to a particular product or service arise where other products or services are necessary for customers using it. This is often known as the 'razor and blade' strategy: once a customer has bought a particular kind of razor, he or she is obliged to buy compatible blades to use it. Apple originally applied a similar strategy when it used Digital Rights Management to ensure that music bought on its iTunes store could only be played on its own iPod players. To switch to a Sony player would mean losing access to all the iTunes music previously purchased.

- *Creating a proprietary industry standard.* Sometimes companies are so successful that they create an industry standard under their own control. Similar to the razor and blade effect, as customers invest in training and systems using that standard, it becomes more expensive to switch to another product or service. However, with industry standards, *network effects* also operate: as other members of the network also adopt the same standard, it becomes even more valuable to stay within it. Microsoft built this kind of proprietary standard with its Windows operating system, which holds more than 90 per cent of the market. For a business to switch to another operating system would mean retraining staff and translating files onto the new system, while perhaps creating communications problems with network members (such as customers or suppliers) who had stuck with Windows.

6.4 INTERACTIVE STRATEGIES

Generic strategies need to be chosen, and adjusted, in the light of competitors' strategies. If everybody else is chasing after cost leadership, then a differentiation strategy might be sensible. Thus business strategy choices *interact* with those of competitors. This section starts by considering business strategy in the light of competitor moves, especially in hypercompetition. It then addresses the option of cooperation and closes with game theory, which helps managers choose between competition and more cooperative strategies.

6.4.1 Interactive price and quality strategies

Richard D'Aveni depicts competitor interactions in terms of movements against the variables of price (the vertical axis) and perceived quality (the horizontal axis), similar to the Strategy Clock: see Figure 6.7.[10] Although D'Aveni applies his analysis to the very fast-moving environments he terms 'hypercompetitive' (see section 2.3.1), similar reasoning applies wherever competitors' moves are interdependent.

Figure 6.7 shows different organisations competing by emphasising either low prices or high quality or some mixture of the two. Graph (i) starts with a 'first value line', describing various trade-offs in terms of price and perceived quality that are acceptable to customers. The cost-leading firm (here L) offers relatively poor perceived quality, but customers accept this because of the lower price. While the relative positions on the graph should not be taken exactly literally, in the car market this cost-leading position might describe some of Hyundai's products. The differentiator (D) has a higher price, but much better quality. This might be Mercedes. In between, there are a range of perfectly acceptable combinations, with the mid-point firm (M) offering a combination of reasonable prices and reasonable quality. This might be Ford. M's strategy is on the first value line and therefore entirely viable at this stage. On the other hand, firm U is uncompetitive, falling behind the value line. Its price is higher than M's, and its quality is worse. U's predicament is typical of the business that is 'stuck in the middle', in Porter's terms. U no longer offers acceptable value and must quickly move back onto the value line or fail.

In any market, competitors and their moves or counter-moves can be plotted against these two axes of price and perceived value. For example, in graph (i) of Figure 6.7, the differentiator (D) makes an aggressive move by substantially improving its perceived quality while holding its prices. This improvement in quality shifts customer expectations of quality right across the market. These changed expectations are reflected by the new, second value line (in green). With the second value line, even the cost-leader (L) may have to make some improvement to quality, or accept a small price cut. But the greatest threat is for the mid-point competitor, M. To catch up with the second value line, M must respond either by making a substantial improvement in quality while holding prices, or by slashing prices, or by some combination of the two.

However, mid-point competitor M also has the option of an aggressive counter-attack. Given the necessary capabilities, M might choose to push the value line still further outwards, wrong-footing differentiator D by creating a third value line that is even more demanding in terms of the price-perceived quality trade-off. The starting point in graph (ii) of Figure 6.7 is all three competitors L, M and D successfully reaching the second value line (uncompetitive U has disappeared). However, M's next move is to go beyond the second value line by making radical

Figure 6.7 Interactive price and quality strategies

(i) Differentiator (D) improves quality

(ii) Mid-point business (M) counter-attacks on price

Note: axes are not necessarily to linear scales.

Source: Adapted with the permission of The Free Press, a Division of Simon & Schuster, Inc., from *Hypercompetition: Managing the Dynamics of Strategic Maneuvering* by Richard D'Aveni with Robert Gunther. Copyright © 1994 by Richard D'Aveni. All rights reserved.

cuts in price while sustaining its new level of perceived quality. Again, customer expectations are changed and a third value line (in red) is established. Now it is differentiator D that is at most risk of being left behind, and it faces hard choices about how to respond in terms of price and quality.

Plotting moves and counter-moves in these terms underlines the dynamic and interactive nature of business strategy. Economically viable positions along the value line are always in danger of being superseded as competitors move either downwards in terms of price or outwards in terms of perceived quality. The generic strategies of cost leadership and differentiation should not be seen as static positions, but as dynamic trajectories along the axes of price and quality. The movement towards more 'local' Starbucks stores demonstrates the need to be continually moving along the trajectory of differentiation (see Illustration 6.3).

A more detailed example of the sequence of decisions and possible options involved in competitive interaction is given in Figure 6.8.[11] This illustrates the situation of a business facing a low-price competitor, for example a high-cost Western manufacturer facing possible attack by cheap imports from Asia. There are three key decisions:

- *Threat assessment.* The first decision point is whether the threat is substantial or not. If there is a threat, the high-cost organisation should not automatically respond to a low-price competitor by trying to match prices: it is likely to lose a price war with its existing cost structure. The high-cost organisation needs a more sophisticated response.

- *Differentiation response.* If there are enough consumers prepared to pay for them, the high-cost organisation can seek out new points of differentiation. For example, a Western manufacturer may exploit its closeness to local markets by improving service levels. At the same time, unnecessary costs should be stripped out. If increased differentiation is not possible, then more radical cost solutions should be sought.

ILLUSTRATION

ILLUSTRATION 6.3

McCafés versus Starbucks

Starbucks coffee chain changes its strategy in response to McDonald's challenge.

Fast food chain McDonald's has launched a world-wide challenge to coffee giant Starbucks with its new concept, McCafés. The McCafé concept had emerged in Australia in the 1990s. McCafés typically operate within or next to regular McDonald's outlets. They use high-quality coffee machines and sell different blends of coffee according to the tastes of local markets. By 2012, there were 1,500 McCafé outlets in the USA, and 600 in Germany. McCafés are spreading rapidly across Europe, from Spain to the Ukraine (in the United Kingdom, McCafé products are still sold under the usual McDonald's brand).

Starbucks is the world's largest coffee chain, with nearly 20,000 stores across 60 countries from Canada to China. Founded in 1971, Starbucks was bought as a small Seattle coffee shop chain by Howard Schultz in 1988. The Starbucks' original concept was good coffee, brewed in an intimate atmosphere by skilled 'barristas'. Schultz expanded rapidly, with his first store outside North America opening in Tokyo in 1996. In 2001, Schultz retired as CEO and under the next two CEOs Starbucks continued its expansion. But in 2007, performance was beginning to flag. Schultz wrote a famous 'Valentine's Day memo' to the then CEO, complaining that growth had led to a 'commoditisation' of the Starbucks' concept. The introduction of automatic espresso machines to speed up service removed the distinctive coffee odour in the shops and deskilled the barristas. The next year, Schultz returned to the helm as CEO.

As he started back in his old job, Howard Schultz proclaimed:

'We are laser-focused on delivering the finest quality coffee and getting the customer experience right every time. We have. . . . been putting our feet into the shoes of our customers and are responding directly to their needs. Our customers are telling us they want value and quality and we will deliver that in a way that is meaningful to them and authentic to Starbucks.'

Schultz famously closed all the stores worldwide for an afternoon in order to retrain the barristas in the skills of brewing good coffee. Starbucks also improved its food offerings: in 2012, the company bought the bakery chain La Boulange for $100 m. So as to access its innovative, quality food products for transfer to Starbucks outlets, the standard Starbucks international store format was relaxed in order to allow more variety according to locality. Local artefacts, bolder colours, bigger community noticeboards and even second-hand furniture were used to create more individual stores. Starbucks stores offered free wi-fi to users.

McDonald's is aiming to match Starbucks' changes. Thus McDonald's too introduced free wi-fi. The quality and price of McDonald's coffees are highly competitive. Thus a McCafé frappé drink cost $3.99 for a 16 ounce drink in 2012 (against $4.20 for a Big Mac burger); Starbucks' equivalent frappuccino cost $5.45. The Canadian *Globe and Mail* reviewed the two companies' products in 2011. The comment on McCafé was: 'It tastes like a combination of damp forest and uncleaned coffee maker.' As for the Starbucks product, it was 'bitter; burnt toast. This is so bad, it's the antithesis of coffee.' Overall, the *Globe and Mail* rated McCafé as slightly superior.

Sources: *Financial Times*, 26 May 2009; smartmoney.com, 23 July 2012; the *Globe and Mail*, 8 November 2011.

Questions

1 Plot the moves of McDonald's and Starbucks on the axes of price and perceived quality, as in Figure 6.7.

2 What should be done by a company with a similar original position to Starbucks, but operating in a market where McCafé has not yet arrived (e.g. Costa Coffee in the United Kingdom)?

Figure 6.8 Responding to low-cost rivals

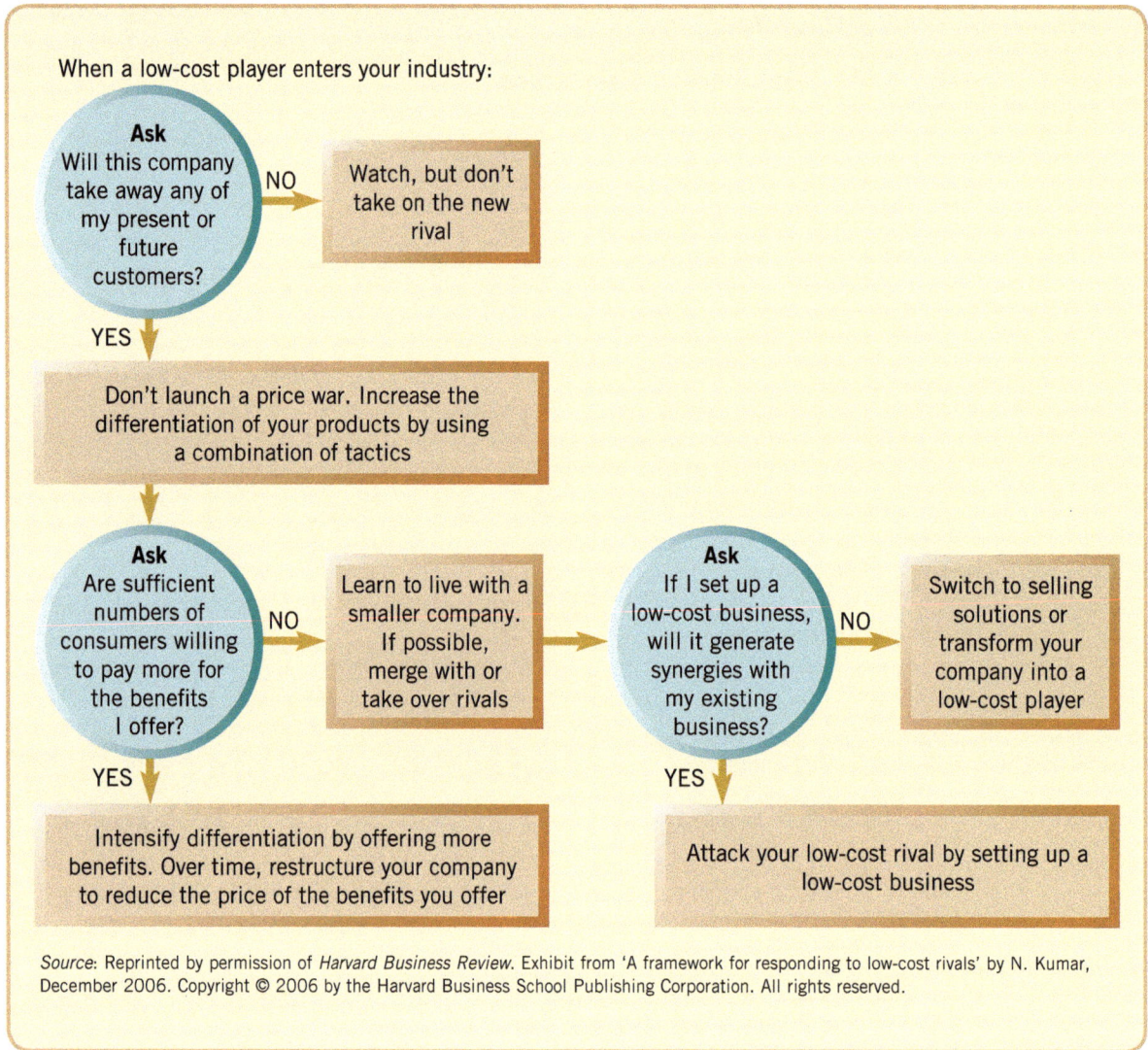

When a low-cost player enters your industry:

Ask
Will this company take away any of my present or future customers?

NO → Watch, but don't take on the new rival

YES ↓

Don't launch a price war. Increase the differentiation of your products by using a combination of tactics

↓

Ask
Are sufficient numbers of consumers willing to pay more for the benefits I offer?

NO → Learn to live with a smaller company. If possible, merge with or take over rivals →

Ask
If I set up a low-cost business, will it generate synergies with my existing business?

NO → Switch to selling solutions or transform your company into a low-cost player

YES ↓

Intensify differentiation by offering more benefits. Over time, restructure your company to reduce the price of the benefits you offer

YES ↓

Attack your low-cost rival by setting up a low-cost business

- *Cost response*. Merger with other high-cost organisations may help reduce costs and match prices through economies of scale. If a low-cost business is synergistic with (in other words, has benefits for) the existing business, this can be an effective platform for an aggressive cost-based counter-attack. If there is neither scope for further differentiation nor synergy between the existing business and a possible new low-cost business, then the existing business must sooner or later be abandoned. For a Western manufacturer, one option might be to outsource all production to low-cost operators, simply applying its design and branding expertise. Another option would be to abandon manufacturing in favour of becoming a 'solutions provider', aggregating manufactured components from different suppliers and adding value through whole-systems design, consultantcy or service.

Equivalent decisions would have to be made, of course, by a low-price competitor facing a differentiator. When Apple entered the phone market with its expensive touchscreen iPhone, established handset manufacturers had first to decide whether Apple was a serious long-term threat, and then choose how far they should either match the iPhone's features or increase the price differential between their products and Apple's expensive ones.

6.4.2 Interactive strategies in hypercompetition

According to Richard D'Aveni, the kinds of move and counter-move outlined in the preceding section are a constant feature of hypercompetitive environments. As in section 2.3.1, hyper-competition describes markets with continuous disequilibrium and change, for example popular music or consumer electronics. In these conditions, it may no longer be possible to plan for sustainable positions of competitive advantage. Indeed, planning for long-term sustainability may actually destroy competitive advantage by slowing down response. Managers have to be able to act faster than their competitors.

Successful competitive interaction in hypercompetition demands speed and initiative rather than defensiveness. Richard D'Aveni highlights four key principles:

- *Cannibalise bases of success*: sustaining old advantages distracts from developing new advantages. An organisation has to be willing to cannibalise the basis of its own success. Intel, traditionally a dominant supplier of microchips for computers, has had to jeopardise its traditional markets by pushing hard into the smart phone and tablet markets.

- *Series of small moves rather than big moves*: smaller moves create more flexibility and give a series of temporary advantages. At the same time, smaller moves make it harder for competitors to detect and counter the overall strategic direction. Apple, for example, tends to make incremental improvements to its products between the launches of major innovations, such as the iPhone in 2007 and the iPad in 2010.

- *Be unpredictable*. If competitors can see a pattern they can predict the next competitive moves and quickly learn how to imitate or outflank an organisation. So surprise, unpredictability, even apparent irrationality can be important. Managers must learn ways of appearing to be unpredictable to the external world while, internally, thinking strategies through. Apple likes to keep competitors guessing about its next major product move: many had been speculating that the company was about to enter the television market when it produced the iPad.

- *Mislead the competition*. Drawing on the lessons of game theory (see section 6.4.4), the organisation might signal particular moves, but then do something else (e.g. talk about alliances, and then make an acquisition). Or the organisation might disguise initial success in a market, until ready to respond to competitor retaliation.[12]

6.4.3 Cooperative strategy

So far the emphasis has been on competition and competitive advantage. However, the competitive moves and counter-moves in section 6.4.1 make it clear that sometimes competition can escalate in a way that is dangerous to all competitors. It can be in the self-interest of organisations to restrain competition. Moreover, advantage may not always be achieved just by competing. Collaboration between some organisations in a market may give them advantage over other competitors in the same market, or potential new entrants. Collaboration can be explicit in terms of formal agreements to cooperate, or tacit in terms of informal mutual understandings between organisations. In short, while organisations need to avoid illegal collusion, business strategy includes cooperative options as well as competitive ones.[13]

Figure 6.9 illustrates various kinds of benefits from cooperation between firms in terms of Michael Porter's five forces of buyers, suppliers, rivals, entrants and substitutes (section 2.3.1). Key benefits of cooperation are as follows:

Figure 6.9 Cooperating with rivals

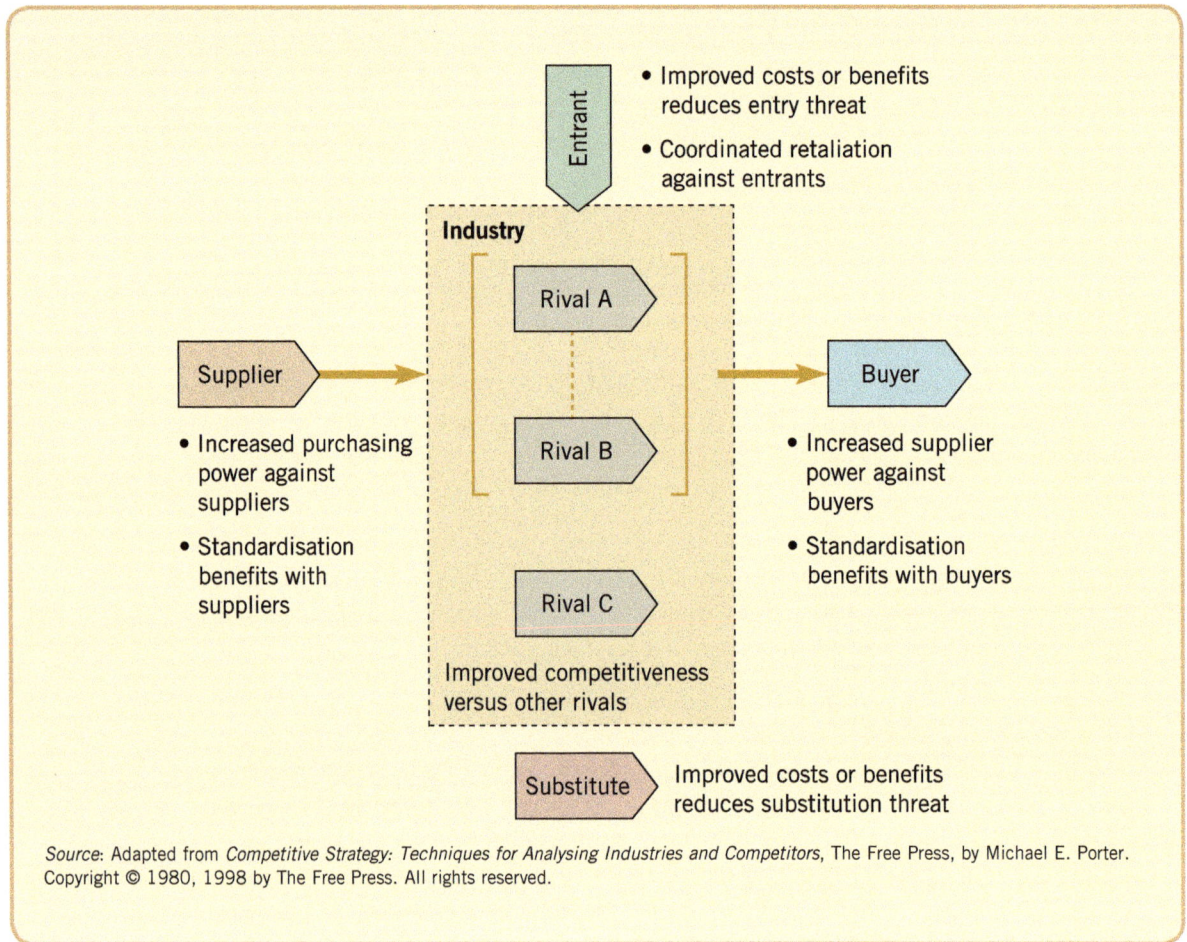

- *Suppliers.* In Figure 6.9, cooperation between rivals A and B in an industry will increase their purchasing power against suppliers. Sometimes this increased cooperation is used simply to squeeze supplier prices. However, cooperation between rivals A and B may enable them to standardise requirements, allowing suppliers to make cost reductions to all parties' benefit. For example, if two car manufacturers agreed on common component specifications, their suppliers could gain economies through production of the standardised part on a greater scale (this kind of *complementarity* is discussed in section 2.3).

- *Buyers.* Conversely, cooperation between rivals A and B will increase their power as suppliers vis-à-vis buyers. It will be harder for buyers to shop around. Such *collusion* between rivals can help maintain or raise prices, though it may well attract penalties from competition regulators. On the other hand, buyers may benefit if their inputs are standardised, again enabling reductions in costs that all can share. For example, if food manufacturers supplying a retailer agree on common pallet sizes for deliveries, the retailer can manage its warehouses much more efficiently.

- *Rivals.* If cooperative rivals A and B are getting benefits with regard to both buyers and suppliers, other competitors without such agreements – in Figure 6.9, rival C – will be at a competitive disadvantage. Rival C will be in danger of being squeezed out of the industry. This was the predicament of Three in Illustration 6.4.

ILLUSTRATION 6.4

Mobile payment systems: cooperating to pay

Cooperative agreements in mobile payment systems may leave some players out.

The opportunities in mobile payment systems ('mobile wallets') attracted a very wide range of competitors and approaches. In 2011, the value of mobile payments worldwide was $240 bn, a sum expected to triple in the following five years. Companies which could skim even a tiny percentage of this total through offering mobile payment services could earn fortunes. Moreover, they would have access to valuable data about which consumers bought what, where and when. It was hardly surprising that companies as diverse as Google, Apple, Facebook, PayPal, Visa, Barclays and Blackberry were crowding into the new market, each with its own particular systems. Indeed, the diversity of possible systems was creating confusion, with retailers and restaurants hesitating to adopt before seeing which system would finally come out on top.

One important initiative was 'Project Oscar', a joint venture launched by the United Kingdom's three leading mobile phone operators Vodafone, Telefónica's O2 and EverythingEverywhere, the merged businesses of DeutscheTelekom and France Telecom. Project Oscar involved giving customers SIM cards that would allow them to store debit and credit card details on their phones and pay for goods or transport either online via their mobile or by tapping the handset on a special reader at the till or ticket barrier, using Near Field Communication (NFC) technology. This contrasted with the Google system, for instance, which involved getting a whole new phone. The three partners in Project Oscar declared: 'If approved, the joint venture will benefit UK plc as a whole. It will promote competition by bringing together the necessary scale to offer a credible alternative to the established online payments and advertising platforms offered by large US-based internet players.'

But not everybody was happy at the prospect of the dominant phone operators collaborating in this way. The United Kingdom's fourth mobile phone operator, Three, complained: 'The JV (Project Oscar) will control and sell access to over 90 per cent of UK mobile subscribers and their data, thus allowing Deutsche Telekom, France Telecom, Vodafone and Telefónica to foreclose the market to third-parties and neatly do away with the inconvenience of competing with each other.' In April 2012, with the support of Google, Three successfully referred the joint venture to the European competition authorities.

The European Commission investigated, aware of a long history of illicit collusion between the various mobile phone operators in Europe. However, the Commission came down in favour of Project Oscar. It declared:

'As a result of its in-depth investigation, the Commission concluded that the joint venture will not likely lead to a significant impediment to effective competition in the EEA within the meaning of the Merger Regulation. The market investigation revealed that a number of alternatives already exist and much more are very likely to emerge in the near future to ensure adequate competitive pressure on the joint venture's mobile wallet platform. Some of these alternatives may rely on a secure access to the SIM card of the mobile handsets in order to store sensitive data like bank account numbers, etc. This access will be controlled by the mobile network operators, including in particular the three parents of the joint venture. However, other alternatives exist which do not store sensitive data on SIM cards and it is unlikely that the creation of the joint venture will allow the parent mobile network operators to block these alternative routes to market using technical or commercial means.'

Sources: *Guardian*, 7 March 2012; *Financial Times*, 8 March 2012 and 29 April 2012; *Communications World*, 5 September 2012.

Questions

1 In terms of Figure 6.9, what are the benefits to the Project Oscar partners of collaboration?

2 What options are available now to the excluded Three?

- *Entrants.* Similarly, potential entrants will likely lack the advantages of the combined rivals A and B. Moreover, A and B can coordinate their retaliation strategies against any new entrant, for example by cutting prices by the same proportions in order to protect their own relative positions while undermining the competitiveness of the new entrant.

- *Substitutes.* Finally, the improved costs or efficiencies that come from cooperation between rivals A and B reduce the incentives for buyers to look to substitutes. Steel companies have cooperated on research to reduce the weight of steel used in cars, in order to discourage car manufacturers from switching to lighter substitutes such as aluminium or plastics.

Further kinds of cooperation will be considered under alliance strategy in section 10.4.

6.4.4 Game theory

Game theory provides important insights into competitor interaction.[14] The 'game' refers to the kinds of interactive moves two players make in a game of chess. **Game theory encourages an organisation to consider competitors' likely moves and the implications of these moves for its own strategy.** Game theorists are alert to two kinds of interaction in particular. First, game theorists consider how a *competitor response* to a strategic move might change the original assumptions behind that move: for example, challenging a competitor in one area might lead to a counter-attack in another. Second, game theorists are sensitive to the *strategic signals*, or messages, their moves might convey to competitors, for example with regard to how fiercely they seem willing to defend their position in a particular market. In the light of possible attacks and counter-attacks, game theorists often advise a more cooperative approach than head-to-head competition.

Game theory is particularly relevant where competitors are *interdependent.* Interdependence exists where the outcome of choices made by one competitor is dependent on the choices made by other competitors. For example, the success of price cuts by a retailer depends on the responses of its rivals: if rivals do not match the price cuts, then the price-cutter gains market share; but if rivals follow the price cuts, nobody gains market share and all players suffer from the lower prices. Anticipating competitor counter-moves is clearly vital to deciding whether to go forward with the price-cutting strategy.

There are two important guiding principles that arise from interdependence:

- *Get in the mind of the competitors.* Strategists need to put themselves in the position of competitors, take a view about what competitors are likely to do and choose their own strategy in this light. They need to understand their competitors' game-plan to plan their own.

- *Think forwards and reason backwards.* Strategists should choose their competitive moves on the basis of understanding the likely responses of competitors. Think forwards to what competitors might do in the future, and then reason backwards to what would be sensible to do in the light of this now.

Game theory insights can be gained through two methods. On the one hand, *war gaming* is helpful where it is important to get stakeholders to deeply appreciate each others' positions through actually playing out their respective roles, and where there is uncertainty about the range of outcomes. Illustration 6.5 provides a public policy example from South Africa. On the other hand, *mathematical game theory* is useful where there is a clear but limited range of outcomes and the values associated with each outcome can be reasonably quantified.

ILLUSTRATION 6.5

War gaming in South Africa

Deloitte proposes war games to develop a strategic solution to a major pollution problem in South Africa.

Deloitte, one of the 'big four' professional service firms, has nearly 200,000 employees offering accountancy, tax, consulting and business advisory services in 150 countries around the world. In 2010, it also got into the war gaming business. In particular, it bought a small simulation company developed by the War Studies Group at King's College, University of London.

War gaming originated with the Prussian Army in the late nineteenth century and developed particularly during the Cold War in the twentieth century. War games place the players in the positions of different actors (e.g. enemies or allies), and ask them to play out a sequence of moves and counter-moves as if they were the actors themselves. Two famous principles help guide the play. The first is from Sun Tzu, the Chinese general who wrote the military treatise *The Art of War* about 500 years BC: 'To know your enemy, you must become your enemy.' The second principle is from the nineteenth-century German General Helmuth von Moltke: 'No plan ever survives the first collision with the enemy.' War games thus help players understand how the various players will act as action unfolds over time. Deloitte uses war gaming simulations to help clients plot strategies for new product introductions, pricing changes and new market entries, all situations where competitor reactions can be highly significant. But they can be used in complex public policy arenas too.

The problem of mine drainage around Johannesburg in South Africa is an example. Gold has been mined there since 1886, but the mining process ends up by mixing water, oxygen and heavy metals to create a diluted sulphuric acid. This acid is seeping out into water sources and is now polluting 10 per cent of the potable water supplied by the local water company. In an area that is short of water, this is potentially disastrous. Worse, the mines must be continuously pumped out in order to avoid flooding the vicinity, including local towns and an important bird sanctuary. The trouble is, many of the mines are no longer owned by their original developers, and current owners dispute their responsibilities, which are liable to be very expensive.

There are clearly many stakeholders involved. First there are the mining companies, whose mines are the source of the problem. There are the various local municipal authorities, threatened by both flooding and polluted water. There are no less than five national government departments involved, from Mining to Agriculture, each with its own interests to defend. Local farmers are very concerned about the threat to the water supply that is vital to their agriculture.

A war game helps players respond to various scenarios. What if there was major pollution? This would be a catastrophe for local communities, but it would also threaten the labour supply for the mining companies: this possible cost should be factored into the calculations of the mining companies as they contemplate the extent to which they would be prepared to pay for solutions. On the other hand, what if the mining companies were forced to solve the problem wholly at their expense? Would the mining companies then prefer simply to abandon the mines, or at least reduce investment in capacity, with knock-on effects on local employment? Putting players into the position of the various stakeholders helps everybody understand fully the interests involved and even, perhaps, to see possibilities for shared solutions.

Source: Based on Deloitte, 'War gaming may just be the answer to solving South Africa's own Chenobyl', 2011.

Questions

1 War games can be used to guide new product introductions, pricing changes and new market entries. Can you think of other business situations where they could be useful?

2 Are there any limits or dangers to comparing business strategy to war?

One of the most famous illustrations of mathematical game theory is the *prisoner's dilemma*. Game theorists identify many situations where organisations' strategic decisions are similar to the dilemma of two prisoners accused of serial crimes together and being interrogated in separate prison cells without the possibility of communicating with each other. The prisoners have to decide on the relative merits of: (i) loyally supporting each other by refusing to divulge any information to their interrogators; and (ii) seeking an advantage by betraying the other. If both stay silent, they might get away with most of their crimes and only suffer some lesser punishment, perhaps for just one or two offences. The interrogators, though, will tempt each of them to divulge full information by offering them their freedom if only they betray their fellow criminal. However, if both betray, then the judge is unlikely to be grateful for the confessions, and will punish them for all their crimes. The dilemma for each of the prisoners is how much to trust in their mutual loyalty: if they both refuse to divulge, they can both get away with the lesser punishment; on the other hand, if one is sure that the other will not betray, it makes even more sense to betray the loyal one as that allows the betrayer to go totally free. The two prisoners are clearly interdependent. But because they cannot communicate, they each have to get in the mind of the other, think forwards to what they might do, and then reason backwards in order to decide what their own strategy should be – stay silent or betray.

The prisoner's dilemma has its equivalence in business where there are two major players competing head-to-head against each other in a situation of tight interdependence. This is the position of Airbus and Boeing in the aircraft business, Sony and Microsoft in the games market, or British Airways and Virgin in transatlantic travel. It would be relevant to the strategic decisions of two such interdependent companies in a range of situations: for example, if one company was thinking about making a major investment in an innovative new product that the other company could match. For two such competitors to communicate directly about their strategies in these situations would likely be judged illegal by the competition authorities. They therefore have to get into each other's minds, think forwards and reason backwards. How will the other company act or react, and, in the light of that, what strategy is best?

The kind of situation two interdependent competitors could get into is represented in the prisoner's dilemma matrix of Figure 6.10. Suppose the two main aircraft manufacturers Airbus and Boeing were both under pricing pressure, perhaps because of falling demand. They each have to decide whether to announce radical price cuts or to hold their prices up. If both choose to hold their prices, neither gets an advantage over the other and they both get the returns represented in the top left-hand quadrant of Figure 6.10: for the sake of illustration, each might earn profits of €500 m. However, if one competitor pursues the radical price cuts on its own while the other does not, the pattern of returns might be quite different: the radical price-cutter attracts a significantly larger share of airline customers and earns €700 m profits through spreading fixed costs over greater sales, while the market-share-losing competitor earns only €100 m (as represented in the top-right and bottom-left quadrants). This situation might tempt one of the competitors to choose radical price cuts for two reasons: first, there is the prospect of higher profits; but, second, there is the risk of the other competitor cutting prices while leaving it behind. The problem is that if each reasons in the same way, the two competitors will *both* cut prices at once. They will thus set off a price war in which neither gains share and they both end up with the unsatisfactory return of just €300 m (the bottom-right quadrant).

The dilemma in Figure 6.10 is awkward because cooperation is simultaneously attractive and difficult to achieve. The most attractive strategy for Airbus and Boeing jointly is for them

Figure 6.10 Prisoner's dilemma game in aircraft manufacture

both to hold their prices, yet in practice they are likely to cut prices because they must expect the other to do so anyway. A distinctive feature of game theory is that it frequently highlights the value of a more cooperative approach to competitor interaction, rather than aggressive competition. The cooperation need not be in the form of an explicit agreement: cooperation can be tacit, supported by the recognition of mutual self-interest in not attacking each other head-to-head. Game theory therefore encourages managers to consider how a 'game' can be transformed from lose–lose competition to win–win cooperation. There are four principles that can help here:

- *Ensure repetition.* The prisoner's dilemma above assumes just one interaction. The thinking forwards is quite limited. In many circumstances, though, it is easier to achieve tacit co-operation if the two players know that they will be making similar interdependent decisions over time. Ensuring repetition makes cooperation much more likely. In a repetitive game, starting with a cooperative approach, and only making more aggressive moves in *response* to the aggression of the other player, has been shown generally to help players maintain a mutually satisfactory position of tacit cooperation. In this approach, both Airbus and Boeing would start by holding their prices; if one cut its prices, the other would simply cut its prices for one period, hoping that the first would move back to the higher price level; if the first company did move back to the higher prices, the second would follow. The idea is that in repeated interactions over time, players can learn from each other's moves and counter-moves the benefits of cooperation.

- *Signalling.* Another insight from game theory is that strategic moves are also signals to competitors. Strategists need to be aware of the messages that their moves convey and read the messages of their competitors' moves. If Airbus failed to punish a price cut of Boeing with its own price cut, then Boeing might decide that Airbus was not serious about the market and would continue its price-cutting strategy. Responding aggressively to an initial price cut may actually support long-term cooperation in a repeated game.

- *Deterrence.* As above, signalling can clearly be about deterring unwanted strategic moves by competitors. During the Cold War, game theorists attribute the lack of direct warfare between the USA and the Soviet Union to the fact that both possessed nuclear deterrents: if one country attacked the other, then the second country would retaliate with a nuclear

KEY DEBATE

To be different or the same?

Can differentiation strategies rebound, making an organisation seem dangerously eccentric rather than delivering competitive advantage?

This chapter has introduced the potential value of differentiation strategies, in which the organisation emphasises its uniqueness. This is consistent also with the argument of the resource-based view (Chapter 3) in favour of the distinctiveness and inimitability of an organisation's resources. But how far should an organisation push its uniqueness, especially if there is a danger of its beginning to be seen as simply eccentric?

McKinsey & Co. consultant Philipp Natterman makes a strong case for differentiation.[1] He tracks the relationship between profitability and differentiation (in terms of pricing and product features) over long periods in both the personal computer and mobile phone industries. He finds that as differentiation falls over time, so too do industry profit margins. Natterman blames management techniques such as benchmarking (Chapter 3), which tend to encourage convergence on industry 'best practices'. The trouble with best practices is that they easily become standard practices. There is no competitive advantage in following the herd.

However, 'institutional theorists' such as Paul DiMaggio and Walter Powell point to some advantages in herd-like behaviour.[2] They think of industries as 'organisational fields' in which all sorts of actors must interact – customers, suppliers, employees and regulators. The ability of these actors to interact effectively depends upon being legitimate in the eyes of other actors in the field. Over time, industries develop institutionalised norms of legitimate behaviour, which it makes sense for everybody to follow. It is easier for customers and suppliers to do business with organisations that are more or less the same as the others in the industry. It is reassuring to potential employees and industry regulators if organisations do not seem highly eccentric. Especially when there is high uncertainty about what drives performance – for example, in knowledge-based industries – it can be a lot better to be legitimate than different. To the extent that customers, suppliers, employees and regulators value conformity, then it is valuable in itself. Being a 'misfit' can be costly.

This institutionalist appreciation of conformity makes sense of a lot of strategic behaviour. For example, merger waves in some industries seem to be driven by bandwagons, in which organisations become panicked into making acquisitions simply for fear of being left behind. Likewise, many management initiatives, such as business process re-engineering, e-business or outsourcing, are the product of fads and fashions as much as hard objective analysis. The insight from institutionalist theory, however, is that following the fashion is not necessarily a bad thing.

Thus institutional theory and the resource-based view appear to have opposing perspectives on the value of differentiation. David Deephouse has investigated this apparent trade-off between differentiation and conformity in the American banking industry and found a curvilinear relationship between differentiation and financial performance.[3] Strong conformity led to inferior performance; moderate differentiation was associated with improved performance; extreme differentiation appeared to damage performance.

Deephouse concludes in favour of 'balance' between differentiation and conformity. He also suggests that the value of differentiation depends on the extent to which key actors in the industry – customers, suppliers, employees, and so on – have converged on institutionalised norms of appropriate strategy. It seems that strategies can be too differentiated, but that how much 'too differentiated' is depends on the kind of industry that one is in.

Notes
1. P.M. Natterman, 'Best practice does not equal best strategy', *McKinsey Quarterly*, no. 2 (2000), pp. 22–31.
2. P. DiMaggio and W. Powell, 'The iron cage revisited: institutional isomorphism and collective rationality in organizational fields', *American Sociological Review*, vol. 48 (1983), pp. 147–60.
3. D. Deephouse, 'To be different or to be the same? It's a question (and theory) of strategic balance', *Strategic Management Journal*, vol. 20 (1999), pp. 147–66.

Questions

1 To what extent do (a) universities and (b) car manufacturers compete by being different or the same?

2 Considering the nature of their industries, and key players within them, why might these organisations adopt these approaches to conformity or differentiation?

attack. This was known as 'mutually assured destruction' (MAD), but it worked. In a similar vein, interdependent competitors have to demonstrate that the costs of an unwanted move will be very high. Two effective forms of deterrent would be maintaining extra capacity that could be used to flood the market, or holding a minor position in a competitor's key market that could easily be expanded. Even if these investments in deterrence are expensive, they may be worthwhile if they encourage cooperation.

● *Commitment*. It is important also to signal commitment. When the Roman invader Julius Caesar burnt his ships on the shores of England, the message was to his adversaries as much as his own invading army. The Britons knew that Caesar would fight to the death: they had strong incentives to negotiate a peace with him. Caesar's signal of commitment was credible because it was costly and irreversible. Similarly, if a company invests heavily in developing its brand in a market, or building up a portfolio of patents, then competitors will know that it is highly committed: they will therefore be cautious about attacking it head-on. Again, additional investments have a signalling value that can help cooperation long-term.

SUMMARY

- Business strategy is concerned with seeking competitive advantage in markets at the *business* rather than *corporate* level.

- Business strategy needs to be considered and defined in terms of *strategic business units* (SBUs).

- Porter's framework and the Strategy Clock define various *generic strategies*, including *cost-leadership*, *differentiation*, *focus* and *hybrid* strategies.

- Managers need to consider how business strategies can be sustained through strategic capabilities and/or the ability to achieve a '*lock-in*' position with buyers.

- In *hypercompetitive* conditions sustainable competitive advantage is difficult to achieve. Competitors need to be able to cannibalise, make small moves, be unpredictable and mislead their rivals.

- *Cooperative strategies* may offer alternatives to competitive strategies or may run in parallel.

- Game theory encourages managers to get in the mind of competitors and think forwards and reason backwards.

VIDEO ASSIGNMENTS

VIDEO
ASSIGNMENTS

Visit MyStrategyLab and watch the CISCO case study for Chapter 6.

1 Explain the concept of generic strategy using either Porter's framework or the Strategy Clock drawing on examples from the IT sector.

2 Using section 6.4, explain how 'hypercompetition strategies' and 'cooperative strategies' are used by CISCO to enhance its competitive advantage.

WORK ASSIGNMENTS

✱ *Denotes more advanced work assignments.*
* *Refers to a case study in the Text and Case edition.*

6.1   What are the advantages and what are the disadvantages of applying principles of business strategy to public-sector or charity organisations? Illustrate your argument by reference to a public-sector organisation of your choice.

6.2   Using either Porter's generic strategies or the Strategy Clock, identify examples of organisations following strategies of differentiation, low cost or low price, and stuck-in-the-middle or hybrid. How successful are these strategies?

6.3✱   You have been appointed personal assistant to the chief executive of a major manufacturing firm, who has asked you to explain what is meant by 'differentiation' and why it is important. Write a brief report addressing these questions.

6.4✱   Choose an industry or sector which is becoming more and more competitive (e.g. financial services or fashion retailing). How might the principles of hypercompetitive strategies apply to that industry or sector?

6.5✱   Drawing on section 6.4 (on cooperative strategies) write a report for the chief executive of a business in a competitive market (e.g. pharmaceuticals* or Formula One*) explaining when and in what ways cooperation rather than direct competition might make sense.

Integrative assignment

6.6✱   Applying game theory ideas from section 6.4.4 to issues of international strategy (Chapter 8), how might a domestic player discourage an overseas player from entering into its home market?

RECOMMENDED KEY READINGS

- The foundations of the discussions of generic competitive strategies are to be found in the writings of Michael Porter, which include *Competitive Strategy* (1980) and *Competitive Advantage* (1985), both published by Free Press. Both are recommended for readers who wish to understand the background to discussions in section 6.3 on competitive strategy and competitive advantage.

- Hypercompetition, and the strategies associated with it, are explained in Richard D'Aveni, *Hypercompetitive Rivalries: Competing in Highly Dynamic Environments*, Free Press, 1995.

- There is much written on game theory but a good deal of it can be rather inaccessible to the lay reader. Exceptions are R. McCain, *Game Theory: a Non-technical Introduction to the Analysis of Strategy*, South Western, 2003; and A. Dixit and B. Nalebuff, *The Art of Strategy: a Game Theorist's Guide to Success in Business and Life*, Norton, 2008.

REFERENCES

1. For a detailed discussion as to how organisational structures might 'address' an organisation's mix of SBUs, see M. Goold and A. Campbell, *Designing Effective Organizations: How to Create Structured Networks*, Jossey-Bass, 2002. Also K. Eisenhardt and S. Brown, 'Patching', *Harvard Business Review*, vol. 77, no. 3 (1999), p. 72.

2. This section draws heavily on M. Porter, *Competitive Advantage*, Free Press, 1985. For a more recent discussion of the generic strategies concept, see J. Parnell, 'Generic strategies after two decades: a reconceptualisation of competitive strategy', *Management Decision*, vol. 48, no. 8 (2006), pp. 1139–54.

3. P. Conley, *Experience Curves as a Planning Tool*, available as a pamphlet from the Boston Consulting Group. See also A.C. Hax and N.S. Majluf, in R.G. Dyson (ed.), *Strategic Planning: Models and Analytical Techniques*, Wiley, 1990.

4. B. Sharp and J. Dawes, 'What is differentiation and how does it work?', *Journal of Marketing Management*, vol. 17, nos 7/8 (2001), pp. 739–59, reviews the relationship between differentiation and profitability.

5. See, for example, D. Miller, 'The generic strategy trap', *Journal of Business Strategy*, vol. 13, no. 1 (1992), pp. 37–42; and S. Thornhill and R. White, 'Strategic purity: a multi-industry evaluation of pure vs hybrid business strategies', *Strategic Management Journal*, vol. 28, no. 5 (2007), pp. 553–61; Heracleous L. and Wirtz J., 'Singapore Airlines' balancing act', *Harvard Business Review*, July–August (2010), pp. 145–151.

6. C. Markides and C. Charitou, 'Competing with dual business models: a contingency approach', *Academy of Management Executive*, vol. 18, no. 3 (2004), pp. 22–36.

7. See D. Faulkner and C. Bowman, *The Essence of Competitive Strategy*, Prentice Hall, 1995.

8. For empirical support for the benefits of a hybrid strategy, see E. Pertusa-Ortega, J. Molina-Azorín and E. Claver-Cortés, 'Competitive strategies and firm performance: a comparative analysis of pure, hybrid and "stuck-in-the-middle" strategies in Spanish firms', *British Journal of Management*, vol. 20, no. 4 (2008), pp. 508–23.

9. W.B. Arthur, 'Increasing returns and the new world of business', *Harvard Business Review*, July–August (1996), pp. 100–9. See also the concept of system lock-in in A. Hax and D. Wilde, 'The Delta Model – discovering new sources of profitability in a networked economy', *European Management Journal*, vol. 19, no. 4 (2001), pp. 379–91.

10. R. D'Aveni, *Hypercompetition: Managing the Dynamics of Strategic Maneuvering*, Free Press, 1994.

11. This analysis is based on N. Kumar, 'Strategies to fight low cost rivals', *Harvard Business Review*, vol. 84, no. 12 (2006), pp. 104–13.

12. For other examples of misleading signals, see G. Stalk Jr, 'Curveball: strategies to fool the competition', *Harvard Business Review*, September (2006), pp. 115–22.

13. Useful books on collaborative strategies are Y. Doz and G. Hamel, *Alliance Advantage: The Art of Creating Value through Partnering*, Harvard Business School Press, 1998; *Creating Collaborative Advantage*, ed. Chris Huxham, Sage, 1996; and D. Faulkner, *Strategic Alliances: Cooperating to Compete*, McGraw-Hill, 1995.

14. For readings on game theory, see B. Nalebuff and A. Brandenburger, *Co-opetition*, Profile Books, 1997; R. McCain, *Game Theory: A Non-technical Introduction to the Analysis of Strategy*, South Western, 2003; and, for a summary, S. Regan, 'Game theory perspective', in M. Jenkins and V. Ambrosini (eds), *Advanced Strategic Management: a Multi-Perspective Approach*, 2nd edn, Palgrave Macmillan, 2007, pp. 83–101. A recent practical example is in H. Lindstädt and J. Müller, 'Making game theory work for managers', *McKinsey Quarterly*, December (2009).

The IKEA approach

Kevan Scholes*

'In times when many nations and people face economic challenges our vision of creating a better everyday life for the many people is more relevant than ever. To make it possible to furnish functionally, individually and sustainably – even when the economy is tight.'

This was Mikael Ohlsson, IKEA's Chief Executive, speaking in 2012[1] while reporting a sales increase of 6.9 per cent (to €25.2 billion), profits of €3 billion and share gains in most markets. At the same time average prices had fallen by 2.6 per cent. IKEA had become the world's largest home furnishings company with 287 stores in 26 countries and employing 131,000 people.

The home furnishings market[2]

By the late 2000s home furnishings was a huge market worldwide with retail sales in excess of $US600 bn in items such as furniture, household textiles and floor coverings. More than 50 per cent of these sales were in furniture stores. Table 1 compares the geographical spread of the market and IKEA sales by region.

Table 1 **The geographical spread of the market and of IKEA sales by region**

	Europe	Americas	Asia/Pacific
% of global market	52	29	19
% of IKEA sales	79	14	7

IKEA's competitors

The home furnishings market was highly fragmented with competition occurring locally rather than globally. In each region that IKEA had stores it would typically face competitors of several types:

- Multinational furniture retailers (like IKEA) all of whom were considerably smaller than IKEA. These included the Danish company Jysk (turnover ~ €2.5 bn).

- Companies specialising in just part of the furniture product range and operating in several countries – such as Alno from Germany in kitchens.

- Multi-branch retail furniture outlets whose sales were mainly in one country such as DFS in the UK. The US market was dominated by such players (e.g. Bed, Bath & Beyond Inc. with revenues of some $US9 bn).

- Non-specialist companies who carried furniture as part of a wider product range. In the UK the largest operator was the Home Retail Group whose subsidiary Argos offered some 33,000 general merchandise products through its network of 340 stores and online sales. Despite this more generalist offering Argos was number one in UK furniture retailing. General DIY companies such as Kingfisher (through B&Q in the UK and Castorama in France) were attempting to capture more of the bottom end of the furniture market.

- Small and/or specialised retailers and/or manufacturers. These accounted for some 90 per cent of the market in Europe.

IKEA's approach

IKEA had been founded by Ingvar Kamprad in 1943 in the small Swedish town of Älmhult. But it did not open its first major furniture store until 1958. The company's success had been achieved through the now legendary IKEA business model – revolutionary in the furnishing industry of its early years (see Table 2). The guiding business philosophy of Kampard was that of improving the everyday life of people by making products more affordable. This was achieved by massive (20 per cent +) reductions in sales prices vs competitors which, in turn, required aggressive reductions in IKEA's costs.

* This case was prepared by Kevan Scholes, Emeritus Professor of Strategic Management at Sheffield Business School. It is intended as a basis for class discussion and not as an illustration of good or bad management practice. © Kevan Scholes 2013. Not to be reproduced or quoted without permission.

Table 2 **IKEA's 'upside-down' business model**

Element of the business model	Traditional furniture retailer	IKEA
Design	Traditional	Modern (Swedish)
Target households	Older, established	Families with children
Style of shop	Small specialist shops	All furnishing items in big stores
Location	City centre	Out-of-town
Product focus	Individual items	'Room sets'
Marketing	Advertising	Catalogue (free)
Price	High	Low
Product assembly	Ready assembled	Flat pack – self-assembly
Sourcing	Local	Global
Brand	Manufacturers'	IKEA
Financial focus	Gross margin	Sales revenue
Overheads	Often high	Frugal – no perks

Reasons for success

In his book *The IKEA Edge*[3] published in 2011, Anders Dahlvig reflected on the reasons for IKEA's success before, during and after his period as CEO (1999–2009). He felt that the success of IKEA was built on a clear and detailed understanding of the furnishing market and IKEA's success criteria:

'IKEA's success has grown from stability and consistency regarding the big picture but with lots of action and innovation in the detail (evolution rather than revolution)'[4] . . . (IKEA's five success criteria were): 1. Design, function, and quality at low prices; 2. Unique (Scandinavian) design; 3. Inspiration, ideas and complete solutions; 4. Everything in one place; 5. "A day out", the shopping experience . . . You may well say that they are similar to those of most companies. The difference, in my opinion, is that IKEA is much better at delivering on these customer needs than are other retailers . . . Most competitors focus on one or at most two of these customer needs. High-street shops focus on design and inspiration. Out-of-town low-cost retailers focus on price. Department stores focus on choice. The real strength of IKEA lies in the combination of all five.[5]

IKEA's competitive strategy

Dahlvig explained IKEA's approach to competition:

'You can choose to adapt your company's product range to the markets you are operating in, or you can choose to shift the market's preference towards your own range and style. IKEA has chosen the latter. By doing this, the company can maintain a unique and distinct profile.

This is, however, a more difficult path to follow.'[6] '. . . A significant understanding of the customer's situation at home is the basis for IKEA's product development and the creation of the main media through which the product is presented to the public.'[7] '. . . For most competitors, having the lowest price seems to mean being 5 to 10 per cent cheaper than the competition on comparable products. At IKEA, this means being a minimum 20 per cent cheaper and often up to 50 per cent cheaper than the competition.'[8]

Global expansion

By 1999 IKEA was operating 158 stores in 29 countries with a turnover the equivalent of €7.6 bn. Despite IKEA's strong global position Dahlvig felt there was much opportunity and need for improvement:

'So far growth has come from going "wide but thin". We have stores in 29 countries but with limited market share in most markets. Now we enter a new phase where the focus will be to go "deep" and concentrate on our existing markets . . . We shall focus on continued strong volume growth, 10 per cent pa for 10 years.'[9]

He explained his reasoning:

'Why make the change? First of all, we were impelled by the changing character of the competition. For many years, the competition had been very fragmented and local in nature. However, many of the very big retail companies were shifting strategy. From being local, they were looking to a global expansion, not least in the emerging markets like China, Russia and Eastern Europe. They were also broadening their product range, moving away from food or traditional DIY products towards more home furnishing. These were big companies with much more muscle than IKEA's traditional competitors. They had both financial resources and operational retailing competence on a par with IKEA. One way to dissuade them from entering into the home furnishing arena was to aggressively reduce prices and increase the company's presence with more stores in all local markets in the countries where IKEA was operating. Market leadership in each market was the objective. Another reason for the shift in strategy was cost efficiency. Growing sales in existing stores is the most cost-efficient way to grow the company.'[10]

Managing the value chain

Dahlvig explained that IKEA's strategy crucially requires the 'design' and control of IKEA's wider value chain in detail:

'The secret is the control and coordination of the whole value chain from raw material, production, and range development, to distribution into stores. Most other companies working in the retail sector have control either of the retail end (stores and distribution) or the product design and production end. IKEA's vertical integration makes it a complex company compared to most, since it owns both production, range development, distribution, and stores.'[11] . . . This included backward integration by extending the activities of Swedwood (IKEA's manufacturing arm) beyond furniture factories, into control over the raw materials, saw mills, board suppliers, and component factories.'[12]

'(The challenge) . . . is how to combine strong specialist functions within "one" company view and approach . . . differentiation through controlling the whole value chain is key to success. There are some very important factors that have helped keep the company together: a strong vision, the business idea, company values, a common store concept, a common product range, and a common distribution and buying organisation.'[13]

'The one disappointment (in my 10 years) was that the cost level did not decrease as much as planned. We'd needed productivity gains of 10 per cent pa or more, and we managed only around a 4 to 6 per cent. Better than planned margins compensated for this, and thus the profit level was in line with the plan. Nevertheless, a low price company must be a low cost company.'[14]

China and India

IKEA first opened in China in 1998 and it had eight stores by 2012. The Chinese market was extremely challenging for a company that had built global success through standardisation.[15] The main problems were that in developing markets IKEA products were expensive relative to local competitors and the consumer shopping expectations were centred on small, local shops and personal service. So inevitably there had to be some flexibility in approach by IKEA. For example, it presented an image as exclusive Western European interior design specialists – popular with younger, affluent, city dwellers. The shops were smaller than usual for IKEA and typically nearer city centres. Because DIY was not well developed in China IKEA offered home delivery and assembly services. Catalogues were only available *in store*. Crucially stores were allowed to source almost 50 per cent locally (against the company average of about 25 per cent) in order to keep prices competitive.

This experience would be useful when IKEA entered India. It was announced in 2012 that IKEA was to invest €1.5 bn in opening 25 stores over 15 to 20 years.[16]

New leaders but same formula?

Michael Ohlsson succeeded Dahlvig as CEO in 2009 – having already worked for IKEA for 30 years. The company commented: 'Mikael Ohlsson has strong implementation skills and is a great ambassador of the IKEA Culture. He is well suited to continue the change process that Anders Dahlvig has initiated.'[17]

Indeed, despite extremely challenging economic conditions the company's success continued, exceeding €25 bn sales by 2012. In September 2012 IKEA announced that Ohlsson would retire in 2013 and be succeeded by another internal appointee – Peter Agnefjäll (18 years at IKEA). Agnefjäll told Reuters that 'under his leadership, the company will increase the number of store openings between 20 and 25 every year, from 2014 to 2015.'[18]

So perhaps the IKEA approach still had a bright future?

Sources
1. 'Welcome inside 2011' from IKEA website: www.ikea.com.
2. Data in this section come from the IKEA website 2012 and from the DataMonitor report on Global Home Furnishings Retail Industry Profile (reference code: 0199-2243, publication date: April 2008).
3. Anders Dahlvig, *The Ikea Edge*, McGraw-Hill, 2011.
4. Reference 3, p. 65.

5. Reference 3, p. 62.
6. Reference 3, p. 63.
7. Reference 3, p. 63.
8. Reference 3, p. 74.
9. Reference 3, p. 120.
10. Reference 3, p. 123.
11. Reference 3, p. 75.
12. Reference 3, p. 83.
13. Reference 3, p. 95.
14. Reference 3, p. 124.
15. U. Johansson and A. Thelander, 'A standardised approach to the world? IKEA in China', *International Journal of Quality and Service Sciences*, vol. 1, no. 2 (2009), pp. 199–219.
16. Reuters, 23 June 2012.
17. IKEA press release, 24 April 2009.
18. Reported by www.valuewalk.com, 18 September 2012.

Questions

1 Identify where (in its value network) and how IKEA has achieved cost leadership.

2 Identify how IKEA has achieved differentiation from its competitors.

3 Explain how IKEA tries to ensure that its 'Hybrid' strategy remains sustainable and does not become 'stuck-in-the-middle'.

4 What are the lessons from China about IKEA's approach?

7

CORPORATE STRATEGY AND DIVERSIFICATION

Learning objectives

After reading this chapter, you should be able to:

● Identify alternative strategy options, including *market penetration*, *product development*, *market development* and *diversification*.

● Distinguish between different diversification strategies (*related* and *conglomerate* diversification) and evaluate *diversification drivers*.

● Assess the relative benefits of *vertical integration* and *outsourcing*.

● Analyse the ways in which a *corporate parent* can add or destroy value for its portfolio of business units.

● Analyse *portfolios* of business units and judge which to invest in and which to divest.

Key terms

BCG matrix p. 244

diversification (related and unrelated/conglomerate) p. 226

dominant logic p. 232

economies of scope p. 232

outsourcing p. 235

parenting advantage p. 226

portfolio manager p. 240

synergy p. 233

vertical (forward and backward) integration p. 235

MyStrategyLab

MyStrategyLab is designed to help you make the most of your studies. Visit **www.pearsoned.co.uk/mystrategylab** to discover a wide range of resources, including:

● A personalised **Study plan** that will help you understand core concepts

● **Audio and video clips** that put the spotlight on strategy in the real world

● **Online glossaries and flashcards** that provide helpful reminders when you're looking for some quick revision.

(7.1) INTRODUCTION

Chapter 6 was concerned with *competitive strategy* – the ways in which a single business unit (SBU) or organisational unit can compete in a given market space, for instance through cost leadership or differentiation. However, organisations may choose to enter many new product and market areas (see Figure PII.1 in Part II introduction). Tata Group, one of India's largest companies, began as a trading organisation and soon moved into hotels and textiles. Since that time Tata has diversified further into steel, motors, consultancy, technologies, tea, chemicals, power, communications. As organisations add new units and capabilities, their strategies may no longer be solely concerned with *competitive strategy* in one market space at the business level, but with choices concerning different businesses or markets. These related choices include which business unit(s) to buy, the direction(s) an organisation might pursue and how resources may be allocated efficiently across multiple business activities. These choices, indicated in Figure 7.1, inform decisions about how broad an organisation should be. This 'scope' of an organisation is central to *corporate strategy* and the focus of this chapter.

Scope is concerned with how far an organisation should be diversified in terms of products and markets. As the opening example shows an organisation may increase its scope by engaging in market spaces or products different to its current ones. Section 7.2 introduces a classic product market framework which uses these categories for identifying different growth directions for an organisation. This indicates different *diversification* strategies open to an organisation, according to the novelty of products or markets. Underpinning diversification choices are a range of drivers, which are discussed in Section 7.3, including increasing market power, reducing risk and exploiting superior internal processes. The performance implications of diversification are, then, reviewed in Section 7.4.

Another way of increasing the scope of an organisation is *vertical integration*, discussed in Section 7.5. It allows an organisation to act as an internal supplier or a customer to itself (as

Figure 7.1 Strategic directions and corporate-level strategy

Scope
How broad to make the portfolio?

Corporate parenting
How should the 'parent' add value?

Portfolio matrices
Which SBUs to invest in?

for example an oil company supplies its petrol to its own petrol stations). The organisation may decide to *outsource* certain activities – to 'dis-integrate' by subcontracting an internal activity to an external supplier – as this may improve organisational efficiency. The scope of the organisation may therefore be adjusted through growth or contraction.

If an organisation has decided to operate in different areas of activity, head office executives, the 'corporate level', need to manage these to add value to the group. Section 7.6 discusses the value-adding effect of head office, termed parenting advantage, to the individual business units that make up the organisation's portfolio. How, then, do corporate-level activities, decisions and resources add value to the actual businesses? As will be seen in the Key Debate at the end of this chapter, there is considerable scepticism about the value-adding role of corporate-level strategy.

In order to decide which industries and businesses organisations should invest in or dispose of, the corporate centre needs to assess whether the *portfolio* of businesses is worth more under its management than the individual businesses would be worth standing alone. Section 7.7 reviews portfolio matrices, which are useful techniques to help structure corporate-level choices about businesses in which to invest and those to divest.

This chapter is not just about large commercial businesses. Even small businesses may consist of a number of business units. For example, a local building company may be undertaking contract work for local government, work for industrial buyers and for local homeowners. Not only are these different market segments, but the mode of operation and capabilities required for competitive success in each also likely to be different. Moreover, the owner of that business has to take decisions about the extent of investment and activity in each segment. Public-sector organisations such as local government or health services also provide different services, which correspond to business units in commercial organisations. Corporate-level strategy is also highly relevant to the appropriate drawing of organisational boundaries in the public sector. Privatisation and outsourcing decisions can be considered as responses to the failure of public-sector organisations to add sufficient value by their parenting.

(7.2) STRATEGY DIRECTIONS

The Ansoff product/market growth matrix[1] is a corporate strategy framework for generating four basic directions for organisational growth: see Figure 7.2 for an adapted version. Typically an organisation starts in the zone around point A, the top left-hand corner of Figure 7.2. According to Ansoff, the organisation may choose between *penetrating* still further within its existing sphere (staying in zone A) or increasing its diversity along the two axes of increasing novelty of markets or increasing novelty of products. This process of increasing the diversity of the range of products and/or markets served by an organisation is known as 'diversification'. Diversification **involves increasing the range of products or markets served by an organisation. Related diversification involves expanding into products or services with relationships to the existing business.** Thus on Ansoff's axes the organisation has two related diversification strategies available: moving to zone B, *developing new products* for its existing markets or moving to zone C by bringing its existing products into *new markets*. In each case, the further along the two axes, the more diversified is the strategy. Alternatively, the organisation can move in both directions at once, following a *conglomerate diversification* strategy with altogether new markets and new products (zone D). Thus conglomerate (unrelated) diversification **involves diversifying into products or services with no relationships to existing businesses.**

Figure 7.2 Corporate strategy directions

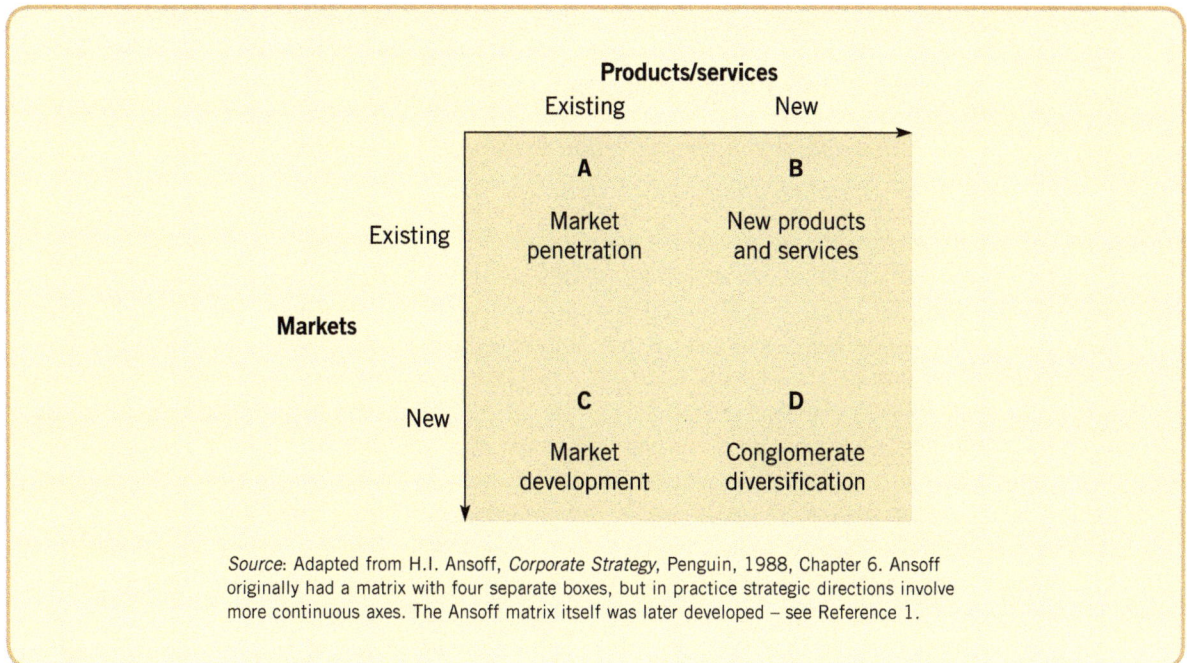

Source: Adapted from H.I. Ansoff, *Corporate Strategy*, Penguin, 1988, Chapter 6. Ansoff originally had a matrix with four separate boxes, but in practice strategic directions involve more continuous axes. The Ansoff matrix itself was later developed – see Reference 1.

Ansoff's axes can be used effectively in brainstorming strategic options, checking that options in all four zones have been properly considered. Illustration 7.1 traces the evolution of a social enterprise raising questions about how businesses might think about Ansoff's matrix in choosing their strategic direction. The next section will consider each of Ansoff's four main directions in some detail. Section 7.5 will examine the additional option of *vertical integration*.

7.2.1 Market penetration

For a simple, undiversified business, the most obvious strategic option is often increased penetration of its existing market, with its existing products. **Market penetration implies increasing share of current markets with the current product range.** This strategy builds on established strategic capabilities and does not require the organisation to venture into uncharted territory. The organisation's scope is exactly the same. Moreover, greater market share implies increased power vis-à-vis buyers and suppliers (in terms of Porter's five forces), greater economies of scale and experience curve benefits.

However, organisations seeking greater market penetration may face two constraints:

- *Retaliation from competitors.* In terms of the five forces (section 2.3.1), increasing market penetration is likely to exacerbate industry rivalry as other competitors in the market defend their share. Increased rivalry might involve price wars or expensive marketing battles, which may cost more than any market-share gains are actually worth. The dangers of provoking fierce retaliation are greater in low-growth markets, as any gains in volume will be much more at the expense of other players. Where retaliation is a danger, organisations seeking market penetration need strategic capabilities that give a clear competitive advantage. In low-growth or declining markets, it can be more effective simply to acquire competitors. Some companies have grown quickly in this way. For example, in the steel industry the Indian

ILLUSTRATION

ILLUSTRATION 7.1

Baking change into the community

How Greyston's diversification transforms a depressed community.

Probably best known for producing the brownies in the famous Ben and Jerry's ice creams, the Greyston Bakery is part of the Greyston Foundation – a $15 m (£9 m; €11.25 m) integrated network of for-profit and not-for-profit entities. The Foundation provides a wide array of services to benefit its local depressed community.

A Zen Buddhist meditation group started the bakery in 1982. They located in the poor neighbourhood of Yonkers, New York, where they perceived a need to create jobs for people in the community who were 'hard to employ' – the homeless, those with spotted employment histories, prison records and past substance-abuse problems. Radically they used an 'open hiring' practice that continues today, in which anybody who applies for a job has an opportunity to work, on a first-come, first-hired basis. Employees have to show up for work on time, perform the job, and have an appropriate attitude for three months and are then automatically made permanent employees. As SVP David Rome says, 'we judge people based on their performance in the operation, not on their background'. There is high initial turnover but the average tenure is about three years. Greyston considers it a success when an employee moves on to a new job using his or her new skills. According to CEO Julius Walls, 'The company provides opportunities and resources to its employees so they can be successful not only in the workplace but in their personal lives. We don't hire people to bake brownies; we bake brownies to hire people.'

As the bakery expanded it realised that providing jobs to the community was not enough. In 1991, working with governmental agencies, Greyston Family Inn was opened to provide permanent housing for homeless people. Currently there are three buildings, providing 50 housing units. A child daycare centre was also started with after-school care as one of the most pressing needs in the community for working parents to fill the gap left by public schools. In 1992 Greyston Health Services was formed, to help poor people with HIV/AIDS, and in 1997 Issan House opened with 35 permanent housing units for those

with HIV/AIDS, mental illness or chemical dependency. Other ventures included Greyston Garden Project, five community-run gardens on neglected properties and a technology education centre. In 2011, a local retail bakery/café was opened and, in 2012, with the help of the Foundation's real-estate division, a new bakery was constructed, for $10 m in a public–private partnership project with the city, on a long dormant brownfield (contaminated) site.

The Foundation is an umbrella for all Greyston organisations, providing centralised management, fundraising, real-estate development, and planning services. It now comprises four interrelated organisations: bakery, healthcare services, child and family programmes, and real-estate development. The Foundation's social mission of supporting low-income people to forge a path to self-sufficiency and community transformation is blended with business collaboration to enable continual growth.

In 2012, Greyston Bakery celebrated its 30th anniversary, and received a fantastic present from New York State: to become a Benefit Corporation, allowing Greyston to demonstrate higher standards of corporate purpose, accountability and transparency. As Foundation CEO Steven Brown says, 'Really, we were a benefit corporation long before the term was coined. You're in business for a much larger community that has a stake in what you are doing. The extent that we can create value and opportunity is the path out of distress for many of these communities. It's not easy, but we're growing.'

Sources: www.greyston.org; http://www.pegasuscom.com/levpoints/ greystonint.html; http://www.huffingtonpost.com/jesse-seaver/ businesses-non-profit-social-enterprise; http://www.youtube.com/ watch?v=2WLzV7JfVSc.

Questions

1 What were the motivation(s) for Greyston Bakery's diversifications?

2 Referring to the Ansoff matrix, how would you classify these diversifications?

company LNM (Mittal) moved rapidly in the 2000s to become the largest steel producer in the world by acquiring struggling steel companies around the world. Acquisitions may reduce rivalry, by taking out independent players and controlling them under one umbrella.

- *Legal constraints*. Greater market penetration can raise concerns from official competition regulators concerning excessive market power. Most countries have regulators with the powers to restrain powerful companies or prevent mergers and acquisitions that would create such excessive power. In the United Kingdom, the Competition Commission can investigate any merger or acquisition that would account for more than 25 per cent of the national market, and either halt the deal or propose measures that would reduce market power. The European Commission has an overview of the whole European market and can similarly intervene. For example, when the German T-Mobile and French Orange companies proposed to merge their UK mobile phone operations in 2010, the European Commission insisted that the merged companies should divest a quarter of their combined share of the key mobile phone 1800 MHz spectrum.[2]

Market penetration may also not be an option where economic constraints are severe, for instance during a market downturn or public-sector funding crisis. Here organisations will need to consider the strategic option of *retrenchment*: withdrawal from marginal activities in order to concentrate on the most valuable segments and products within their existing business. However, where growth is still sought after, the Ansoff axes suggest further directions, as follows.

7.2.2 Product development

Product development is where organisations deliver modified or new products (or services) to existing markets. This can involve varying degrees of diversification along the horizontal axis of Figure 7.2. For Apple, developing its products from the original iPod, through iPhone to iPad involved little diversification: although the technologies differed, Apple was targeting the same customers and using very similar production processes and distribution channels. Despite the potential for benefits from relatedness, product development can be an expensive and high-risk activity for at least two reasons:

- *New strategic capabilities*. Product development strategies typically involve mastering new processes or technologies that are unfamiliar to the organisation. For example, the digital revolution is forcing universities to reconsider the way learning materials are acquired and provided to students and the nature of the student/academic interface. High-quality content available free online and virtual engagement with students now raise the question of how universities should consider redeploying their resources in the future. Success is likely to depend on a willingness to acquire new technological capabilities, to engage in organisational restructuring and new marketing capabilities to manage customer perceptions. Thus product development typically involves heavy investments and can have high risk of project failures.

- *Project management risk*. Even within fairly familiar domains, product development projects are typically subject to the risk of delays and increased costs due to project complexity and changing project specifications over time. An extreme example is Boeing's Dreamliner 787 aircraft: making innovative use of carbon-fibre composites, the Dreamliner had a history of delays even before launch in 2010, and required \$2.5 bn (~ £1.75 bn) write-offs due to cancelled orders. Since then subsequent delamination of the aft fuselage and most recently batteries catching fire in 2013 resulted in fleets being grounded.

Strategies for product development are considered further in Chapter 9.

7.2.3 **Market development**

Product development can be risky and expensive. Market development can be more attractive by being potentially cheaper and quicker to execute. **Market development involves offering existing products to new markets.** Again, the degree of diversification varies along Figure 7.2's downward axis. Typically, of course, market development entails some product development as well, if only in terms of packaging or service. Nonetheless, market development remains a form of related diversification given its origins in similar products. Market development takes two basic forms:

- *New users.* Here an example would be aluminium, whose original users, packaging and cutlery manufacturers are now supplemented by users in aerospace and automobiles.
- *New geographies.* The prime example of this is internationalisation, but the spread of a small retailer into new towns would also be a case.

In all cases, it is essential that market development strategies be based on products or services that meet the *critical success factors* of the new market (see section 2.4.3). Strategies based on simply off loading traditional products or services in new markets are likely to fail. Moreover, market development faces similar problems to product development. In terms of strategic capabilities, market developers often lack the right marketing skills and brands to make progress in a market with unfamiliar customers. On the management side, the challenge is coordinating between different users and geographies, which might all have different needs. *International market development* strategy is considered in Chapter 8.

7.2.4 **Conglomerate diversification**

Conglomerate (or unrelated) diversification takes the organisation beyond both its existing markets and its existing products (i.e. zone D in Figure 7.2). In this sense, it radically increases the organisation's scope. Conglomerate diversification strategies can create value as businesses may benefit from being part of a larger group. This may allow consumers to have greater confidence in the business unit's products and services than before and larger size may also reduce the costs of finance. However, conglomerate strategies are often not trusted by many observers because there are no obvious ways in which the businesses can work together to generate additional value, over and above the businesses remaining on their own. In addition, there is often an additional bureaucratic cost of the managers at headquarters who control them. For this reason, conglomerate companies' share prices can suffer from what is called the 'conglomerate discount' – in other words, a lower valuation than the combined individual constituent businesses would have on their own. In 2012, the shares in French conglomerate Vivendi, with wide interests in mobile telephony and media, were trading down 25 per cent on the previous year and its break-up value was estimated as at least twice the value of the shares. At a shareholder meeting in Corsica in June, senior management stoked speculation when they said 'discussions about whether it should split up its businesses or sell off some assets were "not taboo"'.

However, it is important to recognise that the distinction between related and conglomerate (unrelated) diversification is often a matter of degree. Relationships that might have seemed valuable in related diversification may not turn out to be as valuable as expected. Thus the large accounting firms have often struggled in translating their skills and client contacts developed in auditing into effective consulting practices. Similarly, relationships may change in importance over time, as the nature of technologies or customers change: see, for example, the decision by Zodiac to divest itself of its iconic boat business (Illustration 7.2).

ILLUSTRATION 7.2

Zodiac deflates: from boats to aerospace

For 117 years the Zodiac Group has diversified and then re-centred through de-diversification.

The Zodiac Group is probably best known for its Zodiac inflatable boats, used by Jacques Cousteau and seen in harbours around the world. But by 2012, Zodiac was a world leader in aerospace equipment. How had this transformation come about?

The Zodiac company was founded in 1896 by Maurice Mallet after his first hot-air balloon ascent. Zodiac manufactured only dirigible airships for 40 years until 1937, when the German Zeppelin *Hindenburg* crashed near New York, abruptly halting the airship market. With its traditional activity extinguished, Zodiac decided to leverage its technical expertise and moved to inflatable boats. This proved to be very successful with over one million Zodiac rubber inflatables sold worldwide by 2004.

However, increasing competition from Italian manufacturers led Zodiac to diversify. In 1978, it acquired Aerazur, a company specialising in parachutes, life vests and inflatable life rafts. These products had strong market and technical synergies with rubber boats and their main customers were aircraft manufacturers. Zodiac confirmed this move to a new market in 1987 by taking over Air Cruisers, a manufacturer of inflatable escape slides for aeroplanes. As a consequence, Zodiac became a key supplier to Boeing, McDonnell Douglas and Airbus. This position was strengthened through takeovers of leading manufacturers of aeroplane seats: Sicma Aero Seats (France) and Weber Aircraft (USA) and MAG Aerospace, the world leader for aircraft vacuum waste systems. In 1999, Zodiac took over Intertechnique, a leading player in active components for aircraft (fuel circulation, hydraulics, oxygen and life support, electrical power, flight-deck controls and displays, systems monitoring, etc.). By combining these competences with its traditional expertise in inflatable products, Zodiac launched a new business unit: airbags for the automobile industry.

In parallel to these diversifications, Zodiac strengthened its position in inflatable boats by the takeover of several competitors: Bombard-L'Angevinière in 1980, Sevylor in 1981, Hurricane and Metzeler in 1987. The company also developed a swimming-pool business from its first product line, back in 1981, based on inflatable structure technology. Through takeovers Zodiac now produced rigid above-ground pools, modular in-ground pools, pool cleaners and water purification systems, inflatable beach gear and air mattresses.

However, by 2007, aircraft products accounted for 80 per cent of group turnover. For some airline equipment Zodiac held a 40 per cent market share globally and produced electrical power systems for the Airbus A380 and Boeing 787. Zodiac had even reached Mars: NASA Mars probes *Spirit* and *Opportunity* were equipped with Zodiac equipment.

In 2007 the marine and leisure businesses, which accounted for 19 per cent of turnover, were sold, with Chief Executive Jean-Louis Gérondeau saying 'this would reinforce Zodiac's acquisition capabilities, in the aerospace sector'. It was also a response to pressure from financial analysts, who considered Zodiac too diversified. The sale funded three further acquisitions of aircraft cabin equipment companies, Driessen, Adder and TIA in 2008, and Zodiac renamed itself Zodiac Aerospace. Although subject to a takeover bid from Safran, a French aeronautics group, in 2012, Zodiac rebuffed the bid and announced higher than expected profits of €319 m due to buoyant aerospace demand and two recent acquisitions (Heath Tecna Aircraft (interiors); Contour Aerospace (seats)). Re-pivoted, Zodiac is now a world leader in aerospace equipment and installed systems for commercial aircraft and helicopters.

Source: Based on an illustration by Frédéric Fréry, ESCP Europe Business School.

Questions

1 Explain the ways in which relatedness informed Zodiac's diversification strategy over time.

2 What are the advantages and potential dangers of its decision to focus on the aircraft products market?

(7.3) DIVERSIFICATION DRIVERS

Diversification might be chosen for a variety of reasons, some more value-creating than others.[3] Growth in organisational size is rarely a good enough reason for diversification on its own: growth must be profitable. Indeed, growth can often be merely a form of 'empire building', especially in the public sector. Diversification decisions need to be approached sceptically.

Four potentially value-creating drivers for diversification are as follows.

- *Exploiting economies of scope.* **Economies of scope refer to efficiency gains through applying the organisation's existing resources or competences to new markets or services.**[4] If an organisation has under-utilised resources or competences that it cannot effectively close or sell to other potential users, it is efficient to use these resources or competences by diversification into a new activity. In other words, there are economies to be gained by extending the scope of the organisation's activities. For example, many universities have large resources in terms of halls of residence, which they must have for their students but which are under-utilised out of term-time. These halls of residence are more efficiently used if the universities expand the scope of their activities into conferencing and tourism during holiday periods. Economies of scope may apply to both *tangible* resources, such as halls of residence, and *intangible* resources and competences, such as brands or staff skills.

- *Stretching corporate management competences ('dominant logics').* This is a special case of economies of scope, and refers to the potential for applying the skills of talented corporate-level managers (referred to as 'corporate parenting skills' in section 7.6) to new businesses. The **dominant logic is the set of corporate-level managerial competences applied across the portfolio of businesses.**[5] Corporate-level managers may have competences that can be applied even to businesses not sharing resources at the operating-unit level. Thus the French luxury-goods conglomerate LVMH includes a wide range of businesses – from champagne, through fashion, jewellery and perfumes, to financial media – that share very few operational resources or business-level competences. However, LVMH creates value for these specialised companies by applying corporate-level competences in developing classic brands and nurturing highly creative people that are relevant to all its individual businesses. See also the discussion of dominant logic at Berkshire Hathaway in Illustration 7.4 later.

- *Exploiting superior internal processes.* Internal processes within a diversified corporation can often be more efficient than external processes in the open market. This is especially the case where external capital and labour markets do not yet work well, as in many developing economies. In these circumstances, well-managed conglomerates can make sense, even if their constituent businesses do not have operating relationships with each other. For example, China has many conglomerates because it is able to mobilise internal investment, develop managers and exploit networks in a way that standalone Chinese companies, relying on imperfect markets, cannot. For example, China's largest privately owned conglomerate, the Fosun Group, owns steel mills, pharmaceutical companies and China's largest retailer, Yuyuan Tourist Mart.[6]

- *Increasing market power.*[7] Being diversified in many businesses can increase power vis-à-vis competitors in at least two ways. First, having the same wide portfolio of products as a competitor increases the potential for *mutual forbearance.* The ability to retaliate across the whole range of the portfolio acts to discourage the competitor from making any aggressive moves at all. Two similarly diversified competitors are thus likely to forbear from competing aggressively with each other. Second, having a diversified range of businesses increases the power to *cross-subsidise* one business from the profits of the others. On the one hand, the ability to cross-subsidise can support aggressive bids to drive competitors out of a particular market. On the other hand, knowing this power to cross-subsidise a particular business, competitors without equivalent power will be reluctant to attack that business.

Where diversification creates value, it is described as 'synergistic'.[8] **Synergy refers to the benefits gained where activities or assets complement each other so that their combined effect is greater than the sum of the parts** (the famous 2 + 2 = 5 equation). Thus a film company and a music publisher would be synergistic if they were worth more together than separately – if the music publisher had the sole rights to music used in the film company productions for instance. However, synergies are often harder to identify and more costly to extract in practice than managers like to admit.[9]

Indeed, some drivers for diversification involve negative synergies, in other words value destruction. Three potentially value-destroying diversification drivers are:

- *Responding to market decline* is one common but doubtful driver for diversification. Rather than let the managers of a declining business invest spare funds in a new business, conventional finance theory suggests it is usually best to let shareholders find new growth investment opportunities for themselves. For example, Kodak (see Illustration 5.5 in Chapter 5), the US photo film corporation, spent billions of dollars on diversification acquisitions such as chemicals, desktop radiotherapy, photocopiers, telecommunications and inkjet printers in order to compensate for market decline in its main product. Many of these initiatives failed and the decline of the core business continued until Kodak went bankrupt. Shareholders might have preferred Kodak simply to hand back the large surpluses generated for decades beforehand rather than spending on costly acquisitions. If shareholders had wanted to invest in the chemicals, telecommunications or printers, they could have invested in the original dominant companies themselves.

- *Spreading risk* across a range of markets is another common justification for diversification. Again, conventional finance theory is very sceptical about risk-spreading by diversification. Shareholders can easily spread their risk by taking small stakes in dozens of very different companies themselves. Diversification strategies, on the other hand, are likely to involve a limited range of fairly related markets. While managers might like the security of having more than one market, shareholders typically do not need each of the companies they invest in to be diversified as well – they would prefer managers to concentrate on managing their core business as well as they can. However, conventional finance theory does not apply to private businesses, where the owners have a large proportion of their assets tied up in their company: here it can make sense to diversify risk across a number of distinct activities, so that if one part is in trouble, the whole business is not pulled down.

- *Managerial ambition* can sometimes drive inappropriate diversification. It is argued that the managers of British banks such as Royal Bank of Scotland (at one point the fifth-largest bank in the world) and HBOS (Britain's largest housing-lender) promoted strategies of excessive growth and diversification into new markets during the first decade of the twenty-first century. Such growth and diversification gave the managers short-term benefits in terms of managerial bonuses and prestige. But going beyond their areas of true expertise soon brought financial disaster, leading to the nationalisation of RBS and the takeover of HBOS by rival bank Lloyds.

(7.4) DIVERSIFICATION AND PERFORMANCE

Because most large corporations today are diversified, but also because diversification can sometimes be in management's self-interest, many scholars and policy-makers have been concerned to establish whether diversified companies really perform better than undiversified companies. After all, it would be deeply troubling if large corporations were diversifying simply to spread risk for managers, to save managerial jobs in declining businesses or to generate short-term growth, as in the case of RBS and HBOS.

Research studies of diversification have particularly focused on the relative benefits of related diversification and conglomerate or unrelated diversification. Researchers generally find that related or limited diversifiers outperform both firms that remain specialised and those that have unrelated or extensively diversified strategies.[10] In other words, the diversification–performance relationship tends to follow an inverted (or upside-down) U-shape, as in Figure 7.3. The implication is that some diversification is good – but not too much.

However, these performance studies produce statistical averages. Some related diversification strategies fail – as in the case of some accounting firms' ventures in consulting – while some conglomerates succeed – as in the case of LVMH. The case against unrelated diversification is not solid, and effective dominant logics or particular national contexts can play in its favour. For instance, conglomerate diversification may be particularly effective in developing economies as a form of protection against institutional weaknesses such as poor law enforcement, lack of quality labour, capricious political contexts. The conclusion from the performance studies is that, although on average related diversification pays better than unrelated, any diversification strategy needs rigorous questioning on its particular merits.

Figure 7.3 Diversity and performance

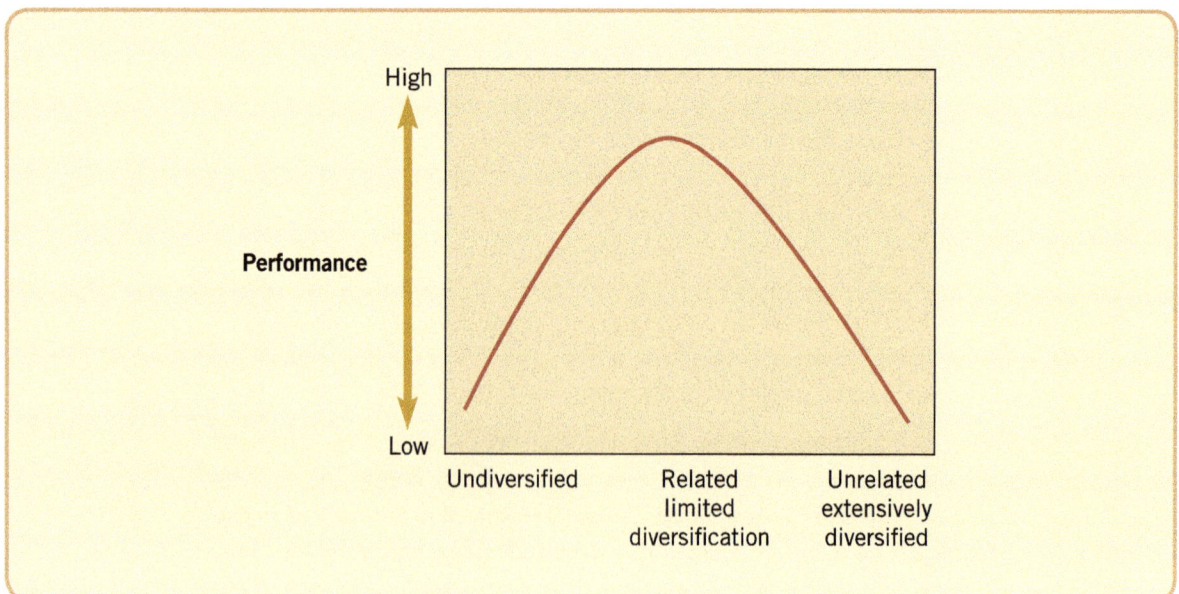

7.5 VERTICAL INTEGRATION

As well as diversification, another direction for corporate strategy can be vertical integration. **Vertical integration describes entering activities where the organisation is its own supplier or customer.** Thus it involves operating at another stage of the value network (see section 3.4.2). This section considers both vertical integration and vertical dis-integration, particularly in the form of outsourcing.

7.5.1 Forward and backward integration

Vertical integration can go in either of two directions:

- **Backward integration** refers to development into activities concerned with the inputs into the company's current business (i.e. they are further back in the value network). For example, the acquisition by a car manufacturer of a component supplier would be a backward integration move.

- **Forward integration** refers to development into activities concerned with the outputs of a company's current business (i.e. are further forward in the value network). For a car manufacturer, forward integration would be into car retail, repairs and servicing.

Thus vertical integration is like diversification in increasing corporate scope. The difference is that it brings together activities up and down the same value network, while diversification typically involves more or less different value networks. However, because realising synergies involves bringing together different value networks, diversification (especially related diversification) is sometimes also described as *horizontal integration.* For example, a company diversified in cars, trucks and buses could find benefits in integrating aspects of the various design or component-sourcing processes. The relationship between horizontal integration and vertical integration is depicted in Figure 7.4.

Vertical integration is often favoured because it seems to 'capture' more of the profits in a value network. The car manufacturer gains the retailer's profits as well. However, it is important to be aware of two dangers. First, vertical integration involves investment. Expensive investments in activities that are less profitable than the original core business will be unattractive to shareholders because they are reducing their *average* or overall rate of return on investment. Second, even if there is a degree of relatedness through the value network, vertical integration is likely to involve quite different strategic capabilities. Thus car manufacturers who forwardly integrate into car service and repair have found that managing networks of small service outlets is very different to managing large manufacturing plants. Growing appreciation of both the risks of diluting overall returns on investment and the distinct capabilities involved at different stages of the value network has led many companies in recent years to vertically *dis*-integrate.

7.5.2 To integrate or to outsource?

Where a part of vertically integrated operations is not adding value to the overall business, it may be replaced through outsourcing or subcontracting. **Outsourcing is the process by which activities previously carried out internally are subcontracted to external suppliers.** Outsourcing

Figure 7.4 Diversification and integration options: car manufacturer example

can refer to the subcontracting of components in manufacturing, but is now particularly common for services such as information technology, customer call centres and human resource management (see Illustration 7.3). The argument for outsourcing to specialist suppliers is often based on strategic capabilities. Specialists in a particular activity are likely to have superior capabilities than an organisation for which that particular activity is not a central part of its business. A specialist IT contractor is usually better at IT than the IT department of a steel company.

However, Nobel prize-winning economist Oliver Williamson has argued that the decision to integrate or outsource involves more than just relative capabilities. His *transaction cost framework* helps analyse the relative costs and benefits of managing ('transacting') activities internally or externally (see also the Key Debate at the end of this chapter).[11] In assessing whether to integrate or outsource an activity, he warns against underestimating the long-term costs of *opportunism* by external subcontractors (or indeed any other organisation in a market relationship). Subcontractors are liable over time to take advantage of their position, either to reduce its standards or to extract higher prices. Market relationships tend to fail in controlling subcontractor opportunism where:

- there are *few alternatives* to the subcontractor and it is hard to shop around;
- the product or service is *complex and changing*, and therefore impossible to specify fully in a legally binding contract;
- investments have been made in *specific assets*, which the subcontractors know will have little value if they withhold their product or service.

Both capabilities and transaction cost reasoning have influenced the outsourcing decisions of the Royal Bank of Scotland, see Illustration 7.3.

ILLUSTRATION 7.3

'Out of sight – out of mind'? Outsourcing at Royal Bank of Scotland

In 2012, Royal Bank of Scotland (RBS) experienced a major crisis when its customers could not withdraw cash. Was this the consequence of outsourcing?

In June 2012 RBS encountered severe problems when 10 million retail and business customers suddenly found they could not access their cash. This was highly damaging to the bank's reputation and could result in significant customer loss. The problem was faulty updating of CA-7 – critical software that controls the batch processing systems dealing with retail banking transactions. Generally regarded as 'a very common and reliable product, it processes accounts overnight via thousands of pieces of work' such as ATM transactions, bank-to-bank salary payments, and so on, and finishes by updating the account master copy with the definitive balance. Described as a huge game of Jenga (the tower game played with interlaced wood blocks), all transactions are related, so everything needs to be processed in order. Thus Tuesday's batch must run before Wednesday's to avoid, for example, penalising someone who has a large sum of money leave their account on Wednesday that might put them in debt but which would be covered by money arriving on Tuesday. In updating CA-7, files were deleted or corrupted so the master copy was wrong for three nights – meaning millions of transactions were not processed. RBS branches had to extend their opening hours to reassure customers about their accounts.

Unions argued the disaster was due to 'offshoring' UK IT jobs to India. 'RBS has 40 years' experience running this system and banks as a rule don't drop the ball like this', remarked one bank employee. However, the general banking crisis had pressured UK banks to reduce their costs. RBS, which had suffered badly from the banking crisis, let thousands of UK staff go and transferred their roles to Chennai, India. As one former employee complained, 'we were having to pass 10–20+ years worth of mainframe knowledge onto people who'd never heard of a mainframe outside of a museum . . .'.

Offshore outsourcing was once heralded as the saviour of UK IT departments, cutting costs without compromising quality. Thousands of IT jobs were axed in the name of 'efficiency', many outsourced to India with much lower wages than the UK. Indeed in February 2012 RBS advertised it was urgently seeking computer graduates with several years' experience of using CA-7.

However, India's staff attrition rates in 2012 were at an all-time high with people changing jobs very quickly for just a few extra rupees, leaving insufficient time for adequate cultural awareness training. Quality at call centres suffered. At the same time the UK was in recession with a devaluing pound greatly reducing wage disparity between India and the UK.

RBS's overseas problems were not uncommon with other banks experiencing loss of private data and in some instances criminal activity. Spanish-owned Santander UK – a bank created from Abbey National, Alliance & Leicester and Bradford & Bingley – also found that outsourced IT systems for these banks could not be trusted and so became the first of the major UK financial institutions to bring back its call centres and software from India to the UK, so that it could take care of its customer base. Ana Botin, Santander UK's Chief Executive, said the move was 'the most important factor in terms of satisfaction with the bank'. This 'inshoring' of strategic assets raises the question of whether strategic assets can afford to be 'out of sight and out of mind'.

Sources: http://www.guardian.co.uk/technology/2012/jun/25/how-natwest-it-meltdown; http://www.hrzone.co.uk/topic/business-life-style/shoring-new-shoring-call-centres-come-back-uk/112654.

Questions

1 In terms of transaction and capability costs, why might outsourcing be attractive to companies?

2 What might be the risks of 'insourcing'?

This transaction cost framework suggests that the costs of opportunism can outweigh the benefits of subcontracting to organisations with superior strategic capabilities. For example, mining companies in isolated parts of the Australian outback typically own and operate housing for their workers. The isolation creates specific assets (the housing is worth nothing if the mine closes down) and a lack of alternatives (the nearest town might be a hundred miles away). Consequently, there would be large risks to both partners if the mine subcontracted housing to an independent company specialising in worker accommodation, however strong its capabilities. Transaction cost economics therefore offers the following advice: if there are few alternative suppliers, if activities are complex and likely to change, and if there are significant investments in specific assets, then it is likely to be better to vertically integrate rather than outsource.

In sum, the decision to integrate or subcontract rests on the balance between two distinct factors:

- *Relative strategic capabilities*. Does the subcontractor have the potential to do the work significantly better?

- *Risk of opportunism*. Is the subcontractor likely to take advantage of the relationship over time?

(7.6) VALUE CREATION AND THE CORPORATE PARENT

Sometimes corporate parents are not adding value to their constituent businesses. Where there is no added value, it is usually best to divest the relevant businesses from the corporate portfolio. Thus in 2012 Rupert Murdoch of News Corporation announced the separation of the troubled newspaper and book publishing assets from the more valuable film and TV business – the latter contributed 90 per cent of group profits. The group could no longer add value to the former businesses, which were mired in public scandals, and these were also causing significant damage to the group's reputation as a whole. In the public sector too, units such as schools or hospitals are increasingly being given freedom from parenting authorities, because independence is seen as more effective. Some theorists even challenge the notion of corporate-level strategy altogether, the subject of the Key Debate at the end of this chapter. This section examines how corporate parents can both add and destroy value, and considers three different parenting approaches that can be effective.

7.6.1 Value-adding and value-destroying activities of corporate parents[12]

Corporate parents need to demonstrate that they create more value than they cost. This applies to both commercial and public-sector organisations. For public-sector organisations, privatisation or outsourcing is likely to be the consequence of failure to demonstrate value. Companies whose shares are traded freely on the stock markets face a further challenge. They must demonstrate they create more value than any other rival corporate parent could create. Failure to do so is likely to lead to a hostile takeover or break-up. Rival companies that think they can create more value out of the business units can bid for the company's shares, on the expectation of either running the businesses better or selling them off to other potential parents. If the rival's bid is more attractive and credible than what the current parent can promise, shareholders will back it at the expense of incumbent management.

In this sense, competition takes place between different corporate parents for the right to own and control businesses. In this 'market for corporate control', corporate parents must show that they have *parenting advantage*, on the same principle that business units must demonstrate competitive advantage. They must demonstrate that they are the best possible parents for the businesses they control. Parents therefore must have a very clear approach to how they create value. In practice, however, many of their activities can be value-destroying as well as value-creating.

Value-adding activities[13]

There are five main types of activity by which a corporate parent can add value:

- *Envisioning.* The corporate parent can provide a clear overall vision or *strategic intent* for its business units.[14] This vision should guide and motivate the business unit managers in order to maximise corporation-wide performance through commitment to a common purpose. The vision should also provide stakeholders with a *clear external image* about what the organisation as a whole is about: this can reassure shareholders about the rationale for having a diversified strategy in the first place. Finally, a clear vision provides a *discipline* on the corporate parent to stop its wandering into inappropriate activities or taking on unnecessary costs.

- *Facilitating synergies.* The corporate parent can facilitate cooperation and sharing across the business units, so improving the *synergies* from being within the same corporate organisation. This can be achieved through incentives, rewards, and remuneration schemes.

- *Coaching.* The corporate parent can help business unit managers develop strategic capabilities, by coaching them to improve their skills and confidence. Corporate-wide management courses are one effective means of achieving these objectives, as bringing managers across the business to learn strategy skills also allows them to build relationships between each other and perceive opportunities for cooperation.

- *Providing central services and resources.* The centre is obviously a provider of capital for *investment*. The centre can also provide central services such as treasury, tax and human resource advice, which if centralised can have *sufficient scale* to be efficient and to build up *relevant expertise*. Centralised services often have greater *leverage*: for example, combining the purchases of separate business units increases their bargaining power for shared inputs such as energy. This leverage can be helpful in *brokering* with external bodies, such as government regulators, or other companies in negotiating alliances. Finally, the centre can have an important role in managing expertise within the corporate whole, for instance by *transferring managers* across the business units or by creating shared *knowledge management* systems via corporate intranets.

- *Intervening.* Finally, the corporate parent can also intervene within its business units in order to ensure appropriate performance. The corporate parent should be able to closely *monitor* business unit performance and *improve performance* either by replacing weak managers or by assisting them in turning around their businesses. The parent can also *challenge and develop* the strategic ambitions of business units, so that satisfactorily performing businesses are encouraged to perform even better.

Value-destroying activities

However, there are also three broad ways in which the corporate parent can inadvertently destroy value:

- *Adding management costs.* Most simply, the staff and facilities of the corporate centre are expensive. The corporate centre typically has the best-paid managers and the most luxurious offices. It is the actual businesses that have to generate the revenues that pay for them. If their costs are greater than the value they create, then the corporate centre's managers are net value-destroying.

- *Adding bureaucratic complexity.* As well as these direct financial costs, there is the 'bureaucratic fog' created by an additional layer of management and the need to coordinate with sister businesses. These typically slow down managers' responses to issues and lead to compromises between the interests of individual businesses.

- *Obscuring financial performance.* One danger in a large diversified company is that the under-performance of weak businesses can be obscured. Weak businesses might be cross-subsidised by the stronger ones. Internally, the possibility of hiding weak performance diminishes the incentives for business unit managers to strive as hard as they can for their businesses: they have a parental safety-net. Externally, shareholders and financial analysts cannot easily judge the performance of individual units within the corporate whole. Diversified companies' share prices are often marked down, because shareholders prefer the 'pure plays' of standalone units, where weak performance cannot be hidden.[15]

These dangers suggest clear paths for corporate parents that wish to avoid value destruction. They should keep a close eye on centre costs, both financial and bureaucratic, ensuring that they are no more than required by their corporate strategy. They should also do all they can to promote financial transparency, so that business units remain under pressure to perform and shareholders are confident that there are no hidden disasters.

Overall, there are many ways in which corporate parents can add value. It is, of course, difficult to pursue them all and some are hard to mix with others. For example, a corporate parent that does a great deal of top-down intervening is less likely to be seen by its managers as a helpful coach and facilitator. Business unit managers will concentrate on maximising their own individual performance rather than looking out for ways to cooperate with other business unit managers for the greater good of the whole. For this reason, corporate parenting roles tend to fall into three main types, each coherent within itself but distinct from the others.[16] These three types of corporate parenting role are summarised in Figure 7.5.

7.6.2 **The portfolio manager**

The **portfolio manager** **operates as an active investor in a way that shareholders in the stock market are either too dispersed or too inexpert to be able to do.** In effect, the portfolio manager is acting as an agent on behalf of financial markets and shareholders with a view to extracting more value from the various businesses than they could achieve themselves. Its role is to identify and acquire under-valued assets or businesses and improve them. The portfolio manager might do this, for example, by acquiring another corporation, divesting low-performing businesses within it and intervening to improve the performance of those with potential. Such corporations may not be much concerned about the relatedness (see section 7.2) of the business units in their portfolio, typically adopting a conglomerate strategy. Their role is not to get closely involved in the routine management of the businesses, only to act over short periods of time to improve performance. In terms of the value-creating activities identified earlier, the portfolio manager concentrates on intervening and the provision (or withdrawal) of investment.

Figure 7.5 Portfolio managers, synergy managers and parental developers

Source: Adapted from M. Goold, A. Campbell and M. Alexander, *Corporate Level Strategy*, Wiley, 1994.

Portfolio managers seek to keep the cost of the centre low, for example by having a small corporate staff with few central services, leaving the business units alone so that their chief executives have a high degree of autonomy. They set clear financial targets for those chief executives, offering high rewards if they achieve them and likely loss of position if they do not. Such corporate parents can, of course, manage quite a large number of such businesses because they are not directly managing the everyday strategies of those businesses. Rather they are acting from above, setting financial targets, making central evaluations about the well-being and future prospects of such businesses, and investing, intervening or divesting accordingly.

Some argue that the days of the portfolio manager are gone. Improving financial markets mean that the scope for finding and investing cheaply in under-performing companies is much reduced. However, some portfolio managers remain and are successful. Private equity firms such as Apax Partners or Blackstone operate a portfolio management style, typically investing in, improving and then divesting companies in loosely knit portfolios. For example, in 2012, Blackstone owned companies in power generation, water treatment, camera manufacture, banking, railway operation and seed development totalling more than 990,000 employees around the world. Illustration 7.4 includes a description of the portfolio parenting approach of Warren Buffett at Berkshire Hathaway.

7.6.3 The synergy manager

Obtaining synergy is often seen as the prime rationale for the corporate parent.[17] The **synergy manager is a corporate parent seeking to enhance value for business units by managing synergies**

ILLUSTRATION 7.4

Eating its own cooking: Berkshire Hathaway's parenting

A portfolio manager seeks to manage a highly diverse set of business units for shareholders.

Berkshire Hathaway's plain-speaking Chairman and CEO is Warren Buffett, one of the world's richest men. With annual sales of $162 bn (£97 bn; €121 bn) in 2012, Buffet founded this conglomerate with a small textile business in the early 1960s. Berkshire Hathaway's businesses now are highly diverse with large insurance businesses (GEICO, General Re, NRG), manufacturers of carpets, building products, clothing and footwear, retail companies and private jet service, NetJets. The company also has significant long-term minority stakes in businesses such as Coca-Cola and General Electric. Aged 83 in 2013, Buffett remains highly active with major acquisitions in 2009 (BNSF, the second largest railway company in the USA for $34 bn), 2011 (Lubrizol, the speciality chemicals company for $9 bn cash), 2013 (Heinz, purchased with 3G Capital Management, for $23.3 bn). Since the mid-1960s, Berkshire has averaged 19.7 per cent growth in book value per year.

Berkshire Hathaway annual reports explain how Buffet and Deputy Chairman Charlie Munger run the business:

'Charlie Munger and I think of our shareholders as owner-partners, and of ourselves as managing partners. (Because of the size of our shareholdings we are also, for better or worse, controlling partners.) We do not view the company itself as the ultimate owner of our business assets but instead view the company as a conduit through which our shareholders own the assets . . . In line with Berkshire's owner-orientation, most of our directors have a major portion of their net worth invested in the company. We eat our own cooking.'

Berkshire has a clear 'dominant logic':

'Charlie and I avoid businesses whose futures we can't evaluate, no matter how exciting their products may be. In the past, it required no brilliance for people to foresee the fabulous growth that awaited such industries as autos (in 1910), aircraft (in 1930) and television sets (in 1950). But the future then also included competitive dynamics that would decimate almost all of the companies entering those industries. Even the survivors tended to come away bleeding. Just because Charlie and I can clearly see dramatic growth ahead for an industry does not mean we can judge what its profit margins and returns on capital will be as a host of competitors battle for supremacy. At Berkshire we will stick with businesses whose profit picture for decades to come seems reasonably predictable. Even then, we will make plenty of mistakes.'

Buffett also explains how they manage their subsidiary businesses:

'We subcontract all of the heavy lifting to the managers of our subsidiaries. In fact, we delegate almost to the point of abdication: though Berkshire has about 257,000 employees, only 21 of these are at headquarters. Charlie and I mainly attend to capital allocation and the care of our key managers. Most are happiest when they are left alone to run their businesses, and that is just how we leave them. That puts them in charge of all operating decisions and of dispatching the excess cash they generate to headquarters. By sending it to us, they don't get diverted by the various enticements that would come their way were they responsible for deploying the cash their businesses throw off. Furthermore, Charlie and I are exposed to a much wider range of possibilities for investing these funds than any of our managers could find.'

Even after Heinz and other acquisitions Berkshire Hathaway still had a huge cash pile in 2013. The billionaire investor had his 'elephant gun loaded for a $15 bn acquisition' – a deal he was 'salivating' to do.

Questions

1 In what ways does Berkshire Hathaway fit the archetypal portfolio manager (see section 7.6.2)?

2 With $20 bn to invest, suggest industries and businesses Warren Buffett is likely never to invest in.

across business units. Synergies are likely to be particularly rich when new activities are closely related to the core business. In terms of value-creating activities, the focus is threefold: envisioning to build a common purpose; facilitating cooperation across businesses; and providing central services and resources. For example, at Apple, Steve Jobs' vision of his personal computers being the digital hub of the new digital lifestyle guided managers across the iMac computer, iPod, iPhone and iPad businesses to ensure seamless connections between the fast-developing offerings. The result is enhanced value through better customer experience. A metals company diversified into both steel and aluminium might centralise its energy procurement, gaining synergy benefits through increased bargaining power over suppliers.

However, achieving such synergistic benefits involves at least three challenges:

- *Excessive costs*. The benefits in sharing and cooperation need to outweigh the costs of undertaking such integration, both direct financial costs and opportunity costs. Managing synergistic relationships tends to involve expensive investments in management time.

- *Overcoming self-interest*. Managers in the business units have to want to cooperate. Especially where managers are rewarded largely according to the performance of their own particular business unit, they are likely to be unwilling to sacrifice their time and resources for the common good.

- *Illusory synergies*. It is easy to overestimate the value of skills or resources to other businesses. This is particularly common when the corporate centre needs to justify a new venture or the acquisition of a new company. Claimed synergies often prove illusory when managers actually have to put them into practice.

The failure of many companies to extract expected synergies from their businesses has led to growing scepticism about the notion of synergy. Synergistic benefits are not as easy to achieve as would appear. For example, in 2012 Hewlett Packard was forced to write down the value of its acquisition of Autonomy, a British software company, by €3.8 bn (£3 bn, $5 bn), as it failed to achieve anticipated integration benefits (the internal politics at HP associated with this decision are described in Illustration 12.4 in Chapter 12). Hewlett Packard blamed the former management team of Autonomy for fraudulent misrepresentation during the due diligence process. Nevertheless synergy continues to be a common theme in corporate-level strategy, as Illustration 7.2 on Zodiac exemplifies.

7.6.4 The parental developer[18]

The **parental developer seeks to employ its own central capabilities to add value to its businesses**. This is not so much about how the parent can develop benefits *across* business units or transfer capabilities between business units, as in the case of managing synergy. Rather parental developers focus on the resources or capabilities they have as parents which they can transfer *downwards* to enhance the potential of business units. For example, a parent could have a valuable brand or specialist skills in financial management or product development. If such parenting capabilities exist, corporate managers then need to identify a '*parenting opportunity*': a business which is not fulfilling its potential but which could be improved by applying the parenting capability, such as branding or product development. Such parenting opportunities are therefore more common in the case of related rather than unrelated diversified strategies and are likely to involve exchanges of managers and other resources across the businesses. Key value-creating activities for the parent will be the provision of central services and resources.

For example, a consumer products company might offer substantial guidance on branding and distribution from the centre; a technology company might run a large central R&D laboratory. There are two crucial challenges to managing a parental developer:

● *Parental focus.* Corporate parents need to be rigorous and focused in identifying their unique value-adding capabilities. They should always be asking what others can do better than them, and focus their energy and time on activities where they really do add value. Other central services should typically be outsourced to specialist companies that can do it better.

● *The 'crown jewel' problem.* Some diversified companies have business units in their portfolios which are performing well but to which the parent adds little value. These can become 'crown jewels', to which corporate parents become excessively attached. The logic of the parental development approach is: if the centre cannot add value, it is just a cost and therefore destroying value. Parental developers should divest businesses[19] they do not add value to, even profitable ones. Funds raised by selling a profitable business can be reinvested in businesses where the parent can add value.

(7.7) PORTFOLIO MATRICES

Section 7.6 discussed rationales for corporate parents of multi-business organisations. This section introduces models by which managers can determine financial investment and divestment within their portfolios of business.[20] Each model gives more or less attention to at least one of three criteria:

● the *balance* of the portfolio (e.g. in relation to its markets and the needs of the corporation);

● the *attractiveness* of the business units in terms of how strong they are individually and how profitable their markets or industries are likely to be; and

● the '*fit*' that the business units have with each other in terms of potential synergies or the extent to which the corporate parent will be good at looking after them.

7.7.1 The BCG (or growth/share) matrix[21]

One of the most common and longstanding ways of conceiving of the balance of a portfolio of businesses is the Boston Consulting Group (BCG) matrix (see Figure 7.6). The **BCG matrix uses market share and market growth criteria for determining the attractiveness and balance of a business portfolio.** High market share and high growth are, of course, attractive. However, the BCG matrix also warns that high growth demands heavy investment, for instance to expand capacity or develop brands. There needs to be a balance within the portfolio, so that there are some low-growth businesses that are making sufficient surplus to fund the investment needs of higher-growth businesses.

The growth/share axes of the BCG matrix define four sorts of business:

● A *star* is a business unit within a portfolio that has a high market share in a growing market. The business unit may be spending heavily to keep up with growth, but high market share should yield sufficient profits to make it more or less self-sufficient in terms of investment needs.

● A *question mark* (or problem child) is a business unit within a portfolio that is in a growing market, but does not yet have high market share. Developing question marks into stars, with high market share, takes heavy investment. Many question marks fail to develop, so the BCG advises corporate parents to nurture several at a time. It is important to make sure

Figure 7.6 The growth share (or BCG) matrix

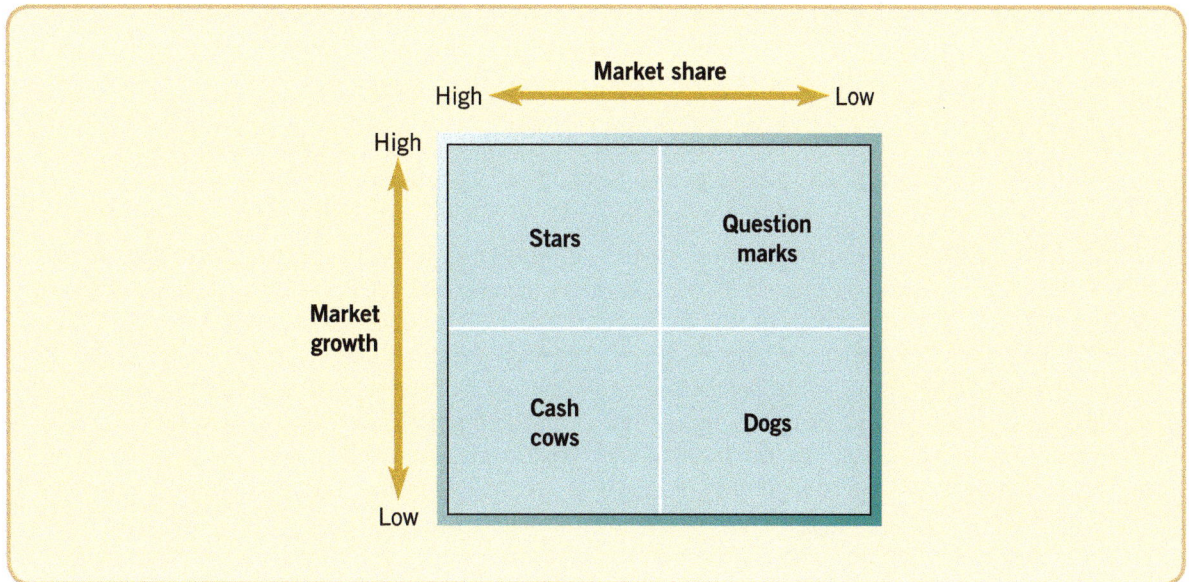

that some question marks develop into stars, as existing stars eventually become cash cows and cash cows may decline into dogs.

- A *cash cow* is a business unit within a portfolio that has a high market share in a mature market. However, because growth is low, investments needs are less, while high market share means that the business unit should be profitable. The cash cow should then be a cash provider, helping to fund investments in question marks.

- *Dogs* are business units within a portfolio that have low share in static or declining markets and are thus the worst of all combinations. They may be a cash drain and use up a dispro-portionate amount of managerial time and company resources. The BCG usually recom-mends divestment or closure.

The BCG matrix has several advantages. It provides a good way of visualising the different needs and potential of all the diverse businesses within the corporate portfolio. It warns corpor-ate parents of the financial demands of what might otherwise look like a desirable portfolio of high-growth businesses. It also reminds corporate parents that stars are likely eventually to wane. Finally, it provides a useful discipline to business unit managers, underlining the fact that the corporate parent ultimately owns the surplus resources they generate and can allocate them according to what is best for the corporate whole. Cash cows should not hoard their profits.

However, there are at least four potential problems with the BCG matrix:

- *Definitional vagueness.* It can be hard to decide what high and low growth or share mean in particular situations. Managers are often keen to define themselves as 'high-share' by defining their market in a particularly narrow way (e.g. by ignoring relevant international markets).

- *Capital market assumptions.* The notion that a corporate parent needs a balanced portfolio to finance investment from internal sources (cash cows) assumes that capital cannot be raised in external markets, for instance by issuing shares or raising loans. The notion of a balanced portfolio may be more relevant in countries where capital markets are under-developed or in private companies that wish to minimise dependence on external shareholders or banks.

ILLUSTRATION 7.5

ITC's diverse portfolio: smelling sweeter

Originally the Imperial Tobacco Company of India, ITC now has a portfolio stretching from cigarettes to fragrances.

ITC is one of India's largest consumer goods companies, with an increasingly diversified product portfolio. Its Chairman, Y.C. Deveshwar, describes its strategy thus: 'It is ITC's endeavour to continuously explore opportunities for growth by synergising and blending its multiple core competences to create new epicentres of growth. The employees of ITC are inspired by the vision of growing ITC into one of India's premier institutions and are willing to go the extra mile to generate value for the economy, in the process creating growing value for the shareholders.'

Founded in 1910 as the Imperial Tobacco Company of India, with brands such as Wills, Gold Cut and John Players, ITC now holds about two thirds of the market for cigarettes in India, with Philip Morris and BAT distant seconds with about 13 per cent each. However, cigarettes in India are highly discouraged by the Indian government, and increasingly heavily taxed.

ITC has a long diversification history. The company's original activities in the growth of leaf tobacco developed into a range of agricultural businesses, including edible oils, fruit pulp, spices and frozen foods. In the 1920s, ITC set up a packaging and printing business originally to supply its cigarette business. By 2012, this was India's largest packaging solutions provider. In 1975, ITC entered the hotel business, becoming the country's second largest operator with over 100 hotels by 2009, ranging from de luxe to economy. In 1979, the company also entered the paperboard industry, and three decades later was the country's largest producer.

The early twenty-first century saw many new diversification initiatives, especially in the booming Fast-Moving Consumer Goods (FMCG) sector. Initially it started in the food business, with Kitchens-of-India ready-to-eat gourmet foods, the *Aashirvaad* wheat-flour business, Sunfeast biscuits and Bingo snacks. ITC's own agri-businesses were an important source of supply for these initiatives. By 2008 *Aashirvaad* reached over 50 per cent Indian market share, and Sunfeast and Bingo had 12 and 11 per cent respectively. At the same time, ITC took advantage of the strong brand values

of its Wills cigarettes to launch Wills Lifestyle, a range of upmarket clothing stores, with its own designs. In 2009, Wills Lifestyle was recognised as India's 'Most Admired Fashion Brand of the Year'. In 2005, ITC launched its personal care business, again using its cigarette brand names: for example 'Essenza Di Wills' (fragrances) and 'Fiama Di Wills' (hair and skin care).

In 2012 Australia announced that cigarette manufacturers have to sell their produce in drab green packages with graphic pictorial warnings. Market research done by the Public Health Foundation of India and Hriday, a health awareness NGO, showed more than 80 per cent of people felt plain packaging would help reduce the attractiveness and appeal of tobacco products. India's Health Ministry officials warned such initiatives may be used in the future. With the cigarette industry facing systemic risk globally and manufacturer share prices being adversely affected, should ITC be concerned about its product portfolio?

ITC segmental sales and profits (Rs in Crores)

Segment	2011 sales	2011 profits	2009 sales	2009 profits
Cigarettes	22,250	6,907	15,115	4,184
Other FMCG	5,537	(195)	3,010	(483)
Hotels	996	279	1,014	316
Agribusiness	3,507	643	2,284	256
Paperboard, paper and packaging	2,579	936	1,719	509

5 Rs in Crores: ~ US $1,000,000; ~ €700,000. Profits are before interest and tax. Figures in brackets are losses.

Sources: ITC annual reports; M. Balaji, *ITC: Adding Shareholder Value through Diversifications*, IBSCDC, 2006; B. Gopal and S. Kora, *Indian Conglomerate ITC*, IBS Research Centre, 2009; *Business Standard*, 6 November 2012.

Questions

1 How well does ITC's portfolio fit in terms of the BCG matrix?

2 Identify and evaluate the various synergies in ITC's business.

- *Unkind to animals.* Both cash cows and dogs receive ungenerous treatment, the first being simply milked, the second terminated or cast out of the corporate home. This treatment can cause *motivation problems*, as managers in these units see little point in working hard for the sake of other businesses. There is also the danger of the *self-fulfilling prophecy*. Cash cows will become dogs even more quickly than the model expects if they are simply milked and denied adequate investment.

- *Ignores commercial linkages.* The matrix assumes there are *no commercial ties to other business units* in the portfolio. For instance, a business unit in the portfolio may depend upon keeping a dog alive. These commercial links are less important in conglomerate strategies, where divestments or closures are unlikely to have knock-on effects on other parts of the portfolio.

7.7.2 The directional policy (GE–McKinsey) matrix

Another way to consider a portfolio of businesses is by means of the *directional policy matrix*[22] which categorises business units into those with good prospects and those with less good prospects. The matrix was originally developed by McKinsey & Co. consultants in order to help the American conglomerate General Electric manage its portfolio of business units. Specifically, the directional policy matrix positions business units according to (i) how attractive the relevant market is in which they are operating, and (ii) the competitive strength of the SBU in that market. Attractiveness can be identified by PESTEL or five forces analyses; business unit strength can be defined by competitor analysis (for instance, the strategy canvas); see section 2.4.3. Some analysts also choose to show graphically how large the market is for a given business unit's activity, and even the market share of that business unit, as shown in Figure 7.7.

Figure 7.7 Directional policy (GE–McKinsey) matrix

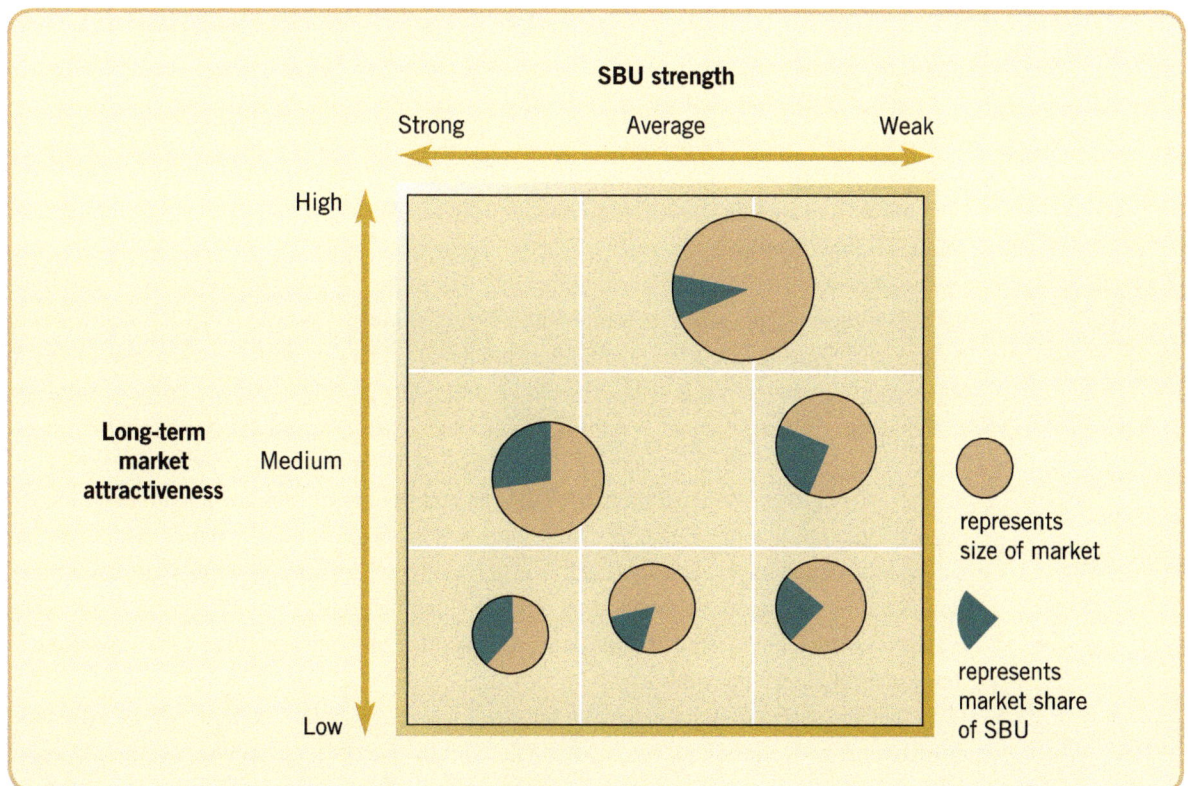

Figure 7.8 Strategy guidelines based on the directional policy matrix

For example, managers in a firm with the portfolio shown in Figure 7.7 will be concerned that they have relatively low shares in the largest and most attractive market, whereas their greatest strength is in a market with only medium attractiveness and smaller markets with little long-term attractiveness.

The matrix also offers strategy guidelines given the positioning of the business units, as shown in Figure 7.8. It suggests that the businesses with the highest growth potential and the greatest strength are those in which to invest for growth. Those that are the weakest and in the least attractive markets should be divested or 'harvested' (i.e. used to yield as much cash as possible before divesting).

The directional policy matrix is more complex than the BCG matrix. However, it can have two advantages. First, unlike the simpler four-box BCG matrix, the nine cells of the directional policy matrix acknowledge the possibility of a difficult middle ground. Here managers have to be carefully selective. In this sense, the directional policy matrix is less mechanistic than the BCG matrix, encouraging open debate on less clear-cut cases. Second, the two axes of the directional policy matrix are not based on single measures (i.e. market share and market growth). Business strength can derive from many other factors than market share, and industry attractiveness does not just boil down to industry growth rates. On the other hand, the directional policy matrix shares some problems with the BCG matrix, particularly about vague definitions, capital market assumptions, motivation and self-fulfilling prophecy and ignoring commercial linkages. Overall, however, the value of the matrix is to help managers invest in the businesses that are most likely to pay off.

So far the discussion has been about the logic of portfolios in terms of balance and attractiveness. The third logic is to do with 'fit' with the particular capabilities of the corporate parent.

7.7.3 The parenting matrix

The *parenting matrix* (or Ashridge Portfolio Display) developed by consultants Michael Goold and Andrew Campbell introduces parental fit as an important criterion for including businesses in the portfolio.[23]

Businesses may be attractive in terms of the BCG or directional policy matrices, but if the parent cannot add value, then the parent ought to be cautious about acquiring or retaining them.

There are two key dimensions of fit in the parenting matrix (see Figure 7.9):

● 'Feel'. This is a measure of the fit between each business unit's critical success factors (see section 2.4.3) and the capabilities (in terms of competences and resources) of the corporate parent. In other words, does the corporate parent have the necessary 'feel', or understanding, for the businesses it will parent?

● 'Benefit'. This measures the fit between the parenting opportunities, or needs, of business units and the capabilities of the parent. Parenting opportunities are about the upside, areas in which good parenting can benefit the business (for instance, by bringing marketing

Figure 7.9 The parenting matrix: the Ashridge Portfolio Display

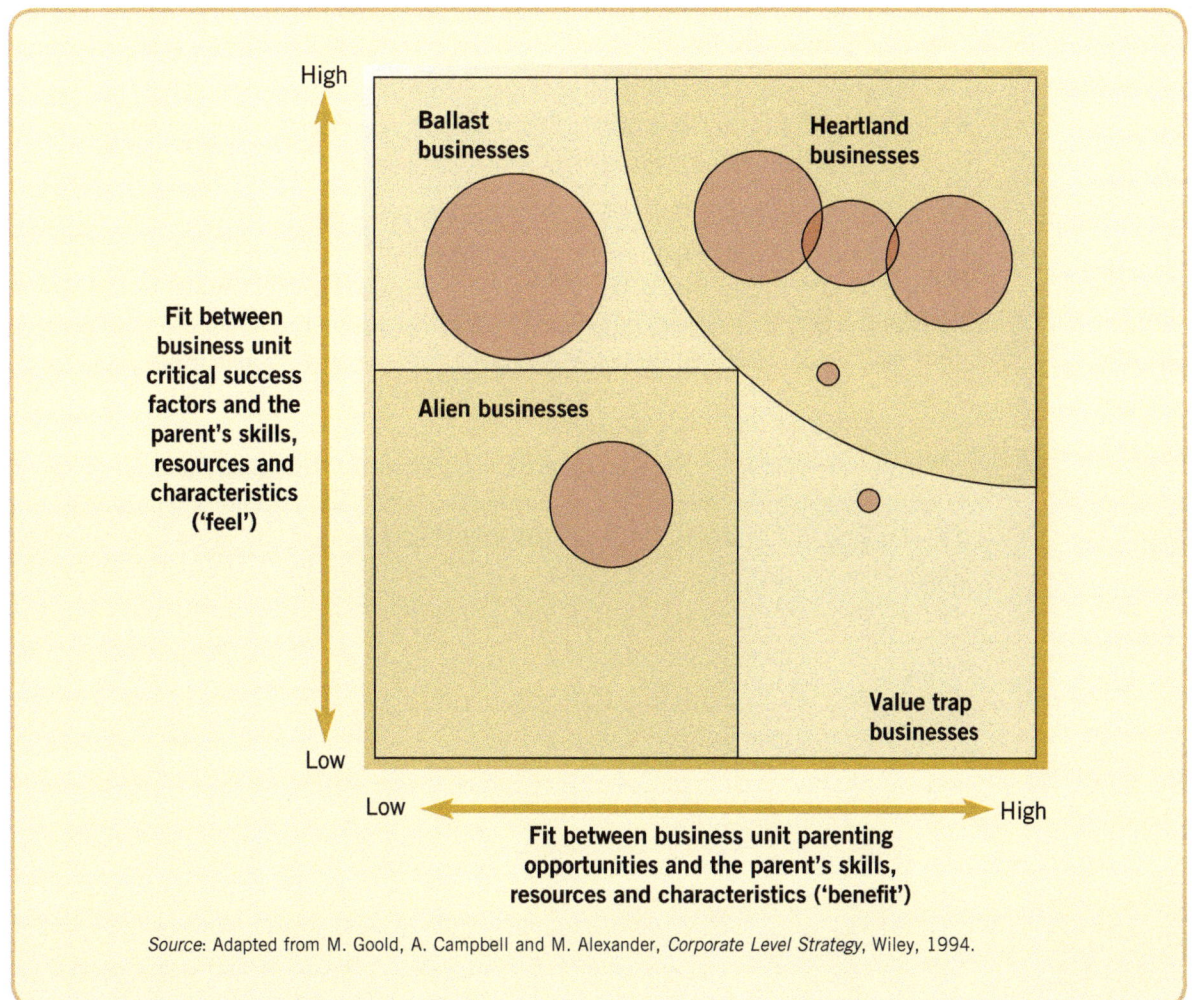

Source: Adapted from M. Goold, A. Campbell and M. Alexander, *Corporate Level Strategy*, Wiley, 1994.

expertise). For the benefit to be realised, of course, the parent must have the right capabilities to match the parenting opportunities.

The power of using these two dimensions of fit is as follows. It is easy to see that a corporate parent should avoid running businesses that it has no feel for. What is less clear is that parenting should be avoided if there is no benefit. This challenges the corporate parenting of even businesses for which the parent has high feel. Businesses for which a corporate parent has high feel but can add little benefit should either be run with a very light touch or be divested.

Figure 7.9 shows four kinds of business along these two dimensions of feel and benefit:

- *Heartland* business units are ones which the parent understands well and can continue to add value to. They should be at the core of future strategy.

- *Ballast* business units are ones the parent understands well but can do little for. They would probably be at least as successful as independent companies. If not divested, they should be spared as much corporate bureaucracy as possible.

- *Value trap* business units are dangerous. They appear attractive because there are opportunities to add value (for instance, marketing could be improved). But they are deceptively attractive, because the parent's lack of feel will result in more harm than good (i.e. the parent lacks the right marketing skills). The parent will need to acquire new capabilities if it is to be able to move value trap businesses into the heartland. It might be easier to divest to another corporate parent that could add value, and will pay well for the chance.

- *Alien* business units are clear misfits. They offer little opportunity to add value and the parent does not understand them anyway. Exit is definitely the best strategy.

This approach to considering corporate portfolios places the emphasis firmly on how the parent benefits the business units. This is the question that observers are asking of the Virgin Group in the end of chapter case. It requires careful analysis of both parenting capabilities and business unit parenting needs. The parenting matrix can therefore assist hard decisions where either high feel or high parenting opportunities tempt the corporate parent to acquire or retain businesses. Parents should concentrate on actual or potential heartland businesses, where there is both high feel and high benefit.

The concept of fit has equal relevance in the public sector. The implication is that public-sector managers should control directly only those services and activities for which they have special managerial expertise. Other services should be outsourced or set up as independent agencies (see section 7.5).

KEY DEBATE

Why have corporate-level strategies anyway?

Do we really need diversified corporations?

The notion of corporate strategy assumes that corporations should own and control businesses in a range of markets or products. But 'transaction cost' economist Oliver Williamson believes that diversified corporations should only exist in the presence of 'market failures' (see also section 7.5.2). If markets worked well, there would be no need for business units to be coordinated through managerial structures. Business units could be independent, coordinating where necessary by simple transactions in the marketplace. The 'invisible hand' of the market could replace the 'visible hand' of managers at corporate headquarters. There would be no 'corporate strategy'.

Market failures favouring the diversified corporation occur for two reasons:

- *'Bounded rationality'*: people cannot know everything that is going on in the market, so perfectly rational market transactions are impossible. Information, for instance on quality and costs, can sometimes be better inside the corporate fold.

- *'Opportunism'*: independent businesses trading between each other may behave opportunistically, for example by cheating on delivery or quality promises. Cheating can sometimes be policed and punished more easily within a corporate hierarchy.

According to Williamson, activities should only be brought into the corporation when the 'transaction costs' of coping with bounded rationality (gaining information) and opportunism (guarding against cheats) are lower inside the corporate hierarchy than they would be if simply relying on transactions in the marketplace.

This comparison of the transaction costs of markets and hierarchies has powerful implications for trends in product diversification:

- Improving capital markets may reduce the relative information advantages of conglomerates in managing a set of unrelated businesses. As markets get better at capturing information there will be less need for conglomerates.

- Improving protection of intellectual property rights may increase the incentives for corporations to license out their technologies to companies, rather than trying to do everything themselves. If the prospect of collecting royalties improves, there is less advantage for corporations keeping everything in-house.

Thus, fewer market failures also mean narrower product scope.

Williamson's 'transaction cost' view puts a heavy burden on corporations to justify themselves. Two justifications are possible. First, knowledge is hard to trade in the market. Buyers can only know the value of new knowledge once they have already bought it. Because they can trust each other, colleagues in different businesses within the same corporation are better at transferring knowledge than independent companies are in the open market. Second, corporations are not just about minimising the costs of information and cheating, but also about maximising the value of the combined resources. Bringing creative people together enhances knowledge exchange, innovation and motivation. Corporations create value as well as minimise cost.

Forty years of empirical research has failed to find unequivocal evidence of the under-performance of diversification although in sophisticated markets the prevailing view is that performance is an inverted 'U'-shape. Nevertheless successful conglomerates such as Berkshire Hathaway and 3M persist in developed markets and elsewhere, such as India and China, diversified businesses are common. The persistence of diversified firms as well as transaction cost economics suggests there is truth in the theory but this may not be whole picture.

Sources: O.E. Williamson, 'Strategy research: governance and competence perspectives', *Strategic Management Journal*, vol. 12 (1998), pp. 75–94; B. Kogut and U. Zander, 'What firms do? Coordination, identity and learning', *Organisation Science*, vol. 7, no. 5 (1996), pp. 502–19; Y.M. Zhou, 'Synergy, coordination costs, and diversification choices', *Strategic Management Journal*, vol. 32, no. 6 (2011), pp. 624–39.

Questions

1 Consider a diversified corporation such as Virgin (end of chapter case): what kinds of hard-to-trade knowledge might be transferred between product and country subsidiaries? Is this likely to be of increasing or decreasing importance?

2 Why might diversified corporations be more common in developing economies than the developed world?

SUMMARY

- Many corporations comprise several, sometimes many, business units. Corporate strategy involves the decisions and activities above the level of business units. It is concerned with the scope of the organisation.

- Organisational *scope* is often considered in terms of *related* and *unrelated* diversification.

- Corporate parents may seek to add value by adopting different parenting roles: the *portfolio manager*, the *synergy manager* or the *parental developer*.

- There are several portfolio models to help corporate parents manage their businesses, of which the most common are: the *BCG matrix*, the *directional policy matrix* and the *parenting matrix*.

- *Divestment* and *outsourcing* should be considered as well as diversification, particularly in the light of relative strategic capabilities and the transaction costs of *opportunism*.

WORK ASSIGNMENTS

✳ *Denotes more advanced work assignments.*
* *Refers to a case study in the Text and Cases edition.*

7.1 Using the Ansoff axes (Figure 7.2), identify and explain corporate strategic directions for any one of these case organisations: CRH*, Marks & Spencer*, SABMiller*.

7.2 Go to the website of any large multi-business organisation (e.g. Google, SABMiller*, Siemens, Tata Group, Virgin Group) and assess the degree to which its corporate-level strategy is characterised by (a) related or unrelated diversification and (b) a coherent 'dominant logic' (see section 7.3).

7.3 For any large multi-business corporation (as in 7.2), Marks & Spencer* or the Virgin Group, explain how the corporate parent should best create value for its component businesses (as portfolio manager, synergy manager or parental developer: see section 7.6). Would all the businesses fit equally well?

7.4✳ For any large multi-business corporation (as in 7.2), SABMiller* or the Virgin Group (end of chapter case), plot the business units on a portfolio matrix (e.g. the BCG matrix: section 7.7.1). Justify any assumptions about the relative positions of businesses on the relevant axes of the matrix. What managerial conclusions do you draw from this analysis?

Integrative assignment

7.5 Take a case of a recent merger or acquisition (see Chapter 10), and assess the extent to which it involved related or unrelated diversification (if either) and how far it was consistent with the company's existing dominant logic. Using share price information (see www.bigcharts.com or similar), assess shareholders' reaction to the merger or acquisition. How do you explain this reaction?

VIDEO ASSIGNMENTS

Visit **MyStrategyLab** and watch the SWAST case study for Chapter 7.

1 Using Figure 7.2 as a starting point, explain how the South Western Ambulance Trust has developed the strategic direction of its activities?

2 What changes in corporate-level strategy has SWAST had to introduce in order to combat the increasing threats in its environment? What further changes do you anticipate in the near future?

RECOMMENDED KEY READINGS

- An accessible discussion of corporate strategy is provided by A. Campbell and R. Park, *The Growth Gamble: When Leaders Should Bet on Big New Businesses*, Nicholas Brealey, 2005.

- M. Goold and K. Luchs, 'Why diversify: four decades of management thinking', in D. Faulkner and A. Campbell (eds), *The Oxford Handbook of Strategy*, vol. 2, Oxford University Press, pp. 18–42, 2003, provides an authoritative overview of the diversification option over time.

- L. Capron and W. Mitchell, *Build, Borrow or Buy: solving the growth dilemma*, Harvard Business Press, 2012, provides a good review of the arguments for and against different modes of growth.

- A good review of the current state of corporate portfolio management research is provided by M. Nippa, U. Pidua and H. Rubner, 'Corporate portfolio management: appraising four decades of academic research', *Academy of Management Perspectives*, November 2011, pp. 50–66.

REFERENCES

1. This figure is an extension of the product/market matrix: see I. Ansoff, *Corporate Strategy*, 1988, Chapter 6. The Ansoff matrix was later developed into the one shown below.

2. For the European Commission competition authority, http://ec.europa.eu/comm/competition; for the UK Competition Commission, see http://www.competition-commission.org.uk/.

3. For discussions of the challenge of sustained growth and diversification, see A. Campbell and R. Parks, *The Growth Gamble*, Nicholas Brealy, 2005; and D. Laurie, Y. Doz and

C. Sheer, 'Creating new growth platforms', *Harvard Business Review*, vol. 84, no. 5 (2006), pp. 80–90.

4. On economies of scope, see D.J. Teece, 'Towards an economic theory of the multi-product firm', *Journal of Economic Behavior and Organization*, vol. 3 (1982), pp. 39–63.

5. See C.K. Prahalad and R. Bettis, 'The dominant logic: a new link between diversity and performance', *Strategic Management Journal*, vol. 6, no. 1 (1986), pp. 485–501; R. Bettis and C.K. Prahalad, 'The dominant logic: retrospective and extension', *Strategic Management Journal*, vol. 16, no. 1 (1995), pp. 5–15.

6. See C. Markides, 'Corporate strategy: the role of the centre', in A. Pettigrew, H. Thomas and R. Whittington (eds), *Handbook of Strategy and Management*, Sage, 2002. For a discussion of recent Chinese diversification patterns, see A. Delios, N. Zhou and W.W. Xu, 'Ownership structure and the diversification and performance of publicly-listed companies in China', *Business Horizons*, vol. 51, no. 6 (2008), pp. 802–21.

7. These benefits are often discussed in terms of 'multimarket' or 'multipoint' competition: see J. Anand, L. Mesquita and R. Vassolo, 'The dynamics of multimarket competition in exploration and exploitation activities', *Academy of Management Journal*, vol. 52, no. 4 (2009), pp. 802–21.

8. M. Goold and A. Campbell, 'Desperately seeking synergy', *Harvard Business Review*, vol. 76, no. 2 (1998), pp. 131–45. See also Y.M. Zhou, 'Synergy, coordination costs, and

diversification choices', *Strategic Management Journal*, vol. 32, no. 6 (2011), pp. 624–39.

9. A. Pehrson, 'Business relatedness and performance: a study of managerial perceptions', *Strategic Management Journal*, vol. 27, no. 3 (2006), pp. 265–82. See also F. Neffke and M. Henning, 'Skill relatedness and firm diversification', *Strategic Management Journal*, vol. 34, no. 3 (2013), pp. 297–316.

10. L.E. Palich, L.B. Cardinal and C. Miller, 'Curvilinearity in the diversification-performance linkage: an examination of over three decades of research', *Strategic Management Journal*, vol. 21 (2000), pp. 155–74. The inverted-U relationship is the research consensus, but studies often disagree, particularly finding variations over time and across countries. For recent context-sensitive studies, see M. Mayer and R. Whittington, 'Diversification in context: a cross national and cross temporal extension', *Strategic Management Journal*, vol. 24 (2003), pp. 773–81; and A. Chakrabarti, K. Singh and I. Mahmood, 'Diversification and performance: evidence from East Asian firms', *Strategic Management Journal*, vol. 28 (2007), pp. 101–20. There are also variations by type of diversification – see M. Geoffrey, G.M. Kistruck, I. Qureshi and P.W. Beamish, 'Geographic and product diversification in charitable organizations', *Journal of Management*, vol. 39, no. 2 (2011), pp. 496–530.

11. For a discussion and cases on the relative guidance of transaction cost and capabilities thinking, see R. McIvor, 'How the transaction cost and resource-based theories of the firm inform outsourcing evaluation', *Journal of Operations Management*, vol. 27, no. 1 (2009), pp. 45–63. See also T. Holcomb and M. Hitt, 'Toward a model of strategic outsourcing', *Journal of Operations Management*, vol. 25, no. 2 (2007), pp. 464–81.

12. For a good discussion of corporate parenting roles, see Markides in reference 6 above. A recent empirical study of corporate headquarters is D. Collis, D. Young and M. Goold, 'The size, structure and performance of corporate headquarters', *Strategic Management Journal*, vol. 28, no. 4 (2007), pp. 383–406.

13. M. Goold, A. Campbell and M. Alexander, *Corporate Level Strategy*, Wiley, 1994, is concerned with both the value-adding and value-destroying capacity of corporate parents.

14. For a discussion of the role of clarity of mission, see A. Campbell, M. Devine and D. Young, *A Sense of Mission*, Hutchinson Business, 1990.

15. E. Zuckerman, 'Focusing the corporate product: securities analysts and de-diversification', *Administrative Science Quarterly*, vol. 45, no. 3 (2000), pp. 591–619.

16. The first two rationales discussed here are based on M. Porter, 'From competitive advantage to corporate strategy', *Harvard Business Review*, vol. 65, no. 3 (1987), pp. 43–59.

17. See A. Campbell and K. Luchs, *Strategic Synergy*, Butterworth–Heinemann, 1992.

18. The logic of parental development is explained extensively in Goold, Campbell and Alexander (see reference 13 above). For more on the dynamics of organisational structure see J. Joseph and W. Ocasio, 'Architecture, attention, and adaptation in the multi-business firm: General Electric from 1951 to 2001', *Strategic Management Journal*, vol. 33, no. 6 (2013), pp. 633–60.

19. J. Xia, and S., Li, 'The divestiture of acquired subunits: a resource dependence approach', *Strategic Management Journal*, vol. 34, no. 2 (2013), pp. 131–48.

20. A good review of the current state of corporate portfolio management research is provided by M. Nippa, U. Pidua and H. Rubner, 'Corporate portfolio management: appraising four decades of academic research', *Academy of Management Perspectives*, vol. 25, no. 4 (2011), pp. 50–66.

21. For a more extensive discussion of the use of the growth share matrix see A.C. Hax and N.S. Majluf in R.G. Dyson (ed.), *Strategic Planning: Models and Analytical Techniques*, Wiley, 1990; and D. Faulkner, 'Portfolio matrices', in V. Ambrosini (ed.), *Exploring Techniques of Analysis and Evaluation in Strategic Management*, Prentice Hall, 1998; for source explanations of the BCG matrix see B.D. Henderson, *Henderson on Corporate Strategy*, Abt Books, 1979.

22. A. Hax and N. Majluf, 'The use of the industry attractiveness business strength matrix in strategic planning', in R. Dyson (ed.), *Strategic Planning: Models and Analytical Techniques*, Wiley, 1990.

23. The discussion in this section draws on M. Goold, A. Campbell and M. Alexander, *Corporate Level Strategy*, Wiley, 1994, which provides an excellent basis for understanding issues of parenting.

Strategic development at Virgin 2013

John Treciokas

Introduction

The Virgin Group is a highly diversified organisation with one of the best-known brands in the UK. Sir Richard Branson, Virgin's charismatic founder, who is one of the UK's richest and highly regarded entrepreneurs, leads the group. However, there are signs that Richard Branson may be stepping back from Virgin's businesses to concentrate on environmental and charity activities. This is causing concern about Virgin's future, as its strategy and business model are not widely understood. Investors are now questioning the extent to which the success of Virgin is due to Branson's entrepreneurial flair rather than the group's structure and business model.

The Virgin Group has grown over the years to become one of the largest private companies in the UK. It has more than 200 branded companies worldwide, employing around 50,000 employees in 34 countries with revenues in excess of £13 billion (approx. US $21 billion) in 2011. Richard Branson has always been integral to the growth of the company from its foundation to the present day. His flamboyant style and flair for publicity generate interest and awareness, which has enabled Virgin to create a brand image, that the group believes, adds value to any business that bears the Virgin name.

The Virgin Group is unusual in many ways, with a unique structure and distinctive image. However, questions are being raised about its sustainability. Does the parent company add value to the wide array of businesses in the group? Does the portfolio itself make strategic sense? It is also suspected the group struggles with profitability. Will the Virgin Group survive should Richard Branson depart?

Virgin's origins and style

The Virgin Group's beginnings can be traced to Richard Branson selling mail-order records in 1970 when he was just 20 years old. This allowed him to easily undercut high street retailers and the business experienced rapid growth. In 1971 Richard Branson opened an Oxford

Richard Branson

Source: Steve Bell/Rex Features.

Street store, which he named 'Virgin Records', to reflect his youth and naivety in business. Further expansion followed as he moved into record publishing with an instant hit album 'Tubular Bells', by unknown musician Mike Oldfield, in 1973. Virgin Records courted controversy by signing the Sex Pistols, a 'punk rock group' whose rude and anti-establishment behaviour brought plenty of public exposure. Risk-taking, optimism, irreverence and attracting publicity epitomised Branson's philosophy from the outset.

This philosophy was very visible when, in 1984, Richard Branson was inspired by an American lawyer to create a low-cost transatlantic airline – Virgin Atlantic. These routes were dominated by British Airways, and so began a long rivalry. When Virgin Atlantic managed to procure landing slots at Heathrow airport in 1991, this rivalry intensified leading to a 'dirty tricks' campaign by British Airways against Virgin Atlantic. The ensuing court battle, which Virgin won, was bitter and fought very publically in the media which often represented Virgin as the underdog fighting an oppressor.

Meanwhile Virgin Atlantic had huge financing needs with initial cash for operations coming from Virgin Records and its subsequent sale to EMI for £500 m. The group then needed an initial public offering of 35 per cent ownership of many Virgin businesses on the London and NASDAQ stock markets. This situation did not last long, however, as Branson's personality was not compatible with the accountability required of a chairman of a public corporation. In 1988 he bought out the external shareholders and returned the group to private ownership.

Virgin growth

Again a private company, the group grew rapidly, through a mixture of acquisitions, joint ventures and new start-ups (Appendix 1, below, lists a selection of new businesses).

Many of the new business initiatives seem to have been pure opportunism or on the whim of Richard Branson. For instance, in explaining why Virgin Records America was established in 1987, he commented: 'We were flying there a lot so it made sense to expand there too.' Since the early 1990s when the group was primarily involved in travel/holidays and music, it expanded into a wide range of businesses. For instance, the development of digital technologies allowed Virgin to grow its retail interests into online sales of music as well as many other products including cars, financial products and wine. The beginning of cellular communications and deregulation of the telecommunications sector in the UK led to the setting up of Virgin Mobile. Deregulation of the railways in the UK provided Virgin with the opportunity to form Virgin Rail, operating a passenger rail service on the West Coast of England, and deregulation in Australia and Nigeria allowed Virgin to set up other low-cost airlines. Branson was also drawn to markets where he perceived undue conservatism, a lack of innovation and an under-served customer. For instance, Virgin entered into health clubs (Virgin Active), biofuels (Virgin Fuels), drinks (Virgin drinks), clothing, cosmetics, comics,

weddings (Virgin Bride) and, in 2012, even a passenger service into suborbital space (Virgin Galactic). Commenting on this latest venture, Richard Branson said, 'Virgin is an adventurous company because I am an adventurer as well as an entrepreneur.' In the same year Virgin Money purchased Northern Rock, a medium-sized UK mortgage provider, from the government (which had nationalised the troubled company in the financial crisis of 2007). The move gave Virgin a much bigger stake in financial services – a growth area. The first new Virgin Money Store opened in July and by the end of the year 75 Northern Rock branches were rebranded to Virgin Money. Virgin paid £747 m for Northern Rock although commentators remarked it was an excellent deal for Virgin at the taxpayers' expense.

Since 2007 Richard Branson has become increasingly interested in environmental issues, launching the 'Virgin Earth Challenge' – to remove large amounts of carbon dioxide from the atmosphere; a 'People & Planet' initiative – to ensure all Virgin companies contribute to a sustainable society; Virgin Unite – to work with partners to improve social and environmental issues; and a Virgin Green Fund to invest in companies in the renewable energy and resource efficiency sectors. It seems that Branson is turning his attention to non-profit and corporate social responsibility issues.

Corporate rationale

In 2013 Virgin had the appearance of a very untraditional multi-business organisation. The group does not provide an organisational structure chart but a discernible grouping of business has become evident within five broad categories (see Figure 1). A cursory inspection of Figure 1 shows that these categories are very broad indeed, for

Figure 1

| | Virgin Group Headquarters | | Entrepreneurs
Forum for new
Ideas |

| **Media &
Mobile**
Includes:
T.V.
Mobiles
Broadband | **Lifestyle**
Includes:
Health
clubs
Wines
Games | **Travel**
Includes:
Airlines
Trains
Holidays | **Money**
Includes
Banks
Financial
services | **Music**
Includes:
Festivals
Radio
stores | **People &
Planet**
Includes:
Earth
Challenge
Unite
Green Fund |

instance 'Lifestyle' includes health clubs, books, games and balloon flights!

The operating companies themselves are all separate entities, financed on a standalone basis. Indeed most of the companies are new start-ups and Branson's approach is for each to succeed within the first year or exit the market. The key rationale to whether Virgin backs a new venture is 'does an opportunity exist for restructuring a market and creating competitive advantage?' The group puts itself in the customer's shoes to see what it could make better. It also considers whether there could be beneficial interaction with other Virgin businesses.

Each business is 'ring-fenced', so that lenders to one company have no rights over the assets of another and financial results are not consolidated. Branson's view is that consolidating income and assets of the companies is misleading and irrelevant for a private company.

Virgin has a mix of privately owned and public listed companies as well as a mix of start-up small businesses and very large corporate ventures. Each may have very different strategic reasoning – some may be an attempt to keep Virgin in the public eye, some are 'anti-establishment' and others about offering customers a better and more fun alternative. The businesses might also be a method of training and developing managers. The larger start-ups are serious strategic moves into new industries.

Each company has no direct lines of reporting or control in a group with minimal management layers and no bureaucracy. This mirrors Richard Branson's disrespect for hierarchy and his preference for informality and individual responsibility from employees. Companies are linked through a complex network of parent subsidiary relations involving 'holding companies' with the ultimate holding company being registered in the British Virgin Islands – a tax haven. The group believes that the separation of businesses enables the group to retain a spirit of entrepreneurialism, which depends on the enthusiasm and commitment of its employees. The group states on its own website that Virgin is a 'leading branded venture capital organisation' and its companies are part of a family rather than a hierarchy. 'There is a tiny board and no massive global HQ, but it works for us!'

The managers of each business are given significant autonomy once the business is up and running. This embodies Branson's ethos of shaping and building businesses around people. Managers are trusted, have high levels of responsibility and have financial incentives that could turn them into millionaires – indeed one of Branson's proudest claims is the creation of many millionaire managers.

One commonality across all the businesses is the Virgin brand, which the group says is about being the consumer's champion for value for money, good quality, brilliant customer service, innovation, anti-establishment and fun. These attributes are the way in which the group differentiates its products and services. In a number of instances observers have commented that Virgin's ventures are driven more by fun than commercial logic. For instance, painting the Union Jack on Virgin Atlantic aircraft when British Airways removed theirs, or positioning an airship with the slogan 'BA can't get it up' over the London Eye, a giant Ferris wheel in central London, which BA was struggling to erect.

In addition to the brand, Richard Branson sees Virgin as adding value in three main ways. These are its public relations and marketing skills; its experience with 'greenfield' start-ups and Virgin's understanding of the opportunities presented by 'institutionalised' markets. Virgin sees an 'institutionalised 'market as one dominated by a few competitors who are not giving good value to customers because they have become inefficient, complacent or preoccupied with rivals. In addition, one might add that the group has an extensive network of contacts and partners.

There is a belief that any type of business could work if Virgin was able to leverage its distinctive capabilities to the new opportunity. There is also a shrewd sense of risk versus reward. As the company says, 'Virgin frequently creates partnerships with others and excels in combining skills, knowledge and operational expertise from a range of industries to build exciting and successful companies'. Virgin invites entrepreneurs to submit their business ideas for consideration and possible Virgin involvement. An example of this was the Virgin Group's move into clothing and cosmetics with an initial outlay of only £1,000 while its partner, Victory Corporation, invested £20 million.

Recent developments

Not all of Virgin's companies are successful and not all meet the standards of customer service that Virgin would like to see. Both Virgin Media and Virgin Rail have had many customer complaints and in the summer of 2012 Virgin Rail seemed to have lost its franchise on the West Coast railway line. Virgin managed to get this decision quashed as serious technical errors were made by the UK's Department of Transport. The company released a statement on 29 October 2012 stating the following:

'This will help ensure we deliver the best result for the passenger and taxpayer, as well as getting the best out of the private sector and the key role it plays in a successful UK rail system.'

Critics have suggested that Rail is a weakness in Virgin's portfolio and it will be interesting to see how committed Branson is to this business.

In February 2013 Liberty Global agreed to purchase Virgin Media for approximately £15 billion. Branson's own share of this was 2 per cent. Virgin will continue earning around £10 million a year for its 30-year brand-licensing agreement. To what extent Liberty will continue to use the Virgin brand and operational expertise is difficult to establish at this stage.

Much of Virgin's brand appeal is linked to Richard Branson himself, his antics, values and personality. His appeal to the British public is his sense of fair play and irreverence. In particular he has created an image of a 'cheeky entrepreneur' who has battled the mighty 'monopoly' of British Airways. But critics suggest that the Virgin brand may now be over-extended, have limited appeal internationally and the UK consumer may be beginning to tire of Richard Branson's stunts. The other lesser-known image of Richard Branson is one of a ruthless, crafty businessman always trying to get one over on his rivals.

It is difficult to discover the overall financial position of Virgin as it is made up of so many individual companies (many private and offshore) and there are no consolidated accounts. Investments in operating companies are also often transferred between group companies. Branson has argued that he pursues growth, not profits, and builds companies for the long term. The group emphasises maximising return to Virgin group equity through high financial leverage and the use of equity partners. None the less, Virgin Atlantic in 2011 posted an £80.2 m loss; Virgin America has yet to post an annual profit and in its first five years of trading made a loss of approximately $500 m. Virgin Media made a profit of £93 m in 2011, but its cumulative profit and loss account stands at a negative £3,259 m. Virgin Trains in the UK made a profit of £41 m in 2011.

In interviews Richard Branson does not mention his departure but states that the company has been carefully groomed to continue without him, and that the brand is now global and sufficiently well known such that his publicity stunts are no longer required. Richard Branson may now be allowing other people to guide the Virgin Group, but observers are divided about the nature of the group's business model with some seeing it as a private equity organisation (though many of the businesses are start-ups), or a branded venture capital organisation (but the group incubates its own businesses). Others suggest it might be a conglomerate but the group rarely makes acquisitions. Recent appointments at the very top of Virgin are former finance experts who are not renowned for the informal, collaborative and personal style epitomised by Richard Branson. If Sir Richard Branson steps aside, what will the future hold for the Virgin group – will it survive?

References and sources
T. Bower, *Branson*, Harper Perennial, 2008.
R. Branson, *Like A Virgin*, Virgin Books 2012.
The Economist, 'Virgin rebirth', 12 September 2008.
S. Goff, Retail Banking Correspondent, 8 January 2010.
J. Treanor, http://www.guardian.co.uk/profile/jilltreanor, city editor, *Guardian*, 1 January 2012.
Virgin Group's Corporate and Sustainable Development Report 2010.
http://www.businessweek.com, November 2007.
http://www.economist.com/blogs/schumpeter/2013/02/libertys-takeover-virgin-media.
http://www.ft.com/cms/s/0/a04c8138-f1f7-11e1-bba3-00144feabdc0.html#axzz2LHmLSkgB.
http://www.guardian.co.uk/media/2013/feb/06/virgin-media-takeover-john-malone-liberty-global.
http://www.redmayne.co.uk/research/securitydetails/financials.htm?tkr=VMED.
http://www.reuters.com, 16 December 2009.
http://www.virgin.com.

Questions

1 What directions of strategic development have been followed by Virgin over the period of the case (use Figure 7.2 as a guide)?

2 What is the corporate rationale for Virgin as a group of companies?

3 How does the Virgin Group as a corporate parent add value to its businesses? To what extent are these parenting skills relevant to the various businesses in the group?

4 What should the future corporate strategy be?

Appendix 1 Strategic developments of the Virgin Group 1970–2012

1970	Branson founds the Virgin business selling records
1971	First Virgin record shop opened
1977	Virgin record label is launched
1984	Virgin Atlantic, a long-haul airline is founded
1985	Virgin Holidays is founded
1986	Virgin Group PLC formed
1987	Virgin Records America is launched
1988–90	Virgin Megastores are opened in prime city locations in Europe, USA and finally Japan in a joint venture with Marui
	Branson takes Virgin Group PLC private for £248 m
1991	Virgin Publishing formed through merging Virgin Books and WH Allen PLC
	Virgin Games formed
1992	Virgin Records sold for £510 m
1993	Virgin Games floated as Virgin Interactive Entertainment PLC with Hasbro and Blockbuster taking minority stakes
	Virgin Radio commences broadcasting
1994	Virgin Retail acquires Our Price chain of shops
	Virgin Vodka and Virgin Cola are launched as joint venture with Cott Corp.
	Virgin City Jet service launched London to Dublin
1995	Virgin Direct launches a financial investment product in joint venture with Norwich Union
1996	Virgin Express Airline, a low-cost short-haul airline starts up
	Virgin Net an internet service provider is launched
1997	Virgin Trains is founded to run West Coast rail franchise in the UK
	Virgin Cosmetics launches with four flagship stores
	Virgin One telephone bank account launched in collaboration with Royal Bank of Scotland
	Virgin Bride retail chain formed
1999	Virgin Mobile is launched in joint venture with Deutsche Telekom
	Virgin Health starts a network of health clubs
	Virgin Cinemas is sold for £215 m
	49 per cent of Virgin Atlantic sold to Singapore Airlines for $500 m
2000	Virgin Mobile launches US wireless phone service (JV with Sprint)
	Virgin Mobile launches Australian wireless phone (JV with Cable and Wireless)
	Virgin Blue launched (low-cost airline – Australia)
	Virgin Cars launched to sell online
2001	50 per cent of Virgin Blue sold
2002	Virgin Bikes launched
2004	Virgin Digital launched to sell online music
2005	Virgin mobile launched in Canada
2006	Virgin acquires the Holmes Place chain of health clubs
	Virgin Media is launched in partnership with NTL-Telewest
	Virgin Mobile and Virgin Money launched in South Africa
	Virgin Fuel launched
	Virgin Cars closed
2007	Virgin Health Bank launched
	Virgin America (airline) launched
	Virgin Earth Challenge and World Citizen initiatives are launched
2008	Virgin Mobile launches in India in a joint venture with Tata Teleservices
2009	Virgin Green Fund launched
2010	Virgin Hotels launches
	Virgin Racing launched (Formula One)
	Virgin Gaming launched
	Virgin Produced launched (film and TV production company)
	Virgin Money US withdraws from the market
	Virgin Money acquires Church House Trust to acquire UK banking licence
2011	Virgin Cosmetics and Virgin Money (USA) are closed
	Virgin launches Virgin Oceanic, a deep-sea exploration submarine
	Virgin Active acquires Esporta for £80 m
	Virgin Unite (charitable foundation) launches Branson's Centre for Entrepreneurship
2012	Virgin Galactic completes hot-fire rocket tests and develops a revolutionary satellite launch vehicle

Source: Based on www.virgin.com.

8

INTERNATIONAL STRATEGY

Learning outcomes

After reading this chapter, you should be able to:

- Assess the *internationalisation potential* of different markets.

- Identify sources of competitive advantage in international strategy, through both exploitation of *local factors* and *global sourcing*.

- Understand the difference between *global integration* and *local responsiveness* and four main types of international strategy.

- *Rank markets* for entry or expansion, taking into account attractiveness, cultural and other forms of distance and competitor retaliation threats.

- Assess the relative merits of different *market entry modes*, including joint ventures, licensing and foreign direct investment.

Key terms

CAGE framework p. 274

global–local dilemma p. 270

global sourcing p. 268

international strategy p. 262

Porter's Diamond p. 266

staged international expansion model p. 281

Yip's globalisation framework p. 264

MyStrategyLab

MyStrategyLab is designed to help you make the most of your studies. Visit www.pearsoned.co.uk/mystrategylab to discover a wide range of resources, including:

- A personalised **Study plan** that will help you understand core concepts
- **Audio and video clips** that put the spotlight on strategy in the real world
- **Online glossaries and flashcards** that provide helpful reminders when you're looking for some quick revision.

8.1 INTRODUCTION

The last chapter introduced market development as a strategy, in relation to the Ansoff axes. This chapter focuses on a specific but important kind of market development, operating in different geographical markets. This is a challenge for many kinds of organisations nowadays. There are of course the large traditional multinationals such as Nestlé, Toyota and McDonald's. But recent years have seen the rise of emerging-country multinationals from Brazil, Russia, India and China. New small firms are also increasingly 'born global', building international relationships right from the start. Public-sector organisations too are having to make choices about collaboration, outsourcing and even competition with overseas organisations. European Union legislation requires public-service organisations to accept tenders from non-national suppliers.

Figure 8.1 identifies the five main themes of this chapter, with international strategy as the core. The themes are as follows:

- *Internationalisation drivers.* Drivers include market demand, the potential for cost advantages, government pressures and inducements and the need to respond to competitor moves. Given the risks and costs of international strategy, managers need to know that the drivers are strong to justify adopting an international strategy in the first place.

- *Geographical and firm-specific advantages.* In international competition, advantages might come from firm-specific and geographical advantages. Firm-specific advantages are the unique strategic capabilities proprietary to an organisation as discussed in Chapter 3.

Figure 8.1 International strategy: five main themes

Geographical advantages might come both from the geographic location of the original business and from the international configuration of their value network. Managers need to appraise these potential sources of competitive advantage carefully: if there are no competitive advantages, international strategy is liable to fail.

- *International strategy.* If drivers and advantages are sufficiently strong to merit an international strategy, then a range of strategic approaches are opened up, from the simplest export strategies to the most complex global strategies.

- *Market selection.* Having adopted the broad approach to international strategy, the question next is which country markets to prioritise and which to steer clear of. The issues here range from the economic to the cultural and political.

- *Entry mode.* Finally, once target countries are selected, managers have to determine how they should enter each particular market. Again, export is a simple place to start, but there are licensing, franchising, joint venture and wholly owned subsidiary alternatives to consider as well.

The chapter takes a cautious view on international strategy. Despite the fashionable talk of increasing 'globalisation', there are many challenges and many pressures for localisation as well.[1] The chapter will therefore also consider the financial performance implications of growing internationalisation and the Key Debate at the end of this chapter considers the controversy around global, local and regional strategies.

The chapter distinguishes between international strategy and global strategy. **International strategy refers to a range of options for operating outside an organisation's country of origin.** Global strategy is only one kind of international strategy. **Global strategy involves high coordination of extensive activities dispersed geographically in many countries around the world.** This chapter keeps open alternative options to full global strategy.

(8.2) INTERNATIONALISATION DRIVERS

There are many general pressures increasing internationalisation. Barriers to international trade, investment and migration are all now much lower than they were a couple of decades ago. Better international legal frameworks mean that it is less risky to deal with unfamiliar partners. Improvements in communications – from cheaper air travel to the internet – make movement and the spread of ideas much easier around the world. Not least, the success of new economic powerhouses such as the so-called BRICs – Brazil, Russia, India and China – is generating new opportunities and challenges for business internationally.[2]

However, not all these internationalisation trends are one-way. Nor do they hold for all industries. For example, migration is now becoming more difficult between some countries. Trade barriers still exist for some products, especially those relating to defence technologies. Many countries protect their leading companies from takeover by overseas rivals. Markets vary widely in the extent to which consumer needs are standardising – compare computer operating systems to the highly variable national tastes in chocolate. Some so-called multinationals are in fact concentrated in very particular markets, for example North America and Western Europe, or have a quite limited set of international links, for example in supply or outsourcing arrangements with just one or two countries overseas. In short, managers need to beware of 'global boloney', by which economic integration into a single homogenised and competitive world is wildly exaggerated (see the Key Debate at the end of this chapter). As in the Chinese retail market (Illustration 8.1), international drivers are usually a lot more

ILLUSTRATION 8.1

Chinese retail: global or local?

In China Carrefour and Walmart have found that internationalisation is not a simple process.

China is a magnet for ambitious Western supermarket chains. With an annual growth rate of 13 per cent a year, the Chinese market is expected to grow to $1.5 (€1.2) trillion in 2015 and 520 million people are expected to join the Chinese upper middle class by 2025.

Two leading Western companies in the Chinese retail market are French supermarket chain Carrefour and the world's largest retailer, the American Walmart. The two companies have had very different strategies. French supermarket chain Carrefour was the first to enter the Chinese market in a substantial fashion, entering in 1995, after six years' experience in neighbouring Taiwan. Although Walmart and Carrefour have expanded rapidly and are among the top 10 retailers in China (Carrefour has around 200 stores and Walmart more than 370), they are far from reaching saturation and are still tiny compared to their respective home countries, where they each have about 4,500 stores. Both chains have encountered challenges including problems adapting to local taste and local competition.

Carrefour is following a decentralised strategy: except in Shanghai, where it has several stores, Carrefour allows its local store managers, scattered across the many different regions of China, to make their own purchasing and supply decisions. In contrast, Walmart's initial approach had been based on its standard centralised purchasing and distribution strategy, supplying as much as it can from its new, state-of-the-art distribution centre in Shenzen. Walmart has, however, moved away from its headquarters-driven approach to give more sway to local store managers and has experimented with a smaller-scale local store format. One early discovery for Walmart was that Chinese consumers prefer frequent shopping trips in contrast to Walmart's home-based experience where customers drive to out-of-town stores and fill their cars with large multi-packs.

Another discovery for Western retailers is the amount of regional variation in this vast and multi-ethnic country and the need to give their Chinese stores a local flavour. In the north of China, soya sauces are important; in central China, chilli pepper sauces are required; in the south, it is oyster sauces that matter. For fruit, northerners must have dates; southerners want lychees. In the north, the cold means more demand for red meat and, because customers are wearing layers of clothing, wider store aisles. Northerners do not have much access to hot water, so they wash their hair less frequently, meaning that small sachets of shampoo sell better than large bottles.

The growth of companies such as Carrefour and Walmart demonstrates that there is a substantial market for the Western retail model. Carrefour, for example, was a pioneer of 'private label' goods in China, while Walmart brings logistical expertise. But progress has been slow as home-grown companies have imitated and proven they often are more flexible and experimental with new store formats. Walmart turned to profit only in 2008 and has decided to slow down its expansion in China and Carrefour's 2–3 per cent margins are significantly below the nearly 5 per cent margins it enjoys in France. In 2011 local authorities accused Walmart of mislabelling ordinary pork as organic and closed down 13 stores for two weeks and Carrefour has repeatedly been obliged to deny that it was considering leaving China.

Sources: Financial Times, Wall Street Journal and Euromonitor (various).

Questions

1 What are the pros and cons of the different China strategies pursued by Carrefour and Walmart?

2 What might be the dangers for a large Western retailer in staying out of the Chinese market?

Figure 8.2 Drivers of internationalisation

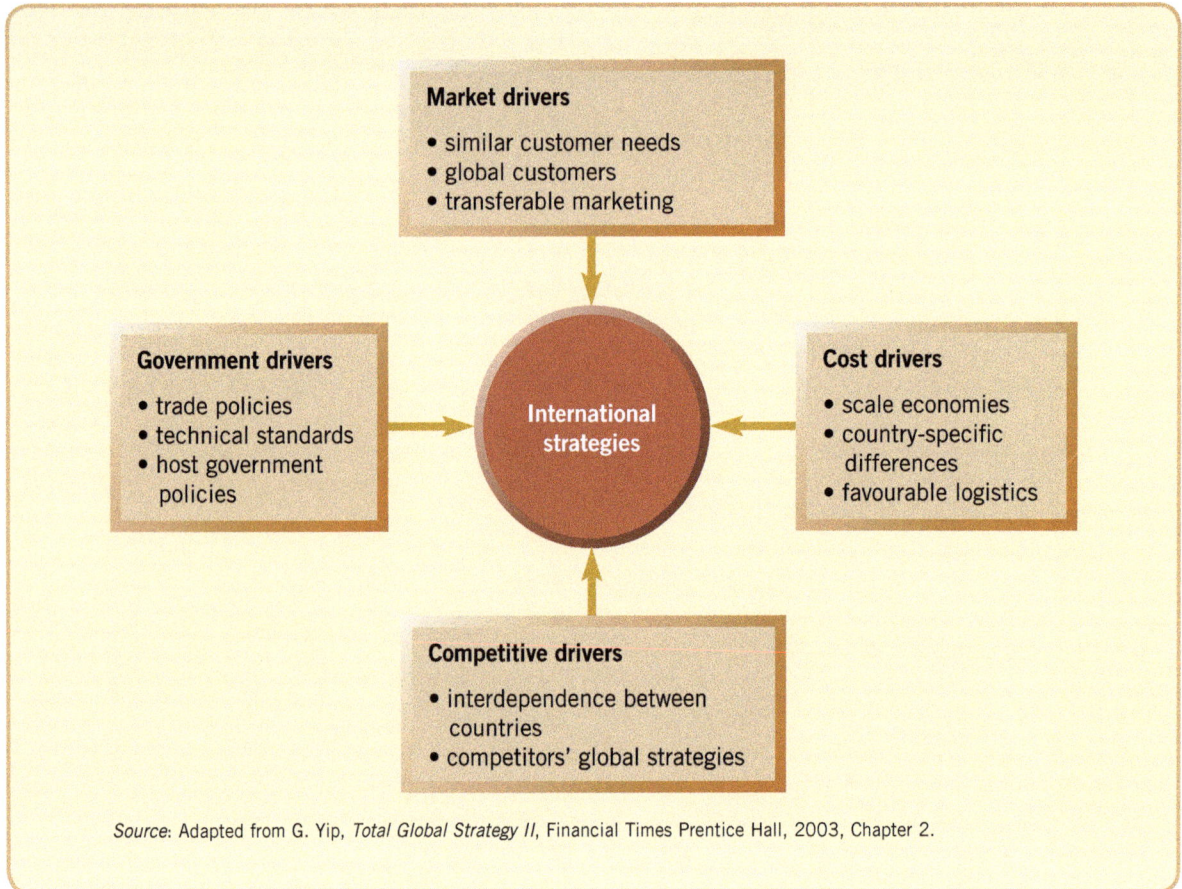

Market drivers
- similar customer needs
- global customers
- transferable marketing

Government drivers
- trade policies
- technical standards
- host government policies

International strategies

Cost drivers
- scale economies
- country-specific differences
- favourable logistics

Competitive drivers
- interdependence between countries
- competitors' global strategies

Source: Adapted from G. Yip, *Total Global Strategy II*, Financial Times Prentice Hall, 2003, Chapter 2.

complicated than that: Chinese markets not only are very different from Western ones, but vary widely within China itself.

Given internationalisation's complexity, international strategy should be underpinned by a careful assessment of trends in each particular market. George Yip provides a framework for analysing 'drivers of globalisation'. In the terms of this chapter, these globalisation drivers can be thought of as 'internationalisation drivers' more generally. In this book, therefore, Yip's globalisation framework sees international strategy potential as determined by market drivers, cost drivers, government drivers and competitive drivers (see Figure 8.2).[3] In more detail, the four drivers are as follows:

- *Market drivers*. A critical facilitator of internationalisation is standardisation of market characteristics. There are three components underlying this driver. First, the presence of *similar customer needs and tastes*: for example, the fact that in most societies consumers have similar needs for easy credit has promoted the worldwide spread of a handful of credit card companies such as Visa. Second is the presence of *global customers*: for example, car component companies have become more international as their customers, such as Toyota or Ford, have internationalised, and required standardised components for all their factories around the world. Finally, *transferable marketing* promotes market globalisation: brands such as Coca-Cola are still successfully marketed in very similar ways across the world.

- *Cost drivers.* Costs can be reduced by operating internationally. Again, there are three main elements to cost drivers. First, increasing volume beyond what a national market might support can give *scale economie*s, both on the production side and in purchasing of supplies. Companies from smaller countries such as the Netherlands, Switzerland and Taiwan tend therefore to become proportionately much more international than companies from the USA, which have a vast market at home. Scale economies are particularly important in industries with high product development costs, as in the aircraft industry, where initial costs need to be spread over the large volumes of international markets. Second, internationalisation is promoted where it is possible to take advantage of variations in *country-specific differences*. Thus it makes sense to locate the manufacture of clothing in Africa or Bangladesh where labour is still considerably cheaper, but to keep design activities in cities such as New York, Paris, Milan or London, where fashion expertise is concentrated. The third element is *favourable logistics*, or the costs of moving products or services across borders relative to their final value. From this point of view, microchips are easy to source internationally, while bulky materials such as assembled furniture are harder.

- *Government drivers.* There are three main factors here that facilitate internationalisation. First, *reduction of barriers to trade and investment* has accelerated internationalisation. During the last couple of decades national governments have reduced restrictions on both flow of goods and capital. The World Trade Organization has been instrumental in reducing trade barriers globally.[4] Similarly, the emergence of regional economic integration partnerships like the European Union, the North American Free Trade Agreement and the Association of Southeast Asian Nations Economic Community has promoted this development. No government, however, allows complete economic openness and it typically varies widely from industry to industry, with agriculture and high-tech industries related to defence likely to be particularly sensitive. *The liberalisation and adoption of free markets* in many countries around the globe have also encouraged international trade and investments. This of course includes the collapse of the Soviet Union and liberalisation of Eastern Europe, China's free market reforms and market-based reforms in numerous Asian and South American economies. A third important government factor is *technology standardisation*. Compatible technical standards make it easier for companies to access different markets as they can enter many markets with the same product or service without adapting to local idiosyncratic standards.

- *Competitive drivers.* These relate specifically to globalisation as an integrated worldwide strategy rather than simpler international strategies. These have two elements. First, *interdependence* between country operations increases the pressure for global coordination. For example, a business with a plant in Mexico serving both the US and the Japanese markets has to coordinate carefully between the three locations: surging sales in one country, or a collapse in another, will have significant knock-on effects on the other countries. The second element relates directly to competitor strategy. The presence of *globalised competitors* increases the pressure to adopt a global strategy in response because competitors may use one country's profits to cross-subsidise their operations in another. A company with a loosely coordinated international strategy is vulnerable to globalised competitors, because it is unable to support country subsidiaries under attack from targeted, subsidised competition. The danger is of piecemeal withdrawal from countries under attack, and the gradual undermining of any overall economies of scale that the international player may have started with.[5]

The key insight from Yip's drivers framework is that the internationalisation potential of industries is variable. There are many different factors that can support it as indicated above, but others can inhibit it. For example, customer needs and tastes for many food products inhibit internationalisation of them and local governments often impose tariff barriers, ownership restrictions and local content requirements on foreign entrants. An important step in determining an internationalisation strategy is a realistic assessment of the true scope for internationalisation in the particular industry. In the Chinese retail case (Illustration 8.1), it may be that the Western entry both includes market and competitive drivers.

(8.3) GEOGRAPHIC SOURCES OF ADVANTAGE

As for any strategy, internationalisation needs to be based on strategic capabilities providing a sustainable competitive advantage. This competitive advantage has usually to be substantial. After all, a competitor entering a market from overseas typically starts with considerable *dis*-advantages relative to existing home competitors, which will usually have superior market knowledge, established relationships with local customers, strong supply chains and the like. A foreign entrant must have significant competitive advantages for it to overcome these inherent advantages of local competitors. Tesco's failure in the USA is an example of this. After seven years and investments of about £1 bn (€1.2 bn) in its US Fresh & Easy business Tesco was forced to withdraw. Unlike in the UK, Tesco had no significant competitive advantage over the strong US domestic retailers. Internationalisation thus requires building on the sources of sustainable competitive advantage that we have discussed earlier in Chapters 3 and 6 including the organisation's unique strengths in resources and capabilities. While these *firm- or organisation-specific advantages* are important, competitive advantage in an international context also depends on *country-specific or geographic advantages*.[6]

As is clear from the earlier discussion of cost drivers in international strategy, the geographical location of activities is a crucial source of potential advantage and one of the distinguishing features of international strategy relative to other diversification strategies. As Bruce Kogut at Columbia University has explained, an organisation can improve the configuration of its *value chain and system*[7] by taking advantage of country-specific differences (see section 3.4.2). There are two principal opportunities available: the exploitation of particular *locational advantages*, often in the company's home country, and sourcing advantages overseas via an *international value system*.

8.3.1 Locational advantage: Porter's Diamond[8]

Countries and regions within them, and organisations originating in those, often benefit from competitive advantages grounded in specific local conditions. They become associated with specific types of enduring competitive advantage: for example, the Swiss in private banking, the northern Italians in leather and fur fashion goods, and the Taiwanese in laptop computers. Michael Porter has proposed a four-pointed 'diamond' to explain why some locations tend to produce firms with sustained competitive advantages in some industries more than others (see Figure 8.3). Specifically, **Porter's Diamond suggests that locational advantages may stem from local factor conditions; local demand conditions; local related and supporting industries; and from local firm strategy structure and rivalry.** These four interacting determinants of locational advantage work as follows:

Figure 8.3 Porter's Diamond – the determinants of national advantages

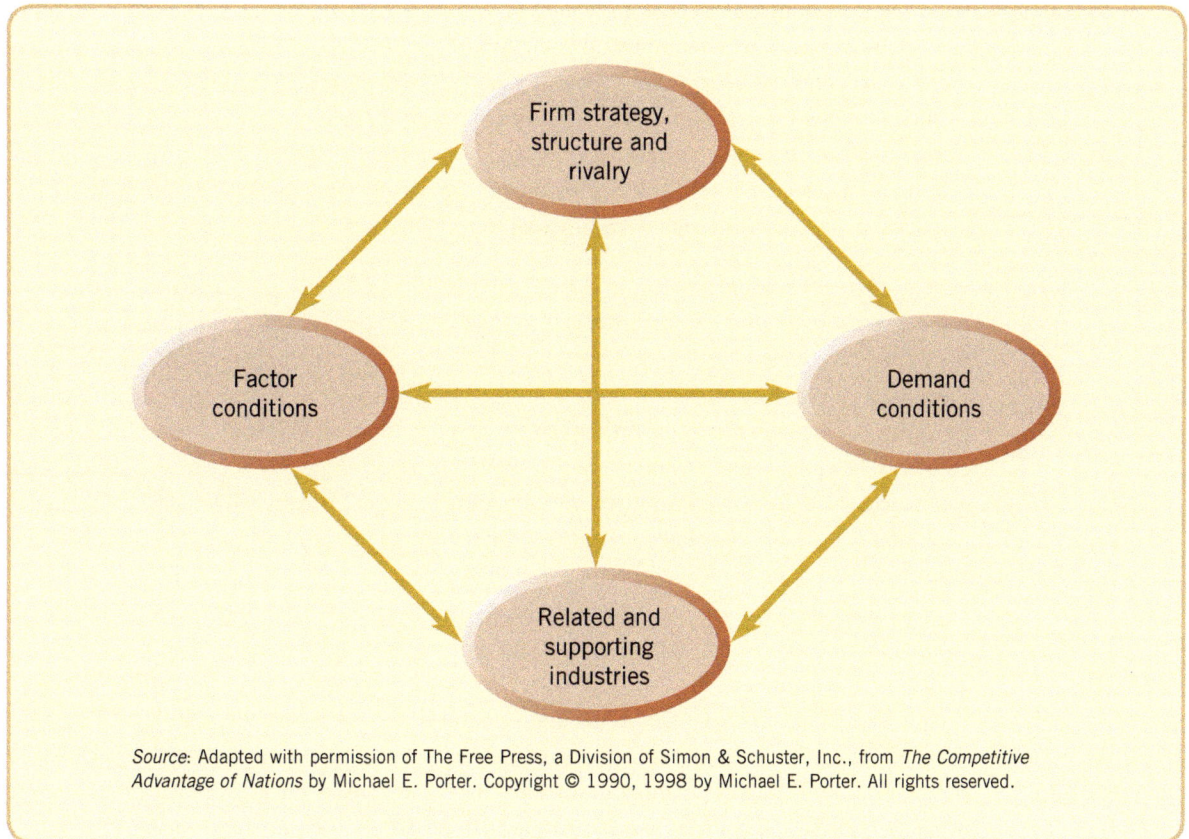

- *Factor conditions*. These refer to the 'factors of production' that go into making a product or service (i.e. raw materials, land and labour). Factor condition advantages at a national level can translate into general competitive advantages for national firms in international markets. For example, the linguistic ability of the Swiss has traditionally provided a significant advantage to their banking industry. Cheap energy has traditionally provided an advantage for the North American aluminium industry.

- *Home demand conditions*. The nature of the domestic customers can become a source of competitive advantage. Dealing with sophisticated and demanding customers at home helps train a company to be effective overseas. For example, America's long distances have led to competitive strength in very large truck engines. Sophisticated local customers in France and Italy have helped keep their local fashion industries at the leading edge for many decades.

- *Related and supporting industries*. Local 'clusters' of related and mutually supporting industries can be an important source of competitive advantage. These are often regionally based, making personal interaction easier. In northern Italy, for example, the leather footwear industry, the leatherworking machinery industry and the design services which underpin them group together in the same regional cluster to each other's mutual benefit. Silicon Valley forms a cluster of hardware, software, research and venture capital organisations which together create a virtuous circle of high-technology enterprise.

- *Firm strategy, industry structure and rivalry*. The characteristic strategies, industry structures and rivalries in different countries can also be bases of advantage. German companies' strategy of investing in technical excellence gives them a characteristic advantage in engineering industries and creates large pools of expertise. A competitive local industry structure is also helpful: if too dominant in their home territory, local organisations can become complacent and lose advantage overseas. Some domestic rivalry can actually be an advantage, therefore. For example, the long-run success of the Japanese car companies is partly based on government policy sustaining several national players (unlike in the United Kingdom, where they were all merged into one) and the Swiss pharmaceuticals industry became strong in part because each company had to compete with several strong local rivals.

Porter's Diamond model underlines the environmental conditions and structural attributes of nations and their regions that contribute to their competitive advantage. It has been used by governments aiming to increase the competitive advantage of their local industries. The argument that rivalry can be positive has led to a major policy shift in many countries towards encouraging local competition rather than protecting home-based industries. Governments can also foster local industries by raising safety or environmental standards (i.e. creating sophisticated demand conditions) or encouraging cooperation between suppliers and buyers on a domestic level (i.e. building clusters of related and supporting industries in particular regions).

For individual organisations, however, the value of Porter's Diamond is to identify the extent to which they can build on home-based advantages to create competitive advantage in relation to others internationally. To compete with local actors, organisations must carefully exploit the distinct environmental conditions and structural attributes illustrated in Figure 8.3. For example, Dutch brewing companies – such as Heineken – had an advantage in early internationalisation due to the combination of sophisticated consumers and limited room to grow at home. Volvo Trucks, the Swedish truck and construction equipment manufacturer, has achieved global success by building on a local network of sophisticated engineering partners and suppliers and a local demand orientated towards reliability and safety. Before embarking on an internationalisation strategy, managers should seek out sources of general locational advantage to underpin their company's individual sources of advantage.

8.3.2 The international value system

The sources of geographic advantage need, however, not be purely domestic. In addition, as companies continue to internationalise, the country of origin becomes relatively less important for competitive advantage.[9] For companies with most of their sales abroad, like the telecom giant Ericsson with 95 per cent of sales outside Sweden, the configuration of the local environments where they operate is at least as important as their domestic environment. This implies that for international companies, advantage also needs to be drawn from the international configuration of their *value system* (see section 3.4.2). Here the different skills, resources and costs of countries around the world can be systematically exploited in order to locate each element of the value chain in that country or region where it can be conducted most effectively and efficiently. This may be achieved through both foreign direct investments and joint ventures but also through **global sourcing**: **purchasing services and components from the most appropriate suppliers around the world, regardless of their location.** For example, in the UK for many years the National Health Service has been sourcing medical personnel from overseas to offset a shortfall in domestic skills and capacity. Smaller organisations can also build on the broader system of suppliers, channels and customers as demonstrated in Illustration 8.2.

ILLUSTRATION 8.2

The international 'Joint Effort Enterprise'

For Blue Skies international strategy is something more than profit alone.

Blue Skies specialises in producing fresh-cut fruit and juice products from a network of factories in Africa and South America. It supplies over 12 major European retailers, including Waitrose in the UK, Albert Heijn in the Netherlands and Monoprix in France. The company has factories in Ghana, Egypt, South Africa and Brazil. Its biggest factory is in Ghana and employs over 1,500 people and sources fruit from over 100 small to medium-sized farms. Blue Skies believes in value adding at source whereby the raw materials are processed within the country of origin rather than shipped overseas and processed elsewhere. By doing this, as much as 70 per cent of the value of the finished product stays within the country of origin, compared to as little as 15 per cent if it is processed outside.

Blue Skies works within a framework it has developed called the 'Joint Effort Enterprise' (JEE). While it is their model for a sustainable business, it is not a model which has been introduced to respond to the growing hype around 'sustainability'. Instead it is a set of principles from the foundation of the business in 1998 to ensure that the organisation would endure. The JEE is principally made up of three strands: a diverse society, a culture of respect and a drive for profit. The latter must not, however, come at the expense of all the other strands. Blue Skies believes that this model ensures that it retains the best people and conserves the resources they rely on, so that they can produce the best quality products and therefore generate the income that keeps the organisation going. Its approach is 'based on fairness in business, respect for each other and above all, trust'. In addition, Blue Skies raised over £400,000 (€480,000) in partnership with two European retailers and completed over 10 projects in Ghana and South Africa including the construction of schools, latrines and community centres. The Blue Skies JEE approach has also been awarded a Queens Award for Enterprise in the Sustainable Development Category in both 2008 and 2011.

During the last few years Blue Skies has encountered several international challenges: a world recession, rising energy prices, exchange rate volatility, shortage of raw materials, etc. It realises that these are challenges that an international operation across three continents must be ready and willing to respond to. Accordingly, it has undertaken a number of initiatives:

- Developing products for local and dollar-based markets to reduce exposure to exchange rate losses and supply chain disruption.
- Expanding its supply base around the world to ensure year-round supply of fruit.
- Helping its suppliers achieve agricultural standards such as LEAF (Linking Environment and Farming) to ensure sustainability of supply.
- Growing the Blue Skies Foundation to strengthen its relationship with staff, farmers and their communities.
- Developing plans to generate renewable energy to reduce electricity costs and greenhouse gas emissions.
- Opening a European-based contingency factory to ensure consistency of supply during supply chain disruption.

Source: Prepared by Edwina Goodwin, Leicester Business School, De Montfort University.

Questions

1 What internationalisation drivers (Figure 8.2) do you think were most important for Blue Skies' decision to enter its specific markets?

2 How does Blue Skies strategy fit into a broader international value system including suppliers, channels and customers (see also Figure 3.5)?

3 To what extent is JEE key to Blue Skies' international strategy and competitive advantage or rather a social entrepreneurship effort?

Different locational advantages can be identified:

- *Cost advantages* include labour costs, transportation and communications costs and taxation and investment incentives. Labour costs are important. American and European firms, for example, have moved much of their software programming tasks to India where a computer programmer costs an American firm about one quarter of what it would pay for a worker with comparable skills in the USA. As wages in India have risen, some IT firms have started to move work to even more low-cost locations such as Thailand and Vietnam.

- *Unique local capabilities* may allow an organisation to enhance its competitive advantage. Gradually value-creating and innovative activity becomes geographically dispersed across multiple centres of excellence within multinational organisations.[10] For example, leading European pharmaceuticals company GSK has R&D laboratories in Boston and the Research Triangle in North Carolina in order to establish research collaborations with the prominent universities and hospitals in those areas. Internationalisation, therefore, is increasingly not only about exploiting an organisation's existing capabilities in new national markets, but about developing strategic capabilities by drawing on capabilities found elsewhere in the world.

- *National market characteristics* can enable organisations to develop differentiated product offerings aimed at different market segments. American guitar-maker Gibson, for example, complements its US-made products with often similar, lower-cost alternatives produced in South Korea under the Epiphone brand. However, because of the American music tradition, Gibson's high-end guitars benefit from the reputation of still being 'made in the USA'.

(8.4) INTERNATIONAL STRATEGIES

Given their organisation-specific advantages and the ability to obtain sources of international competitive advantage through geographic home-based factors or international value systems, organisations still face difficult questions about what kind of international strategy to pursue. The fundamental issue in formulating an international strategy is to balance pressures for *global integration* versus those for *local responsiveness*.[11] Pressures for global integration encourage organisations to coordinate their activities across diverse countries to gain efficient operations. The internationalisation drivers discussed above (section 8.2) indicate forces that organisations can build on to achieve lower costs and higher quality in operations and activities on a global scale. However, there are conflicting pressures that also encourage organisations to become locally responsive and meet the specific needs in each individual country (see section 8.5.1 below). Values and attitudes, cultures, laws, institutions and economics differ across countries, which imply differences in customer preferences, product and service standards, regulations and human resources that all need to be addressed. These two opposing pressures – global integration vs local responsiveness – put contradictory demands on an organisation's international strategy. High pressure for global integration implies an increased need to concentrate and coordinate operations globally. In contrast, high pressure for local responsiveness implies a greater need to disperse operations and adapt to local demand.

This key problem is sometimes referred to as the global–local dilemma: the **extent to which products and services may be standardised across national boundaries or need to be adapted to meet the requirements of specific national markets**. For some products and services – such as televisions – markets appear similar across the world, offering huge potential scale economies if design, production and delivery can be centralised. For other products and

Figure 8.4 Four international strategies

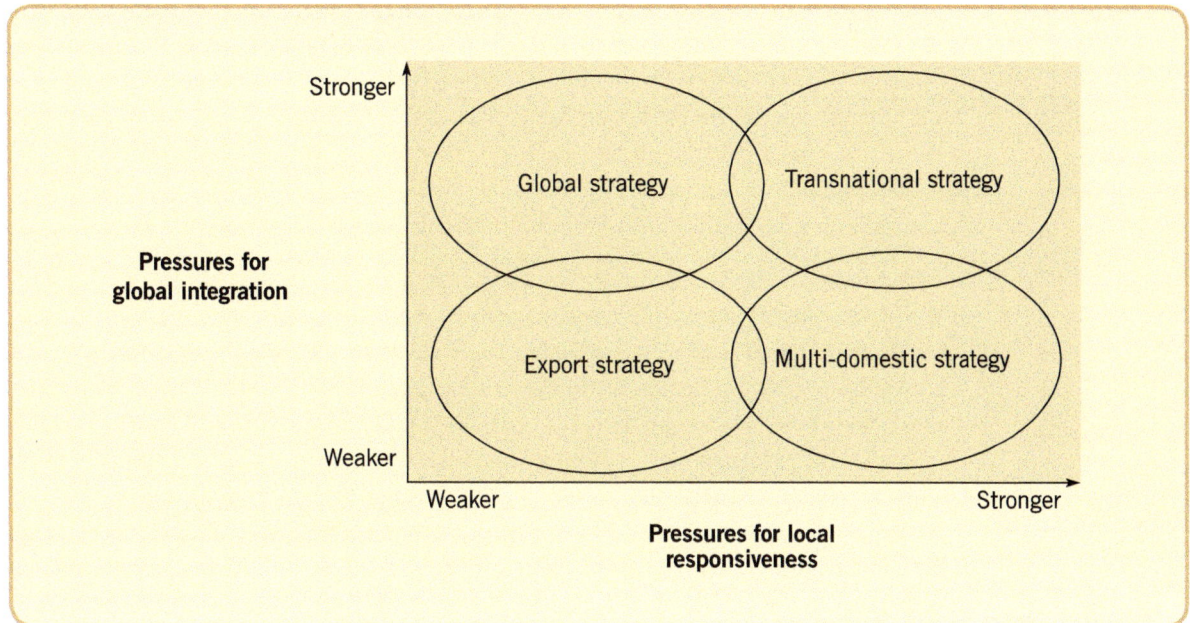

services – such as television programming – tastes still seem highly national-specific, drawing companies to decentralise operations and control as near as possible to the local market.

This dilemma between global integration and local responsiveness suggests several possible international strategies, ranging from emphasising one of the dimensions to complex responses that try to combine both. Organisations need to assess to what degree there are potential advantages of cost and quality of global integration and balance those pressures against the need to adapt products and/or services to local conditions. This section introduces four different kinds of international strategy, based on strategic choices about this balance (see Figure 8.4). The four basic international strategies are:[12]

- *Export strategy*. This strategy leverages home country capabilities, innovations and products in different foreign countries. It is advantageous when both pressures for global integration and local responsiveness are low, as shown in Figure 8.4. Companies that have distinctive capabilities together with strong reputation and brand names often follow this strategy with success. Google, for example, centralises its R&D and the core architecture underlying its internet services at its headquarters in California in the USA and exploits it internationally with minor adaptations except for local languages and alphabets. The downside of this approach is the limits of a home country centralised view of the business with risks of skilled local competitors getting ahead. Google, for example, meets strong local rivals in Baidu in China and Naver in Korea with superior mastery of the language and understanding of consumer behaviour.

- *Multi-domestic strategy*. This is a strategy that maximises local responsiveness. It is based on different product or service offerings and operations in each country depending on local market conditions and customer preferences. Each country is treated differently with a con-siderable autonomy for each country manager to best meet the needs of the local markets and customers in that particular country. As in the export strategy, this strategy is similarly loosely coordinated internationally. The organisation becomes a collection of relatively independent units with value chain activities adapted to specific local conditions. This multi-domestic approach is particularly appropriate when there are strong benefits to adapting to local needs and when there are limited efficiency gains from integration. It is common in food and consumer product industries where local idiosyncratic preferences are significant. Marketing-driven companies often pursue this type of strategy. For example, Frito-Lay, a US branded-snacks company, tailors its global products to local tastes and even creates entirely new snack products for local markets.[13] The disadvantages of a multi-domestic strategy include manufacturing inefficiencies, a proliferation of costly product and service variations and risks towards brand and reputation if national practices become too diverse.

- *Global strategy.* This is a strategy that maximises global integration. In this strategy the world is seen as one marketplace with standardised products and services that fully exploits integration and efficiency in operations. The focus is on capturing scale economies and exploiting location economies worldwide with geographically dispersed value chain activities being coordinated and controlled centrally from headquarters. In these respects this strategy is the exact opposite to the multi-domestic strategy. A global strategy is most beneficial when there are substantial cost or quality efficiency benefits from standardisation and when customer needs are relatively homogeneous across countries. It is a common strategy for commodities or commodity-like products. Mexican Cemex, one of the largest cement companies in the world, follows a global strategy with centralised and shared services in information technology, R&D, human resources and financial services across countries and regions.[14] Non-commodity companies can also follow a global strategy, like Sweden's furniture retailer IKEA. Based on a strong home base they standardise products and marketing with limited local adaptation to gain maximum global integration efficiency. The drawback of the global strategy is reduced flexibility due to standardisation that limits possibilities to adapting activities and products to local conditions.[15] This has, for example, led IKEA to make minor modifications of some furniture offerings to suit local tastes.

- *Transnational strategy.* This is the most complex strategy that tries to maximise both responsiveness and integration. Its aim is to unite the key advantages of the multi-domestic and global strategies while minimising their disadvantages. In addition, it maximises learning and knowledge exchange between dispersed units. In this strategy products and services and operational activities are, subject to minimum efficiency standards, adapted to local conditions in each country. In contrast to the multi-domestic strategy, however, this strategy also leverages learning and innovation across units in different countries. The value chain configuration includes an intricate combination of centralised manufacturing to increase efficiency combined with distributed assembly and local adaptations. Coordination is neither centralised at home nor dispersed in foreign countries, but encourages knowledge flows from wherever ideas and innovations come from. The major advantage of this strategy is its capacity to support efficiency and effectiveness while at the same time being able to serve local needs and leverage learning across units. General Electric has been celebrated as having a transnational strategy that emphasises seeking and exchanging ideas irrespective where they come from. The company swaps ideas regarding efficiency, customer responsiveness and innovation across different parts of the value chain and diverse countries worldwide.[16] However, while it is argued that transnational strategies are becoming increasingly necessary, many firms find it difficult to implement given its complexity and the fundamental trade-off between integration and responsiveness. ABB, the Swiss–Swedish engineering giant, was once identified as the archetypal transnational company, but later ran into serious problems.[17]

In practice, these four international strategies are not absolutely distinct as indicated by the overlapping ovals in Figure 8.4. They are rather illustrative examples of alternative international strategies. Global integration and local responsiveness are matters of degree rather than sharp distinctions. Moreover, choices between them will be influenced by changes in the internationalisation drivers introduced earlier. It is rare that companies adopt a pure form of international strategy; instead they often blend approaches and are located somewhere between the four strategies. As exemplified above, IKEA has a global strategy, but also makes some minor local adaptations, which may take it towards more of a transnational strategy.

Often regions (e.g. Europe or North America) play a larger role in international strategy than individual countries or global expansion. Thus many multinationals compromise between local and global logics by opting for *regional strategies*.[18] The aim of this strategy is to attain some of the economic efficiency and location advantages of more global strategies while simultaneously reaching local adaptation advantages. Regions are treated as relatively homogenous markets with value chain activities concentrated within them. Sales data suggest that many multinational companies follow this type of strategy focused on one or two regions including the triad of the European Union, the North American Free Trade Agreement and/or Japan/Asia.[19] For example, over 85 per cent of all cars sold within each region of Europe, North America and Japan are built in that same region. This regional approach to international strategy emphasises that distances and differences between nations are still relatively large (see section 8.5.1 below), which makes global integration difficult (see also the Key Debate at the end of this chapter).

These differences can, however, be exploited in arbitrage for value creation. *Arbitrage* implies that multinationals take advantage of price differences between two or more markets by purchasing goods cheaply in one market and selling them at a higher price in another. For example, Walmart is known for sourcing much of what the company sells in the USA from China. Not only price differences, but differences in labour costs, in knowledge, capital and taxes can be exploited by operating in diverse countries. Google is known for exploiting tax differences between countries in its international operations, for example the relatively low Irish corporation tax. The potential for arbitrage in multinationals is substantial and it has been suggested as a third significant international strategy dimension, besides integration and responsiveness.[20] Finally, different international strategies require diverse organising requirements for success, which is discussed in Chapter 13 (section 13.2.4).

(8.5) MARKET SELECTION AND ENTRY

Having decided on an international strategy built on significant sources of competitive advantage and supported by strong internationalisation drivers, managers need next to decide which countries to enter. Not all countries are equally attractive. To an extent, however, countries can initially be compared using standard environmental analysis techniques, for example along the dimensions identified in the PESTEL framework (see section 2.2.1) or according to the industry five forces (section 2.3). However, there are specific determinants of market attractiveness that need to be considered in internationalisation strategy: the intrinsic characteristics of the market. A key point here is how initial estimates of country attractiveness can be modified by various measures of *distance*. The section concludes by considering different *entry modes* into national markets.

8.5.1 Market characteristics

At least four elements of the PESTEL framework are particularly important in comparing countries for entry:

- *Political.* Political environments vary widely between countries and can alter rapidly. Russia since the fall of communism has seen frequent swings for and against private foreign enterprise. Governments can of course create significant opportunities for organisations. For example, the British government has traditionally promoted the financial services industry in the City of London by offering tax advantages to high-earning financiers from abroad and providing a 'light-touch' regulatory environment. It is important, however, to determine the level of *political risk* before entering a country. Toyota, for example, found itself the subject of an unexpected consumer boycott in China because of political tensions over a territorial dispute between China and Japan. There is also a risk that governments simply take over companies. In 2012 the Argentinian government nationalised the Spanish oil company Repsol's 57 per cent stake in Argentina's largest oil extractor and refinery.

- *Economic.* Key comparators in deciding entry are levels of gross domestic product and disposable income which help in estimating the potential size of the market. Fast-growth economies obviously provide opportunities, and in developing economies such as China and India growth is translating into an even faster creation of a high-consumption middle class. At the same time entirely new high-growth markets are opening up in Africa including Nigeria and Ghana.

- *Social.* Social factors will clearly be important, for example the availability of a well-trained workforce or the size of demographic market segments – old or young – relevant to the strategy. Cultural variations also need to be considered, for instance in defining tastes in the marketplace.

- *Legal.* Countries vary widely in their legal regime, determining the extent to which businesses can enforce contracts, protect intellectual property or avoid corruption. Similarly, policing will be important for the security of employees, a factor that in the past has deterred business in some African countries.

A common procedure is to rank country markets against each other on criteria such as these and then to choose the countries for entry that offer the highest relative scores. However, Pankaj Ghemawat from Spain's IESE Business School has pointed out that what matters is not just the attractiveness of different countries relative to each other, but also the compatibility of the countries with the internationalising firm itself.[21] Thus Ghemawat underlines the importance of *match* between country and firm. For firms coming from any particular country, some countries are more 'distant' – or mismatched – than others. For example, a Spanish company might be 'closer' to a South American market than an East Asian market and might therefore prefer that market even if it ranked lower on standard criteria of attractiveness. As well as a relative ranking of countries, therefore, each company has to add its assessment of countries in terms of closeness of match.

Ghemawat's 'CAGE framework' measures the match between countries and companies according to four dimensions of distance, reflected by the letters of the acronym. Thus the **CAGE framework** emphasises the importance of **cultural, administrative, geographical and economic distance**, as follows:

- *Cultural distance.* The distance dimension here relates to differences in language, ethnicity, religion and social norms. Cultural distance is not just a matter of similarity in consumer

ILLUSTRATION 8.3

Nordic Industrial Park: bridging distance across international markets

When a resource-constrained firm enters a high-distance market, it helps greatly if it can utilise a low-distance entry point.

The lure of the Chinese market has led several Western companies to venture into a context that is unfamiliar and bewildering, especially for small and medium-sized enterprises (SMEs) lacking the deep pockets of large multinationals. It is useful for SMEs to have a 'bridge' into a high-distance market. One way to accomplish this to use a foreign-owned industrial park (i.e. a space designated for industrial use).

Consider the case of the Nordic Industrial Park (NIP) which provides a physical space for offices and light-manufacturing facilities, and a range of value-added services to set up a business in China. These include legal services (e.g. registering the company and drafting contracts), human resource management (e.g. recruitment, payroll and expat relocation), accounting (e.g. financial reporting), and information and communication technology (e.g. internet access).

NIP was co-founded by Ove Nodland, a Norwegian who first went to China in 1994 to manage a state-owned enterprise that had attracted Norwegian investment. Next, Nodland helped set up a rare-earth magnet venture for another Norwegian concern in Ningbo, a port city in Zhejiang province just south of Shanghai (the commercial centre of China) and renowned for its entrepreneurialism. Nodland knew that even though rules might be set in Beijing (the national capital and political centre of China), they were implemented by local officials – and so they mattered greatly. He invested considerable energies in building close relationships with the city's mayor and other officials, and took care to ensure that the company complied with local regulations and aligned itself with local governmental priorities. Nodland's local guanxi (network connections) grew rapidly. However, the magnet company's target market was the IT industry, and when the dot-com bubble burst, demand collapsed. Nodland was now saddled with a facility to do business in Ningbo, but with little scope to achieve the intended scale of success.

After some thought, Nodland came up with an alternative use for his facility and connections. He reckoned that he was well placed to help European SMEs enter China. He chose to focus on what he knew best: firms from the Nordic region (Denmark, Finland, Iceland, Norway and Sweden) setting up a base in Ningbo. Thus was born the concept of NIP in 2002. It became operational within two years.

From the perspective of a European SME entering NIP, there are multiple benefits:

- *Process:* Lower start-up costs. NIP leverages its knowledge of the Chinese business environment by hand-holding clients through the complexities associated with starting and running a business in China, thereby allowing firms to focus their time and energies on core business activities.
- *Physical environment:* A familiar ambience. NIP's architecture and design mimics Scandinavian features that set it apart from standard Chinese buildings. Not only does this give expat managers a sense of the familiar, it is also a symbolic reminder to Chinese employees that they are part of a Western organisation.
- *People:* A like-minded community. By virtue of being part of the largest concentration of Nordic companies in China, expat managers have the opportunity to share experiences with and pick up 'tricks of the trade' from other managers with a similar cultural background through hallway conversations and lunchtime meetings.

Of course, entering a facility like NIP comes at a cost, but offers benefits in terms of 'reducing distance'.

Source: Prepared by Shameen Prashantham, Nottingham University Business School China.

Questions

1 Consider NIP's services in light of the CAGE framework and analyse how they may help reduce distance.

2 What might be the drawbacks in being located in an industrial park?

Figure 8.5 International cross-cultural comparison

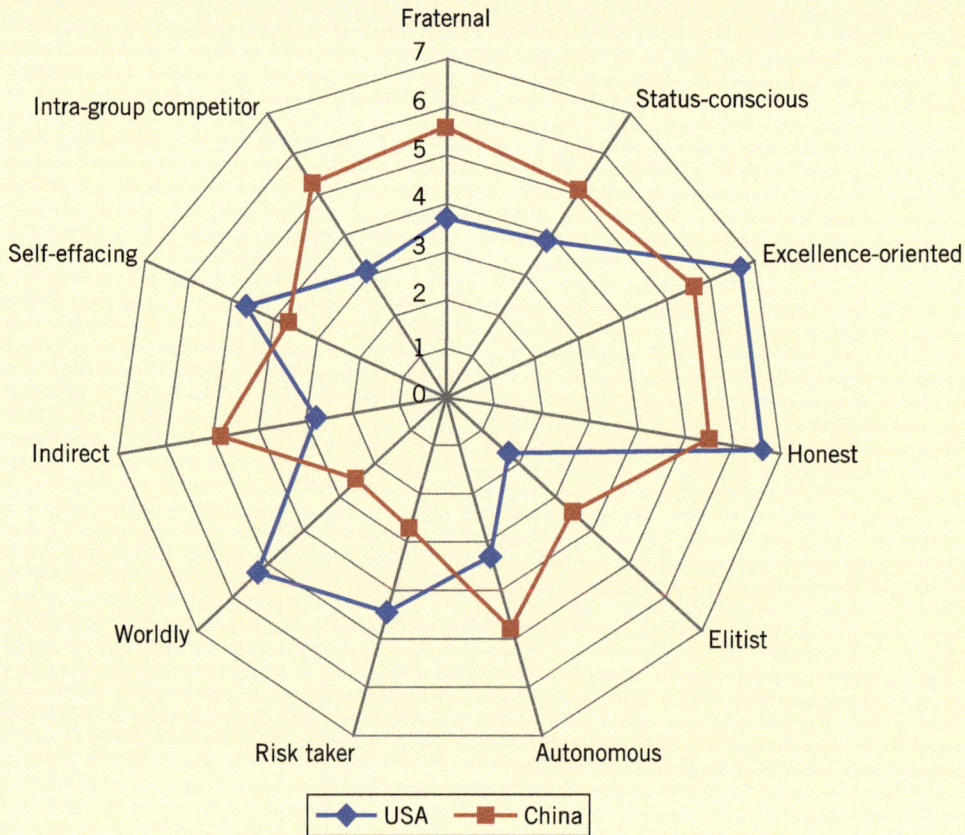

Note: Based on a survey of managers on standard dimensions (selection presented here).

Source: M. Javidan, P. Dorman, M. de Luque and R. House, 'In the eye of the beholder: cross-cultural lessons in leadership from Project GLOBE', *Academy of Management Perspectives* (February 2006), pp. 67–90 (Figure 4: USA vs China, p. 82). (GLOBE stands for 'Global Leadership and Organisational Behaviour Effectiveness'.)

tastes, but extends to important compatibilities in terms of managerial behaviours. Here, for example, US firms might be closer to Canada than to Mexico, which Spanish firms might find relatively compatible. Figure 8.5 draws on the GLOBE survey of 17,000 managers from 62 different societal cultures around the world to contrast specifically the orientations of American and Chinese managers on some key cultural dimensions. According to this GLOBE survey, American managers appear to be typically more risk-taking, while Chinese managers are more autonomous. One way to shrink distance is through cooperation with local partners, which is demonstrated in Illustration 8.3.

● *Administrative and political distance.* Here distance is in terms of incompatible administrative, political or legal traditions. Colonial ties can diminish difference, so that the shared heritage of France and its former West African colonies creates certain understandings that go beyond linguistic advantages. See also, for example, the experience of the Brazilian Vale company in Mozambique, where shared Portuguese heritage made a difference (Illustration 8.4). Institutional weaknesses – for example, slow or corrupt administration – can open up

ILLUSTRATION 8.4

Vale – a Brazilian giant in different cultures

Rapid overseas expansion brings this Brazilian multinational some contrasting experiences.

Until the late 1990s, Brazil's Vale mining company was a state-owned sleeping giant. Vale, the world's largest iron-ore producer and the second-largest miner overall by volume and market value, was privatised in 1997. Since then the company has transformed itself into a dynamic conglomerate and expanded globally. As the former CEO Roger Agnelli commented in 2010: 'Vale used to be fundamentally an iron-ore company. We used to operate essentially in Brazil. Now we are in 36 countries.' Although Vale has been described as 'one of the world's powerful and aggressive mining companies' its international experiences have been mixed as shown in the examples below and consequently the new CEO Murilo Ferreira has somewhat slowed down Vale's global expansion.

Vale's $17.6 bn (€13.2 bn or £10.5 bn) takeover in 2006 of Inco, the world's largest nickel producer, was its first major overseas acquisition. Canada's largest national newspaper, the *Globe and Mail*, described Vale's arrival as 'The great Canadian mining disaster.' Many Canadians resented this takeover by what they regarded as a business from a developing country. Of 29 senior Canadian managers in early 2007, three years later 23 had departed, mostly voluntarily. At one tense meeting a Brazilian manager riposted: 'How come, if you're so smart, you didn't take *us* over?' The clash resulted in a strike that lasted almost a year. While the conflict was finally resolved it was seen as a sign of potential confrontations when companies from emerging economies such as Brazil, China and India expand into new, unfamiliar territories.

The booming demand from China has been a gift and Vale's export of iron ore there account for about 30 per cent of revenues. Compared to main rivals Australian miners BHP and Rio Tinto, Vale, however, has a considerable disadvantage: distance. Vale's solution has been to develop giant iron-ore vessels. A fleet of 100 of the so-called 'Valemaxes' would reduce shipping costs to China by 20 per cent and carbon emission by 35 per cent. The giant ships have, however, ignited controversy among Chinese authorities, especially when one developed a crack in a ballast tank. The struggling Chinese shipbuilding community has been particularly critical as it claims that the mega-carriers would drive freight rates down. All this has resulted in a ban on the Valemaxes to dock at China's ports, forcing Vale to unload in Malaysia and the Philippines instead.

A contrast so far has been Vale's experience in Mozambique. Like many Brazilian companies, Vale has been attracted to the two African countries of Angola and Mozambique because of the shared cultural and linguistic heritage of Portuguese colonialism. About half the 3 million black African slaves sent to Brazil between 1700 and 1850 came from Angola and in the 1820s, settlers in Angola and Mozambique applied to join the newly independent Brazil in a federation. Vale first invested $1.7 bn (€1.3 bn) in Moatize, considered by investors to be one of the world's largest untapped coal reserves. Because of its success Vale has decided to expand Moatize's capacity from 11 million to 26 million tonnes per year with an additional investment of $6 bn (€4.5 bn) including the expansion of railway linkages and infrastructure. Vale's CEO, Murilo Ferreira, confirms Africa's significance for the company's strategy: 'It's a new frontier . . . Africa is very important. We want to grow there.'

Sources: Financial Times, 25 February 2010; Financial Times, 9 February 2010; Financial Times, 11 February 2010; Financial Times, 12 April 2012; Financial Times, 1 October 2012; mining-technology.com, 24 November 2011; miningweekly.com, 18 May 2012.

Questions

1 Suggest three reasons for Vale's different reception in Canada and Mozambique.

2 What can Vale do to mitigate the problems the company encounters when expanding globally?

distance between countries. So too can political differences: Chinese companies are increasingly able to operate in parts of the world that American companies are finding harder, for example parts of the Middle East and Africa.

- *Geographical distance.* This is not just a matter of the kilometres separating one country from another, but involves other geographical characteristics of the country such as size, sea-access and the quality of communications infrastructure. Transport infrastructure can shrink or exaggerate physical distance. France is much closer to large parts of Continental Europe than to the United Kingdom, because of the barrier presented by the English Channel and the latter relatively poor road and rail infrastructure. The possibility for individual companies to reduce geographic distances is illustrated by the development of mega-ship carriers by the Brazilian mining company Vale in Illustration 8.4.

- *Economic.* The final element of the CAGE framework refers particularly to wealth distances. There are of course huge disparities in wealth internationally: around the world, there are 4 billion people beneath the poverty income threshold of less than \$2 a day.[22] Multinationals from rich countries are typically weak at serving such very poor consumers. However, these rich-country multinationals are losing out on large markets if they only concentrate on the wealthy elites overseas. University of Michigan academic C.K. Prahalad pointed out that the aggregated wealth of those at the 'base of the pyramid' in terms of income distribution is very substantial: simple mathematics means that those 4 billion below the poverty threshold represent a market of more than \$2,000 bn per year. If rich-country multinationals can develop new capabilities to serve these numerically huge markets, they can bridge the economic distance, and thereby both significantly extend their presence in booming economies such as China and India and bring to these poor consumers the benefits that are claimed for Western goods. See Illustration 8.5 for examples of innovative base of the pyramid strategies.

8.5.2 Competitive characteristics

Assessing the relative attractiveness of markets by PESTEL and CAGE analyses is only the first step. The second element relates to competition. Here, of course, Michael Porter's five forces framework can help (see section 2.3). For example, country markets with many existing competitors, powerful buyers (perhaps large retail chains such as in much of North America and Northern Europe) and low barriers to further new entrants from overseas would typically be unattractive. However, an additional consideration is the likelihood of retaliation from other competitors.

In the five forces framework, retaliation potential relates to rivalry and entry, but managers can extend this by using insights directly from 'game theory' (see section 6.4.4). Here the likelihood and ferocity of potential competitor reactions are added to the simple calculation of relative country market attractiveness. As in Figure 8.6, country markets can be assessed according to three criteria:[23]

- *Market attractiveness* to the new entrant, based on PESTEL, CAGE and five forces analyses, for example. In Figure 8.6, countries A and B are the most attractive to the entrant.

- *Defender's reactiveness*, likely to be influenced by the market's attractiveness to the defender but also by the extent to which the defender is working with a globally integrated, rather than multi-domestic, strategy. A defender will be more reactive if the markets are important to it and it has the managerial capabilities to coordinate its response. Here, the defender is highly reactive in countries A and D.

ILLUSTRATION

ILLUSTRATION 8.5

Base of the pyramid strategies

Base of the pyramid strategy means more than just low prices. Base of the pyramid involves designing new products, forming partnership, reshaping distribution channels and introducing novel financing solutions.

Product design

A key problem in the developing world is the poor quality of piped water. Unilever Hindustan, India's largest consumer goods company, owned by Anglo-Dutch Unilever, developed a water filter that makes water as safe as boiling. It is marketed and sold through the wide Unilever distribution network. The filter has attracted over three million households, mainly in India's mega- or middle-sized cities. However, at $35 (€26) it is still unattainable for millions of Indians who live on less than a dollar a day. In an effort to reach rural customers Unilever has therefore started to market a light-version (lower capacity) of the filter. The success of the product on the Indian market has led Unilever Hindustan to introduce the water filter in other markets in Asia, Eastern Europe and South Africa.

Partnerships

First Energy Oorja started as a partnership between the Indian Institute of Science Bangalore and British Petroleum (BP) Emerging Consumer Market (ECM) division to develop a stove using the 'power of innovation and a strong understanding of consumer energy needs'. It was later acquired by The Alchemists Ark (TAA), a privately held business consulting firm. The First Energy Oorja stoves are low-smoke, low-cost stoves, which work on pellets – an organic biofuel made of processed agricultural waste. First Energy Oorja works in close partnership with both local non-governmental organisations and dealer networks in rural markets to distribute and market the stove. This distribution model ensures that the product reaches remote Indian locations.

Distribution channels

Bayer CropScience, a global firm that develops and manufactures crop protection products, initiated a Green World venture in Kenya. It introduced small packs of pesticides and trained a network of small, rural agrodealers to guide and educate small farmers on product handling and use. It also provided further support and marketing via radio. Bayer CropScience carefully selected dealers based on their reputation in the community and sales volumes. Today about 25 per cent of its horticultural retail revenues in Kenya now come from Green World stores.

Financial solutions

Cemex, a global cement corporation from Mexico, has been an innovative pioneer in designing a microfinancing system, 'Patrimonio Hoy' (Property Now), for the poor in Mexico and later in the rest of Latin America. In the past, building houses for this group had often proved lengthy and risky because without savings or access to credit, low-income families could only buy small amounts of building material at a time. Patrimonio Hoy is a solution to this. It is a combination of savings and credit schemes in which Cemex provides collateral-free financing to customers via a membership system based on small monthly fees. Customers demonstrate their savings discipline by regular monthly payments and Cemex develops trust in them by delivering building raw materials early on credit. The programme is a success and Cemex reports that it has reached 265 million families so far.

Sources: Swiss Agency for Development and Cooperation, 2011; Institute for Financial and Management Research, 2012; A. Karamchandani, M. Kubzansky and N. Lalwani, 'Is the bottom of the pyramid really for you?', *Harvard Business Review*, March 2011; *Business Today*, December 2011.

Questions

1 Can you imagine any risks or dangers that Western companies might face in pursuing base of the pyramid strategies?

2 Is there anything that Western companies might learn from base of the pyramid strategies in emerging markets that might be valuable in their home markets?

Figure 8.6 International competitor retaliation

Note: Size of bubble indicates defender's relative clout.

Source: Reprinted by permission of *Harvard Business Review*. Exhibit adapted from 'Global gamesmanship' by I. MacMillan, S. van Putter and R. McGrath, May 2003. Copyright © 2003 by the Harvard Business School Publishing Corporation. All rights reserved.

- *Defender's clout*, that is the power that the defender is able to muster in order to fight back. Clout is typically a function of share in the particular market, but might be influenced by connections to other powerful local players, such as retailers or government. In Figure 8.6, clout is represented by the size of the bubbles, with the defender having most clout in countries A, C, D and F.

Choice of country to enter can be significantly modified by adding reactiveness and clout to calculations of attractiveness. Relying only on attractiveness, the top-ranked country to enter in Figure 8.6 is country A. Unfortunately, it is also one in which the defender is highly reactive, and the one in which it has most clout. Country B becomes a better international move than A. In turn, country C is a better prospect than country D, because, even though they are equally attractive, the defender is less reactive. One surprising result of taking defender reactiveness and clout into account is the re-evaluation of country E: although ranked fifth on simple attractiveness, it might rank second overall if competitor retaliation is allowed for.

This sort of analysis is particularly fruitful for considering the international moves of two interdependent competitors, such as Unilever and Procter & Gamble or British Airways and Singapore Airlines. In these cases the analysis is relevant to any aggressive strategic move, for instance the expansion of existing operations in a country as well as initial entry. Especially in the case of globally integrated competitors, moreover, the overall clout of the defender must be taken into account. The defender may choose to retaliate in other markets than the targeted one, counter-attacking wherever it has the clout to do damage to the aggressor. Naturally, too, this kind of analysis can be applied to interactions between diversified competitors as well as international ones: each bubble could represent different products or services.

8.5.3 **Entry modes**

Once a particular national market has been selected for entry, an organisation needs to choose how to enter that market. Entry modes differ in the degree of resource commitment to a particular market and the extent to which an organisation is operationally involved in a particular location. In order of increasing resource commitment, the four key entry mode types are: *exporting*; contractual arrangement through *licensing and franchising* to local partners, as McDonald's does to restaurant operators; *joint ventures*, in other words the establishment of jointly owned businesses; and *wholly owned subsidiaries*, through either the acquisition of established companies or 'greenfield' investments, the development of facilities from scratch.

The *staged international expansion* model emphasises the role of experience in determining entry mode. Internationalisation typically brings organisations into unfamiliar territory, requiring managers to learn new ways of doing business.[24] The staged international expansion model proposes a sequential process whereby companies gradually increase their commitment to newly entered markets, as they build market knowledge and capabilities. Thus firms might enter initially by licensing or exporting, thereby acquiring some local knowledge while minimising local investments. As they gain knowledge and confidence, firms can then increase their exposure, perhaps first by a joint venture and finally by creating a wholly owned subsidiary. For example, the leading Danish wind turbine manufacturer Vestas first entered the US market through exports. Subsequently Vestas established manufacturing and R&D facilities in Eastern Colorado to strengthen its competitive position versus domestic players and now supplies 90 per cent of components required for the assembly of a final turbine within the USA.

However, the gradualism of staged international expansion is now challenged by two phenomena:

- '*Born-global firms*', in other words new small firms that internationalise rapidly at early stages in their development.[25] New technologies now help small firms link up to international sources of expertise, supply and customers worldwide. For such firms, waiting till they have enough international experience is not an option: international strategy is a condition of existence. For example, companies like Twitter and Instagram internationalised quickly from being small start-ups. Other types of companies may also internationalise fast. Blue Skies in Illustration 8.2 with operations across three continents is an example of a small company that started out as a mini-multinational.

- *Emerging-country multinationals* also often move quickly through entry modes. Prominent examples are the Chinese white-goods multinational Haier, the Indian pharmaceuticals company Ranbaxy Laboratories and Mexico's Cemex cement company mentioned above.[26] Such companies typically develop *unique capabilities* in their home market that then need to be rolled out quickly worldwide before competitors catch up. For example, Haier became skilled at very efficient production of simple white goods, providing a cost advantage that is transferable outside its Chinese manufacturing base. Haier now has factories in Italy and the USA, as well as the Philippines, Malaysia, Indonesia, Egypt, Nigeria and elsewhere round the world. The rapid internationalisation made by emerging multinationals from China has largely been based on acquisitions. These are often high-profile acquisitions as illustrated by the Chinese conglomerate Wanda buying the second-biggest movie theatre chain in the USA, AMC (see the end Case example).[27]

Where the demands and pace of international competition rule out more gradualist staged expansion, two fundamental principles can help guide choice of market entry mode:

- *The breadth of competitive advantage* in the target market. This determines whether entry into the market can be done relying upon the company's own capabilities, or whether it must draw on the capabilities of local partners, for instance to access distribution channels or to manufacture locally.

- *Tradability*, in other words the ability to rely on trading relationships, rather than the firm's own presence. Tradability is determined by two factors: ease of transport from home country to target country, and the quality of legal protection in the target country. Legal protection refers for example to the ability to enforce contracts, to safeguard performance standards or to protect intellectual property such as patented technologies. Tradability is low where it is unsafe to trade through market-based contracts with local partners.

Other case-specific factors are liable to enter the calculation of appropriate entry mode as well, not least the availability of suitable local partners. None the less, the two principles of competitive advantage and tradability do suggest the following broad guidelines for entry mode (Figure 8.7):

- *Export* is the baseline option, and is suitable where the product or services are easily transported from country to country and where the home-based competitive advantages are sufficiently broad to minimise reliance on local companies.

- *License or franchise* the product or service where competitive advantages are too narrow to go it alone, but the legal environment is such that licensees and franchisees can be relied on not to abuse their contracts, under-perform on standards or steal the intellectual property.

- *Joint ventures* work where competitive advantages are narrow, but local licensees or franchisees cannot be trusted with intellectual property or long-term performance. A joint venture involving shared ownership gives the foreign company more direct control and ensures that the local partner has an interest in maximising the value of the common enterprise rather than solely its own standalone interests.

Figure 8.7 Modes of international market entry

- *Wholly owned subsidiary* is an attractive route where competitive advantages are sufficiently broad not to depend on local partners, but where nevertheless transport difficulties rule out simple export. Such wholly owned subsidiaries can be via new greenfield investments (as for example many Japanese car companies have entered European markets) or via acquisition, where the integration of a local firm completes the breadth of competitive advantage required.

(8.6) INTERNATIONALISATION AND PERFORMANCE

Just as for product and service diversity discussed in section 7.4 the relationship between internationalisation and performance has been extensively researched.[28] Some of the main findings from such research are these:

- *An inverted U-curve.* While the potential performance benefits of internationalisation are substantial, in that it allows firms to realise economies of scale and scope and benefit from the locational advantages available in countries around the globe, the combination of diverse locations and diverse business units also gives rise to high levels of organisational complexity. At some point, the costs of organisational complexity may exceed the benefits of internationalisations. Accordingly, theory and the balance of evidence suggest an inverted U-shaped relationship between internationalisation and performance (similar to the findings on product/service diversification shown in section 7.4), with moderate levels of internationalisation leading to the best results. However, Yip's research on large British companies suggests that managers may be getting better at internationalisation, with substantially internationalised firms actually seeing performance improving to the point where international sales are above about 40 per cent of total sales.[29] Experience and commitment to internationalisation may be able to deliver strong performance for highly internationalised firms.

- *Service-sector disadvantages.* A number of studies have suggested that, in contrast to firms in the manufacturing sector, internationalisation may not lead to improved performance for service-sector firms. There are three possible reasons for such an effect. First, the operations of foreign service firms in some sectors (such as accountants or banks) remain tightly regulated and restricted in many countries; second, due to the intangible nature of services, they are often more sensitive to cultural differences and require greater adaptation than manufactured products which may lead to higher initial learning costs; third, the services typically require a significant local presence and reduce the scope for the exploitation of economies of scale in production compared to manufacturing firms.[30]

- *Internationalisation and product diversity.* An important question to consider is the interaction between internationalisation and product/service diversification. Compared to single-business firms it has been suggested that product-diversified firms are likely to do better from international expansion because they have already developed the necessary skills and structures for managing internal diversity.[31] At the other end of the spectrum there is general consensus that firms that are highly diversified in terms of both product and international markets are likely to face excessive costs of coordination and control leading to poor performance. As many firms have not yet reached levels of internationalisation where negative effects outweigh possible gains and because of current scepticism with regard to the benefits of high levels of product diversification, many companies currently opt for reducing their product diversity while building their international scope. Unilever, for example, has been combining a strategy of growing internationalisation with de-diversification.

(8.7) ROLES IN AN INTERNATIONAL PORTFOLIO

Just as for product diversification, international strategies imply different relationships between subsidiary operations and the corporate centre. The complexity of the strategies followed by organisations such as General Electric or Unilever can result in highly differentiated networks of subsidiaries with a range of distinct strategic roles. Subsidiaries may play different roles according to the level of local resources and capabilities available to them and the strategic importance of their local environment (see Figure 8.8):[32]

- *Strategic leaders* are subsidiaries that not only hold valuable resources and capabilities, but are also located in countries that are crucial for competitive success because of, for example, the size of the local market or the accessibility of key technologies. Japanese and European subsidiaries in the USA often play this role. Increasingly, subsidiaries are seen as playing important strategic roles with entrepreneurial potential for the whole multinational organisation.[33] Subsidiaries and subunits are either assigned strategic roles or take autonomous strategic initiatives. Hewlett Packard, for example, is known to have used both approaches.[34]

- *Contributors* are subsidiaries located in countries of lesser strategic significance, but with sufficiently valuable internal capabilities to nevertheless play key roles in a multinational organisation's competitive success. The Australian subsidiary of the Swedish telecommunications firm Ericsson played such a role in developing specialised systems for the firm's mobile phone business.

Figure 8.8 Subsidiary roles in multinational firms

● *Implementers*, though not contributing substantially to the enhancement of a firm's competitive advantage, are important in the sense that they help generate vital financial resources. In this sense, they are similar to the 'cash cows' of the Boston Consulting Group matrix. The danger is that they turn into the equivalent of 'dogs'.

● *Black holes* are subsidiaries located in countries that are crucial for competitive success but with low-level resources or capabilities. This is a position many subsidiaries of American and European firms found themselves in over long periods in Japan. They have some of the characteristics of 'question marks' in the Boston Consulting Group matrix, requiring heavy investment (like an astrophysicist's black hole, sucking matter in). Possibilities for overcoming this unattractive position include the development of alliances and the selective and targeted development of key resources and capabilities.

These various subsidiary roles relate to how these subsidiaries are generally controlled and managed, and this is discussed in Chapter 13.

SUMMARY

- Internationalisation potential in any particular market is determined by Yip's four drivers of internationalisation: market, cost, government and competitors' strategies.

- *Sources of advantage* in international strategy can be drawn from both national sources of advantage, as captured in Porter's Diamond, and global sourcing through the international value system.

- There are *four main types of international strategy*, varying according to extent of coordination and geographical configuration: *export strategy*, *multi-domestic strategy*, *global strategy* and *transnational strategy*.

- *Market selection* for international entry or expansion should be based on attractiveness, multidimensional measures of distance and expectations of competitor retaliation.

- *Modes of entry* into new markets include *export*, *licensing* and *franchising*, *joint ventures* and *overseas wholly owned subsidiaries*.

- Internationalisation has an uncertain relationship to financial performance, with an inverted U-curve warning against over-internationalisation.

- Subsidiaries in an international firm can be managed by portfolio methods just like businesses in a diversified firm.

VIDEO ASSIGNMENTS

Visit *MyStrategyLab* and watch the CISCO case study for Chapter 8.

1 Using the concepts in section 8.5, analyse and recommend the appropriate market selection and entry mode for CISCO – refer to both the markets and the mode of entry/development.

2 Using Yip's model (Figure 8.2) and insights from the video, explain and discuss the drivers of internationalisation in the IT industries.

KEY DEBATE

Global, local or regional?

Debate rages over whether companies are really becoming more global, or whether local or indeed regional pressures remain strong.

Ted Levitt, Harvard Business School professor and former non-executive director of the international advertising firm Saatchi & Saatchi, has provocatively made the case for deep commitment to global strategies in all kinds of markets. He argues that modern communications technologies are creating homogeneous market needs, while manufacturing technologies are increasing the benefits of scale. Given the cost advantages of scale, and the diminishing importance of consumer differences, companies that commit to truly global strategies will be able to use low prices to sweep out all competitors still focused on local needs. He argues: 'The global company will seek to standardise its offering everywhere . . . Companies that do not adapt to the new global realities will become victims of those that do.' He cites Coca-Cola, Rolex, Sony and McDonald's as exemplars of the trend. Companies should not hanker over detailed differences left over from the past, but recognise the big picture of coming globalisation.

Levitt's sweeping argument brought a spirited response from American academics Gerry Wind and Susan Douglas, warning of 'the Myth of Globalisation'. They challenge both the trend to homogenisation and the growing role of scale economies. Even apparently global companies adapt to country needs: for example, Coca-Cola sells local products in Japan alongside its classic Coke, and its Dasani bottled water is a success in the USA, but a failure in Europe. As to scale, new flexible automation technologies may even be reducing economic order sizes, allowing short production runs adapted to local needs. Wind and Douglas warn that blind confidence in the inevitability of globalisation will surely lead to business disappointment.

Between the two poles of global and local there is a more recent third position: regional. Pankaj Ghemawat points out that most international trade is intra-regional. European countries trade predominantly with each other. The trend towards intra-regional trade is actually growing, from about 40 per cent of

all trade 40 years ago to 55 per cent at the beginning of the twenty-first century. Alan Rugman calculates that in the early years of the twenty-first century over 300 of the world's largest corporations still have more than half their sales in their home region. An apparently global company like McDonald's is effectively bi-regional, with 80 per cent of its sales concentrated in North America and Europe, and the multinational General Electric has 60 per cent of its sales in North America.

Ted Levitt might be impatient with these empirical details. The essential issue for him is: where are things going in the future? Certainly there are still local differences in taste, but are these declining overall? And are sales really the appropriate proxy for globalisation as the regional advocates suggest? According to this reasoning a US firm that acquires raw materials in one region and country, produces parts in another, offshores its accounting to a third and its R&D in yet another would not be considered global if its majority of sales were in the North American Free Trade Agreement (NAFTA).

Sources: T. Levitt, 'The globalisation of markets', *Harvard Business Review*, May–June (1983), pp. 92–102; S.P. Douglas and Y. Wind 'The myth of globalization', *Columbia Journal of World Business*, vol. 22, no. 4 (1987), pp. 19–29; P. Ghemawat, 'Regional strategies for global leadership', *Harvard Business Review*, December (2005), pp. 98–108; A. Rugman, *The Regional Multinationals – MNEs and 'global' strategic management*, Cambridge University Press, 2005. A. Rugman and A. Verbeke, 'A new perspective on the regional and global strategies of multinational service firms', *Management International Review*, vol. 48. no. 4 (2008), pp. 397–411.

Questions

1 Make a list of products and services which are getting more 'global' over time; then make a list of products and services which are still very 'local'.

2 How many countries in the world have you visited in your lifetime? How many countries had your parents visited by the same age?

WORK ASSIGNMENTS

✱ Denotes more advanced work assignments.
* Refers to a case study in the Text and Case edition.

8.1 Using Figure 8.2 (Yip's internationalisation drivers), compare two markets you are familiar with and analyse how strong each of the drivers is for increased international strategy.

8.2 Visit the websites of the following companies and try to plot their international strategies in one of the four international strategy types of Figure 8.4 (each company primarily fits one strategy): Nestlé, ABB, Louis Vuitton and Lenovo.

8.3 Using the CAGE framework (section 8.5.1), assess the relative 'distance' of the USA, China, India and France for a British company (or a company from a country of your choice).

8.4 Using the diverse modes of international market entry of Figure 8.7 classify the entry mode of H&M*, Tesco* or SABMiller* or any other multinational corporation with which you are familiar.

8.5 Critically evaluate t he suggestion that globalisation is mostly beneficial for companies.

8.6 Take any part of the public or not-for-profit sector (e.g. education, health) and explain how far internationalisation has affected its management and consider how far it may do so in the future.

Integrative assignment

8.7 As in 8.2, use the four international strategies of Figure 8.4. to classify the international strategy of H&M*, Tesco* or any other multinational corporation with which you are familiar. Drawing on section 13.2.4, how does this corporation's organisational structure fit (or not fit) this strategy?

RECOMMENDED KEY READINGS

● A useful collection of academic articles on international business is in A. Rugman and T. Brewer (eds), *The Oxford Handbook of International Business*, Oxford University Press, 2003. For a collection of seminal contributions in research on multinational corporations see J.H. Dunning, *The theory of transnational corporations*, vol. 1, Routledge, 1993.

● An invigorating perspective on international strategy is provided by G.S. Yip and G.T. Hult, *Total Global Strategy*, Pearson, 2012. A comprehensive general textbook is S. Segal-Horn and D. Faulkner, *Understanding Global Strategy*, Southwestern, 2010.

● A critical evaluation of the emphasis on globalisation and global integration contrasted with a regional focus

can be found in A.M. Rugman, *The Regional Multinational – MNEs and 'global' strategic management*, Cambridge University Press, 2005; A.M. Rugman, *The End of Globalisation*, Random House, 2000; and P. Ghemawat, *Redefining Global Strategy*, Harvard Business School Press, 2007.

● An eye-opening introduction to the detailed workings – and inefficiencies – of today's global economy today is P. Rivoli, *The Travels of a T-Shirt in the Global Economy: an Economist Examines the Markets, Power and Politics of World Trade*, Wiley, 2006. A more optimistic view is in T. Friedman, *The World Is Flat: the Globalised World in the Twenty-First Century*, Penguin, 2006.

REFERENCES

1. For another cautious view, see M. Alexander and H. Korine, 'Why you shouldn't go global', *Harvard Business Review* (December 2008), pp. 70–7.

2. T. Friedman, *The World Is Flat: the Globalized World in the Twenty-First Century*, Penguin, 2006; and P. Rivoli, *The*

Travels of a T-Shirt in the Global Economy: an Economist Examines the Markets, Power and Politics of World Trade, Wiley, 2006.

3. G.S. Yip and G.T. Hult, *Total Global Strategy*, Pearson, 2012.

4. Useful industry-specific data on trends in openness to trade and investment can be found at the World Trade Organization's site, www.wto.org.

5. G. Hamel and C.K. Prahalad, 'Do you really have a global strategy?', *Harvard Business Review*, vol. 63, no. 4 (1985), pp. 139–48.

6. For a discussion of firm-specific advantages ('FSAs') and country-specific advantages ('CSAs') see A.M. Rugman, *The Regional Multinational – MNEs and 'global' strategic management*, Cambridge University Press, 2005, A. Rugman and A. Verbeke, 'Location, competitiveness and the multinational enterprise', in A.M. Rugman (ed.), *Oxford handbook of international business*, pp. 150–177, Oxford University Press, 2008; and A. Verbeke, *International business strategy*, Cambridge University Press, 2009.

7. B. Kogut, 'Designing global strategies: comparative and competitive value added changes', *Sloan Management Review*, vol. 27 (1985), pp. 15–28.

8. M. Porter, *The Competitive Advantage of Nations*, Macmillan, 1990; and M. Porter, *On Competition*, Harvard Business Press, 2008.

9. See reference 7 above.

10. J.A. Cantwell, 'The globalization of technology: what remains of the product life cycle model?', *Cambridge Journal of Economics*, vol. 19, no. 1 (1995), pp. 155–74; and A. Rugman and A. Verbeke 'Location, competitiveness and the multinational enterprise', in A.M. Rugman (ed.), *Oxford Handbook of International Business*, pp. 150–77, Oxford University Press, 2008.

11. The integration–responsiveness framework builds on the original works by C.A. Bartlett, 'Building and managing the transnational: the new organizational challenge', in M.E. Porter (ed.), *Competition in Global Industries*, Harvard Business School Press, pp. 367–401, 1986; and C.K. Prahalad and Y. Doz, *The Multinational Mission: Balancing local demands and global vision*, Free Press, 1987.

12. The typology builds on the basic framework of C.A. Bartlett and S. Ghoshal, *Managing across Borders: the Transnational Solution*, The Harvard Business School Press, 1989 (2nd updated edn, 1998); and S. Ghoshal and N. Nohria, 'Horses for courses: organizational forms for multinational corporations', *Sloan Management Review*, vol. 34 (1993), pp. 23–35. The typology was later confirmed in a large-scale empirical investigation by A.W. Harzing, 'An empirical analysis and extension of the Bartlett and Ghoshal typology of multinational companies', *Journal of International Business*, vol. 32, no. 1 (2000), pp. 101–20. For a similar typology see M. Porter, 'Changing patterns of international competition', *California Management Review*, vol. 28, no. 2 (1987), pp. 9–39. For a critical evaluation see T.M. Devinney, D.F. Midgley and S. Venaik, 'The optimal performance of the global firm: formalizing and extending the integration-responsiveness rramework', *Organization Science*, vol. 11, no. 6 (2000), pp. 674–95.

13. For a discussion of companies that build on the multi-domestic route see A. Rugman and R. Hodgetts, 'The end of global strategy', *European Management Journal*, vol. 19, no. 4 (2001), pp. 333–43.

14. For a detailed account of Cemex strategy see P. Ghemawat, *Redefining Global Strategy*, Harvard Business School Press, 2007.

15. For a discussion of the limits of global strategy see A. Rugman and R. Hodgetts in reference 13 above.

16. For a more in-depth discussion of how General Electric (GE) tries to combine a global and multi-domestic ('glocalization') strategy with innovation in emerging markets see J.R.I. Immelt, V. Govindarajan and C. Trimble, 'How GE is disrupting itself', *Harvard Business Review*, October (2009), pp. 57–65.

17. For an analysis of the transnational strategy and ABB as an example, see C.A. Bartlett and S. Ghoshal, *Managing across Borders: the Transnational Solution*, 2nd edn, Harvard Business School Press, 1998, pp. 259–72; and S. Ghoshal and C. Bartlett, *The Individualized Corporation*, Harper Business, 1997.

18. For criticism of the integration–responsiveness framework and its shortcoming in taking regions into account and a detailed discussion of regional strategy see A.M. Rugman, *The Regional Multinational – MNEs and 'global' strategic management*, pp. 48–53 and 201–12, Cambridge University Press, 2005. Further analysis of regional strategies can be found in P. Ghemawat, 'Regional strategies for global leadership', *Harvard Business Review*, December (2005), pp. 98–108.

19. For an in-depth examination of the regional sales data see A. Rugman and A. Verbeke, 'A perspective on regional and global strategies of multinational enterprises', *Journal of International Business*, vol. 35 (2004), pp. 3–18; and A.M. Rugman, *The End of Globalization*, Random House, 2000; A.M. Rugman and S. Girod, 'Retail multinationals and globalization: the evidence is regional', *European Management Journal*, vol. 21, no. 1 (2003), pp. 24–37; and A.M. Rugman, reference 18 above.

20. P. Ghemawat, 'Reconceptualizing international strategy and organization', *Strategic Organization*, vol. 6, no. 2 (2008), pp. 195–206.

21. P. Ghemawat, 'Distance still matters', *Harvard Business Review*, September (2001), pp. 137–47; and P. Ghemawat, *Redefining Global Strategy*, Harvard Business School Press, 2007.

22. C.K. Prahalad and A. Hammond, 'Serving the world's poor, profitably', *Harvard Business Review*, September (2002), pp. 48–55; Economist Intelligence Unit, 'From subsistence to sustainable: a bottom-up perspective on the role of business in poverty alleviation', 24 April 2009.

23. This framework is introduced in I. MacMillan, A. van Putten and R. McGrath, 'global Gamesmanship', *Harvard Business Review*, vol. 81, no. 5 (2003), pp. 62–71.

24. For detailed discussions about the role of learning and experience in market entry see: M.F. Guillén, 'Experience, imitation, and the sequence of foreign entry: wholly owned and joint-venture manufacturing by South Korean firms and business groups in China, 1987–1995', *Journal of*

International Business Studies, vol. 83 (2003), pp. 185–98; and M.K. Erramilli, 'The experience factor in foreign market entry modes by service firms', *Journal of International Business Studies*, vol. 22, no. 3 (1991), pp. 479–501.

25. G. Knights and T. Cavusil, 'A taxonomy of born-global firms', *Management International Review*, vol. 45, no. 3 (2005), pp. 15–35.

26. For analyses of emerging-country multinationals, see T. Khanna and K. Palepu, 'Emerging giants: building world-class companies in developing countries', *Harvard Business Review* (October 2006), pp. 60–9; P. Gammeltoft, H. Barnard and A. Madhok, 'Emerging multinationals, emerging theory: macro- and micro-level perspectives', *Journal of International Management*, vol. 16, no. 1 (2010), pp. 95–101; and the special issue on 'The internationalization of Chinese and Indian firms – trends, motivations and strategy', *Industrial and Corporate Change*, vol. 18, no. 2 (2009).

27. For a detailed analysis of the unique aspects of Chinese multinationals see M.W. Peng, 'The global strategy of emerging multinationals from China', *Global Strategy Journal*, vol. 2, no. 2 (2012), pp. 97–107.

28. A useful review of the international dimension is M. Hitt and R.E. Hoskisson, 'International diversification: effects on innovation and firm performance in product-diversified firms', *Academy of Management Journal*, vol. 40, no. 4 (1997), pp. 767–98. For a meta-analytic review of previous studies of multinationality–performance relationships and what the effects depend on, see A.H. Kirca, K. Roth, G.T.M. Hult and S.T. Cavusgil, 'The role of context in the multinationality-performance relationships: a meta-analytic review', *Global Strategy Journal*, vol. 2, no. 2 (2012), pp. 108–21.

29. For detailed results on British companies, see G. Yip, A. Rugman and A. Kudina, 'International success of British companies', *Long Range Planning*, vol. 39, no. 1 (2006), pp. 241–64.

30. See N. Capar and M. Kotabe, 'The relationship between international diversification and performance in service firms', *Journal of International Business Studies*, vol. 34 (2003), pp. 345–55; and F.J. Contractor, S.K. Kundu and C. Hsu, 'A three-stage theory of international expansion: the link between multinationality and performance in the service sector', *Journal of International Business Studies*, vol. 34 (2003), pp. 5–18.

31. See S.C. Chang and C.-F. Wang, 'The effect of product diversification strategies on the relationship between international diversification and firm performance', *Journal of World Business*, vol. 42, no. 1 (2007), pp. 61–79; and C.H. Oh and F.J. Contractor, 'The role of territorial coverage and product diversification in the multinationality-performance relationship', *Global Strategy Journal*, vol. 2, no. 2 (2012), pp. 122–36.

32. See C.A. Bartlett and S. Ghoshal, 'Tap your subsidiaries for global reach', *Harvard Business Review*, November–December (1986), pp. 87–94; C.A. Bartlett and S. Ghoshal, *Managing across Borders: the Transnational Solution*, Harvard Business School Press, 1989, pp. 105–11; and A.M. Rugman and A. Verbeke, 'Extending the theory of the multinational enterprise: internalization and strategic management perspectives', *Journal of International Business Studies*, vol. 34 (2003), pp. 125–37.

33. For a discussion about the strategic role of subsidiaries see J. Birkinshaw and A.J. Morrison, 'Configurations of strategy and structure in multinational subsidiaries', *Journal of International Business Studies*, vol. 26, no. 4 (1996), pp. 729–94; and A. Rugman and A. Verbeke, 'Subsidiary-specific advantages in multinational enterprises', *Strategic Management Journal*, vol. 22, no. 3 (2001), pp. 237–50.

34. For an analysis of subsidiary and subunit initiatives in multinational corporations, see J. Birkinshaw, *Entrepreneurship and the Global Firm*, Sage, 2000.

China comes to Hollywood: Wanda's acquisition of AMC

Introduction

Chinese acquisitions of US assets and businesses have reached record levels during the last few years, reaching investments of about $35 bn (€26 bn or £21 bn) in 2011. Despite this Wanda's $2.6 bn acquisition of US second-largest cinema chain AMC sent shock wave's through the USA and especially Hollywood. It creates the world's largest cinema company by revenues and Wanda will control about 10 per cent of the global cinema market. It was the biggest Chinese acquisition of a US company ever and marked a new era as Chinese investment reached into the heart of US entertainment and culture. Although Chinese acquisitions in the USA have proven to be controversial before, this one may prove to be even more challenging and it was speculated that a Hollywood ending was far from certain. According to one analyst the deal strengthens Wanda's global status as movie theatre owner:

> 'Wanda has been the largest theatre owner in the second largest film market in the world. Now the deal makes it also the owner of the second largest theatre chain in the largest film market.'

Wanda Cinema Line Corp. is China's largest operator by cinema screens with over 730 screens. Its cinema operations generated $282 m in box office revenue in 2011 at 86 movie theatres cinemas all around China. The plan is to expand to about 2,000 screens by 2015. A month before the deal Mr Wang Jianlin, the Chairman of Wanda, had said that he would announce 'a merger that surprises the world' and when the acquisition was announced he likened the deal to 'airing a huge advertisement on the international stage'. According to Mr Wang the AMC acquisition is a significant step in turning Wanda into a multinational company within 10 years and a truly international business group that will last for a 'century'.

The deal means that Wanda takes a 100 per cent stake in AMC and bears all its debts and the company will also invest $500 m in AMC theatre refurbishments and advertising. AMC is the second-biggest cinema chain operator in North America, which is the world's biggest

Source: Ng Han Guan/Press Association Images.

Gerry Lopez, CEO of AMC Entertainment Holdings, left, shakes hands with Zhang Lin, Vice President of Wanda during a signing ceremony in Beijing, China, Monday, 21 May 2012.

film market with ticket sales of over $10 bn. AMC has more than 5,000 screens in 346 cinema theatres in this market and is the world's largest operator of IMAX and 3D screens including 120 and 2,170 screens respectively.

Although the announced acquisition was huge it is relatively small compared with the rest of the Dalian Wanda real-estate conglomerate. Dalian Wanda Group Corp. Ltd includes assets of over $35 bn, annual revenue of about $17 bn and 55,000 employees. Wanda, which means 'a thousand roads lead here', consists of five-star hotels, tourist resorts, theme parks and shopping malls. The 'Wanda Plaza' complexes that combine malls with housing and hotels have been a huge success in China and can be found in more than 60 Chinese cities.

Mr Wang Jianlin, the Founder, Chairman and President of Dalian Wanda, is the sixth-richest man in China. He joined the army as a teenager and stayed in the military for 17 years. In 1988 he founded Dalian Wanda and rode the wave of China's phenomenal growth by investing in property. His military background and ties to local officials helped him as large commercial land sales are handled by local governments. As he was willing to take on whatever property the local government was ready to give, he became popular with officials. Soon Wanda was the first property company to work in several cities.

A landmark deal

AMC was considered a 'trophy' acquisition in the American entertainment industry and it was described as a landmark deal by analysts and investors. As announced by the Chairman and President, Mr Wang:

> 'This acquisition will help make Wanda a truly global cinema owner, with theatres and technology that enhance the movie-going experience for audiences in the world's two largest movie markets.'

Mr Wang considered the deal to be a springboard to expand Wanda's global cinema presence further with the goal to reach 20 per cent of the world movie theatre market by 2020. He also said that Wanda is considering more acquisitions abroad in entertainment, hotels and retail and said it might try to buy into a global hotel brand or hotel management company as he explained that Wanda wants to be a big company 'not just in China, but in the world'.

At the announcement of the deal AMC's Gerry Lopez, Chief Executive Officer and President, explained:

> 'As the film and exhibition business continues its global expansion, the time has never been more opportune to welcome the enthusiastic support of our new owners. Wanda and AMC are both dedicated to providing our customers with a premier entertainment experience and state-of-the-art amenities and share corporate cultures focused on strategic growth and innovation. With Wanda as its partner, AMC will continue to seek out new ways to expand and invest in the movie-going experience.'

To further expand on its home market Wanda will benefit from the know-how of AMC, which operates on a market five times Chinese annual box office sales. AMC has an established worldwide network of cinema theatres and this will give Wanda a reputable brand. There is also a trend for more foreign movies in China and the transaction may allow Wanda to secure more Hollywood movies for distribution in China. In February 2012 China agreed to open up its cinemas to more American films and through the acquisition Wanda gains more clout in negotiating with major Hollywood studios that are eager to expand into the rapidly growing Chinese market. Wanda is also a contestant in the race for a licence to distribute

foreign films in China, which is now in the hands of two state-owned companies. However, it is uncertain to what degree the acquisition will please the authorities and increase Wanda's chance of winning the licence. There are also opportunities for Wanda in the USA apart from the cinemas themselves, as AMC is considered to be a platform for the development of commercial property, hotels and shopping malls in the USA.

Wanda and the Chinese entertainment industry

Wanda has a history of investing in culture and entertainment and this aligns with China's overall ambition to invest in the sector. When the deal was announced the Chairman and President of Wanda, Mr Wang, accordingly declared:

> 'Wanda has a deep commitment to investing in the entertainment business and is already the largest in this sector in China, with more than US$1.6 billion invested in cultural and entertainment activities since 2005. We share with AMC a passion for the growth of the worldwide movie industry. We look forward to partnering with AMC's management team and employees to build on the many strengths of the company.'

Wanda's press release on the transaction continued:

> 'The Wanda Group began to massively invest in cultural industries in 2005. It has entered five industries, including central cultural district, big stage show, film production and projection, entertainment chain and Chinese calligraphy and painting collection. Wanda has invested more than $1.6 billion in cultural industries and become the nation's largest enterprise investor in cultural industries.'

Wanda's acquisition is part of a more general effort to develop China's own home-grown culture and entertainment industry. Cinema is an increasingly popular recreational activity in China and the film market is booming. China has seen an increase of 30 per cent in box office sales during the last couple of years, reaching $2.1 bn in 2011, and passed Japan as the biggest market for Hollywood films outside the USA in 2012. The country is investing heavily in film, animation and is in the midst of a multiplex building boom to provide entertainment to the expanding middle class. It is adding an average of 8 movie screens a day to its current 9,200 screens. The goal is to build about 25,000 cinema screens nationwide in the next five years. By 2040, the government aims to have 40,000 screens (about the size in the USA in 2012). There are also efforts to build film production companies. In brief, cinema operation is a growing business as people are willing to spend on entertainment as their income increases.

Managing the US entry

Wanda's acquisition of AMC was the largest overseas cultural investment of a Chinese private enterprise ever and raised some concerns in the USA. AMC is a US household name, 'once epitomised as the all-American movie-watching experience'. It is thus a significant expansion of Chinese influence in the American film industry and some were anxious about this effect as many American movies are censored or even banned in China. Mr Wang is after all a Communist Party member, who sits on China's top advisory council. Wanda's acquisition of AMC thus increases concerns that Chinese-style censorship of politically controversial movies may become commonplace also in the USA. As reported by *USA Today*: 'Beijing is investing heavily in projecting its "soft power", or cultural influence, by boosting Chinese state media's presence abroad, including the USA, where the Chinese government has also run advertisements in New York's Times Square.'

Chinese investments in the USA had raised concerns earlier and the US government has rejected investments in the past in the telecommunications and energy industry due to national security concerns. However, cinema is unlikely to be considered a strategic industry for the USA. The acquisition, however, requires regulatory approval both in the USA and China.

Mr Wang also assured that Wanda has 'no plans to promote Chinese films in the United States' and that AMC CEO Lopez 'will decide what movies will be shown' in AMC theatres. It was also made clear that AMC would continue to be operated from its headquarters in Kansas City. Mr Wang said Wanda will retain AMC senior management and would not interfere with everyday operations and programming decisions, which should remain with the US management. He continued to say that the most important part of the deal was securing that more than 40 senior AMC managers would stay after the takeover and he further explained: 'The crucial thing is to keep the enthusiasm of the current management and the workers . . . You have to put the human factors first. The only thing that changed is the boss.'

Sources: *AMC* press release, 20 May 2012, Chinadaily.com, 23 May 2012, *Dalian Wanda* press release, 21 May 2012, *Financial Times*, 22 May 2012, 23 May 2012, 26 May 2012, 28 May 2012, LAtimes.com, 20 May 2012, *New York Times*, 20 May 2012, *Reuters*, 21 May 2012, *The Washington Post*, 21 May 2012, *Wall Street Journal*, 21 May 2012.

Questions

1 Considering Yip's globalisation framework (Figure 8.2), what drivers of internationalisation do you think were most important when Wanda entered the US market through its AMC acquisition?

2 What national sources of competitive advantage might Wanda draw from its Chinese base? What disadvantages derive from its Chinese base?

3 In the light of the CAGE framework, what challenges may Wanda meet as it enters the US market?

9

INNOVATION AND ENTREPRENEURSHIP

Learning outcomes

After reading this chapter you should be able to:

- Identify and respond to key *innovation dilemmas*, such as the relative emphases to place on technologies or markets, product or process innovations, open versus closed innovation, and the underlying business model.

- Anticipate and to some extent influence the *diffusion* (or spread) of innovations.

- Decide when being a *first-mover* or a *follower* is most appropriate in innovation, and how an incumbent organisation should respond to innovative challengers.

- Anticipate both key issues facing entrepreneurs as they go through the *stages of growth*, from start-up to exit, and the choices involved in *entrepreneurial strategies*.

- Evaluate opportunities and choices facing *social entrepreneurs* as they create new ventures to address social problems.

Key terms

business model p. 301

diffusion p. 305

disruptive innovation p. 310

entrepreneurial life cycle p. 312

first-mover advantage p. 308

innovation p. 296

open innovation p. 300

platform leadership p. 301

S-curve p. 306

social entrepreneurs p. 317

tipping point p. 307

MyStrategyLab

MyStrategyLab is designed to help you make the most of your studies. Visit **www.pearsoned.co.uk/mystrategylab** to discover a wide range of resources, including:

- A personalised **Study plan** that will help you understand core concepts
- **Audio and video clips** that put the spotlight on strategy in the real world
- **Online glossaries and flashcards** that provide helpful reminders when you're looking for some quick revision.

(9.1) INTRODUCTION

This chapter is about creating the new – both new products and services and new business models and organisations. Creating value for firms and customers, such innovation and entrepreneurship are fundamental to today's economy. But they also pose hard choices. For example, should a company look always to be a pioneer in new technologies, or rather be a fast follower, as Samsung typically is? How should a company react to radical innovations that threaten to destroy its existing revenues, as the Kodak film business had to with the rise of electronic cameras? How should entrepreneurs handle takeover bids from powerful rich companies: in 2012, photo-sharing site Instagram's founders persuaded Facebook to buy the company for $1 billion (£750 m; €700 m) after just two years of business. The chapter focuses particularly on the choices involved in innovation and entrepreneurship.

Entrepreneurship is a fundamental organisational process. All businesses start with an act of entrepreneurship, but large established firms also practice entrepreneurship in the form of 'corporate entrepreneurship' (section 10.2), while many people pursue 'social entrepreneurship' for the public good. Innovation is a key aspect of business-level strategy as introduced in Chapter 6, with implications for cost, price and sustained competitive advantage. As such, it too is relevant in both public and private spheres. Promoting greater innovation and entrepreneurship is crucial to the improvement of public services.

The two main themes that link innovation and entrepreneurship are *timing* and *relationships* (see Figure 9.1). Timing decisions include when to be first-mover or fast second in innovation; when, and if, an innovation will reach its tipping point, the point where demand takes off; and, for an entrepreneurial new venture, when founders should finally exit their enterprise. The other theme is relationships. Creating innovations or new organisations is very rarely done alone. Successful innovation and entrepreneurship are typically done through relationships. These relationships come in many forms: sometimes relationships between organisations and

Figure 9.1 The innovation–entrepreneurship framework

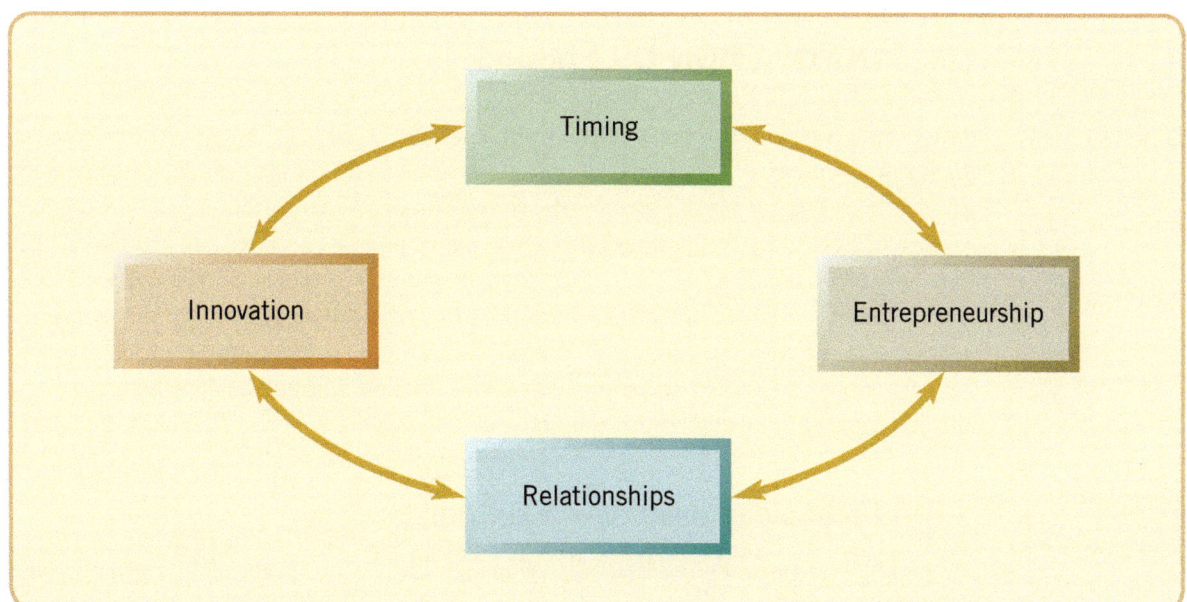

their customers; sometimes relationships between big business and small start-ups; sometimes between business and 'social entrepreneurs'.

Within Figure 9.1's broad framework, this chapter will examine first innovation, then entrepreneurship:

- Section 9.2 starts with four fundamental *innovation dilemmas*: technology push as against market pull; product innovation rather than process innovation; open versus closed innovation; and, finally, technological as opposed to broader business model innovation. None of these are absolute 'either–or' dilemmas, but managers and entrepreneurs must choose where to concentrate their limited resources.

- Section 9.3 considers issues surrounding the *diffusion*, or spread, of innovations in the marketplace. Diffusion processes often follow *S-curve patterns*, raising further typical issues for decision, particularly with regard to tipping points and tripping points.

- Section 9.4 completes the discussion of innovation by considering choices with regard to timing. This includes *first-mover* advantages and disadvantages, the advantages of being '*fast second*' into a market, and the issue of how established *incumbents* should respond to innovative challengers.

- Section 9.5 addresses *entrepreneurship*. The section discusses typical choices facing entrepreneurs as their ventures progress through the uncertain *stages of growth*, from start-up to exit. The section also considers *entrepreneurial strategies*. Finally, it examines the kinds of *relationships* that entrepreneurs may have to form, particularly with larger firms practising 'open innovation'.

- Finally Section 9.6 introduces *social entrepreneurship*, by which individuals and small groups can launch innovative and flexible new initiatives that larger public agencies are often unable to pursue. Again, social entrepreneurs face choices with regard to relationships, particularly with big business.

The Key Debate at the end of this chapter brings entrepreneurship and innovation together again by considering the issue of whether small or large firms are better at innovation.

(9.2) INNOVATION DILEMMAS

Innovation raises fundamental strategic dilemmas for strategists. Innovation is more complex than just invention. *Invention* involves the conversion of new knowledge into a new product, process or service. **Innovation** **involves the conversion of new knowledge into a new product, process or service *and* the putting of this new product, process or service into actual use.**[1] The strategic dilemmas stem from this more extended process. Strategists have to make choices with regard to four fundamental issues: how far to follow technological opportunity as against market demand; how much to invest in product innovation rather than process innovation; how far to open themselves up to innovative ideas from outside; and finally whether to focus on technological innovation rather than extending innovation to their whole business model.[2]

9.2.1 Technology push or market pull

People often see innovation as driven by technology. In the pure version of this *technology push* view, it is the new knowledge created by technologists or scientists that pushes the innovation process. Research and development laboratories produce new products, processes or services and then hand them over to the rest of the organisation to manufacture, market and distribute. According to this push perspective, managers should listen primarily to their scientists and technologists, let them follow their hunches and support them with ample resources. Generous R&D budgets are crucial to making innovation happen. For example, leading pharmaceutical company Pfizer spent $750 m on research on a drug for Alzheimer's disease, before abandoning the effort in 2012.

An alternative approach to innovation is *market pull*. Market pull reflects a view of innovation that goes beyond invention and sees the importance of actual use. In many sectors users, not producers, are common sources of important innovations. In designing their innovation strategies, therefore, organisations should listen in the first place to users rather than their own scientists and technologists. There are two prominent but contrasting approaches to market pull:

- *Lead users*: according to MIT professor Eric Von Hippel, in many markets it is lead users who are the principal source of innovation.[3] In medical surgery, top surgeons often adapt existing surgical instruments in order to carry out new types of operation. In extreme sports such as snowboarding or windsurfing, it is leading sportspeople who make the improvements necessary for greater performance. In this view, then, it is the pull of market experts that is responsible for innovation. Managers need to build close relationships with lead users such as the best surgeons or sporting champions. Marketing and sales functions identify the lead users of a field and then scientists and technologists translate their inventive ideas into commercial products, processes or services that the wider market can use. For example, the Danish toy company Lego runs a special 'Ambassador Program' to keep close to 150 specialised user groups around the world; specialist users in design and architecture were responsible for originating the Lego Jewellery and Lego Architecture ranges.

- *Frugal innovation*: at the other end of the user continuum is the pull exerted by ordinary consumers, particularly the poor in emerging markets.[4] Rather than the expensive research-intensive model of the traditional technology push approach, frugality is the guiding principle here. Frugal innovation involves sensitivity to poor people's real needs. Responding not only to these users' lack of money, but also to the tough conditions in which they live, frugal innovation typically emphasises low cost, simplicity, robustness and easy maintenance. The Tata Nano car is a famous example, a simple car produced for the Indian market for only $2,000. Muruganatham's cheap sanitary towels are another example, this time emphasising opportunities to create employment for the economically disadvantaged too (see Illustration 9.1).

The lead user and frugal innovation approaches are opposite ends of a spectrum, one elitist, the other basic. Many organisations will choose somewhere in between. But fundamentally both approaches share a key insight: innovations do not just come from scientific research, but can be pulled by users in the external market.

There are merits to both the technology push and market pull views. Relying heavily on existing users can make companies too conservative and vulnerable to disruptive technologies that uncover needs unforeseen by existing markets (see section 9.4.3). On the other hand, history is littered with examples of companies that have blindly pursued technological excellence without regard to real market needs. Technology push and market pull are best seen as extreme views, therefore helping to focus attention on a fundamental choice: relatively how much to rely on science and technology as sources of innovation, rather than what people

ILLUSTRATION

ILLUSTRATION 9.1

Frugal sanitary towels

Arunachalam Muruganantham aims to transform the lives of Indian women with a fundamental innovation.

High school drop-out and welder Arunachalam Muruganantham has developed a low-cost sanitary towel the hard way. In India, only 12 per cent of women can afford to use sanitary towels for their monthly periods, the rest making do with old rags and even husks or sand. As Muruganantham's wife explained to him, if she bought the expensive sanitary towels on the market, the family would have to do without milk. But the cost for many women is infections and even cervical cancer.

Muruganantham determined to find a cheap way of supplying Indian women with proper sanitary towels. In Indian society, however, the issue was taboo. The local hospital was unhelpful, and even Muruganantham's wife and sisters refused to talk about the problem. A survey of college girls failed. Muruganantham's prototypes were scorned by his wife. At his wits' end, Muruganantham experimented on himself, carrying a bladder inflated with goat's blood while wearing one of his own sanitary towels and women's undergarments. His tests while walking and cycling around the village created a local scandal. His wife moved out.

Muruganantham characterised the issue as a 'triple A problem – Affordability, Availability and Awareness'. But after four years of research, he finally built a machine for producing sanitary towels at less than half the price of those offered by rivals such as Procter & Gamble and Johnson & Johnson. The machines are cheap and hand-operated, enabling small-scale local production by units employing six to ten women each. Muruganantham believes that the small businesses using his machines could create up to one million jobs: 'The model of mass-production is outdated. Now it is about production by the mass of people.'

Muruganantham sells the machines to local entrepreneurs, charities and self-help groups, who produce the sanitary towels without fancy marketing. Often the women who make the towels are the best marketers, passing on the benefits by word-of-mouth. Resident women dealers are appointed for particular streets or villages, and they inform local women about the dangers of traditional methods at the same time as offering their products. Towels are often sold singly rather than in bulk packets, and are even sold through barter. Muruganantham explains the marketing: 'It's done silently and even the male members of their families don't know.'

By 2012, Muruganantham had machines operating in 23 states within India and was declaring his ambition to make India a 100 per cent sanitary towel using nation. He was also contemplating launch in Africa and spin-off projects such as nappies for babies and incontinence pads for elderly people. Muruganantham was confident about the sustainability of his model: 'We compete very comfortably with the big giants (such as Procter & Gamble). That's why they call me the corporate bomber.' His wife has moved back in with him.

Sources: BBC World Service, 6 August 2012; *Economic Times*, 18 January 2012; *The Hindu*, 9 February 2012.

Questions

1 Identify the various features of Muruganantham's approach that make his sanitary towel business a typical or not so typical 'frugal innovation'.

2 Could a large company such as Procter & Gamble imitate this strategy?

are actually doing in the marketplace. The key is to manage the balance actively. For a stagnant organisation looking for radical innovation, it might be worth redeploying effort from whichever model currently predominates: for the technology push organisation to use more market pull or for the market pull organisation to invest more in fundamental research.

9.2.2 Product or process innovation

Just as managers must manage the balance between technology and market pull, so must they determine the relative emphasis to place on product or process innovation. *Product innovation* relates to the final product (or service) to be sold, especially with regard to its features; *process innovation* relates to the way in which this product is produced and distributed, especially with regard to improvements in cost or reliability. Some firms specialise more in product innovation, others more in process innovation. For example, in computers, Apple has generally concentrated its efforts on designing attractive product features (for instance, the iPad tablet), while Dell has innovated in terms of efficient processes, for instance direct sales, modularity and build-to-order.

The relative importance of product innovation and process innovation typically changes as industries evolve over time.[5] Usually the first stages of an industry are dominated by product innovation based on new features. Thus the early history of the automobile was dominated by competition as to whether cars should be fuelled by steam, electricity or petrol, have their engines at the front or at the rear, and have three wheels or four.[6] Industries eventually coalesce around a *dominant design*, the standard configuration of basic features: after Henry Ford's 1908 Model T, cars generally became petrol-driven, with their engines at the front and four wheels. Once such a dominant design is established, innovation switches to process innovation, as competition shifts to producing the dominant design as efficiently as possible. Henry Ford's great process innovation was the moving assembly line, introduced in 1913. Finally, the cycle is liable to start again, as some significant innovation challenges the dominant design: in the case of cars recently, the emergence of electric power.[4]

Figure 9.2 provides a general model of the relationship between product and process innovation over time. The model has several strategic implications:

- *New developing industries* typically favour product innovation, as competition is still around defining the basic features of the product or service.

- *Maturing industries* typically favour process innovation, as competition shifts towards efficient production of a dominant design of product or service.

- *Small new entrants* typically have the greatest opportunity when dominant designs are either not yet established or beginning to collapse. Thus, in the early stages of the automobile industry, before Ford's Model T, there were more than a hundred mostly small competitors, each with its own combination of product features. The recent challenge to the petrol-based dominant design has provided opportunities to small companies such as the Californian start-up Tesla Motors, which had produced more than 2,000 electric-powered Roadsters by the beginning of 2012.

- *Large incumbent firms* typically have the advantage during periods of dominant design stability, when scale economies and the ability to roll out process innovations matter most. With the success of the Model T and the assembly line, by the 1930s there were just four large American automobile manufacturers, namely Ford, General Motors, Chrysler and American Motors, all producing very similar kinds of cars.

Figure 9.2 Product and process innovation

Source: Adapted from J. Abernathy and W. Utterback, 'A dynamic model of process and product innovation', *Omega*, vol. 3, no. 6 (1975), pp. 142–60.

This sequence of product to process innovation is not always a neat one. In practice, product and process innovation are often pursued in tandem.[7] For example, each new generation of microprocessor also requires simultaneous process innovation in order to manufacture the new microprocessor with increasing precision. However, the model does help managers confront the issue of where to focus, whether more on product features or more on process efficiency. It also points to whether competitive advantage is likely to be with small new entrants or large incumbent firms. Other things being equal, small start-ups should time their entry for periods of instability in dominant design and focus on product rather than process innovation.

9.2.3 **Open or closed innovation**

The traditional approach to innovation has been to rely on the organisation's own internal resources – its laboratories and marketing departments. Innovation in this approach is secretive, anxious to protect intellectual property and avoid competitors free-riding on ideas. This 'closed' model of innovation contrasts with the newer 'open model' of innovation.[8] **Open innovation involves the deliberate import and export of knowledge by an organisation in order to accelerate and enhance its innovation.** The motivating idea of open innovation is that exchanging ideas openly is likely to produce better products more quickly than the internal, closed approach. Speedier and superior products are what are needed to keep ahead of the competition, not obsessive secrecy.

Open innovation is being widely adopted. For example, technology giant IBM has established a network of 10 'collaboratories' with other companies and universities, in countries ranging from Switzerland to Saudi Arabia. Last.fm, the online music service, hosts special 'hack days', when it invites its users for a day of free food, drink and work on developing new applications together. *Crowdsourcing* is an increasingly popular form of open innovation and means that a company or organisation broadcasts a specific problem to a crowd of individuals or teams often in tournaments with prizes awarded to the best solution.[9] Companies such as Procter & Gamble, Eli Lilly and Dow Chemicals use the network company InnoCentive to set innovation 'challenges' (or problems) in open competition over the internet: by 2012, 1,215 challenges had been solved by a community of 260,000 'solvers', winning prizes of up to $1 m.

Open innovation typically requires careful support of collaborators. In particular, dominant firms may need to exercise platform leadership. **Platform leadership refers to how large firms consciously nurture independent companies through successive waves of innovation around their basic technological 'platform'.**[10] Video games console companies such as Microsoft and Sony have to manage relationships with a host of large and small video games publishers in order to ensure that their consoles are supported by an attractive set of games, making full use of the latest technological possibilities. Intel, whose microprocessors are used by a host of computer and mobile phone companies, regularly publishes 'roadmaps' outlining several years ahead the new products it expects to release, allowing customers to plan their own new product development processes (see Illustration 9.2 for Fujitsu's cloud computing roadmap).

The balance between open and closed innovation depends on three key factors:

- *Competitive rivalry.* In highly rivalrous industries, partners are liable to behave opportunistically and steal innovations. Closed innovation is better where such rivalrous behaviours can be anticipated.

- *One-shot innovation.* Opportunistic behaviour is more likely where innovation involves a major shift in technology, likely to put winners substantially ahead and losers permanently behind. Open innovation works best where innovation is more continuous, so encouraging more reciprocal behaviour over time.

- *Tight-linked innovation.* Where technologies are complex and tightly interlinked, open innovation risks introducing damagingly inconsistent elements, with knock-on effects throughout the product range. Apple, with its smoothly integrated range of products from computers to phones, has therefore tended to prefer closed innovation in order to protect the quality of the user experience.

9.2.4 Technological or business model innovation

Many successful innovations do not rely simply upon new science or technology, but involve reorganising into new combinations all the elements of a business. Here innovators are creating whole new *business models*, bringing customers, producers and suppliers together in new ways, with or without new technologies.[11] A **business model describes how an organisation manages incomes and costs through the structural arrangement of its activities.** For the ultra-cheap airline Ryanair, business model innovation involved the generation of revenues via direct sales through the internet, thereby cutting out intermediary travel agents, while also using cheap secondary airports. Internet sales and cheaper airports were much more important than technological innovation. The internet technology itself was not Ryanair's creation and it had the same aeroplanes as most of its competitors. Thus it can be as effective to innovate in terms of business model as in technology.

Opportunities for business model innovation can be analysed in terms of the value chain, value net or activity systems frameworks introduced in sections 3.4.2 and 3.4.3. These frameworks point managers and entrepreneurs to two basic areas for potential innovation:

- *The product.* A new business model may redefine what the product or service is and how it is produced. In terms of the value chain specifically, this concerns technology development,

ILLUSTRATION 9.2

The disruptive cloud

Japanese computer giant Fujitsu plots a roadmap to navigate the transition to cloud computing.

Fujitsu is the world's third-largest information technology services company, after IBM and Hewlett Packard. It offers a range of products and services in the areas of computing, telecommunications and microelectronics. In 2010, it launched a new cloud computing business to take advantage of the transition from the traditional model of in-house business computing. David Gentle, Director of Foresight at Fujitsu's Cloud and Strategic Service Offerings business, describes the transition as a disruptive innovation: 'It's a bit like a salmon that is swimming upstream and then has to make a leap to get to the next smooth stretch of water.'

Cloud computing relies on the internet to deliver computer services from external suppliers direct to users. Dropbox and Apple's iCloud are consumer cloud services. For business, the cloud comes in three main forms: 'Software as a Service' (SaaS), such as Microsoft Office via the internet; 'Infrastructure as a Service' (IaaS), such as Amazon's EC2 virtual computer capacity; and 'Platform as a Service' (PaaS), which provides a computing platform with operating system, web server and database, such as Google's App Engine.

Fujitsu describes the transition from the traditional model to the Cloud Computing Era in a technology 'roadmap' titled 'The Cloud Paradigm Shift'. The roadmap describes the traditional client–server model, where the computing power is supplied by in-house servers, as offering a trajectory of steadily improving *technology* efficiency. This culminates in the so-called Private Cloud, cloud services provided by the business itself. The shift to the 'Public Cloud' (with full adoption of SaaS, IaaS and PaaS) brings a leap in value. By tapping into the shared resources of external suppliers, a business gains access to huge economies of scale and the innovations possible by specialist suppliers. The new trajectory increases value by improving *business* efficiency.

The shift is disruptive, though. Purchasers in IT functions will no longer need such large investments in physical servers and staff. As traditional server products and related services decline, Fujitsu is transitioning its business to meet the demands of the new market. David Gentle explains the function of the roadmap in this context: 'This roadmap is the first slide in any conversation with customers, partners and staff internally. It shows the future, as well as anchoring on the past. It helps get everyone on the same page.'

procurement, inbound logistics, operations and procurement. For example, when Nucor pioneered electric-arc mini-mill technology in the steel industry, it was able to use scrap metal as its raw material rather than pure iron, employ non-unionised labour and outsource a lot of its product development to its equipment supplier Voest Alpine.

- *The selling.* A new business model may change the way in which the organisation generates its revenues, with implications for selling and distribution. In terms of the value chain, this concerns outbound logistics, marketing, sales and service. Nucor, for example, sold its cheap but low-quality steel at standard prices on the internet, in contrast to the traditional steel producers' reliance on elaborate negotiations with individual customers on prices and specifications.

The business model concept emphasises the fundamental features of how business activities are organised. In terms of business models, mature industries therefore often have a lot of standardisation. For example, most accounting firms are organised in similar ways: their business model involves earning the majority of income from audit and relying on a high ratio

Fujitsu's Cloud Roadmap

The cloud paradigm shift

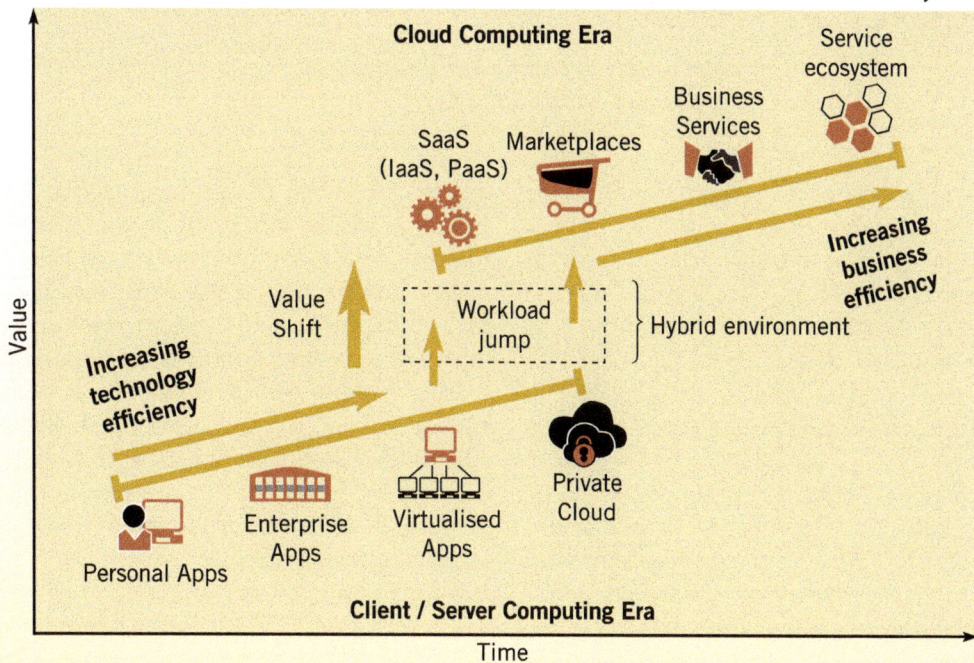

Source: *Making the Transition to Cloud*, Fujitsu Services Ltd. (Gentle, David 2011). With permission from Fujitsu Limited UK.

Questions

1 Why might some groups be apprehensive about the Cloud Computing Era?
2 What are the advantages of a visual roadmap of this kind? What are the limitations to this visual approach?

of junior staff to partners. Business strategy within an industry characterised by standardised business models is mostly about differentiation. Thus accounting firms might differentiate themselves within the same model by emphasising particular kinds of sectoral expertise or international networks.

However, the fundamental nature of business models means that business model innovation tends to imply radical change. Business model innovation is not just a matter of technology, but involves a wide range of the firm's activities. Thus the business model concept helps managers and entrepreneurs consider science and technology as just one part of the whole package that contributes to innovation. Innovation can be drawn from all parts of the value chain, not just technology development. Indeed, radical technological innovation often requires business model innovation too. For example, in order to promote adoption of its innovative electric cars in France, Toyota formed a partnership with electricity supplier EDF and local authorities to create networks of subsidised public charging points. Illustration 9.3 describes the radical repercussions of business model innovation in the movie rental business.

ILLUSTRATION 9.3

Blockbuster's busted business model

Blockbuster's store rental model is challenged by new business models for movie and game distribution.

There are a lot of ways for people to see a movie nowadays. They can go to the cinema. They can buy a DVD from specialist retailers such as HMV or large supermarkets such as Tesco or Lidl. They can order a DVD online and receive it through the post. They can download movies via the internet. They can rent via a kiosk or vending machine. Or they can do it the old-fashioned way and rent it from a video store.

Blockbuster, of course, is famous for its stores: in 2010 it had 7,000 stores in 18 countries around the world. The first Blockbuster store opened in 1985 in Texas. Soon Blockbuster was the world's largest movie rental company, and in 1994 was bought by media conglomerate Viacom for $7.6 bn (€3 bn). Ten years later, as Blockbuster's growth stalled, Viacom spun it off as an independent company again, now valued at $7.5 bn.

Blockbuster's business model had been an attractive one. Two decades ago, in a period of limited television channels, movie rental had given customers unheard-of choice of viewing. Blockbuster used its huge buying power to obtain the latest releases from the film studios at little cost. Blockbuster would give 40 per cent of the rental income to the studios and supply them with information on usage for market research purposes. Studios typically would hold back from releasing the movie to other rental companies or to retailers for an initial period, making Blockbuster the essential outlet for the latest hits. Blockbuster was able to leverage this business model into rapid growth, using a mixture of its own stores, franchising and acquisitions. It also extended the model to the rental of video games.

However, the market is now much more complex. For a start, television channels began to proliferate. In the USA, Netflix emerged in 1997, originally using a rental-by-mail model. By 2009, Netflix had mailed its two-billionth DVD. In the United Kingdom, DVD mail-rental company Lovefilm was founded in 2002,

and by 2010 had 50 per cent of the national market, as well as a strong position in Scandinavia. The mail-rental model offers customers a far greater choice (Lovefilm has 70,000 titles, against the few hundred in a typical Blockbuster store) and needs only a few centralised distribution centres, as against a labour-intensive network of retail stores. Moreover, as internet capacity has improved, both Netflix and Lovefilm have also begun to stream movies straight to customers' computers. Another rental model was pioneered by 2003 start-up Redbox, which had established a network of 22,000 DVD vending machines across the USA by the end of 2009.

Blockbuster responded in several ways. In 2004, it launched its own online rental service, with customers able to return their DVDs simply through a local store. In 2009, Blockbuster launched vending machines in the USA. The company closed more than 1,800 stores. It withdrew from some national markets altogether, for example Spain, Portugal, Ecuador and Peru. But, after continued heavy losses, Blockbuster filed for bankruptcy in 2010. The next year, the company was bought for $233 m by the satellite TV company Dish networks. Store closures continued, and the whole retail management team were dismissed.

Sources: Financial Times, 24 February 2010; The Times, 28 December 2009; The Express on Sunday, 28 February 2010.

Questions

1 Compare the pros and cons of the various business models for movie consumption.

2 What potential competitive advantages did Blockbuster have as a company as the new business models emerged in the last decade or so?

(9.3) INNOVATION DIFFUSION

So far, this chapter has been concerned with sources and types of innovation, for example technology push or market pull. This section moves to the diffusion of innovations after they have been introduced.[12] **Diffusion is the process by which innovations spread among users.** Since innovation is typically expensive, its commercial attractiveness can hinge on the pace – extent and speed – at which the market adopts new products and services. This pace of diffusion is something managers can influence from both the supply and demand sides, and which they can also model using the S-curve.

9.3.1 The pace of diffusion

The pace of diffusion can vary widely according to the nature of the products concerned. It took 38 years for the television to reach 150 million units sold; it took just 7 years for Apple's iPod to reach the same number. The pace of diffusion is influenced by a combination of supply-side and demand-side factors, over which managers have considerable control. On the *supply side*, pace is determined by product features such as:

- *Degree of improvement* in performance above current products (from a customer's perspective) that provides incentive to change. For example, 3G mobile phones did not provide sufficient performance improvement to prompt rapid switch in many markets. Managers need to make sure innovation benefits sufficiently exceed costs.

- *Compatibility* with other factors, for example digital TV becomes more attractive as the broadcasting networks change their programmes to that format. Managers and entrepreneurs therefore need to ensure appropriate complementary products and services are in place.

- *Complexity*, either in the product itself or in the marketing methods being used to commercialise the product: unduly complex pricing structures, as with many financial service products such as pensions, discourage consumer adoption. Simple pricing structures typically accelerate adoptions.

- *Experimentation* – the ability to test products before commitment to a final decision – either directly or through the availability of information about the experience of other customers. Free initial trial periods are often used to encourage diffusion.

- *Relationship management*, in other words how easy it is to get information, place orders and receive support. Google's 2010 launch of its first phone, the Android Nexus One, was hampered because the company was not used to providing the access to help staff that mobile phone customers generally expect. Managers and entrepreneurs need to put in place an appropriate relationship management process to assist new users.

On the *demand side*, simple affordability is of course key. Beyond this, there are three further factors that tend to drive the pace of diffusion:

- *Market awareness*. Many potentially successful products have failed through lack of consumer awareness – particularly when the promotional effort of the innovator has been confined to 'push' promotion to its intermediaries (e.g. distributors).

- *Network effects* refer to the way that demand growth for some products accelerates as more people adopt the product or service. Once a critical mass of users have adopted, it becomes of much greater benefit, or even necessary, for others to adopt it too. With nearly one billion users, Facebook is practically the obligatory social network for most readers of this book. Likewise, people use Microsoft PowerPoint because almost all their collaborators are likely to use it too (see also section 6.3.6).

● *Customer propensity to adopt*: the distribution of potential customers from early-adopter groups (keen to adopt first) through to laggards (typically indifferent to innovations). Innovations are often targeted initially at early-adopter groups – typically the young and the wealthy – in order to build the critical mass that will encourage more laggardly groups – the poorer and older – to join the bandwagon. Clothing fashion trends typically start with the wealthy and then are diffused to the wider population. Managers and entrepreneurs therefore need to target innovations initially at likely early-adopters.

9.3.2 The diffusion S-curve

The pace of diffusion is typically not steady. Successful innovations often diffuse according to a broad *S-curve* pattern.[13] The shape of the **S-curve reflects a process of initial slow adoption of innovation, followed by a rapid acceleration in diffusion, leading to a plateau representing the limit to demand** (Figure 9.3). The height of the S-curve shows the extent of diffusion; the shape of the S-curve shows the speed.

Diffusion rarely follows exactly this pattern, but none the less the S-curve can help managers and entrepreneurs anticipate forthcoming issues. In particular, the S-curve points to four likely decision points:

● *Timing of the 'tipping point'*. Demand for a new product or service may initially be slow but then reaches a tipping point when it explodes onto a rapid upwards path of growth.[14]

Figure 9.3 The diffusion S-curve

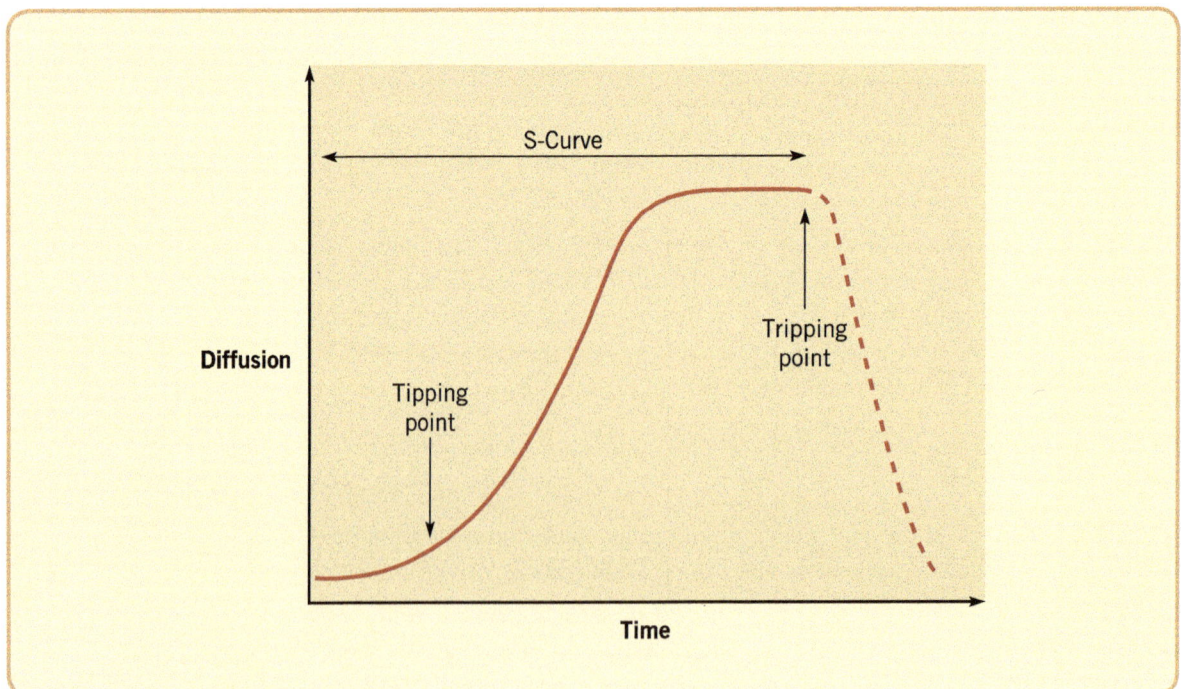

A tipping point is where demand for a product or service suddenly takes off, with explosive growth. Tipping points are particularly explosive where there are strong *network effects*: in other words, where the value of a product or service is increased the more people in a network use them. Being aware of a possible tipping point ahead can help managers plan investment in capacity and distribution. Companies can easily underestimate demand. In the mid-1980s, American companies predicted that by 2000 there would be 900,000 mobile phones worldwide. That year came, and 900,000 phones were sold every 19 hours. The Finnish company Nokia was able to seize worldwide leadership. Failing to anticipate a tipping point leads to missed sales and easy opportunities for competitors.

- *Timing of the plateau.* The S-curve also alerts managers to a likely eventual slowdown in demand growth. Again, it is tempting to extrapolate existing growth rates forwards, especially when they are highly satisfactory. But heavy investment immediately before growth turns down is likely to leave firms with over-capacity and carrying extra costs in a period of industry shake-out.

- *Extent of diffusion.* The S-curve does not necessarily lead to one hundred per cent diffusion among potential users. Most innovations fail to displace previous-generation products and services altogether. For example, in music, traditional turntables and LP discs are still preferred over CD and MP3 players by many disc jockeys and music connoisseurs. A critical issue for managers then is to estimate the final ceiling on diffusion, being careful not to assume that tipping point growth will necessarily take over the whole market.

- *Timing of the 'tripping point'.* The tripping point is the opposite of the tipping point, referring to when demand suddenly collapses.[15] Of course, decline is usually more gradual. However, the presence of network effects can lead to relatively few customer defections setting off a market landslide. Such landslides are very hard to reverse. This is what happened to social networking site MySpace, as American and European users defected to Facebook. The tripping point concept warns managers all the time that a small dip in quarterly sales could presage a rapid collapse.

To summarise, the S-curve is a useful concept to help managers and entrepreneurs avoid simply extrapolating next year's sales from last year's sales. However, the tripping point also underlines the fact that innovations do not follow an inevitable process, and their diffusion patterns can be interrupted or reversed at any point. Most innovations, of course, do not even reach a tipping point, let alone a tripping point. As marketing guru Geoffrey Moore has pointed out, there is often a deep 'chasm' to cross between specialised early-adopters of a product and the mainstream market.[16] The Segway Human Transporter, launched in 2001 as the environmentally-friendly technology that would replace the car, sold 6,000 units in its first two years, despite launch production capacity of nearly 500,000 a year.

(9.4) INNOVATORS AND FOLLOWERS

A key choice for managers is whether to lead or to follow in innovation. The S-curve concept seems to promote leadership in innovation. First-movers get the easy sales of early fast growth and can establish a dominant position. There are plenty of examples of first-movers who have built enduring positions on the basis of innovation leadership: Coca-Cola in drinks and Hoover in vacuum cleaners are powerful century-old examples. On the other hand, many first-movers fail. Even the powerful Microsoft failed with its tablet computer launched in 2001. Nine years later, Apple swept the market with its iPad tablet computer.

9.4.1 First-mover advantages and disadvantages

A **first-mover advantage** exists where an organisation is better off than its competitors as a result of being first to market with a new product, process or service. Fundamentally, the first-mover is a monopolist, theoretically able to charge customers high prices without fear of immediate undercutting by competitors. In practice, however, innovators often prefer to sacrifice profit margins for sales growth and, besides, monopoly is usually temporary. There are five potentially more robust first-mover advantages:[17]

- *Experience curve benefits* accrue to first-movers, as their rapid accumulation of experience with the innovation gives them greater expertise than late entrants still relatively unfamiliar with the new product, process or service (see section 6.3.1).

- *Scale benefits* are typically enjoyed by first-movers, as they establish earlier than competitors the volumes necessary for mass production and bulk purchasing, for example.

- *Pre-emption of scarce resources* is an opportunity for first-movers, as late-movers will not have the same access to key raw materials, skilled labour or components, and will have to pay dearly for them.

- *Reputation* can be enhanced by being first, especially since consumers have little 'mind-space' to recognise new brands once a dominant brand has been established in the market.

- *Buyer switching costs* can be exploited by first-movers, by locking in their customers with privileged or sticky relationships that later challengers can only break with difficulty. Switching costs can be increased by establishing and exploiting a *technological standard* (see section 6.3.6).

Experience curve benefits, economies of scale and the pre-emption of scarce resources all confer cost advantages on first-movers. It is possible for them to retaliate against challengers with a price war. Superior reputation and customer lock-in provide a marketing advantage, allowing first-movers to charge high prices, which can then be reinvested in order to consolidate their position against late-entry competitors.

But the experience of Microsoft with its tablet computer shows that first-mover advantages are not necessarily overwhelming. Late-movers have two principal potential advantages:[18]

- *Free-riding*. Late-movers can imitate technological and other innovation at less expense than originally incurred by the pioneers. Research suggests that the costs of imitation are only 65 per cent of the cost of innovation.

- *Learning*. Late-movers can observe what worked well and what did not work well for innovators. They may not make so many mistakes and be able to get it right first time.

9.4.2 First or second?

Given the potential advantages of late-movers, managers and entrepreneurs face a hard choice between striving to be first or coming in later. London Business School's Costas Markides and Paul Geroski argue that the most appropriate response to innovation, especially radical innovation, is often not to be a first-mover, but to be a '*fast second*'.[19] A fast second strategy involves being one of the first to imitate the original innovator. Thus fast second companies may not literally be the second company into the market, but they dominate the second generation of competitors. For example, the French Bookeen company pioneered the e-book market in the early 2000s, but was followed by Sony's eReader in 2006 and Amazon's Kindle in 2007.

There are three contextual factors to consider in choosing between innovating and imitating:

- *Capacity for profit capture*. David Teece of the University of California Berkeley emphasises the importance of innovators being able to capture for themselves the profits of their innovations.[20] This depends on the ease with which followers can imitate. The likelihood of imitation depends on two primary factors. First, imitation is likely if the innovation is in itself *easy to replicate*: for example, if there is little tacit knowledge involved or if it is embedded in a product that is sold in the external marketplace (unlike many process technologies) and is therefore easy to 'reverse-engineer' (see section 3.3). Second, imitation is facilitated if *intellectual property rights* are weak, for example where patents are hard to define or defend.[21] In 2012, Apple successfully sued Samsung for breaches of its iPhone patents, but the $1 bn fine was less than half of what Apple had originally sought from the courts and was a fraction of the Korean technology giant's $18 bn annual profits.

- *Complementary assets*. Possession of the assets or resources necessary to scale up the production and marketing of the innovation is often critical.[22] Many small European biotech start-up companies face this constraint in the pharmaceuticals industry, where marketing and distribution channels in the USA, the world's largest market, are essential complementary assets, but are dominated by the big established pharmaceutical companies. Small European start-ups can find themselves obliged either to sell out to a larger company with the complementary marketing and distribution assets, or to license their innovation to them on disadvantageous terms. For organisations wishing to remain independent and to exploit their innovations themselves, there is little point in investing heavily to be first-mover in the absence of the necessary complementary assets.

- *Fast-moving arenas*. Where markets or technologies are moving very fast, and especially where both are highly dynamic, first-movers are unlikely to establish a durable advantage. The American electronics company Magnavox was the first to launch an electronic video game console in 1972, the Odyssey. But both the market and the technologies were evolving quickly. Magnavox only survived into the second generation of video game consoles, finally exiting in 1984. The eighth generation is now firmly dominated by Microsoft (entered in 2001), Sony (entered in 1994) and Nintendo (entered in 1983). In slower-moving markets and technologies, such as Coca-Cola's drinks arena, durable first-mover advantages are more probable. Managers and entrepreneurs need, therefore, to assess future market and technological dynamism in calculating the likely value of first-mover advantage.

9.4.3 The incumbent's response

For established companies in a market, innovation is often not so much an opportunity as a threat. Kodak's dominance of the photographic film market was made nearly worthless by the sudden rise of digital photography (Illustration 5.5). Likewise, Blockbuster's network of video stores became redundant with the rise of internet film downloads (see Illustration 9.3).

As Harvard Business School's Clay Christensen has shown, the problem for incumbents can be twofold.[23] First, managers can become too attached to existing assets and skills: understandably, as these are what their careers have been built on. Second, relationships between incumbent organisations and their customers can become too close. Existing customers typically prefer incremental improvements to current technologies, and are unable to imagine completely new technologies. Incumbents are reluctant to 'cannibalise' their existing business by introducing something radically different. After all, as in Figure 9.4, incumbents usually have some scope for improving their existing technology, along the steady upwards trajectory described as Technology 1. Innovations on this trajectory are termed 'sustaining innovations', because they at least allow the existing technology to meet existing customer expectations.

The challenge for incumbents, however, is disruptive innovation. A **disruptive innovation creates substantial growth by offering a new performance trajectory that, even if initially inferior to the performance of existing technologies, has the potential to become markedly superior.** This superior performance can produce spectacular growth, either by creating new sets of customers or by undercutting the cost base of rival existing business models. Such disruptive innovation involves the shift from Technology 1 in Figure 9.4 to Technology 2. Disruptive innovations are hard for incumbents to respond to because poor performance in the early days is likely to upset existing customer relationships and because they typically involve changing their whole business model. Thus, in the music industry, the major record companies were long content to keep on selling traditional CDs through retailers, marketing

Figure 9.4 Disruptive innovation

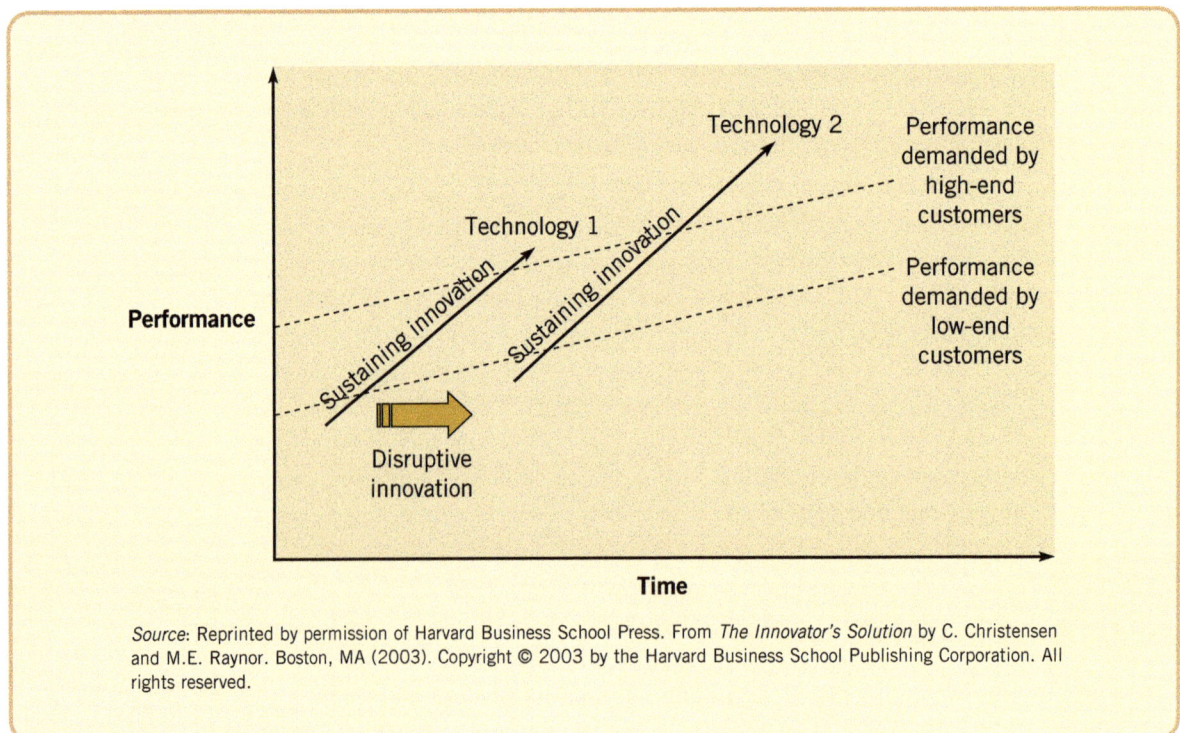

them through promotions and radio-plugging. They responded to online music simply by prosecuting operators such as Napster for breach of copyright and highlighting the relatively poor sound quality of peer-to-peer file sharing. In 2011, the number of online music downloads overtook the number of CD sales in the USA, and control of distribution had passed to services such as Apple's iTunes. Incumbents can follow two policies to help keep them responsive to potentially disruptive innovations:

● *Develop a portfolio of real options.* Companies that are most challenged by disruptive innovations tend to be those built upon a single business model and with one main product or service. Columbia's Rita McGrath and Wharton's Ian MacMillan recommend that companies build portfolios of *real options* in order to maintain organisational dynamism.[24] Real options are limited investments that keep opportunities open for the future (for a more technical discussion, see section 11.3.2). Establishing an R&D team in a speculative new technology or acquiring a small start-up in a nascent market would both be examples of real options, each giving the potential to scale up fast should the opportunity turn out to be substantial. McGrath and MacMillan's portfolio identifies three different kinds of options (Figure 9.5). Options where the market is broadly known, but the technologies are still uncertain, are *positioning options*: a company might want several of these, to ensure some position in an important market, by one technology or another. On the other hand, a company might have a strong technology, but be very uncertain about appropriate markets, in which case it would want to bet on several *scouting options* to explore which markets are actually best. Finally, a company would want some *stepping stone* options, very unlikely in

Figure 9.5 Portfolio of innovation options

themselves to work, but possibly leading to something more promising in the future. Even if they do not turn a profit, stepping stones should provide valuable learning opportunities. An important principle for options is: 'Fail fast, fail cheap, try again.'

● *Develop new venture units.* New ventures, especially when undertaken from a real options perspective, may need protection from the usual systems and disciplines of a core business. It would make no sense to hold the managers of a real option strictly accountable for sales growth and profit margin: their primary objective is preparation and learning. For this reason, large incumbent organisations often establish relatively autonomous 'new venture units', sometimes called new venture divisions, which can nurture new ideas or acquire fledgling businesses with a longer-term view.[25] For example, in 2011, BMW launched a new venture unit called Project i, based in New York and backed by $100 m, in order to acquire innovative new ideas from outside: one of its first investments has been in start-up company Parkatmyhouse, which links people seeking to rent a parking space or garage with those who have one to spare. The risks of such autonomous venture units are twofold.[26] First, the new units may be denied resources that the core business could easily supply, such as branding or management information systems. Second, innovation becomes isolated from the core business: for the core organisation, innovation is something that somebody else does.

Whether by developing real options, internal venture units or equivalent means, it is clear that established incumbents need to be able to support a spirit corporate entrepreneurship (see section 7.2).

⑨.⑤ ENTREPRENEURSHIP AND RELATIONSHIPS

Given the difficulties of large incumbent firms in fostering innovation, many would conclude that the best approach is to start up a new venture from scratch. Independent entrepreneurs such as the Samwer brothers, the creators of Rocket Internet, and Larry Page and Sergey Brin of Google are exemplars of this entrepreneurial approach to innovation (see Case examples for Chapters 3 and 12).[27] This section introduces some key issues for entrepreneurial innovators, and then points to a more complex set of relationships with large firms, raising further choices for entrepreneurs. It concludes by considering the opportunities of social entrepreneurship.

9.5.1 Stages of entrepreneurial growth

Entrepreneurial ventures are often seen as going through four stages of a life cycle: see Figure 9.6. The **entrepreneurial life cycle progresses through start-up, growth, maturity and exit.**[28] Of course, most ventures do not make it through all the stages – the estimated failure rate of new businesses in their first year is more than one fifth, with two thirds going out of business within six years.[29] However, each of these four stages raises key questions for entrepreneurs:

● *Start-up.* There are many challenges at this stage, but one key question with implications for both survival and growth are sources of capital. Loans from family and friends are common sources of funds, but these are typically limited and, given the new-business failure rate, likely to lead to embarrassment. Bank loans and credit cards can provide funding too,

Figure 9.6 Stages of entrepreneurial growth and typical challenges

and there is often government funding, especially for new technologies or economically disadvantaged social groups or geographical areas. *Venture capitalists* are specialised investors in new ventures, especially when there is some track record. Venture capitalists usually insist on a seat on the venture's board of directors and may instal their preferred managers. Venture capitalist backing has been shown to significantly increase the chances of a venture's success, but venture capitalists typically accept only about one 1 in 400 propositions put to them.[30]

- *Growth*. A key challenge for growth ventures is management. Entrepreneurs have to be ready to move from doing to managing. Typically this transition occurs as the venture grows beyond about 20 employees. Many entrepreneurs make poor managers: if they had wanted to be managers, they would probably be working in a large corporation in the first place. The choice entrepreneurs have to make is whether to rely on their own managerial skills or to bring in professional managers. In 2010, Twitter's co-founder Evan Williams handed over as chief executive to Dick Costolo, himself a former entrepreneur but also with experience as a manager in technology giant Google.

- *Maturity*. The challenge for entrepreneurs at this stage is retaining their enthusiasm and commitment and generating new growth. This is a period when entrepreneurship changes to *intrapreneurship*, the generation of new ventures from inside the organisation. An important option is usually *diversification* into new business areas, a topic dealt with in Chapter 7. Amazon.com in the USA has moved from book-selling to automotive parts, groceries and clothing. When generating new ventures at this stage, it is critical to recall the odds on success. Research suggests that many small high-tech firms fail to manage the transition to a second generation of technology, and that it is often better at this point simply to look for exit.[31]

- *Exit*. Exit refers to departure from the venture, either by the founding entrepreneurs or by the original investors, or both. At the point of exit, entrepreneurs and venture capitalists will seek to release capital as a reward for their input and risk-taking. Entrepreneurs may consider three prime routes to exit. A simple *trade sale* of the venture to another company is a common route. Thus in 2012 the founders of photo-sharing site Instagram sold their company to Facebook for $300 m cash and $700 m worth of Facebook shares just two years after starting the company. Another exit route for highly successful enterprises is an *initial public offering* (IPO), the sale of shares to the public, for instance on the American NASDAQ exchange. IPOs usually involve just a portion of the total shares available, and may thus allow entrepreneurs to continue in the business and provide funds for further growth. In 2012, Mark Zuckerberg raised $16 bn in Facebook's IPO, while retaining for himself 28 per cent ownership of the company. It is often said that good entrepreneurs plan for their exit right from start-up, and certainly venture capitalists will insist on this.

Entrepreneurs who have successfully exited a first venture often become *serial entrepreneurs*. Serial entrepreneurs are people who set up a succession of enterprises, investing the capital raised on exit from earlier ventures into new growing ventures. For example, serial entrepreneur Mark Pincus founded and sold three companies before founding the social games giant Zynga in 2007. For serial entrepreneurs, the challenge often is no longer so much funding but good ideas.

9.5.2 Entrepreneurial strategies

Entrepreneurs usually start with one main business, though over time they will often experiment with other ventures and the original business itself may evolve quite radically. Given the importance of a single main business, issues of business strategy (Chapter 6) predominate over issues of corporate strategy (Chapter 7) for most entrepreneurs, at least early on. Thus entrepreneurs will typically have to choose between the generic business strategies of differentiation, cost and focus, for example (section 6.3).

For an entrepreneurial (or small) business, however, business strategy issues are not exactly the same as for more established or larger businesses.[32] There are two characteristics of entrepreneurial businesses that can be particularly influential for strategy choice:

- *Resource scarcity*: start-up enterprises usually face very considerable resource constraints, in terms of finances and managerial capacity especially. Entrepreneurial businesses therefore need to be highly selective in their strategic moves, careful not to waste scarce resources on too many initiatives. They should be extra cautious about competing head-to-head with wealthier players, where there is a risk of wars of attrition.

- *Relative invisibility*: as new and small players, entrepreneurial businesses are typically less visible to larger, established businesses. Lower visibility means that entrepreneurial businesses face less risk of prompt incumbent retaliation for any aggressive strategic moves. Entrepreneurial businesses may therefore have more time to press forward their attack before meeting any counter-attack.

This combination of resource disadvantage and invisibility advantage influences business strategy choices differently according to the kind of market the entrepreneur is operating in:

- *New markets*: entrepreneurial firms in new markets, where products and customer segments are not yet settled, generally do best by exploring potential opportunities fast. Speed of entry is important given the difficulties of competing against larger players in the same product or segment. Even if enjoying a first-mover advantage, it can be better to abandon a market position that is beginning to attract more powerful competitors, and to explore new opportunities instead. In fast-growing markets, large businesses are typically better able to assemble the resources necessary to take advantage of increasing scale. For entrepreneurial firms, therefore, timing is vital: picking the right moments to enter and then to retreat are the crucial decisions.

- *Established markets*: in more established markets, where large firms are already present, entrepreneurial firms are more successful if they can find niches that are still not occupied. These niches are often better supplied by low-cost adaptations of existing products rather than by radical innovations, which are liable to be too risky and expensive for a small-scale enterprise. The key is generally not to attack large incumbents directly and to rely on their inattention to small-scale moves to delay any competitive imitation on their part.

The above strategies are cautious ones, dictated by resource constraints and fear of large-firm retaliation or imitation. These are not the heroic entrepreneurial strategies that capture the headlines, but the strategies that are adopted by the typical new business. For every revolutionary entrepreneur that has created new markets and beaten off well-resourced challengers, there are countless forgotten failures. In this respect, Google and Facebook are exceptions, not the rule. Given the high risks of entrepreneurship, it is important not to generalise from a handful of spectacular successes (see Illustration 9.4 for a failure example).

9.5.3 Entrepreneurial relationships

For many, entrepreneurship is about independence, working for oneself. This pride in independence is reinforced by a common stereotype of entrepreneurs as heroic individuals, starting their businesses at night in a university laboratory, or in the spare room at home or in a local lock-up garage. William Hewlett and David Packard, founders of the famous computing and printer company HP, and Steve Jobs of Apple, are oft-quoted examples of the garage stereotype. But digging beneath the stereotype soon reveals a more complex story, in which relationships with large companies can be important right from the start. Often entrepreneurs have worked for large companies beforehand, and continue to use relationships afterwards.[33] While Hewlett came fairly directly out of Stanford University's laboratories, Packard worked at General Electric and Litton Industries. The HP company used Litton Industries' foundries early on, and later used relationships at General Electric to recruit experienced managers. Steve Jobs worked for William Hewlett for a summer job aged 12, and later was the 40th employee at video games company Atari.

Thus entrepreneurship often involves managing relationships with other companies, especially big companies. Three concepts are particularly influential here:

- *Corporate venturing.* As in section 9.4.3, many large corporations have developed corporate venture units that invest externally in new ventures as safeguards against disruptive innovations and potential drivers of future growth.[34] Entrepreneurs gain by accessing not just capital but also knowledge of large-company thinking in their domain and contacts with other members of the large company's network. It is crucial that both entrepreneurs and corporate venture capitalists continuously monitor the expectations behind the investment: is the investment more profit-driven in terms of expecting good financial returns or is it more strategic, in the sense of being about technological or market development? Shifting expectations on the part of the corporate venture capitalist can lead to the disruption of longer-term plans by the entrepreneurial new venture. Companies such as Ericsson and Diageo have even closed down their venture units entirely.

ILLUSTRATION 9.4

Nearly billionaires

Adam Goldberg and Wayne Ting had the same idea as Facebook's Mark Zuckerberg – and first.

In 2003, Golderg and Ting were engineering students at the prestigious Columbia University, New York. Goldberg was president of his class and hearing lots of complains about lack of community spirit. Over the summer, he designed a social network for his fellow engineers. Unlike other existing social networks such as MySpace and Friendster, this was the first network which overlaid a virtual community on a real community. Mark Zuckerberg would try the same idea at Harvard the next year.

Three quarters of Columbia's engineering students signed up to the Columbia network over the summer. Goldberg improved the network and relaunched it as CU Community in January 2004, open to all the university's students. Most Columbia students signed up within a month. CU Community was sophisticated for its time. When Facebook launched in February 2004, it only allowed members to 'friend' and 'poke' each other. CU Community also allowed blogging, sharing and cross-profile commenting. Goldberg did not worry about Facebook: 'It was totally different. It had an emphasis on directory functionality, less emphasis on sharing. I didn't think there was much competition. We were the Columbia community, they were Harvard.'

Then in March Facebook launched in other elite American universities such as Yale, Stanford and Columbia. Goldberg, now joined by Wayne Ting, transformed CU Community into Campus Network and launched in elite American universities as well. But Facebook outpaced the new Campus Network. By summer 2004, Facebook had already overtaken Goldberg and Ting's network even at Columbia.

Goldberg and Ting now plunged into the competition full-time. They suspended their studies, and moved to Montreal, hiring three other software developers to help them. But resources were tight. Campus Network refused funds from venture capitalists and turned down some large advertisers, including MTV. The two entrepreneurs slept in the office on air mattresses, hiding them away as the three employees turned up for work so they would not know they were homeless.

None the less, Campus Network developed a sophisticated product, with fully customisable pages, multiple designs and backgrounds. Facebook was simpler. The feel of Campus Network was a bit like Dungeon and Dragons, unlike the clean aesthetics of early Facebook. Ting commented on the logic behind the early development of Campus Network: 'Why would you go to a site that only had poking and a photo [like Facebook then] when you can share photos, share music and share your thoughts on a blog?' Looking back, though, he observed: 'A good website should have functionalities that 70 or 80 per cent of users want to use. We had functions that only 10 per cent wanted – nobody blogged, nobody even blogs today.'

Campus Network reached 250,000 users by 2005, but at the same point Facebook had reached one million. Goldberg and Ting decided to wind down the network and returned to Columbia as students in the autumn of 2005. The venture had cost them personally something between $100,000 and $200,000, as well as more than a year of their lives. Ting reflected in 2012, when an MBA student at Harvard Business School: 'There are still moments when you feel a deep sense of regret . . . Could we have succeeded? I think that's a really painful question . . . There are fleeting moments like that. But I'm much prouder that we took a risk and we learnt from it.'

Sources: Slate, 29 September 2010; BBC, 21 December 2010.

Questions

1 What do you learn from the experience of Goldberg and Ting which could be useful to launching a new enterprise?

2 Are there any unmet needs in your community, at college or elsewhere, that could be turned into a business opportunity?

- *Spin-offs (or spin-outs)*. These in a sense go in the opposite direction to corporate venturing, involving the generation of small innovative units *from* larger organisations.[35] Companies such as Fairchild Semiconductor are famous for generating many successful spin-offs, including Intel, AMD and LSI Logic. Spin-off relationships can be mutually supportive, with the larger parent organisation offering the new venture seed capital and access to its marketing or technological resources. The spin-off gains the flexibility of being independent, while the parent retains a stake in any future success. Sometimes parents will seek to buy out the spin-off entrepreneurs, and reintegrate the venture into the original organisation.[36] For entrepreneurial spin-off companies, therefore, there are potential benefits to managing a constructive relationship with their original parent.

- *Ecosystems*. Following the 'open innovation' approach (section 9.2.3), high-technology companies such as Cisco, IBM and Intel often foster 'ecosystems' of smaller companies. These ecosystems are communities of connected suppliers, agents, distributors, franchisees, technology entrepreneurs and makers of complementary products.[37] Thus Apple has created an ecosystem of apps around its iPhone. The superiority of Apple's app offering gives it a competitive advantage over Nokia or BlackBerry, for example. Moreover, Apple app writers get the benefit of a large and often lucrative market. Small entrepreneurial firms wishing to participate in such ecosystems have to be skilled in managing relationships with powerful technological leaders.

9.5.4 Social entrepreneurship

Entrepreneurship is not just a matter for the private sector. The public sector has seen increasing calls for a more entrepreneurial approach to service creation and delivery. Recently too the notion of social entrepreneurship has become common. **Social entrepreneurs are individuals and groups who create independent organisations to mobilise ideas and resources to address social problems, typically earning revenues but on a not-for-profit basis.**[38] Independence and revenues generated in the market give social entrepreneurs the flexibility and dynamism to pursue social problems that pure public-sector organisations are often too bureaucratic, or too politically constrained, to tackle. Social entrepreneurs have pursued a wide range of initiatives, including small loans ('micro-credit') to peasants by the Grameen Bank in Bangladesh, employment creation by the Mondragon cooperative in the Basque region of Spain, and fair trade by Traidcraft in the United Kingdom. This wide range of initiatives raises at least three key choices for social entrepreneurs:

- *Social mission*. For social entrepreneurs, the social mission is primary. The social mission can embrace two elements: end objectives and operational processes. For example, the Grameen Bank has the end objective of reducing rural poverty, especially for women. The process is empowering poor people's own business initiatives by providing micro-credit at a scale and to people that conventional banks would ignore.

- *Organisational form*. Many social enterprises take on cooperative forms, involving their employees and other stakeholders on a democratic basis and thus building commitment and channels for ideas. This form of organisation raises the issue of which stakeholders to include, and which to exclude. Cooperatives can also be slow to take hard decisions. Social enterprises therefore sometimes take more hierarchical charity or company forms of organisation. Cafédirect, the fair-trade beverages company, even became a publicly listed company, paying its first dividend to shareholders in 2006.

ILLUSTRATION 9.5

Sociable rats in search of a model

Rats have proved they can detect landmines in Africa. The problem now is how to make the rats pay.

There are 70 countries around the world affected by landmines left behind from earlier wars. In 2008, these landmines caused 5,200 casualties worldwide. Large areas of land are too dangerous to use for agriculture. But traditional mine-detecting equipment or mine-detecting dogs are very expensive.

Belgian Bart Weetjens had an idea: use rats. Rats have a very sensitive sense of smell, well able to detect the TNT in landmines. As Weetjens told the *Boston Globe*: 'Rats are organised, sensitive, sociable and smart.' In 1998, Weetjens established APOPO as a social enterprise dedicated to developing the potential for rats in de-mining. In 2003, Weetjens began field testing African giant pouched rats in Mozambique, a country with three million landmines. The following year, APOPO's first 11 rats passed their offical test on a real minefield and were ready for action.

The rats work on a Pavlovian basis: for each detected mine, they get a banana or some peanuts. Rats are cheap to train: $4,000 (€2,800) per rat, compared to $40,000 for dogs. They are easier to house and transport than dogs, and also less susceptible to tropical diseases. Because they are lighter than dogs, they do not trip off landmines themselves. Finally, rats are more sociable than dogs: they will work with anyone who rewards them, while dogs are inflexible, only working with those to whom they have formed an attachment. A single rat can inspect 1,000 square feet in about 30 minutes, something that would take a human a whole day working with an electronic mine detector.

Initial funding for APOPO's development phase had come from the University of Antwerp and the Belgian Directorate for International Co-operation. By 2008, more than half of its funding was coming from various government grants, over a third from philanthropic foundations and corporate gifts, some 6 per cent from technical and research institutes and about 5 per cent from APOPO's own fund-raising. Principal among these fund-raising initiatives is the 'Hero Rat'

scheme. For €5 ($7) a month, supporters can adopt a rat, each with a name and picture on APOPO's website.

The problem for APOPO is securing its viability. Because grants are typically just to cover costs, APOPO has never made the kinds of profits necessary to build financial reserves. Now that the rats are a proven concept, research funding is harder to get. As yet, there is no secure business model.

In 2010, financial adviser Alvin Hall visited APOPO on behalf of the BBC. He advised Weetjens to increase the minimum donation for adopting a 'Hero Rat'. He also proposed the creation of an endowment fund, allowing large donations to give APOPO some permanent capital. Hall also encouraged APOPO to think about diversification ventures.

One promising avenue for diversification is tuberculosis (TB) detection. APOPO is running trials in Tanzania using the rats to detect TB in the saliva of sick patients. TB is responsible for 1.7 million deaths each year, mainly in poor countries. Apparently these sensitive rats can process as many saliva samples in a few minutes as a human lab technician can in a whole day. The rats have even detected TB in samples that had been missed by conventional tests. APOPO's 2010 mission statement reflects this widening role: 'to become the centre of excellence in detection rat technologies, to enhance the impact of life-saving actions'.

Sources: www.apopo.org; *Boston Globe*, 23 November 2008; www.bbc.co.uk, 5 March 2010.

Questions

1 What are the advantages and disadvantages of a social enterprise approach in this kind of domain?

2 What would be your advice to Bart Weetjens as he searches for a secure long-term business model?

KEY DEBATE

Are large firms better innovators than small firms?

The famous Austrian economist Joseph Schumpeter proposed that large firms are proportionately more innovative than small firms. This proposition is a controversial one. If true, it would discourage laboratory scientists and engineers from leaving their large-firm employers to set up their own ventures. It would encourage large firms like Google and Cisco to keep on buying up small innovative firms and absorbing them into their own corporate strategies. It would make government policy-makers more tolerant of huge, domineering firms like Microsoft who claim that their large scale is important to continued innovation in computer software.

Schumpeter's proposition for the advantages of large firms in innovation has several points in its favour:

- Large firms have greater and more diverse resources, helping them to bring together all the various necessary elements for innovation.

- Large firms may have a greater propensity for innovation risk, knowing that they can absorb the costs of innovation failure.

- Large firms have better incentives to innovate, because they are more likely to be able to capitalise on innovation, having all the required complementary assets (distribution channels and so on) to roll it out fast and under their control.

On the other hand, there are good reasons why small firms might be more innovative:

- Small firms are typically more cohesive, so that knowledge is more easily shared.

- Small firms are typically more flexible and less bureaucratic, so that they can innovate faster and more boldly.

- Small firms are more motivated to innovate simply to survive, while large firms can simply defend and exploit their dominance of existing markets.

There has been plenty of research on whether small or large firms are proportionately more innovative. Some researchers have focused on the input side, for example measuring whether large firms are more research intensive in terms of R&D expenditure as a percentage of sales. Other researchers have focused on the output side, for example counting whether large firms have proportionately greater numbers of patents for innovations. There is no final consensus on the overall patterns of innovation. However, recent research findings suggest that in general:

- Large firms are relatively less research intensive in high-technology industries, for example electronics and software.

- Large firms are relatively more innovative in service industries than in manufacturing industries.

It seems that the research so far cannot provide any firm rules about whether large or small firms are better innovators in general. However, research scientists, acquisitive large firms and government policy-makers need to consider carefully the specifics of particular industries.

Sources: C. Camisón-Zornosa, R. Lapiedra-Alcani, M. Segarra-Ciprés and M. Boronat-Navarro, 'A meta-analysis of innovation and organisational size', *Organisation Studies*, vol. 25, no. 3 (2004), pp. 331–61.

C-Y. Lee and T. Sung, 'Schumpeter's legacy: a new perspective on the relationship between firm size and R&D', *Research Policy*, vol. 34 (2005), pp. 914–31.

Question

1 What kinds of managerial action might you consider if you were trying to increase the innovativeness of a large firm in a high-technology manufacturing industry?

● *Business model*. Social enterprises typically rely to a large extent on revenues earned in the marketplace, not just government subsidy or charitable donations. Housing associations collect rents, micro-credit organisations charge interest and fair-trade organisations sell produce. Social entrepreneurs are no different to other entrepreneurs, therefore, in having to design an efficient and effective business model. This business model might involve innovative changes in the value chain. Thus fair-trade organisations have often become much more closely involved with their suppliers than commercial organisations, for example advising farmers on agriculture and providing education and infrastructure support to their communities. Illustration 9.5 shows how mine-clearing venture APOPO is struggling to find a viable business model.

Social entrepreneurs, just like other entrepreneurs, often have to forge relationships with large commercial companies. Harvard Business School's Rosabeth Moss Kanter points out that the benefits to large companies can go beyond a feel good factor and attractive publicity.[39] She shows that involvement in social enterprise can help develop new technologies and services, access new pools of potential employees, and create relationships with government and other agencies that can eventually turn into new markets. Kanter concludes that large companies should develop clear strategies with regard to social entrepreneurship, not treat it as ad hoc charity.

SUMMARY

● Strategists face four fundamental dilemmas in innovation: the relative emphasis to put on *technology push* or *market pull*; whether to focus on *product* or *process innovation*; how much to rely on '*open innovation*'; and finally how far to concentrate on technological innovation as opposed to broader *business model innovation*.

● Innovations often diffuse into the marketplace according to *an S-curve model* in which slow start-up is followed by accelerating growth (the tipping point) and finally a flattening of demand. Managers should watch out for 'tripping points'.

● Managers have a choice between being first into the marketplace and entering later. Innovators can capture *first-mover advantages*. However, '*fast second*' *strategies* are often more attractive.

● Established incumbents' businesses should beware *disruptive innovations*. Incumbents can stave off inertia by developing portfolios of real options and by organising autonomous *new venture units*.

● Entrepreneurs face characteristic dilemmas as their businesses go through the *entrepreneurial life cycle* of start-up, growth, maturity and exit. Entrepreneurial strategies are particularly influenced by *resource scarcity* and *relative invisibility*. Entrepreneurs have to choose how they relate to large firms, particularly as they may become involved in their *ecosystems* or strategies for open innovation.

● *Social entrepreneurship* offers a flexible way of addressing social problems, but raises issues about appropriate missions, organisational forms and business models.

VIDEO ASSIGNMENTS

Visit **MyStrategyLab** and watch the Alyssa Smith case study for Chapter 9.

1 Using the video extracts and section 9.5.1, what can we learn about the characteristics needed to be a successful entrepreneur and the challenges that entrepreneurs typically face as they move through the 'entrepreneurial life cycle'?

2 Using Alyssa Smith's experience as a starting point, explain why it is important for entrepreneurs to develop key relationships as part of their approach to business.

WORK ASSIGNMENTS

✱ Denotes more advanced work assignments.
* Refers to a case study in the Text and Cases edition.

9.1✱ For a new product or service that you have recently experienced and enjoyed, investigate the strategy of the company responsible. With reference to the dilemmas of section 9.2, explain whether the innovation was more technology push or market pull, product or process driven, or technological or more broadly business model based.

9.2 Go to a web traffic site (such as alexa.com) and compare over time trends in terms of 'page views' or 'reach' for older sites (such as Amazon.com) and newer sites (such as instagram.com, or any that has more recently emerged). With reference to section 9.3, how do you explain these trends and how would you project them forward?

9.3✱ With regard to a new product or service that you have recently experienced and enjoyed (as in 9.1), investigate the strategic responses of 'incumbents' to this innovation. To what extent is the innovation disruptive for them (see section 9.4.3)?

9.4 With reference to the entrepreneurial life cycle, identify the position of Rovio (chapter Case example), Feed Henry*, Hotel du Vin* or Flight Centre*. What managerial issues might this case company anticipate in the coming years?

9.5 Use the internet to identify a social entrepreneurial venture that interests you (via www.skollfoundation.org, for example), and, with regard to section 9.5.3, identify its social mission, its organisational form and its business model.

Integrative assignment

9.6 Consider a for-profit or social entrepreneurial idea that you or your friends or colleagues might have. Drawing on section 15.4.4, outline the elements of a strategic plan for this possible venture. What more information do you need to get?

RECOMMENDED KEY READINGS

- A. Osterwald and Y. Pigneur, *Business Model Generation*, Wiley, 2010, is an engaging, practical handbook relevant to both innovation and entrepreneurship.

- P. Trott, *Innovation Management and New Product Development*, 5th edn, Financial Times Prentice Hall, 2011, provides a comprehensive overview of innovation

strategy issues. P.A. Wickham, *Strategic Entrepreneurship*, 5th edn, Prentice Hall, 2013, is a standard European text with regard to entrepreneurial strategy.

- Social entrepreneurship is discussed usefully in R. Ridley-Duff and M. Bull, *Understanding Social Enterprise: Theory and Practice*, Sage, 2011.

REFERENCES

1. This definition adapts, in order to include the public sector, the definition in P. Trott, *Innovation Management and New Product Development*, 5th edn, Financial Times Prentice Hall, 2011.

2. A good discussion of the academic theories that underpin these dilemmas is in R. Rothwell, 'Successful industrial innovation: critical factors for the 1990s', *R&D Management*, vol. 22, no. 3 (1992), pp. 221–39.

3. E. von Hippel, *Democratizing Innovation*, MIT Press, 2005; Y.M. Antorini, A. Muniz and T. Askildsen, 'Collaborating with customer communities: lessons from the Lego Group', *MIT Sloan Management Review*, vol. 53, no. 3 (2012), pp. 73–9.

4. D. Nocera, 'Can we progress from solipsistic science to frugal innovation?', *Daedalus*, vol. 143, no. 3 (2012), pp. 45–52; and M. Sarkar, 'Moving forward by going in reverse: emerging trends in global innovation and knowledge strategies', *Global Strategy Journal*, vol. 1 (2011), pp. 237–42.

5. J. Abernathy and W. Utterback, 'A dynamic model of process and product innovation', *Omega*, vol. 3, no. 6 (1975), pp. l42–60.

6. P. Anderson and M.L. Tushman, 'Technological discontinuities and dominant designs: a cyclical model of technological change', *Administrative Science Quarterly*, vol. 35 (1990), pp. 604–33.

7. J. Tang, 'Competition and innovation behaviour', *Research Policy*, vol. 35 (2006), pp. 68–82.

8. H. Chesbrough and M. Appleyard, 'Open innovation and strategy', *California Management Review*, vol. 50, no. 1 (2007), pp. 57–73; O. Gasman, E. Enkel and H. Chesbrough, 'The future of open innovation', *R&D Management*, vol. 38, no. 1 (2010), pp. 1–9.

9. L.B. Jeppesen and K. Lakhani, 'Marginality and problem solving: effectiveness in broadcast search', *Organization Science*, vol. 21, no. 5 (2010), 1016–33.

10. A. Gawer and M. Cusumano, *Platform Leadership: How Intel, Microsoft and Cisco Drive Industry Innovation*, Harvard Business School Press, 2002.

11. See the special issue on business models in *Long Range Planning*, 2010, especially D.J. Teece, 'Business models, business strategy and innovation', *Long Range Planning*, vol. 43, nos 3/4 (2010), pp. 172–94; H. Chesbrough, 'Business model innovation: it's not just about technology

anymore', *Strategy & Leadership*, vol. 35, no. 6 (2007), pp. 12–17; R. Amit and C. Zott, 'Creating value through business model innovation', *MIT Sloan Management Review*, vol. 53, no. 3 (2012), pp. 41–9.

12. Innovation diffusion is discussed in the classic E. Rogers, *Diffusion of Innovations*, Free Press, 1995; C. Kim and R. Maubourgne, 'Knowing a winning idea when you see one', *Harvard Business Review*, vol. 78, no. 5 (2000), pp. 129–38; and J. Cummings and J. Doh, 'Identifying who matters: mapping key players in multiple environments', *California Management Review*, vol. 42, no. 2 (2000), pp. 83–104 (see especially pp. 91–7).

13. J. Nichols and S. Roslow, 'The S-curve: an aid to strategic marketing', *The Journal of Consumer Marketing*, vol. 3, no. 2 (1986), pp. 53–64; and F. Suarez and G. Lanzolla, 'The half-truth of first-mover advantage', *Harvard Business Review*, vol. 83, no. 4 (2005), pp. 121–7. This S-curve refers to innovation diffusion. However, the S-curve effect sometimes also refers to the diminishing performance increases available from a maturing technology: A. Sood and G. Tellis, 'Technological evolution and radical innovation', *Journal of Marketing*, vol. 69, no. 3 (2005), pp. 152–68.

14. M. Gladwell, *The Tipping Point*, Abacus, 2000. Tipping points are also important in public policy and can help anticipate emerging problems, for example crime waves and epidemics.

15. S. Brown, 'The tripping point', *Marketing Research*, vol. 17, no. 1 (2005), pp. 8–13.

16. G. Moore, *Crossing the Chasm: marketing and selling high-tech products to mainstream customers*, 2nd edn, Harper Perennial, 2002.

17. C. Markides and P. Geroski, *Fast Second: How Smart Companies Bypass Radical Innovation to Enter and Dominate New Markets*, Jossey-Bass, 2005; Lieberman, M. and D. Montgomery, 'First-mover (dis)advantages: retrospective and link with the resource-based view', *Strategic Management Journal*, vol. 19, no. 12 (1998), pp. 1111–25; and P.F. Suarez and G. Lanzolla, 'The half-truth of first-mover advantage', *Harvard Business Review*, vol. 83, no. 4 (2005), pp. 121–7.

18. F. Suarez and G. Lanzolla, 'The half-truth of first-mover advantage', *Harvard Business Review*, vol. 83, no. 4 (2005), pp. 121–7. See also S. Min, U. Manohar and

W. Robinson, 'Market pioneer and early follower survival risks: a contingency analysis of really new versus incrementally new product-markets', *Journal of Marketing*, vol. 70, no. 1 (2006), pp. 15–33.

19. C. Markides and P. Geroski, *Fast Second: How Smart Companies Bypass Radical Innovation to Enter and Dominate New Markets*, Jossey-Bass, 2005. See also the discussion of B. Buisson and P. Silberzahn, 'Blue Ocean or fast-second innovation?', *International Journal of Innovation Management*, vol. 14, no. 3 (2010), pp. 359–78.

20. David Teece, the academic authority in this area, refers to the capacity to capture profits as 'the appropriability regime': see D. Teece, *Managing Intellectual Capital*, Oxford University Press, 2000.

21. The key book on intellectual property strategy is A. Poltorak and P.J. Lerner, *Essentials of Intellectual Property: Law, Economics and Strategy*, Wiley, 2009.

22. D. Teece, *Managing Intellectual Capital*, Oxford University Press, 2000.

23. See J. Bower and C. Christensen, 'Disruptive technologies: catching the wave', *Harvard Business Review*, vol. 73, no. 1 (1995), pp. 43–53; and C. Christensen and M.E. Raynor, *The Innovator's Solution*, Harvard Business School Press, 2003.

24. R.G. McGrath and I. MacMillan, *The Entrepreneurial Mindset*, Harvard Business School Press, 2000.

25. C. Christensen and M.E. Raynor, *The Innovator's Solution*, Harvard Business School Press, 2003.

26. V. Govindarajan and C. Trimble, 'Organizational DNA for strategic innovation', *California Management Review*, vol. 43, no. 3 (2005), pp. 47–75.

27. Excellent textbooks on strategic entrepreneurship include J.A. Timmons, *New Venture Creation: Entrepreneurship in the 21st Century*, 6th edn, Irwin, 2004; and P.A. Wickham, *Strategic Entrepreneurship*, 5th edn, Pearson, 2013.

28. D. Flynn and A. Forman, 'Life cycles of new venture organizations: different factors affecting performance', *Journal of Developmental Entrepreneurship*, vol. 6, no. 1 (2001), pp. 41–58.

29. D. Flynn and A. Forman, 'Life cycles of new venture organizations: different factors affecting performance', *Journal of Developmental Entrepreneurship*, vol. 6, no. 1 (2001), pp. 41–58.

30. D. Flynn and A. Forman, 'Life cycles of new venture organizations: different factors affecting performance', *Journal of Developmental Entrepreneurship*, vol. 6, no. 1 (2001), pp. 41–58.

31. For a detailed account of Cisco's policy of taking over high-technology firms, see D. Mayer and M. Kenney, 'Economic action does not take place in a vacuum: understanding Cisco's acquisition and development strategy', *Industry and Innovation*, vol. 11, no. 4 (2004), pp. 293–325.

32. R. Katila, E. Chen and H. Piezunka, 'All the right moves: how entrepreneurial firms compete effectively', *Strategic Entrepreneurship Journal*, vol. 6, no. 2 (2012), pp. 116–132; and M. Chen and D. Hambrick, 'Speed, stealth and selective attack: how small firms differ from large firms in competitive behavior', *Academy of Management Journal*, vol. 35, no. 3 (1995), pp. 453–82.

33. P. Audia and C. Rider, 'A garage and an idea: what more does an entrepreneur need?', *California Management Review*, vol. 40, no. 1 (2005), pp. 6–28.

34. H. Chesbrough, 'Making sense of corporate venture capital', *Harvard Business Review*, vol. 80, no. 3 (2002), pp. 4–11; A. Campbell, J. Birkinshaw, A. Morrison and R. van Basten Batenburg, 'The future of corporate venturing', *MIT Sloan Management Review*, vol. 45, no. 1 (2003), pp. 33–41. See also the discussion of corporate entrepreneurship in Chapter 10.

35. S. Klepper, 'Spinoffs: a review and synthesis', *European Management Review*, vol. 6 (2009), pp. 159–71.

36. A. Parhankangas and P. Arenius, 'From a corporate venture to an independent company: a base for a taxonomy for corporate spin-off firms', *Research Policy*, vol. 32 (2003), pp. 463–81.

37. B. Iyer, C.-H. Lee and N. Venkatraman, 'Managing in a "Small World Ecosystem"', *California Management Review*, 48, 3 (2006), pp. 28–47.

38. A. Nicholls (ed.) *Social Entrepreneurship: New Paradigms of Sustainable Social Change*, Oxford University Press (2006); J. Austin, H. Stevenson and J. Wei-Skillern. 'Social and commercial entrepreneurship: same, different, or both?' *Entrepreneurship Theory and Practice*, vol. 30, no. 1 (2006), pp. 1–22.

39. R. Moss Kanter, 'From spare change to real change', *Harvard Business Review*, May–June (1999).

Rovio Entertainment: Disney of the smart phone age?

Daryl Chapman, Metropolia Business School

Richard Whittington, Saïd Business School

Introduction

Rovio Entertainment Ltd is most famous for its Angry Birds smart-phone game, in which colourful birds are catapulted at egg-stealing pigs. The company is based in Finland, and its management team consist of Mikael Hed, Chief Executive Officer, Niklas Hed, Head of Research and Development, and Peter Vesterbacka, Chief Marketing Officer and self-proclaimed 'Mighty Eagle'. Angry Birds became a top-selling app on Apple's App Store in 2010, the start of a stream of business ventures including broadcast media, merchandising, publishing, retail stores and playgrounds. With about 500 employees at the end of 2012, Peter Vesterbacka told *Wired Magazine* that Rovio could follow the world's largest entertainment company: 'We definitely look to Disney as a model.'

The team

Rovio was founded in 2003 by Niklas Hed and two classmates at Helsinki University of Technology after they won a game-development competition sponsored by Nokia and Hewlett Packard. The company initially did well in work-for-hire jobs, developing games for Electronic Arts, Nokia and Real Networks. Niklas's cousin Mikael Hed, with an MBA from Tulane University in the USA, soon joined. Mikel's father, Kaj Hed, had been a successful software entrepreneur, selling an earlier business for $150 m (£100 m, €110 m). Kaj Hed invested one million euros and became company chairman: Kaj still owns 70 per cent of the equity. Peter Vesterbacka only joined full time in 2010, as Angry Birds began to take off. However, Vesterbacka, a business developer from Hewlett Packard active in the Finnish start-up scene for many years, had been encouraging Rovio and helping from the sidelines since 2003.

Although Rovio had been successful at creating games and selling them to established third-party companies, the company's ambition was to create a major game success of its own. Niklas Hed thought it would take about 15 tries to create a world-beater, but Angry Birds turned out to be Rovio's 52nd attempt. Meanwhile, there were clashes over strategy. In 2005 Mikael Hed left the company after a row with his father, Kaj, whom he accused of being over-controlling. By 2008, Rovio had had to slash employment from 50 to just 12. But in 2009, Mikael came back, making peace with his father and sensing an opportunity with the new Apple iPhone and its App Store. The combination of the striking Angry Bird characters with the success of the Apple iPhone finally created a winning formula.

Rovio used Chillingo, a well-connected British games publisher, to negotiate a deal with Apple and push Angry Birds into world markets. In February 2010, Chillingo persuaded Apple to feature Angry Birds as the game of the week on the Apple App Store's front page: Angry Birds shot to No. 1 in the United Kingdom; five months later, it was top of the US charts as well. Chillingo was bought by Electronic Arts during 2010, and Rovio declared that it would no longer use any publishing intermediaries. In October, 2010, Rovio launched the free Android Angry Birds, winning two million downloads in three days. By 2011, Angry Birds and its various branded spin-offs had earned €50 m, on the back of a game which originally cost only €100,000 to develop. In March 2011 Mikael Hed was cautiously excited, telling *Wired Magazine*: 'I know how fragile the gaming industry is; I'm super-paranoid. But I feel at the moment that we are walking. We should be running.'

The New Disney?

Like Disney with Mickey Mouse, Rovio saw the potential of transferring its powerful brand to other products. Partnering with the American toy manufacturer Commonwealth Toy & Novelty, Rovio was able to place Angry Birds soft toys and T-shirts in US shops as early as 2010. Rovio soon had more than 400 partners, including Coca-Cola, Intel and Kraft. The number of Angry Bird products reached 20,000, including board games, fridge magnets and key chains. *Fast Company* magazine estimated in 2012 that total sales of Angry

Birds merchandise might approach $650 million or so. Rovio receives royalties on sales of its licensed products ranging from 5 to 20 per cent.

Rovio also partnered with Samsung to include a motion-controlled Angry Birds game on its smart televisions. Samsung was aiming to sell 25 million of these TVs in 2012. In November 2012, the company launched the Rovio Channel, letting users of the Samsung TV sets download games as well as the new Angry Birds Toons show and a comic-book series. The Rovio channel builds on the success of the Angry Birds YouTube channel, which has attracted more than 750 million views. The Rovio Channel is also due to launch on Mac, PC, iOS and Android devices, but Rovio prioritised TV as a medium that millions of families use together every day. An Angry Birds 3D movie is planned for release in 2016.

Meanwhile, Rovio has launched its first Angry Birds playground in Finland, in partnership with the Finnish adventure playground designer Lappset, the American entertainment designer BDR Design and the Italian roller coaster manufacturer, Antonia Zamperla. In one sense, the playgrounds strategy mimics Disney's theme parks, but the playgrounds are much smaller. Rovio wants to create a more 'distributed' means of physical interaction with families and children than the occasional visit to Disneyland: the Angry Birds playgrounds are local and can be visited every day. The plan is to roll these playgrounds out internationally, with its first opening in the United Kingdom in the summer of 2012. There are already unlicensed Angry Birds playgrounds in China.

Indeed, export markets have always been important to Rovio, coming from a small northern European country as it does. The company has offices in Shanghai, Stockholm, Tokyo, Seoul, South Korea and Santa Monica, California. The USA is Rovio's largest market, followed closely by China. Rovio launched in China in 2011 and opened three retail stores in Beijing and Shanghai during 2012, with 200 more planned within the next year. Official licensed playgrounds are opening in China too. Peter Vesterbacka told *Fast Company*: 'Over time, China will be our biggest market. It's important for us to be very local. We want to be more Chinese than the Chinese companies.'

Rovio has not neglected its original core gaming business. With 63 levels when first released, Angry Birds now has more than 360. All sorts of variations have been launched, including Angry Birds Star Wars developed in conjunction with Lucasfilm. During 2012, Rovio repeated its success with the launch of Bad Piggies, featuring pigs stranded on a desert island looking for

Table 1 **Top paid iPhone apps, February 2013 (with developer names, countries and foundation dates)**

1. Clear Vision 2 (FDG Entertainment, Germany, 2002)
2. WhatsApp Messenger (Whats App Inc., United States, 2009)
3. Minecraft – Pocket Edition (Mojang AB, Sweden, 2009)
4. Angry Birds Star Wars (Rovio, Finland, 2003)
5. Wood Camera (Bright Mango, United States, 2012)
6. Sleep Cycle alarm clock (Maciek Drejak Labs, Sweden, 2008)
7. Plague Inc (Ndemic Creations, United Kingdom, 2012)
8. Arms Cartel Global (Pixel Addicts, United States, 2001)
9. Fruit Ninja (Halfbrick Studios, Australia, 2001)
10. Bloons TD 5 (Ninja Kiwi, New Zealand, 2007)

Source: AppData, 2013, plus internet search.

eggs: it too reached Number 1 on Apple's App Store. Amazing Alex was also launched in 2012 to create a human character for Rovio, but proved relatively less successful.

A mix of success and failure is to be expected in games. The app market is extremely dynamic, with new games and apps emerging all the time (see Table 1 for top paid apps in early 2013). Disney Mobile had five games at Number 1 on the Apple App Store during 2012. On the other hand, the one-man British developer Ndemic could score a hit with its star Plague Inc. game, at a development cost of just $5,000. Peter Parmentier, Chief Executive of Electronic Arts Mobile (responsible for Tetris, the Sims and Fifa), told the *Guardian* newspaper: 'The marketplace in mobile is arguably the most competitive in the industry. There are more and more apps launching every day, which creates a challenging environment for developers and consumers alike. While I think we will always see that one breakaway hit that takes on a life of its own, we find that consumers seek high quality entertainment and recognisable brands in such a crowded environment.'

Growth plans

Rovio's growth requires investment. In early 2011, the company raised $42 m from three venture capital funds, ceding 21 per cent of the ownership in return (Niklas Hed, Mikael Hed and Peter Vesterbacka between them were left with 8 per cent). One of the venture capitalists was Niklas Zennström, co-founder of Skype, who also joined Rovio's board. The extra capital helped Rovio make two strategic and talent acquisitions that year: first Kombo Animation Studio, then Futuremark Games Studio. During 2012, Rovio had talked of an initial public offering for 2013 with the aim of raising

Table 2 **Selected leading games companies**

	Key businesses	2011 revenues	2011 employees
Activision (US/French)	Computer, social and mobile games	$4.76 bn	7,738
Disney (US)	Film, TV, parks, merchandising, online media, etc.	$42.28 bn	166,000
Electronic Arts (US)	Computer, social and mobile games	$4.44 bn	9,925
Zynga (US)	Social and gambling games (internet and mobile)	$1.14 bn	2,846

$1 bn for further investment. However, in early 2013, Peter Vesterbacka appeared to crush all such talk of an IPO: 'For us right now, we are running a very successful operation, we are growing very, very fast and we are insanely profitable so we can fund our own growth.'

Rovio's growth is building on a new business model for games. The original games model had involved purchasing a disc in a box for €20 or so. Rovio distributes its games over the internet either for about €1 to €4 each via Apple's App Store or, supported by advertising, for free on Android. Where Rovio differs from most other new mobile app companies is its emphasis on brand licensing for other physical products, such as soft toys, drinks and similar items. Revenues from the App Store, advertising and licensed physical products are very roughly equal, but physical products are pulling ahead. Total revenues are estimated at about €150 m for 2012. At the centre of the business are Rovio's brands, especially the Angry Birds themselves. The company believes that the brands will be valuable so long as fans are kept happy with a continuous stream of engaging new games and free upgrades. Rovio concentrates its efforts on game development and brand management: production of physical products is licensed out to partner companies. Although the early physical retail stores are being run by Rovio itself, the virtual store and logistics support are operated by partners that specialise in e-commerce and shipping.

Growth on the back of strong brands is, of course, something that Disney has long been good at (see Table 2 for a comparison with Disney and some competitors). Rovio sees itself as more than a games company, just as Disney saw itself as more than a cartoons company. The target is for more than half its revenues to come from physical products. Mikael Hed explained his ambitions for Rovio to *Fast Company* by drawing two arcs: the first, a narrow curve with a pronounced fall-off from its peak; the second, a much broader curve triple the height of the first. 'A lot of our competitors have an equally myopic view. They've found this hill,' he said, drawing an arrow to the crest of the first arc, 'and say, here's the maximum amount of money you can make with a mobile game. But what we're building' – pointing to the other arc – 'is about the lifetime value of a fan. That picture is much more interesting.'

During 2012, Rovio turned down a $2 bn acquisition offer from Zynga, the US games company famous for Farmville. The Angry Birds company seems determined to aim its catapult directly at US entertainments giant Disney.

Key sources: *Wired Magazine*, 7 March 2011; *Guardian*, Media Network, 15 November 2012; *Fast Company*, 26 November 2012; *The Next Web*, 21 December 2012.

Questions

1 What are the advantages and disadvantages of Rovio's business model?

2 What strategy might Zynga have pursued with Rovio if it had succeeded in its acquisition?

10

MERGERS, ACQUISITIONS AND ALLIANCES

Learning outcomes

After reading this chapter you should be able to:

- Identity key strategic motives for *mergers and acquisitions* and *strategic alliances.*

- Identity key issues in the successful management of *mergers and acquisitions* and *strategic alliances.*

- Identity the appropriate choices between *organic* development, *mergers and acquisitions* and *strategic alliances.*

- Identity *key success factors* of different growth options.

Key terms

acquisition p. 331

collaborative advantage p. 342

collective strategy p. 341

corporate entrepreneurship p. 331

merger p. 331

organic development p. 330

strategic alliance p. 341

(10.1) INTRODUCTION

Mergers, acquisitions and alliances are all common methods for achieving growth strategies and often in the news. For example, in 2012 the largest express carrier and parcel distribution company in the world, UPS, acquired Dutch rival TNT Express for $6.77 bn (€5.2 bn) in a friendly all-cash deal. This acquisition furthered UPS's ambitions to improve its competitive position in European markets and created a global leader in the logistics industry with more than $60 bn (€45 bn) of revenues. In the same year, Tingyi Corporation of Tianjin, China, and PepsiCo Inc., announced the creation of a strategic beverage alliance to manufacture, sell and distribute PepsiCo's carbonated soft drinks in China, which may become the world's largest beverage market.

This chapter therefore addresses mergers, acquisitions and alliances as key methods for pursuing strategic options. It will consider them alongside the principal alternative of 'organic' development, in other words the pursuit of a strategy relying on a company's own resources. Figure 10.1 shows how the main strategic options considered in the previous three chapters – diversification, internationalisation and innovation – can all be achieved through mergers and acquisitions, alliances and organic development. Of course, these three methods can also be used for many other strategies as well, for example consolidating markets or building scale advantages.

The chapter starts with organic development. Organic development is the default option: relying on the organisation's internal resources is the natural first option to consider. The chapter then introduces the two principal external options: first mergers and acquisitions (often abbreviated as M&A) and then strategic alliances. The final section compares the two external options against the internal option of organic development. Given the frequent failures of acquisitions and alliances, the fundamental issue is when to acquire, when to ally or when is it better to 'do it yourself'? The final section also considers key success factors in M&A and alliances. The problematic success record of acquisitions in particular is the subject of the Key Debate at the end of this chapter.

Figure 10.1 Three strategy methods

(10.2) ORGANIC DEVELOPMENT

The default method for pursuing a strategy is to 'do it yourself', relying on internal capabilities. Thus **organic development is where a strategy is pursued by building on and developing an organisation's own capabilities.** For example, Amazon's entry into the e-books market with its Kindle product was principally organic, relying on its own subsidiary Lab126 and drawing on its expertise in book retailing, internet retail and software. For Amazon, this do-it-yourself (DIY) diversification method was preferable to allying with an existing e-book producer such as Sony or buying a relevant hi-tech start-up such as the French pioneer Bookeen as it could work within its own ecosystem for greater synergy gain (see section 7.3).

There are five principal advantages to relying on organic development:

- *Knowledge and learning.* Using the organisation's existing capabilities to pursue a new strategy can enhance organisational knowledge and learning. Direct involvement in a new market or technology is likely to promote the acquisition and internalisation of deeper knowledge than a hands-off strategic alliance, for example.

- *Spreading investment over time.* Acquisitions typically require an immediate upfront payment for the target company. Organic development allows the spreading of investment over the whole time span of the strategy's development. This reduction of upfront commitment may make it easier to reverse or adjust a strategy if conditions change.

- *No availability constraints.* Organic development has the advantage of not being dependent on the availability of suitable acquisition targets or potential alliance partners. There are few acquisition opportunities for foreign companies wanting to enter the Japanese market, for example. Organic developers also do not have to wait until the perfectly matched acquisition target comes onto the market.

- *Strategic independence.* The independence provided by organic development means that an organisation does not need to make the same compromises as might be necessary if it made an alliance with a partner organisation. For example, partnership with a foreign collaborator is likely to involve constraints on marketing activity in external markets and may limit future strategic choices.

- *Culture management.* Organic development allows new activities to be created in the existing cultural environment, which reduces the risk of culture clash.

The reliance of organic development on internal capabilities can be slow, expensive and risky. It is not easy to use existing capabilities as the platform for major leaps in terms of innovation, diversification or internationalisation, for example. However, organic development can be very successful and, as in the example of Amazon's Kindle, be sufficiently radical to merit the term 'corporate entrepreneurship'. **Corporate entrepreneurship refers to radical change in the organisation's business, driven principally by the organisation's own capabilities.**[1] Bringing together the words 'entrepreneurship' and 'corporate' underlines the potential for significant change or novelty not only by external entrepreneurship (see also corporate venture units in section 9.5.2), but also by reliance on internal capabilities from within the corporate organisation. Thus for Amazon, the Kindle was a radical entrepreneurial step, taking it from retailing into the design of innovative consumer electronic products.

The concept of corporate entrepreneurship is valuable because it encourages an entrepreneurial attitude inside the firm. There are many examples of corporate entrepreneurship, such as the creation of low-cost airline Ryanair from inside the aircraft leasing company Guinness Peat. Often, however, organisations have to go beyond their own internal capabilities and look externally for methods to pursue their strategies. The main themes of this chapter, therefore, are first mergers and acquisitions and second strategic alliances.

(10.3) MERGERS AND ACQUISITIONS

Mergers and acquisitions (M&A) frequently grab the headlines, as they involve large sums of money and very public competitions for shareholder support. They can also provide a speedy means of achieving major strategic objectives. However, they can also lead to spectacular failures too. A famous case is that of the Royal Bank of Scotland, whose 2007 takeover of the Dutch ABN AMRO, for $98.5 bn (€71 bn), ended in commercial disaster and the bank's nationalisation by the British government.

10.3.1 Types of mergers and acquisitions

Mergers and acquisitions are typically about the combination of two or more organisations. In an acquisition (or takeover) this generally means an acquirer *taking control* of another company through share purchase. Thus 'acquisition' **is achieved by purchasing a majority of shares in a target company**. Most acquisitions are *friendly*, where the target's management recommend accepting the acquirer's deal to its shareholders. This is good for acquirers as the target management are more likely to work with them to complete the deal and remain to integrate both companies. Sometimes acquisitions are *hostile*, where target management refuse the acquirer's offer. The acquirer therefore appeals directly to the target's shareholders for ownership of their shares. These deals can be very acrimonious with target company management obstructing efforts to obtain key information and not helping integrate the two organisations post-deal. Acquirers are generally larger than target companies although occasionally there may be 'reverse' takeovers, where acquirers are smaller than targets.

A merger is different in character to an acquisition as it is **the combination of two previously separate organisations in order to form a new company**. For example, in 2012 Random House and Penguin, two big publishers, announced a merger to form Penguin Random House to reduce costs and increase their negotiating power with distributors such as Amazon. Merger partners are often of similar size, with expectations of broadly equal status, unlike an acquisition where the acquirer generally dominates. In practice, the terms 'merger' and 'acquisition' are often used interchangeably, hence the common shorthand M&A.

Mergers and acquisitions can also happen in the public and non-profit sectors: for example, the Finnish government created the new Aalto University in 2010 by merging the Helsinki School of Economics, the Helsinki University of Art and Design and the Helsinki University of Technology. Publicly owned institutions frequently build up highly distinctive cultures or systems of their own, as if they were in fact independent organisations. Where there are major cultural or systems differences between organisations, the scale and depth of the managerial issues approximate to those that would be involved in a change of ownership. 'Merger' is therefore often used in such cases because that better reflects the scale of the task involved than simply 'reorganisation'.

10.3.2 **Timing of mergers and acquisitions**

Since records began in the late nineteenth century, mergers and acquisitions have shown a cyclical quality, involving high peaks and deep troughs. Thus 2007 was a record year for global mergers and acquisitions, with transactions taking place worth around $4.14 trn (€2.9 trn), four times the amount of the previous trough in 2002. As the worldwide recession took hold, the value of global M&A in 2011 fell to $2.56 trn (€1.8 trn).[2] These cycles are broadly linked to changes in the global economy but are also influenced by new regulations, the availability of finance, stock market performance, technological disturbances and the supply of available target firms. They may also be driven by over-optimism on the part of managers, shareholders and bankers during upturns, and by exaggerated loss of confidence during downturns. This cyclical pattern suggests that there are better times than others for making an acquisition. At the top of a cycle, target companies are likely to be very highly priced, which may reduce the chances of success for an acquirer. The £5 bn merger between house builders Taylor Woodrow and George Wimpey in 2007 saw the value of the share price crash by nearly 90 per cent in the following year when the recession started. These cycles should warn managers that M&A may have a strong fashion or bandwagon element. Especially in an upturn, managers should ask very carefully whether acquisitions are really justified as prices may be high.

Global activity in mergers has traditionally been dominated by North America and Western Europe, whereas it has been much less common in other economies, for example Japan. Many national governance systems put barriers in the way of acquisitions, especially hostile acquisitions (see section 4.3.2). However, companies from fast-developing economies such as China and India have become very active in large-scale acquisitions in order to access Western markets or technology, or to secure material resources needed for growth. For example, Sinopec's (China Petrochemical Corp) acquisition, in 2012, of US oil and natural gas producer Devon Energy Corp for €1.69 bn (£1.46 bn; $2.2 bn), was the Chinese group's 11th deal in a year. The Indian company Tata has also made many acquisitions including buying UK companies Tetley Tea, British Salt, the car companies Jaguar and Land Rover and the Anglo-Dutch steel company Corus (see Illustration 10.2 later).

10.3.3 **Motives for mergers and acquisitions**

Motives for M&A can be strategic, financial and managerial[3] (see Illustration 10.1).

Strategic motives for M&A

Strategic motives for M&A involve improving the competitive advantage of the organisation. These motives are often related to the reasons for diversification in general (see section 7.3). Strategic motives can be categorised in three main ways:[4]

- *Extension*. M&A can be used to extend the reach of a firm in terms of geography, products or markets. Acquisitions can be speedy ways of extending international reach. Thus in 2010 the Chinese Geely car company bought the Swedish Volvo car company in order to build its global presence. Acquisitions can also be an effective way of extending into new markets, as in diversification (see Chapter 7).

- *Consolidation*. M&A can be used to consolidate the competitors in an industry. Bringing together two competitors can have at least three beneficial effects. In the first place, it

ILLUSTRATION 10.1

Who bought whom?

Movie giant Disney's acquisition of Marvel proves analysts wrong, but problems may lie ahead.

Summer means one thing in Hollywood: big, blockbuster movies. But in 2012 a single superhero film 'ka-powed' all others with $1.5 bn (€1.12 bn, £0.9 bn) global ticket sales, becoming the third-highest grossing title of all time. *The Avengers*, from Disney's Marvel unit, stormed the box office, bringing *Iron Man*, *The Incredible Hulk* and *Thor* together. Its success largely overturned analysts' criticisms of Disney's 2009 $4 bn purchase of Marvel, as overpayment.

On paper, the acquisition looked a perfect fit. Disney was rethinking its entire approach to film making in response to a contracting home entertainment market and falling DVD sales as every studio in Hollywood was under pressure to cut costs. Ready to move to a franchise-led strategy, producing films and brands that could generate sequels and spin-offs, Disney acquired Pixar in 2006, and then Marvel, a brand that could deliver movies with stories that appealed to teenage boys – a demographic Disney found elusive.

The acquisition was not only about movies. Disney planned to use Marvel's vast library of superhero characters throughout its business from theme parks to television shows and consumer products, adding Incredible Hulk underpants and Iron Man lunch boxes to Disney's staple inventory of Mickey Mouse merchandise. In addition the deal retained Marvel's CEO, Isaac 'Ike' Perlmutter. His hard-driving approach to gain a 'big bang for each buck' appealed to Disney; 'Marvel could make a great looking movie for a fraction of the price of a Jerry Bruckheimer (*Pirates of the Caribbean* producer) movie.'

However, the deal also added dramatic tension to the family-oriented company based in Burbank, California – largely, it appears, because of Ike's management style. As Marvel's largest shareholder before Disney, he took much of his $1.5 bn payment in Disney shares, giving him a seat at the decision-making table. Since then he has become a force within Disney. He is a skilled cost-cutter and has been described as obsessive about saving money. 'He used to do this thing in our office that people would laugh at. If there was some used paper lying around he would rip it into eight pieces and would have a new memo pad.'

But Ike's strong opinions and cost-cutting capabilities often put him at odds with colleagues. His interest in merchandising and toy licensing has shaken things up throughout Disney's Consumer Products Division (DCP) – one of Disney's smaller divisions but accounting for 10 per cent of all group profits (2011). The head of DCP had repeated conflicts with Ike over the direction of the division and left in 2012 along with the heads of communications, publishing, HR, Disney stores, and the toys business. Three female executives hired a lawyer to seek individual financial settlements and another filed an internal complaint alleging Ike threatened her. DCP has now been re-organised around Disney's big TV and film franchises rather than individual product categories.

The box office and commercial successes Marvel has produced for Disney have won Ike admirers inside and outside the group. With sequels to *Thor*, *Captain America* and *The Avengers* in the works, analysts are speaking about the upside of the deal. But some former Disney employees warn of culture collisions ahead. 'You would think that Disney, with all its heritage and culture, would prevail, but the common question in the hallways [at DCP] was: remind me who bought who here?'

Sources: *Financial Times*, 1 and 4 September 2009, 7 September 2011, 13 July and 8 August 2012.

Questions

1 Why did Disney acquire Marvel?
2 Critically assess how well these companies fit together in (i) strategic and (ii) organisational terms.

increases market power by reducing competition: this might enable the newly consolidated company to raise prices for customers. Second, the combination of two competitors can increase efficiency through reducing surplus capacity or sharing resources, for instance head office facilities or distribution channels. Finally, the greater scale of the combined operations may increase production efficiency or increase bargaining power with suppliers, forcing them to reduce their prices.

- *Capabilities*. The third broad strategic motive for M&A is to increase a company's capabilities. High-tech companies such as Cisco and Microsoft regard acquisitions of entrepreneurial technology companies as a part of their R&D effort. Instead of researching a new technology from scratch, they allow entrepreneurial start-ups to prove the idea, and then take over these companies in order to incorporate the technological capability within their own portfolio (see section 9.5.2). Capabilities-driven acquisitions are often useful where industries are converging (see section 2.3.1). For example, Google and Apple have made substantial acquisitions in order to gain a foothold in the new high-growth mobile advertising market. Google's €576 m (£500 m; $750 m) acquisition of AdMob and Apple's €212 m (£183 m; $275 m) acquisition of Quattro Wireless in 2010, aimed at achieving a notable presence in the new competitive space where there is convergence between telephony and advertising industries.

Financial motives for M&A

Financial motives concern the optimal use of financial resources, rather than directly improving the actual business. There are three main financial motives:

- *Financial efficiency*. It may be efficient to bring together a company with a strong balance sheet (i.e. it has plenty of cash) with another company that has a weak balance sheet (i.e. it has high debt). The company with a weak balance sheet can save on interest payments by using the stronger company's assets to pay off its debt, and it can also get investment funds from the stronger company that it could not have accessed otherwise. The company with the strong balance sheet may be able to drive a good bargain in acquiring the weaker company. Also, a company with a booming share price can purchase other companies very efficiently by offering to pay the target company's shareholders with its own shares (equity), rather than paying with cash upfront.

- *Tax efficiency*. Sometimes there may be tax advantages from bringing together different companies. For example, profits or tax losses may be transferrable within the organisation in order to benefit from different tax regimes between industries or countries. Naturally, there are legal restrictions on this strategy.

- *Asset stripping or unbundling*. Some companies are effective at spotting other companies whose underlying assets are worth more than the price of the company as a whole. This makes it possible to buy such companies and then rapidly sell off ('unbundle') different business units to various buyers for a total price substantially in excess of what was originally paid for the whole. Although this is often dismissed as merely opportunistic profiteering ('asset stripping'), if the business units find better corporate parents through this unbundling process, there can be a real gain in economic effectiveness.

Managerial motives for M&A

As for diversification (see section 7.3), acquisitions may sometimes serve managers' interests rather than shareholders' interests. 'Managerial' motives are so called, therefore, because they are self-serving rather than efficiency-driven. M&A may serve managerial self-interest for two types of reason:

- *Personal ambition.* There are three ways that acquisitions can satisfy the personal ambition of senior managers, regardless of the real value being created. First, senior managers' personal financial incentives may be tied to short-term growth targets or share price targets that are more easily achieved by large and spectacular acquisitions than the more gradualist and lower-profile alternative of organic growth. Second, large acquisitions attract media attention, with opportunities to boost personal reputations through flattering media interviews and appearances. Here there is the so-called 'managerial hubris' (vanity) effect: managers who have been successful in earlier acquisitions become over-confident and embark on more and more acquisitions, each riskier and more expensive than the one before.[5] Finally, acquisitions provide opportunities to give friends and colleagues greater responsibility, helping to cement personal loyalty by developing individuals' careers.

- *Bandwagon effects.* As noted earlier, acquisitions are highly cyclical. In an upswing, there are three kinds of pressure on senior managers to join the acquisition bandwagon. First, when many other firms are making acquisitions, financial analysts and the business media may criticise more cautious managers for undue conservatism. Second, shareholders will fear that their company is being left behind, as they see opportunities for their business being snatched by rivals. Lastly, managers will worry that if their company is not acquiring, it will become the target of a hostile bid itself. For managers wanting a quiet life during a 'merger boom', the easiest strategy may be simply to join in. But the danger is making an acquisition the company does not really need and it can be one reason for paying too much.

In sum, there are bad reasons as well as good reasons for acquisitions and mergers. The average performance of acquisitions is unimpressive, with evidence suggesting that half of acquisitions fail (see Key Debate at the end of the chapter). However, alternative growth methods also exhibit similar levels of performance. Nevertheless it is worth asking sceptical questions of any M&A strategy. The converse can be true of course: there can be bad reasons for resisting a hostile takeover. Senior managers may resist being acquired because they fear losing their jobs, even if the price offered represents a good deal for their shareholders.

10.3.4 M&A processes

Acquisitions take time. First there is the search to identify an acquisition target with the best possible fit. This process may take years but under some circumstances can be completed very rapidly indeed. Then there is the process of negotiating the deal: to agree on terms and conditions and the right price. Finally managers will need to decide on the extent to which the new and old businesses will need to be integrated – and this will have significant implications for the amount of time required to create value. In other words, acquisition should be seen as a process over time. Each step in this process imposes different tasks on managers (see Figure 10.2). This section will consider three key steps: target choice, negotiation and integration.

Target choice in M&A

There are two main criteria to apply, strategic fit and organisational fit:[6]

- *Strategic fit*: this refers to the extent to which the target firm strengthens or complements the acquiring firm's strategy. Strategic fit relates to the original strategic motives for the

Figure 10.2 The acquisition process

acquisition: extension, consolidation and capabilities. Managers need to assess strategic fit very carefully. The danger is that potential synergies (see section 7.3) in M&A are often exaggerated in order to justify high acquisition prices. Also, negative synergies ('contagion') between the companies involved are easily neglected.[7] An example of negative synergy was when the Bank of America bought the aggressive investment bank Merrill Lynch for $47 bn (~ €33 bn) in 2008. Under its new owner, Merrill Lynch lost business because it was no longer allowed to advise on deals targeting the extensive list of corporations that were already lending clients of Bank of America. Consequently Merrill Lynch was a less valuable business with its new parent than when free to chase any deal it wanted.

● *Organisational fit*: this refers to the match between the management practices, cultural practices and staff characteristics between the target and the acquiring firms. Large mismatches between the two are likely to cause significant integration problems. The acquisition of Marvel by Disney raised many questions of organisational fit (see Illustration 10.1). International acquisitions can be particularly liable to organisational misfits, because of cultural and language differences between countries,[8] although the extent to which there is actual cultural clash will be determined by the extent of integration intended. A comparison of the two companies' cultural webs (section 5.3.6) might be helpful to highlight potential misfit.

Together, strategic and organisational fit determine the potential for the acquirer to add value, the parenting issue raised in section 7.6. Where there is poor organisational fit, attempts by the acquirer to integrate the target are likely to destroy value regardless of how well the target fits strategically. For instance, the merger between French and American telecoms equipment manufacturers Alcatel and Lucent resulted in significant culture clashes for several years post-deal with losses running into billions of dollars and the departure of the two top executives.

The two criteria of strategic and organisational fit are important components of 'due diligence' – a structured investigation of target companies that generally takes place before a deal is closed. In 2012 Hewlett Packard was forced to write down the value of its acquisition of Autonomy, a British software company, by €3.8 bn (£3 bn, $5 bn), alleging the former management team had fraudulently misrepresented the company during due diligence (see end of chapter Key Debate). Strategic and organisational fit can be used to create a screen according to which potential acquisition targets can be ruled in or ruled out. Note that, because the set of firms that meet the criteria *and* that are actually available for purchase is likely to be small, it is very tempting for managers to relax the criteria too far in order to build a large enough pool of possible acquisitions. Strict strategic and organisational fit criteria are particularly liable to be forgotten after the failure of an initial acquisition bid. Once having committed publicly to an acquisition strategy, senior managers are susceptible to making ill-considered bids for other targets 'on the rebound'.

Negotiation in M&A

The negotiation process in M&A is critical to the outcome of friendly deals. If top managements cannot agree because the price is not right, the terms and conditions are unacceptable, or they cannot get on with each other, the deal will not take place. In terms of price, offer the target too little and the bid will be unsuccessful: senior managers will lose credibility and the company will have wasted a lot of management time. Pay too much, though, and the acquisition is unlikely ever to make a profit net of the original acquisition price.

Ways in which the price is established by the acquirer are through the use of various valuation methods, including financial analysis techniques such as payback period, discounted cash flow, asset valuation and shareholder value analysis (see Chapter 11).[9] For acquisition of publicly quoted companies, there is the additional guide of the market value of the target company's shares. However, acquirers typically do not simply pay the current market value of the target, but have to pay a so-called *premium for control*. This premium is the additional amount that the acquirer has to pay to win control compared to the ordinary valuation of the target's shares as an independent company. Depending on the state of the financial markets, this premium might involve paying at least 30 per cent more for shares in a friendly takeover than normal. Especially where the target resists the initial bid, or other potential acquirers join in with their own bids, it is very easy for bid prices to escalate well beyond the true economic value of the target.

It is therefore very important for the acquirer to be disciplined regarding the price that it will pay. Acquisitions are liable to the *winner's curse* – in order to win acceptance of the bid, the acquirer may pay so much that the original cost can never be earned back.[10] This winner's curse effect operated when the Royal Bank of Scotland's consortium competed with Barclays Bank to acquire the Dutch bank ABN AMRO: the Royal Bank of Scotland won, but the excessive price of €70 bn ($98 bn) soon drove the victor into financial collapse and government ownership. The negative effects of paying too much can be worsened if the acquirer tries to justify the price by cutting back essential investments in order to improve immediate profits. In what is called the *vicious circle of overvaluation*, over-paying firms can easily undermine the original rationale of the acquisition by imposing savings on exactly the assets (e.g. brand marketing, product R&D or key staff) that made up the strategic value of the target company in the first place.

Integration in M&A

The ability to extract value from an acquisition will depend critically on the approach to integrating the new business with the old. Integration is frequently challenging because of problems of organisational fit. For example, there might be strong cultural differences between the two organisations (see section 5.3) or they might have incompatible financial or information technology systems (see section 13.3). Poor integration can cause acquisitions to fail (see Illustration 10.2 for difficulties and successes experienced by Indian conglomerate Tata in its integration of British car company Jaguar Land Rover). Getting the right approach to integration of merged or acquired companies is crucial.

ILLUSTRATION

ILLUSTRATION 10.2

Staying power

Hailed a triumph in 2012, Tata's acquisition of Jaguar and Land Rover (JLR) was perceived as extravagant in 2008, saying more about Indian imperial ambitions than commercial logic. How was success achieved?

The largest privately owned Indian company, Tata Group, has interests in steel, hotels, telecommunications and consulting. It has pursued internationalisation with acquisitions including Corus, the Anglo-Dutch steel company, and, in 2008, JLR. At €1.7 bn (£1.4 bn, $2.2 bn) the acquisition from struggling Ford Motors gave Tata two well-known brands and enlarged its global footprint. But critics asked how could a company known for commercial vehicles and cheap cars (the Nano), do better than a gargantuan of the global auto world, which had pumped billions into the brands, when there were no obvious synergies?

Unfortunately the deal coincided with the global financial crisis. Petrol prices spiked, bank collapses spooked consumers, credit markets froze and demand for luxury cars was hit hard. JLR sales plunged 32 per cent in 10 months and lost €807 m in the year. Tata's debt nearly doubled to €12.9 bn hitting its share price and credit rating. With 16,000 employees at five UK sites, there was alarm that some might close and production be sent overseas. As one banker remarked, 'if they carry on operating JLR as it is, it will fail'. Tata pleaded with the British government for assistance, but support for JLR was refused.

Chairman Ratan Tata was quick to reassure with a personal visit to JLR. He recalled his father had bought a classic Jaguar half a century ago and talked about reviving the revered British Daimler brand and returning Jaguar to racing. Further, 600 more skilled staff were hired to help develop environmentally-friendly cars.

JLR still faced challenges. It had relied on Ford Credit to finance its operations and sales and now needed to switch financing to other providers. All its information technology was based on Ford systems and CEO David Smith commented: 'the IT is an absolute hydra'. To improve efficiencies and save the marques, 2,200 jobs were slashed and tough cuts were made to operation costs.

However, Tata did not insist on tight integration into the group. A three-man strategy board, comprising Ratan Tata, the Head of Tata Automotive and David Smith, Overseas JLR. But the JLR executive committee, directly responsible for company operations, had no Tata representatives. Smith commented: 'Tata wants us to be autonomous – I've got all the executive authority I need . . . We can make decisions quickly – very different from life at Ford. Relationships with Tata are based on individual relationships'. Ratan Tata also commanded respect: 'The designers love him, because he's an architect and not only quite capable of telling them what he thinks; he can say it in the right language too' (Smith). JLR has also used Tata Motors' expertise in cost control and Tata Consultancy Division's skills in information technology.

In 2012 JRL introduced new models including the hot-selling Range Rover Evoque – an all-aluminium-bodied car originally started by Ford, boasting improved fuel consumption and better performance. Second-quarter pre-tax profits were up 77 per cent and sales were up 27 per cent on the previous year helped by strong demand in India and China; 1,000 jobs have been added in the UK and new manufacturing capacity is being built abroad. The 'staying power' of Tata has been rewarded.

Sources: Management Today, 1 May 2009; Financial Times, 4 August 2008; The Hindu, 2 September 2012; Financial Times, 7 November 2012.

Questions

1 Using Haspeslagh and Jemison's matrix, assess Tata's integration approach to JLR.

2 How do you explain Tata's success at JLR?

INSEAD's Philippe Haspeslagh and David Jemison[11] argue that the most suitable approach to integration depends on two key criteria:

- *The extent of strategic interdependence.* This is the need for the transfer or sharing of capabilities (e.g. technology) or resources (e.g. manufacturing facilities). The presumption is that significant transfer or sharing through tight integration will enable the 'creation' of value from the acquisition. Of course, some acquisitions 'capture' value purely through the ownership of assets and so there is less need for integration. These unrelated or conglomerate diversifications (see section 7.2) may only be integrated in terms of their financial systems.

- *The need for organisational autonomy.* Where an acquired firm has a very distinct culture, or is geographically distant, or is dominated by prima donna professionals or star performers, integration may be problematic. For this reason some acquisitions need high levels of organisational autonomy. But in some circumstances it is the distinctiveness of the acquired organisation that is valuable to the acquirer.[12] In this case it is best to learn gradually from the distinct culture, rather than risk spoiling it by hurried or overly tight integration.

As in Figure 10.3, therefore, these two criteria drive four integration approaches[13] which have important implications for the length of integration period and choice of top management for the acquired company:[14]

- *Absorption* is preferred where a high level of strategic interdependence is necessary and there is little need for organisational autonomy. Absorption requires rapid adjustment of the acquired company's old strategies and structures to the needs of the new owner, and corresponding changes to the acquired company's culture and systems. In this type of acquisition it is usual to appoint a new top manager in order to manage the organisation differently.[15]

- *Preservation* is appropriate where the acquired company is well run but not very compatible with the acquirer. The high need for autonomy and low need for integration may be found

Figure 10.3 Acquisition integration matrix

Source: P. Haspeslagh and D. Jemison, *Managing Acquisitions*, Free Press, 1991.

in conglomerate deals. The preservation style depends on allowing old strategies, cultures and systems to continue in the acquired company much as before. Changes from the acquirer are generally confined to the essential minimum such as adjusting financial reporting procedures for control. In this situation it is advisable to retain the incumbent top manager.

- *Symbiosis* is indicated where there is strong need for strategic interdependence, but also a requirement for high autonomy – perhaps in a professional services organisation dependent on the creativity of its staff. Symbiosis implies that both acquired firm and acquiring firm learn the best qualities from the other. This learning process takes time and it is often the case that it is best to retain the incumbent top manager in the early stages to stabilise the acquisition before bringing in a new top manager to make far-reaching changes. This is the most complex of the integration approaches.

- *Holding* is a residual category where there is little to be gained by integration. These acquisitions may occur when the acquired company is in poor financial health and rapid remedial action is required.[16] The acquirer will not integrate the company into its own business to avoid contamination but will impose stringent short-term targets and strategies in order to solve its problems. In these cases it is normal to retain the incumbent top managers as they can act more rapidly than a new appointment. These businesses may often be for sale.

Especially for the more active absorption and symbiosis forms of integration, the ultimate success of the acquisition will depend upon how well the integration process is managed. Here methods of managing strategic change explained in Chapter 14 will be relevant. However, because acquisitions often involve the loss of jobs, sudden career changes, management relocations and the cancellation of projects, it is argued that organisational justice is particularly important for successful integration.[17] *Organisational justice* refers to the perceived fairness of managerial actions, in terms of distribution, procedure and information. Thus:

- *Distributive justice* refers to the distribution of rewards and posts: for example, it will be seen as unfair in a merger between equals if the large majority of senior management posts go to one of the partners, and not the other.

- *Procedural justice* refers to the procedures by which decisions are made: for example, if integration decisions are made through appropriate committees or task forces with representation from both sides, then the perception of fair procedures is likely to be high.

- *Informational justice* is about how information is used and communicated in the integration: if decisions are explained well to all those involved, they are more likely to be accepted positively.

Kraft offended principles of both procedural and informational justice when it assured investors and employees before its 2010 takeover of Cadbury that it would keep open the Somerdale chocolate factory near Bristol, with its 400 workers. Within a month of completing the takeover, Kraft announced that production would be transferred to Poland, causing political controversy and a loss of trust among acquired employees.

10.3.5 M&A strategy over time

M&A strategies evolve over time as deals are rarely one-off events for an organisation:

- *Serial acquirers* are companies that make multiple acquisitions, often in parallel. Working on simultaneous acquisitions is very demanding of managerial time and skills. However, repeating the acquisition process does provide an opportunity for acquiring companies to accumulate experience about how to do M&A better. Cisco Systems is well known as a successful serial acquirer. By end of 2012 it had made 157 acquisitions since its first deal in 1993, accounting for at least 50 per cent of revenue. Carrying out lots of M&A means that serial acquirers often develop specialist teams for managing the acquisition process, from target selection through due diligence and negotiation to post-acquisition integration. The amount of work in selecting and evaluating targets is significant. In order to make just 50 software acquisitions, IBM had to assess around 500 different potential acquisition targets, choosing not to proceed in the vast majority of cases. And for those 50 acquisitions, IBM also had to establish 50 different integration teams, with 10 or more teams each working in parallel at any one time.[18]

● *Divesture (or divestment)* is the process of selling a business that no longer fits the corporate strategy.[19] This is obviously a central part of 'asset-stripping' strategy (see section 10.3.2), but ought to be on the agenda of every diversified corporation. The key determinant of divesture is whether the corporate parent has 'parenting advantage': in other words, the corporate parent can add more value to the business unit than other potential owners of the business (see section 7.4). A corporate parent that does not have parenting advantage should divest the business for the best price it can obtain. Corporate parents are often reluctant to divest businesses, seeing it as an admission of failure. However, a dynamic perspective on M&A would encourage managers to view divestures positively. Funds raised by the sale of an ill-fitting business can be used either to invest in retained businesses or to buy other businesses that fit the corporate strategy better. Obtaining a good price for the divested unit can recoup any losses it may have originally made. Sometimes, however, a less positive reason for divesture is pressure from competition authorities, which may force the sale of businesses to reduce companies' market power. For example, in 2012 Vivendi's Universal Music Group sold businesses amounting to 10 per cent of revenue in order to gain European regulators' approval for its €1.9 bn acquisition of EMI's recorded music business.

Acquisitions, therefore, are an important method for pursuing strategies. However, they are not easy to carry out and they are sometimes adopted for misguided reasons. It is important to consider the alternative of strategic alliances.

(10.4) STRATEGIC ALLIANCES

M&A bring together companies through complete changes in ownership. However, companies also often work together in strategic alliances that involve collaboration with only partial changes in ownership, or no ownership changes at all as the parent companies remain distinct. Thus a **strategic alliance is where two or more organisations share resources and activities to pursue a common strategy**. This is a popular method among companies for pursuing strategy. Accenture has estimated that the average large corporation is managing around 30 alliances at any one time.[20]

Alliance strategy challenges the traditional organisation-centred approach to strategy in at least two ways. First, practitioners of alliance strategy need to think about strategy in terms of the collective success of their networks as well as their individual organisations' self-interest.[21] **Collective strategy is about how the whole network of alliances, of which an organisation is a member, competes against rival networks of alliances.** Thus for Microsoft, competitive success for its Xbox games console relies heavily on the collective strength of its network of independent games developers such as Bungie Studios (makers of Halo), Crystal Dynamics (Tomb Raider), Rockstar North (Grand Auto Theft Auto V) and Crytek Studios (Crysis 3). Part of Microsoft's strategy must include developing a stronger ecosystem of games developers than its rivals such as Sony and Nintendo. Collective strategy also challenges the individualistic approach to strategy by highlighting the importance of effective collaboration. Thus success involves collaborating as well as competing. **Collaborative advantage is about managing alliances better than competitors.**[22] For Microsoft to maximise the value of the Xbox, it is not enough for it to have a stronger network than rivals such as Sony and Nintendo, but it must be better at working with its network in order to ensure that its members keep on producing the best games. The more effectively it collaborates, the more successful it will be. Illustration 10.3 describes Apple's approach to collective strategy and collaboration for the iPad.

10.4.1 Types of strategic alliance

In terms of ownership, there are two main kinds of strategic alliance:

- *Equity alliances* involve the creation of a new entity that is owned separately by the partners involved. The most common form of equity alliance is the *joint venture*, where two organisations remain independent but set up a new organisation jointly owned by the parents. For example, Virgin Mobile India Limited is a cellular telephone service provider company which is a joint venture formed in 2008 between Tata Tele service, part of Tata Group, India, and Richard Branson's Virgin Service Group. The joint venture company uses Tata's network to offer its services under the brand name Virgin Mobile. A *consortium alliance* involves several partners setting up a venture together. For example, IBM, Hewlett Packard, Toshiba and Samsung are partners in the Sematech research consortium, working together on the latest semiconductor technologies.

- *Non-equity alliances* are typically looser, without the commitment implied by ownership. Non-equity alliances are often based on contracts. One common form of contractual alliance is franchising, where one organisation (the franchisor) gives another organisation (the franchisee) the right to sell the franchisor's products or services in a particular location in return for a fee or royalty. Kall-Kwik printing, 7-Eleven convenience stores, McDonald's restaurants and Subway are examples of franchising. Licensing is a similar kind of contractual alliance, allowing partners to use intellectual property such as patents or brands in return for a fee. Long-term subcontracting agreements are another form of loose non-equity alliance, common in automobile supply. For example, the Canadian subcontractor Magna has long-term contracts to assemble the bodies and frames for car companies such as Ford, Honda and Mercedes.

The public and voluntary sectors often get involved in both equity and non-equity strategic alliances. Governments have increasingly encouraged the public sector to contract out the building and maintenance of capital projects such as hospitals and schools under long-term contracts. Individual public organisations often band together to form purchasing consortia as well. A good example of this is university libraries, which typically negotiate collectively for the purchase of journals and books from publishers. Voluntary organisations pool their resources in alliance too. For example, relief organisations in areas suffering from natural or human-made disasters typically have to cooperate in order to deliver the full range of services in difficult circumstances. Although public- and voluntary-sector organisations might often be seen as more naturally cooperative than private-sector organisations, many of the issues that follow apply to all three kinds of organisation.

ILLUSTRATION 10.3

Apple's iPad advantage

Gaining competitive advantage through collaboration?

With much fanfare, a new version of Apple's iPad was launched on 16 March 2012. Apple had dominated the tablet market with its iPad for two years. iPad's light-weight touchscreen and new operating system, iOS, designed from the ground up for portable performance, had won may admirers. But among the first customers on 16 March were buyers who just could not wait to tear the gadget apart, to better understand iPad's success.

Market research firm iSuppli's 'teardown' analysis revealed the €622 (£497, $829), 4G 64GB model cost $409 to make, just 49 per cent of its retail price. iSuppli identified Broadcom and Qualcomm as suppliers of Bluetooth and Wi-Fi chips, STMicroelectronics the gyroscope, Cirrus Logic the audio chip, three Taiwanese companies the touchscreen components and Sony the camera CMOS sensor. Samsung, a rival manufacturer of its own tablet, provided a significant portion of the iPad: the expensive display, battery and processor chip.

Apple was therefore at the heart of a network. However, it had always protected its intellectual property. No hardware was licensed, ensuring control of production and maintenance of its premium pricing policy. It was impossible for any independent company to manufacture cheap iPads, in the way for instance Taiwanese manufacturers produced cheap IBM/Microsoft-compatible personal computers in the 1980s.

iPad's success attracted a swarm of companies into the accessory market, with US company Griffin and Logitech from Switzerland supplying attractive add-ons including ultrathin keyboards, cases and touchscreen stylus. Apple licensed them the necessary technology for this and benefited from attractive complementary products and royalties. But the relationship was arm's-length, with no advanced information about new products.

Originally controlling access to iOS, Apple opened up access for the iPad, allowing third-party apps development and stimulating the new App Stores industry. The attractiveness of iOS and strong consumer demand encouraged software developers to produce for Apple first.

Consumers liked the ease of use and vast ecosystem of Apple's iPad but challenges were mounting. Amazon's low-cost 'content consumption device', Kindle, offered a vast library of movies but lacked Apple's beauty and had few apps. Google's low-priced Nexus 10, manufactured by Samsung, aimed to profit from business services use rather than hardware. Its improved screen resolution and Android operating system challenged iPad's technology and it shared many characteristics of other ecosystems with streaming apps and a consistent user experience. Samsung's own tablet, Galaxy Tab, had similar advantages along with compelling design and openness to non-Apple standards. Microsoft aimed to profit from its hardware, Surface, but was not particularly innovative, lacking a comparable software ecosystem and its tie to Windows could be a hindrance.

In September 2012 Apple briefly surpassed Exxon Mobile as the world's largest company by capitalisation. However, problems were surfacing with declining growth rate in iPad sales in a growing market and Apple shares falling 30 per cent in six months. In addition Apple was also embroiled in lawsuits against Samsung over its Galaxy Tablet design. Samsung was also counter-suing. In November 2012 Apple dropped Samsung as its provider of batteries in preference for Chinese manufacturers.

Sources: G. Linden, K. Kraemer and J. Dedrick, 'Who captures value in a global innovation network?', *Communications of the ACM*, vol. 52, no. 3 (2009), pp. 140–5; 'Tablet wars', *Telegraph*, 6 November 2012; F. MacMahon, 'Tablet wars', 4 December 2012, *BroadcastEngineering. com*; A. Hesseldahl, 'Apple's new ipad costs at least $316 to build, IHS iSuppli teardown shows', 16 March 2012, http://allthingsd.com.

Questions

1 What are the pros and cons of Apple's tight control of licensing?

2 What role has 'ecosystem' played in Apple's competitive advantage?

Figure 10.4 Strategic alliance motives

10.4.2 **Motives for alliances**

Strategic alliances allow an organisation to rapidly extend its strategic advantage and generally require less commitment than other forms of expansion. A key motivator is sharing resources or activities, although there may be less obvious reasons as well. Four broad rationales for alliances can be identified, as summarised in Figure 10.4:

● *Scale alliances.* Here organisations combine in order to achieve necessary scale. The capabilities of each partner may be quite similar (as indicated by the similarity of the A and B organisations in Figure 10.4), but together they can achieve advantages that they could not easily manage on their own. Thus combining together can provide economies of scale in the production of outputs (products or services). Combining might also provide economies of scale in terms of inputs, for example by reducing purchasing costs of raw materials or services. Thus health management organisations often combine together to negotiate better prices with pharmaceutical companies. Finally, combining allows the partners to share risk as well. Instead of organisations stretching themselves to find enough resources on their own, partnering can help each partner avoid committing so many resources of their own that failure would jeopardise the existence of the whole organisation.

● *Access alliances.* Organisations frequently ally in order to access the capabilities of another organisation that are required in order to produce or sell its products and services. For example, in countries such as China and India, a Western company (in Figure 10.4, organisation A) might need to partner with a local distributor (organisation B) in order to access effectively the national market for its products and services. Here organisation B is critical to organisation A's ability to sell. Access alliances can work in the opposite direction. Thus organisation B might seek a licensing alliance in order to access inputs from organisation A, for example technologies or brands. Here organisation A is critical to organisation B's ability to produce or market its products and services. Access can be about tangible resources such as distribution channels or products as well as intangible resources such as knowledge and social/political connections.

- *Complementary alliances*. These can be seen as a form of access alliance, but involve organisations at similar points in the value network combining their distinctive resources so that they bolster each partner's particular gaps or weaknesses. Figure 10.4 shows an alliance where the strengths of organisation A (indicated by the darker shading) match the weaknesses of organisation B (indicated by the lighter shading); conversely, the strengths of organisation B match the weaknesses of organisation A. By partnering, the two organisations can bring together complementary strengths in order to overcome their individual weaknesses. An example of this is the General Motors–Toyota NUMMI alliance: here the complementarity lies in General Motors getting access to the Japanese car company's manufacturing expertise, while Toyota obtains the American car company's local marketing knowledge.

- *Collusive alliances*. Occasionally organisations secretly collude together in order to increase their market power. By combining together into cartels, they reduce competition in the marketplace, enabling them to extract higher prices from their customers or lower prices from suppliers. Such collusive cartels among for-profit businesses are generally illegal, so there is no public agreement between them (hence the absence of brackets joining the two collusive organisations in Figure 10.4) and regulators will act to discourage this activity. For instance, mobile phone operators are often accused of collusive behaviour. In 2012 Thailand's three largest mobile phone operators bid 41.63 bn baht (€1.0 bn, $1.3 bn) for a 3G licence, just 2.8 per cent higher than the minimum price, giving rise to criticism that they had colluded. In not-for-profit sectors collusive alliances do take place and they may also be justified politically in sensitive for-profit industries such as defence or aerospace due to national interests and where the costs of development are far greater than an individual firm can sustain.

It can be seen that strategic alliances, like M&A, have mixed motives. Cooperation is often a good thing, but it is important to be aware of collusive motivations. These are likely to work against the interests of other competitors, customers and suppliers.

10.4.3 Strategic alliance processes

Like acquisitions and mergers, strategic alliances need to be understood as processes unfolding over time. Many alliances are relatively short lived although there are examples of some which last for very long periods indeed. For example, General Electric (USA) and SNECMA (France) have been partners since 1974 in a continuous alliance for the development and production of small aero-engines – this arrangement has been recently extended to 2040. The needs and capabilities of the partners in a long standing alliance such as this are bound to change over time. However, the absence of full ownership means that emerging differences cannot simply be reconciled by managerial authority; they have to be negotiated between independent partners. This lack of control by one side or the other means the managerial processes in alliances are particularly demanding. The management challenges, moreover, will change over time.

The fact that neither partner is in control, while alliances must typically be managed over time, highlights the importance of two themes in the various stages of the alliance process:

- *Co-evolution*. Rather than thinking of strategic alliances as fixed at a particular point of time, they are better seen as co-evolutionary processes.[23] The concept of co-evolution underlines the way in which partners, strategies, capabilities and environments are constantly changing. As they change, they need realignment so that they can evolve in harmony. A co-evolutionary perspective on alliances therefore places the emphasis on flexibility and change. At completion, an alliance is unlikely to be the same as envisaged at the start.

● *Trust.* Given the probable co-evolutionary nature of alliances, and the lack of control of one partner over the other, trust becomes highly important to the success of alliances over time.[24] All future possibilities cannot be specified in the initial alliance contract. Each partner will have made investments that are vulnerable to the selfish behaviour of the other. This implies the need for partners to behave in a trustworthy fashion through the whole lifetime of the alliance. Trust in a relationship is something that has to be continuously earned. Trust is often particularly fragile in alliances between the public and private sectors, where the profit motive is suspect on one side, and sudden shifts in political agendas are feared on the other.

The International HIV/AIDS Alliance shows the importance co-evolution and trust: see Illustration 10.5.

The themes of trust and co-evolution surface in various ways at different stages in the life span of a strategic alliance. Figure 10.5 provides a simple stage model of strategic alliance evolution. The amount of committed resources changes at each stage, but issues of trust and co-evolution recur throughout:

● *Courtship.* First there is the initial process of courting potential partners, where the main resource commitment is managerial time. This courtship process should not be rushed, as the willingness of both partners is required. Similar criteria apply to alliances at this stage as to acquisitions. Each partner has to see a strategic fit, according to the rationales in section 10.3.2. Equally, each partner has to see an organisational fit. Organisational fit can be considered as for acquisitions (section 10.3.4). However, because alliances do not entail the same degree of control as acquisitions, mutual trust between partners will need to be particularly strong right from the outset.

Figure 10.5 Alliance evolution

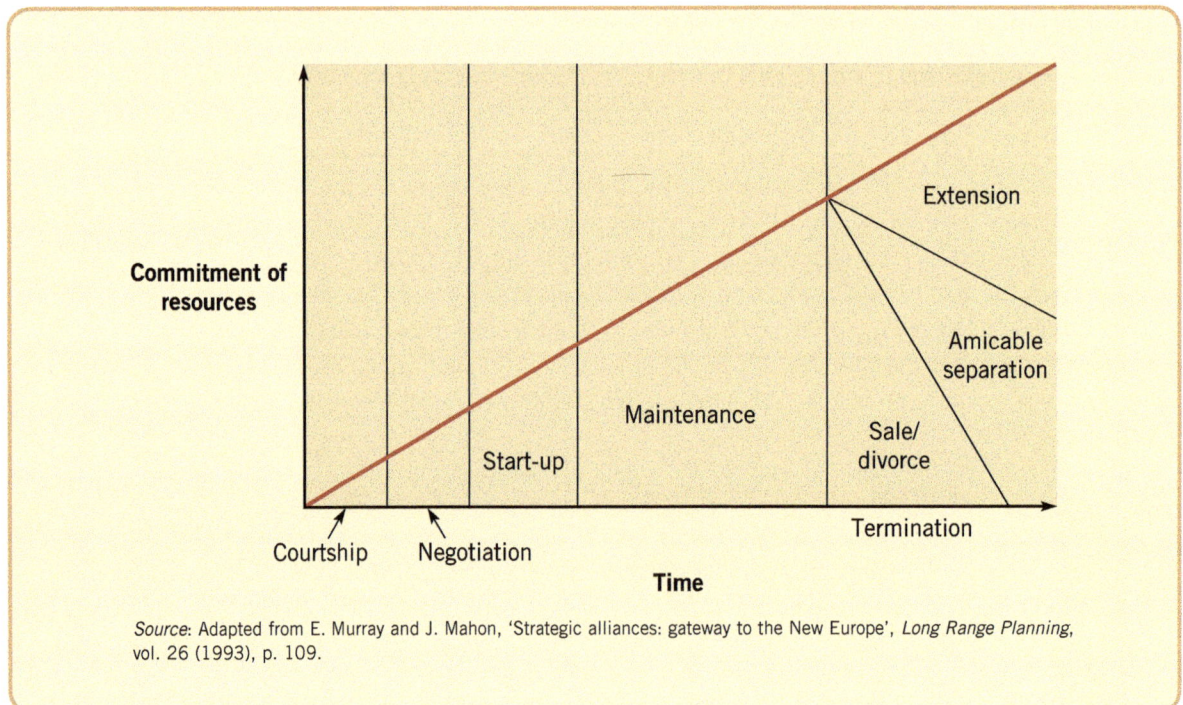

Source: Adapted from E. Murray and J. Mahon, 'Strategic alliances: gateway to the New Europe', *Long Range Planning*, vol. 26 (1993), p. 109.

ILLUSTRATION 10.4

International HIV/AIDS Alliance: trust and co-evolution

An international non-governmental organisation committed to support HIV communities.

Thirty-four million people live with HIV globally and in 2011 the HIV epidemic resulted in 1.7 m deaths. Millions are denied their human rights, resulting in ill-health, isolation, abuse and financial insecurity. Most AIDS deaths can be prevented with access to antiretroviral therapy (ART).

The International HIV/AIDS Alliance ('the Alliance') was formed in 1993 to address this enormous problem. The emphasis has been on developing the capacity for local responses to HIV, rather than direct service provision. The Alliance delivers much of its work – technical expertise and financial support to community-based responses and projects – through nationally based independent not-for-profit Linking Organisations (LOs) that vary in capacity, size and scope. By end 2012 the Alliance was a global partnership of 41 LOs, 7 Technical Support Hubs and an International Secretariat (Secretariat), reaching 4.4 million people. The seven regional Technical Support Hubs, each hosted by a LO, consist of small teams of support providers and regional experts who work with LOs, community-based organisations, governments and other sectors to strengthen their leadership, technical capacity and responsiveness to HIV.

The Alliance is governed by a board of trustees, which has to approve the Alliance's strategy and keep it within mission. The trustees also appoint the Alliance's executive director. The Secretariat is based in Brighton, UK, with offices in Washington, DC, Delhi, Brussels and Geneva. Initially the Alliance acted as a technical support and funding agency, building the capacity of community organisations and dispensing funds from donors to community-based organisations with a technical, project-driven approach. Later strategic activities such as enhancing quality, disseminating best practice, accrediting organisations and working to make more resources available became more important. As LOs developed, the Secretariat role became increasingly one of providing technical support, promoting learning across the Secretariat, LOs and Hubs, policy and advocacy.

The Secretariat also monitored and evaluated programming, and policy, and raised funds largely from government donor agencies. All LOs sign a Charter and Linking Agreement which describes the Alliance's purpose, how it works, its values and commitments and how these will be honoured. An accreditation system evaluates, improves and accredits the LOs as robust organisations operating under certain standards. As Awo Ablo, the Alliance Director of External Relations, pointed out, however, it is important to understand the historic relationship between the LOs and the Secretariat: 'The principle of equality between the LOs and the secretariat is in the DNA of the Alliance. So, the secretariat does not sit above the LOs.' In this sense the Alliance thinks of itself as a 'family' where joint agreement is important.

However, the Alliance's structure is evolving. Ten years ago, Secretariat technical experts flew out to provide support to LOs. This became expensive, and such support increasingly became available as some LOs developed expertise and could act as technical providers to other LOs. These larger LOs have also attracted direct donor support. The Secretariat increasingly acts as an architect of cooperation, binding civil society organisations together to deliver the AIDS mission.

By 2012 funds for fighting AIDS were diminishing and disappearing altogether from countries where donors argue that their economies are rich enough to support themselves. This posed the question: what role should the whole Alliance and Secretariat play in future?

Note: For further information on International HIV/AIDS Alliance strategy development, see the case study in the Text and Cases edition.

Source: http://www.aidsalliance.org.

Questions

1 What role does trust play in the Alliance?

2 What evidence is there that this Alliance has evolved and continues to evolve?

- *Negotiation.* Partners need, of course, to negotiate carefully their mutual roles at the outset. In equity alliances, the partners also have to negotiate the proportion of ownership each will have in the final joint venture, the profit share and managerial responsibilities. There is likely to be a significant commitment of managerial time at this stage, as it is important to get initial contracts clear and correct and it is worth spending time working out how disputes during the life of the alliance will be resolved. In the case of the Areva–Siemens joint venture (Illustration 10.5), Siemens regretted the low share that it originally agreed. Although the negotiation of ownership proportions in a joint venture is similar to the valuation process in acquisitions, strategic alliance contracts generally involve a great deal more. Key behaviours required of each partner need to be specified upfront. However, a ruthless negotiation style can also damage trust going forward. Moreover, co-evolution implies the need to anticipate change. In an acquired unit, it is possible to make adjustments simply by managerial authority. In alliances, initial contracts may be considered binding even when starting conditions have changed. It is wise to include an option for renegotiating initial terms right at the outset.

- *Start-up.* This involves considerable investment of material and human resources and trust is very important. First, the initial operation of the alliance puts the original alliance agreements to the test. Informal adjustments to working realities are likely to be required. Also, people from outside the original negotiation team are typically now obliged to work together on a day-to-day basis. They may not have the same understanding of the alliance as those who initiated it. Without the mutual trust to make adjustments and smooth misunderstandings, the alliance is liable to break up. This early period in an alliance's evolution is the one with the highest rate of failure.

- *Maintenance.* This refers to the ongoing operation of the strategic alliance, with increasing resources likely to be committed. The lesson of co-evolution is that alliance maintenance is not a simple matter of stability. Alliances have to be actively managed to allow for changing external circumstances. The internal dynamics of the partnership are likely to evolve as well as the partners build experience. Here again trust is extremely important. Gary Hamel has warned that alliances often become 'competitions for competence.'[25] Because partners are interacting closely, they can begin to learn each other's particular competences. This learning can develop into a competition for competence, with the partner that learns the fastest becoming the more powerful. The more powerful partner may consequently be able to renegotiate the terms in its favour or even break up the alliance and go it alone. If on the other hand the partners wish to maintain their strategic alliance, trustworthy behaviour that does not threaten the other partner's competence is essential to maintaining the cooperative relationships necessary for the day-to-day working of the alliance.

- *Termination.* Often an alliance will have had an agreed time span or purpose right from the start, so termination is a matter of completion rather than failure. Here separation is amicable. Sometimes the alliance has been so successful that the partners will wish to extend the alliance by agreeing a new alliance between themselves, committing still more resources. Sometimes too the alliance will have been more of a success for one party than the other, with one partner wishing to buy the other's share in order to commit fully, while the other partner decides to sell out. The sale of one party's interest need not be a sign of failure as their strategic agenda may have changed since alliance formation. However, sometimes it can end in bitter divorce, as when Areva threatened to take Siemens to court (see Illustration 10.5). Termination needs to be managed carefully, therefore. Co-evolution

ILLUSTRATION 10.5

Nuclear fission: Areva and Siemens break up

Co-evolution is not easy, as two leading French and German companies discover.

In 2001, Siemens, the German industrial conglomerate, and Areva, the French nuclear industry giant, merged their nuclear reactor businesses into a new joint venture called Areva NP. The joint venture was 34 per cent owned by Siemens, 66 per cent owned by Areva. As the German government had promised to exit nuclear power altogether for environmental reasons, Siemens no longer saw nuclear power as central to its strategy. The joint venture agreement gave the French a right-to-buy option for the Siemens minority stake.

In 2009, the new Siemens CEO, Peter Löscher, sent Areva's CEO Ann Lauvergeon a short email announcing that the Germans would be exercising their right to sell their stake to the French. The email took Madame Lauvergeon completely by surprise: 'It made me think of those men who abandon their wives by leaving a note on the kitchen table.' What had gone wrong in the eight years? Areva NP had been a success. It was the global leader in a market for nuclear reactors that was booming again. Rising oil prices and alarm over global warming made nuclear power increasingly attractive. By 2009, after many years of minimal construction, 51 plants were being built around the world, with 171 more planned. Areva NP was active not only in Europe but in the USA and China.

The recovery of the nuclear industry was in fact one source of the problem: with a new CEO, Siemens wanted back in. Siemens was frustrated by its lack of control as a minority shareholder, and by the slow decision making in Areva NP generally. Moreover, it wanted to get a larger slice of the business than just the nuclear reactors – the big profits were elsewhere in the value chain, in fuel and recycling. Areva, the French parent company, already had a significant presence through the whole value chain.

During 2007, Siemens looked either to increase its stake in Areva NP to 50:50 or to take a direct stake in the French parent, Areva. But, with more than 80 per cent owned by the French government, Areva was not easily for sale. Moreover, Nicolas Sarkozy, then a senior French government minister and soon French President, told German Chancellor Angela Merkel that France could not tolerate a role for Siemens while the German government refused to back nuclear power in its own country. Siemens had to enrol Merkel's support to prevent Areva from exercising its right-to-buy option and forcing Siemens to sell.

In late 2008, Siemens began talks with the Russian nuclear power giant Rosatom. Rosatom had a presence through the whole value chain, including the highly profitable fuel business. With memories of the Soviet nuclear disaster at Chernobyl still live, Rosatom needed Siemens' high reputation for quality. In March 2009, Siemens and Rosatom announced a joint venture with the ambition of displacing Areva NP as world leader.

Ending the Areva NP joint venture was not simple, however. Siemens' strength was in hardware, but Areva owned the software that made it work. Areva was obliged to buy Siemens' stake (~€4 bn; ~$5.6 bn), but lacked the funds to do so. Also, the original joint venture agreement had included an 11-year non-compete clause in case of breakdown. As far as Areva was concerned, Siemens' new joint venture put it in breach of the contract, and so not entitled to the full value of its stake. And the two companies were still working together on various nuclear power stations. Indeed, Areva and Siemens were being jointly sued for €2 bn for cost and time over-runs on a project in Finland. In 2009 Areva took sole control of the joint venture but disputes continued. In 2012 the European Commission ruled the non-compete clause was excessive, anti-competitive and unduly onerous on Siemens – it had to be reduced to three years post joint venture. It was a messy divorce.

Sources: *L'Expansion*, 1 April 2009; *Financial Times*, 28 April 2009; http://www.europa.eu/rapid/press-release_IP-12-618_en.htm.

Questions

1 Why did co-evolution break down in the Areva NP joint venture?

2 Why was the termination of this joint venture messy?

implies that mutual trust is likely to be valuable after the completion of any particular partnership. Partners may be engaged in several different joint projects at the same time. For example, Cisco and IBM are partners on multiple simultaneous projects in wireless communications, IT security, data centres and data storage. The partners may need to come together again for new projects in the future. Thus Nokia, Ericsson and Siemens have had mobile telephone technology joint projects since the mid-1990s. Maintaining mutual trust in the termination stage is vital if partners are to co-evolve through generations of multiple projects.

10.5 COMPARING ACQUISITIONS, ALLIANCES AND ORGANIC DEVELOPMENT

It will be clear so far that all three methods of M&A, strategic alliances and organic development have their own advantages and disadvantages. There are also some similarities. This section first considers criteria for choosing between the three methods, and then draws together some key success factors for M&A and alliances.

10.5.1 Buy, ally or DIY?

Acquisitions and strategic alliances have high failure rates. As in the Key Debate at the end of this chapter, acquisitions are thought to fail about half the time. Acquisitions can go wrong because of excessive initial valuations, exaggerated expectations of strategic fit, underestimated problems of organisational fit and all the other issues pointed to in this chapter. But strategic alliances too have roughly 50 per cent failure rates.[26] Alliances also suffer from miscalculations in terms of strategic and organisational fit, but, given the lack of control on either side, have their own particular issues of trust and co-evolution as well. With these high failure rates, acquisitions and alliances need to be considered cautiously alongside the default option of organic development (Do-It-Yourself).

The best approach will differ according to circumstances. Figure 10.6 presents a 'buy, ally or DIY' matrix summarising four key factors that can help in choosing between acquisitions, alliances and organic development:[27]

- *Urgency.* Acquisitions are a rapid method for pursuing a strategy. It would probably take decades for Tata to build up on its own two international luxury car brands equivalent to Jaguar and Land Rover (Illustration 10.2). Tata's purchase of the two brands gave an immediate kick-start to its strategy. Alliances too may accelerate strategy delivery by accessing additional resources or skills, though usually less quickly than a simple acquisition. Typically organic development (DIY) is slowest: everything has to be made from scratch.

- *Uncertainty.* It is often better to choose the alliance route where there is high uncertainty in terms of the markets or technologies involved. On the upside, if the markets or technologies turn out to be a success, it might be possible to turn the alliance into a full acquisition, especially if a buy option has been included in the initial alliance contract. If the venture turns out a failure, then at least the loss is shared with the alliance partner. Acquisitions may also be resold if they fail but often at a much lower price than the original purchase. On the other hand, a failed organic development might have to be written off entirely,

Figure 10.6 Buy, ally or DIY matrix

	Buy	Ally	DIY
High urgency	Fast	Fast	Slow
High uncertainty	Failures potentially saleable	Share losses and retain buy option	Failures likely unsaleable
Soft capabilities important	Culture and valuation problems	Culture and control problems	Cultural consistency
Highly modular capabilities	Avoid buying whole company	Ally just with relevant partner unit	Develop in new venture unit

with no sale value, because the business unit involved has never been on the market beforehand.

- *Type of capabilities.* Acquisitions work best when the desired capabilities (resources or competences) are 'hard', for example physical investments in manufacturing facilities. Hard resources such as factories are easier to put a value on in the bidding process than 'soft' resources such as people or brands. Hard resources are also typically easier to control post-acquisition than people and skills. As with the Disney takeover of Marvel (see Illustration 10.1), acquisitions pose the risk of significant cultural problems. Sometimes too the acquiring company's own image can tarnish the brand image of the target company. Acquisition of soft resources and competences should be approached with great caution. Indeed, the DIY organic method is typically the most effective with sensitive soft capabilities such as people. Internal ventures are likely to be culturally consistent at least. Even alliances can involve culture clashes between people from the two sides, and it is harder to control an alliance partner than an acquired unit.

- *Modularity of capabilities.* If the sought-after capabilities are highly modular, in other words they are distributed in clearly distinct sections or divisions of the proposed partners, then an alliance tends to make sense. A joint venture linking just the relevant sections of each partner can be formed, leaving each to run the rest of its businesses independently. There is no need to buy the whole of the other organisation. An acquisition can be problematic if it means buying the whole company, not just the modules that the acquirer is interested in. The DIY organic method can also be effective under conditions of modularity, as the new business can be developed under the umbrella of a distinct 'new venture division' (see section 9.5.2), rather than embroiling the whole organisation.

Of course, the choice between the three options of buy, ally and DIY is not unconstrained. Frequently there are no suitable acquisition targets or alliance partners available. One problem for voluntary organisations and charities is that the changes of ownership involved in M&A are much harder to achieve than in the private sector, so that their options are likely to be restricted to alliances or organic development in any case. The key message of Figure 10.6 remains none the less: it is important to weigh up the available options systematically and to avoid favouring one or the other without careful analysis.

10.5.2 **Key success factors**

Figure 10.6 indicates that, despite high failure rates, M&A and strategic alliances can still be the best option in certain circumstances. The question then is how to manage M&A and alliances as effectively as possible.

Strategic fit is critical in both M&A and alliances. The target or the partner should suit the desired strategy. As in section 10.3.4, it is very easy to overestimate synergies – and neglect negative synergies – in alliances as well as M&A. However, organisational fit is vital as well, in both cases. In particular, cultural differences are hard to manage, especially where people resources are important. Because of the lack of control, organisational fit issues are liable to be even harder to manage in alliances than in acquisitions, where the ownership rights of the buyer at least provide some managerial authority. Valuation likewise is a crucial issue in both M&A and equity alliances. Acquisitions are liable to the 'winner's curse' (section 10.3.4) of excessive valuation, particularly where there have been bid battles between competitors. But even alliance partners need to assess their relative contributions accurately in order to ensure that they do not commit too many resources with too little return and too little control.

M&A and alliances each raise some very distinct issues to manage. At the start of the process, alliances rely on courtship between willing partners, whereas that need not be the same for M&A. Mergers do require mutual willingness of course, but, if negotiations go poorly, there often remains the option of the *hostile takeover* bid. The process of a hostile bid is principally about persuading shareholders rather than talking with the target's managers. In M&A, a crucial issue is the right approach to *integration*: absorption, preservation, symbiosis, holding. In strategic alliances, the option to fully integrate the two partners into a single whole does not exist. Rather the task is the continued maintenance of a partnership between independent organisations that must *co-evolve*. Finally, *divesture* of acquired units and the *termination* of alliances tend to differ. Divestures are typically one-off transactions with purchasers, with limited consequences for future relationships. On the other hand, the way in which alliances are terminated may have repercussions for important future relationships, as new projects and simultaneous projects often involve the same partners. In sum, it can be seen that the necessity for courtship, co-evolution and sensitive termination frequently makes the strategic alliance process a much more delicate one than simple acquisition.

KEY DEBATE

Merger madness?

Mergers and acquisitions involve huge sums of money, but how wisely is it being spent?

This chapter has introduced the importance of mergers and acquisitions as a method of development, but also pointed to some challenges. In some cases there have been some spectacular failures. In 2011 Hewlett Packard ('HP') purchased Autonomy, a British software firm specialising in 'unstructured' data analysis, for €8.3 bn (£6.7 bn; $11.1 bn). On 24 November 2012, HP startled analysts who had been expecting an announcement of $2.2 bn net profits for the group that it had made an $8.8 bn loss. HP blamed the Autonomy acquisition for this situation, saying that HP had had to write down its value by €6.6 bn, and ascribing €3.8 bn of this to 'serious accounting improprieties, disclosure failure and outright misrepresentation'. The shares of HP which stood at €22.1 just prior to the deal announcement, now stood at €8.7, their lowest level for 10 years.

Harvard Business School professor Michael Porter has been a prominent sceptic of mergers and acquisitions, noting that half of all acquired companies are sold off again within a few years. The figure shows the aggregate dollar return (i.e. the change in stock price associated with the acquisition announcement) of acquiring companies in the USA between 1993 and 2007. In 2000, acquiring firms' shareholders lost, in all, more than $275 bn. In the whole period of 1993 to 2007, acquiring firms' shareholders lost more than $550 bn.

One interpretation of these large losses is that mergers and acquisitions represent a reckless waste of money by managers who are careless of investors' interests. Indeed there is evidence that CEOs suffer the consequences, over half being replaced within a relatively short time period. It might be appropriate therefore to make mergers and acquisitions more difficult by legislating to help target companies resist or refuse hostile bids. If the law restricted hostile bids, wasteful acquisitions could be cut.

There are drawbacks to restricting mergers and acquisitions, however. Even if acquiring companies often fail to make money for their shareholders, they can improve the profitability of the system as a whole in at least two ways:

● The threat of being taken over if they do not satisfy their shareholders helps keep managers focused on performance. The financial press reports just such threats regularly.

● Mergers and acquisitions can be an effective way of restructuring stagnant firms and industries. The absence of hostile takeovers in Japan is often blamed for the slow restructuring of Japanese industry since the early 1990s.

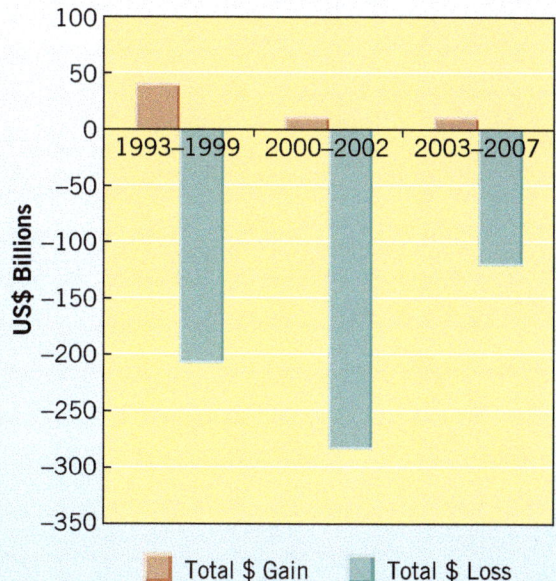

Sources: M. Porter, 'From competitive advantage to corporate strategy', *Harvard Business Review*, May–June (1987), pp. 43–60; S.B. Moeller, F.P. Schlingemann and R.M. Stulz, 'Wealth destruction on a massive scale?', *Journal of Finance*, vol. 60, no. 2 (2005), pp. 757–82; K.M. Lehn and M. Zhao, 'CEO turnover after acquisitions: are bad bidders fired?', *Journal of Finance*, vol. LXI, no. 4 (2006), pp. 1759–810; 'Jump in hostile takeover bids', *Financial Times*, 3 June 2012. G. Alexandridis, C.F. Mavrovitis and N.G. Travlos, 'How have M&As changed? Evidence from the sixth merger wave'. *The European Journal of Finance*, vol. 18, no. 8 (2012), pp. 663–88.

Questions

1 For a recent large merger or acquisition, track the share prices of the companies involved (using www.bigcharts.com, for instance), for several weeks both before and after the announcement. What do the share price movements suggest about the merits of the deal?

2 Identify a hostile takeover threat from press reports. What action did the company's management do to resist the takeover?

SUMMARY

● There are three broad methods for pursuing a growth strategy: *mergers and acquisitions, strategic alliances* and *organic development.*

● Organic development can be either continuous or radical. Radical organic development is termed *corporate entrepreneurship.*

● Acquisitions can be *hostile* or *friendly.* Motives for mergers and acquisitions can be *strategic, financial* or *managerial.*

● The acquisition process includes *target choice, valuation* and *integration.*

● Strategic alliances can be *equity* or *non-equity.* Key motives for strategic alliances include *scale, access, complementarity* and *collusion.*

● The strategic alliance process relies on *co-evolution* and *trust.*

● The choice between acquisition, alliance and organic methods is influenced by four key factors: *urgency, uncertainty, type of capabilities* and *modularity of capabilities.*

WORK ASSIGNMENTS

✱ *Denotes more advanced work assignments.*
* *Refers to a case study in the Text and Cases edition.*

10.1 Write a short (about 10 lines) statement to a chief executive who has asked you to advise whether or not the company should develop through M&A. Write a similar statement to a chief executive of a hospital who is considering possible mergers with other hospitals.

10.2✱ For a recently announced acquisition, track the share prices (using www.bigcharts.com, for example) of both the acquiring firm and the target firm in the period surrounding the bid. What do you conclude from the behaviour of the share prices about how investors regard the bid? Which company's investors are likely to benefit more?

10.3✱ For a recently announced acquisition, or for the acquisitions of Eidos by Square Enix in the end of chapter case, or Jaguar Land Rover by Tata (Illustration 10.2), explain which post-acquisition integration approach might be most appropriate in these situations and why other integration approaches may be less effective.

10.4✱ With reference to either Disney's acquisition of Marvel (Illustration 10.1), SABMiller's* acquisitions, the acquisition of Cadbury* by Kraft, or end of chapter case '*Final Fantasy*', explain why, when the objectives are the mutual creation of value, acquirers chose to make acquisitions rather than alliances.

10.5 Which development approach is a family-owned company likely to prefer? Explain your reasoning.

Integrative assignment

10.6✱ With so many M&A failing, explain why managers continue to transact these deals. In particular consider alternative methods for strategic realignment that may be available to an organisation as well as the possible consequences of a company not using M&A. Now interpret your answer in terms of all the stakeholders who may be affected by an M&A transaction. What conclusions can you draw?

VIDEO ASSIGNMENTS

Visit **MyStrategyLab** and watch the Love Da Pop case study for Chapter 10.

1   What are the main benefits that 'Love Da Pop' might expect to gain from working with Corn Poppers? Are there any risks for Love Da Pop?

2   What does it take for strategic alliances, such as that between Love Da Pop and Corn Poppers, to work effectively and be sustained over a long period?

RECOMMENDED KEY READINGS

- A comprehensive book on mergers and acquisitions is: S. Sudarsanam. *Creating value from mergers and acquisitions: the challenges*, 2nd edn, FT Prentice Hall, 2010. For some alternative perspectives, see the collection by D.N. Angwin (ed.), *Mergers and Acquisitions*, Blackwell, 2007.

- A useful book on strategic alliances is J. Child, D. Faulkner and S. Tallman, *Cooperative Strategy: Managing Alliances, Networks and Joint Ventures*, 2nd edn, Oxford University Press, 2005.

- A book which contrasts the benefits of different modes of expansion is L. Capron and W. Mitchell, *Build, Buy, Borrow: Solving the growth dilemma*, Harvard Business Review Press, 2012.

REFERENCES

1. P. Sharma and J. Chrisman, 'Towards a reconciliation of the definitional issues in the field of corporate entrepreneurship', *Entrepreneurial Theory and Practice*, Spring (1998), pp. 11–27; D. Garvin and L. Levesque, 'Meeting the challenge of corporate entrepreneurship', *Harvard Business Review*, October (2006), pp. 102–12.

2. *Financial Times*, 29 February 2012. It is worth noting that the number of deals only fell to 41,000, which suggests that M&A are an important and constant way in which businesses adjust to changing contexts.

3. D.N. Angwin, 'Motive archetypes in mergers and acquisitions (M&A): the implications of a configurational approach to performance', *Advances in Mergers and Acquisitions*, vol. 6 (2007), pp. 77–105. A useful conceptual model of motives and mitigating variables is J. Haleblian, C.E. Devers, G. McNamara, M.A. Carpenter and R.B. Davison, 'Taking stock of what we know about mergers and acquisitions: a review and research agenda', *Journal of Management*, vol. 35 (2009), pp. 469–502.

4. This adapts J. Bower, 'Not all M&As are alike – and that matters', *Harvard Business Review*, March (2001), pp. 93–101.

5. M. Hayward and D. Hambrick, 'Explaining the premiums paid for large acquisitions: evidence of CEO hubris', *Administrative Science Quarterly*, vol. 42 (1997), pp. 103–27; J.-Y. Kim, J. Haleblian and S. Finkelstein, 'When firms are desperate to grow via acquisition: the effect of growth patterns and acquisition experience on acquisition premiums', *Administrative Science Quarterly*, vol. 56, no. 1 (2011), pp. 26–60.

6. This builds on D. Jemison and S. Sitkin, 'Corporate acquisitions: a process perspective', *Academy of Management Review*, vol. 11, no. 1 (1986), pp. 145–63.

7. J.M. Shaver, 'A paradox of synergy: contagion and capacity effects in mergers and acquisitions', *Academy of Management Review*, vol. 31, no. 4 (2006), pp. 962–78.

8. See J. Child, D. Faulkner and R. Pitkethly, *The Management of International Acquisitions*, Oxford University Press, 2001.

9. A useful discussion of valuation methods in acquisitions is in Chapter 9 of D. Sadtler, D. Smith and A. Campbell, *Smarter Acquisitions*, Prentice Hall, 2008.

10. N. Varaiya and K. Ferris, 'Overpaying in corporate takeovers: the winner's curse', *Financial Analysts Journal*, vol. 43, no. 3 (1987), pp. 64–70.

11. P. Haspeslagh and D. Jemison, *Managing Acquisitions: Creating Value through Corporate Renewal*, Free Press, 1991; P. Puranam, H. Singh and S. Chaudhuri, 'Integrating acquired capabilities: when structural integration is (un)necessary', *Organization Science*, vol. 20, no. 2 (2009), pp. 313–28.

12. G. Stahl and A. Voigt, 'Do cultural differences matter in mergers and acquisitions? A tentative model and examination', *Organization Science*, vol. 19, no. 1 (2008), pp. 160–78.

13. See D.N. Angwin, 'Typologies in M&A research', in D. Faulkner, S. Teerikangas, and R. Joseph (eds), *Oxford Handbook of Mergers and Acquisitions*, Oxford University Press, 2012, pp. 40–70 for a review.

14. D.N. Angwin, 'Typologies in M&A research', in D. Faulkner, S. Teerikangas and R. Joseph (eds), *Oxford Handbook of Mergers and Acquisitions*, Oxford University Press, 2012, pp. 40–70; D.N. Angwin and M. Meadows, 'The choice of insider or outsider top executives in acquired companies', *Long Range Planning*, vol. 37 (2009), pp. 239–57.

15. D.N. Angwin, and M. Meadows (2009) 'The choice of insider or outsider top executives in acquired companies', *Long Range Planning*, vol. 37 (2009), pp. 239–57.

16. D.N. Angwin and M. Meadows, 'Acquiring poorly performing companies during recession', *Journal of General Management*, vol. 38, no. 1 (2012), pp. 1–22.

17. K. Ellis, T. Reus and B. Lamont, 'The effects of procedural and informational justice in the integration of related acquisitions', *Strategic Management Journal*, vol. 30 (2009), pp. 137–61.

18. R. Uhlaner and A. West, 'Running a winning M&A shop', *McKinsey Quarterly*, March (2008), pp. 106–12.

19. L. Dranikoff, T. Koller and A. Schneider, 'Divesture: strategy's missing link', *Harvard Business Review*, May (2002), pp. 75–83; and M. Brauer, 'What have we acquired and what should we acquire in divesture research? A review and research agenda', *Journal of Management*, vol. 32, no. 6 (2006), pp. 751–85; H. Berry, 'When do firms divest foreign operations?' *Organization Science*, vol. 24, no. 1 (2013), pp. 246–61; J. Xia and S. Li, 'The divestiture of acquired subunits: a resource dependence approach', *Strategic Management Journal*, vol. 34, no. 2 (2013), pp. 131–48.

20. Andersen Consulting, *Dispelling the Myths of Strategic Alliances*, 1999.

21. R. Bresser, 'Matching collective and competitive strategies', *Strategic Management Journal*, vol. 9, no. 4 (1988), pp. 375–85.

22. J. Dyer, *Collaborative Advantage*, Oxford University Press, 2000.

23. A. Inkpen and S. Curral, 'The coevolution of trust, control, and learning in joint ventures', *Organization Science*, vol. 15, no. 5 (2004), pp. 586–99; R. ul-Huq, *Alliances and Co-evolution in the Banking Sector*, Palgrave, 2005.

24. A. Arino and J. de la Torre, 'Relational quality: managing trust in corporate alliances', *California Management Review*, vol. 44, no. 1 (2001), pp. 109–31.

25. G. Hamel, *Alliance Advantage: the Art of Creating Value through Partnering*, Harvard Business School Press, 1998.

26. Andersen Consulting, *Dispelling the Myths of Strategic Alliances*, 1999.

27. This draws on J. Dyer, P. Kale and H. Singh, 'When to ally and when to acquire?', *Harvard Business Review*, vol. 82, nos 7/8 (2004), pp. 108–15; and X. Yin and M. Shanley, 'Industry determinants of the merger versus alliance decision', *Academy of Management Review*, vol. 31, no. 2 (2008), pp. 473–91.

'Final Fantasy?' Acquisitions and alliances in electronic games

After several difficult years Japanese games maker Square Enix posted revenues in 2012 of ¥127.9 billion ($1.6 bn; £993 m; €1.23 bn), an increase of 2.1 per cent over the prior year, with net profits of ¥6.1 billion – a marked improvement on the previous year's loss of ¥12 billion. Famous for its role-playing games such as the *Final Fantasy* series, this turnaround in fortunes followed several years of radical strategic initiatives including strategic alliances with the strategy games developers Double Helix and Gas Powered Games in the USA and Wargaming.net in the United Kingdom. Most radically in 2009, it had also acquired the British Eidos Group, famous for the Lara Croft games. Square Enix President Yoichi Wada commented at the time: 'Our goal is to become one of the top ten players in the world's media and entertainment industry. Since the games market is global, both our contact with our customers and our game development must become global too.'

Source: iStockphoto.

The Japanese games industry

Square Enix's strategic moves in 2009 came at a challenging time for the Japanese games industry. The Japanese had enjoyed two decades of domination built on the worldwide success of Japanese consoles such as the Sony PlayStation. But the growing success of Microsoft's Xbox gave an opportunity to American games developers to return to the console market. Indeed, American games developers found that their development skills were more transferable in the new cross-over markets, where games needed to be developed for PCs, consoles and mobile phones alike. Moreover, the Americans had the advantage of proximity to Hollywood, bringing in new creative talent and offering opportunities for film tie-ins. At the same time, Japan's ageing population was shrinking the market for traditional electronic games.

Square Enix's Yōichi Wada recognised the predicament of the Japanese industry vis-à-vis the Americans:

'In the last five to ten years, the Japanese games industry has become a closed environment, with no new people coming in, no new ideas, almost xeno-phobic . . . The lag with the US is very clear. The US games industry was not good in the past but it has now attracted people from the computer industry and from Hollywood, which has led to strong growth.'[1]

At the same time, the basic economics of the games industry is changing, with rising costs due to growing technological sophistication. A typical modern game can cost from $3,000,000 to over $20,000,000 to develop.[2] Games generally take from one to three years to develop. Yet only 1 in 20 games is estimated ever to make a profit. In other words, the risks are very high and the necessary scale to compete is rising.

Square Enix's strategy

Square Enix itself was a merger in 2003 between Square (founded in 1983 and famous for *Final Fantasy* role-playing game) and Enix (founded in 1975 with its role-playing *Dragon Quest* series). Yōichi Wada, President of Square, became the president of the new merged company.

Square Enix's strategy is based on 'polymorphic content'. Its various franchises (*Final Fantasy*, *Dragon Quest* and so on) are developed for all hardware or media, such as consoles, mobile phones, online, PCs rather than any single gaming platform. There are also spin-offs including

TV series, films, comics and novels. In 2005, Square Enix bought the Japanese arcade-game company Taito Corporation, famous for its *Space Invaders* game. *Space Invaders* versions have appeared on PlayStation, Xbox and Wii consoles, as well as PCs.

By 2008, Yōichi Wada was presiding over a company that was increasingly diversified, with sales of ¥136 bn (about €1 bn) and just over 3,000 employees. However, it was still overwhelmingly Japanese (85 per cent of sales at home) and lacked scale by comparison with competitors such as Electronic Arts and Activision. On the plus side, Square Enix reportedly had a 'war-chest' available for acquisitions of about Y40 bn (about €300 m).[3] During the summer of 2008, Square Enix made a friendly bid for the Japanese game developer Tecmo, whose fighting games *Ninja Garden* and *Dead or Alive* were popular in North America and Europe. Tecmo rejected the bid. Wada began to look overseas.

Lara Croft falls

Eidos is a British games company best known for the action-adventure games series *Tomb Raider*, starring the extraordinary Lara Croft. However, during 2008, disappointing sales for *Tomb Raider: Underworld* drove its share price down from £5 (~€5.5; ~$7.5) to around 30 pence. Eidos's founder and Chief Executive, Jane Cavanagh, was forced to resign. The company declared losses of £136 m, on sales of £119 m (down from £179 m two years earlier). In April 2009, Square Enix bought the company for £84 m, a premium of 129 per cent over Eidos's current market value. Given the declining success of the *Tomb Raider* franchise, many speculated that Square Enix had overpaid for its first overseas acquisition.

The acquisition of Eidos did offer Square Enix global reach, however. About one third of Eidos's sales were in the USA and 40 per cent in Europe, excluding the United Kingdom. Eidos also brought Square Enix its first studios outside Japan, with studios in the United Kingdom, Denmark, Hungary, the USA, Canada and China. Yōichi Wada commented: 'It is significant that we have opened a window for creative talents worldwide.'

Wada chose to keep Phil Rogers, the new Eidos Chief Executive, and the rest of his management team in place. Wada described a new group structure, in which Square Enix, the arcade business Taito and Eidos would each be standalone divisions: 'Our aim is to implement a hybrid management structure which avoids the extremes of being either too global or too local.'[4] He

continued: 'The Group's management and administration departments will be integrated, while our product and service delivery will be established locally in each territory to maximise our business opportunities through better understanding of local customers' tastes and commercial practices.' Wada also recognised the new strength that Eidos brought in action-adventure games, by contrast with Square Enix's traditional core of role-playing games. He declared his commitment both to sharing technologies across the businesses and to sustaining particular strengths: 'While promoting shared technology and expertise among our studios, we will also develop products which reflect the unique identity of each studio, regardless of locality.' Wada also commented on the nature of the skilled games developers he was acquiring: 'It is always difficult to manage creatives anywhere in the world. We want to cherish the Eidos studio culture but change it where it is necessary.'[5]

One thing that Square Enix was quick to do was to end the Eidos distribution agreement with Warner Bros for its products in the USA. Square Enix regarded itself as strong enough to do that itself.

Strategic alliances

At the same time as acquiring Eidos, Square Enix cemented three significant strategic alliances. In the United Kingdom, Square Enix tied up with the strategy game developer Wargaming.net (famous for the *Massive Assault* series) in order to produce the World War II game *Order of War*. This would enter the market at the end of 2009 as Square Enix's first global product release. In the USA, Square Enix formed partnerships with Gas Powered Games (producer of the *Supreme Commander* strategy game) and with Double Helix (producer of the *Front Mission* strategy series). Together with the Eidos acquisition, these partnerships significantly extended Square Enix's range beyond its traditional core in role-playing games. They also extended the company's geographical reach. Yōichi Wada commented: 'We see great opportunities in North American and European markets, both of which are expected to be maintaining sustainable growth over these coming years. Therefore it is crucial that we create alliances with proven developers such as Gas Powered Games in order to serve these significant markets better by providing products and services in tune with customer tastes.'[6]

All three of these new partners were relatively small (around 100 employees each), privately owned and had their origins as start-ups during the 1990s. The founders' motivations are explained by Chris Taylor at Gas Powered Games:

> 'I had that dream really from the day I first walked into my first full time job as a games programmer. I wanted to be the guy running the company . . . We've created our own original IPs (intellectual properties) consistently. Some are great, some are not so great, but the fact is you have to keep throwing darts at the board. You have to keep trying to make great stuff, and you can't do that if you're inside of a large megalithic corporation to the same degree . . .'[7]

Chris Taylor described how Square Enix, traditionally a role-playing company, and Gas Powered Games, more a strategy game developer, were working together on their first venture, *Supreme Commander 2*:

> 'One of the things that we took as a cue from Square Enix was the way they embrace character and story. We were all into that, so that was easy. When we asked them, "How should we develop our game to work with their philosophy?", they said, "Don't do that because we want you to do what you do. You make games for the Western market, and we're interested in making games for the Western market." So if we changed, we would be missing the point. Which was terrific, because that meant we could do what we loved to do, make great RTS (real-time strategy) games . . . and if we tried to change them in any way, we'd be moving away from the goal.'[8]

A games enthusiast's view

Through alliances and mergers, Square Enix had transformed its profile. From its base in Japanese-style role-playing games, it was developing a significant presence in strategy and action adventure. It had studios across the world. Its various games titles were big across Asia, Europe and America. Games enthusiast Randy commented:

> 'Square Enix publishing a western-developed game? Is the far-reaching JRPG (Japanese role-playing game) developer dumping the androgynous boy-heroes and shovel-wide swords for WWII fatigues and M1 Carbines? No, not entirely. But they *are* bringing Wargaming.net into the fold to do it for them. First, Square Enix buys out the house that Lara Croft built, and now they're into real-time strategy war games. *Nothing in this life makes sense anymore.*'[9]

Looking forwards

Following the alliances and mergers, Square Enix's financial performance began to suffer, particularly in the increasingly competitive console market. However, in 2012 the digital division was performing well with *Final Fantasy XIII-2*, *Deus Ex: Human Revolution* and the Mobage simulation game *Sengoku Ixa* – with two million registered users – spurring the division to revenues of ¥71.9 billion, up 11.9 per cent year-on-year, and operating profit of ¥12.6 billion, up 11.7 per cent. Square Enix reported it had 'internal reserves' for investments that could 'enhance the company's value'. This could include 'capital investments and M&A to expand and develop new businesses'. Such deals would be a part of a broader strategy to meet the demands of an increasingly digital, networked, multi-device world market.

References

1. M. Palmer, 'Square Enix views Eidos as a jump to next level', *Financial Times*, 28 April 2009.
2. 'Cost of making games set to soar', www.bbcnews.co.uk, 17 November 2005.
3. 'Square Enix needs to show growth scenario to market', *Nikkei*, 9 October 2007.
4. Joint interview with Yoichi Wada and Phil Rogers, www.square-enix.com, 26 May 2009.
5. M. Palmer, 'Square Enix views Eidos as a jump to next level', *Financial Times*, 28 April 2009.
6. 'Square Enix and Gas Powered Games announce strategic partnership', *Newswire Association*, 12 November 2008.
7. P. Elliott, 'Foot on the gas', *gamesindustry.biz*, 19 August 2008.
8. X. de Matos, 'Interview: Chris Taylor on Supreme Commander 2', *joystiq.com*, 9 June 2009.
9. Randy, 'Square Enix tries hand at WWI RTS with Order of War', *Gaming Nexus*, 17 April 2009. Italics in original.

Questions

1 Explain why Square Enix chose alliances in some cases and acquisitions in others.

2 How should Square Enix manage its Eidos acquisition in order to maximise value creation, and how might that management approach change over time?

3 What are the strengths and weaknesses of the alliance strategy, and what problems might Square Enix anticipate over time?

4 What methods of expansion would you recommend to the management of Square Enix now they appear to have the resources and intention to grow?

COMMENTARY ON PART II

The central concern of Part II has been the strategic choices available to organisations, including business strategy, diversification, internationalisation, innovation, acquisitions and alliances. Although the chapters provide various rationales and evidence for these strategic choices, this book recognises that the decisions between them are often not wholly objective and rational. Indeed, the four contrasting 'strategy lenses' (introduced in the Commentary at the end of Part I) each propose very different expectations about strategic decisions. This Commentary applies the same four lenses to the issues raised in Part II, focused on strategic choices. The four lenses raise questions about how to generate the options for strategic choice, assumptions about other organisations, and what is likely to matter in the success of various options.

Design lens

The design lens places high value on extensive information search and analysis for generating strategic options. Logical, optimal choices are important. The design lens therefore recommends you to:

- *Consider all options*: strategy choices should be made between a large initial range, with techniques such as the Ansoff growth matrix (section 7.2) used to generate options.

- *Ensure fit between choice and purpose*: preferred options should be checked carefully for consistency with the purpose, goals and objectives of the organisation (Chapter 4).

- *Maximise returns*: the optimal choice is one that maximises the returns on investment, whether that is investment of capital or effort (Chapter 11).

Experience lens

In this view, strategy develops incrementally based on the past history and culture of the organisation and its members. So the set of strategic options to choose from is unlikely to be comprehensive and cultural factors can generate behaviours different from might be expected on a simplistically rational point of view. You should therefore:

- *Challenge standard responses*: for example, just because a particular diversification option (Chapter 7) or international entry mode (Chapter 8) has always worked before, does not mean that the same should be done again.

- *Respect cultural differences*: in integrating acquisitions (Chapter 10), cooperating with alliance partners (Chapter 10) or going international (Chapter 8), the experience lens suggests it is very important to take account of the other organisation's history and culture, as well as more objective factors.

- *Adjust competitor analysis*: if experience shapes strategy, simple analyses of competitor interaction, as sometimes in game theory (Chapter 6), may need to be adjusted in order to avoid exaggerating the likely speed of competitors' moves or making excessive assumptions about the rationality of their responses.

STRATEGIC CHOICES

This Commentary therefore reconsiders some of the issues of Part II in the light of the four strategy lenses. Note that:

- There is no suggestion here that any one of these lenses is better than the others. It is usually beneficial to explore strategic options using more than one lens, in order to get more than one point of view.
- For a deeper understanding of this Commentary, you might want to review the Part I Commentary, following Chapter 5, which provides a fuller introduction of the four lenses, plus an illustrative case.

Variety lens

The emphasis here is on the variety and spontaneity of strategic options and their possible origins in the organisational periphery. The variety lens is orientated towards innovation. Thus the variety lens encourages you to:

- *Look beyond top management*: from a variety lens point of view, the strategies generated by top management are liable to be limited, so you should look more broadly for ideas about strategic options, for instance by using 'open innovation' or 'market pull' approaches (section 9.2).
- *Learn from acquisitions and partners*: if the top has no monopoly of wisdom, exploring acquired units or alliance partners (Chapter 10) for underappreciated initiatives or capabilities might uncover new strategic options going far beyond what was planned in the original acquisition or alliance.
- *Expect surprises*: in an environment liable to spontaneous innovation, you should be sensitive to the potential for sudden 'disruptive innovations' and consider holding a strong portfolio of 'real options' (section 9.4).

Discourse lens

According to this lens, the strategic options that rise to the surface will typically be shaped by the legitimate discourse of the organisation and the underlying self-interest of various managers. The discourse lens recognises the power of language. So you should:

- *Watch your language*: attend to discursive framing of your strategic options, recognising the emotional resonance of labels such as 'star' and 'dog', or 'heartland' and 'alien', in portfolio analyses for instance (Chapter 7) and the different meanings such labels might have in various national cultures (Chapter 9).
- *Distrust others' language*: strategic options that draw heavily on apparently legitimate or fashionable discourses such as synergy (Chapter 7), innovation and entrepreneurship (Chapter 9) or partnership and ecosystems (Chapter 10) should be probed particularly critically for shaky reasoning or self-interested motives.
- *Look out for managerial interests*: the discourse with which strategic options are framed may hide managerial self-interest, especially in regard to strategies such as unrelated diversification (Chapter 7) or aggressive acquisitions (Chapter 10) that often perform badly for shareholders.

Index